D1351232

Stalking Nabokov

Stalking Nabokov

SELECTED ESSAYS

Brian Boyd

Columbia University Press   New York

Columbia University Press
Publishers Since 1893
New York   Chichester, West Sussex

Library of Congress Cataloging-in-Publication Data
Boyd, Brian, 1952–
Stalking Nabokov : selected essays / Brian Boyd.
p. cm.
Includes bibliographical references and index.
ISBN 978-0-231-15856-5 (cloth : acid-free paper)
ISBN 978-0-231-53029-3 (e-book)
1. Nabokov, Vladimar Vladimirovich, 1899–1977—
Criticism and interpretation. I. Title.

PG3476.N3Z587   2011
813'.54—dc22   2011008348

Columbia University Press books are printed
on permanent and durable acid-free paper.
This book is printed on paper with recycled content.
Printed in the United States of America

c 10 9 8 7 6 5 4 3

To Bronwen
and to my friends in the Nabokov world

CONTENTS

ACKNOWLEDGMENTS

I would like to thank the late Vladimir Nabokov for giving readers, and especially this reader, such pleasure, the late Véra Nabokov for inviting me to sort out her husband's archives and for trusting me enough to tolerate my researching his biography; and Dmitri Nabokov and the late Elena Sikorski for their support, hospitality, and friendship, and Dmitri also for permission to quote all unpublished Nabokov material.

I would like to thank the following writers, editors, publishers, colleagues, students, and friends for inviting me to contribute to conferences, journals, books, talks, or discussions, or for ideas or feedback, or for giving me permission to reproduce the material that follows: Martin Amis, Harold Augenbraum (then of Mercantile Library of New York), André Bernard (then of Harcourt), Marijeta Bozovic (then of *Ulbandus*), Matthew Brillinger, Lisa Browar (then of the New York Public Library), Patricia Carr Brückmann (Trinity College, University of Toronto), Linda Corman (Trinity College Library, University of Toronto), Mo Cohen (Gingko Press), Julian Connolly, Peter Craven (then of *Scripsi*), Galya Diment, Alexander Dolinin, Kristin Eliasberg (then of PEN Center, New York), George Gibian, Jane Grayson (then of SEES, University of London), R. S. Gwynn, Jean Holabird, Don Barton Johnson (including as editor of *Nabokov Studies*), Kurt Johnson, Frederic R. Karl (*Bibliography and Source Studies*), Zoran Kuzmanovich (including as editor of *Nabokov Studies*), Shoko Miura (Nabokov Society of Japan), Akiko Nakata (Nabokov Society of Japan), Fred Neubauer (Einhard Foundation), Will Norman, Mitsuyoshi Numano (Nabokov Society of Japan), Stephen Jan Parker (including as editor of *The Nabokovian*), Rodney Phillips (then of the New York Public Library), Robert Michael Pyle, Stanley J. Rabinowitz, Stanislas Shvabrin, Claudio Soares, Vadim Stark (then of the Institute of Russian Literature and Art, St. Petersburg), Mio Suda (*Gunzo*), Anthony Uhlmann

(Australasian Association for Literature), Deanne Urmy (then of Beacon Press), Frédéric Verger (*La Revue des Deux Mondes*), Olga Voronina (then of the Vladimir Nabokov Museum, St. Petersburg), Tadashi Wakashima (Nabokov Society of Japan), Duncan White, Robert Wilson (*American Scholar*), Dieter E. Zimmer, and Irene Zohrab (*New Zealand Slavonic Journal*). There are many other Nabokovian friends, including some of the most gifted, distinguished, and treasured, with whom I have exchanged ideas and information or from whom I have received invitations, whose names are not listed here only because space is finite and gratitude endless, and because I do not remember specific debts to them in any of *these* pieces. But for other debts, friendship, and common interests, you are certainly included in the dedication, after Bronwen, to whom I owe most.

ABBREVIATIONS

Books by Vladimir Nabokov unless otherwise noted. For full bibliographical details, see the bibliography.

Ada	*Ada or Ardor: A Family Chronicle*
BS	*Bend Sinister*
CE	*Conclusive Evidence*
DBDV	*Dear Bunny, Dear Volodya: The Nabokov-Wilson Letters, 1940–1971*
EO	Alexander Pushkin, *Eugene Onegin*, trans. with commentary by Vladimir Nabokov
Gift	*The Gift*
IB	*Invitation to a Beheading*
KQK	*King, Queen, Knave*
LAS	*Lolita: A Screenplay*
LATH	*Look at the Harlequins!*
LDQ	*Lectures on* Don Quixote
LL	*Lectures on Literature*
Lolita	*The Annotated Lolita*, ed. Alfred Appel Jr. (1st ed., 1970)
LRL	*Lectures on Russian Literature*
MUSSR	*The Man from the USSR and Other Plays*
NAPC	Brian Boyd, *Nabokov's* Ada: *The Place of Consciousness* (2nd ed., 2001)
NG	*Nikolay Gogol*
NPFMAD	Brian Boyd, *Nabokov's* Pale Fire: *The Magic of Artistic Discovery*
N'sBs	*Nabokov's Butterflies*
PF	*Pale Fire*
PP	*Poems and Problems*

RLSK	*The Real Life of Sebastian Knight*
SIC	*The Song of Igor's Campaign.*
SL	*Selected Letters, 1940–1977*
SM	*Speak, Memory* (1967)
SO	*Strong Opinions'*
SoVN	*Stories of Vladimir Nabokov*
TT	*Transparent Things*
VNA	Vladimir Nabokov Archive, Henry W. and Albert A. Berg Collection, New York Public Library
VNAY	Brian Boyd, *Vladimir Nabokov: The American Years*
VNRY	Brian Boyd, *Vladimir Nabokov: The Russian Years*

INTRODUCTION

I was born two generations after Vladimir Nabokov. A butterfly location label in the Cornell Lepidoptera collection tells me that on the day of my birth, at Scout Creek near the "altogether enchanting little town of Afton," Wyoming (*SO* 323), Nabokov stalked and caught a female of a butterfly of a new subspecies he had named three years earlier (*Lycaeides argyrognomon longinus* Nabokov 1949).[1] That day, I could express myself only by squalling, but Nabokov almost certainly added to the manuscript of *Lolita*, perhaps even the passage in the Men's Room of the Enchanted Hunters Hotel— "There a person in clerical black—a 'hearty party' *comme on dit*—checking with the assistance of Vienna, if it was still there, inquired of me how I had liked Dr. Boyd's talk, and looked puzzled when I (King Sigmund the Second) said Boyd was quite a boy"—or the fatal passage describing the next morning: "and for some minutes I miserably dozed, and Charlotte was a mermaid in a greenish tank, and somewhere in the passage Dr. Boyd said 'Good morning to you' in a fruity voice, and birds were busy in the trees, and then Lolita yawned" (*Lolita* 127, 134).[2]

In high school, long before I became Dr. Boyd, I began reading Nabokov so intensely that his way of seeing the world partly shaped mine. I started a doctoral dissertation on his work while he was still alive, but to my shock and consternation learned that he was not time-proof and that I would be writing most of it after his death. For Véra Nabokov I catalogued the paper pile he had left behind in Montreux, Switzerland, and for his biography I followed his trail across Russia, England, Western Europe, and America. Since completing the biography I have explored new fields, but Nabokov keeps pulling me back. By now I have published a pile of my own on him, some of it well known, some not. When recently I had reason to consult one of my less well-known efforts, I decided others might like to see this stuff.

Lately literary critics and scholars tend to avoid a single-author focus, partly because authors have been downgraded as the causes of literary works. That's a mistake, I think:[3] nothing like "The Library of Babel," *Lolita*, or *Waiting for Godot* would have been written in the mid-twentieth century or at any other time had Borges, Nabokov, and Beckett not lived, even had history otherwise run the same course. Nabokov famously denied the influence of any other writer on him and thought "the climate of thought" an "unbelievably spooky" notion (*SO* 128). But for all his insistence on independence he did not suppose writers were self-generated. They owed much, as he knew, to purposes, standards, and tools developed and refined over the ages, and to the boldness of past genius inspiring future risks (see this volume, chapter 15, "Nabokov, Pushkin, Shakespeare: Genius, Generosity, and Gratitude in *The Gift* and *Pale Fire*").

The best criticism, too, is highly individual but also part of highly social processes, and that's another thread that runs through these pieces. Criticism is cooperative: we want to understand the same works, and we learn from others both specific information and ways of understanding and appreciating. And it is competitive: we want to challenge others whose claims we find wrong, and we want *our* efforts and results to be recognized. In my work on evolution and literature, the one line of research after Nabokov I have so far had time to pursue to something near satisfaction, I have explored the interplay of the individual and the social, the collaborative and the competitive, the original insight or the independent effort and the traditions and institutions that make the insight and effort possible and worthwhile.

Another thread running through *Stalking Nabokov* is the range that specialization can entail. Specialists may become too narrow, but Nabokov himself wonderfully evoked to his literature students the magic of discovery that specialization could allow:

The more things we know the better equipped we are to understand any one thing and it is a burning pity that our lives are not long enough and sufficiently free of annoying obstacles, to study all things with the same care and depth as the one we now devote to some favorite subject or period. And yet there is a semblance of consolation within this dismal state of affairs: in the same way as the whole universe may be completely reciprocated in the structure of an atom, . . . an intelligent and assiduous student [may] find a small replica of all knowledge in a subject he has chosen for his special research. . . . and if, upon choosing your subject, you try diligently to find out about it, if you *allow* yourself to be lured into the shaded lanes that lead from the main road you have chosen to the lovely and little known nooks of special knowledge, if you lovingly finger the links of the many chains that connect your subject to the past and the future and if by luck you hit on some scrap of knowledge referring to your subject that has not yet become common knowledge, then you will know the true felicity of the great adventure of learning, and your years in this college will become a valuable start on a road of inestimable happiness.

(*N'sBs* 399)

In his eight years as a professional scientist in the Museum of Comparative Zoology, Nabokov focused on one family of butterflies, the Plebejinae or Blues, and found it hard to tear himself away from the microscope just as, in the next decade, he found it hard to stop researching Pushkin's *Eugene Onegin* ("but what things I'm finding, what discoveries I'm making")[4] until he had amassed over a thousand pages of annotations. He had different specializations—Lepidoptera, literary scholarship and translation, chess problems, and literary composition—and each required a multitude of approaches: in the case of Lepidoptera, for instance, taxonomy, morphology, ecology (and the botany of food plants), geography, evolution; in his literary art, at various times, subordinate specializations, in the life of Nikolay Chernyshevsky, late-nineteenth-century Russian naturalists' explorations of Central Asia, pubescent American girls and their culture, Nordic lore, orchids, the philosophy of time. In the same way, a research specialization like mine on Nabokov has required language learning, interpretation, annotation, bibliography, translation, forays into many literatures and into history, geography, philosophy, science, and psychology. It has meant the continued excitement of discovery; travels to five continents; meetings with the Nabokov family and writers, publishers, scientists, scholars, and librarians who worked with or after him; dialogues with readers famous and obscure; documentary filming; naming new butterflies; and even a law trial. And the best antidote to the confines of one kind specialization can be to follow orthogonal lines of specialization: in my case, Shakespeare, partly as a comparison and contrast to Nabokov within literature and as an alternative delight; as a contrast and comparison to Nabokov within twentieth-century thought, the philosopher Karl Popper, with *his* specializations in the philosophy of science, physics, music, and social philosophy and his preference for ideas over words;

narrative, from Homer and Genesis to the present, across all modes, from epics to comics; and literature and evolution, which has meant exploring across arts and eras and into biology, anthropology, and many fields of psychology. Readers of *Stalking Nabokov* will see these other specializations from time to time crossing my Nabokov trail and offering glimpses of other vistas.

Brian Boyd
Auckland
December 24, 2009

Stalking Nabokov

THE WRITER'S LIFE
AND THE LIFE WRITER

1. A Centennial Toast

In the wake of my Nabokov biographies (*Vladimir Nabokov: The Russian Years*, 1990, *Vladimir Nabokov: The American Years*, 1991), people surfaced with links to Nabokov that I had not traced. Through my work with lepidopterists who had known Nabokov or specialized in the same butterfly families as he had, I learned of John Downey, the expert in the Blues a generation after Nabokov. As a biology student driving a mining truck for his summer job, Downey had met Nabokov collecting butterflies on the slopes of the Wasatch Mountains in 1943, an encounter that inspired him to become a specialist in the Blues himself. Discovering this incident allowed me to reflect on Nabokov as writer and man at a Nabokov Centenary Celebration organized by the PEN American Center, the *New Yorker*, and Vintage Books, on April 15, 1999, at the Town Hall in New York (with Martin Amis, Alfred Appel Jr., Richard Ford, Joyce Carol Oates, and others). That summer, another celebration took place, at the end of a conference at Jesus College, Cambridge, organized by Jane Grayson of the School of Slavonic and Eastern European Studies at the University of London: a centennial dinner in the Hall of Trinity College, Cambridge, where Nabokov dined in his Trinity years (1919–1922). Asked to deliver the centennial toast, I slightly expanded the New York talk.

I would like us all to fix in our minds a famous image captured by Dmitri Nabokov's camera: his father in shorts, bare-chested, with butterfly net at the ready, on a Swiss mountainside, underneath an azure sky. I want us to be able to picture just who it is we are toasting—and not to be distracted by another famous figure showing off *his* famous legs.[1] We shall return in a moment to the man in shorts.

In a much-quoted passage from *Speak, Memory* Nabokov describes a chess problem he composed in such a way that the relationship between composer and solver serves as an analogy for the relationship between author and reader that he aims for in his fiction: an immediate pleasure for the "naïve" solver (the "thesis" of the problem, in the Hegelian terms he invokes); the "pleasurable torments" awaiting the "would-be sophisticated solver" who realizes there's more to the problem (the "antithesis"); and the rush of surprise and delight awaiting the "super-sophisticated solver" who reaches the problem's deepest solution (the "synthesis") (*SM* 290–92). Writing my biography of Nabokov I did not discover in time an incident that I think offers a similar kind of analogy to his literary work, but in terms of butterflies, not chess.

In 1943 a biology student named John Downey was working in his summer vacation in the mountains of Utah. Driving a coal truck one day up the steep Cottonwood Canyon, he found he had to stop every so often to let the engine cool down. After pulling over at a bend, and opening the truck's hood, he noticed a man in shorts and sneakers with no shirt coming down the road with a net in his hand. As the man passed, Downey called out, "Hullo. Whatcha doing? Collecting insects?" The man gave a sharp glance at this stranger covered in coal dust, said nothing, and continued down the road at the same brisk pace. Downey fell in behind him: "'I'm a collector too!' This got a millisecond glance, and one raised eyebrow, as he strolled along. 'I collect *butterflies*.' . . . This rated . . . another raised eyebrow, if not a slight nod of the head; but still no sound, nor slowing of his pace."

"Finally," Downey recalls,

a nymphalid [butterfly] . . . flitted across the road. "What's that?" he asked. I gave him the scientific name as best as I could remember. . . . His pace didn't slacken, but an eyebrow stayed higher a little longer this time. Yet another butterfly crossed the road. "What's that?" says he. I gave him a name, a little less sure of myself, particularly since he had not confirmed the correctness of my first identification. "Hm!" was his only response. A third test specimen crossed his vision, and "What's that?" I gave him my best idea and to my surprise he stopped, put out his arm, and said, "Hello! I'm Vladimir Nabokov."[2]

During the 1940s, while on a research fellowship at Harvard's Museum of Comparative Zoology, Nabokov made himself *the* authority on American Blue butterflies. After completing his major monograph, and no longer needing the stack of index cards he had assembled on the Blues, he sent them on to Downey. In fact, his kindness helped Downey settle on his field of specialization: Downey became the American authority on the Blues in the generation after Nabokov, and his student, Kurt Johnson, has now become the American authority on the Blues for a third generation. With colleagues on three other continents, especially Zsolt Bálint of Hungary and Dubi Benyamini of Chile, he honors Nabokov's pioneer work on the Latin American Blues by naming newly discovered species after his fiction: *humbert* and *lolita*, *luzhin* and *pnin*, *kinbote* and *shade*, *ada* and *hazelea*, and many, many more.[3]

What strikes me about Nabokov's encounter with Downey in Cottonwood Canyon is the demands he makes, the conditions he imposes, on this grimy truck driver: You can walk with me, but I will test you a little. If you pass the test, I will let you see who I am, and I will even offer you all that I have found, so that you can go on to make *your* discoveries in turn. As much as the chess problem, the story suggests Nabokov's demanding but ultimately generous relationship to his readers, which reflects his sense of the demanding but ultimately generous world that life offers us.

That seems to me the key to Nabokov. He was a maximalist: someone who appreciated, as much as anyone has, the riches the world offers, in nature and art, in sensation, emotion, thought, and language, and the *surprise* of these riches, if we animate them with all our attention and imagination. Yet at the same time he felt that all this was not enough, because he could readily imagine a far ampler freedom beyond the limits within which he feels human consciousness is trapped.

He celebrates with unique precision and passion the delights of the visible and tangible world, the tenderness and force of human feelings and relationships, the treasures of memory: the thetic pleasures of life, if you like. He planned to call his first novel *Happiness*—until he realized that might perhaps be just a little too unguarded.

Yet Nabokov also has a deserved reputation for his acid imagination, his savage irony, his trenchant ability to deflate, to register disappointments, humiliations, and horrors. His stories offer endless evidence of the comic, ironic, tragic limitations of human life, and he never lets us forget the absurdity of the very conditions of the human mind: of the solitary confinement of the self, as he defines one central aspect of his work, or of the prison of time, as he defines another.[4] At this level Nabokov registers the "antithetic torments" of life and writes books entitled not *Happiness* but *Laughter in the Dark* or *Despair*.

But readers who stop there, and think that *he* stops there, in modernist irony or a postmodernist *abîme*, miss altogether his positive irony, his attempt to encompass all the negatives, as he suspects life itself does, and reverse their direction in the mirror of death. The search for that possibility is what makes Nabokov different and what makes him write. He believes that the fullness and the complexity of life suggest worlds within worlds within worlds, and he builds his own imagined universes to match. Although we cannot see his hidden worlds at first, he allows us to find our own way to them, just as he thinks whatever lies behind life invites us to an endless adventure of discovery in and beyond life. At this "synthetic" level, Nabokov writes books with titles like *The Gift*, whose hero in turn thinks of writing "a practical handbook: *How to Be Happy*" (*Gift* 340).

"Examples," Nabokov says, "are the stained-glass windows of knowledge" (*SO* 312). I must offer at least one tiny example, not a stained-glass window, but a window even more out of the ordinary, in the opening of John Shade's poem "Pale Fire," in Nabokov's most perfect novel:

> I was the shadow of the waxwing slain
> By the false azure in the windowpane;
> I was the smudge of ashen fluff—and I
> Lived on, flew on, in the reflected sky.

Within this radiant image Nabokov epitomizes his lifelong attention to the particulars of this world and his lifelong desire to have the imagination suggest a way past the world's limits. All his life Shade, like Nabokov, has enjoyed the things of this world and yet searched for something outside the prisons of the self and of time. Here he projects himself into another creature, as it flies, as it dies, and then as he imagines it soaring on in the blue beyond that, in fact, it is death to meet. But behind the immediate "thetic" pleasure of the image, we find ourselves as we *re*-read *Pale Fire* in the "pleasurable torments" of the antithetic phase, haunted and tantalized by the enigmatic relation between Shade's reflected azure here and Kinbote's "blue inenubilable Zembla," that "land of reflections." And if we peer still deeper, we can, as we *re*-re-read, reach the exhilarating discoveries of the synthetic level, as we gradually detect a dozen concealed patterns linking this opening couplet to the rest of the novel, each pattern with its own far-reaching implications.[5]

Like life, Nabokov's art dazzles on the surface, but, like life, it also hides far more behind. Far from mocking and frustrating his audience, he allows us the chance to discover more for ourselves in his work and in our world than any other author I have ever encountered. And his generosity to his readers matches and reenacts and pays tribute to what he senses is the generosity of our world.

Nabokov loved even the little things in life; he could be fascinated and entranced by a row of 9s turning into a row of 0s on an odometer in *Lolita* or, more elegantly, in the line 999 that leads back to line 1 or on to line 1000 of *Pale Fire*, whose three zeros ultimately become a triple infinity. Now that he has turned a hundred, now that he has reached triple figures in a year that will end by turning into a triple zero, it's time to give him thanks:

Thanks for offering an unblinking optimism in this century of blinkered pessimism; for giving us, in Beckett's bizarrely buoyant phrase, "such pleasure that pleasure was not the word";[6] for extending the bounds of what had seemed possible in language and thought, in art and in life, in words and observations and images, in characters and stories and worlds; for making such demands on us and yet being so accessible to us, for inviting us in; for making us perform better than we thought we could and yet also showing us how we sometimes fall short, and how we might do still better; for reminding us how little any of us knows and yet how much we can discover, and how much we all, singly and as a species, still have to find out about life's— and art's—endless surprises.

At the age of twenty-two Nabokov sent his mother a little poem with the comment that it would prove to her "that my mood is as radiant as ever. If I live to be a hundred, my spirit will still go round in short trousers."[7] Back at that age even Nabokov, for all his youthful ambition, would have been astonished to learn how much he would achieve by the time he turned one hundred. Let's raise our glasses to the man whose spirit still wanders around in short trousers: to Vladimir Nabokov.

2. A Biographer's Life

In the years after the Nabokov biography, I was often asked to talk about the experience of researching and writing it. The full talk reached its more or less final form when, on being awarded the Einhard Prize for Biography, on March 17, 2001, I spoke to citizens of the charming medieval town of Seligenstadt, Germany, to which Einhard, a courtier at Charlemagne's court, had retired to write the first life of Charlemagne. I focused on the tribulations and trials of researching Nabokov's life, especially in the unwelcoming world of Soviet Russia, and on the difficulties of intellectual biography. I had spent the previous few years researching the life of Karl Popper and did not realize how long a diversion from that project my work on literature and evolution, begun the previous year, would require.

As a little boy living in a small beach settlement twelve thousand miles from Europe I think I had heard of Charlemagne, but never would I have expected to be awarded a prize in memory of his first biographer.

Einhard not only knew and worked with Charlemagne for decades but also knew the Europe Charlemagne ruled over. I never met Vladimir Nabokov, whose biography I began working on twenty years ago, or another Karl der Grosse, Karl Popper, whose biography I am working on now. I suppose my life at least overlapped theirs, but they lived at the opposite end of the world from me, and they grew up, not in a sandy fibrolite cottage by the sea but at the center of the capitals of Europe's two cosmopolitan continental empires, Russia and Austro-Hungary. Their fathers had libraries of over ten thousand volumes apiece; there was not even a public library in our little settlement. Nabokov and Popper were heirs to the best traditions of European art and thought; I grew up in a country that no humans had yet set eyes on at the time when Einhard gave his cathedral to Seligenstadt, and in the "modern" provincialism of the 1950s, I felt that anything not of the here and now, like the Ireland where I had been born or even the past itself, was not only remote but somehow embarrassing. How on earth did I become a biographer?

How does anyone? First, it might seem, you catch your hare, you choose your subject. But that already presupposes you want to be a biographer. There are distinguished biographers, like Michael Holroyd and Richard Holmes, who began with a passion for biography as a genre, a passion that led them sooner or later even to write biographies of biographers. But perhaps most of us who write biographies begin with a passionate interest in a particular person, and as we ask, what sort of work would best serve my interest in him or her, we suddenly wonder: why not a biography?

For Nabokov, that was certainly my case. I did not choose him; he chose me when I was sixteen. I wrote an essay on Nabokov in my first year at university, when I was seventeen, and then an MA thesis and a doctoral dissertation. I have published thousands of pages *on* him and edited thousands more *by* him. I have tried many times to stop writing about him, but although he has been dead for a quarter of a century, he keeps on setting me new assignments, making me offers I cannot refuse.

Popper, on the other hand, I decided to write about because I already had biography in mind. The two cases could not be more different. I have yet to publish a word on Popper, and although he has been called by one Nobel Prize winner "incomparably the greatest philosopher of science there has ever been," I have never formally studied either philosophy or science.[1] After enjoying so much writing the Nabokov biography, I looked around for another literary figure to write about: a twentieth-century writer, not yet the subject of a good biography, significant enough to keep me passionately interested for the years of work a biography takes. I thought of writer after writer I liked, but none seemed *quite* worth the effort. Popper I had thought of years before, but I had heard that someone else was writing his biography. And I was glad of the fact, as I knew that although I loved his work I didn't have the preparation: German, philosophy, physics, for instance, not to mention Greek, mathematics, music. Somehow, though, his name wouldn't go away, and when I learned that the person who had been writing his biography had died with the project still very far from completion, I found I had not the strength or the sense to resist.

Like Nabokov, Popper had fascinated me from my high school days. Just as well. It can be liberating but also perhaps limiting to have your mind colonized by somebody else at an early age. If you let it happen, you should make sure the person whose spell you fall under is someone with a multifaceted genius, like Nabokov, who worked in Russian, English, and French, as an artist, a scientist, and even a chess composer of world class. And *then* you need a corrective, an alternative, someone to expand your mental horizons in very different directions, and that I found in Popper. Nabokov has been called the greatest novelist of the twentieth century, ahead even of Joyce, and Popper, the greatest philosopher of the century, ahead of Russell or Wittgenstein. But although they overlapped for three quarters of the century they never knew each other and, as far as I know, never even knew *of* each other. Nabokov loved words and hated ideas, or so he said (he meant other people's ideas); Popper loved ideas and hated words. Nabokov found step-by-step argument tiresome; Popper thought the firm tread of logic would always lead us to the brink of new questions, to challenge what we thought we knew. Nabokov loved the world of human experience but felt trapped by not knowing what lies beyond it; Popper insisted only on what was humanly knowable.

I have a student working on a Ph.D. on Nabokov and humor, for Nabokov, after all, was one of the funniest writers of all time. Popper, however, was one of the most serious of thinkers. My Ph.D. student brought me one day an account from a book he had been reading on humor. Someone recalled Popper launching straight into a lecture without the usual joke to relax the audience and not realizing, because he was so intent on the intellectual problem he was trying to solve, that he had failed to connect with the large crowd. Only when he made a slip of the tongue, halfway through the lecture, did the audience at last laugh and relax and open up. So if *I* seem unclear about where I'm headed, you'll know why: Nabokov and Popper are tugging me in opposite directions.

Once you have decided you will write someone's biography, you need to be sure about what others think and know and have written on the subject. What do you want to convince your audience of? Nabokov was widely accepted as one of the great stylists of all time but many thought him rather heartless, with nothing to say, only a brilliant way of saying it. For me, that was quite wrong: he seemed as dazzlingly new as he was because he had such an original and profound way of looking at and responding to his world and because he had gradually found ways original enough to express the full originality of his thought.

Popper was dismissed as either hopelessly radical, denying us any secure knowledge, or hopelessly conservative, rendered outmoded by those since him who showed the irrationality even of what had seemed our most rational pursuit, science. But for me, Popper is the first to describe accurately our state of constantly expanding but always fallible conjectural knowledge. We may sometimes think that we know what we know beyond question, but only because we have not yet discovered what we have not been imaginative enough to realize we do not yet know.

For all that I have stressed the differences between Nabokov and Popper, they also share a sense of gratitude for a world of inexhaustible discovery and endless surprise, a sense of how much has already been discovered and how little, how precarious all that is compared with what we still want to know. Although both were buffeted by the horrors of twentieth-century history, they always swam against the century's prevailing current of fashionable pessimism. Because they were so much at odds with their times, they earned worldwide reputations yet seemed not to be appreciated at the level their work deserved. Biography would offer me a chance to invite the widest possible audience to consider or reconsider their work and their lives.

Once you know not only that you want to write a biography but *why* you want to write it, the real work starts. Although I have researched Popper's life in sixteen countries so far, I know I have only scratched the surface, so from here on I will confine myself to Nabokov. First, you have to locate likely materials and try to obtain access to them.

In Nabokov's case, that was easy. After I finished my Ph.D., I was obliged by the terms of my scholarship to return from Canada to New Zealand. During the Ph.D., I had needed to track down all that Nabokov had written and had discovered that the existing Nabokov bibliography, by Andrew Field, was terribly flawed.[2] As I completed the thesis, I thought that if I could now compile a full bibliography and could add to it whatever I could find about Nabokov's circumstances at the time of writing each work, I could also compensate for the avoidance of fact in the existing Nabokov biography, also by Field.[3] So before returning to New Zealand, I visited the major research libraries in the northeastern United States. Nabokov always insisted that writers should destroy their manuscripts, since only the finished work counted. Scholars had taken that at face value and had not expected there would be anything to find, but I discovered rich materials in the Library of Congress and at Columbia, Cornell, Yale, and elsewhere.

Because my scholarship had ended and I had no money saved after ten years as a student, I bought a monthly Greyhound bus pass. This allowed unlimited travel on Greyhound buses for a surprisingly low fee. To save on accommodation costs, I turned the buses into my hotel. I would work in, say, the Cornell Library all day, and if I didn't need to travel to another library next day, I would still take an interstate bus southward and sit in the bus processing the day's material until midnight, get off the bus at two A.M., and take another bus back north to arrive back at the library at opening time again, not very fresh or very clean but young enough to be still full of energy. I kept that up for two months.

Meanwhile, the Nabokov scholar and Russian-language publisher Carl Proffer, who had examined my Ph.D. thesis, had sent it on to Véra Nabokov. After reading it, she wrote, inviting me to visit her. I had been planning to return to New Zealand across the Pacific but instead flew via Europe and spent four days in Montreux, pumping her with questions until way past what I later learned was her usual bedtime. She discovered from my questions that I knew much about Nabokov's bibliography and his life that no one else but she knew. Two months later she wrote to me asking if I would like to catalogue her husband's archives. It took me a whole loud heartbeat to decide to accept the invitation. I spent two Southern Hemisphere summers or Northern Hemisphere winters sorting out the archives for her while also working on the materials for my bibliography project.

Véra Nabokov was a very private person and, as she was the first to admit, distrustful by nature. She and Nabokov had been badly hurt by their experience with Andrew Field, whose biography of Nabokov had been riddled with envious rivalry, wild guesses, and astonishing errors (he managed to date the Russian Revolution to 1916 and even defended the date when challenged). After Field, I thought Véra would simply not agree to another biography. But once, when she was trying to deflect my insistent requests to be allowed access to Nabokov's letters to his mother, she said to me: "Why do you need to see those, if you're writing only a bibliography? Of course, if you were writing a biography, I would show you everything." I gulped but said nothing: I was a young academic with new courses to teach and no time to write a biography. But I applied for a fellowship and as soon as I was awarded it, I wrote to her reminding her of her words. She could not deny them, and she let me begin. I saw her every day for a year and a half as I worked through the papers in Montreux, but she did not relax her guard. She did not speak to me on first-name terms until after she read the draft of my first chapter, five years after we first met. Much later, in her last year of life when she found the very act of reading had become physically painful for her, I was touched to see that she still kept the biography by her bedside to reread just for pleasure.

For the biography of a living figure, or one not long dead, earning the trust of the subject or the heirs is crucial if you wish to have access to materials and contacts. Of course you also need to maintain intellectual independence at the same time as you sustain trust. That's a delicate task, especially for someone as naturally critical and undiplomatic as I am. Although she had her own strong opinions, Véra respected my independence, partly because she knew how enthusiastic I was about Nabokov, although I could also be bluntly disapproving when I didn't think his work reached his usual standards.

But there is perhaps a more insistent kind of control exerted by your dead subject. If you respect your subject, then you want to respect his or her sense of what matters, as well as your own. Nabokov had an astonishing memory and a no less extraordinary ability to evoke his memories in words. He was reluctant for anything about him to be expressed in ways that differed from his own recollections or formulations. He would ask for interviews to be submitted in writing, and he would answer them in writing and then check the interview in proofs. He could not check *my* material, but his sense of the importance of precise and evocative detail certainly exerted one kind of control over my work. Now, in writing about Popper, I have an opposite kind of pressure since Popper preferred argument to story, ideas to words, explanatory laws to descriptive details, and I will have to resist those preferences without, of course, ignoring the ideas, just as in writing about Nabokov I had to spell out the ideas that he only ever wanted to suggest with the utmost insouciance.

Many a modern biographer must face a problem Einhard never had to contend with. Anyone famous enough to merit a biography is likely nowadays not merely to know how to write, unlike Charlemagne, but to have already written an autobiography. As a biographer, you welcome an autobiography, but you do not want merely to repeat it. Fortunately, autobiographers rarely tell all. Nabokov, with his fierce sense of privacy, refrained from discussing any living person other than himself but movingly ends *Speak, Memory* by addressing its last chapters increasingly overtly to an unnamed "you" that we realize must be his wife. Popper, with his resolute focus on ideas, at one point in *his* autobiography mentions that he has a wife, quickly apologizes for becoming so personal, and moves on.

Just how do you situate your own effort in relation to your subject's "official" life story, especially when it's a performance as superlative as *Speak, Memory*? I adopted two different solutions to the problem: first, to interpret *Speak, Memory* as a work of art—and to show how the artistry, the transforming imagination of the writer, in fact can reveal *more* about Nabokov than a more direct transcription from life would do; and, second, to ferret out those direct transcriptions, the raw facts behind the art, the things that Nabokov would rather we didn't know.

Although Nabokov was often hailed as the finest stylist of his time, many readers have found themselves perturbed by the deliberateness of his style. To them, his phrasing calls attention to itself too much to express genuine emotion or even to *say* anything. I try to show how wrong that is by opening the biography with a close look at one sentence, the end of the first chapter of *Speak, Memory*. There, Nabokov anticipates the day he would look down at his father lying in an open coffin. Again and again throughout his autobiography Nabokov returns obliquely to his father's murder as if it were a wound he cannot leave alone but can hardly bear to touch. For Nabokov the love of those closest to the heart—a parent, a spouse, a child—distends the soul to dwarf all other feeling. The narrowly focused love that marked his life also shapes his fiction, whether positively or negatively, in the desolation of love's absence or the horror of its sham surrogates. Because love matters so much to Nabokov, so, too, does loss. But he had learned from his parents to bear distress with dignity, and when he depicts his father high in the midday air he alludes to his private grief with the restraint taught him as a child. The formality and apparent distance in no way diminish the emotion: he simply feels that even a sense of loss sharp enough to last a lifetime must be met with courage and self-control.

I linger over that sentence to show qualities of mind and tendencies of thought that pervade Nabokov's life and art. But it's enough here to note that he thought that sentence was as much as he could bring himself to write about his father's death. He would *never* have wanted to publish his intensely personal diary account of his and his mother's reaction to the news his father had been shot. But that poignant, heartbreaking document was something I just had to quote in full in the biography (chapter 19 in this volume, "*Speak, Memory*: The Life and the Art," juxtaposes the sentence from *Speak, Memory* and the diary entry). Because I had earned Véra's trust, I had access to that diary even without asking. But the problem of finding materials and of the unevenness of the materials for different phases of a life, are not usually so easily solved.

Each epoch of Nabokov's life presented its own special problems. In 1917, when his family fled Petrograd for the Crimea, and again when they fled the Crimea for London in 1919, they had to leave almost everything of their Russian years behind. Data for the first twenty years of Nabokov's life, other than what he provided in *Speak, Memory*, were extremely difficult to collect, especially as I was researching in the Soviet Union in the days before *glasnost'*, when Nabokov was still persona non grata. I had to travel out to Vyra, the Nabokov family estate, which was further from Leningrad than I was legally entitled to go. On my second excursion to Vyra, I spent the whole day taking photographs. A local came up to me about four o'clock, by which time everybody in the Soviet countryside seemed to be drunk. "How did you get here?" he asked, seeing I was a foreigner and taking photo after photo. He seemed to think that *I* thought the birches and the firs were well-camouflaged missiles. I played the innocent: "By train and bus"—as if I had simply hopped on the wrong ones by accident. We were standing on the bridge across the Oredezh, the river Nabokov had boated on with his first love, the "Tamara" of *Speak, Memory*. The man's face flushed with anger; he leaned toward me, until vodka drowned out the smells of summer. "What are you doing here?" Mention of Nabokov's name might have doomed me—oh, I wouldn't have been thrown into a gulag, but I might have been ejected from the country or at least grilled by the KGB, as had happened to friends much less objectionable than me. I had noticed a police car pass along the highway a few minutes ago and thought my newfound comrade would be shouting for the police again any second now. Then I suddenly realized there was a way out. Nabokov's grandmother's manor house, on the other side of the river, had also been burnt down, but there was a plaque commemorating the fact that the estate had once belonged to Kondraty Ryleev. Ryleev, like the other Decembrists, had been accorded sainthood by the Soviets as a sacred precursor to their holy revolution. So I told my interrogator—it was true enough, though a very small crumb of the truth—"I came to see Ryleev's house." "*Molodets!*" he cried (something like, "You little hero!"), and he embraced me: "You're one of us!" I nearly passed out from relief and from the fumes of his home-brew vodka.

That trip to Vyra told me that, despite Nabokov's quite justified reputation for an extraordinary memory, his own map of the three Nabokov estates in the endpapers of *Speak, Memory* was wrong—as his sister had to concede when I pointed it out. I checked what I could independently of *Speak, Memory*, but for the most part I simply had to rely for that period of his life on Nabokov's own memoirs and to interpret them for all they were worth. I should add that new material for those early years has turned up since *glasnost'* and then the fall of the Soviet system and appears in the French, German, and Russian editions, but not in the English.

For the next two decades of Nabokov's life, from 1919 to 1940, the émigré years, the task was even harder. After devoting twelve chapters of *Speak, Memory* to his childhood, Nabokov allowed himself only three chapters for the émigré years. I was on my own. By the beginning of the 1930s many in the Russian emigration sensed that Nabokov already outshone the acknowledged star of émigré writing, Ivan Bunin, soon to receive Russia's first Nobel Prize for Literature. Throughout the remainder of the decade Nabokov consolidated his position as one of the greatest Russian writers of the century. As German tanks rolled through France in mid-1940, he and his Russian-Jewish wife fled once again. By the time the war ended, the audience and culture Nabokov had written for no longer existed, and its records were either bombed by the Allies (in Berlin), confiscated by the Soviet occupation (in Prague), or destroyed by the Germans—as were many of the papers and a butterfly collection that Nabokov left in Paris with his friend, Ilya Fondaminsky, who was also destroyed.

For this period, I had to search through scores of Russian émigré newspapers and journals where Nabokov's work was published or his name mentioned in a review or the report of a public reading. A single copy of a newspaper, its acidic pages brittle enough to flake at every touch, might contain the only record of a particular event in Nabokov's life. For just one of the most precious newspapers, I had to travel to Helsinki, Uppsala, Lund, Prague, East and West Berlin, Munich, Paris, New York, and Palo Alto to find every issue I could.

Nabokov spent the next two decades in the United States, following four careers more or less simultaneously: writer, teacher, scientist, literary scholar. There are thousands who knew him as a teacher at Stanford, Wellesley, Cornell, and Harvard, but most had no idea he had been famous as a Russian writer and would be famous again as an English one, and so took no special notice.

In Nabokov's first English novel, *The Real Life of Sebastian Knight*, V's search for the past of his half-brother, the novelist Sebastian Knight, becomes a comic nightmare of frustrations, dead ends, and wrong trails because he has no access to the secrets of Sebastian's life—until a magical character who has escaped from one of Sebastian's stories suddenly offers him the kinds of clues sober reality would never have provided. At the end of one chapter, V has visited a friend of his brother's at Cambridge. Just as he leaves his brother's friend, a sudden voice calls out from the mist: "Sebastian Knight? Who is speaking of Sebastian Knight?" There the chapter ends, and the next begins:

The stranger who uttered these words now approached—Oh, how I sometimes yearn for the easy swing of a well-oiled novel! How comfortable it would have been had the voice belonged to some cheery old don with long downy ear-lobes and that puckering about the eyes which stands for wisdom and humour. . . . A handy character, a welcome passer-by who had also known my hero, but from a different angle. "And now," he would say, "I am going to tell you the real story of Sebastian Knight's college years." And then and there he would have launched on that story. But alas, nothing of the kind really happened. That Voice in the Mist rang out in the dimmest passage of my mind. It was but the echo of some possible truth, a timely reminder: don't be too certain of learning the past from the lips of the present. Beware of the most honest broker. Remember that what you are told is really threefold: shaped by the teller, reshaped by the listener, concealed from both by the dead man of the tale.

(RLSK 52)

This was advice I kept in mind. One of the most distinguished of American literary scholars told me of the time he was walking along the corridors of Cornell's Goldwin Smith Hall with his arm in a sling. Other colleagues joshed him about skiing accidents and the like; Nabokov hailed him with an ebullient and delighted "Ah! a duel!" And then I found out that the incident had not happened to this particular professor at all because another professor almost as well known told me in minute detail of the circumstances—and the first professor, I had noticed, had a memory that seemed fuzzy in the extreme away from the books he still remembered with wonderful lucidity. He had simply heard the tale told and in the retelling had forgotten it was not his own memory. And yet this was a great scholar, and Nabokov's colleague for years. You can imagine that along with the masses of anecdote I garnered for Nabokov's American years from those who had stood at the toilet beside him (I kid you not) or heard him in the lecture hall or passed him in the corridor or knew somebody who had passed him once, I was also treated to masses of garbling, misconstruction, and decomposing gossip.

In his last two decades—from 1959 to 1977, to be precise—Nabokov could afford to retire from Cornell and live in a Swiss luxury hotel. He was an international celebrity, his face on the cover of *Newsweek* and *Time*, his books the hottest property on the high literary market, but at the same time he withdrew from the public gaze to the controlled seclusion of his retreat in Montreux, Switzerland. He constructed a literary persona of intimidating arrogance and protested in letters to editors against factual inaccuracies or infringements of his privacy. And although he was interviewed for *Vogue*, *Life*, *Playboy*, *People*, and American and European TV, he agreed to interviews only if the questions were submitted in writing well ahead of time so that he could craft his answers in writing, too. There were advantages of the steadiness of his life in these years—I could interview his secretary and the concierge and under-concierge and under-under-concierge at the Montreux Palace Hotel and use his own private library and sift through the ton of paper that had now accumulated in his archive.

But Nabokov had a reputation for arrogance and aloofness that the rococo fortress of the Montreux Palace Hotel seemed to bear out. I remember dressing for my first meeting with Véra Nabokov there. During the last eight of my nine years as a student, I had worn nothing but purple, tangerine, lime green, or scarlet overalls. Knowing of the Nabokovs' reputation for old-fashioned formality, and sitting in the three-piece suit that my parents had bought in the hope of mending my ways and that I now, in all my gaucheness and diffidence, thought necessary for the occasion, I felt as comfortable as a giraffe on a surfboard. It took years for the awe and the awkwardness to wear off.

The problems of finding the materials and of trying to compensate for the unevenness of the record can occupy a biographer for many months. But then you have to write. Although at the research stage you are desperate to read every scrap, to find out every fact, you also know that readers won't want to read about all these facts any more than you will want to write about them all. You want your readers to have the satisfying illusion of completeness, of unreserved disclosure, of unobstructed access, but you also want them never to be bored: believe it or not, you want to be as brief as possible.

The tension between comprehensiveness and concision is one of many you have to harness as you write. As a biographer, you have to resolve the conflicts between the urge to collect and the urge to select; between the need to set the scene and the need to advance the action; between the desire to explain and the desire to let things speak for themselves; between the impulse to look ahead for distant outcomes or back for remote causes and the impulse to treat the present moment in its own right; between the need to provide as much shape and structure as you can and the need to leave room for life's unruly details; between your wish to remain objective and your knowledge that every phrase creates and colors what you want your readers to see; between allying with your subject and asserting your independence; between attention to your material and attention to your reader.

And in writing the life of someone whose claim on our interest was not in the drama of battle or courts, like Charlemagne, but in the inner drama that unfolds at a quiet desk, you have to find some rhythm to move between the inner and the outer, the work and the life, the timeless image or idea and time ticking away.

But time has ticked away long enough. Thank you, Seligenstadt, for the honor of the Einhard Prize, thank you for bringing me here to talk to you, and thank you for listening.

3. Who Is "My Nabokov"?

After a talk I gave in the Slavic Department of Columbia University, the editors of their graduate journal asked me to write a personal introduction to their forthcoming special issue on the theme "My Nabokov." Later in the same trip, the Nabokov Museum in St. Petersburg, where I happened to have spoken earlier on the day I wrote most of this, had put me up at the Hotel Astoria, 39 Bol'shaya Morskaya Street, just on the other side of St. Isaac's Square from Nabokov's birthplace at number 47, now the Nabokov Museum—details that will help explain the original ending. Back at my own desk, I have now added a coda.

We all have our own Nabokov, and—despite some seeing him as a tyrant to his readers—he would have it no other way. When he said that his ideal audience would be a room filled with little Nabokovs, he did not mean by that a room of identical thinkers but a room full of people who could derive as much pleasure and point from his texts as he had taken the trouble to provide. He always took things in his own way and expected anyone who was properly alive to do the same.[1]

We may each have our own Nabokov, but, like friends or family, he changes for us as well as remaining the same. When I pick up Nabokov after not having read him for a long time (and this *does* happen), I immediately hear his unmistakable voice, see via his singular vision, laugh at his unique humor with recognition and surprise but often, also, with a sense of discovery as I notice nuances, echoes, or implications I have never previously seen. Even when I reread, even though he still says what he said the last time I noticed this page, I hear with new ears, though I had heard and felt I understood before.

We all have our unique associations with favorite writers that accumulate over a lifetime. Nabokov recollects reading *War and Peace* "for the first time when I was eleven (in Berlin, on a Turkish sofa, in our somberly rococo Privatstrasse flat giving on a dark, damp back garden with larches and gnomes that have remained in that book, like an old postcard, forever)" (*SM* 199). I recall reading *Lolita* for the first time in the Weidenfeld and Nicolson edition with a black-and-white Sue Lyon (at fourteen, a year older than me) on the jacket. My parents had both left school at fourteen in the Depression to support their families. They knew I had an appetite for books, but not knowing how to satisfy it, they had bought a bookstore with a lending library both as a business and to offer me somewhere to graze. I soon apprehended that one of the tomes I had to reshelve in the library, *Lolita*, was both "a dirty book" and "a modern classic" and, knowing my parents' Puritanism, snuck it home and hid it under the pillow when I wasn't reading it. It mystified me then, in many ways, and although it mystifies me now in completely different ways, I can still evoke some of those first feelings.

As I can also evoke in a different way the thrill when, three and a half years later, I picked up my next Nabokov. In the bookstore my parents had built up a large stock of magazine orders for regular customers, and it was my job on Saturday to check off against the shipping invoice the bundles sent by the distributor and to place customers' orders in their folders. Had I still been the age when I first read *Lolita*, I would have read almost all that crossed my gaze in this way, from English schoolgirl comics to encyclopedias by weekly installment, but by my last year at high school I had become more careful with discretionary reading. On May 24, 1969, on the narrow mezzanine looking into the rest of the bookshop, I checked off *Time* magazine, which had a cover story on Nabokov to mark the publication of *Ada*. Three years older than when I had tried *Lolita*, I now found fascinating everything that Nabokov said in the red-boxed story with the headline quote "I have never met a more lonely, more lucid, better balanced mad mind than mine."[2] Dazzled by his language, ideas, and attitudes, I rushed to the Palmerston North public library for the latest Nabokov novel. Finding *Pale Fire*, I read it with more enchantment and exhilaration than anything I had ever encountered—and I still regularly recall that sense of explosive discovery and vivid magic when I think of the best in Nabokov or when a fresh blast of discovery shakes me in anyone else's fiction.

At the end of that year my father gave me for Christmas the first English edition of *Ada*, newly arrived in New Zealand, with our bookstore's rubber stamp on the paste-down front endpaper. I still have it beside me at my usual desk, with not only the plastic protective jacket that the bookstore usually added for its library volumes but also a second-generation second plastic layer I've added to hold together what is now my most valuable physical possession, since its marginalia provide the raw data for most of my ongoing *Ada* annotations.[3] I recall re-re-re-reading *Ada* for my doctoral thesis, in a south-facing room in Toronto between 1976 and 1978, with a strange light catching the colored glass on the fanlight above my desk as I added still more marginalia, or reading the "Pale Fire" poem aloud to roommates in the kitchen of that old Edwardian brick house. I recall reading Nabokov's novels in Russian, between 1981 and 1983, over a late-night *thé citron* in the ground-floor café of the Montreux Palace Hotel during breaks between working on the biography up on the sixth floor, in the former laundry storeroom at the end of Véra's corridor where all her husband's manuscripts were housed. I recall arguing with Alexander Dolinin as we walked along the icy Nevsky Prospect, with his wife Galina Lapina, the Russian translator of *Vladimir Nabokov: The Russian Years*, looking agog from one of us to the other as we passionately debated, on December 11, 1990, the dating problem in *Lolita*. I recall reading *Ada* again to my students in the Nabokov Museum, a floor below where Nabokov was born, at the Nabokov 101 Summer School in July 2002. Just as I will remember tonight, where a few hours ago I spoke at the Nabokov Museum, about *Lolita* and evolution, and as I hope I will remember writing this, looking out across my left shoulder to the polished pillars of a spruced-up St. Isaac's gleaming in the lamplight. Late November, and a poor night for mothing.

We all have our unique associations with favorite authors. Strange how recalling them can make memory speak so volubly, when we sometimes fear it can only stammer or stumble.

And strange how, as I expand this for *Stalking Nabokov* beyond the space I was allowed for *Ulbandus*, I think of Nabokov paying tribute to his father at the end of the first chapter of *Speak, Memory* or focusing on Dmitri's developing mind in the last chapter, and of Dmitri, now in his seventies and looking so like his father at that age, telling me he still recalls that experience of "Finding What the Sailor Has Hidden." I look at the photo of my father at the far edge of my desk and at the copy of *Ada* beside me, with his stamp in it, and think of what he gave me—even though he could not read Nabokov, or my Nabokov biography, let alone offer anything like the vast personal library that Nabokov's father was pleased to see his son roam in.

By the time I was seventeen and writing on *Pale Fire* I was already growing a patchy beard. Twenty-five years later, because it was starting to grey before my head hair, I shaved it off and was surprised to see in the mirror what seemed my father's face looking back in surprise at the resemblance. (When, already dying of cancer, he saw me for the first time without the beard, he scrutinized my shaving job and said: "You could have stood a little closer to the razor.") John Shade in the poem "Pale Fire" writes about the inspiration that comes to him as he shaves, and as I now shave each morning, that passage from canto 4 will be more likely than not to spring to my mind. That's how close my Nabokov can be.

Now I've written this, I expect that my morning shave will be linked now not only with my memory of my beardless self looking back at me with my father's face, and my imagining Shade shaving, but also with memories of Nabokov's tributes to his father in *Speak, Memory*, to the inspiration he sensed his father gave him, to the fact that he has Shade shot, just after he finishes writing canto 4, on July 21, 1959, his own father's birthday, in heart-wrenching homage to his own murdered father. My Nabokov builds patterns in time. So does life, as generation gives, and gives way, to generation. Nabokov helps us notice, and care.

NABOKOV'S MANUSCRIPTS AND BOOKS

4. The Nabokov Biography and the Nabokov Archive

Véra Nabokov invited me in 1979 to catalog her husband's archives in Montreux, hoping that they could then more easily be sold to an American institution. Buyers approached in the 1980s offered too little. By the beginning of the 1990s, the New York Public Library was on the point of purchasing the papers for the Henry W. and Albert A. Berg Collection of English and American Literature, famous especially for its Joyce and Woolf collections. As details were being settled, Dmitri Nabokov became anxious about finally parting with his father's archives. Rodney Phillips, director of the Berg Collection, and Lisa Browar, director of the Humanities and Social Sciences Research Libraries at the New York Public Library, fetched me from New Zealand in June 1991 to meet them in Montreux to help reassure Dmitri. Dmitri especially feared further piracy of Russian Nabokov materials by publishers and scholars from Russia. I suggested that the Russian materials in the archive should remain inaccessible for as long as it took for Russians to respect copyright, and the deal went ahead.

Once the archive was installed in New York, the New York Public Library announced the acquisition with an exhibition, a dinner, and a talk that I gave at the Celeste Bartos Forum in the Central Research Library on October 16, 1991. I wanted to suggest how the papers now in the Berg made it possible to understand Nabokov's life and works in new ways and how the papers' preservation by Véra—she had died earlier that year—could serve as a new lens not only on Nabokov's career but also on her dedication to it.

The Nabokov papers are now the most frequently consulted in the Berg Collection.

In *Flaubert's Parrot* Julian Barnes writes:

> You can define a net in one of two ways. . . . Normally, you would say
> that it is a meshed instrument designed to catch fish. But you could,
> with no great injury to logic, reverse the image and define a net as . . .
> a collection of holes tied together with string.

And then, for some strange reason, he proceeds to talk about biography.

In the case of Nabokov's biography, it's a wonder that we're left with anything but holes. He had a hypertrophied sense of privacy. "I hate tampering with the precious lives of great writers and I hate Tom peeping over the fence of those lives—I hate the vulgarity of 'human interest.' I hate the rustle of skirts and giggles in the corridors of time—and no biographer will ever catch a glimpse of my private life" (*LRL* 38). He would deplore the fact that I was allowed to see the manuscript from which I have just quoted, and he would especially deplore the fact that I am about to quote what he first wrote: "no biographer will ever catch a glimpse of my private life—I hope"; he then crossed out the hope, lest a biographer think that there *might* be some hope of peeking behind the scenes.[1] He placed a fifty-year restriction on the papers he deposited at the Library of Congress. He hid behind literary masks and then retreated entirely from the public gaze to the tranquility of Montreux. Ensconced there, he fired off brusque letters to various editors protesting against factual inaccuracies or infringements of his privacy.

In his books Nabokov turned biography upside-down and inside-out. His critical biography of Nikolay Gogol begins with Gogol's death and ends with his birth. His last Russian novel, *The Gift*, contains as an insert the young narrator's 120-page biography of the real writer Nikolay Chernyshevsky, full of genuine scholarly detail but exuberantly defiant of every biographical decorum. In *The Real Life of Sebastian Knight* the narrator's comically frustrated search for the facts of his half-brother's life becomes not only all we can have of Sebastian Knight's biography but also a handbook for all biographers, crammed with precepts and cautionary tales.

Nabokov had least time of all for the biographies of writers, and trying to compose *his* biography seemed at times like preparing a lovingly executed portrait for a Byzantine iconoclast. "Remember that what you are told is really threefold," he intones in *The Real Life of Sebastian Knight*: "shaped by the teller, reshaped by the listener, concealed from both by the dead man of the tale" (*RLSK* 52). Shrewd advice, wise caution. Much more chilling for a potential biographer of Nabokov is this comment that V. makes on Sebastian Knight:

> I soon found out that except for a few odd pages dispersed among other
> papers, he himself had destroyed [his manuscripts] long ago, for he

belonged to that rare type of writer who knows that nothing ought to remain except the perfect achievement: the printed book; that its actual existence is inconsistent with that of its spectre, the uncouth manuscript flaunting its imperfections like a revengeful ghost carrying its own head under its arm, and that for this reason the litter of the workshop, no matter its sentimental or commercial value, must never subsist.

(36)

In his own person, Nabokov stressed "the plain truth of the documents. . . . That, and only that, is what I would ask of my biographer—plain facts, no symbol-searching, no jumping at attractive but preposterous conclusions" (*SO* 156).

All this makes my presence here something of a miracle. I happen to be in North America at the moment for two main reasons: for the publication of the second volume of my Nabokov biography, and for this announcement that the Nabokov Archive has become part of the New York Public Library's Berg Collection. But Nabokov says he wants a biographer to stick to the plain truth of the documents—and then wants all the documents but the published works destroyed. Hardly a promising basis for either a biography or an archive.

As if Nabokov hadn't constructed all these ramparts between himself and the future image of his past, history added moats of its own. The Nabokov family had to flee at short notice from Petrograd to the Crimea in November 1917, leaving behind a young lad's papers, books, and butterfly collection; they had to flee again from the Crimea to London in 1919, in even more desperate haste; and after becoming the most distinguished new writer to emerge in the Russian emigration, Nabokov had to escape Europe in May 1940 as German tanks rolled toward Paris. This time, he left some of his papers in the basement of his friend Ilya Fondaminsky's home. Fondaminsky's apartment was ransacked by the Gestapo, the papers were scattered across the street, and Fondaminsky himself was carried off to die in a concentration camp. Other materials, including the manuscripts of much of Nabokov's unpublished early work, had remained in Prague in the custody of his mother and then passed into the keeping of his rather erratic and unliterary sister, Olga. After the Iron Curtain descended, Olga, conscious of the Soviet bloc's attitude to émigrés, burnt many of her brother's letters to their parents. In the 1950s Nabokov himself, at a time when he was still planning to publish *Lolita* anonymously, burnt each index card of the manuscript as soon as Véra typed it up. Somehow he also simply lost the manuscript of *Pnin*.

But the success of *Lolita* not only earned Nabokov a reprieve from teaching but also saved his papers from the ashcan. Suddenly faced with much more to pay in income tax than ever before, he was approached by the Library of Congress to donate some of his personal papers in return for a tax concession. Despite his abstract convictions, Nabokov readily agreed and continued to donate more material over the next ten years until the tax laws changed. And from the Library of Congress's first approach he began to hoard assiduously his notes, his manuscripts, his galleys, and his page proofs, sometimes in duplicate or triplicate. So much for destroying everything.

For all the drama of abandonment and destruction enacted by Nabokov's papers, other forces had in fact been at work all along to ensure that an unusually high proportion of his work survived. Those forces are easily identified: their names were Elena and Véra, his mother and his wife. For decades his mother gathered, transcribed, and pasted into albums her son's published and unpublished verse, stories, plays, essays. The fat albums she assembled in Prague from his manuscripts and her own transcriptions did not reach Nabokov in Switzerland until the 1960s; now they constitute one of the glories of the Nabokov Archive and the prime tool for establishing the canon of his early work and the development of his art.

Véra Nabokov always denied that she was Zina Mertz in *The Gift,* but if the two women—both Russian Jews, both muses for a Berlin émigré writer—are not identical, they are the only known specimens of their very distinctive species. Fyodor finds out that Zina has been collecting clippings of his verse even before they meet; and Véra's first album of Nabokov's poetry, now in the Archive, begins with clippings of his poems published almost two years before she met him. Already before they were married Véra was preserving everything Nabokov wrote and everything she could find that was written about him. Fifteen years later, when he switched to English and the originality of style he had evolved in the Russian emigration proved an obstacle to publication in America, she began to preserve all of his rejections slips for the amusement of posterity, never doubting that posterity would see things her way. Another twenty years on, as cartoons about *Lolita* began to appear in newspapers and magazines around the world, she collected them all. Two decades later, after her husband's death, she still carried on, despite age and ill health. She even fetched me all the way from New Zealand to Switzerland to sort out the manuscripts. And just this year she died, seventy years after clipping out that first Nabokov poem. Now that clipping and the album she pasted it into are here, in a collection that owes so much to her seven decades of dedication.

Nabokov asked of his biographer just "the plain truth of the documents." I had to violate his sense of biographical method. I interviewed people he would not want me to have seen; I saw papers he had asked to be destroyed; I stalked and I sleuthed; I gathered all the facts I could and then had to move beyond the plain facts into attempts at explanation. But although I knew he would have arched his pale eyebrows at my *methods*, I still wanted to imagine he might not have thought my *results* simply "attractive but preposterous conclusions." He hasn't let me know.

If I couldn't confine myself to the "plain truth of the documents," I also couldn't have done without them: documents Nabokov never dreamed of, documents that turned up in places where he never set foot, but especially the thousands and thousands of notes, letters, diaries, and manuscripts in his own hand that now form part of the Berg Collection.

Biography can be either plain or fancy, straight or crooked: it can follow the life from start to finish, or it can choose its own sweet course. Nabokov had already overturned biographical expectations so thoroughly that to try to outdo or even match him seemed futile. Besides, if I had tried to zig-zag, someone else would have come along to serve all those who crave the straight sequential line. Why *invite* competition?

On the other hand, a biography needs a little more shape than mere sequence. I would like now to trace some of the shape I built into the two volumes of the biography and to illustrate the interplay between the different kinds of material available—the comparatively reliable, enormously copious, but still inevitably gappy archival evidence; the dangerously indirect evidence of the published fiction; the unreliable or perhaps unforthcoming oral evidence of witnesses—and the interplay between what can be found and what can't.

One way to provide shape was to link the life and the art in the right way—not in the manner of the Shakespearean scholar Nabokov refers to "who deduced Shakespeare's mother from the plays and then discovered allusions to her in the very passages he had twisted to manufacture the lady" (*SO* 218).

Another was to establish my biography's relationship to Nabokov's splendid autobiography, *Speak, Memory*, not by trying either to undermine or to ignore it but by deliberately beaming onto it and bouncing off it. And, of course, I also had to define the very different relationship between my biography (or *Speak, Memory*, for that matter) and the work of Andrew Field, which had cost Nabokov so much vexation in his last years.

A third way was to build a second spotlight into each of the two volumes, one, Nabokov's father, growing dimmer through volume 1 as Nabokov himself steps to center stage, the other, Nabokov's wife, glowing brighter throughout volume 2 as they move toward the final long embrace.

So let me describe first a few ways in which materials in the Archive pertinent to Nabokov's father allowed me to establish in volume 1 certain relationships between Nabokov's art and his life and between *Speak, Memory* and *The Russian Years*.

A 1949 letter in the Archive reveals that Nabokov would have liked to travel down from Ithaca to the Library of Congress to carry out research into his father's public career for the first version of his autobiography, but he ran out of money and time (*SL* 95). That letter certainly encouraged my own inclination to feature V. D. Nabokov, especially since I had also found in the Archive a host of family papers relating to Nabokov's father that reached Nabokov from Prague only in 1961. Some of these he used when he revised *Speak, Memory* in 1966, but by this stage he did not want to tamper with the original structure of the book and so said less about his father than the material warranted.

By focusing on V. D. Nabokov, I could not only fill in the gaps his son had left in *Speak, Memory* but could also describe the cultural and political background of later imperial Russia—a world shrouded in myth in the English-speaking world—in a way that would still be intensely personal and that would show how the Nabokovs lived right at the center of Petersburg's swankest street, its artistic animation, its turbulent times. There is other valuable material on V. D. Nabokov in archives and libraries in Moscow and St. Petersburg, Helsinki, Columbia, and the Hoover Institute at Stanford and, of course, historical minutiae in newspapers and journals of the time in research libraries all over the world, but if I had not found in the Archive V. D. Nabokov's memoirs about the St. Petersburg theater of his youth or about the oppressiveness of the state school system, despite his own personal success within it, I would never have been able to paint such a vivid and personalized backdrop of what was, at the time of Nabokov's birth, Russia's immediate past.

All the same, even though V. D. Nabokov filled roles such as parliamentary leader of the largest party in the first Russian Duma, president of Russia's Literary Fund, and drafter of the abdication manifesto that sealed the end of the Romanov dynasty, I would not have been able to justify his having such prominence early in *The Russian Years* unless I could also convey what father and son were like together. But the Archive also provided that: the diary V. D. Nabokov kept all through 1918, when he and his family were taking refuge in a villa on the Black Sea shore, as first Bolshevik, then German, then French, and finally liberal and Tatar nationalist forces took over the

Crimea in that tumultuous year. The Archive contains a complete record of young Vladimir's creative output for this year: an album of his manuscript poems, two small albums of his analysis of classical Russian poems, their meter analyzed according to the diagrams Andrey Bely devised and the poet Maximilian Voloshin had just introduced him to, and then another album with his own new poems late in the year, each composed with a view to the kind of metrical diagram it would yield. Invaluable for me as an archivist, a bibliographer, and a critic, but as a biographer I could do far more with the images in V. D. Nabokov's diary: playing chess with his son, even winning a local tournament with him; hiking up the steep slopes overlooking the Black Sea; standing on guard duty with him through the moonlit Crimean nights; hearing his son read his most ambitious new work and commenting with a connoisseur's taste and a father's pride on the nineteen-year-old Volodya's promise as a writer.

Another reason that Nabokov's father has to loom so large and that his image dims slowly even after his life was switched off so suddenly by an assassin's bullet can be found in the precious stack of letters Nabokov wrote his mother. In some of the letters, for instance, Nabokov makes explicit his conviction that he and his mother will both someday in some inexplicable beyond be reunited with his father. Or he hints at his sense that his dead father may have somehow helped him in the strain of a Cambridge examination room. Nabokov never allows himself to drop the guard of skepticism in his fiction, but at the same time his work never abandons his fascination with the possibility of a life beyond this one. In the light of letters like these, the possibility sketched in *The Gift* that Fyodor's lucky fate and the very idea for his greatest books have been somehow guided by his dead father takes on a new and deeply personal turn (*VNRY* 193, 194, 239, 333–39, 471–72).

Perhaps the most priceless pages in the whole Archive are not in Nabokov's own hand, although they transcribe a fragment from his diary: his account of the night his father was assassinated (*VNRY* 191–93). It was these poignant pages that convinced me I could make V. D. Nabokov's death as handled in one sentence of *Speak, Memory* into the focus of my introduction to volume 1 without robbing the assassination itself of its drama when the story reached that inalterable date.

(To digress for a moment: that diary fragment has its own drama, its own lesson. It is the only evidence we have that Nabokov ever kept any kind of diary before 1943. It covers four pages, two sheets torn from an exercise book, a long transcription in his mother's hand. Whether she asked him to record his impressions of that night or whether he volunteered to show her, perhaps a year later, what he had written after that fateful night, we will never know. It is the only instance in the entire biography where it has been possible to present the kind of running inside view of Nabokov's thoughts that we are used to in following the life of a fictional character. And it survived against the odds because Elena Nabokov saw it, transcribed it, tore the transcription out of the exercise book in which she had written it; because his sister did not destroy *this* particular fragment; and because decades later it found its way from Prague to Montreux. History's juiciest plums can so easily fall and sink without trace into the ground; thank heavens that this one, at least, was preserved.)

As I realized that the biography would take two volumes, not the one I had naively allowed for, I saw that the ideal point to end volume 1 would be at the very moment *Speak, Memory* ends, as the family steps down toward the boat that will take them from the advancing German armies to a safe refuge in America. I could then at the beginning of volume 2 look back at that moment in *Speak, Memory* and ask why Nabokov ended his autobiography's last chapter there, just as I began volume 1 by asking why he picked a foreshadowing of his father's death as the place to end the *first* chapter of *Speak, Memory*.

In both cases, he wanted to show that despite the horrors of history, even *in* the horrors of history, he could find evidence of the harmony and the generosity he still felt behind life. That conviction, which permeates his fiction, also gave him the confidence and the buoyancy to remake himself twice: as a fledgling writer, ejected from the cozy nest of an aristocratic home, cut off from comfort and country and natural audience, he would turn himself by sheer effort and talent into someone who could make Russian soar; then, when even Europe's tiny Russian émigré community had been shattered by Hitler's ambitions and there was no one left to write for, he had to renounce the language he had mastered and restart from scratch as an American writer.

The art and the life are linked, all right, but the links have to be fashioned with the utmost care.

Since this is the year of *The American Years* and of Véra Nabokov's death, I will focus a little longer on the light that the Archive casts on Véra in ways that helped me shape volume 2.

If Nabokov planned to write a chapter on his father in *Speak, Memory*, he had no plans to write a chapter on his wife. Véra once told me: "He had the decency to keep me out of his books." But although he doesn't *describe* Véra in *Speak, Memory*, he nevertheless makes her central: he makes the last chapter an address to Véra, a tribute to her, but only so as to stress how inaccessible their life together would remain to outsiders: "They are passing, posthaste, posthaste, the gliding years—to use a soul-rending Horatian inflection. The years are passing, my dear, and presently nobody will know what you and I know" (*SM* 295).

In fact, Nabokov designs the structure of *Speak, Memory* to position Véra as a culmination of one of his life's key patterns. The whole book has seen a succession of women in his life: mother, pretty governesses, first childhood love, first adolescent love, and a rapid blur of amatory partners in the prime of his youth. Then, as the implicit crown of the series, Véra enters—and suddenly the shutters come down. For she steps into the book only by being addressed as "You," and that is all the glimpse we get.

Nabokov's last novel, *Look at the Harlequins!*, published in 1974, takes the form of an autobiography by a Russo-American writer called Vadim Vadimych N———, whose life is a bleak, barren parody of Nabokov's own until at the end of the book a woman never given any name but "You" steps into his life and turns it from rancor to radiance. Obviously it parodies, among a great deal else, not only Nabokov's life but his own account of his life in *Speak, Memory*.

For a long time after I realized this much about the novel, it still puzzled me. Its self-referentiality seemed sterile and sour. But as I began to sift through the Archive, I came across a fact here and a riddle there that in eventual retrospect added up to a long series of small revelations. In Nabokov's diary for 1971, four years before he died, he recorded on January 28 that he had begun to read the typescript of Field's biography, *Nabokov: His Life in Part*, for which Field wanted feedback within a month. He began reading intensely, and by February 6 he noted: "Have corrected 95 pages of Field's 680 page work. The number of absurd errors, impossible statements, vulgarities and inventions is appalling." (Nabokov's nearly 200 pages of corrections to Field are also in the Archive and a revelation in themselves.) The very day he made that exasperated entry in his diary, he began to write *Look at the Harlequins!*. Still vexed months later, he wrote to his lawyer: "I cannot tell you how upset I am by the whole matter. It was not worth living a far from negligible life . . . only to have a blundering ass reinvent it" (*VNAY* 616).

In the mid-1970s, with perhaps not too many years to live, Nabokov felt that his life had been betrayed. In reply, he served up a deliberately grotesque version of his life that would laugh any unwitting travesty like Field's right out of court. He was painfully aware that this could well be the last book he would ever write. Over the previous thirty years, he had settled into the habit of composing his novels in pencil on index cards. The box of cards containing the manuscript of *Look at the Harlequins!*, now in the Archive, has inside its lid Nabokov's instruction: "To be destroyed *unread* if unfinished."

But even the knowledge that Nabokov feared this novel might be a part-ing shot that he might barely have time to fire still did not redeem it for me. A novel apparently conceived in a spirit of urgent exasperation and cor-rective contempt seemed no better than the narcissistic parody it had first appeared. As I became more familiar with the Archive, however, I came to discover more about *Look at the Harlequins!* The novel begins:

> I met the first of my three or four successive wives in somewhat odd circumstances, the development of which resembled a clumsy conspir-acy, with nonsensical details and a main plotter who not only knew nothing of its real object but insisted on making inept moves that seemed to preclude the slightest possibility of success. Yet out of those very mistakes he unwittingly wove a web, in which a set of reciprocal blunders on my part caused me to get involved and fulfill the destiny that was the only aim of the plot.
>
> (*LATH* 3)

"Three or four successive wives," as if Vadim cannot quite remember how many he has had: an offhand joke within the novel's first lines. (Let me con-fess that I had overlooked the joke until Nabokov's one wife recalled it with a laugh of appreciative pleasure.) As the passage progresses, with its image of fate trying to bring two lovers together after not quite succeeding at first, a keen reader of Nabokov hears an echo of the entire structure of *The Gift*. There Fyodor retrospectively construes what seem to him like repeated, inept moves by fate to bring Zina and himself together as proof that fate persisted until it found the right combination, as if convinced that only Zina would do for him. That theme Nabokov uncharacteristically echoed twice more, in his next two novels, *The Real Life of Sebastian Knight* and *Bend Sinister*.

That much could be gleaned without the help of the Archive. I also discov-ered from interviews and elsewhere that Nabokov liked to tell others about the various ways fate had tried to introduce him to Véra before they were finally brought together and that he insisted that even had there been no revolution they would have somehow met.

In the Archive, in a 1975 letter to his German publisher and friend, Hein-rich Maria Ledig Rowohlt, Nabokov jokingly calls his new novel "Look at the Masks!" (letter of May 1, 1975, VNA). That nickname immediately coalesced in my mind with other facts I had amassed. I had asked Véra if she could tell me anything about her first meeting with Nabokov beyond the one detail he had dropped in an interview, that they met at an émigré charity ball (*SO* 127). "No," she said, firm as a fortress. That did not stop me asking once more and hearing the portcullis again crash down (*VNRY* 558, n. 37). But Nabokov's sister Elena Sikorski told me that her brother had hinted to her that his poem "Vstrecha" ("The Meeting") reflected his first meeting with Véra.

I knew by then that every year in his late diaries Nabokov scribbled a word or two under May 8, and that one could deduce, by collocating all these entries, that he was reminding himself to buy Véra something to commemorate the date they met in 1923. One year, the diary reminder was simply the phrase "profil' volchiy," "wolf's profile" (1969 diary, VNA), a phrase from the poem "Vstrecha," that refers to a wolf's profile mask.[2] The woman in the poem wears a mask throughout and seems to have stepped out from some masquerade into the starry night. The manuscript of this intensely romantic poem, also in the Archive, shows that it was written three weeks after Nabokov and Véra first met. Elena Sikorski's explanation lies behind the summary I give in the biography of the event behind the poem:

> During the course of the ball, he encountered a woman in a black mask with a wolf's profile. She had never met him before, and knew him only through watching over the growth of his poetic talent, in print and at public readings. She would not lower her mask, as if she rejected the appeal of her looks and wished him instead to respond only to the force of her conversation. He followed her out into the night air. Her name was Véra Evseevna Slonim.
>
> (*VNRY* 206–07)

The moment I read that Nabokov had assigned *Look at the Harlequins!* the private nickname "Look at the Masks!" I realized that he was alluding to his meeting with Véra; that the real title of the novel (also, with its imperative verb, an echo of *Speak, Memory*)[3] was a private allusion to the Harlequin mask Véra wore when he first met her; and that in all likelihood the whole novel was a tribute to the kind fate that united them.

All sorts of hints in *Look at the Harlequins!* and throughout the Archive pointed to the possibility that the novel might be an inversion not only of Nabokov's life and of *Speak, Memory* but also specifically of his relationship to Véra. As I examined the novel once more, it became evident that each of the unlovable women Vadim marries was indeed in a different way a pointed inversion of certain of Véra's characteristics, while the "You" who redeems his life distills in a few traits the essential Véra.

Early in the novel, an old aunt tells Vadim, "Stop moping! Look at the harlequins!" "What harlequins? Where?" "Oh, everywhere. All around you. Trees are harlequins, words are harlequins. So are situations and sums. Put two things together—jokes, images—and you get a triple harlequin. Come on! Play! Invent the world! Invent reality!" (*LATH* 8–9)

As I write in the biography, we see almost nothing of You, Vadim's fourth wife. She appears shortly before the end of the novel. Vadim describes the scene of their meeting: As he emerges from his office at Quirn University, the string around a batch of his letters and drafts breaks. Coming from the library along the same path, You crouches down to help him collect his papers. "No, you don't," she says to a yellow sheet that threatens to glide away in the wind. After helping Vadim to cram everything back into his folder she notices a yellow butterfly settle on a clover head before it wheels away in the same wind. "*Metamorphoza,*" she says, in her "lovely elegant Russian."

In this one short scene, she helps a writer assemble his papers (like Véra as typist, secretary, archivist); she notices a butterfly (again like Véra, who in June 1941 caught a specimen of the hitherto unknown species *Neonympha dorothea* just as her husband was catching another a few hundred yards below, inside the Grand Canyon); she cannot help disclosing the alertness of her imagination: she *is* Véra, putting two things together—a joke, an image—to make a triple harlequin. And then Vadim terminates the scene to announce that reality would only be adulterated if he now "started to narrate what you know, what I know, what nobody else knows [a pointed echo of *Speak, Memory*'s "and presently nobody will know what you and I know"], what shall never, never be ferreted out by a matter-of-fact, father-of-muck, mucking biograffitist" (*VNAY* 633; *LATH* 226).

Vadim has been appallingly frank about his other wives, down to their sexual peculiarities. But the moment he introduces You, he insists on privacy. That echo of *Speak, Memory*, that tribute to the *real* privacy of a *real* marriage, as opposed to the three marriages that have left Vadim's life so empty to this point, made me realize for the first time how decidedly Nabokov sees married love as one of the very rare partial escapes that life allows from the solitude of the soul. That escape, he suggests, can exist only where both partners can have absolute confidence that what they share with the other will go no further: only then can there be the kind of frankness, the kind of total sharing of the self, that elsewhere in mortal life is impossible.

Now, I had long understood the importance to Nabokov's work of his frustration at what he calls "the solitary confinement of the soul."[4] In life, he stresses, it is impossible to step outside the self as if into another soul. The only way to achieve this is to step outside life, into the unique conditions of art or perhaps into some state beyond the mortal self that the strange freedoms that art allows somehow foreshadow.

What I now realized, after this succession of discoveries in the Archive—and after having written more than 2,000 pages on Nabokov—was that Nabokov was ready to define one other escape from the terms of our mortal imprisonment: not only in the unrealities of art but in the reality of married love. That unexpected equation between art and married love became especially clear as I looked again at the bizarre marriage proposal Vadim makes to You.

Vadim has a strange mental quirk: although in real life he can easily walk in one direction, turn around, and walk back the opposite way, in imagination he cannot make that turn. A very neurotic individual, Vadim sees this as somehow symptomatic of his overall mental instability and feels honorbound to confess this tell-tale sign to each of the successive women he wants to marry. The first three dreadful inamoratas simply ignore what he has tried to explain; only You understands his irrational anxiety, and manages to allay it.

Vadim gives You a section from the manuscript of his latest novel that describes his inability to contemplate turning around to walk back the way he came. As she reads, he sets off on his evening stroll, but with his recently composed text still fresh in his mind, he can picture every word she reads and keep mental pace with her as her eyes scan each manuscript card. Just as he envisages her at the end of his text, he reaches the end of his walk and prepares to turn and head back to meet her. He cannot. The intensity of his love for her and the vividness of his sense of her have made him so conscious of both ends of the distance separating them that his inability to turn in theory now manifests itself in reality. Rigid, he falls to the ground. Over the next three weeks in hospital, he remains physically paralyzed, sensorially dead, while his mind hurtles through hallucinatory landscapes. Only very slowly do sensation and self begin to seep back.

Until this last confession and proposal, through all of Vadim's previous marriages, there has been no connection whatever between his love and his art as a writer. During this scene, for the first time in his life, these two parts of his existence come together, and in almost miraculous fashion. The scene records a kind of ecstasy, a standing outside the self: knowing the depths of her artistic responsiveness, Vadim can follow You's thoughts as she reads over his index cards. Art always allows for a kind of transcendence of the self as one person participates in the visions of another imagination, but here the force of Vadim's love for You grants him a still more immediate transcendence of the self, a virtual entry into her mind as she reads.[5]

At their highest, both art and the mental harmony of married love suggest to Nabokov a kind of foretaste of what death may bring: the release of the self from its prison. But in life even these glimpses of a freedom beyond must remain highly conditional. Just at the moment where Vadim's last confession-cum-proposal seems to blur the boundary between life and art (You reads from Vadim's novel as he acts out the novel's scenario), self and other (Vadim seems to be *in* her mind reading his own text even as he heads away from her), life and death—just at that moment he has to turn around and face the anxiety that after all he does not know You's thoughts, that she might be repelled by his confession, that she might reject his proposal (*VNAY* 637–38).

Julian Moynahan once criticized Andrew Field's first and best book on Nabokov for arguing that Nabokov's works were all concerned primarily with art. That, Moynahan suggested, was a drastic diminution of their force.[6] For Moynahan, Nabokov was above all the great celebrator of married love.[7] If we look closely at *Look at the Harlequins!*, we can see the extent to which both are right since there Nabokov links art and married love as different means toward one of his central themes, the transcendence of the self.

A novel that appears compulsively self-referential turns out to focus on the transcendence of self; a novel that seems terminally narcissistic turns out to be a love song, and no less passionate for all its play. And what especially interested me as a biographer was that Nabokov's career, dedicated unrelentingly to his art, and his life, devoted utterly to Véra, had begun to make a new sort of sense together.

By the time I had reached this conclusion—in the second-to-last of fifty chapters—I could finally appreciate the full measure of what the privacy of their married lives meant to the Nabokovs. By now, having solved the riddle of their first meeting and Nabokov's sense of the difference that meeting made to his life and his art, I could afford to mind less than ever that Véra had so flatly refused to tell me how she and Nabokov had first met or what happened next. There is a hole at the center of Nabokov's biography, and there always will be: it is part of the romance of his story. Perhaps the hardest part of my task as a biographer was to find the right frame for that hole, the right knots for my net. And it was in the Archive—in a letter to Rowohlt, in a sequence of cryptic diary entries, in the manuscripts of a poem written in 1923 and a novel begun half a century later—that I found most of the strands I needed.

I returned to Montreux in June 1991 to help with the transfer of the Archive. I had spent years working on the manuscript materials, seeing Véra every day. Usually each time I return to the town, I am struck by the constancy of the place: the same familiar figures in the Grand-Rue, the same faces and furniture and food in the Montreux Palace Hotel. This time, I was struck by change. Véra was no more; the Palace Hotel, where she had lived for three decades, had just been radically renovated and the Nabokovs' suite, and the small former linen room where I had sorted out the Archive, had vanished. But now the manuscripts are here in New York, in the city where Vladimir and Véra Nabokov arrived from Europe and at last found a new home, a haven from exile. Now, the Archive that Véra began when she was not yet twenty and watched over until she was almost ninety has at last found *its* permanent home.

5. From the Nabokov Archive
Nabokov's Literary Legacy

In 2009 the Japanese magazine *Gunzo* published a special Nabokov issue on the occasion of the imminent publication of *The Original of Laura*, which Tadashi Wakashima, professor of American literature at Kyoto University, will translate. I was asked to write on *Laura*. Because Dmitri Nabokov, his agent, and the publishers wanted the novel's contents to be strictly embargoed, and the special issue was to appear before the novel, I asked to write about my encountering *Laura* in the context of other materials in the archive that had been or would also be published posthumously. My focus became the changes to my and our perception of Nabokov as new parts of his archives became available.

Many writers and readers now consider Vladimir Nabokov to be least *among* the greatest novelists of the twentieth century. Martin Amis, in New York in November 2009 to celebrate Nabokov on the eve of the publication of his last, unfinished novel, *The Original of Laura*, told me that he would rate *Ulysses* ahead of any Nabokov novel (as I would, some of the time), but rightly stressed that Nabokov comes out far ahead of Joyce in grand slams.

In the 1920s and 1930s Nabokov, always a prodigious worker, was at his most prolific, although writing mostly for the small, shrinking, and isolated audience of the Russian emigration. By the time of his arrival in the United States in 1940, he had a huge backlog of acclaimed Russian works. He wanted them urgently to appear in English, but not until after *Lolita* made him famous in 1958 did publishers solicit his Russian output. His son, Dmitri, recently graduated from Harvard, was just then becoming old enough to serve as his principal translator. By the 1960s a stream of old work joined the steady flow of new to make a flood. His books began to appear with exhilarating but almost exhausting rapidity, despite his slow, superscrupulous habits of composition: fifteen new or thoroughly revised books appeared in the decade before his death. Six of these volumes were translated by Dmitri—by this time an opera singer and, to his parents' relief, no longer a race-car driver—in conjunction with his father.

Keeping up with translations of his own expanding backlist, adding to his frontlist, and his declining health from 1975 ensured that Nabokov's last work, *The Original of Laura*, remained unfinished at his death. Although he had asked Véra to destroy the manuscript should he not complete it, she could not bear to. A third of a century later, Dmitri decided to publish the novel. My own initial recoil from *The Original of Laura* and my later reversal I describe in detail in chapter 26 of this volume, "A Book Burner Recants." What else has been found in Nabokov's papers after his death and his prolific life? Why should I of all people be asked to write about the new or little-known parts of Nabokov's literary legacy, when I recommended to Véra and Dmitri, after reading the manuscript of *The Original of Laura*, that they should destroy it? And what difference can works published or collected since Nabokov's death make to our sense of the writer and the man?

I wrote my M.A. thesis on Nabokov and ended up sending it to him (no one, he had complained, had solved the puzzle of *Transparent Things*; I had, and wanted to show him it could be solved independently). Véra returned the thesis with Nabokov's encomium and one marginal cross and three corrections in his blunt pencil hand: my first treasured sample of a handwriting that would become almost as familiar to me as my own. Soon after, I started a Ph.D. thesis on Nabokov, having become bored with the one I had begun on John Barth. In the summer of 1976, visiting Europe for the first time and all but resolved to switch from Barth to Nabokov's *Ada*, I visited Montreux, where Nabokov had been living since 1961. I ventured inside the imposing Montreux Palace Hotel and left a note for Nabokov but did not dare ask to meet him. I did not know that already that summer he was in hospital and would never fully recover. I can remember how stunned I was, eleven months into my thesis, to hear of his death on July 2, 1977. In photographs he still looked fit, striding up mountain slopes in pursuit of butterflies. His prose seemed invulnerable. How could death have claimed *him*?

In the course of my research, the interlibrary-loan service at the University of Toronto helped me glean all Nabokov's published work I could lay my hands on, including even his first book, published when he was seventeen. Although the one known copy in the Americas had recently been sold to Harvard for $10,000, an interlibrary-loan copy arrived for me by ordinary mail from the Lenin Library in Moscow. Some of the material I gathered then has still not appeared in book form, has not been consulted by even some of the best Nabokov scholars, yet offers priceless insights into his thinking and wonderful instances of his imagery. Take this review of a book by a now-forgotten philosopher that Nabokov wrote for a now-defunct New York newspaper in his first year in the United States. He notes

> the old pitfall of that dualism which separates the ego from the non-ego, a split which, strangely enough, is intensified the stronger the reality of the world is stressed. . . . [W]hile the brain still pulses one cannot escape the paradox that man is intimately conscious of Nature because he is walled in himself and separated from her. The human mind is a box with no tangible lid, sides, or bottom, and still it is a box, and there is no earthly method of getting out of it and remaining in it at the same time.[1]

The excitement of discovering passages like this kept me searching for far-flung Nabokoviana all through my dissertation years. When I came to write the biography, an uncollected interview offered the ideal epigraph for the book, in this succinct and luminous metaphor: " 'What surprises you most in life?' . . . 'the miracle of consciousness: that sudden window opening onto a sunlit landscape amidst the night of non-being.' "[2] Nabokov's reflections on literature and life and on his own work and thought in his collected interviews have proved fascinating for readers, memorable for dictionaries of quotations, and invaluable for critics. Now, more than thirty years after I started amassing stray Nabokoviana, I am delighted to be preparing an edition of his uncollected prose and interviews, which should be published in the next few years as *Think, Write, Speak*—after the opening sentence of his foreword to his own collection, *Strong Opinions*: "I think like a genius, I write like a distinguished author, and I speak like a child."

Excitement remained a constant in my Ph.D. studies. As work advanced, I also built a modest collection of Nabokov first editions. At an antiquarian book fair in Toronto I was astonished to find that a stall representing Serendipity Books, Berkeley, offered a stack of Nabokov first editions, especially of the early Russian works. Most bore Nabokov's inscriptions to Anna Feigin, Véra's cousin and the family's closest friend, with whom they lived in Berlin from 1931 to 1937. With beating pulse and bated breath, I held for the first time a page inscribed in Nabokov's neat Russian hand, a title page dedication to "Anyuta," in a copy of his first novel, *Mashen'ka* (*Mary*). After fingering each of the precious tomes—far beyond what I could afford as a student—I continued to loiter around the Serendipity counter for hours, transcribing the inscriptions and taking all the data I could for a bibliographical analysis of these books.

I would have been astonished then to look ahead to the access I would soon have to material in Nabokov's hand—and delighted to know that I would eventually help to make much of this material available. When I finished the Ph.D. at the end of 1978, I joined my girlfriend for a weekend unwinding in New York. As soon as we met there, she mentioned she'd chanced on *The Nabokov-Wilson Letters* in a bookstore. I made her take me straight there, opened up Simon Karlinsky's elegant edition, saw that the original letters were at the Beinecke Library at Yale, and immediately knew where I'd be heading the next week. Nabokov had happily cultivated an air of Olympian remoteness as a shield to his privacy during his post-*Lolita* years of fame, and he had long expressed his disdain for writers who preserved their manuscripts. Along with everybody else I had assumed that there would be no chance of finding Nabokov papers. At Yale, I found hundreds of letters from Nabokov to Edmund Wilson, his closest literary friend in the 1940s, and twenty-five letters—including the most vivid of all—omitted (by mistake, I soon found out) from the book. Electrified by these discoveries, I spent the next two months flitting back and forth among libraries at Wellesley College, Harvard, and Cornell, where Nabokov had taught, the Bakhmeteff archive of Russian émigré papers at Columbia, the Library of Congress, and elsewhere.

The Nabokov-Wilson Letters offered the first real insight into Nabokov's casual human side. Its trove of literary detail confirmed me in my decision to compile a bibliography that would record the circumstances and processes of composition and publication of Nabokov's books and that could serve as a kind of surrogate biography and as compensation for the dearth of fact and the glut of error in Andrew Field's 1973 bibliography and 1977 biography.

After finishing my dissertation, I had sent a copy to Véra Nabokov. Just before I was due to return to New Zealand, as the terms of my scholarship required, she invited me to Montreux. I spent four days there, grilling her for the bibliography. Two months after I returned to New Zealand, she asked if I would sort out her husband's archive. Naturally I said yes, and for two consecutive Southern Hemisphere summers came to work through the ton of papers and Nabokov books in room 69, the *chambre de débarras*, across the corridor from room 64, the Nabokovs' sitting room—from where, in their suite in the Cygne wing of the Montreux Palace Hotel, they had overlooked Lake Geneva for decades.

The papers in Montreux did not cover Nabokov's whole legacy. In 1959, suddenly facing a massive tax bill on his *Lolita* income, Nabokov took advantage of the tax relief awarded for donating papers to the Library of Congress. Although he had always thought manuscripts should not distract attention from finished works, the concrete financial incentive conquered his abstract antipathy. Over the next few years he sent the Library of Congress the manuscripts of his Russian novels and stories and his English works up to *Pale Fire* in 1962. To allay his misgivings, he placed a fifty-year ban on access to the materials, despite the Library of Congress's attempts to persuade him otherwise—a ban that expired only in 2009. During my first winter in Montreux, I extracted from Véra a promise to allow me access to the papers he had deposited in Washington. With Dmitri's help, I held her to her promise and had my first foray into the Nabokov papers at the Library of Congress—badly catalogued, as I found—in January 1980.

In Montreux, Véra allowed me to come and go as I liked into room 69 and the unheated former laundry storeroom at the end of the corridor, which we made into the new manuscript room. There I arranged and catalogued everything Nabokov had kept after settling in Montreux—all the manuscripts on index cards, the typescripts, galleys, page proofs, editorial correspondence, and material from his early years, especially the albums his mother had lovingly compiled of his first fifteen years' work as a writer. These had arrived in the 1960s from Prague, where his mother had died in 1939, by way of his sisters, one still in Prague, one now near him in Geneva.

I soon found in the Montreux archives first one, then two manuscripts of *Volshebnik* (*The Enchanter*), the novella that we might now call "The Original of Lolita," which Nabokov had written in Russian in 1939 but been advised not to publish. After writing *Lolita* itself, he thought he had destroyed its Russian precursor but then rediscovered it and considered translating and publishing it in the wake of *Lolita*'s international success. But the manuscript had again been misplaced for decades when I *re*-rediscovered what would be published in 1985, in Dmitri's translation, as *The Enchanter*.

Despite my free access to everything in the Montreux archive room and controlled access to the Library of Congress Nabokoviana, I could not see other materials that Véra guarded in her bedroom: Nabokov's letters to his parents and to her, his diaries, and *The Original of Laura*. Véra knew that as well as sorting the archive for her I was gathering information for a bibliography. She did not know that old photostats—negatives, on paper now turned brown—of some of the letters from Nabokov to his parents were among the material I was sorting. I transcribed them painstakingly by holding their reversed script up to a mirror, but Nabokov had crossed out personal details on the photostats, made for Field's inspection in 1970, and many letters were missing altogether. I kept pressing Véra for access to what I had not yet been able to see.

In 1981 Véra formally agreed to condone a *bio*graphy project. In November I returned to Montreux to begin. Several months later, I discovered, at the bottom of a pile of otherwise empty boxes behind a cupboard in room 69, a cardboard box full of manuscripts of Nabokov's lectures on Russian literature from its origins to the twentieth century, all the material *other* than the authors (Gogol, Dostoevsky, Tolstoy, Turgenev, Chekhov) taught in his Masterpieces of European Fiction course and featured in the 1981 *Lectures on Russian Literature*. Véra had always been perturbed that her husband's lectures on Russian poetry could not be found. "*Eureka!*" I wrote in headline-size capitals on a note I left for her to find the next morning.

The material found in that box almost thirty years ago has still not been published. Part of the problem of dealing with Nabokov's legacy is that it is so vast that it can be hard to know where to turn next. I have worked on subjects other than Nabokov for most of this millennium, but in preparing a paper for a Nabokov conference three years ago, I was sent back to my notes on the unpublished Russian lectures and immediately stumbled on a paragraph I could not resist transcribing and sending to Dmitri Nabokov:

> When examining a writer and his work, three points of view interest me above all. Individual genius, the position his work holds in the historical evolution of artistic vision and the artist's struggle *against* public opinion and the current ideas of his time. Such things as Realism and Romanticism and the rest of the lot mean nothing to me. Absolute objective reality cannot exist or rather cannot be apprehended by the human mind. It is the approximation to it that only matters; and the reality with which human genius deals, be it the buffalo which the caveman painted on a rock or the lullaby sung by an Indian squaw, is but a series of illusions becoming more and more vivid according to the artist's power and his position in time. What must always be remembered is that the reality of the world as imagined and conveyed by a writer is but the individual reality of his individual world. When people find this or that writer's world to be true to nature, as the saying goes, it means that either 1) the writer has adopted a popular point of view—and that is the way of all second-rate writers from [Virgil,] the minor poet of Rome[,] to Mr Hemingway of Spain, —or 2) that the writer has made the general public see the world in his own terms—and this is the way of all great writers from William Shakespeare to James Joyce.[3]

As I wrote to Dmitri, the passage, although crossed out by Nabokov, seems invaluable for anyone with an interest in him—or in literature—and deserves publication, along with the rest of these lectures. Dmitri agreed. (This and similar passages in these lectures in fact led me to formulate a new appreciation of the role that a belief in cultural evolution plays in Nabokov's thought and artistic judgments; see chapter 14, "Nabokov's Transition from Russian to English: Repudiation or Evolution?") The subjects covered by these "new" Russian lectures run all the way from saints' lives to Vladislav Khodasevich, whom Nabokov considered the greatest twentieth-century Russian poet. They cover the literary material that Nabokov knew best, that he devoured as a boy, that he studied at Cambridge, and that he was brought to Cornell to teach. In these lectures he opens up the whole range of Russian literature and injects all his passion and imagination into discussions of Pushkin or digressions on literature, art, and life like the one above.

By the time I unearthed this treasure, Véra had already let me see Nabokov's diaries and his letters to his parents. But it was not until I returned to Montreux in the winter of 1984–85, after she had seen the first chapters of my biography and realized she would not regret trusting me, that she allowed me oblique access to Nabokov's letters to her. She would not let me read or hold them, but sat at the small round dining table in her sitting room—the one where she and Vladimir were photographed playing chess—while I sat opposite. In her eighties, still coughing and husky from a recent cold, she read aloud from the letters into my tape recorder, session after session, skipping endearments and anything else she thought too personal, announcing "*propusk*" ("omission") at each cut. Now these splendid letters are being produced in their own volume, transcribed and translated from the Russian by Olga Voronina, former deputy director of the Nabokov Museum, and by me, with Dmitri Nabokov adding the final polish and familial tone. They will also be released in the original Russian.

Late in 1984 Véra had told me she would "of course" eventually let me see *The Original of Laura*, but she offered such concessions mainly to buy time. But in February 1987, as I was writing on Nabokov's American years, she at last handed me the little box of index cards. My awe at holding Nabokov's manuscripts had long passed. For seven years I had been cataloguing and rearranging them for Véra and transcribing and indexing them for my own purposes, letting myself into the archive room and the "library" in the Nabokov rooms of the Montreux Palace Hotel's Cygne wing, often working there from morning till after midnight.

I explain in this book's last chapter the unpropitious circumstances of my reading *The Original of Laura* at last, and my negative reaction. Not long after I read it, Véra and Dmitri asked me what I thought they should do with it. Though I had religiously preserved every relic of paper, envelope, or cardboard in the archives that bore his handwriting, I now said, to my own surprise, "Destroy it." A whole *novel!* I will explain in that chapter why I changed my evaluation of *Laura* so radically and how glad I am now that my original advice went unheeded.

While I worked in the archives, Véra told me many times how keenly she wanted to assemble a volume of Nabokov's verse translations. I promised to keep track of all I discovered as I sorted and sifted. But Véra had neither the health nor the time to edit the translations. She was already seventy-seven when I met her, frail after the shock of Nabokov's death, and always busy as agent for the Nabokov estate and as translator or indefatigable checker of translations into Russian, English, French, and German.

When Stanislav Shvabrin, in the course of his doctoral research on Nabokov's verse translations, discovered in 2003 some unpublished Nabokov verse translations in Harvard's libraries, he asked Dmitri Nabokov whether he could publish them. Dmitri asked my advice. I pointed out all the other uncollected verse translations and suggested to Stas that we edit together a volume of Nabokov's collected verse translations. He and Dmitri readily agreed. At 441 pages, the resulting volume, *Verses and Versions* (2008), is not skimpy, but even so it could not include a large fraction of Nabokov's verse translations: those before 1923, those into Russian (including Ronsard, Shakespeare, Goethe, Byron, Baudelaire, Rimbaud), and those into French (especially Pushkin). That reflects one constraint on all Nabokov's posthumous publications. Since the volumes can sell well, trade publishers naturally prefer selectiveness to the exhaustiveness that eager scholars would like and that some university presses might permit.

Another constraint is manpower. Véra Nabokov had a hands-on approach to all the Nabokov material published in her lifetime. She was even a meticulous first editor for me on the half-million words of the Nabokov biography. After a high-speed crash in one of his Ferraris in 1982, leading to severe burns, a broken neck, and ten months in hospital, Dmitri Nabokov—already his father's main translator into English during his lifetime—decided to set aside his career as an opera basso profundo and to dedicate the remainder of his life to serving the Nabokov literary legacy.

In the 1970s Matthew Bruccoli, a former student of Nabokov's at Cornell and already the leading Fitzgerald scholar, set up a publishing company that, in partnership with an established New York publisher, published four volumes of Nabokov's Cornell and Harvard lectures in swift succession: *Lectures on Literature* and a facsimile edition of one part, *Lectures on* Ulysses

(1980); *Lectures on Russian Literature* (1981); and *Lectures on* Don Quixote (1983). Two important lectures on drama did not fit into these volumes. Recovered from his accident, Dmitri Nabokov took it upon himself as his first major task to translate four of Nabokov's one-act plays and one three-act play into English and publish them with the essays and his own introduction (*The Man from the USSR and Other Plays*, 1985).

His next task was to translate the manuscript of *Volshebnik* (*The Enchanter*, 1986) that I had rediscovered while sorting out the archive for Véra. While he was translating, I was beginning to write the biography, very conscious that other Nabokov scholars would benefit enormously from the archival material that only I had access to in Montreux and Washington. I was determined to make available in the biography as much as I could that was relevant to Nabokov scholars, while not overloading other readers—not that *they* would object to more unpublished Nabokov.

During my research on the biography I had come to know and love Nabokov's favorite sibling, Elena Sikorski, who was living in Geneva and published her fascinating correspondence with her brother in 1986 (in Russian, of course). A much larger but much more selective *Selected Letters, 1940–1977*, chosen rather hastily by Matthew Bruccoli and Dmitri Nabokov, appeared three years later.

Véra Nabokov's decline and her death in 1991 slowed the flow of Dmitri's work as translator and editor. He had translated in 1985 one story Nabokov had chosen not to republish, and he now translated another eleven in his edition of *The Stories of Vladimir Nabokov* (1995). The sale of his father's remaining manuscripts to the New York Public Library and of his father's books inscribed to his mother, usually with wonderful drawings of invented butterflies, and his dealing with the duties of the estate, the persistent problem of Russian piracies, and a ten-volume collected works in Russian took up much of his time. Nabokov scholarship was also powering ahead elsewhere, in the Pléiade edition of Nabokov in France (begun in 1986, with the second of the projected three volumes published only in 2010), and Dieter E. Zimmer's annotated twenty-five-volume German edition.

In the early 1990s I teamed up with lepidopterist Robert Michael Pyle to edit Nabokov's butterfly writings. The thick tome that resulted included not only the scientific papers but also many unpublished notes from the 1940s, when Nabokov was working at Harvard's Museum of Comparative Zoology; an abandoned *Butterflies of Europe* from 1963–65; all the lepidopterological references in his creative works; an abandoned story, his last, "The Admirable Anglewing"; and his longest story still unpublished at the time, "Father's Butterflies," an appendix to his longest and greatest Russian novel, *The Gift*.

The incompletely revised and sometimes barely legible manuscript of this complex appendix proved Dmitri's most difficult translating task, occupying him on and off through the late 1990s. *Nabokov's Butterflies* (2000) was preceded, in 1999, the centenary of Nabokov's birth, by my Knopf edition of Nabokov's *Speak, Memory* with, for the first time, chapter 16, a key to the rest that Nabokov had written immediately after the other chapters but then decided not to publish.

For much of the last decade Dmitri's health has been under serious assault. At seventy-six he has slowed from five Ferraris and a Dodge Viper to a wheelchair. Nevertheless, alongside his editing and translating his father's fiction, he has continued to enjoying translating and publishing his father's Russian poems, a diversion that began in the 1980s. Nabokov had published his own translations of thirty-nine Russian poems, along with fourteen English poems and some of his chess problems, in *Poems and Problems* (1970). In 1975 and 1976, often bedridden, he had selected the Russian poems he thought worth collecting, and these were published, two years after his death, as *Stikhi* (*Poems*, 1979). Dmitri has translated for the first time many other poems in *Stikhi* and "A University Poem," his father's longest Russian poem, for an imminent *Collected Poems*, along with the last, previously unrecovered or unpublished, Russian stories, including "Natasha," for an expanded and final version of *The Stories of Vladimir Nabokov*.

I had more than enough projects of my own and was pleased to see Dmitri preparing for publication whatever he could. But now Dmitri has recognized that he cannot deal with all the business of the estate, all the scores of countries interested in publishing, translating, or adapting Nabokov works, *and* translate the primary literary texts—there still remain other poems and Nabokov's longest and most exuberant play, *Tragediya Gospodina Morna* (*The Tragedy of Mister Morn*, not published even in Russian until 1997)—*and* edit the remaining texts, the uncollected prose and interviews, the remaining lectures, and the remaining letters. I did not initiate *Nabokov's Butterflies*, or *Verses and Versions*, but I have been interested for many years in editing Nabokov's uncollected prose and am happy also to edit his remaining Russian lectures and his Russian letters, and eventually the still-unpublished English letters.

What difference can Nabokov's posthumous literary legacy make? What has changed in our understanding of Nabokov since his death, and what chances for further change do we have?

Perhaps the first was our growth in knowledge of Nabokov the man. Field's *Nabokov: His Life in Part* was published in 1977, in the month Nabokov died, but what one reviewer called its "incompetence and malice" meant that despite Nabokov's hundreds of pages of corrections to Field's typescripts, it still offered very little knowledge of or insight into the man.[4] The editing of *The Nabokov-Wilson Letters* (1979) had begun while Nabokov was still alive. This rich correspondence showed the back story to the fierce public rift in the mid-1960s between Nabokov and Edmund Wilson, the leading American critic from the 1930s to the 1960s, and Nabokov's close involvement in American literary life from 1940, despite to many seeming to arrive like a bolt from the blue in the late 1950s. *Selected Letters, 1940–1977* offered more glimpses of Nabokov while leaving many gaps, but as John Updike wrote in response: "What a writer! And, really, what a basically reasonable and decent man." My *Vladimir Nabokov: The Russian Years* (1990) and *Vladimir Nabokov: The American Years* (1991) benefitted from years in Nabokov's and other archives from Moscow to Stanford and from interview leads the archives suggested. The two volumes allowed a full treatment of Nabokov's Russian context; his Russian writing; his other American careers as a lepidopterist and a teacher, translator, and scholar; and the protective withdrawal of his final European years from 1959 to 1977. Stacey Schiff's *Véra (Mrs. Vladimir Nabokov)* offered another perspective. When *Letters to Véra* appears in 2011 it will finally correct the image some still have, despite all the evidence in his literary work and outside, of Nabokov as somehow cold and aloof. When his letters to his family—to his parents, sister, and brother—appear a little later, they will show a loving and playful son, a supportive and sometimes critically corrective brother. When his letters to his other Russian friends, especially other writers, artists, and musicians, appear—usually much more intense and intimate than the equivalent letters in English—they will illuminate his intense engagement in, as well as his self-protective creative detachment from, Russian émigré cultural life.

Many have read *Lolita* but little else of Nabokov. Even many much better acquainted with his work knew little, for a long time, beyond his prose fiction and his memoirs. In his own late years Nabokov wanted to make less-prominent sides of his achievement visible when he translated his Russian poems, collected his English poems, republished his chess problems in *Poems and Problems*, and, with Dmitri's help, translated three volumes of Russian stories in the 1970s. When he was too unwell to write more, in his last years, he selected his Russian poems, published as *Stikhi* two years after his death. Nabokov's poetry has always divided readers. Some see it as light, brittle, old-fashioned. Georgiy Adamovich, the most influential émigré critic, regularly dismissed it, only to fall into Nabokov's trap and hail as works of a new genius two poems Nabokov published not under his regular Russian pseudonym, Vladimir Sirin, but under the pseudonym

Vasily Shishkov. Some keen readers of Nabokov think the poetry he writes for John Shade intentionally poor. Other excellent readers of poetry, such as the critic Helen Vendler and the poet R. S. Gwynn, consider his poetry first-rate, hiding depths of concealed design under its glittering surface patterns. A forthcoming publication of Shade's "Pale Fire" unencumbered by Kinbote (see chapter 24, "'Pale Fire': Poem and Pattern"); a pseudo-facsimile edition of the poem, on index cards, as if Shade's own manuscript; and the translations Dmitri continues to produce, including his excellent version of his father's longest Russian poem, "A University Poem," should help in the reappraisal of Nabokov's lifelong commitment to poetry launched in Paul Morris's hefty *Vladimir Nabokov: Poetry and the Lyric Voice* (2010).

Nabokov translated one of his plays, *The Waltz Invention*, at a publisher's invitation in the mid-1960s. Dmitri translated four more for *The Man from the USSR and Other Plays*. Once Tommy Karshan and Anastasia Tolstoy complete their translation of the longest and most colorful of the Russian plays, *The Tragedy of Mr. Morn*, and it is published with the long and short versions of his *Lolita* screenplays, readers will have about 800 pages of Nabokov's dramatic writing to factor into their sense of his work.

Nabokov also wished to collect his verse translations but, like Véra, did not find the time. Now *Verses and Versions*, although it omits his translations into Russian and French verse, allows the Anglophone reader to appreciate easily the hundreds of pages of verse he translated from Russian into English *outside* those already published in separate books, the anonymous medieval *Song of Igor's Campaign* (1959) and Pushkin's *Eugene Onegin* (1964, revised 1975). The thousand pages of notes to his translation into English of *Eugene Onegin* have been translated into Russian as the best commentary available in any language.

Nabokov as a reader of other writers was known in his lifetime from his highly personal and penetrating study *Nikolay Gogol*. Thanks to the enthusiasm of former students like Alfred Appel Jr., Hannah Green, and the New York journalist Ross Wetzsteon, his lectures were already renowned before the publication of the four volumes in the early 1980s. Those have now become talismans for writers and readers, if not for academic critics. The impression created by the existing volumes of lectures, that Nabokov focused only on the peak of his homeland's output, will be corrected in the new volumes of Russian literature. His *Eugene Onegin* displays his scholarly precision but little of the warm personal passion for Pushkin visible in his Russian fiction, especially *The Gift*. This warmth saturates the new lectures, where his interest in Pushkin as writer and man and icon of artistic freedom radiates from page after page. Nabokov's own artistic credo, often tantalizingly oblique in his fiction, poetry, and drama, here receives its most direct expression in his comments on other writers. With the forthcoming lectures, we will have three volumes of Nabokov's translations of Russian verse, the two volumes of *Eugene Onegin* annotations, and soon two or three volumes of his Cornell lectures on Russian literature: seven or eight volumes from the man who forms a natural bridge between Russian and English literature.

Another aspect of Nabokov's extraordinary output was his passion for butterflies and his work as a professional lepidopterist. Field was so little interested in this side of his subject that he imagined Nabokov climbing trees to catch butterflies. My biography established the seriousness of Nabokov's science. About the time it appeared, lepidopterists working in South America were discovering new species of Blues, Nabokov's specialty, in the Andes. They also discovered that Nabokov, who had worked out the specific and generic relationships of Latin American Blues from the very few specimens available to him in wartime Cambridge, Massachusetts, had determined them perfectly.

In just over a decade, Nabokov's lepidopterological work went from seeming a mere personal quirk that had led to a few inconsequential amateur publications to being widely available in the 800-page *Nabokov's Butterflies*, annotated minutely by Dieter E. Zimmer (see chapter 9, "Netting Nabokov"); narrated and contextualized by lepidopterist Kurt Johnson and his cowriter Steve Coates, in *Nabokov's Blues: The Scientific Odyssey of a Literary Genius* (1999); updated, cited extensively, and commemorated in fifteen-odd papers by Johnson, Zsolt Bálint, and Dubi Benyamini; and even featuring in *Natural History*. Naomi Pierce, curator of Lepidoptera at Harvard's Museum of Comparative Zoology, and therefore Nabokov's successor, agreed in the early 2000s to organize an exhibition at the MCZ in commemoration of Nabokov's butterflies. Herself an expert in the Blues, even she had assumed he was merely a gifted amateur, but she ended the project in awe at Nabokov's insight. (Stop Press: January 2011. A new paper by a team led by Pierce suggests that DNA analysis—undreamed of, of course, in Nabokov's day—supports his hypothesis about the evolution of Latin American Blues.)[5]

In *Speak, Memory* Nabokov uses the nickname of a local bog, "America," where he collected butterflies as a child, as a way to prefigure the America he would sail for at the end of his autobiography. In a poem, he foresaw in this America refuge, *per contra*, that he would one day be recognized in the land of his birth: "a Russian branch's shadow shall be playing upon the marble of my hand."[6] It did not happen in his lifetime. Even when Véra Nabokov edited the Russian poems he had selected just before his death for inclusion in *Stikhi* 1979, she had no inkling that his books would be published in the Soviet Union, with official blessing, a few years later. Now Nabokov's verse has earned a volume in the prestigious Biblioteka Poetov series; his work has been collected in a ten-volume annotated edition and glossed by Russian scholars like Alexander Dolinin; it is being reissued by Azbuka, for whom Andrey Babikov has produced an exemplary edition of all his Russian plays.[7]

Nabokov had a long-standing interest in infinity. One of the many paradoxes of infinity is that although there can be larger and smaller infinities, infinity equals infinity times two. Nabokov's work seemed inexhaustible even in his own lifetime. Now it seems twice as inexhaustible and, for all its increased diversity, even more seamless. *The Original of Laura* will be almost the last new Nabokov fiction we will ever see. But there are hundreds, even thousands more pages to come of Nabokov in full flow, and not dammed up by death.

NABOKOV'S METAPHYSICS

6. Retrospects and Prospects

I wrote my M.A. thesis between November 1973 and January 1974 at the University of Canterbury, Christchurch, New Zealand, on what were then Nabokov's last three novels, *Pale Fire*, *Ada*, and *Transparent Things*. A few months later, when *Strong Opinions* reached New Zealand, I read a 1972 interview where Nabokov, talking about *Transparent Things*, expressed surprise that neither the "careful readers [who] have published some beautiful stuff about it . . . nor, of course, the common criticule discerned the structural knot of the story. May I explain that simple and elegant point?" He continues: "The solution, my friend, is so simple that one is almost embarrassed to furnish it. But here goes." I had already reached that solution—that it is the ghost of the novelist Mr. R., who dies in the course of the novel, who narrates it and in its last sentence welcomes the hero, Hugh Person, over the threshold of death. To reassure Nabokov that readers could realize this unaided, I sent him my only copy of the thesis, with return postage paid. Véra wrote back on his behalf with generous praise, but what I treasured most was the occasional cross or indignant correction in Nabokov's thick pencil hand.

By the time I received the thesis back, late in 1974, I was studying for a Ph.D. in English at the University of Toronto. For my dissertation I had considered other periods and authors, and even began working on John Barth, but I shifted back to Nabokov, focusing on *Ada*, annotating it line by line but also examining it in the context of his work and thought. In early 1977 I suddenly saw how to map Nabokov's philosophical—and especially metaphysical—world (also see chapter 7; for a more detailed original version, see part 2 of my book *Nabokov's* Ada: *The Place of Consciousness*). Another fifteen months later, in mid-1978, I saw how Nabokov had made Lucette central to the novel even as vain Van and arrogant Ada seem to push her to the periphery and to suicide (for a later reflection on this aspect of the novel, see chapter 25, "*Ada*: The Bog and the Garden") and how he suggests that from beyond death she somehow intervenes in Van and Ada's life, as Sybil and Cynthia Vane, pointedly evoked in *Ada*, had done much more directly in the 1951 story "The Vane Sisters."

Later that year I learned from the Nabokov scholar and publisher Carl Proffer that in her introduction to her husband's posthumous collected poems in Russian, Véra had identified *potustoronnost'*, "the beyond," as his main theme. This both heartened me and seemed an oversimplification. Proffer showed my thesis and passed on Véra's remark to William Woodin Rowe, whose book *Nabokov's Deceptive World* had occasioned Nabokov's most furious and hilarious denunciation of a critic's work (see *SO*). Rowe quickly wrote *Nabokov's Spectral Dimension*, in which spooks, not sex, had become the new key to Nabokov, and Proffer's press, Ardis, published it in 1981. Indignant, I returned the contract for the book version of my thesis to Ardis. Already consumed by my first years as a university teacher and working on the Nabokov biography, I did too little to seek publication elsewhere and sheepishly returned to Ardis in 1984. *Nabokov's* Ada: *The Place of Consciousness*, was published in 1985, with a critique of *Nabokov's Spectral Dimension* as an appendix.

By now other more responsible scholars such as Don Barton Johnson, Pekka Tammi, and Sergey Davydov had also begun to follow Véra Nabokov's lead.[1] I, too, added more about Nabokov's testing the boundaries of life and death in my readings of his style in general and of some of his novels, especially *The Defense* and *The Gift*, in *Vladimir Nabokov: The Russian Years* (1990). The next year Vladimir Alexandrov published *Nabokov's Otherworld*. As I wrote in a review, I thought it "immeasurably superior to Rowe's in intelligence and argument. But is the 'otherworld' Nabokov's 'main theme'?"

To my surprise, in defending my interpretation of *Pale Fire* in *Vladimir Nabokov: The American Years* in a Nabokv-L listserv discussion at the end of 1997, I found more conclusive flaws in my earlier arguments than others had suggested and discovered evidence that seemed to demand a quite different—and decidedly otherworldly—solution that I had never expected. I set this forth in *Nabokov's* Pale Fire: *The Magic of Artistic Discovery*, where I ensure that readers cannot reach the otherworldly without the full engagement with this world, and with the invented world of the novel, that *Pale Fire* wonderfully inspires.

In 2000 I was invited to give the keynote for a small conference on Nabokov's metaphysics at the Nabokov Museum in St. Petersburg. This talk reflects the novelty and excitement of discovering Nabokov's metaphysics; the suspicion that it could become a routine key to the work of someone who always hated the routine; and the questions that I felt needed to be asked both within Nabokov's framework and outside it—where my evolutionary interests begin to show.

In 1977 I visited Russia for the first time. My Russian had just become fluent then, though it has silted up since, and I was walking and talking in the countryside with some new friends. At the time I was writing my Ph.D. dissertation on Nabokov and had recently worked out what I still think a fair analysis of his metaphysics.[2] Somehow this came up, and one person wanted to quiz me further while the others walked on ahead. When we rejoined them, one of the others asked: "What did he say about Nabokov's philosophy?" The woman I had been talking to answered: "Nothing."

Five years later I was at Harvard, researching Nabokov's biography and interviewing Harry Levin, one of the great American critics of the twentieth century, who had been, through his Russian wife, Elena, a friend of the Nabokovs for many decades. Levin asked what particularly interested me in Nabokov's work. "I suppose, his philosophy." He laughed, puzzled at my response but sure of his own: "But he doesn't *have* a philosophy!"

Things have changed. At the Cambridge Nabokov centenary conference in 1999, I arrived from a lecture at the Nabokov Museum just as Zoran Kuzmanovich, the editor of *Nabokov Studies*, was arguing that all the critical attention paid to Nabokov's metaphysics left out *this* world in Nabokov's work. After his paper we had the liveliest discussion I have been part of at any Nabokov conference. Kuzmanovich raised a real issue: now that so much has been said about Nabokov's metaphysics, what else remains to be said, or what are we forgetting to talk about?

But perhaps that is jumping the gun. What has been established about Nabokov's metaphysics?

It was in late 1977 that Véra Nabokov wrote for her introduction to *Stikhi* that no one seemed to have noticed the main theme of his work: the beyond (*potustoronnost'*).[3] She didn't know that earlier that year I had written about this, or perhaps she wouldn't have said what she did. But I think she was wrong then, as I later told her, and I still think so. I think Nabokov's main theme was, in his own words, the position of consciousness in the universe (*SM* 218: "To try to express one's position in regard to the universe embraced by consciousness, is an immemorial urge"). That certainly *includes* asking about what might lie behind or beyond consciousness, but the beyond itself, in Nabokov's own terms, is too unknowable to be the main theme of a novelist's work.

I argued in 1977, and I would still argue, that Nabokov's own image in *Speak, Memory* and elsewhere of a kind of Hegelian spiral of being provides the basic framework of his metaphysics: a first, inner, thetic, arc, *space without time*; a larger, antithetic, arc, *time without consciousness*; a still more open, synthetic, arc, *human consciousness in time*; and beyond that, ampler and still ampler arcs that include, beyond human death, as a new thesis, perhaps, *a consciousness beyond time*, and somewhere further out still, perhaps after several more twists, some more or less ultimate synthesis, *a conscious designing force* (see *SM* 275, 301). I also suggested that on each arc of the spiral, two complementary poles of Nabokov's mind point in opposite directions (*NAPC*, 67–108; *VNRY*, 294–95). He has a passion for independence, for the individuality of things, which leads him to delve deeper into the details of isolated particulars, and a passion for pattern, which leads him to search for new connections and combinations in things.

In the world of space, he attends, on the one hand, to the particularity of natural objects (butterflies, famously, but much else besides) and, on the other, to the unique combinations of things and especially to the designs of mimicry, which, as he says, "had a special attraction for me" (*SM* 124). In the world of time, he focuses, on the one hand, on the freedom, the openness of time and, on the other, on the mysteries of the patterns we can see in time that might seem like fate. In the world of human consciousness, he focuses on the unique freedom of the mind within the moment and on its power to reach beyond its time or place by connecting one thing with another in memory or imagination.

He knows we cannot see any form of consciousness beyond death, but he imagines the next arc of the spiral in terms of overcoming the confinement of human consciousness to the present moment and gaining a free access to the past; in terms of being able to detect the designs of time; and in terms of overcoming the confinement of personality and somehow being able to form free combinations with other souls. Still further out, beyond even a human consciousness that has transcended death, he suspects other levels of consciousness, culminating eventually in a form of mind that actually creates our world, allowing for the independence of things it creates yet imparting whatever designs it chooses, inviting lesser forms of consciousness to develop their own freedom and to exercise their own creative power in recombining the parts of their world or in discovering the freedom and the design that lie behind it.

I have tried to explain, especially in the "Nabokov the Writer" chapter in *VNRY*, how this metaphysics also helps explain the peculiarities of Nabokov's style: the distinct detail and the verbal design; the unpredictables of the present and the patterns of the past; the power of the mind, especially as it tries to peer beyond itself through the heightened control he imparts to his sentences, in a kind of escape from the muddle of the moment into the freedom of timelessness; and everything that he hides in the texture of a verbal world to be rediscovered by our inquiring minds.

I have also tried to probe the expression of Nabokov's metaphysics in some of his major works: *The Defense*, *The Gift*, *Speak, Memory*, *Pale Fire*, *Ada*, and *Transparent Things* (see especially *NAPC*, *VNRY*, *VNAY*, and *NPFMAD*). Others have joined me in exploring the metaphysical system revealed in these and other books, but I know that I, for one, am still baffled by such other major works as *Invitation to a Beheading* (where the otherworldly quality seems too dominant, even, paradoxically, despite its emphatic absence) and *Lolita* (where it seems too recessive, even as Humbert celebrates his island of entranced time).

Apart from working out how his metaphysics manifests itself in individual works there are other tasks still to pursue. One is to identify the sources of Nabokov's metaphysics. Some obvious sources are his mother's noninstitutional religious sensibility; the pre-Darwinian, early-nineteenth-century tradition of natural theology in George Paley and others, who felt that the intricacy of natural design was clear evidence of a supernatural designer, an attitude that had powerful after-echoes in the poetry of Browning, a lifelong favorite of Nabokov's; the antipositivism of the late nineteenth and early twentieth centuries, especially in artistic circles in the symbolists of Western Europe and Russia: the world of Mallarmé, Yeats, and Blok; and the late-nineteenth-/early-twentieth-century development by Bergson of an indeterminist and nonmaterialist explanation for evolution. Others have looked at Berkeley,[4] whom Nabokov at least mentions, and Uspensky, to whom he never once refers.[5] There is much to be done in this area—we need to look, for instance, at Pascal, Leibniz, Kant, Schopenhauer—although in view of our ignorance of *what* Nabokov read *when*, and Nabokov's reluctance to cite sources and his inclination to find his own terms, this seems likely to remain contested territory.

Another task is to trace the development of Nabokov's metaphysics. To judge by a note he wrote in 1918 (quoted in *VNRY* 154), his attitudes were clearly established by then, and he already sounds the independent and, in a sense, skeptical note that we hear in his later works: as Michael Wood has aptly commented, his metaphysics is "a theology for sceptics."[6] But in Nabokov's early poems and early stories there is a tendency for the otherworldly to break into this world that is at odds with the subtler methods of his later work. Perhaps this early tendency was merely the result of his reaching for convenient and conventional models, or perhaps it is evidence that his early thinking was indeed more shaped by traditional sources than his later work suggests.

But by about 1925, Nabokov started to stick to the world we see and know and to suggest something more beyond this world only as if by inversion. In "The Return of Chorb," for instance, the husband's attempt to retrace the route of his brief life with the wife he has just lost stresses only the impossibility, in human terms, of travelling back in time as we can in space and the desperation of the human craving for a freer kind of time. My guess, but it is only that, is that Nabokov's sense of a designing force that creates a world for us to rediscover develops into a central part of his metaphysics mostly after the 1920s, perhaps as a result of his deepening knowledge of mimicry or of his exposure to the surprises of his scientific discoveries. Or perhaps this is an illusion, and the change simply reflects his own increasing capacity in his work to create a world that we as readers have to rediscover.

In the 1969 article in *Time* that led to my reading *Pale Fire* and my "conversion" into a passionate Nabokovian, Nabokov's own words provided the headline: "I have never met a more lucid, more lonely, better balanced mad mind than mine."[7] That combination of lucid, lonely, and mad almost suggests to me, now, that Nabokov thought he had buried his metaphysical secrets—the secrets of Fyodor's dead father's participation in Fyodor's life, or dead Hazel Shade's participation in Kinbote's and Shade's lives, for instance, if these readings are right—had buried them so deep that they would perhaps never be discovered. Was it for this reason that, although the skeptical note sounds more and more strongly in his later works, there are also more explicit pointers past the skeptical reading, at least in the acrostic of "The Vane Sisters" and the ghostly narrator or narrators of *Transparent Things*? Did Nabokov write these two works partly *in order to* provide the key to what is safely stored but locked away in his other work?

But what I want to focus on here is not questions about the nature of Nabokov's metaphysics, its impact on his style or works, or its origins and development, but some quite different kinds of questions that seem appropriate now that so much has been done on his metaphysics, now that it threatens to settle into an orthodoxy in Nabokov criticism.

The first question is: What difference does his metaphysics make? Or, less crudely: Why stress the metaphysics so much, as such a central part of his work, when it is possible to respond with great pleasure to Nabokov and not even *notice* his metaphysics—as Harry Levin and, at least in Véra Nabokov's eyes, everybody before she wrote her introduction to *Stikhi*, had done? There are utterly committed Nabokovians, like Dieter E. Zimmer—who has worked on Nabokov longer and more selflessly than anyone else—who find Nabokov's work astonishingly fertile but who have no interest in or sympathy for his metaphysics. How can a response like this be possible, if, as I have argued, Nabokov's metaphysics shapes his style *and* structures many of his stories, and if one of his claims to originality is the originality of his philosophical world and of the artistic measures he has found to express it?

What if, simply, we dislike or disagree with his metaphysics? Can we then like what he writes? We can easily *not* share Homer's metaphysics, or Dante's, and still admire his work. I'm not sure it's so easy closer to our own times. I know I would prefer Yeats much more, although I value him highly, if he were not so often "away with the fairies," and I know that T. S. Eliot's craving for traditional belief, especially traditional Christianity, is at least one strong obstacle to my responding to his work (as it was, too, for Nabokov).

I happen not to share Nabokov's metaphysics, yet I find it a fascinating intellectual achievement—as I do *not* find the irrationalist credulism of Yeats or the traditionalism-as-refuge of Eliot. Nabokov's metaphysics seems, indeed, an intellectual achievement like Homer's or Dante's, a comprehensive vision that, unlike theirs, of course, can reflect and incorporate modern skepticism even as it refines and fulfils age-old human ways of making ultimate sense of our world.

Being agents ourselves, and particularly attuned to social action, we human beings tend to think of cause in terms of agency and to explain unknown causes in terms of unseen agents: hence all the gods, spirits, witches, fairies, and so on that have appealed to humankind for as long as we have had language capable of telling stories.[8] Nabokov knows he cannot *know* directly whether there is unseen agency behind this world, but something in the world's inexhaustibleness, which he reads as generosity, and in its intricacy, which he reads as design—even design seemingly hidden for rediscovery by our intelligent eyes—suggests to him there is some mindlike agent ultimately behind things.

And because we explain things in terms of the difference between the material and the mental, or between the physical and the spiritual (we can cause a material object to move by touching it in the right way, but we can cause a "mental object," another person, to move without our needing to physically touch them), we also have an age-old conviction that the spiritual is not subject to the same laws as the physical. That being so, and the mental or spiritual being unseen, we have often come to the conclusion that perhaps our spirits, our nonmaterial parts, survive, unseen, the material decay brought on by death. Nabokov again knows he cannot *know* that we survive death, but as in the case of conscious agency as ultimate cause, he uses the very fact that we have no direct evidence of the survival of mortal consciousness as the beginnings of his argument. We cannot know because an existence beyond death would have to be so inconceivably different from the conditions of mortal consciousness that it is beyond our apprehension.

This is why I find it so annoying when readers of Nabokov, aware of the ways in which the shape and structure of his metaphysics have been described, tend at once to look for explanations in terms of the metaphysics.[9] This is not at all how Nabokov has written since his work began to mature, in 1925, apart from the unique exception of *Transparent Things*, where we see the story through the eyes of the dead narrator. In the vast bulk of his work, there is no *presumption* of the otherworldly. He presents a seemingly self-sufficient material world, with human beings in it who are certainly mental agents, who may have a conviction or a strong curiosity about something mindlike behind or beyond matter (as in the case of, say, Fyodor or Shade), but whose conviction never seems supported, or whose curiosity never seems answered, within the fiction. Fyodor imagines fate on his and Zina's side, but they are then locked out of the apartment where they could be together at last. Shade feels as confident that his daughter is somewhere alive as that he will wake up the next morning, but he is killed that very day. It is only after we have mastered all the details of the particular world of a novel, forming a relationship to its parts and its time quite unlike that of the characters as they live it, that we can see that the very evidence that seems to refute the hopes of a Fyodor or a Shade actually testifies to their being fulfilled in a way greater than even they could imagine.

Another reason Nabokov's metaphysics seems to me such an amazing intellectual achievement is that in his efforts to encompass modern skepticism, he finds himself prompted to such extraordinary *artistic* achievements. His metaphysics forces Nabokov to invent worlds that are self-sufficient, on one level, more or less akin to our normal modern way of reading our world—although of course he sees these worlds more exactly and more imaginatively than the rest of us—but worlds that nevertheless, the more closely we look, seem to require a deeper and utterly unexpected level of explanation. No one else has ever been able to create such hidden worlds of discovery within stories so fascinating and original and moving on a first reading.

Whether or not one shares Nabokov's sense of a designer behind the world and some sort of deliverance beyond death, it seems to me, does not matter artistically. Of course *personally* it would be wonderful if Nabokov's metaphysics were true and one could believe it, but I cannot do so: it seems to result from hopes rather than sober recognitions. The mimicry, for instance, that Nabokov took as such strong evidence of a conscious design concealed behind nature, a cosmic hide-and-seek, can in fact now be explained perfectly well, even in its most intricate forms, in terms of evolution by Darwinian natural selection.

But as a matter of attitude, Nabokov's response to his world is wonderfully refreshing and fertile. If the optimist sees a glass half filled with water as half-full and the pessimist sees it as half-empty, Nabokov sees the empty glass as overfull: merely looking at the reflections of the scene around the glass and the refracted distortions of the scene behind the glass are more than enough to quench the mind's thirst. But he also sees the full glass as empty: his thirst to savor and understand the world is infinitely greater than even the full glass can provide.

Nabokov has a sense of the inexhaustible riches of the world, even a small aspect of the world (the butterfly genus *Lycaenidae*, for instance), yet this, nevertheless, seems to drive him in quest of an even more inexhaustible relationship to his world. "Though I personally would be satisfied to spend the whole of eternity gazing at a blue hill or a butterfly," he wrote in 1940, "I would feel the poorer if I accepted the idea of there not existing still more vivid means of knowing butterflies and hills."[10] We may or may not share his sense that the very riches of the world amount to a generosity offering hope that there is some even more inexhaustible surprise beyond what our mortal minds can see. But whether we share that sense or not, we can appreciate the power of his drive to know this world and to know what might lie beyond it and his capacity to awaken us to the surprise of this world and the surprises that perhaps lie behind it, if only we could know more.

What matters in Nabokov's metaphysics is not so much his answers, then, although these are wonderfully elegant, intellectually and artistically, as the fact that both his questions and his answers arise from such a full appreciation of this world and from such a desire for more.

7. Nabokov's Afterlife

Don Barton Johnson, who was a cryptologist and a Slavic linguist before the Russian literary scholar, editor, and publisher Carl Proffer invited him to solve Nabokovian puzzles, had become by 1985, with the publication of *Worlds In Regression: Some Novels of Vladimir Nabokov*, the leading American Nabokovian of his day. He later founded the journal *Nabokov Studies* and the electronic listserv, Nabokv-L, both still running.

Despite his own work on the relation between this world and a next or other world in Nabokov, this natural skeptic came to feel that the metaphysics was almost superfluous icing on the Nabokovian cake. At the Nabokov centenary conference in Cambridge in 1999—where Zoran Kuzmanovich stirred so much discussion when he asked about the place of the metaphysics in Nabokov—Jane Grayson, the conference organizer, invited a concluding discussion on future directions in Nabokov scholarship. Among other things, Don Johnson and I addressed Zoran's question, and I later persuaded Don that we should write up our remarks for a dialogical prologue to the two-volume record of the conference. Here's my contribution. I try to explain the relationship between Nabokov's imagination, as we see it in his writing, and his ethics, metaphysics, and psychology—or to show the depths beneath the dazzling surface and the surface as an entrance to the depths.

Don Johnson concludes with a series of linked questions about responding to and evaluating Nabokov. Let me follow his cue and start with my own series. Do we respond to Nabokov, and do we rate him highly, because of his ethical seriousness or his metaphysical range or his epistemological depth? Or do we respond to him and rate him rather for his gifts of word and image, character and story, fictional detail and form? Or for less usual literary values, such as his unique relationship to his curious readers, the challenges and rewards he offers us? Or for his humor, his irony, his pathos? Or for his alertness to nature or art, to individual cognition or social interaction?

In fact, of course, readers respond to authors and rate them in different ways. Some, like Don himself, will particularly enjoy the local puzzles in Nabokov's work; others, like Ellen Pifer, will pay these little heed but be passionately interested in his ethics.[1] Yet all readers are likely to have their imaginations caught first, if at all, at the level of word, character, story, feeling. Some, of course, may be deterred by obscure words like "granoblastically," by repellent characters like Axel Rex, by slow stories like Smurov's, by perverse feelings like Humbert's, or by a sense that Nabokov demands too much of his readers or dismisses or refuses to care for too many of us and our kind. A proportion of readers who reject Nabokov out of such considerations may gradually be won back by adequate explanations of the ethical, epistemological, metaphysical, aesthetic, scientific, psychological, or sociological reasons for this or that feature or characteristic of his work, while others who might otherwise enjoy a story once and then set it aside might be encouraged to return, to linger, and to discover more as they perceive these dimensions for themselves or with the help of others.

A classic has to appeal to many readers over many readings and many changes in taste, personal and historical. No work can satisfy every taste (a Vermeer can do things that a Breughel cannot and vice versa), but the more dimensions of excellence and interest a work has, the more likely it is to endure, to invite us to keep returning to something that somehow still remains new. The ethical, epistemological, and other dimensions, in other words, are not extraliterary but enrich the literary experience. Their multiplicity and consistency add to the value of a literary work as their absence or inconsistency diminish it—although, again, it must be stressed that readers will respond differently to these different dimensions, as well as to their multiplicity or paucity or their consistency or inconsistency. Of course, Nabokov's special gift is to suggest so many dimensions without ponderous system building, with the lightest and fastest of touches, keeping our imaginations off guard, jumping from one sudden foothold to another, rather than plodding along a predictable path.

Don seems to imply that one side of Nabokov's art (the ethical, say, or the metaphysical) is readily detachable from another (in particular, the aesthetic). This was not Nabokov's attitude ("the forces of imagination . . . in the long run, are the forces of good";[2] "the inherent morality of uninhibited art" [*SL* 57]), nor is it mine.

The imagination tries to see things from many different points of view, and that has ethical consequences. It is no accident that Shakespeare, the greatest verbal imagination the word has known, was also the greatest creator of human character. One of the many reasons he remains so perpetually fresh is that he can see from the side of an Aaron as well as a Titus, of an Angela as well as an Isabella, a Bernardine as well as a Duke Vincentio, a Caliban as well as a Prospero. For that reason he has done as much as anyone to extend our sense of humanity, to make us see the depth, flaws, and strengths in people high and low, like us or not. Nabokov works differently, depicting the egotism of the ego from within, in a way that makes us confront our own egotism, as well as encouraging us to transcend it, to exercise the full freedom of our imaginations. His work would be vastly poorer if he did not invite us to see from Lucette's point of view and Ada's, as well as from Van's; from Shade's point of view and Hazel's, as well as from Kinbote's; from Lolita's point of view and Charlotte's, as well as from Humbert's.

Not only does Nabokov see and *realize* in his fiction both the freedom and the confinement of the ego—of those characters at the periphery as well as at the centers of his stories—but his imagination also tries to look at and, again, to *realize* human life not only from within but from without. He talks of Gogol's religion as "imaginative, humanly imaginative (and thus metaphysically limited)" (*NG* 22), and he tries to avoid such limits, to pass beyond the desperate attachment to the official version of Western metaphysics we find in T. S. Eliot or the uncritical acceptance of any not currently official version we find in Yeats.

Hence it is for good reason that Don's remarks focus particularly on the metaphysical side of Nabokov, a subject, as he points out, increasingly dominant in Nabokov studies over the last twenty years. He modestly underplays his own invaluable part, in *Worlds in Regression* and after, in this development. But he asks if it would make any difference whether Nabokov's otherworldly philosophy were shopworn. To me it certainly would. Eliot's craving for the authority of tradition and Yeats's refuge in the irrational to me seriously diminish their art. Nabokov is of such interest partly because he is such a clear and independent thinker, and his style is the way it is because he has such clarity and independence of thought. You cannot detach the style or the wit from the rest.

Don now speaks of a plurality of "levels" or "worlds." Advisedly so, in my view. I found his older "two-world" terminology unsatisfactory because, first, Nabokov stresses in numerous ways that the "other" world he suspects surrounds the one we see is somehow *in* as well as *beyond* this one. Second, the idea of two worlds collapses or ignores several possible levels in the Nabokovian "beyond": a more or less personal afterlife; a more or less personal fate, designing force or forces, or series of such forces not responsible for the world but creatively contributing to or attempting to contribute to the designs of time; and a more or less ultimate conscious creative power, or god, more or less emergent, more or less responsible for and more or less providentially predesigning "this" world. Third, "two worlds" overdefines as it undercounts. Nabokov suggests possibilities and possibilities within possibilities or, if you like, worlds within worlds: worlds in regression.

Nabokov was fascinated by the possibility of a beyond and rightly felt it would make all the difference to our sense of our lives if we could know whether there *is* anything beyond. But he also knew that despite all his own searching he had no "conclusive evidence." Only in private intuitions could he feel this possibility; only in the analogies he could fashion in his art could he express it; and even then he could do so only covertly, only through indirection and concealment. In order not to falsify human experience, he never (outside the more or less explicit ghost story of *Transparent Things*) violates the rule that for his mortal characters and for all but those rereaders who have transcended the linear time of the characters, this world is all there is.

This means, of course, that Nabokov's ethics and epistemology, like his politics and sociology and psychology, must operate within the constraints of this world. This also means that although his metaphysics, his otherworld, is a vitally important aspect of his work, and in some senses its deepest level, its most recently discovered, and its most secret until discovery, he creates his fiction to work perfectly self-sufficiently, to have its principal life upon the surface tension of the here and now.

Good work is being done on Nabokov's metaphysics by younger scholars, and there is more to be done. But Nabokov was never reductive and never uninterested in this world. May I offer some advice? Do not look for Nabokov's otherworld just because it is a critical fashion but because you think the evidence compels you to, and do not overlook all his other worlds, his Russia, his Germany, his France, his England, his America, his Switzerland, his dream and nightmare Europes, his Zemblas and Antiterras. If he could not make this world exist so well in fiction, his otherworlds would matter much, much less.

NABOKOV'S BUTTERFLIES

8. Nabokov, Literature, Lepidoptera

In writing the biography I knew I needed to examine closely Nabokov's passion for Lepidoptera because it was so early, deep, and long-lasting, because it dominated his working life for much of the 1940s, and because it must have appealed to and intensified something worth understanding in his mind. In researching *Vladimir Nabokov: The American Years* I interviewed those who had worked alongside Nabokov at his bench at the Museum of Comparative Zoology, like graduate student Charles Remington, later head of entomology at Yale. Shortly after the biography, I met Kurt Johnson, then at the American Museum of Natural History. Johnson, the American apex of an international triangle of scholars reexamining the South American Plebejinae, a subfamily of butterflies of which Nabokov had been first reviser, could not stress enough how highly they rated Nabokov's work, and he has remained unwavering in this admiration for twenty years.

In the early 1990s Princeton University Press, which had published my Nabokov biographies, approached me to edit a volume of Nabokov's butterfly papers because a historian of Lepidoptera they had contracted for the project years earlier had not delivered. I agreed but was shortly afterward asked by the nature writer Robert Michael Pyle, also editor of the *Audubon Guide to the Butterflies of North America*, whether I could put him in touch with Dmitri Nabokov for the rights to Nabokov's butterfly papers for a volume for which he was signed with Beacon. I suggested we pool resources, and since Beacon's editor, Deanne Urmy, was keen to venture well beyond the scientific papers into fiction, memoirs, poetry, letters, and notes, we moved to Beacon with *Nabokov's Butterflies: Unpublished and Uncollected Writings*.

I introduced the volume by looking at Nabokov's life in art and science, discussing his work as butterfly collector and scientist as both intimately connected with *and* perfectly separable from his literary output.

My pleasures are the most intense known to man: writing and butterfly hunting.

—Vladimir Nabokov, *Strong Opinions*

The problem is this. Scientists think of VN as an important entomologist who wrote fiction. Literary critics think of VN as one of the most important twentieth century literary figures who somehow fancied insects.

—Ronald Wilkinson[1]

Let me pin Vladimir Nabokov into place between several superficially similar specimens.

Nabokov and Beckett seem likely to be remembered as the foremost writers of the mid-twentieth century. Both published over six decades, from just after the heyday of the great modernists, Joyce, Proust, and Kafka, to the emergence of postmodernism as a fashion and a formula. Both wrote major works in two languages (Russian and English, English and French) and translated them from one language into another. Both wrote with great eloquence, intelligence, learning, wit, and originality. But their visions were polar opposites.

Or, rather, Beckett's was polar, Nabokov's tropical. Beckett saw life as a terminal illness and human thought, speech, and action as a babble amid meaninglessness. Nabokov saw life as "a great surprise" (*PF* 225) amid possibly greater surprises. Four years after the best friend of his childhood was shot and he was forced to leave forever the country he loved, a year after the father he adored was murdered, he has a character, a man whose young son has recently died, speak for him: "Everything in the world is beautiful, but Man only recognizes beauty if he sees it either seldom or from afar" (*SoVN* 45). Nabokov looked at his world tirelessly and at close range, and for all the horrors he could evoke in his darker books, he found it swarming with inexhaustible diversity and delight. Not the least of his delights was Lepidoptera.

In a game that asks us to associate natural kinds and famous people, "butterflies" would yield the answer "Nabokov" as surely as "hemlock" would trigger "Socrates." But while Socrates did not *choose* to be forever linked with hemlock, Vladimir Nabokov made butterflies his lifelong personal mark. He succeeded more than he could ever have imagined at the time when St. Petersburg's best portrait photographer came to record him, a boy of eight, surrounded by butterfly books. Although those who know just one fact about Nabokov know him as the author of *Lolita*, the familiar icon of Sue Lyon as Lolita licking her lollipop never graces books about him. But designers who would not dream of picking hemlock for the cover of a new book on Socrates again and again pin butterflies to the lapel of Nabokovian jackets.

Nabokov's singular attraction to butterflies attracts us as an image and an enigma. Consider this third contrast. In the margins of his manuscripts Pushkin sketched hundreds upon hundreds of human faces in profile, a high proportion of them a stylized and embellished version of his own striking silhouette. Nabokov drew thousands of butterflies for his scientific papers, for his unfinished catalogue of the butterflies of Europe, on the title pages of dedication copies of his novels, and in signing his most playful letters. Pushkin's case needs no explanation: we can expect poets to be interested in people and a romantic poet to be interested in himself above all. But why should someone with Nabokov's great gift as a writer be so obsessed with something so peripheral as butterflies are to most readers?

Does his passion for *papillons* indicate that he is insufficiently interested in people? Or should we argue the opposite, that the way he used the butterfly net of his boyhood has no bearing on the way he flourished his pen? After all, Humbert pursued nymphets, not Nymphalids; Luzhin captured chessmen, not Checkerspots; Pnin accumulated sorrows, not Sulphurs. Why did butterflies so fascinate Nabokov, and why should that so fascinate us? He became the world's most famous lepidopterist, but was he a serious scientist or little more than an enthusiastic collector? Did he leave any legacy in lepidoptery as he did in literature? And are the butterflies and moths in his works no more than a sly authorial signature?

When Nabokov caught his first butterfly in 1906, aged seven, his mother showed him how to spread it. She herself had a passion for collecting mushrooms and came from a family long interested in science. Her mother's father had been president of the Russian Academy of Medicine and her mother had arranged to have a chemical laboratory built for herself. But it was Nabokov's father who had been a keen lepidopterist in his youth. A man of exacting scholarly standards, he was one of Russia's leading criminologists, along with much else (in politics, publishing, public life) that left him little time to wield a net. Nabokov adored both of his parents and the summer estate of Vyra, forty miles south of St. Petersburg, where he caught and collected his first butterflies. His parent's example and encouragement and the chance to see and savor Vyra in a new way sparked an explosive interest in butterflies.

Other elements in his makeup kept the fire burning. Sharp-eyed, sure of hand and foot, a zealous and accomplished sportsman (soccer, tennis, boxing), he always enjoyed the physical thrill of the butterfly chase. But the intellectual challenge appealed just as much to this precocious child. A mathematical prodigy at five, he lost the capacity for complex computation during a bout of pneumonia before he was eight. As he recovered, his mother surrounded his bed with butterflies and butterfly books. Decades later Nabokov would curiously rework that memory by having Humbert bring Lolita, convalescing from influenza, a bouquet of wild flowers collected from a mountain pass and a book called *Flowers of the Rockies*. That child, for good reason, is unresponsive to *that* "parent" and, in fact, escapes before Humbert can see her again. But Nabokov thrived on *his* mother's love, "and the longing to describe a new species completely replaced that of discovering a new prime number" (*SM* 123).

From this point on, literature and Lepidoptera dance an elaborate pas de deux through seventy years of Nabokov's life.

As a boy of nine, still enjoying Wild West games, Nabokov wrote to the great lepidopterist Nikolay Kuznetsov proposing a new subspecies name for a poplar admiral he had found (Kuznetsov scribbled back a two-word reply, the existing subspecies name and the name of its author). A year or two later Nabokov would translate Mayne Reid's Western novel *The Headless Horseman* into French verse. In his twin passions exhilaration merged with ambition and determination. Even before he read and reread all of Tolstoy, Flaubert, and Shakespeare in the original languages as he entered his teens, he had mastered the known butterflies of Europe and "dreamed his way through" the volumes so far published of Adalbert Seitz's *Die Groß-Schmetterlinge der Erde*.[2]

"Few things indeed have I known in the way of emotion or appetite, ambition or achievement, that could surpass in richness and strength the excitement of entomological exploration," Nabokov writes in his autobiography (*SM* 126). His lepidopterological ambitions seemed more haunting than his literary aspirations because they took so much longer to realize. At twelve or so, he sent off the description of a "new" moth to the British journal *The Entomologist*, whose editor did not recognize the species but found out it had already been described by Kretschmar. Twenty years later Nabokov had still discovered no new species but had become the leading writer of the Russian emigration and could recoup his adolescent disappointment by assigning Kretschmar's name to the unfortunate hero of *Camera Obscura*, unwittingly preempted in his love for Magda by another, slyer lover.

At fourteen Nabokov had prepared and distributed to friends and family his first "publication," a romantic poem of which he could later recall only one line, evoking a hawkmoth hovering over a rhododendron. Real publication soon followed. Just turned seventeen, he had a poem accepted by Russia's most august literary journal, *Vestnik Europy*. That same summer,

1916, he had his first book of poems privately printed, and after inheriting his uncle's considerable estate, he began to contemplate seriously an expedition to Central Asia, perhaps with the great explorer and naturalist Grigory Grum-Grzhimaylo.

But when the Bolshevik coup came, he had to flee Petrograd. He could take with him his manuscript albums of verse and the slim volumes of his favorite poets, but he had to leave his butterfly collection behind. In the Crimea with his family, his rhymes nostalgically mourned Vyra and northern Russia even as he exulted in the opportunity to explore the almost Asiatic fauna in the cliffs above Yalta and on the Crimean plateau.

In the spring of 1919 the advance of the Bolshevik army forced the Nabokovs to abandon Yalta, and another butterfly collection, and head for England. In his first term at Cambridge, Nabokov compiled a record of his butterfly collecting in the Crimea that "at last"—he was all of twenty—earned him his first publication in *The Entomologist*. Like the literary work of his Cambridge years—a Russian essay on Rupert Brooke, a translation of a difficult Romain Rolland novel from French into Russian, and, day after day, his own Russian poems—the butterfly article bore no relation to his nominal course of study.

Installed from 1922 in Berlin, by then the center of the Russian emigration, Nabokov soon evolved from imitative poetry to increasingly original prose. Except during a stint as a farm worker at Solliès-Pont near Toulon in the summer of 1923, he had few chances to collect butterflies: writing and tutoring earned him enough only to keep him in Berlin, not to pay for travel further afield. But imagination offered a passe-partout. At the end of 1924 his first story about Lepidoptera, "Christmas," drew on his early and very late memories of northern Russia: the collection he had been forced to forsake at Vyra and the one exception, a hawkmoth pupa that he had kept in a box for seven years and that had hatched in the overheated railway carriage taking him from Petrograd down to Simferopol. Nabokov knew he could not overload and imbalance his fiction with entomological detail, but in "Christmas" a moth that unexpectedly emerges crowns a very human story: A father, presumably a widower, cannot cope with the death of his only child, a son, the little lepidopterist who yearned to see that moth emerge. Just as the father decides life is no longer worth living, the glorious atlas moth cracks open its cocoon, and its huge wings dilate in a sign of new hope, perhaps even of resurrection.

But neither literature nor life offered Nabokov other significant outlets for his love of Lepidoptera until, at the end of 1928, German translation and serial rights for his second novel, *King, Queen, Knave*, paid well enough for him to take his wife, Véra, on their first butterfly expedition together, in the eastern Pyrenees, from February to April 1929 at Le Boulou then until June at Saurat.

As would often happen in later years, in seeking butterflies Nabokov also found inspiration. While collecting above Le Boulou, the idea for his first masterpiece, *The Defense*, suddenly sprang to mind.[3] Able to write in the late afternoons and evenings or on wet or dull mornings, he finished the novel by August. Back in Berlin, he checked his new catches against the records of the Entomological Institute at Dahlem in preparation for a report of his finds that he published in *The Entomologist*. In the course of this research he came across a detail that evolved into a key image in his next novella, *The Eye*, and may even, it has been suggested, have provided the first spark for the whole story.[4]

Certainly the four-month expedition in the south of France seems to have awakened Nabokov's sense that his science could play a larger part in his art. As soon as he had completed *The Eye*, in the spring of 1930, he started "The Aurelian," a story about the owner of a Berlin butterfly store, who, after selling his prize collection, hopes to escape his frustrating domestic life and fulfill his one dream of a collecting expedition to Spain and beyond.

By the end of 1932 Nabokov prepared to climb new heights in his art as he moved toward *The Gift*. In this new novel, far longer, denser, and wider in scope than anything else he had yet written, he would fuse his passions for literature and Lepidoptera, art and nature, country and family, life and art; ten years after the assassination of his father, he now felt ready to commemorate him in print. The novel is the story of the development of a young Russian émigré writer in Berlin, Fyodor Godunov, an ardent lepidopterist who as a youth dearly longed to join his father on the last of his entomological expeditions into Central Asia, from which Count Godunov never returned. In real life, Nabokov's father had been an amateur lepidopterist and a celebrated statesman; Fyodor's father has no time for politics but is renowned as a scientist. Yet to Elena Nabokov he seemed an exact portrait of her husband. Fyodor tries to write a biography of his father, and in recounting the expeditions gradually includes himself in the party, at last even taking over his father's voice.

For Fyodor, as for Nabokov, these imagined expeditions are both a wish-fulfillment compensation for a dream that history had forever quashed and a product of painstaking research in the writings of actual Russian naturalists like Grum-Grzhimaylo and Nikolay Przhevalsky. Although he had been producing novels at a rate of one a year, Nabokov began research for *The Gift* early in 1933 and did not complete the book until five years later.

At the beginning of 1937, with much of its final draft still to write, he fled Germany for France. Living in Moulinet, high in the Maritime Alps, in the summer of 1938, he caught a butterfly that seemed the long-delayed realization of his thirty-year-old dream: a new species. Three years later he would be able to describe and assign a species name to his catch—which would eventually prove, as he himself suspected could be the case, to be a hybrid rather than a new species.

In the meantime, like his collecting in the Pyrenees in 1929, the new find intensified further his desire to explore entomology within his art. Sometime in 1939, it seems, Nabokov wrote a long appendix to *The Gift*. Here Fyodor recounts his own early love for Lepidoptera and expounds his father's incisive but cryptic ideas on speciation and evolution, supposedly noted down in outline on the eve of his departure for his final expedition. This appendix, translated from the Russian by Dmitri Nabokov and published for the first time in any language in *Nabokov's Butterflies*, is, with the exception of *The Enchanter*—also a fifty-page typescript, also written in 1939, and also left unpublished in the author's lifetime—the longest piece of Nabokov fiction to appear between his death and the publication of *The Original of Laura* in 2009. Here Nabokov's art, science, and metaphysics meet more unguardedly than anywhere else. Perhaps he did not publish it at the time because his other plans for continuing or expanding *The Gift* were never realized after the outbreak of the Second World War and his shift from Europe to America and from Russian to English. But perhaps, too, he had misgivings about mixing hard science with the kind of free speculation he had allowed himself from behind the mask of the Godunovs, father and son.

Nabokov ends his autobiography with the image of himself and his wife walking their son through a park in St. Nazaire, the port where they boarded the *Champlain* in May 1940 to escape to the United States. They know that Dmitri is about to glimpse the ship, to feel "the blissful shock, the enchantment and glee . . . [of] discovering ahead the ungenuinely gigantic, the unrealistically real prototype of the various toy vessels he had doddled about in his bath . . . to make out, among the jumbled angles of roofs and walls, a splendid ship's funnel, showing from behind the clothesline as something in a scrambled picture—Find What the Sailor Has Hidden—that the finder cannot unsee once it has been seen" (*SM* 309–10). Nabokov sets that ship and the America it implies in this key position at the book's close as the solution of a much larger puzzle, his long experience of exile.

America solved another problem, realized another dream, in allowing him a chance to discover new species and to become not just an informed amateur but a scientist who could make a lasting contribution to lepidopterology. He began to write his autobiography in 1947, just after completing the first draft of his major lepidopterological monograph. No wonder he makes America shine through, ahead of time, here and there in *Speak, Memory*, never more riddlingly or triumphantly than at the end of his chapter on butterflies. In Europe, and in his first two entomological publications, he had been merely a talented collector. After arriving in New York, he turned into a scientist at the same time as—and partly because—he stopped writing in Russian.

In the fall of 1940, Nabokov approached the American Museum of Natural History and asked to be allowed to check the status of his Moulinet catches (almost everything else in his European collection, the third he had lost to history, he had been forced to leave behind in Paris as German tanks advanced). Although he was unfamiliar with microscopes and dissection, he learnt as he went along. Two years earlier, in Paris, he had written his first novel in English, setting much of it in the England he knew from Cambridge days. Then he had still hoped to find an academic or publishing job in Great Britain, but nothing turned up. Now in the United States he did not yet consider himself ready to begin writing fiction for an American audience, but he felt he had to renounce writing fiction in Russian if he was to develop as an American novelist. Meanwhile he spent the winter of 1940–41 preparing the lectures he would give at Stanford that summer and anywhere else that might hire him as a Russian lecturer. But he happily took time off to work for nothing at the AMNH. This resulted in another short paper in the issue of the *Journal of the New York Entomological Society* that published his description of the Moulinet butterfly, which he now named *Lysandra cormion*.

He had supported his family over his first winter in America partly by giving Russian tuition to several women associated with Columbia University. One, Dorothy Leuthold, offered to drive the Nabokovs across the continent to Stanford. Delighted, Nabokov collected all along the way. On June 7, 1941, he discovered a butterfly he recognized as new, and he would name it in Leuthold's honor *Neonympha dorothea* (subsequent work has reclassified it as a subspecies, *Cyllopsis pertepida dorothea*, of a species that had not been known to extend from Mexico into the United States). Here, on the south rim of the Grand Canyon, he realized his dream of discovery even more vividly than he had in Moulinet.

After the summer, Nabokov returned east to a one-year engagement as visiting lecturer in comparative literature at Wellesley College, near Boston. From October 1941 he began to work, unpaid, setting in order the butterfly collections of the Harvard Museum of Comparative Zoology. By the middle of 1942 he had written his first major paper, on the genus *Neonympha*, and was appointed to a one-year position as research fellow at the MCZ, an appointment that would be extended, a year at a time, until he left Cambridge for Cornell in 1948.

During these six years he became the MCZ's de facto curator of Lepidoptera and one of the authorities on South and especially North American polyommatine butterflies, the Blues. He wrote four key papers. In the fifteen-page "Nearctic Forms of *Lycaeides Hüb[ner]*," completed over the winter and spring of 1943, he established principles still used in analyzing the genitalia of the Blues. Between the fall of 1943 and the fall of 1944 he completed a thirty-five-page paper on the morphology of the genus *Lycaeides* that drew on the collection he had built up at the MCZ, now the most representative series of American *Lycaeides* anywhere; here for the first time he developed the technique of describing wing markings by counting scale rows under the microscope. His sixty-page paper on the Blues of Central and South America, "Notes on Neotropical Plebejinae" (written 1944–45), constituted what taxonomists call a "first revision"—a comprehensive reconsideration—of what he called the subfamily Plebejinae and is now known as the tribe Polyommatini. His final and longest paper, the ninety-page monograph on the Nearctic members of the genus *Lycaeides*, took him from 1945 to 1948, since during this time he also wrote most of *Bend Sinister* and added a course in Russian literature to his two Russian-language courses at Wellesley. His paper, in the words of another entomologist, "entirely rearranged the classification of this genus."[5]

The long paper on Neotropical Plebejinae stands out from the rest for several reasons. Nabokov often dreamed of chasing tropical butterflies, but he never had the opportunity. He did, on the other hand, collect zealously in North America. Why, then, did he choose to write a paper on *South American Blues*? For the simple reason that he had already mastered North American Blues and wished to compare the northern groups, as he now understood their relationships, with their southern counterparts. A colleague he greatly respected, Paul Grey, felt a similar impulse with fritillaries, and borrowed all of the AMNH's specimens of South American fritillaries to see how they compared under the microscope with the North American species he knew so well. "He came to a grinding halt, however," notes Kurt Johnson, "when he saw how complex the southern stuff was. Nabokov saw how complex the southern stuff was and chose to do a seminal (generic) nomenclature for it."[6]

Nabokov's work on North American *Lycaeides* transformed the understanding of a particularly difficult genus and has proved extremely durable, but there are many scientists who have undertaken such intrageneric revisions within the well-known Nearctic and Palearctic butterfly fauna. Nabokov's work on South American Blues, though, constitutes the first revision of a whole tribe of butterflies. As such, it took him to the frontiers of lepidopterological knowledge and would prove "seminal" even if the seeds took another half-century to sprout in the recent work of Zsolt Bálint, Kurt Johnson, Dubi Benyamini, and their colleagues.

Nabokov worked as a laboratory scientist in the 1940s in a way he would never do again. Why did he feel driven to spend up to fourteen hours a day at the microscope? Chiefly because he could not stop. He found it bliss to be able to make far-reaching discoveries that he had in one sense long dreamed about and in another hardly anticipated since his earlier work had been so confined to collecting. He was piecing together a whole new world. Those who have worked at the microscope with butterfly genitalia are inclined to say, "Show me a butterfly and I can't tell you what it is, but show me the genitalia and I'll identify anything you have." Nabokov learnt to enjoy the deceptiveness and the difficulty of genitalic identification almost as much as the thrill of exploration and the triumph of discovery.

He also had few demands from the job that provided his basic income, teaching Russian language at Wellesley, until the fall term of 1946 when he was able to add his first literature course. For once his science could advance because his art retreated. Although he began writing *Bend Sinister*, his first American novel, in 1941, he found it agony to renounce his Russian prose. Rather than suffer the throes of writing a full-length work of fiction in a language other than Russian—although he was also writing stories and a critical book on Gogol in English—he could return to entomology, where his working language had always been English and his sense of mastery, far from being diminished, was now vastly expanded.

At the end of *Bend Sinister* he pictures himself as both author of the novel we are reading and as lepidopterist. "Twang," the book ends, "A good night for mothing," as another moth hits the wire screen over his window and he closes down his hero's painful life. In the season the novel was published, its author, now an *Atlantic Monthly* and *New Yorker* regular, was photographed by *Time* and *Vogue* at his desk in room 402 of the MCZ. That year, 1947, he began to write his autobiography and to build into it an explicit celebration of his life as a lepidopterist and its pattern of a dream fulfilled, if not in the Europe where the story began then in the America that *Speak, Memory* foreshadows.

Although he had been eager to explore the fauna of as many states as he could from the moment he arrived in the United States, Nabokov had no car and little money during his first eight years in the country and had to depend on the offers of others. His friend Mikhail Karpovich of Harvard invited him to his summer home in Vermont in 1940 and 1942; Dorothy Leuthold drove him across the country in 1941; a whistle-stop lecture tour by train in late 1942 took him through much of the South; James Laughlin, his publisher, let him have low-cost accommodation at his alpine lodge above Sandy, Utah, in 1943, where he caught a number of previously unknown species of moths for his colleague James McDunnough, who in gratitude named one of them *Eupithecia nabokovi*. Not until 1947 did the advance for *Bend Sinister* again provide enough money to allow the family to travel west by train, to Estes Park, Colorado, where they were able to stay until September only because of the *New Yorker's* enthusiastic response to the first installment of Nabokov's autobiography.

That year things began to change. Late in the fall he was offered a permanent position at Cornell. After taking it up for the fall term of 1948, he would now have no leisure for serious entomological work but would need, and could afford, a car. Never a driver himself, he was chauffeured west by Véra every summer between 1949 and 1959 except for the three years (1950, 1955, 1957) when work pressure ruled it out. The motels they stayed at would provide material for *Lolita*, which he began writing in 1950, and his success at discovering the first known female of *Lycaeides sublivens* above Telluride, Colorado, in the summer of 1951, led him to commemorate the locale in the celebrated "final" scene in the novel, Humbert's vision from a mountain road of the mining town below, its tranquility broken only by the sounds of children at play.[7]

Even before *Lolita* made him famous, the image of Nabokov as lepidopterist was becoming well known. His autobiography, with its evocation of the onset of his "obsession," was extremely popular in its *New Yorker* instar, and when *Pnin* began to appear there, too, in serial form, he had a character point out a score of small blue butterflies—actually the rare northeastern subspecies of *Lycaeides melissa*, identified and named *samuelis* by Nabokov from museum specimens and encountered by him in the wild in upstate New York in June 1950—and remark "Pity Vladimir Vladimirovich is not here. He would have told us all about these enchanting insects." Nabokov wrily has Pnin reply: "I have always had the impression that his entomology was merely a pose."[8]

In the wake of his autobiography, *Life* approached Nabokov for a photo essay on his butterfly hunting; he was asked to review butterfly books for the *New York Times* as well as to send along what he could to the much more modest *Lepidopterists' News*; he was even approached by Edmund Wilson's daughter, Rosalind, to write a book on mimicry for Houghton

Mifflin. In all cases he was happy to oblige, although in the first and last instances the very scale of his enthusiasm frightened the proposals away. But apart from the short pieces in the *Times* and the *News* he published nothing more on butterflies throughout the 1950s. His research interests had shifted to his enormous project of translating and annotating Pushkin's *Eugene Onegin*. Arising out of the needs of his Russian literature students, and serving also as a means of establishing his academic credentials, this project, like his butterfly work in the 1940s, drew him deeper and deeper as the sheer excitement of discovery intensified. The whole effort took seven years (1950–57) and produced four five-hundred-page volumes before he was through.

When *Lolita* caught the attention of America in 1958, Nabokov had just finished his work on *Eugene Onegin* and now had the first opportunity in many seasons to spread the thousands of butterflies he had caught in his summer hunts since 1952. As he did so, he hit on the idea for a new story, "The Admirable Anglewing," his first purely entomological tale since "The Aurelian" in 1930 and the last short story he ever worked on. Although abandoned at the pupal stage, despite several years of on-and-off work, it was published for the first time in *Nabokov's Butterflies* and offers remarkable glimpses of Nabokov at both writing desk and laboratory bench.

Lolita allowed Nabokov to take leave from Cornell early in 1959, a leave that soon solidified into retirement. The novel's triumph also prompted Doubleday to issue his *Poems*, with a butterfly on the cover and title page in honor of both the poem "A Discovery" and his image as lepidopterist, more widespread than ever now that his afterword to *Lolita* ("Every summer my wife and I go butterfly hunting . . .") appeared in every copy of the novel. He was horrified at the designer's sketches, "as meaningless in the present case as would be a picture of a tuna fish on the jacket of *Moby Dick*" (*SL* 285). When he travelled west for the summer, reporter Robert H. Boyle was sent by *Time-Life* to cover Nabokov the lepidopterist for *Sports Illustrated*. His write-up provides the best minute-by-minute account we have of Nabokov the man and certainly of Nabokov the collector.

In the fall of 1959, Nabokov left with his wife for what they thought would be a short visit to Europe, primarily to be nearer their son, Dmitri, who was training as an opera singer in Milan. As it happened, apart from seven unexpected months in Hollywood in 1960 to write the *Lolita* screenplay and, of course, to re-sample Californian butterflies, they would never again live in the United States. After two decades away, Nabokov found Europe unappealing and overrun with cars, but once he had his first successful butterfly hunting there (he spent four hours chasing *Callophrys avis* Chapman in the south of France on behalf of the American Museum of Natural History), and especially once he had his first taste of collecting in the High Alps in 1962, he settled comfortably back into a part of the world that he had never felt to be a proper home during the émigré years, when he could so rarely afford to pursue his passion.

In early 1948, just as he was putting the last touches to his longest lepidopterological monograph, Nabokov had suggested to Cyril dos Passos and Paul Grey that the three of them write a guide to the butterflies of North America. With his teaching at Cornell about to start and the *Onegin* project it spawned not far off, Nabokov would in fact have almost no time to pursue Lepidoptera research for the next fifteen years, let alone something on this scale. But in the early 1960s, after finishing *Pale Fire*, Nabokov found that his next novel—still tentatively entitled *The Texture of Time* and a long way from the *Ada* it would become—posed problems he could not yet solve. With no financial worries, no teaching duties, and for once no pressure from his muse, he was free to think of other projects.

His English publisher, George Weidenfeld, whose publishing firm had been virtually *made* by the staggering success of *Lolita*, agreed at the end of 1962 to publish his complete catalogue of the *Butterflies of Europe*, covering all species and significant subspecies. From late 1963 through to late 1964, Nabokov worked hard on what would have been his lepidopterological magnum opus. Like *Eugene Onegin*, it continued to expand as he worked on it, to the point where Weidenfeld became daunted by its size and could not guarantee publication even if it became a multinational, multilingual venture. Unable to settle to a new novel while the uncertainty persisted, Nabokov regretfully called off the project late in 1965. Had he been able to complete it, it would have been a work of natural history without parallel in the way it fused art and science in both its layout and its text. Left unfinished, and now obsolete, it can never be published in the form Nabokov envisaged, but his plans and the samples of the text included in *Nabokov's Butterflies* offer some hint of its magic.

As the *Butterflies of Europe* moved back, *Ada* could advance. A first flash of inspiration in December 1965, apparently unconnected to the *Texture of Time* project, and another in February 1966, which established the connection, soon had Nabokov writing at a rapid rate. Occupying a place within his English works like that of *The Gift* within his Russian oeuvre, *Ada* was long in gestation, large in scale, and voracious in curiosity, except that this time, everything was lighter, more playful, more disruptive. In *The Gift* Nabokov represented his sense of dislocation between Russia and Berlin almost literally, with meticulous realism; in *Ada* the dislocation of two worlds, Europe and America, becomes the disjunction between Terra and Antiterra, marked by disconcertingly or delightfully detailed distortions of our everyday world. As if he had reflected in the crazy mirror of the imagination his short-lived hopes of coauthoring a *Butterflies of North America* and his recent plans for the *Butterflies of Europe*, Nabokov places Ada on an Old World estate somewhere in New England and then makes her a precocious naturalist, an ardent lepidopterist, whose world of Antiterra he stocks with invented but possible species belonging to real genera.

By the mid-1960s, Nabokov had begun to contemplate another project, *Butterflies in Art*. Ever since 1942, when Florence Read, president of Spelman College in Atlanta, had given him a reproduction of a Theban wall fresco in honor of his love of butterflies, he had considered one day using the representation of butterflies in art to test whether evolutionary changes had been recorded within the span of human history. In his travels around Italy and its museums in the early 1960s, the idea had returned, and in 1965 he began a more systematic search. Although he deeply cherished as an ideal the fusing of art and science, this project, too, failed to materialize, even if he never quite abandoned it. But it, too, permeated *Ada*, where Nabokov straddles the boundaries of art and life, art and nature, by making Ada a flower painter and Lucette a student of art history who stumbles on some of her own creator's discoveries about butterflies in art.

In the 1970s, and in his own seventies, Nabokov still collected butterflies every summer, still hoped to complete *Butterflies in Art*, and still dreamed of writing a *Speak on, Memory* or *Speak, America*, which would devote a chapter to his researches at the Harvard Museum of Comparative Zoology. Instead of continuing his autobiography, however, he ended his career with a savagely inverted fictional autobiography, *Look at the Harlequins!*, whose hero, a novelist called Vadim Vadymich, is a reduced shadow of himself:

> I spent what remained of the summer exploring the incredibly lyrical Rocky Mountain states, getting drunk on whiffs of Oriental Russia in the sagebrush zone and on the Northern Russian fragrances so faithfully reproduced above timberline by certain small bogs along trickles of sky between the snowbank and the orchid. And yet—was that all? What form of mysterious pursuit caused me to get my feet wet like a child, to pant up a talus, to stare every dandelion in the face, to start at every colored mote passing just beyond my field of vision? What was the dream sensation of having come empty-handed—without what? A gun? A wand?
>
> (*LATH* 155–56)

In 1975, at seventy-six, he was still working assiduously, starting at six o'clock every morning, to revamp the French translation of *Ada*, still chasing butterflies in the Alps. That summer, sapped of strength by the rush to transpose *Ada*, he had a serious fall down a steep slope at Davos. His butterfly net slipped still further, lodging on the branch of a fir, as he said, "like Ovid's lyre" (*SL* 552).

That image seems a perfect emblem of the link between literature and Lepidoptera that lasted to the end. For after this fall, Nabokov was never the same. He spent much of the next two years in hospital, in the summer of 1976 reading with delight, when his delirium lifted, the new Doubleday *Butterflies of North America* and mentally rereading, as it were, the still unwritten text of his own next novel, *The Original of Laura*. But a year later, as another summer approached and he sank toward his death, *Laura* remained largely unwritten, and in his last recorded words, he told his son tearfully that he knew "a certain butterfly was already on the wing; and his eyes told me he no longer hoped that he would live to pursue it again."[9]

How fitting, then, that Dmitri Nabokov should have compensated for these twin plans his father's death cut short by translating from Russian into English his father's most intense amalgam of literature and Lepidoptera, his afterword to *The Gift*, itself cut short by his switch from Russian to English and from Europe to America at the midpoint of his life.

I have retold Nabokov's life as a dance in which science suavely partners art. But it would be perfectly possible to read a thousand pages of his best fiction—*The Defense*, *Invitation to a Beheading*, *The Real Life of Sebastian Knight*, *Lolita* without its afterword, *Pale Fire*, and *Transparent Things*—and another five hundred pages of his short stories and not even realize he was a lepidopterist. What, then, can his passion for butterflies explain in his art? How did it reflect or affect his mind, his thinking, his writing?

From as far back as we can see, Nabokov had a love of both detail and design, of precise and unpredictable particulars and intricate, often concealed patterns. Aware of how little most people know about nature, of how much effort it took to master all he had learned about the butterflies of the world, and of how much more there always was to discover even about the Blues he specialized in, he disliked the impulse to impose easy meaning—a generalization, an allegorization, a handy quick-stick label—

on a complex and recalcitrant reality. "As an artist and a scholar," he once proclaimed, "I prefer the specific detail to the generalization, images to ideas, obscure facts to clear symbols, and the discovered wild fruit to the synthetic jam" (*SO* 7).[10]

But if he rejected anything that quashed the live independence of things, he nevertheless, like any scientist, delighted in the patterns that ordered their relationship. Pattern has its purely aesthetic side, of course, and Nabokov is celebrated for his mastery of phonic and fictive design. But understanding pattern also allows us some degree of control over the unruliness of life, and in Nabokov that urge to control was powerfully developed: witness his refusal to submit to interviews unless he could have questions in advance, write out his answers, and check the final text; his insistence that his characters were his "galley slaves" (*SO* 95); his famous comparison of the relationship between author and reader to that between chess problemist and problem solver (*SM* 290); and his command of form at all levels, from phrase to finished fiction. Not for him the world as a big, booming, buzzing confusion. The world is there to be teased out by the inquiring mind, as in his fiction it is there to be shaped by the imaginative one.

Nabokov nevertheless had a strong sense of the limits of human knowledge: He thought that no matter how much we can find out, there is always more behind things—beyond our human sense of space and time, beyond the limits of personality and mortality, beyond our ignorance of ultimate origins and ends—that consciousness as we know it seems unable to penetrate. He had a lifelong urge to probe "the beyond," which Véra Nabokov has gone so far as to call—a slight overstatement in my judgment—"the main theme" of his work.[11] This impulse may have derived from his mother's unconventional religious sense, even before he could be aware of the antipositivism in the air in the Europe and especially in the Russia of his childhood (Bergson, Blok, Bely). But his passion for butterflies attests to and surely helped develop his respect for *this* world, no matter how strong his curiosity about what might lie beyond it. As he wrote rather gnomically in his last novel: "*This* was the simple solution, that the brook and the boughs and the beauty of the Beyond all began with the initial of Being" (*LATH* 16).

His love of Lepidoptera drew upon and sharpened further his love of the particular and the habits of detailed observation that gave him such fictional command over the physical world—biologically (birds, flowers, trees), geographically (localities, landscapes, ecologies), socially (manorial Russia, boardinghouse Berlin, motel America), and bodily (gesture, anatomy, sensation). He thought that only the ridiculously unobservant could be pessimists in a world as full of surprising specificity as ours, and he arranged his own art accordingly.

Still deeper than the pleasures of immediate observation were the delights of discovery. As a child exploring on his own his parents' butterfly books, he preferred the small type to the main text, the obscure to the obvious, the thrill of finding for himself what was not common knowledge. That impulse became a positive addiction when he peered into the microscope in Harvard's laboratories in the 1940s or prowled the stacks of its libraries while compiling his *Onegin* commentary in the 1950s. His fiction had always invited readers to discover things for themselves, but from the time he began *Bend Sinister* in 1941, he encouraged his readers more and more to become researchers in increasingly intricate labyrinths of internal and external references and relationships.

Nabokov's science gave him a sense of the endless elusiveness of reality that should not be confused with modern or postmodern epistemological nihilism. Dissecting and deciphering the genitalic structure of lycaenids, or counting scale rows on their wings, he realized that the further we inquire, the more we can discover, yet the more we find that we do not know, not because truth is an illusion or a matter of mere convention but because the world is infinitely detailed, complex and deceptive, "an infinite succession of steps, levels of perception, false bottoms" (*SO* 11).

He found this not frustrating but challenging, not niggardly of nature, in hoarding its secrets, but fantastically generous, in burying such an endless series of treasures for the human mind to unearth. This sense of design deeply embedded in nature's detail, of a playful deceptiveness behind things, of some kind of conscious cosmic hide-and-seek is fundamental to Nabokov, though hardly unique to him. Almost 3,000 years ago, the Bible declared, "It is the glory of God to hide a thing, but the glory of kings to search things out" (Proverbs 5:2); at the dawn of modern science, Francis Bacon liked to repeat and refashion the phrase; and in *Bend Sinister* Nabokov himself playfully half-reveals and half-conceals both sources for us to rediscover as he cites, "not for the first time," "the glory of God is to hide a thing, and the glory of man is to find it" (*BS* 106).

Throughout his later fiction Nabokov shapes his own worlds to match the munificence he senses behind our world's complexity. But although this feeling arose in good measure out of his science, he could not express it there. Only in mimicry did he suspect that the design behind things was apparent enough and explicit enough to be treated *as* science. No wonder, as he writes in his autobiography, "the mysteries of mimicry had a special attraction for me" (124); no wonder he has Konstantin Godunov in *The Gift* expound to his son "about the incredible artistic wit of mimetic disguise, which was not explainable by the struggle for existence . . . and seemed to have been invented by some waggish artist precisely for the intelligent eyes of man" (122). Although he reported in the fall of 1941 that he was "writing a rather ambitious work on mimetic phenomena," and although he leaped at the chance to write a whole book on the subject a decade later, the first does not survive and the second was never written. It seems likely that, had he begun serious work on mimicry, he would have found sufficient evidence of purely physical explanations to be forced to abandon his dearly held metaphysical speculations.

Just as Nabokov suspected there was some conscious design behind the world, he also thought it likely that there was some transformation of human consciousness beyond death. Insect metamorphosis hardly provided a model, yet it seems strikingly apt that the journal in which his lepidopterological writings appeared most frequently, *Psyche*, was named after the Greek word for "butterfly, moth, soul." Nabokov adverted often to the immemorial association between overcoming gravity and transcending death, and the change of form from a caterpillar's earth-bound beginnings to winged freedom and beauty at least offered an appealing image of the soul's expansion beyond death. He could use it half-playfully ("we are the caterpillars of angels," he wrote in a 1923 poem). He could rudely reject it as a symbol: when a Russian Orthodox archbishop suggested that his interest in butterflies might be linked with the highest state of the soul, he retorted that a butterfly is not at all a half-angelic being and "will settle even on corpses."[12] But in a series of stories, although increasingly more obliquely—in "Christmas," "The Aurelian," *Invitation to a Beheading*, *The Gift*, and *Pale Fire*—Nabokov repeatedly links butterflies with the transcending of death.[13]

Although the possibility of a metamorphosis beyond death had everything to do with Nabokov's art, it bore little relation to his science. What was, and is, his position as a scientist? Nabokov had a reputation for arrogance. In literature he was supremely sure of himself and greatly enjoyed the shock value of his strong opinions about other writers. But as a lepidopterist he was different, if hardly diffident.

As a boy, he mastered butterflies and moths early and developed a complementary interest in beetles, the most diverse animal order of all. But at Cambridge he had only brief exposure to zoology and none at all to entomology, and he remained little more than an ardent and ambitious collector, an encyclopedic amateur, until his arrival in the United States. There he had much to learn even from veteran collectors like Don Eff and Don Stallings, from the most efficient way of killing his catch (pinching the thorax immediately, rather than putting the butterfly in a carbona-soaked jar) to the most efficient way of finding it.

In the laboratory, he had everything to learn, but he learned it quickly. He worked happily with other lepidopterists, especially William Comstock and Cyril dos Passos, and was eager to share information and propose collaboration. In his work on *Eugene Onegin* he insisted on his own findings and poured scorn on his rivals; in his entomology, although still frank in disagreement, he could be generous in praise, even of those who had completed projects he would dearly have liked to undertake himself (see his reviews of Klots's *Field Guide to the Butterflies of North America* and Higgins and Riley's *Field Guide to the Butterflies of Britain and Europe*, and his acclaim, in the year before his death, for Doubleday's *Butterflies of North America*, illustrated and edited by William Howe).[14]

Nabokov's laboratory work focused almost entirely on the American representatives of one tribe, the Polyommatini, or Blues (in his day, classified as the subfamily Plebejinae) of the Lycaenidae, the largest of butterfly families, which includes Coppers and Hairstreaks as well as Blues. Although his output as a lepidopterist is small in comparison with that of scientists who spend a lifetime in the laboratory and the field, it is of lasting importance and worth within its domain.

His methods were advanced for his time: more than most, he insisted on dissection rather than on superficial characteristics, and in a group as notoriously difficult as the Polyommatini this stance was particularly well justified. His own findings at the microscope confirmed for him the modern recognition that the genitalia "differed in shape from species to species" and so "offered tremendous utility for taxonomy."[15] Writing his "Second Addendum" to *The Gift* in 1938, before he had worked in a laboratory himself, he had seemed to share Count Godunov-Cherdyntsev's dismissal of those the Count

subtly berated . . . [as] "genitalists": it was just the time when it became fashionable to accept as an unerring and adequate sign of species differentiation distinctions in the chitinoid structure of the male organ, which represented, as it were, the "skeleton" of a species, a kind of "vertebra." "How simply various discussions would be resolved" [the Count] wrote, "if those who concentrated on splitting similar species according to this one criterion, whose absolute stability has, moreover, never been proven, turned their attention, in the first place, to the entire radiation of doubtful forms in their overall Palearctic aspect instead of concentrating on a handful of long-suffering French *départements*."

Five years later, working with as wide a range of samples as he could obtain, and at an entirely new level of detail, Nabokov himself had become one of the most advanced of "genitalists." Where others tended to consider "only the general features of the clasping parts of the male organ," he emphasized "the multiple differences in all the parts of the genital anatomy, in females as well as males. And by being extremely specific about the shapes of the various structures along the contour of the male clasper, as well as many other organs, Nabokov introduced many new structures into the study of Blues."[16] He named new micro-organs, developed new techniques to analyze the genitalia, and offered new interpretations of the diagnostic value of their structure. He was "among the first researchers to picture more than a single genital illustration for each species," his "multiple illustrations buttressing his hypotheses concerning ranges of variation in one species and the hiatuses, or breaks, in those characters that distinguished different species."[17]

Since he also analyzed wing markings more minutely than anybody else had done in any group of butterflies, even counting the numbers of scale rows, "it was clear that no one else was applying such detailed analysis to Blue butterflies in the 1940s."[18] Although he was working in and just after the Second World War and had fewer specimens, less advanced equipment and techniques, and fewer diagnostic characters than would be available to modern researchers, he had a superb eye for relationships, and his classifications have stood the test of time.

His work in clarifying Nearctic (North American) Polyommatini was immediately appreciated by lepidopterists of the caliber of Don Stallings ("We name this distinctive race after V. Nabokov who is contributing so much to our American literature on Lepidoptera"),[19] Alexander Klots ("The recent work of Nabokov has entirely rearranged the classification of this genus"),[20] Cyril dos Passos ("I have followed . . . Prof. VLADIMIR NABOKOV in the PLEBEJINAE to the extent that he has revised the genera and species"),[21] and John Downey.

As a student working in a summer job in Utah in 1943, Downey, already a keen lepidopterist, chanced to meet Nabokov with his net and was taken by him to the haunt of the curious subspecies *L. melissa annetta*. He later stressed that Nabokov "strongly influenced me to take up the study of the 'blues' and their relatives."[22] By the late 1960s, Downey had become the authority in the Blues and found Nabokov's research indispensable: "Nabokov had put the study of North American Blues on a strong taxonomic footing, and the work he had produced had created a context for researching the evolution of this group in the complex environs characterizing the Rocky Mountains and Great Basin regions."[23] Downey's former graduate student

Kurt Johnson recalls Downey in 1968 discussing the section on the Blues he was writing for Howe's *Butterflies of North America* (which Nabokov would read and reread with great pleasure in his hospital bed, in the interstices between delirium, during his last full summer). They were considering the problem of whether *Everes comyntas* (the eastern tailed Blue) and *Everes amyntula* (the western tailed Blue) were separate species. Johnson suggested writing to Harry Clench, the associate curator of entomology at the Carnegie Museum of Natural History in Pittsburgh. Clench, who by this time had become a hairstreak authority and a specialist in the Blues, had been Nabokov's benchmate at the MCZ as a student in the early 1940s and was influenced by his colleague's example in choosing his areas of specialization.[24] Downey snapped: "Clench doesn't know. If anybody knows, Nabokov would know!" Although Clench named a large number of new species and, as Johnson later judged, had come to fancy himself the authority on the Blues, he thought that little more needed to be done and therefore did not dissect much. Nabokov, by contrast, in Johnson's estimate, was a meticulous morphologist whose detailed work on wing patterns and genitalic structure showed a rigor and range Clench lacked despite being a professional with graduate training in zoology.[25]

Although Nabokov's North American work was drawn on immediately, there was little further research for many years on Neotropical (Central and South American) Polyommatini. The recent collaborative studies of Kurt Johnson of the AMNH and Zsolt Bálint of the Hungarian Museum of Natural History amply testify to the high regard in which Nabokov's single major paper on Neotropical Polyommatini is held. In the 1940s Nabokov was often thought to be a generic "splitter"—or, as Johnson explains from the standpoint of the present: "His good eye had brought him to a level of taxonomic sophistication beyond that of many of his contemporaries, but in a sense it also made it easier for his work to be overlooked or misunderstood by those who weren't disposed to look quite as deeply."[26] He wrote his 1945 paper only a couple of years after two well-established AMNH lepidopterists, William Comstock and E. Irving Huntington, published *Lycaenidae of the Antilles*. "Unlike Nabokov two years later, Comstock and Huntington brought nothing new to the general taxonomy for the region; in the case of the Neotropic Blues, they deviated little from Draudt's rudimentary arrangement from 1921." Yet because of their established names, their work was considered authoritative for decades to come.[27] As late as 1975 the distinguished lepidopterist Norman Riley, longtime editor of *The Entomologist* and keeper of the Department of Entomology at the British Museum, could follow the lead of Comstock and Huntington and sink the genus *Cyclargus*, which Nabokov had proposed in 1945, back to part of *Hemiargus*, because to his expert eye, wing patterns in both groups looked too much the same; others in turn followed Riley. But scientists have recently reinstated Nabokov's *Cyclargus* after cladistic analysis of many anatomical features revealed that *Cyclargus* and *Hemiargus* are not even immediate sister genera, despite their apparent resemblance.[28] The many new species and specimens Johnson and Bálint have recorded in Latin America, especially in the Andes, confirm all of Nabokov's generic divisions (although not all of his names) and show that far from its being the case that he was an excessive splitter, there are, in fact, more lycaenid genera and many more species than even he could have suspected.

Johnson and Bálint announce that they "follow the methods of NABOKOV (1945) (the first reviser of the Neotropical polyommatines), who underlined the taxonomic importance of the genitalic armatures in lycaenid systematics,"[29] and Balint declares his paper "the cornerstone of modern knowledge concerning polyommatine butterflies occurring in Latin America."[30] In honor of Nabokov's work as first reviser, they have named many new species after people, places and things in his life and art, lately in consultation with leading Nabokov scholars (for example: *Itylos luzhin, Pseudolucia vera, Nabokovia ada, Paralycaeides shade, Madeleinea vokoban, Polytheclus cincinnatus, Leptotes krug*), and plan to dedicate their forthcoming volume on the Blues in the *Atlas of Tropical Lepidoptera* to his memory. So much for the idea that Nabokov was a mere dilettante and no serious scientist.

To write his papers on the Polyommatini, Nabokov had to clarify his sense of species, a seemingly natural notion—until nature confronts one with the complexities of the particular case. His agonized tussles with the problems of identity and relationship involved in speciation produced some of his most fascinating scientific writing, apparently prepared for a talk before the Cambridge Entomological Club and hitherto unpublished. Attacking the biological species concept then being advanced by ornithologist Ernst Mayr, also of the MCZ, he not only rejects it as more suitable for birds than butterflies, and rightly insists on the logical priority of distinguishing on morphological grounds exactly *which* population one is counting, but also goes so far as to suggest that the sense of specific distinction in Lycaenidae might need to be different from even that of other closely related families. Elsewhere, after suggesting some possible causes of divergence within the genus *Lycaeides*, he comments: "This scheme of course is not a phylogenetic tree but merely its shadow on a plane surface, since a sequence in time is not really deducible from a synchronous series."[31] He could not foresee the theoretical advances leading to modern phylogenetic systematics or the multiplication of characteristics of Lepidoptera anatomy that researchers would learn to consider, or the power of computer-assisted cladistic analyses that could factor in all these diagnostic variables and make it possible to construct species lines reflecting or suggesting evolutionary descent, but he shows himself to be acutely aware of the issues and, of course, brilliantly up to the task of articulating them.[32]

(Stop Press: January 2011.) This month a paper was published online by Roger Vila and others, including Kurt Johnson, Zsolt Bálint, Dubi Benyamini, and Naomi Pierce, that grew out of Nabokov's 1945 paper and demonstrates his astonishingly accurate and far-reaching insight.[33] The driving force behind the research was Naomi Pierce, Hessel Professor of Biology at Harvard and curator of Lepidoptera at the MCZ. Pierce had assumed Nabokov was a competent but conservative and old-fashioned taxonomist when she began preparing an MCZ exhibition for his centenary in 1999, but she changed her mind when she read Kurt Johnson and Stephen Coates's account of his 1945 paper in their *Nabokov's Blues*.

On the strength of the meager number of specimens he had at his disposal at the MCZ under wartime conditions, Nabokov was able to work out taxonomic divisions that seemed radical at the time but would be completely vindicated decades later by Bálint, Johnson, et al. But still more startling, from the extremely limited evidence available to him Nabokov hypothesized that the Blues in the Americas evolved from ancestors arriving from Asia across the area now known as the Bering Strait (at times connected by a land bridge) in five successive waves: first, colonization by the ancestors of the Plebejinae (now *Polyommatus*) section, which produced the current neotropical taxa but then died out in North America; second, the ancestors of the *Icaricia-Plebulina* group; and then *Lycaiedes*, *Agriades*, and *Vacciniina* in that order (*N'sBs* 378). Reading this, Naomi Pierce realized the hypothesis could be tested with the computational and molecular methods now available. She and her team drew together data from Old and New World Blues, especially DNA, and from host plants and climate records. The Harvard team had to develop a new technique, using the thermal tolerances of modern species to infer the thermal tolerances of their ancestors. They show five separate waves of colonization, corresponding with the cooling climate of Beringia over 9 million years: the oldest colonists were warm adapted, their later relatives increasingly cold adapted.

Nabokov's hunch was exactly right: "Our results show that Nabokov's inferences based on morphological characters (primarily of the male genitalia) were uncannily correct in delineating not only species relationships but also the historical ordering of these key five events in the evolution of New World blues" (Vila et al., 4). Kurt Johnson commented that the results confirm "that Nabokov's contribution was significant, historic, and displayed remarkable, uncanny biological intuition."[34]

Within butterflies, the Blues are "among the largest and most systematically challenging tribes within the family Lycaenidae (the blues, coppers and hairstreaks). . . . With more than 400 species, the cosmopolitan *Polyommatus* section (equivalent to 'Plebejinae' in older classifications) is the most diverse of these" (Vila et al., 1). All the more kudos to Nabokov, then, for not only sorting out taxonomic relationships correctly in such a complex group but for having developed a hypothesis that proved fertile sixty years later in driving a groundbreaking research project that uses methods (DNA sampling, computer-assisted cladistics) that neither he nor anyone else could have imagined in 1945. (End of Stop Press.)

With only something like two full working years at the microscope, Nabokov had become a major lepidopterist, and a first-rate one. "He was *the* authority on blues," attests Johnson.[35] If scientists are measured in part by their ability to inspire new generations of workers in their field, Nabokov's achievement again seems remarkable. Never a professor of entomology, but only a research fellow in Lepidoptera, and then only from 1942 to 1948—a position without power, renewed only on a year-by-year basis, and competing for his time with his fiction, verse and criticism, and Russian language and literature classes—he nevertheless influenced Downey and Clench, two of the leading figures in the next generation of specialists in the Blues and, through Downey, Johnson, a leading figure in the generation after that.

Normally experts are more captious and begrudging of one another than outsiders. It seems telling that the sheer quality of Nabokov's lepidopterology has been appreciated most by those working closest to his particular field. In tribute to his work, colleagues at other American museums began to name butterflies after him in the late 1940s, soon after his first major papers appeared, and he would have been thrilled by the recent spate of species names that celebrates his contribution to both literature and Lepidoptera.

He seems, in fact, to have had a curiously intense desire for—and an exaggerated sense of—the fame accruing to those whose names become part of the taxonomic record. From his childhood he had dreamed of discovering a new species, and when he thought he had, with his Moulinet discovery,[36] he exulted in print:

I found it and I named it, being versed
in taxonomic Latin; thus became
godfather to an insect and its first
describer—and I want no other fame.

Wide open on its pin (though fast asleep).
and safe from creeping relatives and rust,
in the secluded stronghold where we keep
type specimens it will transcend its dust.

Dark pictures, thrones, the stones that pilgrims kiss,
poems that take a thousand years to die
but ape the immortality of this
red label on a little butterfly.

(PP 155–56)

He was never anxious about literary fame, because he knew by the age of
thirty that he had done enough to assure it, but he prized immortality as
a lepidopterist precisely because it seemed so unattainable. Yet the mere
naming of a single taxon hardly constitutes fame when there are, so far,
about a million and a half known biological species, and current estimates
suggest there may be ten—perhaps even fifty—times as many names still
to bestow.[37]

Although in his adult years Nabokov's collecting often led to or arose naturally from his papers and was always guided by an instinct for the scientifically revealing, it is Nabokov's major papers of the 1940s, rather than any of
his catches, that will ensure his niche in entomological history. But if within
the science of Lepidoptera his collecting was of secondary importance, it
was one of his most intense and lasting pleasures throughout his years in
Russia, in a few short seasons in his émigré years, and again throughout
his American and final European years. In his first seasons in America, he
searched for butterflies and moths wherever he could. From the late 1940s,
with a car of his own, he repeatedly chose the Rockies, partly because alti-
tude increases the variety of butterfly species one is likely to encounter and
partly because the alpine vegetation reminded him of old Russia. He particularly sought out localities likely to yield lycaenids, especially those he
had described from museum specimens but not caught for himself, those
for which only one sex had so far been found, or those that might reveal an
intergrade between one subspecies and the next.

He had lost three collections in Europe, moved from house to house in
America, and had no desire to keep his new collections himself. He gave
them to the institutions with which he was associated, first the AMNH,
then the MCZ, and finally Cornell. In Europe he continued to confine
himself to collecting in montane areas, regularly in Switzerland, often in
Italy (including Sicily), occasionally in France (including Corsica), once in

Portugal. He would spend long stretches at a single mountain resort, a summer holiday for his wife and a writing retreat and a hunting ground for himself. Although he would catch anything uncommon, he still sought out lycaenids above all, managing, for instance, to net 90 percent of Swiss lycaenids from only five (the most alpine) of the twenty-two cantons. Knowing exactly what he wanted, he would collect long series only in genera where he knew species were difficult to distinguish except in the laboratory. He bequeathed his European collection to the Musée Cantonal de Zoologie in Lausanne.

Exhibitions of his butterfly collections have been held in Milan and Lausanne and at Harvard and Cornell. Had Nabokov not been famous as a novelist, these commemorations would never have taken place. But had he not become a writer, he repeatedly said—had he not been able, for instance, to escape from Soviet Russia—he would have spent his life as a lepidopterist. As it was, other professionals have rated as extraordinary his achievement in the small time he was working professionally in the field.

As a lepidopterist he had hoped to do much that he never achieved: neither the expedition to Central Asia he envisaged in his teens nor, fifty years later, the forays to Peru, Iran, or Israel "before I pupate"; neither the *Butterflies of North America* nor the book on mimicry that he contemplated in the United States; neither the *Butterflies of Europe* nor the *Butterflies in Art* that he began in Europe came to fruition. But in his seventies, he replied to an interviewer's question: "My life thus far has surpassed splendidly the ambitions of my boyhood and youth. . . . At the age of twelve my fondest dream was a visit to the Karakorum range in search of butterflies. Twenty-five years later I successfully sent myself, in the part of my hero's father (see my novel *The Gift*) to explore, net in hand, the mountains of Central Asia. At fifteen I visualized myself as a world-famous author of seventy with a mane of wavy white hair. Today I am practically bald" (*SO* 177–78). Literature may have prevented him realizing some of his dreams as a lepidopterist, but it also provided a way of realizing others far more fully than he could ever have imagined as a child.

It is one thing to know of Nabokov as a lepidopterist from his superbly poetic evocation of his passion in *Speak, Memory*. It is another thing entirely to see the results of his research, so rigorous and so painstaking, vivid proof of a whole side of his life and a whole sphere of knowledge remote from most of us but home to him. He knows our world; he can even describe parts of it better than those who have lived there all their lives. But most of us exploring this part of *his* world will find it another planet and find that we can never directly breathe its air or palpate its soil. And even the lepidopterists who know Nabokov's articles of the 1940s have been unaware of the prodigious amount of work he expended on the much larger scale of his *Butterflies of Europe*.

The entire selection of Nabokov's lepidopterological writings, published and unpublished, scientific and literary, polished and provisional, can be read as a singular case study in specialization and diversity, in development and metamorphosis. The chronological sequence, from a letter written by Nabokov's father two years after the boy discovered butterflies to a memoir by Dmitri Nabokov two years after his father's death, lets us track the development of the writer's art, the evolution of the naturalist's science, and the interplay between the two. The shifts of scale, from microscopic samples to entire organisms, from a line or two to fifty pages of continuous text, also serve their purpose. Removed from their old haunts, the scores of short excerpts refocus the part and refresh the whole. Whenever a butterfly plucked from its natural habitat in a particular novel demands attention, identification, and explanation, the anthologist's net suddenly becomes the reader's lens.

Not only in date and scope but in genre, too, no other volume of Nabokov's writing encompasses as much variety as *Nabokov's Butterflies*, from novels, stories, poems, a screenplay, autobiography, criticism, lectures, and articles to annotations, reviews, interviews, letters, drafts, notes, diaries, drawings. The very restrictedness of subject matter throws into striking relief the range of Nabokov's styles, strategies, contexts, and mental modes: troubled reflection, painstaking description, lovingly fanciful sketches, comradely exchanges: the surreally false flatness of the world of *Invitation to a Beheading*, the majestic exoticism of *The Gift*, the lyric evocativeness of *Speak, Memory*, the haunting charms of *Pale Fire*, the dizzy density of *Ada*. And when we remember that outside his scientific work Nabokov limits severely what he allows himself to write about butterflies, it seems staggering that he can ring so many changes on this one theme—exactly what he might have said about "that other V.N., Visible Nature" (*SO* 153).

9. Netting Nabokov

Review of Dieter E. Zimmer, *A Guide to Nabokov's Butterflies and Moths, 2001*

In 1994 I wrote a review-article on Dieter E. Zimmer's 150-page section, "Nabokov's Lepidoptera: An Annotated Multilingual Checklist," in Michel Satoris's *Les Papillons de Nabokov* (1993), which accompanied an exhibition at the Lausanne Canton Museum, to which Nabokov had bequeathed all the butterflies he had caught in his final European period, from 1959 until his death in 1977.

Dieter E. Zimmer has been translating, editing, and annotating Nabokov since 1959, especially as general editor of the collected works in German (twenty-five volumes to date) and as documenter of Nabokov's Berlin, of his imagined trip in *The Gift* to Central Asia, and of the impact of *Lolita*. By 1994 Dieter and I had been in touch by mail for years. I praised his checklist as "fertile and full of fact" and wrote of him now, after naming his other roles, as "the first thorough explicator of Nabokov's second major career. What makes Zimmer's work all the more remarkable is that it has all been accomplished for the sheer love of his subject. A distinguished essayist and journalist, a literary editor at *Die Zeit*, he has earned no promotions, no research grants, no sabbaticals for his devotion to Nabokov's work." But I also pointed out what I thought were shortcomings. I concluded, though, that if his labor of love was not yet an exhaustive checklist, "if it seems sometimes provisional, that is because he has attempted to provide so much. No one else has had the imagination or the energy even to try. Let us hope—it is too much to ask, but let us hope—that he now has the energy to be his own First Reviser."

Dieter indeed continued to revise and expand his checklist along lines I had suggested and others I had not dreamed of. What became *A Guide to Nabokov's Butterflies and Moths* passed through numerous revisions during the 1990s, provoking continued and heated discussion between Dieter and me on Nabokov's taxonomy and Nabokov's Darwin. When Dieter published the final version, privately printed, like the rest, in 2001, it had swelled to over

400 pages and become an incomparable field guide to the butterflies and moths of Nabokov's invented lands and worlds.

I was very happy to describe Zimmer's *Guide* with the kind of rapt awe that Fyodor Godunov-Cherdyntsev expresses in describing his father's *Butterflies and Moths of the Russian Empire* in "Father's Butterflies." But I also had to voice my disagreements with Dieter's reading of Nabokov's relation to twentieth-century taxonomic principles and to Darwin (see also chapter 8).

To know more about where butterflies fit into Nabokov's life than he disclosed in *Speak, Memory*, readers had to wait for *Vladimir Nabokov: The Russian Years* (1990) and *Vladimir Nabokov: The American Years* (1991). To know where Nabokov's work on butterflies fit into science, they had to wait for Kurt Johnson and Steve Coates's *Nabokov's Blues: The Scientific Odyssey of a Literary Genius* (1999). To know what Nabokov wrote about butterflies, and when and where, they had to wait for *Nabokov's Butterflies: Unpublished and Uncollected Writings* (2000).

And to *understand* Nabokov's butterflies, and where they fit into his work, they have had to wait for Dieter E. Zimmer's stupendous labor of love, thirteen years in the making, *A Guide to Nabokov's Butterflies and Moths 2001* (2001).

The "2001" in the title differentiates this *Guide* from four previous published versions, "Nabokov's Lepidoptera: An Annotated Multilingual Checklist" (1993) and two 1996 prototypes and a 1998 revamp of *A Guide to Nabokov's Butterflies and Moths*. The 2001 model, while of course not definitive—nothing that treats a rich and rapidly changing body of scientific knowledge can claim this—easily outperforms its forebears (392 pages and 21 color plates to the 146 pages of the 1993 "Checklist") and seems unlikely ever to be surpassed.

In a review article in *Nabokov Studies* 2 (1995), I focused on Zimmer's "Checklist," hailing it as an immeasurable advance on everything else in the field to date but also noting omissions, limitations in presentation, and shortcomings in the discussion of Nabokov's science and its context. Not only has Zimmer plugged the few omissions I mentioned, as well as innumerable others no one else had been aware of, he has also thought out carefully and discovered how to provide whatever non-lepidopterists might need to know about Nabokov's butterflies. Even lepidopterists will learn much and find much they could not easily have checked.

In 1995 I discussed the "Checklist" in a review article because it provided an occasion to draw the attention of Nabokovians, including Zimmer, to the work being done since the late 1980s by Zsolt Bálint, Kurt Johnson, Gerardo Lamas, Dubi Benyamini, and their associates on the Latin American Blues of which Nabokov had been first reviser, and to the work done by Nabokov himself in his then unpublished writings at the Henry W. and Albert A. Berg Collection of the New York Public Library. Already that time when literary Nabokovians knew so little of their lepidopterological counterparts seems long ago. Since then, Kurt Johnson has written of Nabokov's butterflies, with others or alone, in *Nabokov Studies*, in a stream of submissions to Nabokv-L, in *Nabokov's Blues* and elsewhere, and in papers at both literary and scientific conferences, as well as in new technical papers where he and his colleagues have named new species in honor of Nabokovian people and places, in close cooperation with Nabokov scholars.

Everyone who knows Nabokov knows of his passion for butterflies, and after the work of Johnson and others no one now has an excuse for thinking he was merely a passionate dilettante. He was a first-rate, although never a major, scientific lepidopterist. At the same time he was also too good a writer, too astute a student of human psychology, and too staunch a defender of individual difference to wish to impose his particular passion on readers of his fiction. For that reason, there are some otherwise gifted Nabokovians who have no interest in his lepidopterology.

That is a mistake. Remaining aloof from the lepidopterological detail is as misguided and self-defeating as a Russian scholar's ignoring the English literary contexts of Nabokov's work, or an English critic's ignoring his Russian context, Pushkin and all, or an English or Russian reader's ignoring his French context. To be a serious Nabokovian—and that also means, of course, to enjoy the work to the full—you simply have to know the butterflies, and Zimmer's *Guide 2001* is the place where you will find what you need to know.

The *Guide 2001* contains

(1) an introduction to Lepidoptera, to taxonomy and systematics, to mimicry, to evolution, and to Nabokov's attitudes to all of these;
(2) catalogues of the taxa named by and for Nabokov, with detailed discussions and explanations;
(3) a 190-page alphabetical catalogue of all the butterflies mentioned by Nabokov in his published work and occasional unpublished pieces. This, the invaluable core of the volume, identifies butterflies whether or not Nabokov named them directly or only implied their identity; provides an immense amount of vivid natural and scientific history about hundreds of species and genera; astutely discusses, where appropriate, Nabokov's artistic purposes in using these taxa in this or that work; supplies translators with the equivalent popular names in

other major European languages and provides stress accents to assist readers in pronunciation; establishes the current scientific names of each taxon named, which can and frequently do change, for general (and extremely interesting) reasons that Zimmer discusses under (1) and for specific reasons that he explains in each case;

(4) a sequential list of all the butterflies in Nabokov's work, chronologically by book and then by page, with cross-references to (3);

(5) a copiously detailed biographical index of lepidopterists with Nabokov connections;

(6) an annotated bibliography of Nabokov's scientific papers and the interviews where he refers to butterflies;

(7) a species list, allowing a cross-reference to the catalogue (where many of the generic names under which the butterflies are listed have been revised since Nabokov's day);

(8) twenty-one color plates of illustrations.

Zimmer's long introductory essay is a mine of information for those who know little about taxonomy, a scientific subdiscipline with ramifications not only in biology and evolutionary theory but also in linguistics, philosophy, and psychology. Despite a few bumps in the English, the introduction is as well written as we would expect of one of Germany's foremost postwar essayists and reveals a zeal for connecting art and science that has long infused his columns in *Die Zeit*. Zimmer's contrast of Nabokov's precise use of natural detail with the sloppy symbolism of a Herman Hesse poem that most readers might have thought lepidopterologically sophisticated demonstrates stunningly how Nabokov has raised literature's standards of honesty to nature.

My strongest criticism of the 1993 "Checklist" was its treatment of Nabokov's attitude to the species concept and evolution, where Zimmer argued that Nabokov was behind the times scientifically. The *Guide 2001* has a much more nuanced and fairer evaluation, although it could still be clearer. The history of the species concept in the twentieth century is far more complex than Zimmer seems aware of even now, the biological species concept that Mayr advanced in the 1940s being only one of a succession of such concepts. Nabokov's various attempts to work out a species concept for himself, moreover, is in some ways closer not to what Zimmer once thought a pre-evolutionary morphological concept but to Hugh Paterson's recognition concept of species of the 1980s.

Zimmer does not distinguish sufficiently sharply among Nabokov's attitude to the species concept, his taxonomic practice, his attitude to evolution, and his attitude to Darwinian natural selection as the principal mechanism of evolution. Nabokov's taxonomy not only "did not lag behind the times" (43) but was ahead of the standard lepidopterological practice of his day in its insistence on microscopic examination and the insufficiency of external characteristics, on the need for large samples where possible, on the role of female as well as male features, and on the aim of phylogenetic reconstruction. After leaving the laboratory, Nabokov unsurprisingly fell gradually behind in his knowledge of the newest techniques for taxonomic determination, but this occurred only *after* he had stopped writing scientific papers. Writing in 1939, he showed Konstantin Godunov-Cherdynstev in 1917 as hostile to genitalic dissection, but by 1943, after two years at the microscope, he was himself extending the scope of genitalic and alar description, and there is no reason to think that had he returned to the laboratory in the 1950s or later that he would not again have welcomed and extended new taxonomic tools.

Nabokov fully accepted evolution and enjoyed the challenge of trying to work out phylogenetic relationships within the Blues through the evolution of both genitalia and wing markings. But what certainly did place him at odds with the direction of twentieth-century biology was his attitude to Darwin's theory of natural selection as the core explanation for the mechanism of evolution. On the one hand, one could argue that even here Nabokov, when seen in the context of his times, was not that out of step with the pace of evolutionary theory. The new synthesis of Darwinian natural selection and Mendelian particulate genetics was being worked out in the late 1930s and the 1940s and was finally consolidated only in the 1950s, after Nabokov left the laboratory.

On the other hand, despite his antipathy to formal religion and his sense that "God" was a hopelessly anthropomorphic term, Nabokov was committed to what had seemed for millennia the natural explanation for the origins of life, a top-down, mind-first explanation. Although he accepted evolution as a principle and Darwin as a scientist of genius, he strongly resisted the intellectual revolution of Darwinian natural selection and its bottom-up principles.

One of his main props for still retaining, a century after Darwin, his deep conviction that there was some form of Mind or Design behind life was the case of mimicry. He was convinced mimicry could not be accounted for by its protective role because it exceeded predators' powers of perception and seemed almost designed by some waggish artist for human discovery. But research from the 1950s to the present on many facets of the subject and in many species has presented conclusive evidence for the protective advantages of mimicry, the extraordinary perceptual discrimination of predators, and the power of natural selection to account completely for even the most complex instances of mimicry. What Nabokov's attitude to these findings would have been—fascination, resistance, admission that his favorite prop for a mind-first version of evolution had been knocked away?—remains impossible to know. I suspect he was too emotionally attached to a top-down explanation for existence to have accepted Darwinism, although he would probably have accepted many of the local advances in Darwinian theory and especially the clarifications of the power of natural selection in mimicry.

Zimmer treats these complicated matters in depth, perhaps a little too much depth, even, for an introduction to his *Guide*. I, too, have treated them here in too much depth. For although this is the most complex and controversial aspect of Nabokov's work as a scientist, and closest to the metaphysical issues in his art, Zimmer is nevertheless right that both Nabokov's science and his art depend above all on an inspired command of detail. And that detail is where Zimmer also excels, in the catalogues that are the chief and lasting treasure of his *Guide*.

David Sexton, reviewing *Nabokov's Butterflies*, ended with the comment that whatever your starting point, you would think more of Nabokov after reading the book.[1] The same could be said of Zimmer's *Guide*. You will also think more of Zimmer, even if you already know how selflessly he has worked for Nabokov since 1959, translating volume after volume into German, compiling the first Nabokov bibliography, editing and annotating the twenty-plus volumes of the Rowohlt edition of the collected works, contributing to the Nabokov website Zembla, and putting the final touches to a book on Nabokov's Berlin.

Anyone who teaches Nabokov, and especially anyone who supervises or hopes to supervise graduate students working on him, should ensure that they have their own copy of *A Guide to the Butterflies and Moths 2001* and that they order another copy for their university library. Those who missed out on Michael Juliar's *Vladimir Nabokov: A Descriptive Bibliography* for themselves and their library and now find it quite unavailable should not make the same mistake again.

Nabokov the commentator on *Eugene Onegin*, as well as Nabokov the researcher of "Notes on Neotropical Plebejinae" and Nabokov the author of *The Gift*, "A Discovery," and *Pale Fire*, would have welcomed and applauded Zimmer's invaluable *Guide 2001*. And Nabokov the lifelong lover of Lepidoptera would have had to blink back or wipe away tears of gratitude.

NABOKOV AS PSYCHOLOGIST

10. The Psychological Work of Fictional Play

When my friends in the very active Nabokov Society of Japan, Tadashi Wakashima, Akiko Nakata, and Shoko Miura, organized an international Nabokov conference in Kyoto in 2010, partly as a result of my cajoling—and my offering to organize a return conference in Auckland in 2012—they asked me to present a plenary paper. I had been reading a great deal of psychology over the previous decade and thought that this, as much as my reading in evolution (which dominates chapter 11, shapes chapter 23, and inflects chapters 8, 14 and 24), could offer me a fresh perspective on Nabokov. He is a formidable psychologist, but apart from studies of his relationship to Freud, far too little research has been done in this area. And, as I argue, psychology has grown to the point where it can now focus on much about human minds and behavior of central concern to literature. Nabokov's psychology, like his ethics and metaphysics, is another of those dimensions of his work that I think we cannot separate from his work as literature.

Vladimir Nabokov once dismissed as "preposterous" Alain Robbe-Grillet's claims that his novels eliminated psychology: "The shifts of levels, the interpenetration of successive impressions and so forth belong of course to psychology—psychology at its best" (*SO* 80). Later asked, "Are you a psychological novelist?" he replied: "All novelists of any worth are psychological novelists" (*SO* 174). Since he evidently did not consider himself a novelist of no worth, we can infer he saw himself as a psychological novelist.

Psychology fills vastly wider channels now than when Nabokov, in the mid-twentieth century, refused to sail between the Scylla of behaviorism and the Charybdis of Freud. It deals with what matters to writers, readers, and others: with memory and imagination, emotion and thought, art and our attunement to one another, and it does so in wider time frames and with tighter spatial focus than even Nabokov could imagine. It therefore seems high time to revise or refresh our sense of Nabokov by considering him as a serious (and, of course, playful) psychologist and to see what literature and psychology can now offer each other.

I offer no definitive chart of the terrain, just prompts to exploration. We could move in many directions, a fact itself a tribute to Nabokov's range and strengths as a psychologist: the writer as a reader of others and himself; as an observer and introspector; in relation to the psychology he knew from fiction (Dostoevsky, Tolstoy, Proust, Joyce), nonfiction, and professional psychology (William James, Freud, Havelock Ellis); as a psychological theorist, in his fiction and nonfiction; and as a psychological "experimenter" in his fiction, running thought experiments on the characters he creates and on the effects he produces in readers. We could consider him in relation to the different branches of psychology, in his own time and now: abnormal, clinical, comparative, cognitive, developmental, evolutionary, individual, personality, positive, social; in relation to different functions of mind, whose limits he happily tests (attention, perception, emotion, memory, imagination, and pure cognition: knowing, understanding, inferring, discovering, solving, inventing); in relation to different states of consciousness (waking, sleeping, dreaming, delirium, reverie, inspiration, near-death experience, death experience). And we could consider what recent psychology explains in ways that Nabokov foresaw or all but ruled impossible to explain.

He used to tell his students: "The whole history of literary fiction as an evolutionary process may be said to be a gradual probing of deeper and deeper layers of life. . . . the artist, like the scientist, in the process of evolution of art and science, is always casting around, understanding a little more than his predecessor, penetrating further with a keener and more brilliant eye" (*LRL* 164–65). As a young boy he desperately wanted to discover new species of butterflies, and he became no less avid as a writer for new finds in literature: not only in words, details, and images, in structures and tactics, but also in psychology.

He declared that "next to the right to create, the right to criticize is the richest gift that liberty of thought and speech can offer" (*LRL* ii), and he liked to criticize, utterly undaunted by reputation. He especially liked to correct competitors. He was fascinated by psychological extremes, as his fiction testifies, but he deplored Dostoevsky's "monotonous dealings with persons suffering from pre-Freudian complexes" (*LRL* 104). He admired Tolstoy's psychological insight and his gift of rendering experience through his characters, but while he availed himself of Tolstoy's techniques for scenic immersion, he sought to stress also, almost always, the capacity of our minds to transcend the scenes in which we find ourselves. Nabokov admired Proust's capacity to move outside the moment, especially in untrammeled recollection, but he allotted more space to the constraints of the ongoing scene than Proust. In *The Gift* he gives Fyodor some of Proust's frustration with the present, but he also locates the amplitude and fulfillment even here, for those who care to look. And where Proust emphasizes spontaneous, involuntary memory in restoring our links with our past, Nabokov stresses memory as directed by conscious search. He revered Joyce's verbal accuracy, his precisions and nuances, but he also considered that his stream-of-consciousness technique gave "too much verbal body to thoughts" (*SO* 30). The medium of thought for Nabokov was not primarily linguistic: "We think not in words but in shadows of words" (*SO* 30). Thought was for him also multisensory and, at its best, multilevel. As cognitive psychologists would now say, using a computing analogy foreign to Nabokov, consciousness is parallel (indeed, "massively parallel"), rather than serial, so cannot translate readily into the emphatically serial mode that a single channel of purely verbal stream-of-consciousness can provide.

Famously, Nabokov could not resist deriding Freud. And for good reason: Freud's ideas were enormously influential, especially in Nabokov's American years, but his claims hollow. The Nobel laureate Peter Medawar, perhaps the greatest of science essayists, declared, in terms akin to Nabokov's, that Freudianism was "the most stupendous intellectual confidence trick of the twentieth century."[1] Nabokov saw the intellectual vacuity of Freudian theory and its pervasiveness in the popular and the professional imagination. He thought it corrupted intellectual standards (*SO* 47), infringed on personal freedom (Guérin interview), undermined the ethics of personal responsibility (*SO* 116), destroyed literary sensitivity (Guérin interview), and distorted the real nature of childhood attachment to parents—as has been amply confirmed by modern developmental psychology.

Nabokov treasured critical independence, but he did not merely resist others: he happily imbibed as much psychology as he could from the art of Tolstoy and the science of William James. He also looked for himself. He was a brilliant observer not only of the visual and natural worlds but also of the world of human nature. We can see his acute eye for individuals throughout his letters and memoirs, in others' recollections of *his* sense of *them*, even many years later, and, of course, in his fiction.

Let's turn there now: to the fiction, to one short passage, a mere sixty-seven words. I want to interweave the psychology Nabokov observes and experiments with in his fiction and the modern psychology about whose possibilities he was so skeptical. I also want to show just how much psychological *work* fiction can involve, or how much Nabokov's swift shifts *make* it involve.

In *Ada*'s fourth chapter, we see Van Veen at his first school, the elite River-lane, and at his first sex, with the young helper at the corner shop, a "fat little wench" whom another boy at the school has found can be had for "a Russian green dollar." The first time, Van spills "on the welcome mat what she would gladly have helped him take indoors." But "at the next mating party" he "really beg[a]n to enjoy her . . . soft sweet grip and hearty joggle," and by the end of term he has enjoyed "forty convulsions" with her. The chapter ends with Van leaving to spend the summer at Ardis, with his "aunt" Marina:

> In an elegant first-class compartment, with one's gloved hand in the velvet side-loop, one feels very much a man of the world as one surveys the capable landscape capably skimming by. And every now and then the passenger's roving eyes paused for a moment as he listened inwardly to a nether itch, which he supposed to be (correctly, thank Log) only a minor irritation of the epithelium.
>
> (*Ada* I.4:33)

Nabokov writes fiction, not psychology, but this typically exceptional passage depends on, depicts, and appeals to psychology. These lines and psychology have much to offer each other.

The "elegant first-class apartment" and the "gloved hand" make the most of a cognitive bias, the contrast effect: our minds respond to things much more emphatically in the presence of a contrast. Through the suddenness of the switch, Van and VN contrast the tawdriness of the "fat wench" possessed "among crates and sacks at the back of the shop" with the opulence of the train and Van's fine dress.

"One feels very much a man of the world": we can all recall and imagine sudden moments of self-satisfaction, especially at points where life steps up a level in childhood and adolescence. We can unpack this several ways. Life-history theory in recent evolutionary biology focuses on species-typical patterns of development and their consequences across species—although before life-history theory showed our human life patterns in a comparative light, we knew the importance of, and the unique delay in, the onset of human sexual activity. Psychology long neglected emotion. Now it explores even the social emotions, like those associated with status. Taking a step up on the staircase of life marks a rise in status, and recognizing that boosts levels of the neurotransmitter serotonin in the brain. This rise in turn, past puberty, raises the inclination to sexual activity—as in Van, on his way to

Ardis, who wakes up there early the next morning to a "savage sense of opportune license" (*Ada* 46) when, in his skimpy bathrobe, he encounters the nineteen-year-old servant Blanche.

In "*one's* gloved hand . . . *one* feels very much a man of the world," Van invites us to a common human emotion through the generalizing pronoun "one." We take this appeal to shared experience for granted. Recognizing shared experience, and wanting to, are at the basis of fiction and the social life fiction feeds on. But psychology should do more than just take these facts for granted: it should help us explain them.

Mirror neurons, discovered in the 1990s, fire in the same part of my motor area that would be activated if, say, I grasp something, when I merely *see* someone else grasping. This unforeseen component of neural architecture, especially elaborate in humans, helps us to understand and to learn from others, and perhaps to cooperate or compete with them.[2] We also have from infancy a far stronger motivation to share experience than have other animals, even chimpanzees: think of an infant's compulsion to point to draw others' attention to something just possibly of interest. This heightened motivation to share experience seems to lay the foundation for human ultrasociality.[3]

We understand the actions of others when we see them by partially reactivating our own experience of such actions, stored in our memories.[4] But more than that: we also attune ourselves to others' actions and empathize with them, unless we perceive them as somehow opposed to us. Over the last fifteen years, psychology has begun to study the remarkably swift and precise ways we attune ourselves rapidly, and often unconsciously, to what we see in others.[5] Van and Nabokov appeal here to our shared experience, to our recollection of our pride in reaching a new stage in life, like learning to walk, starting school, or, here, mastering the rudiments of sex.

Research in grounded cognition in recent neuroscience shows that thought is not primarily linguistic, as many had supposed, but multimodal, partially reactivating relevant multimodal experiences in our past, involving multiple senses, emotions and associations. Just as seeing someone grasp something activates mirror neurons, even hearing the *word* "grasp" activates the appropriate area of the motor cortex.[6] Our brains encode multimodal memories of objects and actions, and these are partially reactivated as percepts or concepts come into consciousness.

Nabokov rightly stressed that imagination is rooted in memory: indeed, that was the very point of entitling his autobiography *Speak, Memory*. Since the early 1930s it has been known that we store episodic memories, memories of our experiences, as *gist*, as reduced summaries of the core sense or feel of situations, rather than all their surface details.[7] Our stored knowledge of past situations and stimuli allows us later, as it were, to unzip the compressed file of a memory and to reconstruct an image of the original. Recent evidence shows that memory's compression into gist evolved not only to save space on our mental hard drives but also to make it easier to activate relevant memories and to recombine them with present perception or imagination of future or other states not experienced.[8] If memories were stored in detail and the details had to match exactly, mental search would be slow and rarely successful. But once memories have been compressed into gist, many memories can be appropriate enough to a new situation or a new imaginative moment to be partially reactivated, as it were, according to their common mental keywords or search terms.

Minds evolved to deal with immediate experience, and although human minds can now specialize in abstract thought or free-roaming imagination, we still respond most vividly and multimodally to immediate experience. For that reason more of our multimodal memories can be activated by language that prompts us to recreate experience, as fiction does, rather than more abstract, less personal, less sequential texts.[9] Nabokov was right to insist on the power of the specific in art to stimulate the imagination. Here, he and Van appeal to the groundedness of cognition through their use of details like the velvet side-loop and the gloved hand to activate our multimodal memories of the look and feel of gloves, velvet, and side-loops in trains or cars.

So far I have stressed how these first few words appeal to what we share in experience. But despite its appeal to what we share, the passage also implies different kinds of distance. There's the distance between Van as adult narrator—as by this stage we already know him to be, despite his third-person presentation of young Van as character—and Van as a fourteen-year-old feeling himself "very much a man of the world." The word "one," which generalizes from his situation, as if adolescent Van can now grandly sum up a new truth he has reached from his lofty vantage point of experience, can only seem absurd to Van many years later, after much more sexual exploration than a few furtive convulsions with a shop girl. As nonagerian narrator, he can see a fourteen-year-old's pride in his experience as proof of his past self's relative innocence. But that distance between Van as character and Van as narrator *also* sets up something for us to share with Van as narrator: we have all reflected ironically later in life upon satisfactions that had seemed robust when we first felt them. We see here how memory compression into gist may help us retrieve a whiff of similar episodes we have experienced or witnessed.

But apart from this multiple appeal to what we share, Van and especially Nabokov behind him also know that his way of wording his recollection will also establish a different kind of distance between Van and reader. Many readers never travel first class, and few men, however "elegant," now wear gloves on a summer's day. Van, in his "elegant first-class compartment," with his gloved hand in a velvet loop, has a strong element of dandified class consciousness mingling with his pride at being "very much a man of the world." The generalizing pronoun "one," which on one level invites readers to share a common experience, on another also discloses Van's intellectual pride in arriving at the new generalization and his foppish indulgence in his sense of superiority to others. The upper-class English use of "one" applied to oneself, seen as a mark of high-toned speech, reinforces the snobbery that amplifies Van's self-satisfaction and complicates the appeal to our identification with him—although we, too, will recognize moments when we have felt superior to others.

We're not far into this passage yet. Let's move on one clause: "one feels very much a man of the world as one surveys the capable landscape capably skimming by." Here Van and VN comically evoke our human tendency to see the world through the tinted lenses of our emotions, or even to project our emotions onto what we perceive. "Capable" applies legitimately only to agents; Van and VN absurdly apply it to the landscape and then, adverbially, to the way the landscape skims past Van's train window. Narrator and author know the comedy of twice misapplying this term, which suits only Van's sense of himself, to the landscape. Nabokov suddenly confronts us in this surprising, vivid, ironic, amusing way with an instance of our human tendency to project our emotions onto our world. Psychologists study this kind of projection through priming, in terms, say, of what we notice or think of first if we have been primed with (just exposed to) either positive or negative images. Yet despite the comedy of Van's emotional "priming," Nabokov and Van also appeal to our imaginations through our memories, in that landscape "skimming by."

We're hurtling along now, at the last sentence already: "And every now and then the passenger's roving eyes paused for a moment as he listened inwardly to a nether itch." Van-and-VN activate our own multimodal memories and awareness: our proprioceptive sense (our awareness, from inside, of our bodily positions and sensations) of the ways our eyes move as we attend to an inner discomfort or pain and our memories of others glancing sideways in thought or hurt. The surprise and yet the naturalness of the metaphor, "*listened* to a nether *itch*," trigger another multimodal activation (roving eyes, inner ears, touch) of multimodal memories of monitoring our inner sensations—and perhaps arise out of the synesthesia that Nabokov rendered so exactly in *Speak, Memory* that his description has become a classic of synesthesia studies.[10]

But Van, attending to this nether itch, supposed it "to be (correctly, thank Log) only a minor irritation of the epithelium." We are invited to infer that Van has a few momentary worries about a venereal disease he could have contracted from the "fubsy pig-pink whorelet" at the shop near his school and that some time later, when the itch does not recur, he confirms to himself that there was no cause for alarm. Nabokov stresses the importance in the development of modern fiction of writers' learning to trust readers' powers of inference because we prefer to imagine actively, to see in our mind's eye much more than what the page spells out explicitly. We intuit Van's concern through our familiarity with his context: because we now share that common ground with him, things *don't* have to be spelled out for us to infer the whole situation, and that successful inference further confirms our sense of the ground we share with Van.

Van's unfounded fears of venereal disease may add another note of comedy, but they also prepare us structurally both for the romance of love and sex with Ada at Ardis, where Van's train will take him, a romance highlighted by contrast with the schoolboy line-up for paid sex, and the tragic aspects of Ardis as sexual paradise, not least in the venereal disease that, through Blanche, enfolds itself into the romantic myth of Van and Ada at Ardis.

This brief paragraph, immediately accessible, immediately evocative of multiple senses, emotions, and memories, typically embodies a multiple awareness: of Van at fourteen on the train; of him a little later that summer, when he can feel sure he has not caught a venereal disease; of him as a much older narrator recalling his young self and inviting his readers to sense what we share with him but also to recognize young Van's cocky sense of what makes him privileged and apart. As narrator Van evokes and reactivates the experience, yet he also sees himself from outside: "And every now and then *the passenger's* roving eyes paused." Psychologists distinguish between a field and an observer relationship to an experience or a memory: an inner view, as if amid the field of experience, and an outer view, observing oneself as if from outside. Ordinarily we experience life in the "field" condition, but precisely because we can compress memories into "gist," we can also afterward recall our experience as if from the outside, as in the radical recombinations of our memories in our dreams. As we read, we also tend to toggle or glide between imagining ourselves within the experience of a focal character— Van seeing the landscape swimming by or listening to his nether itch—and an outer view: seeing Van with gloved hand in the velvet side-loop.

A number of times in his works Nabokov makes explicit one of his personal psychological observations about the casual, insignificant impressions suddenly locked into permanent memory when they happen to be caught in the forehaze of a major change. Here he does not refer explicitly to the forehaze, but that's what he portrays: Van unaware that the visit to his "cousins," from which he does not expect much, will transform his life—and, of course, will cast an entirely different light on his pride in being a man of the world merely because of a few paid orgasms with a fubsy whorelet.

As rereaders we can be highly conscious of the structural role of this scene, of the contrasts between Van in the shop with the pig-pink wench and at Ardis, in passionate embrace with Ada; between the cheap whorelet and the fancy whores he resorts to when away from Ada or when he flees Ardis, appalled at her infidelity; or between the comically fleeting anxiety about venereal disease that the whorelet causes Van and the venereal disease that Blanche, the prime celebrant of the romance of the Veen venery at Ardis, tragically passes on to her child.

Ada's complexities and charms invite multiple rereadings, and rereaders can sense all these multiple contexts surrounding the immediate scene. We also seek to explain anything unaccounted for by its local or larger context. I had laughed at the "capable landscape capably skimming by" but never felt it problematic. But the Kyoto Reading Circle recognized something in the conjunction of "capable" and "landscape" that anyone who knows the English eighteenth century well should recognize. Van and VN allude here to the greatest of English landscape architects, Lancelot "Capability" Brown (1716–1783), particularly appropriate since Ardis, where Van is headed, is an eighteenth-century estate whose grounds display the kind of gentle naturalness Brown introduced, between earlier English formality and later romantic preferences for the wild and sublime. I find the fact that Van and VN smuggled this allusion in, and that I didn't see it, but that it was eminently discoverable, very funny. Nabokov loves the psychology of attention, of memory, of discovery, and of humor.

On rereading we can be aware not only of what we know now but also of what we think we were being led to expect or being mentally and emotionally prepared for on a first reading, or what the author has devised to work one way for first-time readers and more richly still for rereaders. We are immediately aware here of Van as fourteen-year-old character and less vividly but still consciously aware of him as mature narrator looking back with amusement but also with pleasure at his young self and of the intricate combination of appeal to shared experience and proud Van's sense of his own specialness. And after discovering the hidden as well as the overt joke in "capable," we can also recall our discovery of the allusion and our state of innocence before the discovery. We can be aware, therefore, of these multiple times and levels: Van, (1) here in June 1884, (2) a few weeks later, when he can be sure he has picked up no disease from the shop girl, (3) recalling this in later life, and (4) at the moment of writing this; (5) Nabokov behind Van Veen; and readers, (6) first-time and recalling train journeys we have taken or stages in life we have triumphantly reached, (7) rereading and placing the scene in relation to Ardis, and even (8) expert enough to see the landscape architect hidden in the landscape.

Think how different this is from our experience as readers of Tolstoy characters on trains. In Tolstoy we seem to enter immediately into the minds and experience of the focal characters because he conjures up all the relevant elements of the situation, the physical presence, the personalities of those involved, the interactions between them, and relevant information about their past relations. Our imaginations seem contained entirely within the scene: we feel ourselves within the space the characters occupy. But Nabokov prefers to evoke and exercise our recognition of the manifold awareness of consciousness: the different Vans here, character now, character slightly later, narrator much later, felt from inside or seen from outside; the different appeals to recognize what we share and what holds us at a distance from Van; and the awareness, on rereading, of the appeal to first-time readers and to our accumulated knowledge of the rest of the book on rereading or our awareness of specific puzzles we can now recognize as puzzles because we have seen the solution. Tolstoy also builds up scenes gradually, coordinating characters' actions and perceptions. Nabokov speeds us into his railroad scene without warning, without explicitness (only "first-class compartment," "skimming," and "passenger" specify the situation), without lingering (the scene ends here), and without spelling out the when or where until we infer them at the beginning of the next chapter. He has confidence in our pleasure in imagination, inference, and orientation.

Clinical, comparative, developmental, evolutionary, and social psychology over the past thirty years have devoted a great deal of attention to theory of mind and to metarepresentation.[11] Theory of mind is our capacity to understand other minds, or our own, in terms of desires, intentions, and beliefs, and metarepresentation, our capacity to understand representations *as* representations, including the representations other minds may have of a scene. While some intelligent social animals appear to understand others of their kind in terms of desires and intentions, only humans have a clear understanding of others in terms of what others *believe* and factor these beliefs effortlessly into their inferential systems. By adolescence, we can readily understand four degrees of intentionality: A's thoughts about B's thoughts about C's thoughts about D's. As adults, we start to make errors with but can still manage five or six degrees: our thoughts as rereaders, say, about our thoughts as first-time readers about Nabokov's thoughts about Van the narrator's thoughts about Van's thoughts at Ardis about Van's thoughts on the train to Ardis.

Nabokov finds fascinating the multilevel awareness of the mind and worked to develop it in himself and in his readers and rereaders—as he discusses most explicitly through Fyodor in *The Gift*. Fyodor deliberately sets himself exercises of observing, transforming, recollecting, and imagining through the eyes of others. Frustrated at earning his keep by foreign-language instruction, he thinks: "What he should be really teaching was the mysterious thing which he alone—out of ten thousand, a hundred thousand, perhaps even a million men—knew how to teach: for example—multilevel thinking"—which he then goes on to define (*Gift* 176). The very idea of training the brain in this way, as Fyodor does for himself, as he imagines teaching others, as he learns to do for his readers, as Nabokov learned over many years to do for *his* readers, fits with neuroscience's recent understanding of brain plasticity, the degree to which the brain can be retrained, fine-tuned, redeployed.[12]

Play has been nature's main way of making the most of brain plasticity. It fine-tunes animals in key behaviors like flight and fight—hence the evolved pleasure animals take in chasing and frisking and in rough-and-tumble fighting, nature's way of ensuring they'll engage in this training again and again. In *On the Origin of Stories* I look at art as a development of play, and as a way of fine-tuning minds in particular cognitive modes that matter to us: in the case of fiction, our expertise in social cognition, in theory of mind, in perspective taking, holding multiple perspectives in mind at once. As I made that case, I was not thinking of Nabokov, but he takes this kind of training of the mind—perception, cognition, emotion, memory, and imagination—more seriously, and more playfully, than any other writer.

I have used one brief and superficially straightforward example from *Ada* to show how much psychological work we naturally do when we read fiction, especially when we read Nabokov's fiction, and how much light psychology can now throw on what we do naturally when we read fiction. Literature's aims differ considerably from those of research psychology. Nevertheless literature *draws on* human intuitive psychology (itself also a subject in recent psychology) and *exercises* our psychological capacities. Literature aims to understand human minds only to the degree it seeks to move human minds. It may move readers' minds, in part, by showing with new accuracy or vividness, or at least with fresh particulars, how fictional minds move and by showing in new ways how freely readers' minds can move, given the right prompts. Psychology, too, wants to understand minds, both simply for the satisfaction of knowing and also in order to make the most of minds, to limit mental damage or to extend mental benefits. It uses the experimental method. We can see fictions, too, as thought experiments, experiments about how characters feel, think, and behave and about how readers feel, think, and behave and how they can *learn* to think more imaginatively, feel more sympathetically, act more sensitively.[13] Fictions are experiments whose results will not be systematically collected and peer reviewed—and then perhaps read by a few psychologists—but will be felt vividly by a wide range of readers.

Nabokov thinks that at their best art and science meet on a high ridge. Psychology, after wandering along wrong paths to Freud Falls or the Behaviorist Barrens, has just emerged onto the ridge. Nabokov may have doubted psychology could crest this particular ridge, but I think he has met science there.

NABOKOV AND THE ORIGINS
AND ENDS OF STORIES

11. Stacks of Stories, Stories of Stacks

In 2010 I gave the Frederic Alden Warren Lecture at Trinity College, University of Toronto. Its regular theme, Literature/Libraries/Culture, prompted me to consider stories and other aspects of culture in relation to the accumulation, preservation, and innovation epitomized in library holdings. I decided to explore also, on the one hand, Nabokov's relation to evolution and to the ideas in my evolutionary account of stories, and, on the other, the ways libraries feature in his fiction.

Others have written books on Nabokov and trains, cars, and planes (Leving), Nabokov and geography (Manolescu); Nabokov and painting (De Vries et al.; Shapiro); Nabokov and cinema (Appel; Wyllie); Nabokov and science (Blackwell); Nabokov and translation (Grayson); Nabokov and Berlin (Zimmer); Nabokov and Central Asian exploration (Zimmer); Nabokov and politics (Rampton); Nabokov and Freud (Green); and Nabokov and, of course, butterflies (Zimmer; Johnson and Coates); and much else. Books on Nabokov and food or humor or play or symbols or liberalism have been proposed or written, and books on Nabokov and birds or flowers or trees or light or gesture or personality disorders would seem among the many that *could* be written. A whole volume on Nabokov and libraries, though, might push too far. Or would it?

Once I accepted the invitation to speak here at Trinity College, I was asked for a title and an abstract based on my recent work on stories. *Work?* I happened to feel like play. Playing with the occasion and topic of the lectures, I added libraries to my literature and culture game, to produce what seemed an appealing abstract:

What can the long perspective of evolution suggest about the past and future of stories—and multi-story library stacks? How do stories—

and the libraries that stack up more stories than any mind can hold—preserve and generate knowledge and imagination? How will stories and libraries stack up in the digital age?

This sounds rather fun, but it's not quite what transpired. If you put some bite into abstracts written in advance they have a nasty habit of biting back.

Tonight, returning to the University of Toronto, I want to combine my new work and my old: the new, evolution and literature, and the old, my Nabokov work, which reached orbit when I came here. But I also wanted to keep to the occasion: libraries, but seen within the trajectory of evolution and the work of Nabokov. This may only have produced a grotesque hybrid, like the mouse with a human ear growing in its back.

The highlight of the coursework in my first two years of the Ph.D. was taking Professor Patricia Brückmann's Scriblerus class. A Circe of a scholar, Pat bewitched us into becoming allusion bloodhounds: we could spend weeks on Swift's *A Tale of a Tub* or *Gulliver's Travels* without getting past the allusions on the title pages. I had an even better next two and a half years working on my dissertation under Pat, exploring Nabokov's longest and most complex novel, *Ada*, in the context of all his other work and his styles, strategies, and thought. For more than a year I worked day after day in the Reference Room of the Robarts Library sniffing through the allusions and the arcana in *Ada*, line by line, discovery by discovery. Oddly enough, I'm still annotating *Ada*, now in journal form and online, with hypertext links between text, notes, illustrations, and motifs, and in this form I'm only a third of the way through the novel but already up to 900 pages of annotations. All happy scholars, as Vladimir Tolstoy might have said, are mad in their own way.

Now I use Google, although my main source for *Ada*Online is still the penciled marginalia on the copy of *Ada* I would take every day to the Robarts Reference Room along with my boxes of index cards. I was young and hairy, not fifty-plus and ideally bald and endearing like Nabokov's Professor Pnin, but Nabokov's description of Pnin researching at the Waindell University Library wonderfully evokes aspects of researching in the days before computers ousted index cards:

> He then returned to his carrell for his own research.
>
> He contemplated writing a *Petite Histoire* of Russian culture, in which a choice of Russian Curiosities, Customs, Literary Anecdotes, and so forth would be presented in such a way as to reflect in miniature *la Grande Histoire*—Major Concatenations of Events. He was still

at the blissful stage of collecting his material; and many good young people considered it a treat and an honor to see Pnin pull out a catalogue drawer from the comprehensive bosom of a card cabinet and take it, like a big nut, to a secluded corner and there make a quiet mental meal of it, now moving his lips in soundless comment, critical, satisfied, perplexed, and now lifting his rudimentary eyebrows and forgetting them there, left high upon his spacious brow where they remained long after all trace of displeasure or doubt had gone. He was lucky to be at Waindell. Sometime in the nineties the eminent bibliophile and Slavist John Thurston Todd (his bearded bust presided over the drinking fountain), had visited hospitable Russia, and after his death the books he had amassed there quietly chuted into a remote stack. Wearing rubber gloves so as to avoid being stung by the *amerikanski* electricity in the metal of the shelving, Pnin would go to those books and gloat over them: obscure magazines of the Roaring Sixties in marbled boards; century-old historical monographs, their somnolent pages foxed with fungus spots; Russian classics in horrible and pathetic cameo bindings, whose molded profiles of poets reminded dewy-eyed Timofey of his boyhood, when he could idly palpate on the book cover Pushkin's slightly chafed side whisker or Zhukovski's smudgy nose.

(*Pnin* 76–77)

There will be a kind of pas de deux on the library floor between Nabokov and evolution throughout this talk, perhaps ending with them, or me, falling between two stools.

In the 1940s Nabokov was a scientist, a world-class lepidopterist, *the* authority on a small family of butterflies, the Blues. He happily researched the evolution of speciation within the Blues, and the evolution of their main diagnostic characteristics, their genitalia and their wing markings. But while he accepted evolution, as he wrote, "as a modal formula" (*LL* 378), and while he admired Darwin as a scientist, he also objected strongly to natural selection as a sufficient explanation for evolution. In his autobiography, *Speak, Memory*, he writes:

There is also keen pleasure (and, after all, what else should the pursuit of science produce?) in meeting the riddle of the initial blossoming of man's mind by postulating a voluptuous pause in the growth of the rest of nature, a lolling and loafing which allowed first of all the formation of *Homo poeticus*—without which *sapiens* could not have been evolved. "Struggle for life" indeed! The curse of battle and toil leads man back to the boar, to the grunting beast's crazy obsession with the search for food. You and I have frequently remarked upon that maniacal glint in a housewife's scheming eye as it roves over food in a grocery or about the morgue of a butcher's shop. Toilers of the world, disband! Old books are wrong. The world was made on a Sunday.

(*SM* 298)

Nabokov once wrote that "next to the right to create, the right to criticize is the richest gift that liberty of thought and speech can offer" (*LRL* ii), and he was happy to criticize anybody: in this paragraph, even if playfully, he takes on Darwin, Marx, and the Bible at once. Here the crucial point to note is his dislike of natural selection's stress on competition and his preferred emphasis on stepping outside competition into play, the free play of the imagination.

Nabokov thought, in particular, that natural mimicry was too complex, too perfect, too artful to be explained in terms of natural selection. Earlier in *Speak, Memory*, describing his early passion for butterflies, he notes:

The mysteries of mimicry had a special attraction for me. Its phenomena showed an artistic perfection usually associated with man-wrought things. Consider the imitation of oozing poison by bubble-like macules on a wing (complete with pseudo-refraction) or by glossy yellow knobs on a chrysalis ("Don't eat me—I have already been squashed, sampled and rejected"). Consider the tricks of an acrobatic caterpillar (of the Lobster Moth) which in infancy looks like bird's dung, but after molting develops scrabbly hymenopteroid appendages and baroque characteristics, allowing the extraordinary fellow to play two parts at once (like the actor in Oriental shows who becomes a pair of intertwisted wrestlers): that of a writhing larva and that of a big ant seemingly harrowing it. When a certain moth resembles a certain wasp in shape and color, it also walks and moves its antennae in a waspish, unmothlike manner. When a butterfly has to look like a leaf, not only are all the details of a leaf beautifully rendered but markings mimicking grub-bored holes are generously thrown in. "Natural selection," in the Darwinian sense, could not explain the miraculous coincidence of imitative aspect and imitative behavior, nor could one appeal to the theory of "the struggle for life" when a protective device was carried to a point of mimetic subtlety, exuberance, and luxury far in excess of a predator's power of appreciation. I discovered in nature the nonutilitarian delights that I sought in art. Both were a form of magic, both were a game of intricate enchantment and deception.

(SM 124–25)

If man as a species has made God in his own image, Nabokov made God or Nature in his own personal image: as a subtle cosmic and comic prankster, hiding elegant and playful surprises for the observant and curious mind. In *The Gift* the hero and narrator, Fyodor, reports that his lepidopterist father

> told me about the incredible artistic wit of mimetic disguise which was not explainable by the struggle for existence (the rough haste of evolution's unskilled forces), was too refined for the mere deceiving of accidental predators, feathered, scaled and otherwise (not very fastidious, but then not too fond of butterflies), and seemed to have been invented by some waggish artist precisely for the intelligent eyes of man.
>
> (*Gift* 122)

Nabokov was no Christian, but he did believe in his own brand of Intelligent Design, design somehow hidden for "the intelligent eyes of man" to rediscover.

In the 1940s a scientist could legitimately think that natural selection could not explain mimicry, but experimental work on the survival rates of camouflaged animals in the 1950s, and work on animal perception and cognition after that, confirmed that even elaborate mimicry could be perfectly explained by natural selection. But Nabokov's sense of human evolution as not being explicable in terms of competition and as needing to stress imagination anticipates some recent shifts in our understanding of our distant past. While Nabokov was alive, but after he had stopped working as a scientist, modern neo-Darwinism took shape. The new insights into genes and DNA possible after Crick and Watson combined with William Hamilton's notion of inclusive fitness: that *my* evolutionary fitness depends on the survival and reproduction of the genes not only *in me* but also in others *closely related to me*. In 1975 Richard Dawkins memorably showed the power of a gene's-eye view of life in *The Selfish Gene*. Many who have never read the book suppose it must be about genes as selfish, but it actually explains how cooperation could arise from genes that, metaphorically, serve only their own interests. As Dawkins later wrote, he could have called his book *The Cooperative Gene* without needing to change a word.[1]

Recent work in human evolution has shown cooperation to be increasingly central to what we have become. In the 1970s and 1980s, competition was still seen as a key to the emergence of intelligence. A major driving force in intelligence, it was realized, was the ability to understand other minds, the most volatile and usually the most consequential kind of information in the environment. With chimpanzees, a highly competitive species, as a prime research focus, the idea was called the Machiavellian intelligence hypothesis. In the 1990s came the recognition that social *cooperation* as well as social competition could drive intelligence. In the last decade, with detailed comparative studies of chimpanzee and human development, researchers have seen the unique extent and importance of human cooperativeness as the key to the emergence of language and complex cognition and to the unique extent of human culture.

Michael Tomasello and his team have compared human and chimpanzee development more closely than anyone else. Tomasello stresses that humans have evolved a unique motivation to engage with and understand others of our kind and a unique capacity to do so. Our intense engagement with others begins at birth. Human mothers and infants have evolved so that they can and want to share their gaze while the infants suckle, unlike in any other species. Human eyes have evolved to *reveal* the direction of their attention, whereas other primate eyes have evolved to *conceal* eye direction. Human one-year-olds engage in joint attention—following others' hands or eyes and checking to see that the others follow theirs—and in proto-declarative pointing—indicating objects or events simply for the sake of sharing attention toward them, which apes never do. They expect others to share interest, attention, and response: "This by itself is rewarding for infants— apparently in a way it is not for any other species on the planet."[2]

Why? I said that primatologists originally named the social intelligence hypothesis the Machiavellian intelligence hypothesis because they assumed that the competition they observed in chimpanzees was a key driver of intelligence. But flexible cooperation requires even more intelligence than competition. To compete with others in ways apart from the purely physical usually needs little more than concealing your knowledge and intentions. To cooperate in flexible ways, you need to know in detail what the others you wish to cooperate with know and plan. You need to pay close and continuous attention to what others are seeing, feeling, and doing.

Tomasello stresses that our minds have evolved a unique capacity to understand one another because we have evolved a unique disposition to engage and cooperate with one another: somehow we have crossed a cooperation divide. We *want* to share attention and intentionality, to direct our minds toward the same things, and to share similar responses—without which art and story would be impossible. In fact, stories can be one of the richest ways of sharing intentionality with authors, with characters, and with others in the audience.

Our cooperative disposition has made us uniquely capable of social learning. All social animals can learn from others rushing from a threat or toward an opportunity. Highly social animals can cut down on information search time. Honeybees with their waggle dances and ants with their pheromone trails act as superorganisms, each individual almost like a neuron firing in an extended social brain. Bees and ants are eusocial, adapted for hypersociality, even to the point of having specialized breeders and non-breeding workers; biologists have recently begun to characterize humans, uniquely, as ultrasocial. Our cooperative disposition and our desire for joint attention and shared intentionality led to the emergence of language, probably out of gesture and mime, and ultimately to our occupying, uniquely, the cognitive niche.

As a result we therefore learn all sorts of fine-grained information from one another. We have even evolved a uniquely long childhood to help us learn. "Even in a school-less hunter-gatherer society, individuals learn more than 99 percent of fifty core skills with help from others."[3]

We not only pass on information, we actively seek it out. Why? A vast amount of research has been done in cognitive ethology and in comparative and developmental psychology to understand theory of mind, the capacity to understand other minds. It seems that only humans have evolved to become capable of understanding others not only in terms of desires and intentions, which many animals intuit, but also in terms of beliefs. By the age of five, we can realize that if another person lacks a key piece of information, they may have a wrong belief, which may then affect their desires and intentions. But that understanding of the possibility of false belief also alerts us to the possibility that *we* may not know enough, that *we* may be missing key pieces of information, that we need to seek more.

Chimpanzees are more curious than any other nonhuman animal, but humans take curiosity to a whole new level. Human curiosity, most momentously, allowed us to understand how plant cycles work, how to help them work, how to start agriculture, how to generate food surpluses. From there we could build settlements with some of the features of a beehive or an ant colony, with more scope for information search and sharing. We can send out, as it were, not food seekers laying down food trails but specialized information seekers laying down knowledge trails that then feed back into the colony. In these more complex societies, we learn not just from elders, as in hunter-gatherer societies, but from specialized teachers, from writing, from printed books, from libraries, and now the Internet. There is,

I think, in Darwin's words, "grandeur in this view of life," in seeing sociality and social learning from their simple origins to the present.

I started that line of inquiry in answering Nabokov's dislike for the stress on competition, on the struggle for life, in Darwinian natural selection and in showing recent developments in understanding cooperation. What about the other aspect of Nabokov's misgivings about natural selection: his sense that play is crucial to understanding "*Homo poeticus*—without which *sapiens* could not have been evolved"? Or to put another question, which will lead to the same answers: if information has been so powerful for humans, how is it that we also spend more of our time and energy on *mis*information than any other species? Why do our libraries store not only nonfiction but also fiction and the scriptures that are considered fictive at least by most outside any given faith?

In *On the Origin of Stories* I build on the findings I have already discussed to try to answer the question, why does a species that derives so many of its advantages from mastering information have a compulsion to spend time engaged in fiction, in telling one another stories that teller and listeners know to be untrue? It's no biological puzzle at all why we should have evolved to tell *true* stories. If we can comprehend events, if we have language, and if we are highly social animals, then, without needing to add anything else, we will tell true stories. Chimpanzees monitor each other intensely, and one chimp will bring to the attention of another the fact that this male and that female are copulating behind that tree. Humans, too, have every reason to want to know who's doing what to whom, and with true narrative we can also point who *has* done you-know-what to whom or who has had a successful kill and where and so on.

But in a world of unsparing biological competition—which our world still is, despite the evolution of cooperation—how could a successful species afford an unflagging appetite for stories we know to be *un*true? To answer that we have to answer the question why do we expend time and resources, across cultures, epochs, classes, life stages, and intellectual levels, on music, dance, design, and stories.

I say this because it seems highly likely that the literary arts were the last of the arts to emerge. Analogues of music and dance exist in many species, in birds, in intelligent nonprimates like whales and dolphins, and in primates like gibbons and chimpanzees. Chanting and rhythmic movement and perhaps rhythmic stick or rock banging—in other words forms of proto-song, proto-dance and proto-instrumental music—are likely to stretch back a million years or more. And the earliest signs of the visual arts date back hundreds of thousands of years, with the first over-refinement of Acheulean hand axes for purely aesthetic reasons. (Some of these stone tools were made much larger or much smaller or much more symmetrical than appropriate for use, and these impractical hand axes, unlike the practical ones, show no signs of use.)[4] Although the matter is a very long way from being decided, a full modern language adequate for telling stories seems to date back only a hundred or a hundred and fifty thousand years. Other proto-arts had probably been developing for hundreds of thousands of years before the first full-scale fictions.

In *On the Origin of Stories* I try to offer a comprehensive explanation for the arts, especially the art of fiction. Art, I argue, is a kind of high play. Play exists in many species, and the amount of play in a species correlates with its flexibility of behavior. Flexibility of behavior solves the problem of coping with unpredictable, complex circumstances, so by definition it cannot be entirely genetically programmed. A flexible behavior has to be *learned* to maximize flexibility. If a behavior is hardwired, there would be no point in exercising it in a way as expensive in energy and risk (injury, predation) as play. But if there is room for flexibility, then individuals who can improve their execution of complicated behaviors and their judgment of situations in which they are needed will fare better. This is especially the case in critical behaviors like flight or fight.

If in moments of security animals practice the behaviors that make the greatest life-and-death difference, like flight and fight, they can then perform better in moments of high urgency. For that reason play has developed in many species, especially those with the security that parental care provides: in birds and in perhaps all mammals. (And it seems highly significant that the two most common forms of play, chasing and rough-and-tumble fighting, indeed exercise exactly the skills needed for flight and fight.) The motivation to try out these behaviors has been selected for as those more inclined to practice survive more often until species after species loves play, until they have a compulsion to run, chase, twist, roll, or engage in rough-and-tumble. What we experience as the sheer fun of play overcomes the deeply rooted inclination not to expend energy if effort can be avoided.

Because we have the longest childhood of any species, play is particularly important for us, and because we now can produce food surpluses and live in settlements safe from predation, children have still more scope for play than the young of any other animals. But humans depend not just on physical skills but even more on mental power. Information matters for any species, but for no others is it so decisive as for ours. So for us the problem arises: How can we make more of our information-processing skills?

For animals to process information quickly, to make rich rapid inferences that can guide action, information needs to form patterns that minds can recognize almost automatically. Information falls into patterns, in most cases, when there are regularities in the world, regularities that make it more possible to predict what is about to happen. All animals seem to prefer patterned information (symmetry, for instance, distinct colors and shapes, clear-pitched sounds) over more chaotic information arrays: we therefore perceive as particularly beautiful phenomena like rainbows and sunsets in the world of physics and flowers and butterflies in the biological world. We especially crave information that falls into the kinds of patterns our minds have found most useful and have learned to process especially efficiently, like information about other plants or animals or fellow humans.

We crave information. But because we have a much more open-ended curiosity than other animals, we have a special appetite for pattern. We crave the high yield of novel kinds of pattern. So we not only chase and tussle, we not only play physically, but we also play cognitively, with patterns of the kinds of information that matter most to us: sound, sight, and, in our ultrasocial species, social information. We play with the rhythm and pitch and shape of sounds in music and song; with colors and shapes in drawing and painting and mudpies or sandcastles; and with patterns of social information in pretend play and story. In the social world, we see patterns of identity (who are they?), personality (what are they like?), society (whom are they related to? whom do they team up with? how do they rank?). In the world of events, we see patterns of cause and effect. In the world of social events, we see patterns of intention, action, and outcome.

Art and fiction start here. Because intense repetition and concentrated attention can rewire brains incrementally, the compulsiveness of music, images, and story reshapes human minds. We process aural, visual, and social information more rapidly, accurately, and flexibly through playing in a self-rewarding way with the high-density information, the cognitive play, of art. In this light Nabokov's hunch that what makes us most human is not competition but "lolling and loafing," the security of parental care and the *play* of the imagination within it—stressed so beautifully in the first and last chapters of *Speak, Memory*—seems not so wide of the mark.

Our minds are most finely tuned for understanding agents—any creature that can act, animal, human, and even, by extension, unseen agents like spirits. In ancient environments, the agents we evolved to track were other animals as well as people, and even in modern urban environments children have a compulsive desire to learn the names of animals and to play or attend to stories with animals. Our minds want to and easily can track and differentiate agents since other agents, human or not, offer the most complex, volatile, and high-stake information we regularly encounter. We carry that motivation and capacity into pretend play and story. Very young children do not readily think offline, away from the here and now. They do not easily recall their recent past, but they can easily use the present props of toys, whether homemade or manufactured, to conjure up scenarios involving agents that hook their attention. They learn to think in a sustained fashion in ways decoupled from the here and now, first by using physical props as fellow agents, then gradually by raiding the readymade stories and characters of their culture. By building on our sociality, fiction stretches our imaginations, taking us from our immediate present along tracks we can easily follow offline because they are the fresh tracks of agents.

In *On the Origin of Stories* I discuss the other functions that derive from stories as cognitive play with patterns of social information. Not only does their compulsiveness improve our social cognition, but stories also stretch our imagination, our capacity to think away from the here and now, our capacity to see from multiple perspectives in time, place, person, and mode. They offer a series of social thought experiments and ways to share values and understandings, ways to amplify our attunement, motivate our assembly, and therefore improve social cohesion. Like the other arts, fiction becomes a kind of high play that also offers a sense of human mastery, a sense we can shape the world on our own terms. Homer, the greatest of early storytellers, unfolds the world as humanly knowable, from the minds of the gods to the minds of humans, from the panorama of the known world down to a detail like the latch on a door. Homer's stories, classicists have argued, may even have provided the incentive to develop the first alphabet;[5] they certainly promptly provided the core of Greek education and, arguably, the confidence in the mind's capacity to encompass the world that inspired Greek thought.

In the real world of biological evolution, as opposed to the world of the stories we shape for ourselves, every benefit has a cost. Our capacity to understand other minds so well, which arises especially from our cooperative disposition, allows us to understand false belief: we appreciate clearly that others may not know information relevant to the situation that we happen to know. That also means that we realize *we* may not know what we need to know, and that realization drives human curiosity. But it also drives our unique human anxiety. There may be things we feel we need to know about that we know we do not know. That shapes stories: dramatic irony, what some of us know about a situation that others do not.

But it also shapes our real-world anxieties. We want to understand the causes of things, and we want to understand the consequences. Where do we come from? Where do we go to? Uncertainty and indecision are biologically unproductive. Better at least to think we know and make a move than to stay stalled. Because our imaginations naturally play with agents, we have ways to plug the gaps in our knowledge. We have a natural tendency to over-read rather than underread agency: better to suppose that bush a bear than vice versa. We want to do things, and we do: we see agency as the prototype of cause. We are fascinated by powers different than ours: animals stronger or swifter than us, birds that fly by day, owls or bats that fly by night and "see" in the dark.

Our uncertainty produces anxiety, anxiety that, throughout history, our predisposition to think in terms of agency has allayed. We engage in a kind of social confabulation rather than having to confront our failure to understand.[6] We have coped with our anxiety about not knowing enough by inventing stories involving agents who know what we don't. As research shows, we especially notice and remember creatures with powers that are *minimally* counterintuitive—gods or spirits who can see but be unseen, say, rather than those who exist only on Wednesdays. Such stories pervade all known cultures, and the sense of control they help give human lives means they have been handed down through the generations in compelling stories often reinforced by compelling ritual, music, dance, costume, and architecture. For a long time, much of the power of art has been commandeered by religion. And even someone as little disposed to conventional religion as Nabokov can be prone to overread agency in the unknown and, in his case, to see a cosmic playfulness behind things.

So the species that thrives most on information also generates the acknowledged fictions of story and the apparent explanations in the stories that have congealed into belief, into religion. Although true information can be invaluable biologically—if I want to kill prey, I need to know where it is—information need not invariably be true to be biologically advantageous. So long as it leads to biologically advantageous behavior it can be favored: a belief, say, in an unseen being who would witness and punish my uncooperative conduct, even if no others in my group could see what I was up to, will benefit the cohesiveness of my group and therefore, on average, our capacity to overcome competing groups.

Religion offers explanations beyond what we can see. It allays our anxieties about what we recognize we do not know, and it does so via the inclination to understand in terms of agency so natural for our ultrasocial selves. Eventually our awareness that there are things we do not know and should find out leads to science, to explaining things without agency. Science, too, uses our ultrasociality, although in a different way, through the competitive and cooperative advancing and testing of ideas. But whereas agency comes naturally to us, systematically challenging and testing the ideas that seem to have allowed us to survive so far seems comparatively unnatural. Unlike stories with agents, which we have evolved to be predisposed to, the agentless explanations of scientific stories seem draining both emotionally, in that they require us to put our best explanations to the test, and imaginatively, in that they require us to think about mechanisms not at the level of agency.

Despite Nabokov's own hunch that natural mimicry could be explained only as the invention "of some waggish artist precisely for the intelligent eyes of man"—a hunch he gives to the lepidopterist Konstantin Godunov-Cherydntsev in *The Gift*—he knew to keep this kind of explanation out of his science. In the fictional addendum to *The Gift* published in English as "Father's Butterflies," Godunov-Cherdynstev, though a distinguished scientist, proposes an explanation for evolution that passes beyond material causes. But once Nabokov himself became a research scientist, his own papers remain resolutely within the parameters of science, eschewing any appeals to ultimate agents or metaphysical drives.

I've tried to suggest why, from an evolutionary perspective, libraries store fictions and scriptures as well as nonfictions in their stacks. I've also suggested that without the capacity we have to understand and imagine other minds, without the capacity to move about in imaginative space that we develop in pretend play and story, without the confidence that we can shape things to please ourselves as we do in art generally and in fiction in particular, we might not have libraries or books to put in them.

Or to put this in Nabokovian rather than Darwinian terms: without freedom from incessant competition, without lolling and loafing in ideas, without the play of the mind, we would not have Nabokov's *Lolita* or his Lepidoptera papers or his speculations about what might lie behind and beyond life. Room to play matters to us as human beings, even if for those of us who have the privilege of working primarily with information, playing with ideas can become compulsive hard work—ninety hours a week for Nabokov in his prime. The Nobel Prize–winning Turkish novelist Orhan Pamuk, perhaps the most distinguished of those to have learned from Nabokov, writes ten hours a day: "Yes, I'm a hard worker. . . . I'm in love with what I do. I enjoy sitting at my desk like a child playing with his toys. It's work, essentially, but it's fun and games also."[7] Few filmmakers have produced such searing explorations of the human condition as Ingmar Bergman, but he described filmmaking as like returning to childhood, a game, a kind of play.[8] And not just art needs play. Nabokov would have been delighted with the work of Robert Root-Bernstein, who shows that leading scientists in many fields insist on the element of play that they need to be able to invent new ideas and on the element of imaginative identification that makes them able if they are chemists, say, to imagine themselves as one kind of molecule interacting with others.[9] Without the unruliness of play we would not have the hush and the order of libraries.

One of the great libraries in fiction, by the greatest librarian among fiction writers, is Jorge Luis Borges's "Library of Babel." Borges imagines a universe that is an infinite library. The philosopher and evolutionary theorist Daniel Dennett takes Borges's story as a way of picturing the infinity, what he calls the Vastness with a capital V, of "Design Space," as he calls it, or possibility space.[10] Imagine that one section of the library contained copies of only *Moby Dick* but contained copies with just the first letter different, in each of fifty-one different ways (not the capital *C* of "Call me Ishmael," but any other capital or minuscule), or the second, or the third, and so on, or with any combination of the first letter and any other letter in the novel different, or any two combinations, or any number of combinations. And other sections of the library would include every other actual or possible book, in every possible variant. That suggests the space of possibility, and as Dennett observes, once we start to concretize that as a library with books, with endlessly trivially different variants of books, it's actually mostly empty or uninteresting.

Evolution doesn't roam through infinite possibility space. It cannot venture into the void but starts with variations on what it has already generated so far. And in our human case, it works with a highly social primate, with minds shaped for social understanding, stretching them through the pretend play and story that fine-tune social understanding.

Evolution needs to conserve to be able to innovate. DNA appears to be fantastically well conserved for as far back as we can trace life, yet it can recombine into many trillions of possibilities even from the same two sexually reproducing parents. And natural selection automatically tracks each of those possibilities actually realized, favoring whatever yields more descendants.

Humans, too, need to accumulate to innovate. Our genome has accumulated our unique predisposition for sharing attention for others, for social learning, for culture. Individually we store experiences that provide the elements we can recombine in imagination. Not for nothing did Nabokov call his autobiography *Speak, Memory*, an invocation to Mnemosyne, to Memory as the mother of the muses. And socially, humanly accumulated traditions, like the traditions of the sonnet or the novel, the fresco, the canvas, the installation, become the basis for innovation.

Libraries, like memories at the individual level, preserve our accumulated possibilities to date and become the basis for new variations. Nabokov, with his sense of the evanescence of things in time and his passion for the particular, saw this preservation of fleeting particulars as the role of art. In his 1925 story "A Guide to Berlin" he writes:

> The horse-drawn tram has vanished, and so will the trolley, and some eccentric Berlin writer in the twenties of the twenty-first century, wishing to portray our time, will go to a museum of technological history and locate a hundred-year-old streetcar, yellow, uncouth, with old-fashioned curved seats, and in a museum of old costumes dig up a black, shiny-buttoned conductor's uniform. Then he will go home and compile a description of Berlin streets in bygone days. Everything, every trifle, will be valuable and meaningful: the conductor's purse, the advertisement over the window, that peculiar jolting motion which our great-grandchildren will perhaps imagine—everything will be ennobled and justified by its age.
>
> (*SoVN* 157)

He adds: "I think that here lies the sense of literary creation: to portray ordinary objects as they will be reflected in the kindly mirrors of future times; to find in the objects around us the fragrant tenderness that only posterity will discern and appreciate in the far-off times when every trifle of our plain everyday life will become exquisite and festive in its own right: the times when a man who might put on the most ordinary jacket of today will be dressed up for an elegant masquerade."

Unlike Borges, who likes to hover near infinity, with its rather rarefied atmosphere, Nabokov prefers the here and now as a springboard for infinite possibility. Once he demolished a critic who looked for sexual undersides of every innocent Nabokovian detail, explaining that "the fatal flaw in Mr Rowe's treatment of recurrent words, such as 'garden' or 'water,' is his regarding them as abstractions, and not realizing that the sound of a bath being filled, say, in the world of *Laughter in the Dark*, is as different from the limes rustling in the rain of *Speak, Memory* as the Garden of Delights in *Ada* is from the lawns in *Lolita*" (*SO* 305–6). Libraries for Nabokov vary as much from work to work as gardens or water. He offers accurate information, he observes and he conserves, he "portrays ordinary objects as they will be reflected in the kindly mirrors of future times," but he also plays. He plants exact details into the unique imaginative ecologies of different novels. He recombines observed facts and invented fictions, preserving the details in a clear light but transforming them under the special illumination of a new fictional world, to offer a basis for further recombination and innovation as long as libraries remain. A few more examples to close.

In the rich fact-based realism of *The Gift*, the writer-hero first resorts to the Berlin Library for material to construct a biography of his father, a naturalist-explorer of Central Asia who never returned from his last expedition: "Scientific books (with the Berlin Library's stamp always on the ninety-ninth page), such as the familiar volumes of *The Travels of a Naturalist* in unfamiliar black and green bindings, lay side by side" (110): notice the familiar volumes—familiar from his father's prerevolutionary library—in unfamiliar library bindings. Fyodor has to abandon the project but decides, unexpectedly to himself and everyone else, to write a biography not of the father he idealized but of the father of so-called socialist realist fiction, the real nineteenth-century novelist Nikolay Chernyshevksy, whom he derided:

> But now, taught by experience, he did not allow himself his former slovenliness in the use of sources and provided even the smallest note with an exact label of its origin. In front of the national library, near a stone pool, pigeons strolled cooing among the daisies on the lawn. The books to be taken out arrived in a little wagon along sloping rails at the bottom of the apparently small premises, where they awaited distribution, and where there seemed to be only a few books lying around on the shelves when in fact there was an accumulation of thousands.
>
> (*Gift* 211)

In the stylized hyperliterary world of *The Real Life of Sebastian Knight*, the narrator V. addresses and dismisses the previous biography of his half-brother, the writer Sebastian Knight, by a vacuous hack called Goodman:

I, for one, would have ignored that book altogether had it been just another bad book, doomed with the rest of its kind to oblivion by next spring. The Lethean Library, for all its incalculable volumes, is, I know, sadly incomplete without Mr Goodman's effort. But bad as the book may be, it is something else besides. Owing to the quality of its subject, it is bound to become quite mechanically the satellite of another man's enduring fame. As long as Sebastian Knight's name is remembered, there always will be some learned inquirer conscientiously climbing up a ladder to where *The Tragedy of Sebastian Knight* keeps half awake between Godfrey Goodman's *Fall of Man* and Samuel Goodrich's *Recollections of a Lifetime*.

(61)

Both of these books, by the way, happen to be real: Nabokov knows how to use a library catalogue. Sebastian leaves his true love for a femme fatale shortly before his heart gives out, but when V. meets the woman, he does not yet know *she* is the one: "I had wished to ask her whether she ever realized that the wan-faced man, whose presence she had found so tedious, was one of the most remarkable writers of his time. What was the use of asking! Books mean nothing to a woman of her kind; her own life seems to her to contain the thrills of a hundred novels. Had she been condemned to spend a whole day shut up in a library, she would have been found dead about noon" (174).

Nabokov says he learned most of what he knew about literature from the 11,000 volumes in his father's library, whose catalogue was twice published by their private librarian. But in his autobiography he records that "not once in my three years of Cambridge—repeat: not once—did I visit the University Library, or even bother to locate it (I know its new place now), or find out if there existed a college library where books might be borrowed for reading in one's digs" (*SM* 268). In fact, he never kept much of a personal library after leaving Russia, reading books and journals he could not afford to pay for while standing up browsing in Russian émigré bookstores in Berlin or later luxuriating in American university libraries but mostly just consulting the books in the ample library in his head.

I'll skip Humbert's almost hallucinatory self-referential prison library and poor Pnin lugging back a heavy tome that has been recalled, only to find that the person who issued the recall was himself. Let's move to *Pale Fire* and the Wordsmith University Library, into whose stacks mad Charles Kinbote thinks the shadowy Zemblan agent and would-be regicide Jakob Gradus has pursued him—the real him, as he thinks, Charles the Beloved, the last king of Zembla:

"I don't know where he lives," said the girl at the desk. "But I know he is here right now. You'll find him, I'm sure, in North West Three where we have the Icelandic Collection. You go south [waving her pencil] and turn west, and then west again where you see a sort of, a sort of [pencil making a circular wiggle—round table? round book-shelf?]—No, wait a minute, you better just keep going west till you hit the Florence Houghton Room, and there you cross over to the north side of the building. You cannot miss it" [returning pencil to ear].

Not being a mariner or a fugitive king, he promptly got lost and after vainly progressing through a labyrinth of stacks, asked about the Icelandic Collection of a stern-looking mother librarian who was checking cards in a steel cabinet on a landing. Her slow and detailed directions promptly led him back to the main desk.

"Please, I cannot find," he said, slowly shaking his head.

"Didn't you—" the girl began, and suddenly pointed up: "Oh, there he is!"

Along the open gallery that ran above the hall, parallel to its short side, a tall bearded man was crossing over at a military quick march from east to west. He vanished behind a bookcase but not before Gradus had recognized the great rugged frame, the erect carriage, the high-bridged nose, the straight brow, and the energetic arm swing, of Charles Xavier the Beloved.

Our pursuer made for the nearest stairs—and soon found himself among the bewitched hush of Rare Books. The room was beautiful and had no doors; in fact, some moments passed before he could discover the draped entrance he himself had just used. The awful perplexities of his quest blending with the renewal of impossible pangs in his belly, he dashed back—ran three steps down and nine steps up, and burst into a circular room where a bald-headed suntanned professor in a Hawaiian shirt sat at a round table reading with an ironic expression on his face a Russian book. [This is Pnin, offered a happier fate in *Pale Fire* than he was ever allowed in *Pnin* itself.—BB] He paid no attention to Gradus who traversed the room, stepped over a fat little white dog without awakening it, clattered down a helical staircase and found himself in Vault P. Here, a well-lit, pipe-lined, white-washed passage led him to the sudden paradise of a water closet for plumbers or lost scholars where, cursing, he hurriedly transferred his automatic from its precarious dangle-pouch to his coat and relieved himself of another portion of the liquid hell inside him. He started to climb up again, and noticed in the temple light of the stacks an employee, a slim Hindu boy, with a call card in his hand. I had never spoken to that lad but had felt more than once his blue-brown gaze upon me, and no doubt my academic pseudonym was familiar to him but some sensitive cell in him, some chord of intuition, reacted to the harshness of the killer's interrogation and, as if protecting me from a cloudy danger, he smiled and said: "I do not know him, sir."

(PF 281–82)

There's more—like the library of forbidden books administered by a comically unforbidding librarian in the erotic paradise of the Ardis Manor library in *Ada*—much, much more. But you see what libraries, and agents and the work of accumulation and the play of the imagination, can offer up for our past, our present, and our creative futures.

NABOKOV AS WRITER

12. Nabokov's Humor

The intensity and variety of Nabokov's humor have always been among his chief appeals for me, as for others, but humor does not yield easily to academic analysis. Nevertheless I was supervising an Auckland doctoral dissertation on Nabokov's humor when I was invited to speak at the Mercantile Library in New York on November 19, 1996. The main reason for that trip to New York was to launch the three Library of America volumes of Nabokov's English-language novels and memoirs that I had edited. The launch was celebrated by a reading of *Lolita* from start to finish. When Dmitri Nabokov, despite elaborate planning and precautions, could not find his limousine in time to arrive for the unpostponable start of the reading, Stanley Crouch opened, reciting part 1, chapter 1 of the novel from memory. I chose to read the chapter of the *Enchanted Hunters* scene from which I quote here.

I tend to want to connect everything with everything else, and hence, here, to connect Nabokov's humor with his personality, his thought, and his art. I hope that doesn't detract from the fun. A few years later I investigated laughter from an evolutionary perspective, and later still, in *On the Origin of Stories*, made play central to my explanation of art and storytelling.

"Van," said Lucette, "it will make you smile" (it did not: that prediction is seldom fulfilled). . . .

—*Ada*, 371

I've written the odd thing about Nabokov, but there are times when I don't get to read him for a long stretch. Some chance circumstance or stray impulse will send my hand toward a page of Nabokov—I have a number of his books in my study—and I dip in and purr and chuckle and wonder: Why does he write so well? Why is he so funny, line for line? Why are his humor and his style so inextricable when he is not simply a "humorist"? Why is the magic of his work so inseparable from its humor?

Nabokov stressed that we should remember that the difference between the comic and the cosmic depends on just one little sibilant (*NG* 142). In one story, which was to have been part of his last, unfinished, Russian novel, *Solus Rex*, he has his narrator write in a letter to his dead wife—and already we're very much in Nabokov's world:

> My angel, oh my angel, perhaps our whole earthly existence is now but a pun to you, or a grotesque rhyme, something like "dental" and "transcendental" (remember?), and the true meaning of reality, of that piercing term, purged of all our strange, dreamy, masquerade interpretations, now sounds so pure and sweet that you, angel, find it amusing that we could have taken the dream seriously (although you and I did have an inkling of why everything disintegrated at one furtive touch—words, conventions of everyday life, systems, persons—so, you know, I think laughter is some chance little ape of truth astray in our world).
>
> (*SoVN* 499)

That sentence seems to me a key to Nabokov's sense of humor and to the *sense* in his humor. Sineusov, the narrator, has recently met someone from his past, a man named Falter, who has perhaps become insane, or at least somehow utterly remote from "conventions of everyday life, systems, persons," after he has had a mental explosion in which the truth of things was revealed to him (within the story, Nabokov makes this seem quite plausible). Because Falter happens to be physically strong, this explosion of truth didn't quite shatter him completely, but when he passed on to someone else the solution to the riddle of life, the other person died of insight or fright. In the bothersome aftermath of that death, Falter won't pass on his secret to anyone else, especially not to Sineusov, who's desperate to find out if there is something beyond mortal existence, something that will suggest he isn't forever separated from his dead wife.

When Sineusov writes to his wife, then, about their shared inkling that laughter "is some chance little ape of truth astray in our world," it seems a kind of analogy to the experience of Falter, who seems himself a chance *big* ape of truth astray in our world. Laughter, Nabokov suggests along with Sineusov, is something let loose in our world that bespeaks a much richer but inarticulate truth about things than our little understandings can have within this world. What could that mean?

Nabokov wanted to be funny at every level, and in every way. That doesn't mean he was a standup comedian, or an Oscar Wilde, who has to get in a certain number of *similar* laughs or of precious paradoxes per minute or per page. He once said "All writers that are worth anything are humorists. I'm not P. G. Wodehouse. I'm not a funny man, but give me an example of a great writer who is not a humorist. . . . Dostoevsky's slapstick is wonderful, but in his tragedy he is a journalist" (Meras interview).

What Nabokov tried for in his own fiction was to mingle laughter and its opposites: humor and horror, laughter and loss. He insisted that "genuine art mixes categories." He also tried to find as many different *kinds* of humor as possible, some fast, some slow-release, some local, some global, some verbal, some situational, some sympathetic, some barbed.

He never thought much of his spontaneous powers because he felt he could do so much better if he had time to prepare. But his spontaneity had its own moments. When Alfred Appel Jr. was visiting in the late sixties, he told Nabokov about a nun who complained to him after class that a couple in the back of the lecture theater wouldn't stop spooning. Pleased with his response, Appel told Nabokov he had had replied: "In this day and age you're lucky that's all they were doing." Nabokov let out a mock groan: "What an opportunity you missed: you should have said 'You're lucky they weren't forking!'" Or when Lionel Trilling interviewed him in New York for a live television broadcast—in the days before he began to insist on only written questions submitted in advance, to which he would supply written answers he would read from during the "interview"—he was talking about *Lolita* and used the word "philistine." Trilling asked him to explain what he meant by philistines. He shot back: "Readymade souls in plastic bags."

But it's the humor of his *art*, his *planned* play, that really deserves our attention. Humor runs all through his work. Nabokov was a respected composer of chess problems, and his problems are famous not for their difficulty—the usual measure of a good chess problem—but for their wit, their startling novelty of conception. So, for instance, he devised a problem in which the queen was the obstacle to the successful solution—"such a powerful piece—and in the way!" (*Glory* xiii), as he himself commented. Or another that seems to have an obvious solution but that the sophisticated solver is invited to doubt because there's the shadow of a fashionable chess theme planted—but it's an exotic wild goose chase, ultimately sending the "by now ultrasophisticated solver" back to something like the original solution (*SM* 291).

The same playful originality of overall conception characterizes all his novels. His first, *Mary*, rests on one simple joke: the heroine of the novel, whose arrival the whole book builds toward, doesn't appear after all. His second, *King, Queen, Knave*, already a good deal more complex, leads up to a murder, but the victim survives. One of the murderers dies instead, and her death paradoxically brings the other would-be murderer back to life.

His longest and greatest Russian novel, *The Gift*, starts on April Fool's Day (and that turns out to be a joke with several false bottoms) and ends with a marvelous situational joke half-hidden for the good reader to find. And it takes a Nabokov to invent a novel in the wildly unnovelistic form of poem and line-by-line commentary and then to have the commentary bear no relation to the poem, or to write a long lyrical novel about a long-lasting, lyrically happy incestuous love.

Nabokov offers humor at every level from the pun (Humbert's "pin," his name for gin and pineapple, or "Parkington," one of those nondescript American towns whose center and soul is a parking lot), to the allusion (in *Ada*, Antiterra's randy nineteenth-century King Victor replaces our history's prim Queen Victoria), to character (pseudo-seductive Charlotte Haze, mishappy Pnin, Kinbote frantically spying on his neighbor and force-feeding him the story of Zembla), to situation (Humbert stuffing Lolita with sleeping pills, which don't work, or stuffing Quilty with bullets, which also don't seem to work), to structure and social satire.

Why so much humor? To show he's funny, to impress others? Some read Nabokov's compulsion to be original—which he certainly had—as a compulsion to demonstrate his superiority to others. This kind of reader responds to Nabokov's deliberateness, to his *display* of style, as evidence that he has no substance. It was to combat this response to Nabokov, more than any other misconception, that I was motivated to write his biography, to reach the wide audience a biography could command.

To me—I'm a simple man—it seems fairer to say that Nabokov is funny because he wants to amuse us, just as he's stylish because he wants to excite our imaginations and to make us realize what the imagination can do.

One of his characters refers to "knight moves of the mind." That's just what Nabokov offers again and again: "I guess it's your father under that oak, isn't it?" Greg Erminin asks Ada. "No, it's an elm," she answers (*Ada* 92). "I was born in 1910, in Paris" Humbert tells us. "My father was a gentle, easy-going person, a salad of racial genes: a Swiss citizen, of mixed French and Austrian descent, with a dash of the Danube in his veins. I am going to pass around in a minute some lovely, glossy-blue picture postcards. He owned a luxurious hotel on the Riviera. . . . My very photogenic mother died in a freak accident (picnic, lightning) when I was three" (*Lolita* 11–12; the greatest parenthesis in all of literature, Tom Stoppard has said).

Nabokov makes these and other knight moves of the mind because he wants to wean us from the habitual and to show us the room for surprise everywhere in our world. One character in *Look at the Harlequins!* tells the hero, a kind of mock Nabokov, when he's still just a boy: "Stop moping! . . . Look at the harlequins!" "What harlequins! Where?" "Oh, everywhere. All around you. Trees are harlequins, words are harlequins. So are situations and sums. Put two things together—jokes, images—and you get a triple harlequin. Come on! Play! Invent the world! Invent reality!" (*LATH* 8–9). Since Nabokov has called the image or the figure of speech "the main, sacred quiddity and eye-spot of a poet's genius" (*SO* 234), the juxtaposition here of "jokes, images" proves it's no mean role he assigns to humor.

In both imagery and humor we bring things together in unexpected ways. Now, it's possible to do that quietly, and Nabokov can be stealthy indeed. But it's also possible to foreground what is being done, to stress the power of the mind behind an image or a joke. Like the metaphysical poets, Nabokov often displays the power of his own artifice, in images often deliberately playful and far-fetched.

Let me give just one instance of the overlap of joke and image in Nabokov. Charles II of Zembla, not yet crowned, is homosexual and misogynistic but under half-hearted amorous siege from the wonderfully named Fleur de Fyler, the daughter of the ambitious Countess de Fyler, who has set her daughter on the king.

She wore on the second day of their ridiculous cohabitation nothing except a kind of buttonless and sleeveless pajama top.

The sight of her four bare limbs and three mousepits (Zemblan anatomy) irritated him.

(*PF* 110)

By foregrounding themselves, Nabokov's images often suggest the presence of the mind behind them, and often, curiously enough, the presence of the mind—or the possibility of its presence—in things themselves: "The rain would stop one moment and the next start pouring again, as if practicing" (*KQK* 248).

Nabokov highlights presence of mind and contrasts it with absence of mind, what he calls *poshlost'*: a taking things for granted, an unquestioned acceptance of things, ideas, judgments, especially when they pretend to mental distinction, to classiness. Both his imagery and his jokes stress the activity of mind, in himself as their inventor, in his audience, and often in what he writes about, whether animate or a playfully personified inanimate.

He stresses the unruly freedom and power of the mind, as opposed to the glossy parade of *poshlost'*. For that reason, he is pointedly original in his imagery and his humor. He once suggested, "Perhaps humor is simply seeing things in a singular, unique, extraordinary way. This almost always sounds funny to the average person" (Meras interview). He is also compulsively disconcerting: and he once defined humor as "loss of balance—and appreciation of losing it" (*Newsweek* interview).

His refusal to accept the way things have commonly been perceived, his urge to see new juxtapositions, no matter how incongruous, unites his sense of humor to something that might not seem to fit with the humorist: his rigorous, painstaking scholarship, whether devoting a year to his hilarious but meticulously researched *Life of Chernyshevsky* in *The Gift*, or a decade and his eyesight to the laboratory study of butterflies, or another decade to translating and annotating *Eugene Onegin*.

He refuses to accept fixed categories. For that reason he confounds the distinction between humor and horror in the nightmare of *Bend Sinister* or the sick fairytale of *Lolita*. Humor saturates what ought to be tragic scenes. Humbert has lusted after Lolita but left her untouched until the morning after the night at the Enchanted Hunters when she enters Humbert's "world, umber and black Humberland" (*Lolita* 168). It's a scene of great tension and disastrous consequence, but because of Nabokov's humor and Humbert's we are tense on Humbert's behalf more than Lolita's. The sleeping pills *haven't* put Lolita to sleep; the loud noises in the hotel make ironic comments from the wings on Humbert poised over his prey,

Lolita curved with her spine to Humbert, Humbert resting his head on his hand and burning with desire and dyspepsia.

The latter necessitated a trip to the bathroom for a draft of water, which is the best medicine I know in my case, except perhaps milk with radishes; and when I re-entered the strange pale-striped fastness where Lolita's old and new clothes reclined in various attitudes of enchantment on pieces of furniture that seemed vaguely afloat, my impossible daughter sat up and in clear tones demanded a drink, too.

(*Lolita* 132–33)

The night of unbearable tension, of oscillating hope and frustration, at last draws to an end, and Humbert addresses us: "Frigid gentlewomen of the jury! I had thought that months, perhaps years, would elapse before I dared to reveal myself to Dolores Haze; but by six she was wide awake, and by six fifteen we were technically lovers. I am going to tell you something very strange: it was she who seduced me" (134).

She wakes, and shortly bends over to whisper in his ear,

> and gradually the odd sense of living in a brand new, mad new dream world, where everything was permissible, came over me as I realized what she was suggesting. I answered I did not know what game she and Charlie played. "You mean you have never—?" her features twisted into a stare of disgusted incredulity. "You have never—" she started again. I took time out by nuzzling her a little. "Lay off, will you," she said with a twangy whine, hastily removing her brown shoulder from my lips. (It was very curious the way she considered—and kept doing so for a long time—all caresses except kisses on the mouth or the stark act of love either "romantic slosh" or "abnormal".) . . .
>
> She saw the stark act merely as part of a youngster's furtive world, unknown to adults. What adults did for purposes of procreation was no business of hers. My life was handled by little Lo in an energetic, matter-of-fact manner as if it were an insensate gadget unconnected with me.
>
> (*Lolita* 135–36)

A childhood has just been destroyed, and still we can't help smiling.

"Invent reality!" the mock muse of *Look at the Harlequins!* tells Vadim, our mock Vladimir. Nabokov's refusal to accept the fixity of common categories, received evaluations, and rigid frameworks of all kinds, his subversion of standard notions, far from constituting an evasion of the real, has direct implications in the real world. "Curiosity," he proposes in *Bend Sinister*, "is insubordination in its purest form" (46), and laughter, he suggests in "Tyrants Destroyed," is the way to defeat tyrants, to stop our minds being colonized or tyrannized.

Nabokov claims he has "no moral in tow" (*Lolita* 316). "Satire is a lesson," he says, "parody is a game" (*SO* 75), and it's parody he admits to. Not because he has nothing to teach, in fact, but because he believes that games get us closer to truth than stolid lessons: the surprise of the game or the imagination can reveal more than the earnest plod of instruction or the strict sequence of logic.

Although he would not have accepted the old definition of comedy as corrective, showing, as Sir Philip Sidney put it, "the common errors of our life" "in the most ridiculous and scornful sort that may be; so as it is impossible that any beholder can be content to be such a one,"[1] he did in fact have a very strong corrective impulse.

His critical humor, his barbs, could be directed even at friends. After noticing that Harry Levin always implied he had read absolutely everything, Nabokov as he talked to him one night invented a nineteenth-century novelist and elaborated in great detail upon his life and works while Levin nodded as if *of course* he knew this person and his work. Nabokov's could also turn his corrective humor on literary enemies. In the emigration, the critic Georgy Adamovich regularly panned Nabokov's work, so Nabokov published two poems under the name of "Vasily Shishkov," and when Adamovich hailed them as works of genius Nabokov then rubbed salt in the wound by publishing a story called "Vasily Shishkov" that toyed with the question of the relationship between Shishkov and Nabokov.

If really provoked, Nabokov could aim his critical humor at his own critics. When William Rowe insisted on seeing sexual allusions everywhere, Nabokov denounced his "torrent of Freudian drivel, which allows him to construe 'metrical length' as an erection and 'rhyme' as a sexual climax. No less ludicrous is his examination of Lolita's tennis and his claim that the tennis balls represent testicles (those of a giant albino, no doubt)" (*SO* 306). He could apply caustic correctives to literary reputations, to snobbery or racism or pretentiousness, to *poshlost'*, to Freud, to Marx, to Hitler, to all he saw as opponents of freedom.

For Nabokov a sense of humor is closely related to a capacity for freedom, to the mind's consciousness of its own freedom. He felt strongly the tension between the extraordinary freedom of the mind and its entrapment within the limits of the human: the powers of the mind are triumphant, its limits absurd and humiliating. He explores that tension and that irony again and again, in a Herman, a Humbert, a Kinbote, or, in a different way, in his own person.

In the opening chapter of his autobiography he describes the shock of becoming aware of time, "so boundless at first blush," the shock of "the awakening of consciousness." He recalls the particular scene, with his father in the resplendent uniform of the Horse Guards, and adds: "My father, let it be noted, had served his term of military training long before I was born, so I suppose he had that day put on the trappings of his old regiment as a festive joke. To a joke, then, I owe my first glimpse of complete consciousness— which again has recapitulatory implications, since the first creatures on earth to become aware of time were also the first creatures to smile" (*SM* 22).

His humor, like his style, offers a chance to see and savor the freedom of the mind, to see how easily we leap from invention to invention, how our minds can twist in midair. Nabokov wants to suggest that we should respond to our world not passively but actively, that we should not dully impose standard expectations on things but notice with surprise and delight when they do not fit what we expect. That incongruity between expectation and actuality is fundamental to humor. "The unusual is funny in itself," he once said. "A man slips and falls down. It is the contrary of gravity in both sense" (Meras interview).

He wants to show us how active, how nimble, how unexpected our minds can be—how we can put our own spin on our world when we put two things together, a joke, an image, and invent reality, when we become not the passive products of our immediate world but its active shapers. Yet at the same time he asks us to respect our world and let *it* catch *us* by surprise, if we watch closely enough.

Beyond that, Nabokov wants his humor to connect us with the surprises that might lie beyond the understanding of the world that our minds trap us within. "Life is a great surprise," he makes John Shade say, "and I do not see why death should not be an even greater one." As a child, Nabokov notes, in the passage where he describes that first flush of excitement at being "plunged into a radiant and mobile medium that was none other than the pure element of time," he was "unaware that time, so boundless at first blush, was a prison" (*SM* 21, 20). He came to feel that beyond the prison of conscious time, beyond the "solitary confinement of the self," there must be freer, less restricted modes of existence, which perhaps we might reach through the doorway of death.

But existence beyond time and the self would have to be so surprising that the only way we can know it is *through* surprise. Nabokov had a hunch that humor, by making us suddenly conscious of the disparity between expectation and outcome, is one of the most promising signposts to this realm of surprise. At the end of *The Real Life of Sebastian Knight*, the narrator, Sebastian's half-brother, describes Sebastian's last book, which builds up to the promise of a great revelation, somehow connected with the afterlife. When he hears Sebastian is dying, V. rushes by overnight train to Paris and then to Sebastian's hospital, but a series of mishaps delay him so he doesn't arrive until late at night and is directed towards the bedside of the sleeping patient. Sitting beside his brother in the dark, listening to his breathing, he feels a great sense of communion with Sebastian, a rapture of revelation— only to discover that the nurses had misunderstood whom he was asking for. That was the wrong bedside: Sebastian died the previous day.

In *Pale Fire*, the poet John Shade has a near-death experience during a heart attack and in it has a vision of a tall white fountain. He reads a magazine article in which someone else has also had a near-death experience, and in it she, too, saw a white fountain. Agog, he tracks her down but realizes at once that this garrulous sentimentalist will be all over him if he mentions his vision. Later, when he checks with the journalist who wrote up the story, he finds out that the article was accurate: "I've not changed her style." But: "There's one misprint—not that it matters much. / Mountain, not fountain" (PF 62).

In one light, these comically frustrated glimpses of the beyond might seem to suggest only a wry metaphysical skepticism, a cruel debunking of desperate human hopes. Some people do think of Nabokov as a savage ironist. An émigré critic wrote in 1929: "How terrible, to see life as Sirin [Nabokov's émigré nom de plume—BB] does! How wonderful, to see life as Bunin does!" Nabokov reported to a friend: "I read the article and had a good laugh—not at Zaitsev, but at the fact that in life and in my whole mental makeup I am quite indecently optimistic and buoyant, whereas Bunin, as far as I know, is rather inclined to dejection and black thoughts— but in Zaitsev's article it comes out the other way round" (VNRY 343). In the 1960s an interviewer suggested to Nabokov that he saw life as a very funny but cruel joke. Nabokov answered: "You must be confusing me with Dostoevsky" (SO 119).

Although the frustrations at the end of The Real Life of Sebastian Knight's or in John Shade's probing of the beyond may look like cruel jokes, when we look deeper we find that the joke is not so much that there's nothing ahead— although Nabokov does leave that as one possibility—as that that all we can know is the surprise, the enormous and absurd distance between mortality and beyond, between whatever we expect and what we might get if our minds could escape the prison of time and self. In this sense laughter is indeed a chance ape of truth astray in our world. Or as Nabokov wrote to Véra before they were married: "Only through laughter do mortals get to heaven."[2]

Beyond this, beyond the idea of some almost comically unimaginable state perhaps awaiting us outside the prison of the mortal mind, is a further level of the beyond: a sense of some conscious design, some ultimate playfulness, behind things.

As a naturalist, a lepidopterist, Nabokov insisted on "the incredible artistic wit of mimetic disguise" (Gift 122). Natural mimicry for him was too complex, too perfect, too playfully deceptive to explain in terms of natural selection: it "seemed to have been invented by some waggish artist for the intelligent eyes of man" (Gift 122). Nabokov had a sense of some playfully benign design behind the cosmic cyclorama, perhaps some impish fate, perhaps something more, some artistic and gamesome god. In The Gift Fyodor watches the stray delights of a summer morning, ending with a glimpse of two elderly postal workers "grown suddenly playful." He sees them sneak up to tickle a colleague basking with eyes closed on a bench in the sun, and he asks: "Where shall I put all these gifts with which the summer morning rewards me—and only me? Save them up for future books? Use them immediately for a practical handbook: *How to Be Happy*? Or getting deeper, to the bottom of things: understand what is concealed behind all this, behind the play, the sparkle, the thick green grease-paint of the foliage? For there really is something, there is something! And one wants to offer thanks but there is no one to thank. The list of donations already made: 10,000 days—from Person Unknown" (*Gift* 340).

Nabokov presents as the first scene of *Speak, Memory* his first taste of consciousness and time, which he attributes to his father's "joke" in putting on an outdated uniform for a festive occasion. When he had this first flash of self-consciousness, he was holding his parents' hands and walking along a garden path. The *last* scene of *Speak, Memory* shows Nabokov and his wife walking along another garden path with Dmitri between them, holding their hands. They spot the boat that will take them to America from a France that Germany has already invaded, but they do not immediately point it out

> to our child, so as to enjoy in full the blissful shock, the enchantment and glee he would experience on discovering ahead the ungenuinely gigantic, the unrealistically real prototype of the various toy vessels he had doddled about in his bath. There, in front of us, where a broken row of houses stood between us and the harbor, and where the eye encountered all sorts of stratagems, such as pale-blue and pink underwear cakewalking on a clothesline, or a lady's bicycle and a striped cat oddly sharing a rudimentary balcony of cast iron, it was most satisfying to make out among the jumbled angles of roofs and walls, a splendid ship's funnel, showing from behind the clothesline as something in a scrambled picture—Find What the Sailor Has Hidden—that the finder cannot unsee once it has been seen.
>
> (*SM* 309–10)

Placing this as the very close of the story of his life, Nabokov suggests here that life itself has a playfulness, that it offers us games of surprise, akin to these two parents wanting to maximize their son's shock of amazement. He suggests that there is something behind life that invites our imaginations to discovery as generously as doting parents wanting to foster the imagination of their little boy. He suggests that life invites us to play the game, to notice our world and the possibilities it offers us to see things in surprising and playful ways and to take that as a token of further surprises ahead ("authentic humor," as he once wrote, "comes from the angels" [*LDQ* 65]). And he suggests that as a novelist he tries to match life's own game by maximizing the play and the surprises ahead as we read, by inventing his own equivalents for the inexhaustibility of life's surprise

Nabokov's humor stands at the opposite pole from that of Beckett, the other great literary humorist of the middle of last century, of the prepostmodern era (and the absolute antithesis between these two writers, whose output overlapped for half a century, is the most marvelous proof of the meaninglessness of those period labels). Beckett's astonishing humor springs (not a Beckettian verb) from a sense of the absurdity, the meaninglessness of human life, the futility of human hope, and the cracked powers of the human mind in its attempts to cope. He shows the awfulness of things yet makes it awfully funny. Nabokov's humor springs (and here it is the *mot juste*) from his sense of the endless creativity of life, of the pleasures it plants, of the comedy of life's mismatching our expectations, even from a sense that life's pleasures and play and surprise might suggest surprises behind and beyond life. If Beckett is our great cosmic comic caustic, Nabokov loves and laughs at life even amid loss.

At the end of *Speak, Memory*, in that ship in the harbor, Nabokov sketches in the promise of America ahead. He was carrying in his suitcase the manuscript of his first English novel, which he couldn't get published in England or America, a comic novel about the tragic gap between a Russian-born writer's background and the books he writes in English. When he arrived in New York, Nabokov took another year and a half to get *The Real Life of Sebastian Knight* published, and more than a decade and a half to arrange the first translation of one of his major Russian novels. Now in the Library of America he sits on the same shelf as Lincoln, whom he would translate into Russian, or Melville, whom he revered. There's only one occasion on which I can recall him placing himself alongside his favorite American writer: when he was about to take to task the critic who sought out subliminal sex in his fiction. Before objecting to Rowe's "manipulating my most innocent words so as to introduce sexual 'symbols' into them," to all his nudges and winks at sex supposedly *between* the lines, Nabokov conceded begrudgingly that it might be legitimate, if hardly necessary, to indicate the sex actually *in* the lines of some of his books. But picking out the "erotic bits" in *Lolita* and *Ada*, he wrote, was "a process rather like looking for allusions to aquatic mammals in *Moby Dick*." Picking *comic* bits out of Nabokov is even easier than picking out the *erotic*—but, I hope, not quite so pointless.

13. Nabokov as Storyteller

As an undergraduate I was probably excited most, apart from Shakespeare and Dickens, by Nabokov (who did not feature in any of my courses, although I was allowed to write about him for American Studies) and John Barth. Barth's explorations of the origins of stories in the Sanskrit *Ocean of Stories*, early Greek myth, and the *Thousand and One Nights* must in some way have precipitated the graduate course in narrative that I began to teach at the University of Auckland in 1993, running from Homer to Art Spiegelman, from epics to comics. When that interest coalesced with a developing interest in evolution, I found myself in 2000 writing the book that became *On the Origin of Stories*.

For a keynote at the Nabokov conference at the Nabokov Museum in St. Petersburg in July 2002, I linked these interests by talking about Nabokov as a storyteller. In comparing the openings of Nabokov's first novel, *Mary*, and his penultimate completed novel, the mini-masterpiece *Transparent Things*, I may have drawn as much on my comparison of the openings of *Anna Karenina* and *Lolita* in chapter 17 as on my reflections on narrative before and after adding an evolutionary dimension.

In the quarter century since his death, much has been made of Nabokov as a thinker, as a metaphysician and moralist.[1] We have learned a great deal, but D. Barton Johnson has recently challenged readers of Nabokov by asking, wouldn't we still be fascinated by his work even without his ideas?[2] Although Nabokov would write differently in all sorts of ways if his metaphysics and ethics were thinner and poorer, Johnson surely is right: we would still read Nabokov without them.

Why would we? The obvious first answer is style. Nabokov is widely and justly regarded as a high-water mark of literary style. But although we admire the style of *Speak, Memory* or Nabokov's forewords and afterwords or even *Strong Opinions*, we would not be drawn back to Nabokov again and again if there were just style and no story in his work. The dazzling detail, the inventive imagery, the patterned prose, the sinuous sentences, the thrill of the thought are all very well—very, very well—but even they are not enough.

Nabokov famously declared that "there are three points of view from which a writer can be considered: . . . as a storyteller, as a teacher, and as an enchanter. A major writer combines these three—storyteller, teacher, enchanter" (*LL* 5). In his own terms, his metaphysics and ethics fall within his role as teacher; his style, within his role as enchanter, which he himself ranks highest in his holy trinity. Perhaps, but as a species we are so shaped as to be especially entranced by stories. We follow the fates of others, real or invented, far more readily and for far longer than we follow either pure ideas or pure expression. Nabokov attracts us in the first place, and keeps us returning, by his power as a storyteller.

But for that very reason, how can we describe him as a storyteller without saying what we have all known from the start? And how can we describe him as a storyteller without referring to his style or without referring to the ideas that shape his way of telling stories?

Or how can we describe him as a storyteller when one of his hallmarks is that his strategies can differ so much from work to work, when he could write his most fantastic novel, *Invitation to a Beheading*, in the midst of his most densely realistic, *The Gift*? Austen, Dickens, and Tolstoy each have a narrative manner common throughout their canons. Joyce differs even more than Nabokov from work to work, but in his case he steadily matures, to the point of overripeness, even, in *Finnegans Wake*, whereas Nabokov makes deliberate choices from work to work so that even at similar times (*Ada* and *Transparent Things*) or with similar themes (Zoorland and Zembla) one of his works can be deeply unlike another.

Much, of course, has been written about Nabokov as storyteller, and much has been written about narrative and narratology in general over the last forty years.[3] But can we describe Nabokov as a storyteller in a way that keeps close to the feel of his work, that doesn't trap the telling of tales in a tangle of terminology? Can we also do this in a way that doesn't move too quickly from description to explanation?

THE NATURE OF NABOKOVIAN NARRATIVE

Let me first set out in stark, almost tabular form, Nabokov's features as a storyteller and then compare the openings of novels from each end of his career to see how these characteristics play out in particular cases.

Nabokov is a master of language, but like late (and unlike early) Shake-speare, his aims as a storyteller predominate over detachable delights of style. Unlike other major modernist novelists, Nabokov did not disparage *plot*; although he rarely offers formal stories within stories, in the manner of Cervantes, Fielding, or Barth, he likes to offer hints of or vistas on other stories, or even a second main story concealed behind the first.[4] For all his compulsive originality, he relies on the salient events of story that arise out of the biological necessities of reproduction and survival: love or death—or both—intense, consuming, sometimes perverse passion; and murder, sui-cide, execution, assassination, and violent death by fire, water, or air.

Like many writers from Sterne and Austen on, Nabokov drives stories by means of *character* rather than plot. But his stories are unique in their intense focus on one character. Nabokov respects individual experience as primary, as all that any of us can know from the inside. Each of his nov-els highlights the centrality and isolation of the consciousness of the hero. Usually there will be a marked disparity between the individual and his (it is almost without exception *his*) environment. The environment itself, whether as real as Fyodor's Berlin or as fanciful as Kinbote's Zembla, will be superbly evoked, but the hero will have a tragic or comic or tragicomic disjunction from it. He will usually be driven by an obsession—love, chess, art, murder, a real or imagined lost homeland—which gives an urgency to the story and an edge to the irony of the disjunction between the individual and his world.

Nabokov evokes *scenes* as few can do. His scenes are tightly consistent, exact, literal, specific, surprising, economical, evocative, quickly set up, and often quickly dismissed. Nabokov uses detail with the eye of a naturalist, a photographer, a painter, and a poet: visual, natural, social, locomotory, and gestural particulars seen from the outside but also felt from the inside. But despite his precision, he is sparing. He operates not by steady accumulation of detail but by swooping and swerving in ways that catch our attention, stir our imagination, and prod our memory, for the detail is highly selective, highly open-ended, highly diverse, highly correlated. And despite his focus on one central consciousness, he *peoples* his scenes with characters limned with the same quick exactness and surprising individuality as everything else and evaluated for their capacity to see their world for themselves and to imagine it from the point of view of others.

But while Nabokov evokes scenes and people from without and within, he can also *shift* readily at any point *from* the scene. He may establish scenes almost as vividly as Tolstoy, but he can glide away from them at any moment in ways Tolstoy never does: to a metaphor or an abstraction, to another time or place or mind, real or imagined, within the story or elsewhere, to the mind evoking the scene in words, or to the mind of the reader recreating it. His scenes are always saturated by mind, by the hero's or, briefly, by another character's, by the narrator's or author's or reader's, able to move with grace and speed within or behind or away from the scene.

Beyond the scene, Nabokov handles stories with an inventive and critical awareness of narrative convention and possibility. He challenges and questions and refreshes every aspect of narrative, from *exposition* of new material, *preparation* for later developments, *transition* from one element to another, to the *conclusion* of stories.[5]

He does not impose technical innovations for their own sake, but nor will he accept a convention like first- or third-person narration simply because it exists as a convention. When one of his first-person narrators tells his own story, Nabokov will always supply him with a motive, a means, an occasion, and an audience, and the relationship between the telling and the tale will transform both. As his oeuvre expands he seldom uses third-person narration, but if he does he will question or complicate it according to the needs or opportunities of the story.

Nabokov pays especially close attention to what both his characters and his readers can know at a particular point in the story. He has a superb command of *anticipation* and *recapitulation*, so central to the traditional impetus and impact of story and heightened in his work by the hero's often obsessive quest after a goal. Because his stories focus on a single life, there are rarely secrets to be unearthed, à la *Oedipus* or Dickens or Ibsen, or any reason for multiple narrators or disjoined narratives, à la Faulkner or Erdrich or DeLillo. To Nabokov, such devices falsify the unfolding of individual experience, and in his stories, the *siuzhet* (the events in the order they are related) therefore largely follows the sequence of the *fabula* (the events in the order they happen). But Nabokov explores time from many sides and knows how present experience may be modified by what we *have* lived and *will* live through, and he can add time's details and designs in many ways, internally (through a character's recollection or discovery) or externally (through a narrator's disclosure), overtly or covertly, smoothly or joltingly, in advance or arrears, in a trickle or a deluge, without the least anxiety that this will dispel the force of the current scene.

Nabokov rethinks story, scene, structure, and narrative situation out of an impatience with convention, a desire for artistic originality, a search for a singular way of revealing the singular circumstances of a new story, and a unique sense of both the scope and the limits of consciousness that inspires him to make the most of the gaps and the links between character, reader, and author. And because the human mind's capacity to represent, or meta-represent, is central to its power,[6] and because he is always preoccupied with the relationship between the inner (the individual consciousness) and the outer (the world outside the individual consciousness), Nabokov also incorporates in his stories an extraordinary number and variety of metarepresentations of the story, of parts that reflect the whole.

While it engages our curiosity and emotions as a story, a Nabokov novel always intimates that the narrative is also something else, a strategy as much as a story: an image or a metaphor, a joke, a problem, a design, a playful puzzle, or a series of interlocking puzzles prepared by the author for us somehow to solve. The riddling strategy nevertheless arises out of the particular circumstances of the story, out of some special constraint or situation in the story, rather than being imposed on it arbitrarily, and is therefore different from work to work.

Throughout his stories, from the local to the global level, Nabokov attends to what we and his characters can know at a particular point and to the difference between the characters' knowledge and what we as readers might be able to infer from our position outside their world. He stokes our expectations and rewards our capacity to notice, imagine, infer, recall. He becomes a kind of personal trainer in mental flexibility, his novels workouts that stretch our capacity for attention, curiosity, imagination, and memory not to stress our limits, as so often in twentieth-century literature, but to extend them.

FAMILY LIKENESSES

Nabokov's stories may resemble others in their timeless preoccupation with love and death, and they may be different from one another because of the special strategy he devises for each, but they also have a family likeness that sets them apart from other fiction.

A recurrent plot structure can identify an author's key concerns. In Austen, for instance, it is the difficult and potentially dangerous choice of marriage partner, because in her world nothing matters more than people reading other people with maximum care, and never do we need to read others more carefully than when considering the commitment of marriage. In Dickens, it is a legacy, contested, denied, or imposed, because he senses that the world's real riches are often cruelly hoarded from those who deserve them. As we follow the characters' approach to a more equitable redistribution of life's bounty at the end of the novel, Dickens's exuberant invention dispenses for *us* imaginative riches to match those he finds in his world.

In Nabokov the key structure is the hero's obsession. On the one hand, it fires up an invaluable private intensity in the protagonist; on the other, it keeps him apart both from his immediate world and from the world of freedom and fulfillment he compulsively imagines—and here lies the source of so much of the humor, poignancy, and irony of Nabokov's fiction and the emotional charge of his unreliable narrators.

Partly because of the dominating role of the hero's obsession, Nabokov's stories tend to avoid what we think of as a "dramatic" development of plot, plot advancing through conflict, through the clash of character actions, reactions, and interactions. Precisely because conflict catches our attention so easily, Nabokov feels, it has become a convention and a trap for storytelling. It generates a false picture of life as a series of forced moves leading to an inescapable outcome. And it seems to imply that our lives are shaped by our engagement, and especially our clashes, with others, when for him there is so much more to the mind's involvement in and detachment from its world.

Instead of the standard drama of action and reaction, Nabokov's plots tend to show the accumulating pattern of a single life, the whole distinctive pattern of a hero's past, the unique rhythms of his "fate," the special design of a person's individuality that extends through a life and often into the moment of death. His stories are not biographies; they do not attempt to cover the whole of a life with the same consistency. They tend to focus on a key time, often not short enough to be a crisis, usually not long enough for a lifetime.

In Nabokov's fiction each life follows its own distinct pattern, indiscernible in advance, ever clearer in retrospect. But certain moves recur again and again. First, the myth of return: the futile attempt to return to or relive the past. Next, the myth of arrival: the futile attempt to foresee or control the future. Third, the surprise of the ending, a new possibility that undercuts what we and the heroes have foreseen but in a way that sends us, and perhaps them, back to the beginning. The ending may mark the failure to reach a coveted past or a coveted future or both at once. Often, it can crack the solid surface of the work's world, yet it may also send us spinning back to the beginning, returning to all that accumulates in the course of the hero's life but with an answer to the puzzle of the whole perhaps somehow nearer and a way of closing the gap between character, author, and reader somehow more possible.

MARY: ZOOM IN ON OPENING

How does Nabokovian narration operate at the local level? Let us focus on two opening scenes: the first chapter of Nabokov's first novel, *Mary* (1926), where Ganin and Alfyorov are stuck in the elevator, and the first two chapters of his second-to-last novel, *Transparent Things* (1972), where Hugh Person is hailed by the narrator as he arrives at a hotel in a Swiss mountain resort. These examples of Nabokov's very early and very late work are not his strongest stories and have little of the force of *The Defense* or *Pnin*, let alone *Lolita* or *Pale Fire*, but much of what is true here should therefore be true a fortiori elsewhere in Nabokov.

Uncharacteristically, *Mary* starts with direct speech: "Lev Glevo. Lev Glebovich? A name like that's enough to twist your tongue off, my dear fellow."[7] Helmut Bonheim has shown that in the search for dramatic immediacy in narrative, direct speech, once a rare start for stories, became almost the normal beginning for fiction in the twentieth century.[8] Nabokov rarely conforms to twentieth-century norms, but this was his first book—and as he said, its autobiographical basis, its offering the writer "the relief of getting rid of oneself" in a first novel, "is one of the very few common rules I have accepted" (*Mary*, xi). Yet although Nabokov was much less original in *Mary* than even in the start of his next novel, he was already inventive, already himself. Ganin's tongue-twister name is funny, of course, and Nabokov's humor will never be far from his storytelling. But beneath the immediate humor lies more.

Stories, Aristotle says, must have beginnings, middles, and ends, and the beginnings of stories need exposition to orient us. Exposition had become stylized and slick on the stage, as Nabokov knew well. He writes in "The Tragedy of Tragedy":

A more sophisticated form of the French "dusting the furniture" exposition is when, instead of the valet and the maid discovered onstage, we have two visitors arriving on the stage as the curtain is going up, speaking of what brought them, and of the people in the house. It is a pathetic attempt to comply with the request of critics and teachers who demand that the exposition coincide with action, and actually the entrance of two visitors is action. But why on earth should two people who arrived on the same train and who had ample time to discuss everything during the journey, why must they struggle to keep silent till the minute of arrival whereupon they start talking of their hosts in the wrongest place imaginable—the parlor of the house where they are guests? Why? Because the author must have them explode right here with a time-bomb explosion.

The next trick, to take the most obvious ones, is the promise of somebody's arrival. So and-so is expected. We know that so-and-so will invariably come.

(*MUSSR* 334–35)

Mary's ending overturns that last expectation, and its beginning radically reworks the "dusting the furniture" exposition through dialogue. The dialogue does take place, but comically, in the dark, with neither participant able to see the other, and it involves an effusive Alfyorov, whose very cheerfulness and garrulity irritate the peevish Ganin still further. The situation in the lift, with time to kill and with Alfyorov happily prattling away, introduces on the first page the name of his wife, Mary, due to arrive in six days' time. And since the scene, although it records the speech of both, clearly focuses on Ganin and his perceptions and thoughts, since it therefore identifies him as the likely protagonist, and since the novel is called *Mary*, we are primed to expect that some relationship will link Ganin and Alfyorov's wife.

Nabokov's economy, his comic inventiveness of situation, his critical attitude to narrative convention even in this exposition, his ability to rework exposition by way of the personalities and moods of the two characters are all already in evidence long before we discover how the story's ending undermines the expectation that a novel called *Mary* and the announcement of her arrival in its exposition will lead to her arriving, as it were, "on stage." Nabokov's attention to exposition and preparation and the wit with which he reworks them already operate at a high level.

Nabokov pays keen attention to what characters and readers can know at a particular point: his epistemology is very much present in the texture of his telling. The second paragraph of *Mary* is this, in response to Alfyorov's comment that Ganin's name is a tongue twister:

> "Yes it is," Ganin agreed somewhat coldly, trying to make out the face of his interlocutor in the unexpected darkness. He was annoyed by the absurd situation in which they both found themselves and by this enforced conversation with a stranger.
>
> (*Mary*, 1)

Nabokov does not spell out at once *what* the absurd situation is, but offers us a little challenge and lets us have the pleasure of deducing, if not immediately, then within a few lines, that what has caused this "unexpected darkness" must be a stalled elevator. At the same time, he is true to Ganin's inability to see Alfyorov or recall what he looks like, and in being true to this, he cheerily toys with the expectation that a novelist will describe characters as they step on stage and shows that the self-contained Ganin has paid no heed, before they found themselves stuck in the elevator together, to this newcomer to his *pension*.

Nabokov attends closely to and makes the most of what his characters can know: think of Albinus's ignorance of Axel Rex's presence, Krug's blindness to the pressure being exerted on those near to him, the inability of the narrator of "The Vane Sisters" to see the message Cynthia and Sybil spell out for him, Humbert's cluelessness as to the identity of Lolita's "abductor," or Van's uncertainty about Ada's involvement with Percy de Prey despite his seeing all too clearly the evidence of Percy's interest. Nabokov also attends to what we as readers cannot yet know but might be able to infer from our position outside the characters—unable to know as soon as Ganin and Alfyorov do that they are stuck in an elevator but able as soon as Mary is mentioned to see that in a novel entitled *Mary* she will somehow connect these two men. He stokes our expectations and rewards us for our inferences, our capacity to notice, imagine, deduce, and remember. Joyce, by contrast, pays too little attention to what the reader knows; Faulkner tries to match Joyce by being deliberately difficult; Robbe-Grillet thwarts the reader's accumulating knowledge; but nobody else shows such alertness to what the reader can know and infer or dripfeeds such constant rewards for attention.

But despite the glimpses of Nabokov at his future best we catch in *Mary*'s superb opening, the novel settles from its second chapter into a rather conventional description of the *pension* and Ganin's situation within it. A finely observed report of a Russian émigré milieu, with Nabokov's naturalist's eye and artist's hand working closely together, it sketches a revealing picture of Ganin's dissatisfied life, but it is the sort of thing many writers could have managed or come close to. Nabokov has not yet quite become the unique writer he soon would be.

TRANSPARENT THINGS: ZOOM IN

By the time of *Transparent Things*, Nabokov had long been a nonpareil. The novel opens:

> Here's the person I want. Hullo, person! Doesn't hear me.
> Perhaps if the future existed, concretely and individually, as something that could be discerned by a better brain, the past would not be so seductive: its demands would be balanced by those of the future. Persons might then straddle the middle stretch of the seesaw when considering this or that object. It might be fun.
> But the future has no such reality (as the pictured past and the perceived present possess); the future is but a figure of speech, a specter of thought.
> Hullo, person! What's the matter, don't pull me. I'm *not* bothering him. Oh, all right. Hullo, person . . . (last time, in a very small voice).
> (*TT* 1)

So far as we can make out, this is not one character speaking to another but the narrator trying to speak to a character, although why the character should be hailed in that clumsy "Hullo, person!" fashion is quite unclear. Nor is it clear why the person doesn't hear, nor why the sudden shift to this interesting philosophical discussion of the future should occur here, nor what the relationship between "Persons" in the second paragraph might be to the "person" hailed in the first, nor who it is who doesn't want the speaker or narrator to bother this person or why. Here we cannot make out, even though we want to, speaker, addressee, bystanders, setting, or situation, although we can sense that these are all present, if only we knew how. The "exposition" exposes little but our uncertainty about where we are.

Never before has Nabokov pushed quite so far, and he's too much of a storyteller not to know that we couldn't stand much of this, that we need a story. He gives us one, at the start of the second chapter: "As Hugh Person extricated his angular bulk from the taxi that had brought him to this shoddy mountain resort from Trux, his eyes went up to check the aspect of the Ascot Hotel against an eight-year-old recollection. A dreadful building of gray stone and brown wood, it sported cherry-red shutters which he remembered as apple green." Here is storytelling as we know it: an identifiable character named and described, performing an identifiable action in a recognizable world, in a setting described and named. What, then, is so special about Nabokovian storytelling, even late Nabokov storytelling, after the disconcerting chapter 1?

What's special is everything I have omitted. Here's how chapter 2 of *Transparent Things* actually begins, with all the Nabokovian peculiarity reinstated:

As the person, Hugh Person (corrupted "Peterson" and pronounced "Parson" by some) extricated his angular bulk from the taxi that had brought him to this shoddy mountain resort from Trux, and while his head was still lowered in an opening meant for emerging dwarfs, his eyes went up—not to acknowledge the helpful gesture sketched by the driver who had opened the door for him but to check the aspect of the Ascot Hotel (Ascot!) against an eight-year-old recollection, one fifth of his life, engrained by grief. A dreadful building of gray stone and brown wood, it sported cherry-red shutters (not all of them shut) which by some mnemoptical trick he remembered as apple green. The steps of the porch were flanked with electrified carriage lamps on a pair of iron posts. Down those steps an aproned valet came tripping to take the two bags, and (under one arm) the shoebox, all of which the driver had alertly removed from the yawning boot. Person pays alert driver.

(*TT* 3)

Earlier I contrasted Nabokov the stylist with Nabokov the storyteller. It may be an artificial distinction, certainly not an absolute one, but it is true that a story's needs may be at odds with sheer style. This is high-energy prose, yet it will never appear in any anthology of fine flourishes: it's no "Lolita, light of my life, fire of my loins," or "the cradle rocks above an abyss." This is what I mean by saying that Nabokov, like late Shakespeare, subordinates style to story. Shakespeare was an immeasurably more sophisticated dramatic storyteller in his late play *Cymbeline* than in his youthful *Romeo and Juliet*. He had to write with more compression to achieve more complex aims, but where the *Oxford Dictionary of Quotations* includes phrases from *Romeo and Juliet* as early as the play's first speech and then from scene after scene, it cites nothing of *Cymbeline* until almost a thousand lines into the play and then not dialogue but an inset song. Like Shakespeare, Nabokov can exude eloquence but subdues it to the local needs of his story. His language works wonders in situ but does not necessarily seem stylish out of its situation.

"As the person, Hugh Person (corrupted 'Peterson' and pronounced 'Parson' by some)" would be off-putting as an isolated line of prose but is beguiling in context. We notice with surprise, amusement, and relief the echo of the "person" of "Hullo, person" in chapter 1: this is presumably the person whom the disembodied voice was addressing, and his name, absurdly, is actually Person. The parenthetical aside about Person as a surname is comically clumsy pedantry, when the protagonist and his name have just been introduced, but it proves of a piece with the clumsiness of "Hullo, person" in the first line of the novel or "easy, you know, does it, son," in the last, or Mr. R.'s awkward and pedantic introduction of his editor Mr. Person and his secretary Mr. Tamworth:

> "I don't think you met Mr. Tamworth. Person, pronounced Parson; and Tamworth: like the English breed of black-botched swine."
> "No," said Hugh, "it does not come from Parson, but rather from Peterson."
> "O.K., son."
>
> (*TT* 31)

We can eventually discover, therefore, that that ungainly parenthesis is one more clue that the unidentified speaker or narrator at the start of the novel is none other than the ghost of Mr. R.—who, when alive, learned the information it imparts from Hugh in this very scene.

A crucial and unique aspect of Nabokov's storytelling, especially in a tale like this, is that the strategy is as important as the story, that in this case the riddle of who tells the tale is as important as the role of the hero. It's crucial, too, that the strategy nevertheless arises out of the story, that this is a story of someone finding his way out of a life of mounting frustration when he is welcomed across the threshold of death by perhaps the only person in his recent life who had taken an interest in him and who cares enough now to tell his story. And it's crucial, as so often in Nabokov, that there is a story behind the story—although Nabokov, with his love of surprise, of posing new *kinds* of problems in novel after novel, begins *Transparent Things*, paradoxically and unprecedentedly, with the story *behind* the story ("Hullo person. Doesn't hear me"), and in *this* case the immediate riddle the novel poses is to discover that the speaker in the story *behind* the story was a character in the story while he was alive.

But long before we can see that, we see long-limbed Hugh clambering out of the taxi. Nabokov renders the scene vividly. He attends, as always, to human movement, seen from the outside but also felt from the inside, here in the irritation of "an opening meant for emerging dwarfs" that infects the narrating voice. He attends to visual detail, not that there's much of it— Hugh's "angular bulk," the driver's "helpful gesture," the hotel's "gray stone and brown wood," "cherry-red shutters," and "electrified carriage lamps on a pair of iron posts"—just enough to render in full color and movement the scene of arrival and the pseudo-chalet setting, but he also attends to the character registering the details, to Hugh's distaste for the town, his effort in emerging, his recoil at the "dreadful" building, his memory of the shutters as green.

Not that the narration confines itself to Hugh's perspective. Although visually alert to the outer details of the scene and alert to Hugh's mind within the scene at all sorts of levels (his larger context, "one fifth of his life, engrained by grief"; his current mood of distaste for "this shoddy mountain resort"; his bodily ungainliness, which will prove so unfortunately important; his sudden perception of a misrecollection), although it pays such attention to the outer and inner within the scene, the paragraph also shifts easily from the scene, to an aside on etymology or to highlight its own verbal surface ("the aspect of the Ascot Hotel," "cherry-red shutters (not all of them shut)": and in this second case, notice how the visual attention to the scene and the verbal attention to the sentence do not at all exclude each other).

The long first sentence moves effortlessly back and forth from outer to inner, from locomotion to perception, from scene to language, from the long term ("one fifth of his life") to the immediate and even the instant (the sudden snort of derision in that parenthetical "(Ascot!)"—presumably at the inappropriateness of the name's social pretensions for an alpine hotel). The sentence renders the scene, but even as it does so, it draws attention to the mind of Hugh within the scene, the mind of the narrator recording the scene, the mind of the reader registering the scene both with and beyond Hugh and with and yet somehow behind the narrator, but able to catch up.

In the sentence that follows, what "mnemoptical trick" causes Hugh to remember the cherry-red shutters as apple-green? It doesn't matter. It's amusing in itself, the complementary color, the contrasting fruit; but two pages later the person introduced as "an aproned valet" will be described slightly more fully as "the apple-green-aproned valet," and we can recognize with more amusement what has caused Hugh's confusion and what a game of attention Nabokov is playing with his audience, what rewards he can hide behind any detail.

We have to keep attention up across a gap like this, but we have to exercise attention even within the sentence: the aproned valet came tripping down those steps "to take the two bags, and (under one arm) the shoebox, all of which the driver had alertly removed from the yawning boot." Are we alert enough to notice the *alert* driver versus the *yawning* boot, or the *shoebox* removed from a *boot*? And to see the humor in the driver so pointedly alert just when he can earn a tip?

As an observer, a naturalist, and an artist, Nabokov renders the scene of Hugh's arrival in Witt with precision—the milieu, the occasion, the activity, the character as he takes in the scene or moves his awkward body within it or imposes his temperament and mood on it—but what makes it so uniquely Nabokovian is that at the same time as he renders the inner and outer scene so sharply, he can shift from the scene to the mind evoking it in words or to the mind of the reader, engaged with the scene seen from outside Hugh and seen and felt from within him, engaged with the unseen storyteller behind the words, and engaged with the words seen on the page. That multiplicity of levels we already sense here will only be compounded when we become aware both of the layers of Hugh's past that fold over onto this moment and of exactly what level of being the transparent things observe him from.

Every mature Nabokov novel is a demanding but exhilarating workout in what Fyodor calls "multilevel thinking" (*Gift* 175). What especially distinguishes Nabokov's stories, on small scale and large, is that they are saturated by mind: the hero's, the narrator's, the author's, and the reader's. Nothing could be further from Hemingway's presentation of a story through objective actions and utterances that only *imply* the subjective.

Hemingway was writing partly against the fashion, by the early 1920s, for the deep representation of mind in the moment, in the stream of consciousness of a Dorothy Richardson, a Joyce, a Woolf. Nabokov, too, differs markedly from stream of consciousness, but in another direction. He is interested chiefly not in the mind within the moment—although he gives this its due (Hugh's surprise as he looks up at the Ascot Hotel)—but in minds able to transcend the moment, the mind of a character, a narrator, an author, or a reader able to flash or soar beyond a scene through a sudden shift of thought or perspective, consciousness able either to enfold or escape a scene.

Transparent Things is an extreme example of Nabokov as storyteller. In his previous novel, *Ada*, he had created a whole new world, a long, passionate, rapturous, and tragic story amid bright settings and brighter characters. In *Transparent Things*, despite the cherry-red shutters and the apple-green aprons, we enter a grey and gloomy world where not much happens to poor Hugh except that he strangles the woman whom for some reason he loves, no matter how unlovable she is, then loses his own life in a pathetic attempt to revisit the scene of his first humiliations with her, which are all he has left. Nabokov can sweep us up in the emotions of his characters, as in the case of Van's enthusiasm for Ada or Kinbote's for Zembla or even, to our discomfort, Humbert's for Lolita, but he deliberately leaves us unmoved by Hugh's love for Armande or Hugh's pilgrimage back to his past, and he has to use all his virtuosity as a storyteller to make this story on the brink of a death come to life. But the storytelling skills so concentrated even in the uneventful opening scene of *Transparent Things* can help suggest what makes Nabokovian narrative so special.

MARY AND TRANSPARENT THINGS: ZOOM OUT

How do *Mary* and *Transparent Things* reflect Nabokov as storyteller at the large scale rather than the small? In terms of plot, each novel focuses on love—indeed, love compounded by adultery—and death: Ganin's love for Mary and his planned elopement with her from Berlin, an adultery anticipated, assumed, but left untried, and placed in pointed counterpoint with Podtyagin's planned escape from Berlin, which will be thwarted by his approaching death; Hugh's abject love for Armande, despite her flagrant infidelities, and his strangling her in his sleep not because of but despite her unlovableness, and *his* death by fire on his pathetic pilgrimage to the scene of his past with her.

Each novel is *driven by character*: *Mary*'s plot depends on Ganin's love, his self-enclosed nature, his arrogance, his restlessness. And although neither the strangling of Armande nor his own suffocation in a hotel fire are Hugh

Person's choices, the plot of *Transparent Things* depends on his abjectness, his frustration, his doggedness, his misplaced sentimentality.

Each hero is *obsessed* to the point of disjunction from his world and in a uniquely Nabokovian way that maximizes the tension between obsession and freedom. Although Ganin chafes at the confines of his room in a cramped pension, his obsession with Mary lets him exult in his capacity to roam Berlin streets while inhabiting his spacious past, until to his surprise and ours he walks away from Mary and memory into an open future. The much less happy Hugh, as soon as he is released from prison for killing his wife in a dream, makes the free decision to return across the Atlantic to where Armande first obsessed him, but although in Witt he still seems trapped by inimical space and oppressive time, his chance death there liberates him at last into the ampler dimensions of his future.

Each novel deploys *anticipation* and *recapitulation* in new ways, and each exposes the myths of return to the past and arrival at the future. The numbered doors from April 1 to April 6 and the countdown from Sunday to the Saturday of Mary's advent provide a stark and insistently unilinear means of stalking the expected climax of Nabokov's first novel. In *Transparent Things* the anticipation of the future is much more multichanneled, saturated with apparent foreshadowings of Hugh's imminent death, from the failed warning of the opening chapter, and even the narrators' "perhaps if the future existed," through the throng of images, real, fictional, and dreamed, of deaths, fires, and falls.

In *Mary*, recapitulation plays a key structural role as the novel alternates present time, the days marking Mary's approach, with Ganin's memories of their past, again in rather rigid linear form, the memories proceeding with a chronological neatness that serves the novelist's needs rather than his hero's psychic reality.[9] In *Transparent Things*, recapitulation takes flamboyant form in the hands of narrators, who can trace a mere pencil back centuries to the tree from which its wood was made. The story folds into Hugh's present trip to Switzerland an account of his first trip and his father's death and his first whore and on top of *that* past scene, a bravura recollection of a writer who enjoyed a whore in the same room almost a century earlier, and on top of that Hugh's second trip, to meet the novelist R., when he also found himself sitting opposite Armande in a train.

Ganin thinks he can *return to his past* with Mary or resume where he left off. But the central surprise of the novel's plot, the essential twist of the novel's *strategy*, is that the title character does not arrive, despite the steady countdown. When Ganin realizes that he has his past with him in memory and need not return to it, he heads away from Mary toward an open future.

The novel's title seemed to guarantee her arrival, but as the novel ends it is left unrealized and no longer matters.

Hugh feels less sanguine about returning to his past with Armande, especially as it was so often torment, yet he feels compelled to try to revisit the first and only summer of their "love." But his foray through space in search of lost time fails dismally, to the point where the narrator taunts: "What had you expected of your pilgrimage, Person? A mere mirror rerun of hoary torments?" (*TT* 94).

If *Transparent Things* mocks the myth of the return to the past, it undermines the myth that we can know the future we will arrive at. As readers, outside Hugh's world and aware of the narrators' failed attempt to divert him from the hotel where he plans to stay, we can see images of death, fire, and falling that appear to signal that Hugh will die by jumping to escape a fire that the narrators have already seen in the making. But because of a last-minute change of room, his death does not happen as so insistently foreseen. Hugh does die in the fire, but by suffocation, and he is welcomed, in a dizzying and unexpected final scene, onto the level of being of the spectral narrators, especially the ghost of R., whom he had been visiting when he first met Armande. Again, the novel as strategy depends on the surprise of the ending: not a plunge into death but a heady dance of imagery that leads Hugh to a threshold beyond the story and onto the level of its tellers.

Since adultery, planned or performed, sets the tone for both *Mary* and *Transparent Things*, one might expect it to result in the clash of wills so familiar in story from Agamemnon and Clytemnestra to Anna and Karenin and beyond. But Nabokov writes in "The Tragedy of Tragedy":

> The idea of conflict tends to endow life with a logic it never has. Tragedies based exclusively in the logic of conflict are as untrue to life as an all-pervading class-struggle is untrue to history. Most of the worst and deepest human tragedies, far from following the marble rules of tragic conflict, are tossed on the stormy element of chance.
>
> (*MUSSR* 340)

For Nabokov, conflict is a convenient but conventional trap for story and one that he springs open again and again. Ganin plans to take Mary from her husband, but neither Alfyorov nor Mary will ever know, after Ganin quietly slips away, having changed his mind, with no one but himself the wiser. Hugh Person kills Armande not as a consequence of her infidelities, for which he has never reproached her, but only in the throes of the dream of someone who has always been as lurching and lumbering in sleep as in waking life.

In "The Tragedy of Tragedy" Nabokov envisages "the higher form of tragedy"—but it could in fact be the higher form of plot, whether tragic or not or theatrical or not—as

> the creation of a certain unique pattern of life in which the sorrows and passions[10] of a particular man will follow the rules of his own individuality, not the rules of the theatre as we know them . . . a writer of genius may discover exactly the right harmony of . . . accidental occurrences, and . . . this harmony, without suggesting anything like the iron laws of tragic fatality, will express certain definite combinations that occur in life.
>
> (*MUSSR* 341)

In his own work Nabokov does not impose the character's individual mark with the stark irony of Hardyesque fate but with a delicacy that it can often take the eye of sensitive retrospection to spot, in a pattern that once seen, cannot be unseen, like Ganin in stasis and then suddenly moving again or Hugh awkwardly emerging to cross a new threshold.

In *Mary* Nabokov establishes a stiff rhythm to Ganin's existence as he alternates between present and recollections of the past, but in fact he fails to provide Ganin with much of a past beyond his love for Mary, much of a present beyond his reminiscences of her and plans for escape with her, much of a future except his no longer needing Mary to help him cope with the present and beyond. These are not deliberate decisions, like Tolstoy's refusal to give his characters background lives, but simply youthful inexperience. As early as the Franz of his next novel, Nabokov will use backfill and infill to build up the patterns of a life that can extend even into the moment of death. In Hugh's case, the aggressive overtness and humiliating insistence of the patterns, from his unhappy years as a youthful somnambulist to his waking to death by fire, disturb us, as does so much about the novel. The overt patterning of time here stands in stark contrast to the complex, covert, celebratory layering of past on past in Nabokov's immediately previous novel, *Ada*.[11] The difference reflects the gulf between Van's character, his love, his triumphant fate, and his role as fond retrospector, with Ada, of the past he shares with her, and Hugh's character, his love, his sad fate, and the power the narrators of his story have to search his past with a more than human, indeed quite inhuman, freedom.

THE IMPLIED WORLDS OF NABOKOVIAN NARRATIVE

Because he rejects determinism, because he refuses to see life in terms of action and counteraction meshing like teeth on interconnecting cogs, Nabokov's stories minimize the conflict that ticks its way through so much of story. He constructs *his* stories to reflect the unique, unpredictable rhythm of an individual character's life.

He also shapes his stories so that each poses an overarching problem where the force of characters' moves and countermoves often seems less significant than their combining into an artfully playful and puzzling authorial design. He famously explains this by analogy with chess-problem composition (*SM* 288–93), and some chess-problem aficionados indeed feel that in his problems he is too ingenious, that he does not maximize the tension between black and white but instead focuses too much on the tension between problemist and solver, between the solver's expectations and the problemist's radical inventiveness. In the same way, resistant readers of his fiction prefer the simpler rhythm of action and reaction—the powerful clash of character and character, which, after all, our ancestors evolved to notice even before they were hominids or humans—to Nabokov's focus on the subtle tension between author and reader.

As plot became less central to literary storytelling in the twentieth century, there was a general tendency, at least early in the century, to pay less attention to the clash of characters over time and to focus instead on the inner experience of the mind within the moment. But Nabokov rejects that, too, as a primary focus because he is interested in the mind as much *beyond* as *within* the moment or the self. What makes his work unique at the local level is his capacity to be true to the details of a scene but also to shift within or beyond the scene and to take responsive readers with him.

He does not eschew situations in the here and now, and in fact he can render them, a stalled elevator, a taxi outside a hotel door, with stunning immediacy, not by the sheer accumulation of detail but by catching our imaginations off guard. He knows that attention fades if we habituate to stimuli, so he refreshes and provokes it by shifting it from one point to another within a scene: not by shifting from one character's mind to another, since life rules that out, but by retaining a focus on one mind yet freely sliding or soaring this way, aside or ahead, to another scene, another time, another plane, as smoothly or abruptly as he chooses, and expecting the reader can do so, too.

Nabokov's storytelling allows a free choice at every moment, a perpetually open series of surprises, and his innovative subjects, structures, and stratagems, in works like *The Gift*, *Lolita*, *Pale Fire*, *Ada*, *Transparent Things*, anywhere at all, really, even as early as *Mary*, show him again and again opening up new dimensions of possibility and inviting us to enter and explore these strange new spaces. But his very desire for freedom, on the small scale and the large, at the level of the sentence, the life, and the work, means that his imagination is present and active everywhere. Some readers resist what they feel as his imposing himself throughout his fictional worlds. Others appreciate his work as inviting both readers and characters, in line after line and life after life, into something freer than even the ample and opulent prison of space, time, and the self.

Unlike so many serious storytellers of the twentieth century, Nabokov can give us the pleasures of extraordinary characters and events: Luzhin and the madness that impels him to his suicide; Humbert and the obsession that drives him to abduction and murder; Kinbote and his fantastic relocation of a thoroughly realistic poem; Van and Ada and their eighty-year-long forbidden love. But even without extraordinary events, in the quiet worlds of a Ganin or a Hugh Person, Nabokov tells his stories with so much imaginative mobility and surprise that he gives us a new confidence in what our imaginations can do to apprehend our world and to step right outside it. In a sense, he tells the same story each time, since each life leads from a similar beginning to a similar end, but he also ensures, as life does, that it could not be more different each time.

14. Nabokov's Transition from Russian to English

Repudiation or Evolution?

I met Alexander Dolinin in 1990 in St. Petersburg, and within a couple of minutes realized he knew Nabokov better than almost any Western Nabokovian. We have since had many delightful arguments in person and in print. But his 2005 essay suggesting that in his years of world fame Nabokov deliberately mythologized his past, downplayed his Russianness, and denigrated his Russian achievements seemed to me both deeply wrong and deeply unfair to Nabokov. Invited to a Nabokov conference at Oxford where Sasha was speaking, I decided to issue a challenge in person and, at more length, in print. I also wanted to turn the essay from the critical to the constructive. I found a way to do so by explaining the exacting standards Nabokov applied to his own work as well as that of others. No one had noticed that behind his strong critical opinions stands his strong sense of cultural evolution, his conviction that civilization in general and art in particular have extended and will continue to extend human possibilities and sensitivities.

Nabokov was unsparing in criticism, but outsiders—and perhaps even insiders—are surprised how sparing Nabokovians tend to be to other Nabokovians. As editor of *Nabokov Studies*, Zoran Kuzmanovich would like more controversy in the Nabokov world. I don't believe in controversy for his sake, or for its own sake, but I do believe we should always be ready to challenge our own and others' strong opinions and confident claims by testing them against the evidence.

Five years ago in the *Cambridge Companion to Nabokov*, Alexander Dolinin offered a "strong" reading of Nabokov's career.[1] He characterized Nabokov's early years as a period of creatively combative engagement with the Russian literary tradition but his later years, some time after his switch to English, in terms of, first, a disavowal of that former engagement; second, a diminution of his own Russian achievement; and third, a "mythmaking" self-portrayal as "a born cosmopolitan" never attached to anything (53). Given that these claims were made by the foremost Russian Nabokovian in an authoritative series from a major academic press, given that they would rewrite our sense of Nabokov's late career and his character, they deserve scrutiny. Dolinin's claims prove far more mythical than Nabokov's pronouncements on his own career: the evidence contradicts them at every turn.

After showing this, I pass beyond the negative to explain in a new way why Nabokov continually drove himself to develop artistically and why he was hard not just on some of his own past work but also on the work of authors he revered. High standards lurk behind his strong opinions, and these high standards are far from narrowly literary or even artistic: they derive from a broad sense of cultural development not sufficiently recognized in Nabokov.

REPUDIATING THE RUSSIAN?

Nabokov, Dolinin asserts, "worked out a peculiar strategy of presenting his earlier writings as inferior 'outlines' or 'dress rehearsals' for his English masterpieces" (50); he "never misses a chance to sneak in a favorable reference to his English writings and to subtly pit them against their Russian counterparts" (51). "Sirin fell victim to the tricky mythmaking and playacting Nabokov indulged in during his later years" (53); "this scenario automatically, by definition, sends all Nabokov's Russian writings downhill, relegating them to a secondary role of immature, imperfect antecedents" (54). "It would be wrong . . . to follow Nabokov in downgrading them to the rank of apprenticeship" (56).

Dolinin finds this supposed strategy of downgrading "peculiar," but he never questions his own scenario. He does not feel any need to *explain* why someone like Nabokov—not unappreciative of his own work, to say the least, and not unaware that the income from sales ensured his future freedom to write—would persistently diminish the value of his old work to a new audience much larger than any he had previously had, especially in forewords that might sway browsers' decisions to purchase or not.

Let me cite some obvious counterevidence to the claim that Nabokov devalued his Russian work—counterevidence Dolinin knows. In September 1958 Nabokov wrote to his sister Elena, "*Lolita* is having an unbelievable success—but all this ought to have happened thirty years ago" (*SL* 259). All this international success and recognition ought to have happened, that is, in 1928, if we count exactly, or, if we take "thirty" as only the nearest round number, in 1929, the year of *The Defense*, which always remained one of Nabokov's favorite novels. Would he have expected extraordinary international critical and commercial success from apprentice work, from "immature, imperfect antecedents"? Does he not imply here that his Russian work had long *deserved* the acclaim that had suddenly arrived for one of his English novels?

Perhaps Nabokov believed privately in the value of his Russian work but chose to downgrade it publicly for, as Dolinin says, some "peculiar" reason, and despite the effect such deprecation would have had on his sales? No. Consider a 1964 remark to *Playboy*, at a time when, according to Dolinin, Nabokov's mythmaking should be at its height. In an interview, Alvin Toffler asked him whether in view of *Lolita*'s becoming such a cause célèbre he ever regretted writing it: "No, I shall never regret *Lolita*. . . . Of course she completely eclipsed my other works—at least those I wrote in English: *The Real Life of Sebastian Knight*, *Bend Sinister*, my short stories, my book of recollections" (*SO* 20–21). This is exactly the converse of Dolinin's claim. Nabokov here diminishes by comparison with *Lolita* the achievement of his early English fiction and even *Speak, Memory*, but not that of his best Russian fiction, which he evidently sees as reaching the level of his most successful novel. Or consider a public pronouncement from 1970, where Nabokov responds to a reminiscence by James Joyce's and his own friend Lucie Léon Noel.[2] In Mme Léon's account of a dinner where Joyce and Nabokov met at her house, Nabokov writes, "She pictures me as a timid young artist; actually, I was forty, with a sufficiently lucid awareness of what I had already done for Russian letters preventing me from feeling awed in the presence of any living writer" (*SO* 292). Remember what Nabokov says earlier in *Strong Opinions*: "*My* greatest masterpieces of twentieth century prose are, in this order, Joyce's *Ulysses*; Kafka's *Transformation*; Biely's *Petersburg*; and the first half of Proust's fairy tale *In Search of Lost Time*" (*SO* 57). Nabokov not only stresses his age, that he was far past his apprentice years, but also declares himself aware enough of what he had done for Russian literature not to feel awe even before the writer of the greatest novel of the twentieth century. In the way he words this, it can only mean that he thought then—and he refers to his thought as "a sufficiently *lucid* awareness," so *not* as a misapprehension he now renounces—that what he had written in Russian was in the same class as what he and so many others have named the greatest novel of the century. Where is Dolinin's "tricky mythmaking"? How is Nabokov "sending all [his] Russian writings downhill"?

True, Nabokov points out flaws in some of his Russian work. Dolinin cites Nabokov's regret in the foreword to *The Gift* that "here and there history shows through artistry" and that he "did not have the knack of recreating Berlin and its colony of expatriates as radically and ruthlessly as I have done in regard to certain environments in my later, English, fiction" (51). That history occasionally shows through artistry, that Nabokov's indignation at Hitler's Germany darkens his canvas of Berlin, seems a very human and even touching admission. And it is true that in *Lolita*, *Pnin*, and *Pale Fire* Nabokov does recreate America at home and on the road and on campus more radically and in some ways more ruthlessly than he "recreates" German and émigré Berlin. But that doesn't mean that he downgrades to the level of apprentice work the book he repeatedly called the best of his Russian novels. Shakespeare could quite truthfully have noted that he did not have the knack of recreating Eastcheap and Elsinore as radically and ruthlessly as he did Sicilia and Bohemia in *The Winter's Tale*, but this would not mean he dismissed the *Henry IV* plays and *Hamlet* as mere apprentice work.

Nabokov points out flaws of *many* kinds in *Ulysses*—stylistic flaws (giving too much verbal body to thought [*LL* 289]); structural flaws (overelaborating the Odyssean parallels [*LL* 288]; "poorly balanced" chapters [*LL* 320]); psychological flaws (making Bloom over-preoccupied with sex almost to "the verge of insanity," even after the masturbation scene, in a way that seems "artificial and unnecessary," or making Stephen too artistically controlled in casual speech [*LL* 287, 286]); ethical flaws (presenting, as Nabokov saw it, an unduly coarsened image of woman in Molly [*LL* 286]), social flaws (overstressing the racial aspect in Bloom [*LL* 287]), esthetic flaws ("needless obscurity" [*LL* 290])—far more serious and numerous than the single humanly admirable flaw he notes in *The Gift*. Yet he thought *Ulysses* the greatest novel of the century and in the early 1930s volunteered to translate it into Russian at the peak of his own productivity as a writer.[3] Nabokov also points out flaws in *Madame Bovary*, yet for much of his adult life had prized it as the greatest of all novels.[4] He points out flaws in *Eugene Onegin* despite thinking it the masterpiece of Russian poetry and, once again, worth devoting five of his own most creative years to (*EO*, passim). Nabokov thought *Hamlet* "the greatest miracle in all of literature," but he did not consider it flawless.[5]

But take the first example Dolinin adduces after claiming Nabokov had "worked out a peculiar strategy of presenting his earlier writings as inferior" (50): "His verdict was strict: 'Not all of that stuff is as good as I thought it was thirty years ago'" (citing *SO* 88). Is that such an odd judgment? Do we not all tend to judge our work more harshly later than in the first flush of completion? And notice Dolinin's first example in its context in *Strong*

Opinions, where Nabokov goes straight on to talk only about *Glory* in these terms: "It is the story of a Russian expatriate, a romantic young man of my set and time, a lover of adventure for adventure's sake, proud flaunter of peril, climber of unnecessary mountains, who merely for the pure thrill of it decides one day to cross illegally into Soviet Russia, and then cross back to exile. Its main theme is the overcoming of fear, the glory and rapture of that victory" (*SO* 88). That is all Nabokov adds, and it reads more like advertising copy than artistic disparagement.

Dolinin does not specify exactly when Nabokov began to "indulge in" "tricky mythmaking" but locates it "during his later years" (53), not immediately after his transition from Russian to English. He claims that the poems Nabokov wrote in Russian in the late 1930s and the 1940s were "before he created a new persona for himself," some time in the 1950s or later, apparently. But long before Nabokov purportedly adopted his new persona, he responded to Edmund Wilson's reference to *Glory* with this remark in early 1943 (Wilson had also just read all Pushkin's longer poems, and declared himself "disappointed in the patriotic *Poltava*, though I can see it is finely written"): "You are quite right about 'Poltava.' Incidentally, 'Poltava' in Pushkin's output is on the same level as *Podvig* in mine. I wrote it twenty years ago—and you know how one feels about one's *blevotina* [vomit]" (*DBDV* 104, 105). Wanting to maximize distance between himself and the novel, Nabokov dates it to twenty years previously, when he had actually written it only thirteen years earlier. As late as 1966 he could say that translating *Podvig* as first published was not worth the effort, and that he would have to change a great deal.[6]

So from at least 1943 to 1966, the year of the interview where he said, "Not all of that stuff is as good as I thought it was thirty years ago," Nabokov appears to have looked back on *Glory* with some distaste, as a patriotic effusion—yet in the 1966 interview, all that he actually says about the novel makes it sound attractive. But listen to what Nabokov writes in 1970 in his foreword to *Glory*, after he had reread it closely in revising Dmitri's translation and discovered he did not need to make strategic changes. This was the last of his novels to be translated, his last foreword to a Russian novel, and should therefore show his "mythmaking" in its most potent form. He writes:

It would make things too easy for a certain type of reviewer (and particularly for those insular innocents whom my work affects so oddly that one might think I hypnotize them from the wings into making indecent gestures) were I to point out the faults in the novel. Suffice it to say that, after all but lapsing into false exotism or commonplace comedy, it soars to heights of purity and melancholy that I have only attained in the much later *Ada*.[7]

Since Nabokov points out faults in the novels he thinks the greatest ever written, his being ready to point out faults in *Glory* hardly seems a dismissal of apprentice work. Nabokov writes scornfully here of "a certain type of reviewer" in the same year as his foreword to *Mary*, where he refers without elaborating to that novel's "flaws, the artifacts of innocence and inexperience, which any criticule could tabulate."[8] Since nobody wants to be thought a criticule, the effect is not to draw attention to *Mary*'s weaknesses but to invite critics not to do so, lest they prove themselves mere "criticules," and to lower expectations somewhat so that readers do not expect in his first novel something on the level of his maturer masterpieces. It's not self-sabotage but a preemptive strike against potential attack.

But *Glory* is not Nabokov's first novel, and his strategy here is both similar and quite different. "It would make things too easy for a certain type of reviewer"—for a prejudiced criticule, as it were, Nabokov implies— "were I to point out the faults in the novel." But he will *not* do so. Yet in the next sentence he adds: "Suffice it to say that, after all but lapsing into false exotism or commonplace comedy . . ." These seem hardly grave faults, especially as he refers to "all but lapsing"—not quite lapsing, therefore— and the exotism of the novel often has real charm. And he continues: "It soars to heights of purity and melancholy that I have only attained in the much later *Ada*." Not to heights that he has *topped* in *Ada*, but to heights that since *Glory* he has only attained there. In this respect at least, he claims that *Glory* outdoes his other work before *Ada*, including his other English masterpieces.

Everything else Nabokov writes in the foreword makes *Glory* sound humanly appealing and artistically accomplished: "It is the glory of high adventure and disinterested achievement; the glory of this earth and its patchy paradise; the glory of personal pluck; the glory of a radiant martyr" (xiii). Nabokov famously divided the novelist into three facets, the storyteller, the teacher, and the enchanter, and declared the enchanter the greatest of these (*LL* 5). He writes that "The hero of *Glory* . . . is not necessarily interested in politics—that is the first of two mastertricks on the part of the wizard who made Martin" (xii). Later he adds: "My second wandstroke is this: among the many gifts I showered on Martin, I was careful not to include talent. How easy it would have been to make him an artist, a writer; how hard not to let him be one" (xiii). In other words, he twice acknowledges himself the enchanter behind *Glory*. He then compares *Glory* to a chess problem he composed, whose "beauty" he explains, and adds: "The problem was diabolically difficult to construct. So was *Podvig*" (xiv). How can Dolinin claim that Nabokov is trying to distance himself from imperfect apprentice work?

Nabokov concludes the foreword by warning readers not to seek for glimpses of the author's autobiography:

> The fun of *Glory* is elsewhere. It is to be sought in the echoing and linking of minor events, in back-and-forth switches, which produce an illusion of impetus: in an old daydream directly becoming the blessing of the ball hugged to one's chest, or in the casual vision of Martin's mother grieving beyond the time-frame of the novel in an abstraction of the future that the reader can only guess at, even after he has raced through the last seven chapters where a regular madness of structural twists and a masquerade of all characters culminate in a furious finale, although nothing much happens at the very end—just a bird perching on a wicket in the grayness of a wet day.
>
> (xiv)

That is the last word of Nabokov's last foreword to his Russian novels, and it is haunting, beguiling, and a marvelous insight into the subtleties of the novel, which certainly provided me with clues to my reading of *Glory* in *The Russian Years*. Far from diminishing his Russian novels, Nabokov offers us keys to their artistry and appeal.

Glory taps into a rich humus of Russian myth and fairytale and literature that makes it a favorite for many Russian readers. Nabokov knew it would be counterproductive to tell non-Russian readers what we are missing, but he hints at enough of the human and artistic appeal of the novel to entice us to enjoy all we can respond to. The Nabokov who dismissed *Glory* as patriotic "vomit" in 1943, before Dolinin says he adopted the tricky persona of a disparager of his earlier work, introduces his last-translated Russian novel in terms of respect, affection, pride, and subtle enthusiasm.

The evidence contradicts Dolinin's claims at every point. Nabokov also devalues his work in *English*, like the English poems he collects in *Poems and Problems* ("they are of a lighter texture than the Russian stuff, owing, no doubt, to their lacking that inner verbal association with old perplexities and constant worry of thought which marks poems written in one's mother tongue" [*PP* 14]). He dismisses his early verse translations of Pushkin and others, before he adopted his later strict literalism.[9] He disparages the "frivolous little book" on Gogol, before he developed his later strictly scholarly approach to Pushkin (*EO* 2.314). As in his comments on his Russian work, his criticisms come from the vantage point of new techniques or approaches or simply from his admission of the limitations of his second language, not from any perverse persona.

And he also *praises* his Russian works: *Priglashenie na kazn'* (he gives it its Russian title) is the one of his works he holds in "the greatest esteem" (*SO* 92) in 1966, at the supposed peak of his mythmaking. From 1945 to his death, in private and in public, he unwaveringly designated his Russian poems of the late 1930s and especially the early 1940s as his best.[10] He repeatedly draws attention to the challenges and beauties of his Russian works. The story "Terror" "preceded Sartre's *La Nausée*, with which it shares certain shades of thought, and none of that novel's fatal defects, by at least a dozen years" (*SoVN* 644). He describes "The Circle" as a satellite of *The Gift* but asserts that "a knowledge of the novel is not required for the enjoyment of the corollary which has its own orbit and colored fire," while he also suggests that "the story will produce upon readers who are familiar with the novel a delightful effect of oblique recognition" (*SoVN* 649–50). I could go on and on.[11]

From before his arrival in America, and during his early years there, Nabokov passionately and persistently sought to arrange translations into English of what he thought his three best Russian novels—*The Defense, Invitation to a Beheading*, and *The Gift*. He gave up in the face of the difficulty of finding a translator up to his standards and the difficulty of finding publishers even for his English-language novels (*The Real Life of Sebastian Knight, Bend Sinister, Lolita*, and *Pnin* were all rejected by American publishers). He lamented in the afterword to *Lolita*, "None of my American friends have read my Russian books and thus every appraisal on the strength of my English ones is bound to be out of focus" (*Lolita* 318). Despite finding many errors of fact, interpretation, and translation in Andrew Field's 1967 *Nabokov: His Life in Art*, he welcomed it enthusiastically for opening up his still untranslated Russian works and for treating the Russian and English work as a seamless whole, for breaking down what Field calls "the meaningless and harmful division of Nabokov's art into 'Russian works' and 'English works.'"[12]

If the evidence is so decidedly against Dolinin's claims, how can he even argue his case? The keystone of his argument is his reference to the poem "We So Firmly Believed":

At the center of the Nabokov myth lies the very idea of his life in art as an uninterrupted path, a continuous ascension, to use the images of the poem "We So Firmly Believed" (*PP*, 89) from the "damp dell" of promising juvenilia up to the "alpine heath" of faultlessly crafted masterpieces, a history of triumphant emergence unimpeded (and maybe even furthered) by the painful switch to a different language. It is clear that this scenario automatically, by definition, sends all of Nabokov's Russian writings downhill, relegating them to a secondary role of immature, imperfect antecedents.

(54)

Yet the poem does not support Dolinin's argument as he claims it does. It does not refer to Nabokov's art at all. It was written in 1938, *before* Nabokov switched to English, and therefore "by definition" *before* he had written his English masterpieces and before he could have possibly entertained any thought of presenting his Russian oeuvre as apprentice work. Let me cite an earlier, unpublished translation Nabokov made of the poem, which renders its sense more clearly than the version in *Poems and Problems*:

To My Youth

We used to believe so firmly, you and I, in the unity
of existence; but now I glance back—and it is
astounding—how impersonal in color, how unreal in
pattern you have become, my youth.

When one examines the matter, it is like the haze of
a wave between me and you, between the shallows and the
drowning—or else I see a receding highway, and you
from behind as you pedal right into the sunset on your semi-racer.

You are no more myself, you're a mere outline, the subject
of any first chapter—but how long we believed
in the oneness of the way from the damp gorge
to the mountain heather.[13]

Dolinin implies that this poem "at the center of the Nabokov myth" talks about a writer's progress. It does no such thing. He implies that the poem suggests "a continuous ascension . . . up to the 'alpine heath' of faultlessly crafted masterpieces." Nabokov says nothing about artistic achievement. In fact, the poem is a deeply moving reflection on the gaps in memory, the gulfs in time within the self, the sense that as you look back at yourself you realize that despite the illusion of continuous identity, you may no longer feel a live connection with your younger selves. In this context, and in view of the immemorial image of a life as a river taking one at death out to the sea, it seems more likely that Nabokov is thinking of the journey back in thought from the "damp gorge" of the present to the mountain heather, to the source and spring of one's life: the way *back* from the present to the origins of the self. It's not a glorious *ascension* to future achievement: after all, heather hardly grows on mountain summits, but it can flourish on slopes where springs start to flow down continuously to lower "damp dells."

This poem was written before Nabokov changed languages, before he had written any of the English works that Dolinin tries to imply the poet implies with the "ascension" to the "alpine heath" and "this scenario" that "automatically, by definition, sends all Nabokov's Russian writings downhill." A page later Dolinin writes: "To quote and paraphrase his poems of the late 1930s and the 1940s written before he created a new persona for himself," (55), but when he quotes "We So Firmly Believed" and refers to "this scenario" and its consequences "by definition," he does not note the fact that the poem was actually written in 1938, long before the supposed "alpine heath" of flawless English masterpieces and long before the new persona that he presents the poem as confirming. Who is the mythmaker?

I would like to move to subsidiary claims that Dolinin makes that are just as obviously unfounded and even more obviously unfair. According to Dolinin, the later Nabokov looking back at his Russian self "pretended that he had always stood apart from literary battles and discussions of the day" (53). Once again, Dolinin does not ask himself why Nabokov might have done such a thing—when Nabokov could declare that "next to the right to create, the right to criticize is the richest gift that liberty of thought and speech can offer" (*LRL* ii); when he so loved being a provocateur, in his jibes at Freud and at Soviet propaganda, in his debunking of esteemed authors, in his fierce polemics on literary translation; and when he showed such recognition that this was good copy, a sure way of provoking critics' and readers' attention.

Let me cite just a few instances of Nabokov insisting on his part in literary skirmishes. No scholar had approached Nabokov about his Russian work until Andrew Field in 1966. That year, reading Field's discussion of the 1931 story "Lips to Lips" in the manuscript of *Nabokov: His Life in Art*,

Nabokov, unprompted, volunteered the information—and suggested "one might mention" it—that "the story is based on an actual event in connection with a certain Alexander Burov being milked by the clique of *Chisla*."[14] In the same note, he also offers an explanation that the 1944 Russian poem "No Matter How" "was aimed at those émigré Russians whom Russian victories led to forget and forgive Soviet iniquities." Field duly used the information, and reported on other literary feuds he had recognized, with Nabokov's approval.[15]

When Nabokov began collecting his Russian stories and poems for McGraw-Hill in the late 1960s and the 1970s, he did not miss a chance to highlight past polemics. He explains the narrative emphasis of his poetry of the late 1920s and early 1930s as expressing "my impatience with the dreary drone of the anemic 'Paris school' of *émigré* poetry" (*PP* 14). He refers to what had become by then the main émigré newspaper, the Paris "*Poslednie Novosti*, with which I conducted a lively feud throughout the 1930s" (*SoVN* 648). He explains the 1939 poem "The Poets" thus:

The poem was published in a magazine under the pseudonym of "Vasily Shishkov" in order to catch a distinguished critic (G. Adamovich, of the *Poslednie novosti*) who automatically objected to everything I wrote. The trick worked: in his weekly review he welcomed the appearance of a mysterious new poet with such eloquent enthusiasm that I could not resist keeping up the joke by describing my meetings with the fictitious Shishkov in a story which contained, among other plums, a criticism of the poem and of Adamovich's praise.

(*PP* 95)

When he introduced the translation of the story, he again reprinted the whole poem and explained the tussle with Adamovich at still greater length. Dolinin may not know Nabokov's letters to Field, but he knows Nabokov's references to his feuds with Paris poets, critics, and periodicals. He has a copious and exact memory. How can he claim that Nabokov "pretended that he had always stood apart from literary battles and discussions of the day" (53)?

I could go on, but the point is made. No, I *will* go on, because Dolinin keeps impugning Nabokov, despite the evidence:

Like those unhappy expatriates who leave their native country in search of a better life and then are doomed again and again to prove to themselves that their decision was right, Nabokov had to justify his emigration from his native language and literature to their acquired substitutes. For this purpose, he would argue that "the nationality of a worthwhile writer is of secondary importance" (*SO*, 63) and present himself as a born cosmopolitan genius who has never been attached to anything and anybody but his autonomous imagination and personal memory.

(53)

"For this purpose," Dolinin says—to justify his leaving first Russia and then Europe—Nabokov would argue that "the nationality of a worthwhile writer is of secondary importance." I would have thought it did not take much to justify fleeing death for yourself and your family, and I would have thought Nabokov's arguments about the transnational quality of the best writing deserved serious consideration rather than dismissal as spurious self-justification. In the Russian survey lectures that he taught at Wellesley and Cornell (for the first time in 1947, so before he had written any of the English masterpieces that Dolinin claims provided the pretext for Nabokov's belittling his Russian masterpieces), Nabokov had this to say:

> *Individuals* not *nations* create literature. The term "national literature" is a contradiction in terms. . . . for me literature is *not* the echo of a nation but the echo of individual genius. . . . *Literature* is not created by the average Russian or the average American. It is created by a dispersed and universal family of great men. The art of Pushkin or Gogol or Tolstoy is considerably closer to that of Flaubert or Dickens or Proust or Joyce than to anything an average Russian could think up; . . . Dostoevsky's divagations were much closer to the sentimental and crude phantasms of English and French mystery novels of the 18th and early 19th centuries than to any national psychology of Russian murderers and monks.[16]

This sounds like Nabokov's authentic voice and his authentic convictions. It even sounds like an opinion worth taking seriously, and advice well directed at literarily unsophisticated students. What does it have to do with justifying flight from Bolshevized Crimea or Nazified France? If Nabokov concocted such ideas to consolidate the persona of a born cosmopolitan genius, why did he say this to a class mostly unaware that he was a writer and, according to Dolinin's dating, before he adopted this late persona?

Let us turn to Nabokov's "present[ing] himself as a born cosmopolitan genius" (53) , in Dolinin's words. Did he *not* present himself as a Russian, in every major work he wrote except *Lolita*, where he intended to hide his authorship? Asked by an interviewer in 1962, by which time the persona was supposed to be in place, "Do you still feel Russian, in spite of so many years in America?" Nabokov answered without hesitation, "I do feel Russian and I think that my Russian works, the various novels and poems and short stories that I have written during these years, are a kind of tribute to Russia. . . . I have just finished revising a good translation of my novel, *The Gift*, which I wrote about thirty years ago. It is the longest, I think the best, and the most nostalgic of my Russian novels" (*SO* 13).

Still on this same Dolinin sentence: Nabokov would present himself as someone "who has never been attached to anything but his autonomous imagination and personal memory" (53). Not true. As always, Nabokov insisted on his independence and distanced himself from any group response or period perspective, but he "presented himself" eloquently and intensely as attached to Russia, the Russian liberal tradition, the Russian literary tradition (including particular writers of his youth like Blok, Bely, Gumilyov, and Voloshin), the Russian emigration as a continuer of both, to his family and to figures in the literary world like the critic Aykhenvald, the poet Khodasevich, and the patron and editor Fondaminsky. He kept out of the public gaze individuals he knew only in a private capacity, but the intensity of his affection for friends like his schoolmate Samuil Rosov, Georgy Hessen, the companion of his early manhood, and later Russian friends in France and America like the Marinel sisters saturates his letters. Why does Dolinin distort and insult Nabokov so?

Alexander Dolinin is a major scholar, to whom all who read Nabokov carefully now owe a great deal. Why does someone with his fund of exact knowledge overlook so much of what he knows and fall so stubbornly short by making a case for which he so rarely cites evidence but for which counterevidence lies so readily at hand?

This has genuinely puzzled me ever since I first read Dolinin's piece. One answer can be glimpsed in the essay's recurrent irritation at the critical stress on Nabokov's English oeuvre at the expense of his Russian. Sometimes his irritation may be justified, although it also seems perfectly natural that scholars without Russian, like Maurice Couturier and Michael Wood, should focus primarily on Nabokov's English works rather than his Russian, and since the proportion of the academic world that is Anglophone greatly exceeds the Russophone portion, that imbalance is likely to persist. Still, that should leave rich opportunities for Russian scholars. To the best of my recollection I have not published on Nabokov's Russian work, except for material I have edited, since I have met Sasha because I know I can never compete with his knowledge of Nabokov's Russian literary contexts. I have been happy to pass the ball to his usually safe hands.

I also agree with Dolinin that Elizabeth Klosty Beaujour is wrong to consider the English versions of Nabokov's Russian works the definitive replacements of the Russian texts "to all intents and purposes" (cited at 53n. 6). Nabokov did intend the English versions of his Russian texts to be the definitive basis for all "foreign" (non-Russian) editions.[17] In them he explained matters of Russian culture or émigré life obvious to a Russian émigré (and now to most post-Soviet Russian readers aware of the emigration) and found approximately equivalent allusive effects in Western European culture to those the Russian allusions would have had for the original audience and sometimes, especially in *Despair*, *The Eye*, *King, Queen, Knave*, and *The Waltz Invention*, invented additional effects. Nabokov quite naturally insisted that the new English translations should become the basis for future translations since the same problem of the inaccessibility of recherché Russian allusions and details was common to all non-Russian audiences.

But he did not intend the translations to supplant the Russian originals. When Radio Liberty selected *The Defense* and *Invitation to a Beheading* for publication and clandestine distribution in the Soviet Union, Nabokov did not think of suggesting the novels should incorporate Russian equivalents of the changes he had made in English (see *VNAY* 504–5). Except for the revisions in *Laughter in the Dark* and *Despair*, the Russian texts are artistically definitive. As translations, the English versions of Russian originals are inevitably compromises, unable to exploit the phonic, lexical, idiomatic, syntactic, associational, and allusive resources that partly shaped the content of the originals. The more artists make of their medium the more they stand to lose when their works are transposed into another, even the medium of another language. In composing his original texts Nabokov had a consistent system of artistic intentions; in translating them he had to balance what he could retrieve of those intentions against the incommensurate intention of appealing to a different audience—two different audiences, indeed, a specifically Anglophone and a generically non-Russian audience—and whatever new artistic habits, resources, and inclinations he happened to have developed by the time the translation happened to be ready to be tackled.

Dolinin has a legitimate claim, then, when he says that for artistic purposes the Russian originals have priority, although for publishing for non-Russian audiences, the English versions provide the new compromise source.

He has another legitimate grievance when he protests against the judgments of non-Russian readers that Nabokov's English style may be richer than his Russian would have become. Nabokov's Russian was an extraordinary instrument for at least his last fifteen years as a Russian writer and during those years became ever more so, and there is no reason to suppose that he would not have continued to develop it in ways we cannot now know. Here I have to agree with Dolinin (54–55) against Michael Wood. There may have been gains from Nabokov's being so ready to pick up the crutch of English, but there is no reason to think they more than compensated for the loss of his natural Russian gait.

I have suggested one partial reason for Dolinin's advancing a thesis that contradicts evidence he knows: his frustration, as a Russian scholar, and despite his own background as an Americanist, with Anglophonocentric scholarship. I will suggest two more.

Dolinin often seems to construe Nabokov's situation in terms of his own. He moved from Russia to the United States and started writing in English, but he also returns to Russia and continues to write in Russian and to write about the Russian literary tradition in both places and both languages. Dolinin writes that "Nabokov led his English readers into believing that the switch to English was a necessity, an unavoidable stage of . . . evolution rather than a free choice ('I *had* to')" (54). But Nabokov's supposedly "free" first choice was either to stay in Europe, where he had almost no income and fewer prospects and would risk the lives at least of his wife and son, or to escape from Europe. Once in America, his supposedly "free" second choice was either to become a writer of English, supporting his family that way, or to remain a writer of Russian, with no income, or to take a job that made nothing of his singular talents and inclinations. The one way he knew to earn a living was through writing, and he could not earn a living by writing for a Russophone audience in the United States. He looked for university positions but could not find a permanent academic job until 1948, by which time he was writing his sixth book in English and at last making good money from doing so. For a man in his situation and with his gifts, there was no choice.

A third reason for Dolinin's misreading lies in his belief that as Sirin, Nabokov's theme was "the life of Russian literature and the life of genres, styles, and themes within its framework" (59). He thinks that Nabokov's engagement with the Russian literary tradition was the core of his work, shaping his theory and his practice, his form and his content, his themes and his techniques. A Nabokov who underplayed the Russian subtexts when translating Sirin into English, who criticized his Russian work, and who no longer in his English work focused overwhelmingly on the Russian tradition could only be betraying his old self.

But the fact that there are writers in the background or foreground of much of Sirin's Russian fiction hardly makes the Russian literary tradition the principal theme of his Russian work, any more than the fact that writers are even more prominent in his English work makes the life of English literature, or literature in general, the principal theme of his English work. When Dolinin asserts Sirin's theme was "the life of Russian literature," he creates a Sirin in his own image—and a Sirin of less interest to readers than the work actually offers.

Nevertheless, the fate of Russian literature *did* matter a great deal to Nabokov as a Russian writer, although Dolinin claims that this preoccupation "went more or less unnoticed by . . . émigré criticism" (59)—hardly surprising, before his last Russian novel, *The Gift*, where it really does become central.

But I would link Nabokov's concern with the fate of Russian literature with a wider motivation that has been little recognized. Nabokov was deeply concerned with the Russian literary tradition, in his Russian years and, pace Dolinin, in his American years. But we need to see this as part of a much broader motivation that explains far more of his behavior, before and after the transition from Russian to English.

EVOLVING INTO CULTURE

From his father Nabokov imbibed a strong sense of cultural meliorism, a sense that culture had evolved to make humans more humane, that it could continue to evolve much further, and that art had played and could continue to play a key role in this process. V. D. Nabokov grew up in an intellectual climate pervaded by late-nineteenth-century notions of evolution and progress, individual, cultural, and biological. Encouraged by the rapid growth in productivity and in material well-being for unprecedented numbers of people in Europe and North America, intellectual notions of biological evolution and cultural progress that had begun with Lamarck and Hegel early in the century expanded at midcentury through Herbert Spencer, even before Darwin, and at the end of the century took new forms in the work of Ernst Haeckel, William James, and Henri Bergson, all of whom Nabokov read. Both Spencer and Haeckel believed culture evolved through successive stages. Spencer's ideas in particular seem close to those of the Nabokovs, father and son. His model of cultural evolution contrasted a primitive militaristic state of society, dominated by compulsion, force, and repression and by the collective, the good of the group, with a modern industrial state, where the good of the individual was paramount and individual initiative and independence central to new possibility. Spencer coined the term "survival of the fittest" as a summary of Darwin, but while committed to progressive evolution, he did not accept the relentless competition he thought Darwinism implied. Before Nabokov, Spencer had in a sense snorted, "'Struggle for life' indeed!"

V. D. Nabokov and his son shared Spencer's sense of cultural evolution as progress, if without his mid-nineteenth-century confidence in the *inevitability* of progress. Vladimir especially sided with Bergson, who stressed indeterminacy, free will, and the ongoing openness of creative evolution. But both father and son felt the importance of trying to improve one's own cultural level, partly in the hope that that could help raise the cultural level around one not by compulsion but by the example one set to responsive others.

One of his close political colleagues observed that V. D. Nabokov had entered politics more for cultural reasons than ordinarily political ones.[18] Nabokov's father believed that cultural development was an effortful process by which individuals could increase their distance from brute origins and societies could move beyond barbarism. He hoped to help Russia to rise to the level of the West, especially of England, and humanity to rise to higher individual levels of genuine culture (cf. *VNRY* 156). As a criminologist, he accepted the claims of the social sciences of his day that there were objective markers of the different levels of cultural development in different societies and that societies and individuals could raise their cultural level through effort and application. He thought that art at its best could raise the level of culture at large, so that in opposing the death penalty he naturally turned not to legal arguments but to the pity aroused by novelists like Hugo, Dickens, Turgenev, Tolstoy, and Dostoevsky.[19] He also took seriously the idea of individual development, responsibility, and freedom. When his politics sent him to prison he followed a physical exercise regime, taught himself Italian, and pursued a rigorous reading schedule in his other four languages. Improving one's own cultural level might offer an example to others but should never be *imposed* on them as a model. Although he went into politics in the hope that he could help bring Russia to the level of British constitutional monarchy, as a politician he was so averse to compulsion that he even felt qualms about trying to sway voters' minds during election campaigns (*VNRY* 130).

Vladimir Nabokov learned much from his father, most important, perhaps, this sense of cultural development as the effortful striving for a maximal evolution beyond the brutish. Nabokov's cultural meliorism begins with the free individual. Unfettered individual efforts can open up new possibilities that expand the freedom and scope of culture, offering us better access to the values Nabokov sees in art: creativity and complexity and "curiosity, tenderness, kindness, ecstasy" (*Lolita* 317). Individuals should preserve and extend the gains of culture to the degree that they can.

The idea of the evolution of consciousness and culture saturated and structured Nabokov's thought. In the first chapter of his autobiography, he introduces as the first concrete scene his dawning self-consciousness his sense of his father and of his father's and mother's ages and identities as distinct from his own:

All this is as it should be according to the theory of recapitulation [in other words, the theory that "ontogeny recapitulates phylogeny" proposed in 1866 by Darwin's German champion Ernst Haeckel: that the different stages of individual development reenact the evolution of the species]; the beginning of reflexive consciousness in the brain of our remotest ancestor must surely have coincided with the dawning of the sense of time. . . .

My father . . . had that day put on the trappings of his old regiment as a festive joke. To a joke, then, I owe my first gleam of complete consciousness—which again has recapitulatory implications, since the first creatures on earth to become aware of time were also the first creatures to smile.

(*SM* 22)

That ends the first section of the first chapter, and the next section begins, extending the evolutionary and "recapitulatory" imagery: "It was the primordial cave (and not what Freudian mystics might suppose) that lay behind the games I played when I was four" (*SM* 22–23).

The last chapter of the autobiography again focuses on the dawn of consciousness at the individual (ontogenetic) and species (phylogenetic) levels, but with Nabokov as not son but father: pointedly, I think, a recapitulation in another key. Again, Nabokov thinks about the evolution of mind and culture, with a special Nabokovian twist on Darwin:

There is also keen pleasure (and, after all, what else should the pursuit of science produce?) in meeting the riddle of the initial blossoming of man's mind by postulating a voluptuous pause in the growth of the rest of nature, a lolling and loafing which allowed first of all the formation of *Homo poeticus*—without which *sapiens* could not have been evolved. "Struggle for life" indeed! The curse of battle and toil leads man back to the boar, to the grunting beast's crazy obsession with the search for food. You and I have frequently remarked upon that maniacal glint in a housewife's scheming eye as it roves over food in a grocery or about the morgue of a butcher's shop. Toilers of the world, disband! Old books are wrong. The world was made on a Sunday.

(*SM* 298)

We can note here a Spencerian sense that the survival of the fittest fails to explain evolution; a symbolist sense that imaginations and dreams offer the likeliest route to the deepest truths; an aristocratic sense that real refinement requires leisure rather than the coarsening effect of unremitting toil; and a purely Nabokovian sense of play.[20] And poetry. A few years previously, in an essay on Lermontov, he had written: "It might be said that what Darwin called 'struggle for existence' is really a struggle for perfection, and in that respect Nature's main and most admirable device is optical illusion. Among human beings, poets are the best exponents of the art of deception."[21]

After "'Struggle for life,' indeed!" in the last chapter of *Speak, Memory*, the evolutionary themes persist tellingly as Nabokov goes on, and out of his way, to contrast the culturally evolved with the brutal backwardness of Hitler. Describing the various prams and baby carriages and other wheeled vehicles for Dmitri, Nabokov writes:

A new wave of evolution started to swell, gradually lifting him up again from the ground, when, for his second birthday, he received a four-foot-long, silver Mercedes racing car operated by inside pedals . . . and in this he used to drive . . . down the sidewalk of the Kurfürstendamm while from the open windows came the multiplied roar of a dictator still pounding his chest in the Neander valley we had left far behind.

The next paragraph immediately makes the evolutionary imagery explicit again via the idea of ontogeny recapitulating phylogeny: "It might be rewarding to go into the phylogenetic aspects of the passion male children have for things on wheels, particularly railway trains" (*SM* 300). In a Parisian park Nabokov is appalled as he sees a little girl parading a live butterfly on a thread and directs his son's gaze away; he reflects:

I may have been reminded, in fact, of the simple, old-fashioned trick a French policeman had—and no doubt still has—when leading a florid-nosed workman, a Sunday rowdy, away to jail, of turning him into a singularly docile and even alacritous satellite by catching a kind of small fishhook in the man's uncared-for but sensitive and responsive flesh. You and I did our best to encompass with vigilant tenderness the trust-ful tenderness of our child but were inevitably confronted by the fact that the filth left by hoodlums in a sandbox on a playground was the least serious of possible offenses, and that the horrors which former generations had mentally dismissed as anachronisms or things occur-ring only in remote khanates and mandarinates, were all around us.

(SM 306)

Notice the combination of the evolution of the species and the evolution of culture (in this case, the local atavistic return to earlier cultural stages)—and the sense Nabokov shared with his father that the Orient ("khanates and mandarinates") represented earlier stages in the evolution of civilization, like "medieval" within the Occidental context, which for Nabokov was also almost invariably a term of reproach. In view of his comment that in terms of the "struggle for perfection, . . . Nature's main and most admirable device is optical illusion," and that "among human beings, poets are the best expo-nents of the art of deception,"[22] it is no wonder he ends the final chapter of *Speak, Memory* with a kind of optical illusion provided by life for Dmitri. "Find What the Sailor Has Hidden" is an illusion carefully left unbroken by his parents and carefully relived and made poetic by Nabokov in the retell-ing, so as to point toward the ship that would take them all from a Europe sliding back into barbarism and toward an America that he thought offered a new stage in the evolution of freedom.

Nabokov's concern for the evolution of consciousness, the evolution of culture, and the evolution of art pervades his work. It reflects his sense that "every *accepted* form tends to become rigid, lose its elasticity, and deterio-rate into a tight-fitting coffin, for life is growth, improvement, elaboration, change."[23] (Pure Bergson, to my ear.) He thought that art has evolved, that it needs to keep evolving, and that it has a long way still to evolve. He declares in an unpublished lecture that "in the course of the historical evolution of liter-ature . . . the various senses . . . become keener, probe deeper. . . . Shakespeare saw colors more distinctly than Homer and a poet of today sees color more distinctly than Shakespeare."[24] (Notice that Nabokov drew on these inter-national examples before he had published his first American novel: before, on Dolinin's own account, he adopted the persona of the internationalist.) Tolstoy, he claims, was the first Russian writer to see lilac shades; Bunin saw them still more finely than Tolstoy.[25] On the scene of Kitty's giving birth in *Anna Karenina* he responds in a uniquely Nabokovian way: "Mark incidentally that the whole history of literary fiction as an evolutionary process may be said to be a gradual probing of deeper and deeper layers of life. It is quite impossible to imagine either Homer in the ninth century B.C. or Cervantes in the seventeenth century of our era—it is quite impossible to imagine them describing in such wonderful detail childbirth" (*LRL* 164–65). In another lecture Nabokov looks back: "How different is this world of Dickens from the world of Homer or the world of Cervantes. Does a hero of Homer's really feel the divine throb of pity? . . . let us nurse no doubt about it: despite all our hideous reversions to the wild state, modern man is on the whole a better man than Homer's man, *Homo homericus*, or than medieval man. In the imaginary battle of *americus* versus *homericus*, the first wins humanity's prize" (*LL* 86–87). But if art and culture have evolved a long way from Homer or medieval times, they still have a long way to go: as he once exclaimed, "Art is in its infancy!" (Lucas interview).

Nabokov had such a strong sense of human possibility, and of the scope for the future evolution of human possibility, in art and in life, that he could be angry or scornful at any shortfall. As he once remarked in a deleted passage in a lecture: "I [am] so passionately fond of the good thing when I find it, that my passionate hatred for what I deem to be bad art or even worse— second-[rate art]—is on the whole, the same kind of passion."[26]

He believed that the evolution of culture, art, and literature depended on individual talent and strenuous individual effort and that the most he or any artist could do for the evolution of civilization was to stick to the integrity of his art: to offer the highest standards, to open up new possibilities, which others could rise to or move beyond:

> The mission of the poet to listen intently to the voice of the inner judge and never to deviate from the road which that judge points out to him was never betrayed by the best Russian poets and writers. Never betray what your artistic conscience tells you is right, never sacrifice your artistic purpose to the intellectual urgings, to the dictates of a party or to the [conventionality?][27] of a publisher. Somehow, therein lies the inherent apostolism of art. For only by adhering strictly to the bidding of the artist within him can a poet or writer achieve that degree of artistic persuasiveness which can make his message effective, and since *true* art also automatically

happens to be *good* art it is but a betrayal of the purpose to try and artificially force upon it an extra message of goodness which, being not integrated with the artistic purpose does nothing but upset the whole delicate structure and compromise both the initial and the additional message.[28]

Or as he says in another lecture:

I am not telling you that art does not improve and enlighten the reader. But it does all this in its own special way and it does it only then when its own single purpose remains to be good, excellent art, art as perfect as its creator can make. The moment this *only* real and valuable purpose of art is forgotten, the moment it is replaced by a utilitarian aim, art stops being[29] art, and through this loss of its ego, loses not only its sense and its beauty but also the very object to which it has been sacrificed: bad art neither teaches nor improves nor enlightens.[30]

Nabokov confesses to a close sympathy with Chekhov and cites with approval Chekhov's "conclusion . . . that pure art, pure science, pure learning, being in no direct contact with the masses, will, in the long run, attain more than the clumsy and muddled attempts of benefactors" (*LRL* 250).

His idea that those artists who insist on their own creative freedom and follow the dictates and the integrity of their own art will open up new possibilities for all who choose to respond is elitist but not exclusive or complacent. It places serious responsibilities on anyone with talent. For that reason he could reproach even his beloved Pushkin on the occasions when he thought Pushkin accepted easy formulae rather than searching for new ways of seeing and saying. And just as he championed individual efforts to revise the accepted and readymade he excoriated what he saw as the opposite of genius and creative evolution: *poshlost'*, conformism, not thinking for oneself, not trying for the best, or falling for false gods or false goods.

Like his father studying Italian in prison, he felt determined to improve himself, in the ways he saw fit. As a child, he "dreamed" his way through Seitz's multivolume *Die Gross-schmetterlinge der Erde* (The macrolepidoptera of the world) (*SM* 123). As a young man at Cambridge, already determined to be a writer, he did not pay attention to his studies as his father expected and not only wrote poetry compulsively but also dreamed his way assiduously through Dal's four-volume Russian dictionary, as in later adulthood he would playfully work or workfully play his way through Webster's *New International Dictionary Unabridged* (*VNRY* 171; *VNAY* 461). All his mature literary life he studied intently the works of others, questioning clichés of thought, perception, language, and narrative strategy, consciously seeking new means partly by critiquing and correcting and caricaturing the old.

Nabokov, in other words, values all cultural advance beyond the "wild state" and saw this embodied in the rapid development of Russian culture in the nineteenth century—and its converse in the tragedy of Russia's regression after 1917. Nabokov was committed to the Russian literary tradition not only when he wrote as Sirin but also when he signed himself Nabokov, although by then his commitment reflected the ways available to him as a writer and teacher in an English-speaking environment. When he moved to English he did not lose contact with or a sense of responsibility to the Russian tradition, as Dolinin seems to imply, but he realized his English readers were starting from a very different position in relation to Russian literature than that of his émigré audience, especially if they had only the existing translations of, say, Pushkin and Gogol. He therefore translated the least accessible material: first, nineteenth-century verse, Pushkin, Lermontov, Tyutchev, and Fet; then, what he could of the least accessible nineteenth-century prose, in his *Nikolay Gogol*; and more Russian poetry from the medieval *Slovo o polku Igoreve* to the person he thought the best Russian poet of the twentieth century, Khodasevich. Once he had begun to work intensively on Pushkin for his *Eugene Onegin* translation and commentary—once he knew he could make Pushkin part of the heritage of world and not just Russian literature—he incorporated Pushkin in key ways in his fiction, in *Pnin* and *Ada*. And, indeed, he includes Russian language and literature as much as he can for an initially Anglophone audience in all his English-language novels from *The Real Life of Sebastian Knight* to *Look at the Harlequins!*, with the sole exception of *Lolita*, the one novel where he planned, while he wrote, to keep his authorship concealed.

Nabokov also displayed throughout his American and final European years a strong desire to keep alive the memory of the Russian liberal tradition, before the revolution in Russia and after the revolution *outside* it, and to oppose Soviet propaganda that downplayed both. He did this both as a teacher of literature, in pieces like "The Triumphs and Trials of Russian Literature,"[31] and as a writer, in the forewords to his own books in translation.[32] He wanted to stress the development toward freedom during (and despite) Tsarism, the regression toward intensified oppression under the Soviets, and the emigration as the preserver of the Russian liberal tradition and of the tradition of freedom in Russian literature.

Nabokov's sense of the free growth of literature and culture—of their evolution to date, of their need to keep evolving, of the best of the past as a basis for still further evolution—lies behind his strong opinions, his commitment to the freedom that allows creation and criticism, and his distaste for what he sees as cliché, conformity, complacency, or the control of art by extra-artistic forces. But it does not apply only to the Russian literary tradition. During his Russian years Nabokov was also engaged with the Western tradition: with Theodore Dreiser in *King, Queen, Knave*, despite his later disclaimer;[33] with Spengler and other prophets of the decline of civilization in *Glory* (*VNRY* 353); with Joyce and Proust in *The Gift* (*VNRY* 466–67).[34]

And during his American years he did not cease challenging current literature as well as past traditions: T. S. Eliot and Pound; Sartre, Camus, and existentialism; Mann, Faulkner, Pasternak, Steinbeck, Borges; or, further in the past, Lawrence, Galsworthy, George Eliot, Dostoevsky, eighteenth-century conventionalism; and so on. If in his Russian works he had exalted the Russian literary tradition from within his fiction and verse, in his English years he continued to exalt the Russian tradition in his roles as scholar and translator and, when he could, as storyteller; paid tribute in his English fiction and verse to Shakespeare, Donne, Marvell, Pope, Wordsworth, Coleridge, Shelley, Keats, Browning, Hardy, and Housman within the English verse tradition; celebrated Shakespeare as example and inspiration to English literature as he had celebrated Pushkin as inspiration for Russian literature (see chapter 15); and invoked Austen, Pushkin, Dickens, Flaubert, Tolstoy, Proust, and Joyce as sources of the traditions of the novel in *Ada*.

Because of his high standards, his sense of the need and duty of art to evolve, Nabokov weighed carefully even the work of writers he esteemed as much as Shakespeare, Pushkin, and Tolstoy and readily dismissed whole swathes of art: the primitive, the Oriental, the *hochmodern*, the *poshliy*. He criticized his own Russian work in the same spirit, not because he was trying to diminish Sirin or distance himself from him but because he thought that art needed to keep rising to the highest standards possible, by making the best of past art an inspiration and a challenge and a basis for critique and new discovery.

Nabokov's post-1940 critiques of aspects of his Russian work and his changing treatment of Russian matters were not inexplicable denigrations of his earlier work or denials of its deep Russianness. Rather, they reflected his high expectations of literary and cultural traditions in Russia and elsewhere and of his own contribution to those traditions over the years. If we see this we can see the *range* of his behavior—beyond his concern for only the Russian literary tradition—and its reasons: his consistent attitudes to cultural and individual development.

NABOKOV AND OTHERS

15. Nabokov, Pushkin, Shakespeare

Genius, Generosity, and Gratitude in *The Gift* and *Pale Fire*

Nabokov may have rejected attributions of the influence of other writers on him, yet he also paid generous homage to the way writers of genius animate their traditions and extend the possibilities of literary art. I had written (but not published) much of a book on Shakespeare in the early 1990s, and in the late 1990s wrote a book on *Pale Fire*, a novel whose title comes from two Shakespeare plays at once. When invited by the Institute of Russian Literature (Pushkinskiy Dom) to speak in St Petersburg in April 1999 at their conference celebrating the centenary of Nabokov's birth and the bicentenary of Pushkin's, I chose to speak on Nabokov's sense of the life-giving and almost eerie reverberations of Shakespeare within English and Pushkin with Russian literature.

I did not originally note in this essay but think it worth adding here, in light of the relation between parent and child that Nabokov mingles with the influence of Pushkin and Shakespeare in *The Gift* and *Pale Fire*—so as to link the personal and the impersonal or the familial and the social handing-on of tradition—that Nabokov prompted his son to write his Harvard B.A. honors thesis on Pushkin and Shakespeare, a prompt for which Dmitri always remained grateful.

Shakespeare strews his plays with portents; Pushkin probes his life for fatidic dates; but no writer can have been more fascinated by patterns in time than Nabokov. How appropriate, then, that he should share a birth year with Pushkin, '99, and a birthday that, only after he left Russia, aligned with Shakespeare's, April 23, as if to mark the unique role that Pushkin would play in his Russian works and Shakespeare in his English.

Shakespeare and Pushkin are special for Nabokov in terms of quality—he calls Pushkin "the greatest poet of his time (and perhaps of all time, excepting Shakespeare)" (*NG* 29)—and in terms of influence: as he said in an interview,

"Pushkin's blood runs through the veins of modern Russian literature as inevitably as Shakespeare's through those of English literature" (*SO* 63). Indeed, his sense of the unique creative legacy Pushkin leaves in Russian literature and Shakespeare leaves in English results in a series of extraordinary parallels running through what many think are his two greatest novels in his two main languages: *Dar* (*The Gift*) and *Pale Fire*.

Although Nabokov often invents failed or twisted artists or near-artists, Luzhin, Hermann, Humbert, Van Veen, on two occasions he invents as a central character an artist who is *not* a failure or a freak, Fyodor Godunov-Cherdynstev and John Shade, and has each of them draw his own artistic self-portrait, write his own artistic autobiography, within the work we are reading. Both artist-heroes are almost exactly Nabokov's age, Fyodor a year younger, Shade a year older; Fyodor is an émigré writer when Nabokov is one, Shade an American literature professor when Nabokov had just been one. In both cases, this artist-hero tries to comes to terms with the loss of someone he has loved—a parent or a child—and to discern the design in a life that he finds astonishingly rewarding despite all that he has lost.

Both novels mingle poetry and prose to an unusual degree, *Dar* through the gliding into and out of the verse that Fyodor often composes in the midst of a scene, *Pale Fire* through the breach and bond between poem and line-by-line commentary. Both contain a radically detached inset work, Fyodor's *Life of Chernyshevsky*, a trial run before he handles the role fate plays in his *own* life, and Shade's "Pale Fire," his verse autobiography, a foil to Kinbote's commentary. Both of these insets have a ricorso structure, circling around on itself: the concluding sestet of the sonnet that begins the *Life of Chernyshevsky*, the opening octet that ends it; the unended couplet that closes or at least breaks off "Pale Fire" at line 999 and invites us to complete the couplet, and fill in the apparently intended line 1,000 by returning to line 1.

Both novels juxtapose a closely observed real world (an émigré's alien capital, a stay-at-home American academic's cozy campus town) and an imagined, romantic elsewhere (Central Asia, Zembla) that has persistent overtones of the beyond. In both novels, an unbalanced figure who has also suffered devastating loss urges upon the central artist figure a subject for his work that is absurd from the artist's point of view—and yet ends up as part of the whole work. In *The Gift* Alexandra Yakovlevna Chernyshevsky all but commissions Fyodor to record the story of her son's death in an uncompleted suicide pact while her increasingly deranged husband prompts him to undertake a life of Nikolay Chernyshevsky. Both proposals Fyodor can only reject, yet he nevertheless ends up writing both, the second in his inset *Life of Chernyshevsky*, the first in *The Gift* itself. In *Pale Fire*, Kinbote urgently and insistently implores Shade to immortalize in verse the story of Charles the Beloved's escape from Zembla, which again Shade cannot but which becomes part of the first edition of "Pale Fire."

Each of the novels also engages with an entire literary tradition: *Dar*, with the whole of modern Russian literature, from Pushkin to Fyodor's émigré present; *Pale Fire*, with literature in English, from Shakespeare through Pope and Swift to Frost and T. S. Eliot. And in each case, one individual talent stands out within that tradition: Pushkin in *Dar* and Shakespeare in *Pale Fire*.

In both cases, although in different ways, the source of the artist's work becomes problematic—more deeply so, the more we reread. Why does Fyodor write what he does? Why does he feel that "divine stab" prompting him to record his father's life and travels? Why does someone of his esthetic inclinations experience such an irresistible impulse—after his initial bemused distaste—to write a *Life of Chernyshevsky*? Why does he suddenly feel a powerful urge to preserve the story of Yasha Chernyshevsky and his parents and then conclude, "There was a way—the only way" (*Gift* 349), in a manner that somehow seems to help release *The Gift* itself? In *Pale Fire*, the problem of identifying immediate and ultimate sources is rather different. Where does the title of the poem "Pale Fire" come from? Kinbote, of course, has no clue. But is there anything to his apparently absurd claim to being the "only begetter" of Shade's "Pale Fire" (*PF* 17), to his sense that his pressing on Shade the claims of the Zembla story "acted as a catalytic agent upon the very process of the sustained creative effervescence that enabled Shade to produce a 1000-line poem in three weeks" (*PF* 81)? And once we have enjoyed the comedy of the discords between Shade's Appalachian poem and Kinbote's Zemblan commentary, why do we keep detecting more and more concords between part and part, as if one owes something to the other?

In the lives of both invented writers we can discern a similar pattern, although the details and the rhythm could not be more different: a fate superficially seems to mock and frustrate but discloses a deep underlying generosity. In Fyodor's case the frustrations begin when he cannot accompany his father on his next expedition into Central Asia and are compounded when he and family flee Petrograd and the October Revolution and when his father fails to return from his last expedition. They continue through the novel as exile settles into a round of petty tedium and dislocation, and Fyodor has to abandon the projected life of his father that seemed to offer an imaginative consolation for his losses. Offsetting these frustrations are two great compensations, the flowering of his literary gift and the gift of his love for Zina. Yet even his love is frustrated in the final sweep of the novel, which moves not to the consummation that Fyodor anticipates with such longing, but to their both being locked out of their apartment penniless, as he had been locked out of new lodgings alone on the first night of the novel.

In Shade's case the frustrations are fewer but more absolute: the lifelong frustration of his search for something beyond death; the birth of a daughter whose life is made such a misery by her physical unattractiveness that she commits suicide; a heart attack that at last seems to offer him a vision of a beyond but then appears only to turn into a cosmic joke, when the fountain that he glimpsed seems confirmed by another woman's near-death experience until he finds her "fountain" was a misprint for "mountain"; his senseless murder, just before he can put the last line to his poetic testament; and even after that, the theft and appropriation of his poem by the megalomaniac next door, who imposes his own irrelevant designs on the greatest achievement of Shade's life.

In both novels we are invited to recognize the ultimate kindliness of the fate in which the writer within the story trusts, despite all his disappointments. We are even invited to discover eventually that the person whose death obsesses the writer plays some part from beyond death in the protective pattern of his fate.

Fyodor finds the generosity of fate in his own life in exactly what had seemed his most acute frustrations. His being locked out of his lodgings on the first night of the novel triggers off a new poem; the very move to these cramped quarters seems in retrospect a first attempt by fate to bring Zina and him together; when his landlady asks him to move again, it brings to an end his work on the life of his father—although this had in any case been headed for an impasse—but the shift to a new room also introduces him to Zina, his future fiancée, already living in this apartment; and even the frustration of the last night of the novel, implied beyond the final paragraph, turns out in the long run to be the perfect place to end his account of his own life: *this* time being locked out supplies him not just with a poem but with a whole book.

We can recognize all this shortly after reaching the last page of the novel, but as we reread we can see still deeper. Fyodor repeatedly tries to *see* and *be* his father, to imagine traveling on his expeditions into Central Asia; he records his father's sense of the innate strangeness of human life (*Gift* 131) and again and again associates him with patterns of rainbow and shade and paradise that he highlights at turning points in his own life. The last of these turning points comes on the eve of the book's last day, in a dream in which his disconcertingly vivid image of his father seems to give a clue to his death, to give Fyodor approval for what he has written about him, and to lead to his full recognition, the next day, of the generous role of fate in his life, which gives him the key idea for *The Gift* (*VNRY* 470–77). And now the biography of his father, which could never have stood alone, will find a perfect part in his own life's story. As we reread, we can see that the patterns in the novel do not merely imply a generalized, somewhat playful fate but record Fyodor's own sense that his father's spirit has guided him toward Zina and the achievements of his art.

In *Pale Fire*, as I explain elsewhere (*NPFMAD*), Nabokov similarly allows us to see that Shade himself has been helped by his daughter Hazel after *her* death. When a suicidal and crazily egocentric Russian named Botkin moves into the house next door to her father's, she helps stabilize his fancies into the imagined refuge of Zembla and the image of himself as Kinbote, disguised former king of Zembla. He feels so elated by this vision that he presses it on John Shade as the subject of a long poem he must write. Shade, of course, cannot write such a saga, but Hazel appears to have designed Zembla to satisfy not only Kinbote's needs and her own but also her father's. Details that Kinbote passes on, especially the escape through the tunnel, trigger Shade to write an autobiographical poem about his attempt to explore the passage to death. Some Zemblan scenes even precipitate specific images, such as the waxwing of the poem's opening line. When Shade dies, he joins his daughter beyond death and from there adds a new element to Kinbote's Zemblan fantasies, the Gradus story, developed from the Jack Grey who has killed Shade. In prompting Kinbote to imagine Gradus, Shade provides a close structural counterpoint between the composition of the poem and the approach of the poet's killer that offers Kinbote's commentary a shape and tension it would otherwise lack.

But beyond the roles of the familiar dead in the lives of the living—a pattern that can be seen more overtly in other Nabokov fiction, such as "The Vane Sisters" and *Transparent Things*—stands a more remote source of creative energy, still personal, not yet ultimate. In *Dar* that source is identified with Pushkin. Fyodor's father "took little interest in poetry, making an exception only for Pushkin: he knew him as some people know the liturgy, and liked to declaim him while out walking" (160). When he dismisses the modern poetry Fyodor once devoured, Count Godunov's "mistake was not that he ran down all 'modern poetry' indiscriminately, but that he refused to detect in it the long, life-giving ray of his favorite poet" (161). On the last day of his mother's visit, Fyodor reads some Pushkin prose—the *Journey to Arzrum*—"when suddenly he felt a sweet, strong stab from somewhere. Still not understanding, he put the book aside" (107). After his mother's departure, he feels "vaguely tormented by the thought that somehow in his talks with his mother he had left the main thing unsaid" and again picks up his one-volume Pushkin. "Again that divine stab! And how it called, how it *prompted* him. . . . Thus did he hearken to the purest sound from Pushkin's tuning fork—and he knew already what this sound required of him. Two weeks after his mother's departure he wrote her about what he had conceived" (108): the plan of writing a life of his father. He cannot start immediately, and, "continuing his training program during the whole of the spring, he fed on Pushkin, inhaled Pushkin (the reader of Pushkin has the capacity of his lungs enlarged). . . . To strengthen the muscles of his muse he took on his rambles whole pages of *Pugachyov* learned by heart as a man using an iron bar instead of a walking stick. . . . Pushkin entered his blood. With Pushkin's voice merged the voice of his father. . . . From Pushkin's prose he passed to his life, so that in the beginning the rhythm of Pushkin's era commingled with the rhythm of his father's life" (109–10).[1]

Early in this chapter, Fyodor has been traveling to work on a Berlin tram and has been filled with the usual revulsion: "He was going to a lesson, was late as usual, and as usual there grew in him a vague, evil, heavy hatred for the clumsy sluggishness of this least gifted of all methods of transport"— "least gifted" (*bezdarennyy*): a strangely loaded word in a novel called *The Gift* (*Dar*)—"for the hopelessly familiar, hopelessly ugly streets going by the wet window, and most of all for the feet, sides and necks of the native passengers" (92). He knows that his Russian contempt for Germans is "a conviction unworthy of an artist," but he cannot stop himself fixing his hatred on one archetypal German who bumps him as he makes his way to the seat in front, while Fyodor stares at him and silently ticks off all the reasons *why* he hates the Germany that this man so perfectly embodies. Then this passenger takes out a Russian émigré newspaper and coughs with a Russian intonation, and Fyodor thinks: "That's wonderful. . . . How clever, how gracefully sly, and how essentially good life is!" (94). Here in miniature is the pattern of the whole novel: initial frustrations and vexations compensated for by the playfully deceptive generosity behind life.

That this reversal offers a paradigm for *The Gift* as a whole is indicated by the word "ungifted" oddly applied to tramcars. This passage, in a chapter so saturated with Pushkin, seems to confirm Alexander Dolinin's suggestion that the very title of the novel comes from Pushkin, from his great lyric:

Dar naprasnyy, dar sluchayniy,
Zhizn', zachem ty mne dana?
Il' zachem sud'boyu taynoy
Ty na kazn' osuzhdena?

Vain gift, chance gift,
Life, why were you given to me?
Or why by some secret fate
Were you sentenced to death?[2]

Just as Fyodor fuming at the "ungifted" tramcar system is then made to realize "how clever, how gracefully sly and how essentially good life is," so Pushkin, desolately bemoaning life as a vain gift in this poem, answers himself in a poem that Fyodor soon quotes:

O, net, mne zhizn' ne nadoela
Ya zhit' hochu, ya zhit' lyublyu.
Dusha ne vovse ohladela,
Utratya molodost' svoyu.

Oh, no, life has not grown tedious to me,
I want to live, I love to live.
My soul, although its youth has vanished,
Has not become completely chill.

So far it has been genuine Pushkin, but now comes an addition that Pushkin is supposed to have added in an album and that a memoirist whom Fyodor reads has recalled:

Eshchyo sud'ba menya sogreet,
Romanom geniya upyus',
Mitskevich pust' eshchyo sozreet,
Koy chem ya sam eshchyo zaymus'—

Fate yet will comfort me; a novel
Of genius I shall yet enjoy,
I'll see yet a mature Mickiéwicz,
With something I myself may toy—[3]

Just as Fyodor finds himself fostered rather than frustrated by fate, and even finds that fate has bestowed on him the gift of a novel of genius, so Pushkin himself continues to toy with life, perhaps by, for instance, *becoming* in part the fate that helps Fyodor to *his* gift, his life neither in vain, nor chance, nor sentenced to death.

When at last Fyodor introduces Zina into the novel, by way of a poem in her honor that he composes as he waits for her, he comments: "And not only was Zina cleverly and elegantly made to measure for him by a very painstaking fate, but both of them, forming a single shadow, were made to the measure of something not quite comprehensible, but wonderful and benevolent and continuously surrounding them" (189). Fyodor turns that sense of a very painstaking and benevolent fate into the structure of *The Gift* itself and saturates the sense of life's and art's gifts with the implied presence of his father and of Pushkin behind him as the source of all that flowed from him in Russian literature, as an example of creative perfection, as a font of personal inspiration, flowing all the way from the "Pushkin Avenue" of the first apartment, through which fate hoped to bring Fyodor and Zina together and in which Fyodor writes his Pushkinesque Journey to Asia, to the "Gogol Street" of the second apartment, in which Zina actually lives and into which they are about to enter together when the story breaks off with a final *Eugene Onegin* stanza.[4]

As John Shade nears the end of his poem, he announces as if offhandedly: "*this* transparent thingum does require / Some moondrop title. Help me, Will! *Pale Fire*." Kinbote glosses: "Paraphrased, this evidently means: Let me look in Shakespeare for something I might use for a title. And the find is 'pale fire.' But in which of the Bard's works did our poet cull it? My readers must make their own research. All I have with me is a tiny vest pocket edition of *Timon of Athens*—in Zemblan! It certainly contains nothing that could be regarded as an equivalent of 'pale fire' (if it had, my luck would have been a statistical monster)." If Kinbote does not know or bother to find out, Nabokov's alert readers have already been given many clues, pointing in the same direction as this one: the phrase indeed comes from *Timon of Athens*, from the disenchanted Timon's hysterical denunciation of the cosmos as a chain of theft:

> I'll example you with thievery:
> The sun's a thief, and with his great attraction
> Robs the vast sea; the moon's an arrant thief,
> And her pale fire she snatches from the sun;
> The sea's a thief, whose liquid surge resolves
> The moon into salt tears.

(4.3.438–43)

A few lines later in his poem, Shade, who has tried all his life to probe the riddle of death and who has centered his poem on the death of his daughter Hazel, writes:

> I'm reasonably sure that we survive
> And that my darling somewhere is alive,
> As I am reasonably sure that I

> 980   Shall wake at six tomorrow, on July
> The twenty-second, nineteen fifty-nine,
> And that the day will probably be fine.

But instead he is killed that very evening by a madman, killed before he can write the thousandth line he had probably planned for his poem. Like Fyodor he has trusted in the ultimate benevolence of things, despite the losses we mortals must endure, but his trust seems to be shattered and even mocked as if by some malevolent fate.

But as I have already intimated, as we reread we can discover the evidence for both Hazel's and then her father's survival after death—evidence I do not have time even to summarize here, although Nabokov prepares it with all his usual exactness (see *NPFMAD*, part 3). Hazel dies in 1957, and a year later, apparently under her influence, although not knowing the source of his inspiration, her father writes a poem, "The Nature of Electricity," that suggests playfully how the dead may light up the lives of the living:

> The dead, the gentle dead—who knows?—
> In tungsten filaments abide,
> And on my bedside table glows
> Another man's departed bride.

> And maybe Shakespeare floods a whole
> Town with innumerable lights, . . .

After Botkin arrives as her father's neighbor in early 1959, Hazel sees in him a kindred spirit, a desperate man on the brink of suicide. Recognizing his troubles, she offers him a consolation in the visions of Zembla that she develops in his mind, a fantasy in which he is a deposed king who escapes from his former castle, carrying with him a tiny volume of *Timon of Athens*, and emerges near the Royal Onhava Theater, then into Timon Alley and Coriolanus Lane, a fantasy, in other words, where Shakespeare pervades, as he does already in New Wye, where a landscaper of genius has planted an avenue of all the trees mentioned by Shakespeare (a wonderful echo, in this context, of the "Pushkin Avenue" in *The Gift*). Hazel devises the Zemblan fantasy to soothe Kinbote's disturbed mind, to express her own new radiant confidence, and to stimulate her father to write a verse autobiography that will commemorate his lifelong attempt to see past the mirror world of death.

Curiously, even Shade's dead parents seem to join with his dead daughter in influencing the poet. I do not have room to explain, but part of the evidence is a famous passage in *Hamlet*—one Nabokov translated into Russian—where the Ghost of King Hamlet declares to his son, "The glow-worm shows the matin to be near, And 'gins to pale his ineffectual fire." Alongside Shade's dead parents Hazel seems to stand, and alongside her, after *his* death, stands Shade himself, adding his own contributions to Kinbote's commentary. And behind them seems to stand the Shakespeare who pervades this whole world.

Let me quote from one of my earliers books, *Nabokov's* Pale Fire:

> From start to finish of *Pale Fire* Shakespeare recurs as an image of stupendous fecundity, someone from whom we continually borrow and through whom we can continually pass on our experience of the unending bounty of things, as Shade's parents and his daughter pass on the *Timon* in the tunnel to Kinbote and then to Shade himself. In this novel of worlds within worlds, this "system of cells interlinked within / Cells interlinked within cells interlinked / Within one stem," death borrows endlessly from life and life from death, one level of creativity takes from another and endlessly gives. "I'll example you with thievery," Timon says, . . . but Nabokov steals from this speech to express not Timon's contempt for universal thievery but his own vision of an unfathomable creative generosity behind our origins and ends.
>
> (NPFMAD 245–46)

In both *The Gift* and *Pale Fire*, Nabokov creates artists who despite their frustrations and losses sense the ultimate bountifulness of things. As readers we are eventually allowed to see, even more clearly than the writers themselves, how they have been influenced by the spirits of their beloved dead, and, beyond them, by the colossal creative energies radiating out from a Pushkin or a Shakespeare, and, beyond them, in a sense, by the Nabokov who creates Fyodor's and Shade's worlds—and who suspects the role in his own work and life of his father's spirit, of forces he can best imagine in terms of the creative radiance of a Pushkin or a Shakespeare, and of still more unfathomable sources of energy and design beyond them in nature, in the design of life itself. Readers who know Nabokov will know that one of his main examples of the playful creative design behind nature is natural mimicry. In the "Second Addendum to 'The Gift,'" Nabokov's afterthought to the work where he invokes Pushkin with the deepest metaphysical resonance, he refers again to natural mimicry and links it with Shakespeare, when he writes "of the fantastic refinement of 'protective mimicry,'" which, in a world lacking an appointed observer endowed with artistic sensitivity, imagination, and humor, would simply be useless (*lost upon the world*), like a small volume of Shakespeare lying open in the dust of a boundless desert" (*N'sBs* 219).

In an unpublished lecture Nabokov distinguishes the *toska* running through Pushkin's poetry from Oneginesque *spleen* and defines it as "a feeling of aimless longing permeating one's whole being," "an acute dissatisfaction with one's surroundings"; it "presupposes a high goal, contempt for compromise, and that irrational sense of worlds beyond worlds which is so characteristic of true mysticism."[5] Nabokov, too, can express a sense of dissatisfaction with his surroundings, but he expresses much more deeply a sense of endless gratitude for the generosity of the world that he finds in nature, in a butterfly or a bird, or in art, in Shakespeare or Pushkin. Fyodor on a bus feels exasperated that he is "wasting his youth on a boring and empty task, on the mediocre teaching of foreign languages—when he has his own language, out of which he can make anything he likes—a midge, a mammoth, a thousand different clouds. What he should really be teaching was . . . the constant feeling that our days here are only pocket money, farthings clinking in the dark, and that somewhere is stocked the real wealth, from which life should know how to get dividends in the shape of dreams, tears of happiness, distant mountains" (*Gift* 175). For Nabokov, the most accessible account, the most tangible tally, the most concrete image of that "real wealth" beyond the pocket money of the here and now is the legacy of Shakespeare or Pushkin—and perhaps, he hopes, the legacy they have helped him, too, to bequeath.

16. Nabokov as Verse Translator
Introduction to *Verses and Versions*

I was always touched by Véra Nabokov's enthusiasm for overlooked aspects of her husband's literary art. Since she was particularly eager to assemble a volume of his verse translations, I made a point of noting down every one I came across as I catalogued the Montreux archives. But she was too busy with other things, as I was, until it was too late for her to complete the task. In 2004 Dmitri Nabokov referred to me a request from Stanislav Shvabrin, then working on a Ph.D. at UCLA. Shvabrin had found at Harvard some unpublished Nabokov translations of Tyutchev and others and had asked Dmitri could he publish them. I suggested that we should combine forces, using the material I had gathered over the years with Véra in mind. Stas patiently identified and transcribed the texts Nabokov had used and transliterated them for our website for the book, http://www.nabokovversesandversions.ac.nz/. I introduced the volume, explaining the surprises of Nabokov's changing attitudes to translating Russian verse.

Translation, like politics, is an art of compromise: inevitable compromise between the resources of From-ish and those of To-ish.[1] When the unique riches of From-ish—all the accidents of its associations and accidence—have been exploited to the full by a poet of genius, the compromise must be all the greater.

"Vladimir Adamant Nabokov," as he once signed himself, was a man singularly averse to compromise. Artists usually are: within the work, as nowhere else in life, they can choose their own conditions. Nabokov notoriously eschewed compromise by translating the unquestioned masterpiece of Russian verse, Aleksandr Pushkin's *Eugene Onegin*, into an English version that allows readers to understand the exact sense of Pushkin's lines, especially through notes eight times as long as the poem, but renounces any attempt to provide an equivalent of Pushkin's poetry, his perfect placement of words, his seemingly effortless mastery of rhythm and rhyme. Rather than trying to replicate Pushkin's landscape in another medium, another place, Nabokov provides detailed signposts to Pushkin's precise terrain.

But before 1951, when he arrived at this austerely unpoetic method of translating *Eugene Onegin*, Nabokov had been a brilliant translator of verse into verse, always with a strong loyalty to accuracy of sense but accepting in this one instance the compromises that must be made to find some match for the verse of From in the linguistic resources and verse conventions of To. He translated from French and English—and even German, of which he knew little—into Russian, from Russian and French into English, and from Russian into French.

Fluently trilingual by the age of seven, he translated at twelve Mayne Reid's Wild West novel, *The Headless Horseman*, into French alexandrines. That translation does not survive, but much of his prolific early verse and verse translation does, although neither Nabokov himself nor his son Dmitri has judged this juvenilia worth publishing. In his last years Nabokov was ruthless in selecting his early verse for his collection *Stikhi* (Poems), published two years after his death. His first nine years as a poet are represented there by only slightly more poems than the single year of 1923, his last year as predominantly a poet, his first year of real poetic maturity. That year, therefore, provides the starting point for this collection of Nabokov's verse translations.

There is another reason for choosing 1923. That was the year Nabokov met Véra Slonim, whom he married two years later. Fluent in Nabokov's three languages, and also in German, an avid reader of his verse before they met, and already herself translating and publishing in *Rul'*, the Russian émigré newspaper where Nabokov had published most of his early work, Véra remained particularly attached sixty years later to the notion of assembling a volume of her husband's verse translations and would have edited it herself in her eighties had she had the strength and time.

Nabokov, too, had often thought of collecting his verse translations, even after he had insisted so firmly in *Eugene Onegin* on the need for unyielding literality. In November 1958 the young Jason Epstein, who had eagerly published *Pnin* and *Nabokov's Dozen* for Doubleday, flew from New York to Ithaca to secure Nabokov for the firm he had just joined, Random House, and proposed publishing three books: *Eugene Onegin*; an anthology of Russian poetry, including the masterpiece of Russian medieval poetry, the *Song of Igor's Campaign*, and "some Pushkin, some Lermontov, Tyutchev, possibly Blok & Hodasevich"; and Nabokov's greatest Russian novel, *The Gift*.[2] Nabokov signed an agreement for an "Anthology of Russian Verse in translation,"[3] which he expected to include, apart from the Igor epic, "three short dramas by Pushkin and poems from Lomonosov (XVIII century), through Zhukovski, Batyushkov, Tyutchev, Pushkin, Lermontov, Fet, to Blok."[4]

But after spending a productive spring in Arizona, Nabokov realized by June 1959 that *The Song of Igor's Campaign* had become "a book in itself which cannot be combined with the kind of second half we had planned. That second half . . . would throw the book completely out of balance because it would necessarily lack the copious notes the first half has." Since the second half was "supposed to cover the entire century of Russia's renaissance in poetry, the commentary should have taken at least twice as many pages as that on *The Song*."[5] Nabokov realized he did not have the time, and Random House happily published *The Song of Igor's Campaign* on its own.

In the wake of *Lolita*'s triumph, Nabokov was kept busy both writing new novels and translating or supervising translations of his old Russian work. In 1968, dissatisfied with Putnam, the publisher of *Lolita*, he was ready to move to McGraw-Hill, which offered a large advance for a multibook contract that included *Ada*. Late in the year he proposed delivering a translation of his first novel, *Mary*, and "An Anthology of Russian Poets" by mid-January 1970.[6] Other books, however, replaced that proposed anthology, and when a second multibook contract was being negotiated with McGraw-Hill late in 1973, Nabokov proposed delivering an "Anthology of Russian Poetry in English" in 1978. By 1975 he had become too weak to advance the project, and by 1977 he was dead. When Véra recovered from the shock of his death, she wanted to compile the volume herself but did not know where to locate all she had in mind or how to find the time.

Verses and Versions contains the anthology of Russian poets Nabokov proposed to McGraw-Hill and more. It also includes some of Nabokov's discussions of translation (others are readily available in *Eugene Onegin* and *Strong Opinions*); the entire texts, both notes and translations, from his first anthologies of Russian verse (*Three Russian Poets* [1944], expanded in the British edition of 1947 into *Pushkin, Lermontov, Tyutchev*); and selections of notes and verses from the *Eugene Onegin* commentary, talks to fellow Russian émigrés, his still-unpublished Cornell lectures on Russian verse, and his translations of verse by Mandelshtam and Okudzhava, which are more recent than the translations he originally intended to include. Still left in the archives are Nabokov's Russian translations, early and late, from English, French, and German (Shakespeare, Baudelaire, Goethe, and others) and his translations from Russian (Pushkin, Tyutchev) into French.

This volume therefore serves three linked purposes: as a treasury of Russian verse, as a workshop in translation, and as another showcase in the library of Nabokov's literary diversity. First, it is an introduction to the classics of Russian lyric verse—an anthology of texts, translations, and pointed pen portraits of poets—by the person who has already done more than anyone else to introduce to the Anglophone world the narrative masterpieces of medieval and modern Russian verse, *The Song of Igor's Campaign* and *Eugene Onegin*. Russia's prose and drama have been readily enjoyed and admired outside her borders, but it has taken the greatest writer working in both Russian and English to convince the English-speaking world through his translation and commentary that Pushkin is, as all Russians know, central to the Russian literary pantheon. As Korney Chukvosky writes, thanks to Nabokov's *Eugene Onegin*, "Pushkin, whose genius has until recently been concealed from a 'proud foreign gaze,' has at last become for readers abroad an established classic."[7]

In *Verses and Versions* we can see other sides of Pushkin: his incomparable love lyrics, his verse dramas, his pungent epigrams, and his range of emotions, forms, and themes. As translator and commentator, Nabokov places Pushkin in time and space, introducing first the origins of the Russian iamb in Lomonosov, then Pushkin's great predecessor Derzhavin, then Pushkin himself amid his contemporaries, and the successors he inspired even as they established new directions over the century that followed his early death.

To offer the reader maximum access to poems in another language and script, Nabokov first intended his *Eugene Onegin* translation to be published interlinearly, with each line of the translation beneath its transliterated and stress-marked Russian counterpart. He abandoned the idea when he correctly foresaw that the sheer bulk of his text—it turned out to be four printed volumes—would make publication difficult enough even without the extra expense of such an expanse of transliteration. But within the 1,200 pages of his commentary, Nabokov always transliterates and stress marks any Russian verse. And in 1966, for the last Russian verse translation he attempted (and failed) to publish, by the youngish Soviet poet Bulat Okudzhava, he carefully prepared a transliterated and stressed Russian text.

I had intended to follow Nabokov's practice in *Eugene Onegin*, but he himself found that for the sake of readers who know some Russian, from students to native speakers, the publisher of *Poems and Problems* required the originals of his own Russian poems that he translated for the volume to be printed in Cyrillic. For the same reason, we also present the originals of all Russian texts in Cyrillic. For those without Russian but an interest in the placement of the original words and sounds, the *Verses and Versions* website contains transliterated and stress-marked texts of all the Russian poems here. Written Russian does not normally indicate stress, but stressed syllables are marked on the transliteration since even for intermediate students of Russian syllabic stress can often be difficult. Readers with little or no Russian can therefore engage with the originals, in print and on screen, with a reliable sense of the music and magic of their sound.

Had Nabokov lived to complete the anthology of Russian poetry, he would no doubt have affixed to each poet an introductory sketch as pithy and witty as those he wrote on Pushkin, Lermontov, and Tyutchev for *Three Russian Poets* in his first years in America. Those introductions are printed in *Verses and Versions*, along with other astute commentaries, sometimes directed at fellow Russians for whom nothing needs to be explained, sometimes at Anglo-American readers or students of whom nothing can be assumed, sometimes to Anglo-American or Russian scholars.

The selection of poems is also more accidental than it would have been had it been entirely Nabokov's own. Nevertheless, it includes the range of poets he intended for his Russian anthology, like Pushkin, Lermontov, Tyutchev, Fet, and Hodasevich, whom he had already published, and other literary peaks. Nabokov translated poetry over many years, for many reasons and many different audiences: to introduce a new enthusiasm to a wider audience; as a personal tribute or an exercise in the possibilities of translation because he thought the model a masterpiece and a challenge (Shakespeare, Goethe, Baudelaire, Rimbaud); to have work to sell to periodical and book publishers in the early 1940s, when he still had no widespread American reputation and, despite his command of English, found it painful to write fiction other than in Russian; to introduce Russian literature to a wider audience; to teach Russian literature, from 1947 to 1958; to establish his scholarly credentials during his academic years, in his copiously annotated and exact *Eugene Onegin* and *The Song of Igor's Campaign*; and as part of a polemic critique of other translators in the 1950s and 1960s (Pushkin, Mandelstam, Okudzhava).

Verses and Versions is not, therefore, Nabokov's selection of the top third or so of the three hundred perfect poems he believed had been written in Russian. He had selected more than thirty of those in the poems from Pushkin to Hodasevich that he translated in 1940s. About as many again in *Verses and Versions* might also sit in his top tier. Others are included simply because he translated them, especially as part of his vast *Eugene Onegin* apparatus.

Pushkin's predecessors and contemporaries, and fragments of Pushkin's own minor poetry that merely happen to have some strong association with this or that part of *Eugene Onegin*, are all slightly overrepresented yet allow invaluable views of the context, life, and personality of Russia's greatest poet. And throughout the selection of the Pushkin poems we can see Nabokov's particular interest—evident also in his still-unpublished lectures on Russian poetry—in Pushkin's poems about art and the artist, about freedom, and about the freedom of art and artist.

Not included are poems by four older Russian contemporaries Nabokov preferred not to translate but to parody, as he parodied T. S. Eliot in *Lolita*, *Pale Fire*, and *Ada*: Vladimir Mayakovsky, whom he thought "fatally corrupted by the regime he faithfully served"; Boris Pasternak, whose early poetry he respected but thought marred by clumsy lapses; Marina Tsvetaeva, whom he considered a flawed genius and compromised in her relationship to Stalin's Soviet Union;[8] and Anna Akhmatova, whom he rated, along with Ezra Pound, as "definitely B-grade," and parodies in *Pnin*.

Second, *Verses and Versions* is a master class in the possibilities and problems of literary translation. Nabokov became not only one of the most renowned writers of the twentieth century but also the most celebrated translator—even though he ended up *not* translating *Ulysses* into Russian or *Anna Karenina* into English, as he had at various times intended. His *Eugene Onegin* provoked "what can be called the great debate on translation norms of the 1960s,"[9] which embroiled Edmund Wilson, Robert Lowell, George Steiner, and Anthony Burgess and caused more uproar than anything on the subject since the famous polemics of Matthew Arnold and Francis Newman on translating the *Iliad* a hundred years earlier. Nabokov's extreme position on translating *Eugene Onegin* with unflinching literalism still polarizes. The Pushkinist Alexander Dolinin writes that "everyone who has tried to teach *Eugene Onegin* in rhymed translations knows all too well that they make it a futile enterprise to convince even the most gullible students that Pushkin, to quote Edmund Wilson, 'is the only modern poet in the class of Shakespeare and Dante.'"[10] But Douglas Hofstadter, writing two years later in his *Le Ton beau de Marot: In Praise of the Music of Language*, saw the eschewal of rhyme in translating rhymed verse as a betrayal, and he demonizes "the rabid Nabokov," "the devil," "the implacably Nazistic Nabokov," for his "unrelenting verbal sadism" and "hardball savaging" that "goes way beyond bad taste."[11] Nabokov in reply might have quoted his "Problems of Translation: *Onegin* in English": "To translate an *Onegin* stanza does not mean to rig up fourteen lines with alternate beats and affix to them seven jingle rhymes starting with pleasure-love-leisure-dove. Granted that rhymes can be found, they should be raised to the level of *Onegin*'s harmonies"—but no ukulele can ever replicate a Stradivarius.

Although he developed an uncompromising literalism in teaching American students of Russian literature at Cornell and Harvard, in order to allow them to appreciate great originals directly, not via pseudosurrogates, Nabokov *had* been a superb translator of verse into verse, from four and into three languages. At Cornell he began translating *Onegin* in rhyme (no text survives) before deciding at the beginning of the 1950s that this was "sinful" and hopelessly misleading. Yet even in the *Eugene Onegin* commentary, he offers rhymed translations of short poems by Lomonosov, Karamzin, Zhukovski, Batyushkov, and Pushkin. As late as 1959 and 1962, after completing his unversified *Onegin*, he entered *Sunday Times* poetry competitions, translating formally intricate French verse into formally intricate English verse (he also signed the later submission "Sybil Shade": in *Pale Fire*, published that year, Sybil, the wife of the poet John Shade, translates English verse into French). Nabokov's early verse translations attain rare heights of fidelity. In a comparative and strictly quantitative study of nineteen translations of *Eugene Onegin*, Ljuba Tarvi assesses Nabokov's verbal accuracy at between 98 and 100 percent, well ahead of the competition, but even in her sole example of his other translations from Russian (Tyutchev's "Silentium") she assigns him an unmatched combined score for combined verbal and formal equivalence of 97 percent.

But *Verses and Versions* does not pretend to be a collection of perfect or near-perfect translations. Some of Nabokov's translations come close: some of the poems of Pushkin, Lermontov, Tyutchev, Fet, and perhaps especially Hodasevich, which he translated for publication in the 1940s, before the needs of teaching students drove him to total fidelity to sense even at the cost of style. His others translations work as ideal cribs for accessing the originals. But the tribulations of translation, even for a writer with such a command of prose and verse style and history in three languages, are as fascinating as the triumphs. Nabokov's successive tries at translating a particular poem, with and without rhyme, show the sheer magnitude of the task, the impossibility of perfection, the possibility only of offering improved access to the original but not of creating its image and equal.

Nabokov painstakingly worked and reworked his fiction to a state of serene finality. His translations were different. As he writes in an unpublished note, "translations fade much more rapidly than the originals, and every time I re-read my versions I tend to touch them up here and there."[12] So *Verses and Versions* is not only an anthology of two centuries of Russian poetry but also a sampler of the problems and possibilities of literary translation, as demonstrated by someone who wrote and translated in three languages for over sixty years. The prose essays and talks that begin the volume articulate Nabokov's theory of translation, first in the 1940s, before he developed his provocative literalism, then in the 1950s, when he first began to formulate his new principles. Because the poems are arranged chronologically not by the date of Nabokov's translations but according to the poet's date of birth and the poem's dates of composition, readers will find themselves moving from a poem translated into melodious verse, in Nabokov's own early manner, to another in his later exact but unpoetic manner, or vice versa. Sometimes the translation shifts to another version of the same poem, the gains and the losses of each method bright on the page. Readers should therefore take note of the date of Nabokov's translation: anything after 1950 is likely to display the unrhymed literalism of his later style.

Having concluded that it was impossible to translate poetry *as* poetry with total fidelity to both sense and verse form, Nabokov at the end of the 1960s decided to show the exception that proved the rule by composing a short poem simultaneously in English and Russian with the same complex stanza structure: a poem about the very act of walking simultaneously on these two separate linguistic tightropes, each swinging to its own time. Even he found he could write only stiltedly under these disconcerting conditions, and he wisely abandoned the effort.

Much more successful was his earlier attempt to create in English two stanzas in the strict form that Pushkin created for *Eugene Onegin*, in a poem about his translating *Onegin*. Pushkin's fourteen-line *Onegin* stanza ingeniously reworks the pattern of the sonnet so that, as Nabokov notes, "its first twelve lines include the greatest variation in rhyme sequence possible within a three-quatrain frame: alternate, paired, and closed."[13] The stanza offers an internal variety of pace, direction, and duration that forms part of the poem's magic for Russian readers. To show non-Russian readers the variability of this variety, Nabokov composes two stanzas in English that, like Pushkin's, modulate tone, pace, subject, imagery, and rhyme quality within the stanza and from stanza to stanza, so that the stanzas are both self-contained and internally changeable and, in the movement from one to another, both continuous and contrasting. The first quatrain of stanza 1 stops and starts, with question and answer after abrupt dismissive imagistic answer; the first quatrain of stanza 2 skims on unstopped, like a camera zooming through a fast-forward nightscape. Nabokov knows he cannot combine Pushkin's sense and pattern while exactly transposing Pushkin's precise thought into the different structures and associations of English, but at least he can impart to Anglophone readers a sense of the coruscating enchantment of Pushkin's stanza form.

On Translating "Eugene Onegin"

1

What is translation? On a platter
A poet's pale and glaring head,
A parrot's screech, a monkey's chatter,
And profanation of the dead.
The parasites you were so hard on
Are pardoned if I have your pardon,
O, Pushkin, for my stratagem:
I traveled down your secret stem,
And reached the root, and fed upon it;
Then, in a language newly learned,
I grew another stalk and turned
Your stanza patterned on a sonnet,
Into my honest roadside prose—
All thorn, but cousin to your rose.

2

Reflected words can only shiver
Like elongated lights that twist
In the black mirror of a river
Between the city and the mist.
Elusive Pushkin! Persevering,
I still pick up Tatiana's earring,
Still travel with your sullen rake.
I find another man's mistake,

I analyze alliterations
That grace your feasts and haunt the great
Fourth stanza of your Canto Eight.
This is my task—a poet's patience
And scholiastic passion blent:
Dove-droppings on your monument.

(*PP* 175)

Third, *Verses and Versions* offers another facet of one of the greatest and most multifaceted writers of the twentieth century—not only a major author in two languages and in fiction, nonfiction, poetry, and drama but also, as readers have come to realize, a world-class scientist, a groundbreaking scholar, and a translator.

Nabokov once said that he called the first version of his autobiography *Conclusive Evidence* because of the two *V*s at the center, linking Vladimir the author and Véra the anchor and addressee, as she proves to be by the end of the book. *Verses and Versions* similarly links Vladimir and Véra, who wanted to assemble a book like this as a monument to her husband's multifacetedness. It also pays homage to *Poems and Problems*, which, late in his career, introduced readers to Nabokov's Russian verse as well as his English and to still another facet of his creativity, his world-class chess-problem compositions.

Pushkin has a special place in the hearts of all Russians who love literature. He has a particularly special place for Nabokov in his Russian work (Pushkin is the tutelary deity of his last and greatest Russian novel, *The Gift*, which even ends with an echo of the ending of *Eugene Onegin*, in a perfect Onegin stanza, cast in prose) and in his efforts as an English writer to make Pushkin known. Pushkin is also a byword for the untranslatability of poetic greatness: unquestioned in his preeminence in his native land yet long almost unrecognized within any other. Flaubert, one of the brightest stars in Nabokov's private literary pléiade, famously remarked to his friend Turgenev: "He is flat, your poet."

Nabokov himself discusses the untranslatability of one of Pushkin's great love lyrics in the first of his essays on translation. I would like here to consider *another* great love lyric, "Ya vas lyubil" ("I loved you"), which Nabokov translated three times, in three different ways: in an awkward verse translation of 1929 and in a literal translation and a lexical (word for word) translation, accompanied by a stress-marked transliteration and a note, about twenty years later. None of these quite works (the lexical is not even meant to work, merely to supply the crudest crib); none of these can quite convince the English-language reader that this is one of the great love lyrics—one of the great lyrics of any kind—in any language.

Yet Nabokov is not alone. For the bicentennial of Pushkin's birth—and coincidentally the centennial of Nabokov's—Marita Crawley, a great-great-great-granddaughter of Pushkin and chairman of the British Pushkin Bicentennial Trust, asked herself how she could convince the English-speaking public that Pushkin's genius is as great as Russians claim. She answered herself: she would invite a number of leading poets to "translate" Pushkin poems, or rather to make poems out of Pushkin translations. In a volume for the Folio Society, she includes poets of the stature of Ted Hughes, Seamus Heaney, and Carol Ann Duffy. Duffy took "Ya vas lyubil":

> I loved you once. If love is fire, then embers
> smoulder in the ashes of this heart.
> Don't be afraid. Don't worry. Don't remember.
> I do not want you sad now we're apart.
>
> I loved you without language, without hope,
> now mad with jealousy, now insecure.
> I loved you once so purely, so completely,
> I know who loves you next can't love you more.

Duffy is a fine poet, but I suspect few will think this one of literature's great lyrics—not that she is not as successful as other poets in *After Pushkin*.[14] What is it that makes Pushkin's poem great?

I offer a plain translation into lineated prose:

> I loved you; love still, perhaps,
> In my heart has not quite gone out;
> But let it trouble you no more;
> I do not want to sadden you in any way.
>
> I loved you wordlessly, hopelessly,
> Now by timidity, now by jealousy oppressed;
> I loved you so sincerely, so tenderly,
> As God grant you may be loved by someone else.

My translation, if undistinguished, is acceptable, though I almost sinned by ending, "As God grant you may be loved again." In Pushkin the last word is "*drugím*" and means "by another" (in context, "by another man"): "As God grant you may be loved by another." I should not have thought of closing with "again" and would not have done so had I not been intending to supply a literal translation and a lexical one. On its own, "again" might be ambiguous, might suggest the speaker has perhaps ended up anticipating a complete revival of his own feelings. What is needed is a short, strong, decisive ending, and "again" at first seemed to supply some of this, though without the shift and precision of thought and feeling in Pushkin's "*drugím*," where "As God grant you may be loved by another" ended too intolerably limply for me to tack it to the rest of the translation.

The poem starts with what might seem banal, "Ya vas lyubíl," except that it is in the past, and that gives it its special angle. As Pushkin treats of the near-universal experience of having fallen out of love, he gradually moves from the not unusual—the change from present love to near past, the aftershock of emotions, the shift from desire to tender interest and concern—to the unexpected closing combination, the affirmation of the past love in the penultimate line, "I loved you so sincerely, so tenderly," then to the selfless generosity of the last line, the hope that she will be loved again as well as *he* has loved her, which in its very lack of selfishness confirms the purity of the love he had and in some sense still has.

Where Duffy's "who loves you next" almost implies a line-up of lovers, Pushkin offers a surprise, yet utter emotional rightness and inevitability. Where Duffy's line becomes a near boast, emphasizing that the speaker's love is unsurpassable, Pushkin's speaker dismisses self to focus on and pray for his former love.

This is what Pushkin is like, again and again. He cuts directly to the core of a human feeling in a way that makes it new and yet recognizably right and revelatory. He creates a complex emotional contour through swift suggestion, a scenario all the more imaginatively inviting by being unconstrained by character and event. His expression seems effortless and elegant, but his attention and ours is all on the accuracy of the emotion. In this poem Pushkin allows just one shadow of one metaphor, in the verb in the second line, *ugásla*, which can mean "gone out" or "extinguished," where Duffy feels the need to embellish and poeticize the image into "If love is *fire*, then *embers / smoulder* in the *ashes* of this heart," with a pun on "heart" and "hearth." This is inventive translation, but it is not Pushkin's steady focus on feeling. Duffy's lines draw attention to the poet, to the play. In other moods Pushkin can himself be supremely playful and playfully self-conscious in his own fashion, but here he offers an emotional directness and a verbal restraint amid formal perfection that is alien to English poetry and that to Duffy feels too bald to leave unadorned.

With your attention now engaged, ready to slow down and savor this poem, I offer below Pushkin's own words, transliterated and stressed, with an italicized word-for-word match below (a "lexical translation" in Nabokov's terms) and my strictly literal translation below that.

Ya vas lyubíl: lyubóv' eshchyó, bït' mózhet,
I you loved: love   yet,   be may,
I loved you; love, perhaps, has not yet

V dushé moéy ugásla ne sovsém;
In soul my   gone-out not altogether
Quite gone out in my heart;

No pust' oná vas ból'she ne trevózhit;
But let   it [my love] you more not trouble;
But let it trouble you no more;

Ya ne hochú pechálit' vas nichém.
I not want to-sadden you in-any-way
I do not want to sadden you in any way.

Ya vas lyubíl bezmólvno, beznadézhno,
I you loved wordlessly, hopelessly.
I loved you wordlessly, hopelessly,

To róbost'yu, to révnost'yu tomím;
Now by-timidity, now by-jealousy tormented.
Now by shyness, now by jealousy oppressed;

Ya vas lyubíl tak ískrenno, tak nézhno,
I you loved so sincerely, so tenderly,
I loved you so sincerely, so tenderly,

Kak day vam Bog lyubímoy bït' drugím.
As give you God   loved to-be by-another.
As God grant you may be loved by someone else.

Nabokov's note comments perceptively on the sound-link between *"lyubí-moy"* and *"drugím"* in the last line, which makes the inevitability and the surprise both greater. *"Drugím,"* coming last, rhyming quietly and expect-edly with *"tomím"* but also happening to echo the *"lyubímoy"* it is linked so closely to sense, sets off the whole poem's explosive emotional charge in its final word, without resorting to anything conventionally "poetic." As Alexander Zholkovsky notes, moreover, a Russian might well expect a short poem beginning "Ya vas lyubíl" and leading up to a rhyme with *"tomím"* to end with the word *"lyubím,"* "(be)loved"; instead it ends with *"drugím,"* "by another," as if to compress the difference between the *"ya,"* the "I" who *used to* love you in the poem's first word and this *"drugím,"* this "other" in the poem's last word, who perhaps *will* love you so well.[15]

Nabokov first tried to translate this poem, uncharacteristically, in 1929, when he was developing as a Russian writer and almost always translat-ing into rather than from Russian. (The occasion was the centenary of the poem's composition, and since Nabokov was born a hundred years after Pushkin, he was translating it at the age at which Pushkin wrote it.) The translation opens with the eyebrow-raising "I worshipped you." Although not strictly equivalent to Pushkin, this phrase reflects the sense that the speaker has indeed worshipped the beloved "wordlessly, hopelessly," pas-sively, and distantly rather than actively and intimately, and its stress pro-vides a reasonably close match for the metrical force of Pushkin's opening "Ya vas lyubíl." But "I worshipped you" becomes increasingly a liability as the poem progresses and it has to be repeated each time "loved" or "love" would normally return. In general, the translation sacrifices too much sense to keep Pushkin's stresses and his alternating feminine/masculine rhymes. Nabokov chooses the same "ember"/"remember" rhyme that Duffy indepen-dently arrives at, but maintains the rhyme where Duffy abandons the effort halfway through. But his rhymes are trite (fashion-passion, true-you) and the whole poem too compliantly follows tired English verse conventions.

By the 1940s, Nabokov's verse translations into English were far more assured and often superb. By the 1950s he had committed himself to lit-eralism, but sometimes with uneasy compromises, if not for the sake of rhyme then for the sake of rhythm. In the case of "Ya vas lyubíl," his "lexi-cal" translation often seems closer than the literal translation not only to Pushkin's words but to his power. The line "now by shyness, now by jealousy oppressed," which I have gladly drawn on, captures the order, the sense, and, except for the tight sound patterns, the impact of Pushkin's "To róbost'yu, to révnost'yu tomím." For some reason Nabokov "improved" this into a literal version, "either by shyness irked or jealousy," supposedly better English and no less accurate, yet in fact both less accurate and more awkward. The last line of the literal version does improve the last line ("as give you God to be loved by another") of the lexical, but only into "as by another loved God grant you be," which has the sense but neither the clarity nor the éclat of Pushkin's line.

Nabokov writes that he regularly felt the urge to tinker with his translations, and he may well have continued to do so here had he prepared his own *Verses and Versions*. But the difficulties he had translating his favorite Russian poet—difficulties he expresses eloquently and ironically in his own voice—are as interesting as, and deliberately more challenging than, his successes. Nabokov uncompromisingly translates the second line of "Ya vas lyubíl" as "not quite extinguished in my soul." I rendered it as "in my heart has not quite gone out." In Russian, "*dushá*," "soul," is far more common than its English equivalent and covers much of the territory of the heart as the conventional seat of the emotions. Nabokov, in refusing to compromise on "soul," points to a difference between Russian and English that lies at the core of the difference between an English speaker's and a Russian's sense of self and other and of life and death.

Pushkin famously compared translators to horses changed at the post houses of civilization. In his earlier and more accessible translations, Nabokov makes us feel the post-horses have arrived, that we are meeting Pushkin, Lermontov, Tyutchev, or Hodasevich almost face to face. In his later work, translation is not the illusion of arrival but the start of a journey—glimpses of the destination but also of the bracing rigors of the intervening terrain. Through the contrasting strategies within *Verses and Versions*, as through the special methods of *Eugene Onegin*, Nabokov continues to prod English-speaking readers into persisting on our journey toward the peaks of Russian poetry.

17. Tolstoy and Nabokov

I adore Tolstoy, but as a member of an English rather than a Slavic department did not teach him until I launched a graduate course in narrative in 1993,
which included both *Anna Karenina* and *Ada*—whose first sentence Nabokov
lifts from the first sentence of *Anna Karenina*.

   In the Laurence and Suzanne Weiss Lecture at Amherst College in 1992,
I compared Tolstoy and Nabokov. To offer examples that presupposed no
other knowledge of the works, I opted for the opening of *Anna Karenina* and
the start not of *Ada* but the better known and less complex *Lolita*. I wanted
to show how great writers say things so differently, even as they learn from
their predecessors, because they see so differently.

Nabokov once recalled the novelist and Nobel laureate Ivan Bunin telling
him about visiting Tolstoy for the first time and being almost shocked "to
see suddenly emerge from a small door a little old man instead of the giant
he had involuntarily imagined." Nabokov added in his own voice: "And I have
also seen that little old man. I was a child and I faintly remember my father
shaking hands with someone at a street corner, then telling me as I continued our walk, 'That was Tolstoy.'"[1] The only other overlaps I have found
between these two lives was that both were photographed in the same year
by the great Petersburg photographer Karl Bulla, Tolstoy in his seventies or
eighties, Nabokov at seven or eight, each with his own trademark, a peasant costume or a butterfly book, and that both lived at Gaspra, the estate of
Countess Sophia Panin, Tolstoy during a spell of ill health in 1902, Nabokov
when his family was fleeing the revolution in Petrograd in 1918.

   So much for biography. I wish it was always so easy to dispose of.

   I'd like to compare Tolstoy and Nabokov by looking at the openings
of *Anna Karenina* and *Lolita*. When I contrast the two novels, it will be to
highlight the individuality of the two novelists, not to set an example of

"classical realism" against an example of "postmodernism." Tolstoy's realism is very much his own, as Gary Morson argues so persuasively in his superb book on *War and Peace*.[2] And Nabokov's manner, whether you want to call it realistic or not, is his own: he is not a modernist (despite affinities with aspects of Joyce and Proust), nor a postmodernist (despite the influence he has had on some writers so labeled, he has never shared the common epistemological presuppositions, whatever they are, that are supposedly possible in "this era," whatever that means). And although he does share some traits with the symbolists, he is mostly just himself.

As a young man, Nabokov thought *Madame Bovary* "2000 metres higher than *Anna Karenina*."[3] By the end of the 1940s he had reversed the rankings and had come to think *Anna Karenina* the greatest of all novels (Meras interview). He taught it and agreed to annotate it and to retranslate it, and although that project remained incomplete because of the pressure of other work, he went on to pay tribute to the novel in his own fiction.

In line with his general reestimation of *Anna Karenina*, Nabokov's response to its first two paragraphs changed revealingly over twenty years. In late 1939 or early 1940, before arriving in the United States, he began to prepare lectures on Russian literature in the hope he would find a university literature post much sooner than he did. He jotted down: "*Anna Karenin*: Grand looseness of style: The word 'house' is repeated *8 times* in the course of the first paragraph—17 lines."[4] But in the annotations he began for the Modern Library *Anna Karenina* fifteen years later, we find this: "the word *dom* (house, household, home) is repeated eight times in the course of six sentences. This ponderous and solemn repetition, *dom*, *dom*, *dom*, tolling as it does for doomed family life (one of the main themes of the book), is a deliberate device on Tolstoy's part" (*LRL* 210). From grand looseness to deliberate design.

But I'm not sure that this is entirely correct. I've translated the start of the novel myself in order to highlight the startling, dogged insistence of Tolstoy's verbal repetitions that surely can't all be explained as sounding one's theme in the first few bars.

"All happy families are like one another, every unhappy family is unhappy in its own way": all right, repetition, but only for the sake of pointing a contrast.

Then:

All [remember what we were told at school: don't start consecutive sentences and especially consecutive paragraphs with the same word] was confusion in the Oblonsky household. [I have used "house" here as a kind of chemical marker for the Russian syllable "*dom*"] The wife had found out that the husband was linked [I picked this word because Tolstoy recycles the same word two sentences later: normally we would translate "was having an affair"] with the former French governess in their house, and told her husband that she couldn't live in the same house as him. This situation had been going on for three days now and was felt painfully by the couple themselves and all the members of their family and the household staff. All the members of the family and the household staff [a very characteristic repetition: Nabokov himself defines it, in an unpublished note in quite a different context: "the phantom of Tolstoy's style: the bringing over of the last definition of one phrase into the beginning of the next one, as solid supports for the development of a logical sequence"[5]] felt [and that was the last verb used in the previous sentence] that there was no sense in their cohabitation and that people who had accidentally converged at any wayside inn were more linked [there's *that* repetition] to one another than they [and here it comes again], the members of the Oblonsky family and household. The wife did not come out of her rooms, the husband had not been in the house for three days now. The children ran all over the house; the English governess had argued with the [housekeeper][6] and had written a note to a friend asking her to find her a new place; the cook had gone out yesterday right at dinner time; the under-cook and the coachman had given notice.

What we have here is not so much the sounding of a theme as Tolstoy's relentlessly analytical mind in action, his ruthless, uncompromising desire to define. He likes to turn something over patiently, facet by facet, and refuses to stop where ordinary decorum expects. Here it leads, I think we have to admit, to some awkwardness, but this awkwardness is intricately allied to his own special greatness, his readiness to take things apart, his ignoring received explanations, his rejecting ordinary limits.

Though he admired Tolstoy above all other novelists, Nabokov was very different. He was quick to spot the logical flaws in the arguments of others and held that "next to the right to create, the right to criticize is the richest gift that liberty of thought and speech can offer" (*LRL* ii). But he was highly impatient with analysis as a means of arriving anywhere: he thought that logic could lead you in a straight line all the way around the globe, only to bring you back to where you started, to mark out once more the closed circle of human thought. And given the odd conclusions Tolstoy could argue himself into by patient logic—that sex is immoral even within marriage, for instance, in the afterpiece to "The Kreutzer Sonata"—Nabokov has a point. Nabokov preferred the aside of consciousness, the knight move of mind, the sidestep of fancy, to the dogged step-by-step of analytical thought.

I chose the opening of *Anna Karenina* partly to take issue with Nabokov. In teaching Tolstoy, Nabokov stressed the visual detail. "What one would like to do," he told his students, "would be to kick the glorified soapbox from under [Tolstoy's] sandalled feet and then lock him up on a desert island with gallons of ink and reams of paper—far away from the things, ethical and pedagogical, that diverted his attention from observing the way the dark hair curled above Anna's white neck" (*LRL* 140). When he taught, he focused on detail and expected his students to "caress the details"; the most notorious of his notorious exam questions was: "Describe the wallpaper in the Karenins' bedroom" (*VNAY* 358).

But if you look at the opening of *Anna Karenina*, Tolstoy incorporates far less visual detail than so-called classical realists are supposed to employ. There is nothing corresponding to the description of Verrières on the opening page of *The Scarlet and the Black*; or the description of the new schoolboy, Charbovari, at the start of *Madame Bovary*; nothing to match the view from Miss Pinkerton's academy at the beginning of *Vanity Fair*; or the description of Dorothea as *Middlemarch* opens; or any of Dickens's views of London— although if there were space to quote these, you would detect a cast of mind in each of these authors sufficiently distinct, even if they all happen to start with description, to make you suspect that a label like "classical realism" seems hardly a classification.

There is no physical detail at the beginning of *Anna Karenina*, and that seems appropriate. What distinguishes Tolstoy is not a concentration on the visual minutiae Nabokov savors but his concern to establish situations in all their complexity. Just as the objects in a painting by Vermeer are all perfectly related to one another in space and in the picture plane, and perfectly related to the overall tone of ambient light and the reflected light off surfaces nearby, so in Tolstoy people and predicaments are coordinated with an exactness and truth we don't find matched in any other writer. By introducing Vermeer I don't mean to suggest this is a visual phenomenon. We have no direct description here of the Oblonsky home: instead we find the perfect coordination of actions and reactions, of the effects of the discovery of infidelity on the household, on father, mother, children, governess, under-cook, in fact, on "all the members of the Oblonsky family and the household staff."

In this description of the Oblonskys we perhaps begin to see what Tolstoy means by that uncharacteristic opening aphorism: it's not so much that all happy families are alike, all *Cosby Show* clones, all happy Huxtables, and unhappy families interestingly different. It's more that happy families are somehow united, in themselves and to other such families, and unhappy families divided in themselves—the mother in her room, the father out, the children running loose—and divided from other families: Tolstoy's idea that all things are united in God and separated in evil.

I remember I used to have a sense of a Tolstoy novel unfolding before your eyes as if you were just watching a film. I happened to see the 1965 Bondarchuk *War and Peace* again recently, and that confirmed my growing suspicion that the film analogy was hopeless. What happens is much more immediate than film. In a film, we sit before an image. In Tolstoy, we are invited into the character.

> On the third day after the quarrel Prince Stepan Arkadievich Oblonsky—Stiva, as he was called in society—at his usual time, that is at eight A.M., woke up not in his wife's bedroom but in his own study, on a morocco couch. He turned his full, well-tended body on the sofa springs, and as if wanting another long sleep, hugged the underside of his pillow and pressed his cheek into it; but he suddenly started, sat on the sofa, and opened his eyes.
>
> "Yes, yes, how was it?" he thought, recalling his dream. "Yes, how was it? Yes! Alabin was giving a dinner in Darmstadt; no, not in Darmstadt, but something American. Yes, but this Darmstadt was in America. Yes, Alabin was giving a dinner on glass tables, yes,—and the tables were singing *Il mio tesoro*, no, not *Il mio tesoro* but something better, and there were some little decanters, and they were women," he remembered.

Tolstoy describes Stiva's situation—sleeping, and not in his wife's bedroom—just enough for us to understand; he describes his "full, well-looked-after body" just enough so we don't imagine him lean or gaunt with worry. And then he invites us *into* Stiva by describing his last turn in bed, his last pressing of cheek to pillow, and his start awake: Tolstoy invites us to imagine Stiva not by projecting him before our eyes—not by Dickens's fixing on a striking external characteristic—but by inviting us to project ourselves into Stiva, by inviting us to trust what is common in human experience, and there's nothing more common than sleeping and waking with a dream on one's mind.

Nabokov describes the way the dream defines Stiva's character (*LRL* 151). Once we know just what he is like, we can indeed see that the dinner, the glass tables, the decanters that are somehow women, are appropriate to this bon vivant, who treats women as something he can pour out for his pleasure. But before we can see that significance, we register that Tolstoy has captured perfectly the process of attempting to recall a dream. There have been dreams in literature for millennia, but how often before Tolstoy has a writer refused to convert a dream to a lucid story and showed a character simply groping for dissolving fragments, as each of us does perhaps several times a week?

But if I am right about Tolstoy's invitation to what is common in human experience, how do we account for the wonderful particularity, the unmistakable individuality of his characters? Tolstoy's brilliant analytical mind allowed him to dissect the essential particularity of things, people, moments, events, but it is precisely because he had such an extraordinary sense of the difference between things, the apartness of things—and because his own analytical imagination made him aware of how the very act of analysis kept him apart from things—that he had such an overwhelming urge towards mystic unity, such a drive to seek out the secrets we all share, such a desire to invite us into one another, or at least into the characters he created.

In the dream, Tolstoy selects details that are perfectly illustrative of Stiva's character, once we learn his character. But he doesn't force Stiva's idiosyncrasies on us at first: after all, almost anybody could have that sort of dream, and anybody at all will know that sense of groping for a dream.

Tolstoy's ideal of art, as he explains in *What Is Art?*, is to *infect* the audience with an emotion the artist wants to convey. By inviting us into Stiva, he succeeds; we share Stiva's sense of pleasure in the aftereffects of a pleasant dream and in the retrieval of bits of the dream and—a very Tolstoyan touch—in Stiva's satisfaction at being able to put into thoughts the elusiveness and intangibility of dream sense.

Oblonsky's eyes began to sparkle merrily, and he lapsed into thought, smiling. "Yes, it was good, very good. There was a lot there that was marvelous but I can't say in words or even put into thoughts now I'm awake." And, noticing a strip of light breaking through one of the cloth blinds from the side, he cheerfully lowered his feet to search for the slippers (last year's birthday present) his wife had worked in gold morocco, and according to his long-standing, nine-year-old custom he stretched his arm, without getting up, to the place where his dressing-gown hung in the bedroom. And here he suddenly remembered how and why he was sleeping not in his wife's bedroom, but in the study; the smile vanished from his face and he frowned.

"Ahh, ahh, ahh! Ooh! . . ." he groaned, remembering all that had happened. And his imagination replayed all the details of the quarrel with his wife, all the inescapability of his situation, and most torment-ing of all the fact that it was his own fault.

"Yes! she won't forgive me, she can't forgive me. And worst of all is that it's my fault, my fault, but I'm not to blame. That's the whole trag-edy," he thought. "Ahh, ahh, ahh!" he added in despair as he remem-bered the most unbearable impressions in the quarrel.

We are inside Stiva as he sees the strip of light, as he gropes for his slippers—though Tolstoy darts in for *our* benefit that pointed description of the slip-pers fashioned by the wife who remembered his birthday but whom Stiva has momentarily forgotten—and we are inside him as he automatically reaches for the dressing gown that's in fact hanging in another room. That shock of the failure of an automatic action after something has changed, or that other shock as the glow of a sweet dream or the chill of a grim one fades—these again appeal to common experience, to what we share with Stiva or one another, although we may not give voice to these things that link us.

Suddenly Stiva's situation rushes back on him, and Tolstoy can intro-duce the exposition of the past—the moment Stiva knew he was caught out in his infidelity—as a memory in the mind of a character with whom we already involuntarily identify. And then comes Tolstoy's strange unsparing truth of analysis: that most torturing of all for Stiva is that he is to blame, that he can't escape into the luxury of anger at anyone else.

As Tolstoy describes the scene through Stiva's memory, there is again no visual detail, just that one marvelous huge pear that Stiva has brought home for the theater, which seems somehow lush, plump, satisfied, as in Wordsworth's "The Old Cumberland Beggar":

> The easy man
> Who sits at his own door,—and, like the pear
> That overhangs his head from the green wall,
> Feeds in the sunshine.

A marvelous image of somebody lazily contented at his own home, growing fat like the pear, sucking up the goodness from the sun, turning ripe and juicy—very like Stiva. Stiva comes home with the pear for his wife, a mark of his spontaneous generosity, on the one hand, and a sop, on the other, to the woman who's had to stay home while he's out on the town, and the pear is something Nabokov would want you to imagine Stiva holding, incongruously, awkwardly, at this moment of high drama.

But if we picture the pear, we are not asked to picture Dolly: there is no physical description of her at all.

> Most unpleasant of all was that first minute, when he returned from the theater, cheerful and content, with a huge pear for his wife in his hand, and didn't find his wife in the drawing room; to his surprise, he didn't find her in the study either, and at last, he caught sight of her in the bedroom with the unfortunate note that explained everything in her hand.
>
> Dolly, always preoccupied, fussing, not too bright, as he thought her, sat motionless with the note in her hand and looked at him with an expression of horror, despair, and anger.
>
> "What's this? What is it?" she asked, pointing at the note.

Tolstoy again explains exactly what the situation needs: there she is with the tell-tale letter in her hand, "always preoccupied, fussing, none too bright, as he thought her." That is the implicit evaluation of her that Stiva brings into the room and that is suddenly shattered by the image of her with the letter: again, Tolstoy describes this very particular scene not by multiplying details but by suddenly inviting us to recall the experience of seeing that we have typecast and dehumanized another person whose pain, whose live reality, suddenly shames us.

"And, *as so often happens*, what tormented Oblonsky most about this memory was not so much the event itself as the way he had answered his wife." The implicit tendency to psychological generalization now becomes explicit. This "as often happens" points to our liability to reproach ourselves not for what deserves reproach but for the way we have come off less well than we would have liked: Tolstoy's analytical scalpel slices away at our egotism at the same time as he pays a compliment to our shared humanity.

Here Tolstoy's gift for "infecting" us reaches its peak. He evokes in us a state of mind he has experienced, and he makes his character alive not so much by any particularizing device as by our sense of fundamental human kinship with him, through our sharing what Tolstoy calls "the secrets that are common to us all."[7] Our sense of embarrassment at having someone know us so well is more than balanced by our sense of pleasure in the "Ah ha!" of recognition, *and* by our realizing, "It's not *only* me," *and* by our sense of relief that, after all, no one has actually caught us out.

Then comes that fatal, instinctive response, the smile, and even before we reach it, another Tolstoyan complexity: Stiva's self-satisfaction, as he pins a technical term on the reaction that he now remembers with such vivid, immediate embarrassment, and then easily back to the smile that outpaces what the mind can tell the body to do, that alertness to the body that made Dmitri Merezhkovsky call Tolstoy "the seer of the flesh":

> At that minute there happened to him what happens to people when they are unexpectedly caught out in something disgraceful. He didn't have time to prepare his face for the situation he found himself in before his wife now that she had discovered his guilt. Instead of taking offence, denying it, offering excuses, asking forgiveness, even staying indifferent—anything would have been better than what he did!— his face quite involuntarily ("reflexes of the brain," thought Oblonsky, who loved physiology), quite involuntarily smiled suddenly his usual kind and therefore silly smile.

That smile has an instant effect on Dolly:

> He couldn't forgive himself for this silly smile. Seeing this smile, Dolly shuddered, as if from a physical pain, and breaking out with all her usual vehemence into a torrent of harsh words, she ran out of the room. Since then she had not wanted to see her husband.
> "It's all the fault of that silly smile," thought Oblonsky.
> "But what's to be done? What's to be done?" he asked himself despairingly and found no answer.

Dolly shudders; she cries out bitterly as she rushes from the room. And this would be my fourth principle of Tolstoyan style; after the analytic mind, the integrity of situation, and the invitation to perceive the common humanity one shares with a character, comes this minute attention to interactions. The reading and frequent misreading of other people's responses, especially their involuntary ones, the reactions that can move faster than our conscious thoughts direct us, are familiar to anyone who has ever lived with anyone else, but the experience is so familiar that it usually precedes or outstrips language. It has never been described better than in this book—and it has never been more painful than in the series of ghastly misreadings of each other that Vronsky and Anna make as Anna slips toward her death.

For me these are the things that makes Tolstoy's style so unique, not his visual details. When he lectured on *Anna Karenin*, Nabokov would spend some time drawing for his students a model of the first-class cars on the St. Petersburg–Moscow night express trains. Useful to know, but what matters much more is the situation that Tolstoy so carefully prepares: Anna on the train all night listening to Vronsky's mother talk proudly of her son, Anna stepping off the train in Moscow, seeing Vronsky waiting for his mother, trying to suppress her sense of amused recognition because she has seen him before and sees he doesn't recognize her and yet unknown to him he has been a main subject of conversation all night long. And there is something about that discreet look of interest and suppressed amusement from Anna that beguiles Vronsky—who evidently hasn't particularly noticed her before—to the point where he immediately makes the first move in his long campaign to win her.

I began dissecting the start of *Anna Karenina* with a look at insistent repetitions of word and phrase. I explained them as evidence of Tolstoy's exceptional predilection for analysis. Nabokov describes the mark of the "groping purist" in Tolstoy: "what we might call creative repetitions, a compact series of repetitive statements, coming one immediately after the other, each more expressive, each closer to Tolstoy's meaning. He gropes, he unwraps the verbal parcel for its inner sense, he peels the apple of the phrase, he tries to say it one way, then a better way, he gropes, he stalls, he toys, he Tolstoys with words" (*LRL* 238). There Nabokov parodies Tolstoy, he plays with Tolstoy, he strikes images off Tolstoy—and in doing so he deliberately undermines his own parody because Tolstoy does not play.

That leads to another reason for those insistent repetitions. Tolstoy the moralist has misgivings about Tolstoy the artist, let alone about other artists or about art that involves parody, play, imagination, invention. Nabokov writes of the "rejection of false elegancies" in Tolstoy's style "and its readiness to admit any robust awkwardness if that is the shortest way to sense" (*LRL* 228). Rather than succumb to the false elegancies of conventional art, Tolstoy preferred to be uncompromising to the point of gracelessness.

If we turn now to *Lolita* we find in its author someone who revels in art, in artifice, in pattern. There's a wonderful television documentary of Nabokov being asked to read the start of the Russian *Lolita*.⁸ He agrees to do so, but turns to the camera, peers over his glasses, and as he reaches for the *English* text of *Lolita* declares: "Incrrredible as it may seem, not everybody remembers the opening of *Lolita* in *English*"—and he begins to read:

Lolita, light of my life, fire of my loins. My sin, my soul. Lo-lee-ta: the tip of the tongue taking a trip of three steps down the palate to tap, at three, on the teeth. Lo. Lee. Ta.

That is fun: the extravagance of the profession of passion, the extravagance of the phrasing. But the artifice seems so pronounced by that third sentence that while it captivates by its lilt and amuses by its comic clatter, it seems to drown out sense. In fact, Christopher Ricks points out that what sense you can see seems suspect: in an English "t" the tongue taps the alveolar ridge, not the teeth. Julian Barnes takes up Ricks's point in *Flaubert's Parrot* when he quotes this sentence in a catalogue of mistakes in literature. But the mistake is theirs: there is very meticulous sense here: Nabokov is defining as patiently as Tolstoy—OK, not that patiently, but as patiently as he can—or rather he has Humbert explain in his exuberant way that Lolita's name is to be pronounced with a Spanish "t," not a thick American one: Low-leed-uh.

Behind the pattern, there is sense. And behind that, more sense: Lolita was conceived on a honeymoon in Vera Cruz, and her name is her parents' memento of the occasion, along with "a white-eyed wooden thingamabob of commercial Mexican origin" and "some more Mexican trash" in the hallway of the Haze home that confirm Humbert's repugnance at the idea of lodging there until he sees Lolita herself. And those words that had seemed all pattern prove as aptly related to *source* as to *sense* or *subject*: Humbert fusses over the pronunciation of Lolita's name because he is a scholar of Romance languages and literatures, and a pedant, at the same time as he also romanticizes himself as a lover and a poet.

Nabokov foregrounds the artifice here as much as possible, but behind that extravagance, which he has obviously enjoyed concocting (surely no other novel starts off with a fancier verbal flourish), he nevertheless distances himself from Humbert's style (he never began a book in his own voice with anything like this flamboyance)—which only adds another level of camouflage, another level of artifice.

Nabokov believed that there is something deeply artful about the world not in the sense of Wilde's patter of paradoxes, not in the sense of the postmodern cliché that all knowledge is a fictional construct, but in the sense that there seems to be detail and design that endlessly proliferate the deeper one looks into things, as if reality is almost playfully deceptive in concealing so much and allowing so much to be discovered by human eyes. And Nabokov's sense of the artifice behind nature came from looking closely at nature as a specialist in butterflies. In foregrounding artifice as he does in *Lolita*'s opening lines, he is true to his sense of the ultimate reality of things, but his truth could hardly be more different from Tolstoy's.

As John Bayley observes, Tolstoy had an obsessive desire to see life steadily and see it whole.[9] Nabokov could see that that was impossible. As a lepidopterist, he knew that the world was too rich, too endlessly specialized in every direction, to allow for the mastery Tolstoy sought. The human mind has to work at discovering its world, and the more it discovers of the excitement of detail, the more mysterious seems its inability to understand what lies behind it all. Rather than try to capture the whole, Nabokov tries to vivify the part. So he chooses an off-center, unexpected detail: "She was Lo, plain Lo, in the morning, standing four feet ten in one sock."

In Stiva, or even in Lyovin, Tolstoy shows the natural egotism of the human mind and by showing it shows us with a sense of both surprise and recognition how much unites us even in what divides us. But where Tolstoy opts for the common ground, Nabokov chooses a patch of rare earth: not someone in whom we want to recognize anything of ourselves but a perverse obsessive, an eccentric, a monster. Nabokov believes in the inalienable difference of person from person, and in that he again reflects his biological training. As Stephen Jay Gould puts it, "All evolutionary biologists know that variation is itself nature's irreducible essence. Variation is the hard reality, not a set of imperfect measures for a central tendency. Means and medians are abstractions."[10]

Humbert sees how others see Lolita: "She was Lo, plain Lo, in the morning. . . . She was Lola in slacks. She was Dolly at school. She was Dolores on the dotted line." But he wants to see her in his own way, his own terms— "But in my arms she was always Lolita"—just as he chooses his own kind of sexual pleasure in defiance of social norms.

"But in my arms she was always Lolita": Humbert presents himself as a romantic, a lover whose love elevates Lolita to heights beyond her mundane world of teenage moods and modes. But Nabokov, who can celebrate love as a way of partially transcending the essential isolation of the soul, introduces a love affair where Humbert pays no attention to Lolita herself, simply worshipping the image that he has fabricated and enslaving the live child whose independence he ignores. She might be called Lo to her mother, or Dolly to herself and her friends, but Humbert sees and celebrates her, appropriates her, as Lolita, a name no one else ever uses, a name Leona Toker insists we should refuse to employ if we don't want to be complicit in Humbert's crime.[11]

> Did she have a precursor? She did, indeed she did. In point of fact, there might have been no Lolita at all had I not loved, one summer, a certain initial girl-child. In a princedom by the sea. Oh when? About as many years before Lolita was born as my age was that summer. You can always count on a murderer for a fancy prose style.

Nabokov chooses to portray an exceptional, obsessive mind, fixated on his one object. But at the same time he gives Humbert astonishing mental freedom, the freedom to write with such flair, in the opening paragraph; with such a capacity for seeing other points of view while insisting on his own, as in the second paragraph; or with such self-awareness, and such a capacity for self-detachment, as he now discloses in the third paragraph. He is fixated yet free; blinded by his passion yet extraordinarily clear sighted; trapped yet uncannily mobile. And for Nabokov that is an image of us all: he perpetually celebrates the munificence, the power, the freedom of human consciousness, and he perpetually protests against its imprisonment in the self and in the here and now.

"You can always count on a murderer for a fancy prose style." But the first-time reader hasn't known until this line that the narrator is a murderer. Quite a clanger to find dropped on the first page. Nabokov has a very strong sense of the reader, as does Humbert himself, where Tolstoy tends to provide the illusion of transparency, a sense that we are sharing in or even living out the unmediated experience of the characters. Nabokov by contrast reminds us of our distance and continues to do so: Humbert discloses that he has murdered someone but plays a game with us as he misleads us as to *whom* he has murdered, thereby upending the detective story pattern and, as I suggested in the biography (*VNAY* 227–54), thereby also introducing the important theme of the difference between a forward and a rearward view of time, simultaneously one of the novel's most playful and its most morally serious themes.

"You can always count on a murderer for a fancy prose style" strikes me as an inverted echo of Ivan Karamazov in the courtroom saying: "*S ubiitsa nel'zya zhe sprashivat' krasnorechiya*" (*Brothers Karamazov*, 12.5), which we could translate as, "You can never count on a murderer for eloquence," an echo that can perhaps be explained by Nabokov's thinking of Dostoevsky as a writer of detective fiction. At any rate, it's no accident that this first invocation of the inverted detective-story pattern of the book comes between two allusions to the founder of the detective story, Edgar Allan Poe.

"In a princedom by the sea. . . . Ladies and gentlemen of the jury, exhibit number one is what the seraphs, the misinformed, simple, noble-winged seraphs, envied." Since Humbert is about to present us with his account of his traumatic first love, on a Riviera beach—whom he names Annabel Leigh in honor of Poe's poem "Annabel Lee," about a girl torn away as a child from her lover—here he twice echoes Poe's poem. The man he murders, Clare Quilty, will take on, in Humbert's telling, the quality of a grim double, again like a character out of Poe. And Humbert, as a scholar of French and English poetry, is very familiar with Poe, a writer championed by Baudelaire and more celebrated in French literary culture than in English.

Humbert sees his life, quite self-consciously, in terms of works of art. Nabokov employs these images quite differently. Although he sees life as inherently artistic, he also signals the difference between life and art, in fact tries to define the limitations on human life by their contrast with the possibilities of art, where you can enter the mind of a character or revisit endlessly a story's past. But Humbert tries to turn other people in his life, on his own level of being, into works of art: Lolita, as an object of celebration, a sort of miraculous willed revival of Annabel Leigh, and Quilty, as the victim of a carefully staged murder. Humbert travesties the values Nabokov sees in art: Humbert inflates his ego and reduces other people to the level of his creations, where art for Nabokov allows a kind of transcendence of the self. Humbert reduces Lolita to his creation, where Nabokov does all he can to show, behind Humbert's rhapsodies, the live reality of her appalling life. Humbert tries to reduce Lolita to the object of his fancies, but she remains utterly remote from him, utterly inaccessible. For Nabokov art is about respecting and yet being able to enter the otherness of others, as we cannot do in life. *That* is what he means when he says in the afterword to *Lolita*: "For me a work of fiction exists only insofar as it affords me what I shall bluntly call aesthetic bliss, that is a sense of being somehow, somewhere, connected with other states of being where art (curiosity, tenderness, kindness, ecstasy) is the norm" (*Lolita* 316–17).

"I was born in 1910, in Paris. My father was a gentle, easy-going person, a salad of racial genes." As John Bayley points out, Tolstoy eschews biography: he refuses to give background information on his characters' past.[12] Bayley explains this as part of Tolstoy's distaste for invention, his reluctance to create characters over whom he can have control. To put it another way, perhaps, Tolstoy can present truth to life when he shows all the complexities of a scene, the integrity of a situation, the openness of a moment, but he cannot keep that complexity, that integrity, that openness when he has to reduce to a summary. So he simply avoids biographical résumés.

Nabokov, on the other hand, was compulsively biographical about his heroes. He might not tell a character's history in linear sequence, but he almost invariably traces a novel's hero somehow from birth to death or at least to his exit from the book. He was too interested in the unique pattern of human personality, the mystery of identity, the design of individual distinctiveness *not* to allow readers to trace in their own way the subtle and often subterranean repetitions of a protagonist's past.

One last sip of *Lolita*. Humbert tells us his father was

> a Swiss citizen, of mixed French and Austrian descent, with a dash of the Danube in his veins. I am going to pass around in a minute some lovely, glossy-blue picture-postcards. He owned a luxurious hotel on the Riviera. His father and two grandfathers had sold wine, jewels and silk, respectively. At thirty he married an English girl, daughter of Jerome Dunn, the alpinist, and granddaughter of two Dorset parsons, experts in obscure subjects—paleopedology and Aeolian harps, respectively. My very photogenic mother died in a freak accident (picnic, lightning) when I was three, and, save for a pocket of warmth in the darkest past, nothing of her subsists within the hollows and dells of memory, over which, if you can still stand my style (I am writing under observation), the sun of my infancy had set: surely, you all know those redolent remnants of day suspended, with the midges, about some hedge in bloom or suddenly traversed by the rambler, at the bottom of a hill, in the summer dusk; a furry warmth, golden midges.

In 1956 Roman Jakobson distinguished between two linguistic devices, one characteristic of verse, one of prose: metaphor and metonymy: the principle of similarity, in an image, and the principle of contiguity, of natural connectedness, in a narrative: "My love is like a red, red rose," an image from a line of verse, and Anna Karenina's red handbag in the scene of her death, a detail typical of prose.[13] In fact, even a novelist like Dickens, famous for creating carriages or costumes that are metonymic extensions of character, also swarms with metaphor and simile. Of all great novelists, none eschews imagery as assiduously as Tolstoy, none keeps as faithfully as he to pure contiguity, to the particulars of the scene before his eyes.

Nabokov, on the other hand, disrupts scenes with the greatest of glee. Where Robbe-Grillet or Donald Barthelme does so programmatically, to undermine or explode what they decree to be no longer relevant habits of narrative connection, Nabokov doesn't deny the particulars of his scenes: Humbert *is* writing under observation, in a prison psychiatric ward, after the murder of Quilty, and he is attempting to set down his remote past to explain his recent life. But within that he darts this way and that with the utmost ebullience and ease, in the process upsetting the distinction between metaphor and metonymy in a phrase like "I am going to pass around in a minute some lovely, glossy-blue picture-postcards" (that feigns to be metonymic, an aspect of Humbert's situation as narrator, but is really metaphoric, only to serve a metonymic function of describing his father's Riviera hotel). Or again, that crazily compacted aside, "picnic, lightning," whose picnic landscape generates that crazily extended metaphor of hollows and dells that start to take on a solid, "metonymic" life of their own.

In a paragraph like this Nabokov revels in invention, in the sheer mobility of the mind, in the endless proliferation of the quirkiest particulars, in the eccentricity and centrifugality of things and facts: "two Dorset parsons, experts in obscure subjects—paleopedology and Aeolian harps, respectively." And he pays us the compliment of expecting that we will follow his imagination with all the speed and delight of his prose. Just as Humbert here remains trapped in his psychiatric ward and in the aftermath of the past he describes, so we stay with him in his situation, but within the constraint of the here and now we find that we can be freer than we thought.

Nothing could be further from Tolstoy's scenic method than Nabokov's, yet in both of them, I think, we discover ourselves.

I have compared Tolstoy and Nabokov by close analysis—although obviously not solely by deducing from the passages in front of us. But I could do it another way—for instance, by comparing trains in *Anna Karenina* and cars in *Lolita*—and I think the conclusions will be much the same.

In Tolstoy the trains, despite Nabokov's diagram, are the background for the wonderful situations he prepares: Anna's meeting with Vronsky after her arrival in Moscow and the ominous crushing by a train of the peasant whose widow Vronsky offers money in order to impress the woman who has just made such an impression on him; the romantic scene of the return to St. Petersburg, with Vronsky deliberately pursuing Anna and declaring his love on a station platform in the midst of a snowstorm, and Anna's catching sight of her husband's big ears as she descends from her train in St. Petersburg; and the final catastrophe of Anna's suicide. Again, it's the integrity of the situations, the reflections and the involuntary interactions, that carry us into the characters' experiences.

Tolstoy did say that "the railroad is to travel as the whore is to love,"[14] and certainly he does associate trains with the encroachment of Western ways, a loosening of the old values, an invasion that won't be as quickly turned back as Napoleon's. It is no accident that when Lyovin has the glimpse of Kitty returning to Russia that starts him in pursuit of her again, she is riding in a carriage, not a train. But trains are not symbols, or even obtrusive settings, so much as the place where situations evolve. Tolstoy has unusually strong opinions about many things he describes—the army in which Vronsky serves, the restaurants in which Stiva eats, the trains in which characters meet—but in this novel he presents things objectively, whatever his private judgments, and allows situations to speak for themselves.

Nabokov never learned to drive a car any more than Tolstoy learnt to drive a train, but in *Lolita* cars are everywhere, from the taxi in Paris where the cabdriver proves to be Valeria's new beau, to the car that kills Charlotte, and to all that follows from her death. Humbert takes Lolita by car around the whole of the United States; on their apparent reprise of that long excursion, Quilty follows them in a prismatic series of rented roadsters; and in a final flourish, after killing Quilty, Humbert drives on the wrong side of the road. If trains in *Anna Karenina* seem associated with Europe, cars in *Lolita* represent in a sense American mobility and freedom and variety but simultaneously become a prison for Lolita as Humbert forces her to remain on the move. But again cars are not so much a symbol as a fact of the novel's world, a fact that Nabokov renders with acute detail or eerie pattern (the spectrum of cars that Quilty hires in pursuit of Humbert), or a mixture of the real and the fantastic (the scene of Charlotte's death, turned into a toy diagram by a driver anxious to escape charges), or a blend of the comprehensive and the wildly centrifugal—like Humbert's catalogues of "the curious roadside species, Hitchhiking Man, *Homo pollex* of science," or "all cars on the road—behind, before, alongside, coming, going, every vehicle under the dancing sun"—but never with an unobtrusive Tolstoyan solidity. There's the town with the improbable but brilliant name of "Parkington"; or the close of the murder scene ("With a heavy heart I left the house and walked through the spotted blaze of the sun to my car. Two other cars were parked on both sides of it, and I had some trouble squeezing out": as Craig Raine says, you commit a murder, and you still have to worry about parking);[15] or Humbert's mad final fling, after the murder, as he drives along the wrong side of the road: "Cars coming towards me wobbled, swerved, and cried out in fear." His drives the way he writes, breaking all the rules.

Let me now offer another reason for focusing primarily on the opening of *Anna Karenina* and *Lolita*. If Tolstoy would have hated *Lolita*, he would have been simply unable to read *Ada*, which starts like this:

> "All happy families are more or less dissimilar; all unhappy ones are more or less alike," says a great Russian writer in the beginning of a famous novel (*Anna Arkadievitch Karenina*, transfigured into English by R. G. Stonelower, Mount Tabor Ltd., 1880). That pronouncement has little if any relation to the story to be unfolded now, a family chronicle, the first part of which is, perhaps, closer to another Tolstoy work, *Detstvo i Otrochestvo* (*Childhood and Fatherland*, Pontius Press, 1858).

And in *Ada*, although there are nineteenth-century trains and twentieth-century cars, there are also "jikkers," petrol-powered magic carpets that swoop low over hedges, causing cyclists to wobble and dive into ditches.

I have been stressing the differences between these two writers, and in that sense, my argument seems to ally me more closely with Nabokov, who focuses on the wild divergences of the world, than Tolstoy, who searches for a common humanity. But at the same time I have also been trying to suggest that both writers do share something profound: a passion for truth that makes them rethink what fiction can do—and if I had space I could show that same passion for truth even in the flamboyant artifice of *Ada*—a passion for working out their *own* ways of expressing their own truths.

Isaiah Berlin uses the old proverb of the fox who knows many little things and the hedgehog who knows one big thing (how to roll itself in a protective ball) to characterize Tolstoy as a brilliant fox who thought it was more important to be a hedgehog.[16] Tolstoy had an instinctive mastery of the little things, the details of situation, as I have termed it, and searched for the one big thing, which was usually nothing less than the meaning of life. (Stephen Hawkings was reputedly lazy at school until he came on the problem of cosmology and thought that *there* was something big enough and hard enough to be worth the effort; Tolstoy comes back to the meaning of life as if it were the only problem big enough to tackle and he were the only person big enough to tackle it.) But his answer was generally a way of overcoming the apartness of things by honest living and working together, like Lyovin's day in the hay harvest, and as I have tried to suggest, every detail of his fiction seems based on the premise that the way he can portray fundamentally similar human beings in their different situations offers a way of overcoming our apartness.

Nabokov, on the other hand, was a hedgehog who knew it was more important to be a fox. He felt that he had found what the hedgehog was after, so instead of a sense of relentless quest he had a Cheshire cat smile because he had found it: "it" being a quiet conviction that beyond the prison of self and time and understanding in which mortal consciousness is confined there are greater freedoms to be had, and that precisely because of the limits on human understanding there is no way we can reach whatever these freedoms are, except through the endless particulars that seem to differentiate and recombine in a way that he sees as inherently artistic, somehow related to the deceptive artistry behind things.

To reduce these highly individual notions to preprinted, easy-peel labels like realism or postmodernism would be to rob literature of all its magic.

18. Nabokov and Machado de Assis

I had learned of the great Brazilian novelist Joaquím Maria Machado de Assis (1839–1908) through John Barth's enthusiasm for him and bought a number of his novels in 1975 just before switching from Barth back to Nabokov for my doctoral dissertation. The Brazilian writer and social-networking commentator Claudio Soares, inspired in composing his hypertext novel, *Santos Dumont No. 8*, by *Pale Fire* and by my website *Ada*Online, wrote to me asking what, if anything, Nabokov thought of Machado. I had only sipped a mouthful of Machado's sparkling but bitter waters but answered that as far as I knew, Nabokov had not known of Machado's existence but would have loved him. Soares arranged for me to talk at the Brazilian Academy of Letters, of which Machado de Assis was the founding president, on September 17, 2009. I had rashly suggested I could talk on Nabokov and Machado and as the time approached had to devour Machado in great gulps. What a feast. To my taste he ranks among the great fiction writers of the second half of the nineteenth century. He would have made Joyce write differently. His closest literary kin could be Beckett and especially Nabokov.

Other pairings I might like to tackle, if life lasts forever and no one else beats me to them: Nabokov and Darwin; Nabokov and William James; Nabokov and T. S. Eliot.

For me to come to Rio de Janeiro to talk about Machado at the Casa de Machado seems as foolhardy as traveling back in time to ancient Athens, without knowing Greek, to talk about Plato to an audience of Aristotles. I hope you can accept my tentative foray into your home territory in the spirit in which it's intended.

Vladimir Nabokov, so far as I know, was unaware of the existence of Joaquím Machado de Assis. Had he read him, he would surely have said so in no uncertain terms and ranked him among the pinnacles of nineteenth-century fiction with Dickens, Flaubert, and Tolstoy.

Nabokov liked to claim that after his juvenilia he was never influenced by anybody. If Machado were as well known outside the Lusophone world as he deserves, critics would no doubt have claimed to see his influence on Nabokov. On the evidence of the astonishing similarities in their work, and disregarding the minor detail that Nabokov knew nothing of Machado, such critics would seem to have had more in their favor than those who have proposed Pushkin, Gogol, Tolstoy, Joyce, Proust, or Kafka as influences on Nabokov. The Brazilian and the Russian could almost have thought up some of each other's works: Nabokov could easily have developed the ideas behind Machado stories like "Those Cousins from Sapucaia," "Final Prayer," and "Dona Paula," just as Machado might have taken as premises the ideas behind stories like "A Nursery Tale," "An Affair of Honor," or "Lips to Lips." Nabokov played again and again with the central paradox of Machado's breakthrough novel, *The Posthumous Memoirs of Brás Cubas*,[1] written from beyond the grave. In Nabokov's novella *The Eye*, Smurov, the narrator, tells us early in the story that he has committed suicide, but he continues to narrate. In *Transparent Things*, the narrator is a novelist who dies in the course of the story and welcomes the hero over the threshold of death in the last line. In *Look at the Harlequins!*, the narrator cites a little rhyme, "The I of the book / Cannot die in the book" (239), but describes a three-week delirium that he feels as a traverse through death, not unlike the delirious vision from outside human time that Brás Cubas has just before *he* dies.

Machado never traveled far from Rio de Janeiro, and Nabokov never visited Latin America, although he did say in his late years that he would like to visit Peru before he pupated. In Nabokov's other career, as a lepidopterist, his greatest work was the reclassification of the Blues of Latin America, work that has been extended over the last twenty years and celebrated in *Nabokov's Blues: The Scientific Odyssey of a Literary Genius*. Nabokov would have been thrilled by Machado as a writer, even if he might have been frustrated sometimes to find that he'd been beaten to ideas he might have wanted to use.

He would have found it an extra pleasure that Machado had a rich strand of African ancestry. In 1942 he spoke at what was then called a Negro women's college in Atlanta, in the segregated American South, and delighted his audience by lecturing on Pushkin and Pushkin's pride in his one-eighth African heritage. He told them that Pushkin, the greatest poet since Shakespeare, "provides a most striking example of mankind at its very best when human races are allowed to mix" (*VNAY* 51).

As a lepidopterist, Nabokov was regarded as temperamentally a splitter rather than a lumper: in other words he placed more stress on *differences* between what might look like representatives of the *same* species or genus rather than similarities, so he would be inclined to split them into different species or genera. He gives perhaps his most gifted creation, the poet John Shade in *Pale Fire*, the remark: "Resemblances are the shadows of differences. Different people see different similarities and similar differences" (*PF* 265). How do the similarities and differences between Machado and Nabokov throw light on the resources of fiction and the range of literary vision?

First, what *are* the similarities? I could spend an entertaining hour just pulling verbal rabbits out of hats to illustrate moments when Machado and Nabokov seem part of the same magic act.

Self-conscious fiction stretches from at least Lucian and Apuleius through Cervantes and Sterne into postmodernism, but Machado and Nabokov seem particularly close in their quick comic asides to readers. Early in *Lolita*, Humbert writes that he somehow sensed Lolita was ready to be kissed by him: "I cannot tell my learned reader (whose eyebrows, I suspect, have by now traveled all the way to the back of his bald head), I cannot tell him how the knowledge came to me" (*Lolita* 50). At a much later stage in his stalking Lolita, Humbert playfully appeals to part of his audience: "Frigid gentlewomen of the jury!" (*Lolita* 134) Machado's narrators, too, address readers who shift from male to female according to context or impulse. Although Nabokov has a reputation for teasing his readers, Machado much more overtly berates his imagined bad readers ("the main defect of this book is you, reader" [*BC* 111]; "Good Lord! Do I have to explain everything?" [*BC* 183])—and thereby instructs, amuses, and compliments his actual good readers.

Both Machado and Nabokov wring comedy, drama, and psychological revelation from the narrator's processes of composition and publication. Bento Santiago confesses, as his control over his story starts to slip, "Right here I should be at the middle point of my book, but inexperience has made me lag behind my pen, and I arrive almost at the end of my supply of paper, with the best of the story yet to tell."[2] Humbert writes at yet another moment of desperation, "Don't think I can go on. Heart, head—everything. Lolita, Lolita, Lolita, Lolita, Lolita, Lolita, Lolita, Lolita, Lolita, Lolita. Repeat till the page is full, printer" (*Lolita* 111). Brás Cubas notes in chapter 130 that: "This chapter is to be inserted between the first two sentences of Chapter 129." In his foreword to *Pale Fire*, Kinbote writes, "Frank has acknowledged the safe return of the galleys I had been sent here and has asked me to mention in my Preface— and this I willingly do—that I alone am responsible for any mistakes in my commentary. Insert before a professional. A professional proofreader has carefully rechecked the printed text of the poem" (*PF* 18).

Machado and Nabokov both make their readers conscious of the book as book. Tolstoy might conjure up the beauty of Natasha or Anna at a ball, but only Machado could write of Sofia: "She was wearing a dark blue dress, very low-cut—for the reasons cited in Chapter XXXV."[3] Like Machado, Nabokov was a foe of capital punishment, and he begins *Invitation to a Beheading* with the hero having his death sentence pronounced, according to the custom of this nightmare world, with a nightmare discreetness, in a whisper. The second paragraph starts: "So we are nearing the end. The right-hand, still-untasted part of the novel, which, during our delectable reading, we would lightly feel, mechanically testing whether there were still plenty left (and our fingers were always gladdened by the placid, faithful thickness) has suddenly, for no reason at all, become quite meagre: a few minutes of quick reading, already downhill, and—O horrible" (*IB* 12).

In Machado and Nabokov the undermining and overturning of the conventions of fiction bespeak a skeptical, independent intelligence that can also be directed to challenges to extraliterary conventions and assumptions. Both writers can be caustically critical and mordantly ironic. Machado may not be quite the "peevish pessimist" that Brás Cubas calls himself, but he remains always alert to the ironies and imperfections of life beneath accepted commonplaces and practices. Nabokov's view of life could also seem bleak and unsparing. One critic responding to his first great Russian novel, *The Defense*, wrote, "How terrible, to see life as [Nabokov] does" (*VNRY* 343), and in the afterword to his first great English novel, *Lolita*, Nabokov reports a close friend worried that he lived "among such depressing people" (*Lolita* 318). Both Machado and Nabokov hated cruelty enough to depict it in its raw horror, in the nightmarish vivisections of first rats, then prisoners, then philosophers in Machado's "Alexandrian Tale" or the senseless, tasteless, agonizing, and appallingly cheery torture of the hero's son at the close of Nabokov's *Bend Sinister*.

Both Machado and Nabokov can ground their fiction in the particulars of their worlds yet can also shift at any moment to a view from far outside the apparent solidity of the characters' situations. Machado writes of the heroine of *Quincas Borba*: "Sofia put her soul into a cedar casket, closed the cedar one up in the lead casket of the day, and left it there, sincerely deceased. She didn't know that the deceased think, that a swarm of new notions comes to take the place of the old, and that they emerge criticizing the world the way spectators come out of the theater criticizing the play and the actors" (*QB* 222). The Nabokov scholar Alfred Appel Jr., who became a friend of his former teacher, told Nabokov of staging a puppet show for his children and catching the expression of horror and then hilarity on their faces when in the excitement of the climax of the story he knocked over the stage of the puppet world they had been so engrossed in—a shift in perspective that he felt akin to what readers face in Nabokov. Nabokov told him: "You must put that in your book" (*Annotated Lolita* xxxii).

Time has been a subject of literature since Ecclesiastes, if not since time immemorial. But both Machado and Nabokov not only obsess about time as loss but also show how the passage of time can make what had been reviled or barely noticed in its day seem infinitely precious if it lasts. In Machado, a politician's unsparing tell-all memoirs will cause a justified outcry for its breaches of trust, "but after a century has passed, the same book will become a valuable historical and psychological document. With cool objectivity readers will study the intimate life of our times: how we loved, how government cabinets formed or dissolved, if women were open or dissimulating, how we held elections and courted women, if we wore shawls or capes, what kind of carriages were in vogue, if watches were worn to the right or the left."[4] In exactly the same spirit, Nabokov's story "A Guide to Berlin" observes, "The horse-drawn tram has vanished, and so will the trolley, and some eccentric Berlin writer in the twenties of the twenty-first century, wishing to portray our time, will go to a museum of technological history and locate a hundred-year-old streetcar, yellow, uncouth, with old-fashioned curved seats, and in a museum of old costumes dig up a black, shiny-buttoned conductor's uniform. Then he will go home and compile a description of Berlin streets in bygone days. Everything, every trifle, will be valuable and meaningful: the conductor's purse, the advertisement over the window, that peculiar jolting motion which our great-grandchildren will perhaps imagine—everything will be ennobled and justified by its age" (*SoVN* 157).

Love has been an even more irresistible theme in literature than time. Not only does it dominate all of Machado's novels and most of Nabokov's, but both writers often explore the self-love entangled with the love of another: in the many adulteries in Machado or his chilling delineation of Carlos Maria's faithful but utterly narcissistic married love in *Quincas Borba*, or in Humbert's supposition that his adoration of Lolita elevates her, or in Van and Ada Veen's glorying in each other as magnifying mirrors of their mutual vanity. The perversity of jealousy fascinates Machado again and again, not least in adulterous lovers' jealousy of their mistresses' husbands or passing admirers. Humbert, too, becomes murderously jealous of the man who takes Lolita from him yet thinks nothing of showing Lolita his very active interest in other young girls (*Lolita* 163).Nothing will stop Van Veen's urge to duel or maim the two men with whom Ada has betrayed him, but even as he rushes by train after his rivals he caresses another willing girl under the table of the dining car.

Both Machado and Nabokov focus on jealousy as a prime case of conflicted human motives. More generally, both revel in psychological contradiction and psychological extremes, like the madness of Quincas Borba and Rubião, or the alienist in the story of that name, or the madness of Nabokov's heroes Luzhin, Hermann, Krug, and Kinbote.

Machado and Nabokov in strikingly similar ways resist the determinism of literary naturalism, from Machado's 1878 review of Eça de Queirós' *O Primo Basilio* through all the novels that followed, and from Nabokov's anti-deterministic parody of Theodore Dreiser's *An American Tragedy* in his own *King, Queen, Knave*. In Machado's story "Funeral March," Cordovil becomes obsessed with what he interprets as signs that he will die that evening, yet he lives on many years, just as in Nabokov's "A Busy Man" Grafitski recalls a dream that he will die in his thirty-third year and lives out the year in increasing panic only to find that he has been reprieved.

Time and love may be common literary themes, but darting a hundred years ahead to reevaluate what seems valueless in the present or analyzing jealousy as hypocritical vanity are rarities. Such specific overlaps testify to a singular congruence between Machado's imagination and Nabokov's.

Both novelists attend with the same care to often-unremarked aspects of the art of fiction or independently arrive at similar artistic ploys. Nabokov loved Chekhov and even named him as his desert-island author. But he also thought that in his drama Chekhov was caught "by the very conventions he thought he had broken— . . . he had not studied the art of drama completely enough, . . . was not critical enough about certain aspects of his medium" (cited in *VNAY* 31). Nabokov did not make the same mistake in his apprenticeship for fiction, nor did Machado. Nabokov paid close attention, in the work of other writers, and in his own practice, for instance, to what he calls the "art of preparation and transition" (*SIC* 10). He can make preparation singularly stealthy and transition remarkably fluid or comically or tragically jolting. Machado too explicitly and parodically deals with both preparation and transition: Brás Cubas writes at one point, "And now watch the skill, the art with which I make the greatest transition in this book" (*BC* 22) just before a would-be elegant but in fact comically forced transition; Bento Santiago raises the level of apprehension when he announces, "Let this chapter serve as preparation—and preparation is important, dear reader" (*DC* 116). One transition Machado and Nabokov particularly like to disguise or blur, to decisive effect, is the shift between objective reality and imagination: without any warning, description segues into conversations that can last for pages, as in Machado's story "Mariana" or Nabokov's novel *The Gift*, before we discover that these scenes have taken place only in the heroes' imaginations.

Both Machado and Nabokov distort chronological order to introduce their heroines before or after we are ready. Virgilia features teasingly in the first chapter of Brás Cubas's memoirs, only to be announced later in regular chronological order, and then delayed chapter after chapter. In Nabokov's *Mary*, the name of Mary, the great love of the hero's life, is mentioned on the first page of the novel without the hero realizing it, but Mary herself, despite providing the novel's title, never appears on its stage. In *The Defense*, Luzhin's future wife appears unannounced and unexpected at the end of one chapter, only for the narrative to have to backtrack, in a key move, before resuming the interrupted scene in the next chapter but one. Similarly the opening chapter of *Quincas Borba* introduces Rubião filled with hope that Sofia feels as keenly for him as he does for her, only for Machado to interrupt ("Come with me, reader. Let's have a look at him months earlier") before returning us to the same morning thirteen chapters later.

Machado and Nabokov independently invent or at least deploy one authorial device after another. Both repeatedly issue memory tests to the reader. Brás Cubas, for instance, reports that Virgilia's father "introduced me to his wife—an estimable lady—and his daughter, who in no way belied my father's panegyric. I swear to you, in no way. Reread Chapter XXVII" (89). In *Ada*, Van Veen in 1892 describes a series of photographs of 1884 that require us to recollect in similar detail events from three hundred pages earlier, then in 1967 refers back to that early summer one final time, after *five* hundred pages, in precise but oblique details that challenge our powers of recollection.

Both writers can dangle clues in front of our noses but seem to dismiss them, as Bento Santiago in the opening chapter of *Dom Casmurro* tells us, "Don't consult your dictionaries" for the special meaning of "*casmurro*" that has supplied his nickname, or Kinbote twice divulges the context in Shakespeare that provides the title for *Pale Fire*, without his or our realizing it. Like magicians, both writers slip in key information after engaging our attention elsewhere, like the casual reference to slave trading when we are waiting for Brás Cubas as a boy to avenge himself in some spectacular way on Villaças, or Van's disclosing in a subordinate clause his vile treatment of a would-be blackmailer while we are preoccupied with the agony of his parting from Ada.

And both writers explicitly conceal deeper meanings beneath dazzling surfaces. Machado explains that he writes "one utterance but with two meanings";[5] Nabokov tells the *New Yorker* that "most of the stories I am contemplating (and some I have written in the past—you have actually published one with such an 'inside' . . .) will be composed on these lines, according to this system where a second (main) story is woven into, or placed behind, the superficial semitransparent one" (*SL* 116–17).

Both writers challenge and reward their readers. Nabokov stressed that he wrote for "the artistic reader" (*SO* 40), "the creative reader" (*NG* 140). "The authentic writer of genius," he maintained, "writes for an ideal audience, for readers or spectators whom he would like to possess the same power of comprehension as his own power of expression."[6] He prefers the reader with "some artistic sense—which I propose to develop in myself and others whenever I have the chance" (*LL* 3). Machado's playful tweaking of imagined incompetents in his audience both deters the uncreative reader and instructs creative readers in exactly Nabokov's spirit.

More conventional novels, even those of major writers, build to dramatic crises and climaxes. Both Machado and Nabokov thought this falsified life. Brás Cubas writes: "in order to titillate the nerves of fantasy I should have suffered great despair, shed a few tears, and not eaten lunch. It would have been like a novel, but it wouldn't have been biography" (*BC* 160). Nabokov explicitly stated his opposition to the conventions of drama: "The idea of conflict tends to endow life with a logic it never has" (*MUSSR* 340). He proposes instead "the creation of a certain unique pattern of life in which the sorrows and passions[7] of a particular man will follow the rules of his own individuality" (*MUSSR* 341). Both Nabokov and Machado in their best fiction tend to follow not the contours of rising dramatic conflict but the unique pattern of a life: the life rhythms of a Brás Cubas, a Dom Casmurro, a Humbert, or a Van Veen.

What makes Nabokov and Machado, who knew nothing of each other, more alike than either of them was to writers they *did* know? Each of them, I think, had a powerful independence of mind and spirit and a powerful sense that independence matters. Both of them detested the iron-clad determinism in literary naturalism. But even realism, even as perfected by Flaubert and Tolstoy, did not satisfy them. Realism at its best seems to place us right inside the situations of the characters. Like all animals, we have evolved to respond to our immediate surroundings, especially, in the case of our ultrasocial species, to our immediate social environment. Our senses have evolved to pick up cues from this immediate world and our emotions have evolved to assign them instant value.

But unlike other animals, we have uniquely evolved ways to step outside our here and now, to remember the remote past, to imagine possible futures or different perspectives, to generalize or connect, and to direct others to these remote vistas, improbable options, and unprecedented images. Machado and Nabokov always want to keep, as Nabokov once wrote, "all the shutters and lids and doors of the mind . . . open at once" (*RLSK* 67) and to develop that imaginative openness in their styles and their readers. They can engage us intensely in situations, but they also remind us always of the power of thought to make what Nabokov calls knight moves of the mind.[8] Their natural sense of independence explains their self-conscious awareness of not just the scenes before them but the worlds of actuality and possibility around them. It explains their gleeful challenges to literary and intellectual conventions. It explains their readiness to step beyond the immediate or the sudden leaps into distant perspectives that simultaneously testify to our freedom and expose our vulnerability in the infinitude of time and space.

The high value Machado and Nabokov set on independence finds its reflection in their social attitudes. Machado offers a critical analysis of economic dependence in clientelist nineteenth-century Brazil, and, of course, a particularly stinging critique of slavery, still in force in Brazil until 1888. Nabokov, by contrast, living in a more economically liberal world, could celebrate independence—even in the poverty he and his fellow émigrés experienced in Russian Europe—and denounce the authoritarian regimes he escaped from in Russia and Germany. To an early reader of his book on Nikolay Gogol who noted Gogol did not object to serfdom, Nabokov replied, maybe not, but "the interior moral standards of [*Dead Souls*] bristle against it" (*VNAY* 56).

Being so independent of mind, Machado and Nabokov tended to swim against the tide: as Nabokov instructed young writers, "Avoid the cliché of your time" (Givan interview). But since in the nineteenth and twentieth centuries the prevailing tides of thought flowed in opposite directions, Machado and Nabokov faced in contrary ways.

Machado's independence made him an instinctive critic of the widespread nineteenth-century confidence in inevitable progress. In his delirium, Brás Cubas sees the cavalcade of folly in human history and beyond and the delusions of the nineteenth century, "in the end as miserable as the ones before" (*BC* 20). Machado satirizes would-be improvers in stories like "The Alienist" and "Alexandrian Tale" or in his critique of positivism and social Darwinism in Quincas Borba's humanitism. Throughout his work he stresses the mixed nature of humanity, the egotism and vanity likely to taint even the rare acts of altruism, and the tangle of good sometimes emerging from bad and bad from good. Even the competition between different possible versions of what we see as good can lead to disaster or distress in the fever of indecision that kills Flora in *Esau and Jacob* (1904) or the young love that triumphs at the cost of the godparents' happiness in *Counselor Ayres' Memorial* (1908).

If Machado was a pessimist in a century of optimism, Nabokov was an optimist in a century of pessimism. The carnage of World War I, the tyrannies of communist Russia and fascist Europe, the Holocaust, the threat of nuclear warfare, and the prospect of technological apocalypse have made gloom the dominant mood of modern intellectual life. Where Machado resisted the optimism of his century, the still darker Beckett resonated perfectly with the pessimism of the next. Nabokov, by contrast, remained an optimist, despite exile and poverty, a father assassinated by Russian monarchists, and family and friends at risk or killed in the Holocaust. Nabokov's strong disagreement with Spengler's *Decline of the West* and similar fare inspired him to write a novel set in the present, *Glory*, which he first planned to call *Romanticheskiy vek* (*Romantic Age*). By having the insanely erratic Quincas Borba endorse Pangloss, Machado marks his own distance from optimism. Nabokov, by contrast, declared himself ready to agree with the eighteenth-century philosophers who thought humans are fundamentally good (*PF* 225, *LL* 375).

Yet many have understood Nabokov differently: "How terrible, to see life as [Nabokov] does" (*VNRY* 343); why does he live "among such depressing people" (*Lolita* 318)? His novels swarm with prominent suicides (five of seventeen novels) and violent deaths, including prominent murders and on- or offstage executions (eleven of seventeen novels). In *Lolita* even murder pales beside child abuse. How can I, and how can Nabokov, read Nabokov as an optimist?

Here the chase hots up as we focus on not the similarities but the differences between Machado and Nabokov. Machado stresses, never more clearly than in "The Devil's Church," that human lives are inevitably mixed. Even positive forces can conflict, as in his most serene mature novel, *Counselor Ayres' Memorial*. In his emphasis that even the clash of positive factors can compound human sorrow Machado anticipates the twentieth-century philosopher Isaiah Berlin, who emphasizes that even ideals we may agree on, like love, freedom, justice, and tolerance, may conflict rather than converge.

Nabokov, by contrast, focuses squarely on suffering and evil but nevertheless sees grounds for optimism beyond. In the essay "The Art of

Literature," composed during World War II, Nabokov wrote that if we reject false common sense,

> the irrational belief in the goodness of man . . . becomes something much more than the wobbly basis of idealistic philosophies. It becomes a solid and iridescent truth. . . . goodness becomes a central and tangible part of one's world, which world at first sight seems hard to identify with the modern one of newspaper editors and other bright pessimists, who will tell you that it is, mildly speaking, illogical to applaud the supremacy of good at a time when the police state, or communism, is trying to turn the globe into five million square miles of terror, stupidity, and barbed wire.
>
> (LL 373)

Nabokov's surface irony can sting but can also hide deeper positive ironies. The Nabokov character closest to his maker, John Shade, writes at the end of his poem "Pale Fire," where he probes the question of death and an afterlife, and recounts the story of his daughter's suicide:

> And if my private universe scans right,
> So does the verse of galaxies divine
> Which I suspect is an iambic line.
> I'm reasonably sure that we survive
> And that my darling somewhere is alive,
> As I am reasonably sure that I
> 980 Shall wake at six tomorrow, on July
> The twenty-second, nineteen fifty-nine.

Shade can read his world positively despite the raw pain of his daughter's loss, but despite his confidence, he will be killed by a madman that very afternoon: he will *not* wake at six the next morning or ever again. Nabokov's emphatic irony seems to deny that "the verse of galaxies divine" can scan right, or that Shade has any reason to suppose that his daughter, despite her suicide, is somewhere, somehow, in some sense alive. Yet Nabokov allows the curious reader to see a "second (main) story . . . woven into, or placed behind, the superficial semitransparent one," where both Shade's daughter and Shade himself survive beyond death and contribute their creative energy to what from this side of death may look like a cruelly mocking world (see *NPFMAD*).

Again and again Nabokov sets up positives, counters them with ironic neg-atives, then allows still deeper positives to incorporate but reverse the nega-tive. Although he had no time for organized religion and thought the very idea of God revealed the limitations of human thought, he suspected some cre-ative consciousness behind the world. He also supposed that the world's inex-haustible details offer human minds the chance to discover more and more and in that process of discovery to share much of the magic of creation. And while he felt strongly the limitations of human consciousness, the absurdity of our not being able to escape the prisons of the present and the self, he also felt that love, kindness, curiosity, imagination, and art offer intimations of a freer and ampler world beyond the confines of mortal consciousness.

Nabokov's optimistic metaphysics supported not only an optimistic epis-temology but also an optimistic ethics, a confidence that by dint of effort individuals and humanity could become more sensitive to their world, kinder, freer, more creative.[9] For him, the forces of good *do* converge, even if at a point beyond human sight. He ends his introduction to *The Eye*, whose hero tries to commit suicide: "The forces of imagination which, in the long run, are the forces of good remain steadfastly on Smurov's side, and the very bitterness of tortured love proves to be as intoxicating and bracing as would be its most ecstatic requital" (*Eye* 10).

Like all great artists, Nabokov constructed his imagined worlds to match his sense of the real world around him. He tried to make his fiction inex-haustible and to allow the curious and creative reader the chance of discov-ery after discovery, even to discover positive ironies that could encompass and repolarize earlier negatives and strike deeper into the heart of things.

Machado's and Nabokov's differences in outlook help highlight new dif-ferences in detail. In his delirium, Brás Cubas hears Nature tell him: "You're alive: that's the only torment I want" (*BC* 17). Nabokov, by contrast, has one of his narrators describe death as "the wrench of relinquishing forever all one's memories—that's a commonplace, but what courage man must have had to go through that commonplace again and again and not give up the rigma-role of accumulating again and again the riches of consciousness that will be snatched away!" (*Ada* 585). Nabokov acknowledges the pain and the loss in death, but he also stresses the magnitude of what consciousness amasses in the course of a life—and that very magnitude seems to him to intimate more.

Machado sees time as loss, as mishap: wasted by Brás Cubas; blighted, even after high good fortune, in Rubião's fall; a seeming paradise that turns into its own hell for Bento Santiago. We squander even life's best gifts or have them snatched from us by time and death. For Nabokov time also involves loss, but he sees our inability to reenter the rich reality every moment of our past once had as only more proof of the limitedness of human consciousness. Nevertheless, for Nabokov we can access the past, albeit indirectly, through the controlled power and precision of memory.

Emphasizing humanity as flawed, Machado appeals to his readers, too, as flawed creatures who may fail to remember or infer or to expect more than what convention prompts. Nabokov, by contrast, invites his good readers to become fellow artists who can help reconstitute the complex worlds of his fictions. Machado and Nabokov both famously compare the relationship of authors, characters, and readers to chess, but their differences are revealing. In *Esau and Jacob*, Machado writes, "There is an advantage in having the characters of my story collaborate in it, aiding the author in accordance with a law of solidarity, a kind of exchange of services between the chess-player and his men."[10] Where Machado sees solidarity between the author and the characters he moves about on the board, Nabokov by contrast focuses on chess *problems* rather than chess games and locates the real drama not "between White and Black but between the composer and the hypothetical solver (just as in a first-rate work of fiction the real clash is not between the characters but between the author and the [reader])" (*SM* 290).[11] Machado interrupts his narratives in a jarring, wary engagement with his flawed characters, his flawed readers, and his flawed world. Nabokov sees his novels, like his chess problems, as enclosed worlds, like lives bracketed off by death, upon which we can look as if from outside life or beyond death, enjoying not only our empathetic engagement with the characters in their worlds but especially our creative engagement with the creator of these miniature worlds.

Machado frequently sounds notes of failure or undercuts outbursts of eloquence: "No, that's not a good comparison" (*BC* 24); "One of the ancients has said he loathed a guest with a good memory. Life is filled with such guests, and I perhaps am one of them, though proof of having a weak memory may be the very fact that the name of that ancient does not occur to me at the moment, but he was one of the ancients and that's enough" (*DC* 119); "bewitched at the feet of my Crippled Venus. Bewitched is just a way of enhancing style" (*BC* 85). Nabokov, by contrast, tends to stretch language to its utmost, to maximize the mind's motility in space, time or thought. The rare hints of failure will usually be recouped by proof of success. In his autobiography, he cannot recall the name of the dog of the girl he loved on the beach of Biarritz in the summer of 1907, when he was eight, but then, near the end of the chapter, "triumphantly, along those remote beaches, over the glossy evening sands of the past, where each footprint slowly fills up with sunset water, here it comes, here it comes, echoing and vibrating:

Floss, Floss, Floss!" (*SM* 151–52). Even the ineptitudes of Nabokov's leading characters, like Pnin's comically flawed English or Kinbote's appalling verse, tend to be matched by aptitudes, Pnin's precise and erudite Russian and Kinbote's flamboyant prose.

Both Machado and Nabokov linger over love. Machado mocks the hopes that the intensity of love might testify to its permanence in stories like "Eternal!" or Brás Cubas's passion for the fickle fortune hunter Marcella. He regularly exposes the vanity so often lurking in love. And if we do not cease to love, we cease to live, like Helena, Nhan-Lóló, or Flora. On the other hand, although Nabokov can show love as monstrous egotism or narcissism, in Humbert and in Van and Ada Veen, he can also show the joys of fulfilled and faithful love, in Fyodor and Zina or John and Sybil Shade. Machado focuses again and again on jealousy not only to show the pains that can complicate the pleasures of love but also as an emblem of the conflict between competing goods: Pedro and Paulo both have qualities that Flora loves, but she cannot have both of them; Flora has qualities that both Pedro and Paulo love, but each resents the other's love; and ultimately the tension between competing positives leaves everyone unfulfilled. In Nabokov the bitter jealousy Van feels toward Ada's infidelities destroys their early bliss, just as it destroys Bento's feelings for Capitú in *Dom Casmurro*, but after many years apart Van and Ada resume their passionate amour for almost another half-century, where Bento and Capitú remain apart, and as if in separate worlds, for the rest of their lives.

Nabokov was a maximalist in a century of minimalism. Some of his most flawed characters have tried to maximize themselves, to transcend ordinary limits, in entirely wrong ways. Hermann tries to escape the prison of his self through stealing another's identity and life. Humbert tries to retrieve the past even at the cost of the frail and delicate present. Kinbote seeks to impose his ego on the world and on his neighbor's poetic work. Nabokov creates monsters of egotism, as he says, to show the demons that have been booted out of his private cathedral. Most memorably, he inverts his own positives, he tests them against their magnified negatives, but in ways that allow the positives to show through.

That leads me to a final cluster of questions. Is Machado as much of a peevish pessimist as Brás Cubas? Or is he more like Nabokov, ready to express or test his own positives by means of their negatives, or so committed to what he takes as good that he cannot help indignantly confronting the bad? Machado often depicts lives wasted (Brás Cubas, Quincas Borba, Rubião, Dom Casmurro). but his own life could hardly have been more resolutely without waste. When his heroes complain of life as an empty pageant, do they speak for him or does he indict them for not having made more of themselves? He depicts idleness, fickleness, greed, jealousy, envy, and vanity, but he also introduces characters who represent values he himself embodied: faithful love, committed and conscientious work, care for others, and creativity. Indeed, his positives can seem so strong, even in the acerbic *Quincas Borba* ("universal sympathy" is "the soul of" Dona Fernanda, [*QB* 262]) or a late novel like *Counselor Ayres' Memorial*, that they can come close to romantic idealizations. And if even the best of human achievements will erode in time, Machado cites writers like Homer, Virgil, and Lucian, whose contribution to human thought and life has lasted for millennia and whose names he is happy to pass on to readers to come—as readers and writers to come will no doubt pass on *his* name.

Both Machado and Nabokov can vividly portray human shortcomings, the transience of human lives, and the minuteness of our world in the perspectives beyond our own that human imaginations can readily adopt. Both had an independence of mind that made them resist the commonplaces of their time, but it was more than that, surely, that meant they had such different evaluations of the ultimate place of human life, even if they often used such similar means. Machado, without Nabokov's metaphysical hopes and his confident maximalism, did live in a darker world, but both held onto values like love, kindness, work, play, and art, ordinary human values that both knew how to turn into very similar and very different works of extraordinary art.

NABOKOV WORKS

19. *Speak, Memory:* The Life and the Art

When I wrote my biography of Nabokov, I had to deal with the Pegasus in the room: Nabokov's own autobiography. I mined *Speak, Memory* as much as I could for inimitable evocations and for factual details (except in the rare cases where documentary evidence proved Nabokov's attempt at fidelity to the facts had failed), but I also analyzed his artful shaping of his life in order to throw new light on his mind and art.

The first section of the introduction to my *Vladimir Nabokov: The Russian Years* (1990) quickly surveys Nabokov's life; the second shows how much the artfulness he displayed in recounting his life could teach us. In a talk in Moscow in May 1990, a few months before the biography's publication, at the first Nabokov conference in what was still the Soviet Union, I juxtaposed that second section of the introduction, the analysis of *Speak, Memory*'s art, which in the sentence I focus on foreshadows Nabokov's father's death, with the rawness of the diary account that Nabokov wrote up the day after the killing.

I visited Russia in 1990, after hair-raisingly clandestine researches in 1982, only at the encouragement of the late Simon Karlinsky, the finest of émigré Nabokovians (he began reading "Sirin" in Harbin, Manchuria, the émigré capital of the east, in his early teens, in the 1930s).[1] When I happened to talk to him in early 1990, he encouraged me, despite my wariness, to revisit Russia's libraries and archives: "They'll show you everything!" They certainly showed me whatever I knew to ask for, and I was able to squeeze some of what I found into the proofs of *The Russian Years*.

Nabokov always insisted that audiences needed to know the details of artists' work but had no right to know the details of their lives. True to that principle, he made his own autobiography more a work of art than any other autobiography has ever been, and he left out almost all his adult life.

One problem for a biographer of someone who has written such a superlative autobiography as *Speak, Memory* is to situate one's own effort in relation to the author's "official" version of his life. In *Vladimir Nabokov: The Russian Years*, I tried two different solutions to the problem: the first, to interpret *Speak, Memory* as a work of art—and to show how the artistry, the transforming imagination of the writer, in fact can reveal *more* about Nabokov than a more direct transcription from life would do—and the second, to ferret out those direct transcriptions, the raw facts behind the art, the things that Nabokov would rather we didn't see. I want to take as my example the death of Nabokov's father in *Speak, Memory* and in real life.

Although Nabokov was often hailed as the finest stylist of his time, many readers have found themselves perturbed by the deliberateness of his style. To them, his phrasing calls attention to itself too much to express genuine emotion or even to *say* anything. This puts Nabokov in good company, since it was exactly the reaction Shakespeare provoked in Tolstoy. Surely no old man on a heath in a storm would ever cry out

Blow, winds, and crack your cheeks! rage, blow!
You cataracts and hurricanoes, spout
Till you have drench'd our steeples, drown'd the cocks!
You sulph'rous and thought-executing fires,
Vaunt-couriers to oak-cleaving thunderbolts,
Singe my white head! and thou, all-shaking thunder,
Strike flat the thick rotundity o' th' world!

From his premises, Tolstoy is quite correct. Shakespeare's lines testify to an impressive verbal mastery but they do not represent any plausible human speech. There is not one reader in a thousand, though, who does not feel that if Tolstoy had just turned his stiff neck a fraction he could have espied in Shakespeare all the life and truth he could have wished. A considered style may not convey what naturally comes first to mind or mouth, but for that very reason it can express so much more.

At the end of the first chapter of *Speak, Memory* Nabokov describes how the villagers living on the fringes of the family estate where he spent his childhood often subjected his father to a spontaneous Russian rite of gratitude. After Vladimir Dmitrievich Nabokov had settled some dispute or granted some request, five or six men would toss him high in the air and catch him in their arms. Young Vladimir at lunch inside would see only his father aloft and not the men below:

Thrice, to the mighty heave-ho of his invisible tossers, he would fly up in this fashion, and the second time he would go higher than the first and then there he would be, on his last and loftiest flight, reclining, as if for good, against the cobalt blue of the summer noon, like one of those paradisiac personages who comfortably soar, with such a wealth of folds in their garments, on the vaulted ceiling of a church while below, one by one, the wax tapers in mortal hands light up to make a swarm of minute flames in the midst of incense, and the priest chants of eternal repose, and funeral lilies conceal the face of whoever lies there among the swimming lights, in the open coffin.

(SM 31–32)

Some will enjoy that sentence enough to trust its author. Others might suppose it a tour de force too accomplished to be aiming at any response but meek acclamation. To those with an open mind, I would like to suggest that the first reaction may be right.

Despite the generalized nature of the church scene that materializes beneath the sky's blue vault, Nabokov in fact anticipates here (as the good reader may intuit at once, as any reader of *Speak, Memory* should gradually recognize) a precise moment later in his own life, the day he looks down at his father lying in an open coffin. Though that first image of a man soaring against the sky seems to start careening away from its occasion, there is nothing haphazard or indulgent in the way the sentence drops down from the figure poised as if forever in the air to the dead man on his bier. For even as Nabokov envisages the funeral he also half-affirms his father's immortality: "like one of those paradisiac personages who comfortably soar." But style cannot charm the facts away: the body still lies there motionless in the church, the candle flames swim because of the tears in young Nabokov's eyes.

Nabokov ends the chapter this way to add his own tribute to that of the villagers—the oldest of whom, incidentally, still revered the memory of Nabokov's father after more than sixty years of Soviet rule. Vladimir Dmitrievich died a hero's death, bravely defending his chief ideological opponent within his own liberal Kadet party from two right-wing thugs and being shot in the scuffle. Nabokov's verbal glide from the villagers' gratitude to his father's last rites foreshadows the fact that in the very manner of his death his father justified the high esteem in which he was always held.

Again and again throughout *Speak, Memory* Nabokov returns obliquely to his father's death as if it were a wound he cannot leave alone but can hardly bear to touch. For Nabokov the love of those closest to the heart—a parent, a spouse, a child—distends the soul to dwarf all other feeling. The narrowly focused love that marked his life also shapes his fiction, whether positively (Fyodor and Zina, Krug and his son, John and Sybil Shade) or negatively, in the desolation of love's absence (Smurov or Kinbote) or the horror of its sham surrogates (Albinus and Margot, Humbert and Lolita). Because love matters so much to Nabokov, so too does loss (Krug and his wife or son, Fyodor and his father). But he had learned from his parents to bear distress with dignity, and when he depicts his father high in the midday air he alludes to his private grief with the restraint taught him as a child. The formality and apparent distance in no way diminish the emotion: he simply feels that even a sense of loss sharp enough to last a lifetime must be met with courage and self-control.

Some conclude that since his stylistic originality announces itself with such force, Nabokov therefore can have only style to offer. I find another explanation more convincing: his style stands out so boldly because he has rethought the art of writing deeply enough to express all his originality of mind.

In the sentence I am scrutinizing, two opposite aspects of Nabokov's style reveal two counterpoised tendencies in his thought. On the one hand, he admits to an "innate passion for independence" (Feifer interview, 22). He reveres the particularity of things, all that can break away from generalization and the blur of habit; he values the freedom of the moment, the possibility of the freakily unexpected that derails the iron mechanism of cause and effect; he celebrates the capacity of the mind to move about within the present. All these impulses make his style a perpetual declaration of independence: in this case, he chooses to stress the unconstrained mobility of the mind as his sentence loops off from the summer sky to church ceiling—and refuses to return.

On the other hand, Nabokov prizes pattern and design, things united in new combinations rather than considered in isolation. He is entranced and puzzled by the chance harmonies of the moment, the complex artistry of mimicry in the natural world, the designs of time or fate, the patterns lurking within memory. When he lets a new scene materialize under the flimsy awning of a simile he seems to have yielded to mere momentary whim. But before the sentence ends we discover that it was always under control, and as we read on in *Speak, Memory* we can make out that that image of church and funeral forms part of a pattern at the core of the book: again and again Nabokov foreshadows his father's death, reticently but ineluctably, as if he had no choice but to reconstitute the insidious designs of fate.

Independence and pattern function like the complementary twin hemispheres of Nabokov's mind. He searches out pattern in the music of a phrase or the spell of an anagram, in the shapes of time or the weave of the universe. He pursues independence in everything from his own sense of self to his philosophy of history, from his politics or esthetics to his way of looking at a face or a tree.

As Nabokov well knew, the manifest artistry of the sentence on his father—or of his style in general—carries its own metaphysical implications. Consciousness at full stretch can pass beyond its impromptu range; here it can also transcend time by compressing together a past occasion and what was then the future by freezing the moment to leave someone suspended in that cobalt sky. Through the force of his art Nabokov answers the question with which he began the first chapter of *Speak, Memory*, the question he confesses has always bewildered and harassed him: what lies outside the prison of human time, our entrapment within the present and our subjection to death? Typically, he chooses to display rather than efface the power of a mind working *un*spontaneously and so able to create an image or a thought out of the ordinary. The energy mortal consciousness can have when it vaults over the barrier of the moment suggests more than anything else its kinship with some other form of consciousness lurking beyond human limits.

In the last chapter of *Speak, Memory* Nabokov writes:

> Whenever I start thinking of my love for a person, I am in the habit of immediately drawing radii from my love—from my heart, from the tender nucleus of a personal matter—to monstrously remote points of the universe. . . . I have to have all space and all time participate in my emotion, in my mortal love, so that the edge of its mortality is taken off, thus helping me to fight the utter degradation, ridicule, and horror of having developed an infinity of sensation and thought within a finite existence.
>
> (*SM* 296–97)

This states the problem Nabokov addresses throughout his art: what can we make of the breach between the limitless capacity of consciousness and its absurd limitation? To answer this, he has searched relentlessly for some consciousness beyond the boundaries of the human.

This interest in the beyond stems not from any denigration or repudiation of the here and now: quite the contrary. Nabokov had two great gifts as a writer and a man: literary genius and a genius for personal happiness. The hero of *The Gift*—whose giftedness is twofold in just this way—actually anticipates in a rush of gratitude and joy that he will compile "a practical handbook: *How to Be Happy*" (*Gift* 328). But even sunny genius knows another side of experience, for to the degree that the world makes happiness possible it also primes us for the ache of loss. The key to Nabokov is that he loved and enjoyed so much in life that it was extraordinarily painful for him to envisage losing all he held precious, a language, a love, this instant, that sound.

Nabokov extols the freedom we have within the moment, the richness of our perceptions and emotions and thought. Nevertheless, we are all imprisoned within ourselves, trapped in the present, doomed to die. It seems brutal and senseless that we must store up such wealth of recollection—and even agonies like bereavement in time become a kind of wealth, a measure of having lived—when we know that it will all be snatched away by death. But *perhaps* at its very best consciousness itself hints at a way out. In art or science, in memory, in the exercise of imagination and attention and kindness, the mind seems almost able to peer past the prison bars of selfhood and time.

Nabokov's sentence tosses his father so high he almost condenses into pigment and dries out on a ceiling fresco. Such sudden, disturbing transitions from life to art occur often in Nabokov. Why? A fashionable conundrum? Art for art's sake?

No: Nabokov believed in art for *life's* sake. Cast your eyes around a crowded room: a meeting, a party, a classroom. No artist could create people so individual—in appearance, manner, character, history—or render so flawlessly all the nuances of their interaction. But that does not make art second-rate, a poor imitation of life: on the contrary, Nabokov says, art has awakened us to such qualities as detail, integrity, and harmony that we can now recognize as part of the inherent artistry of life. See the world this way, and everything—a crumpled leaf, the smoke above an ashtray—becomes miraculous, a token of the inexhaustible creativity of the world.

Often when Nabokov jolts us from life to art he also tilts us from life to death. In the sentence about his father or at the end of half a dozen novels, he opens the trapdoor of terra firma and reminds us not to accept stolidly "the marvel of consciousness—that sudden window swinging open on a sunlit landscape amidst the night of non-being" (Feifer interview 22). In life we can never escape being who we are and what we are, but in art we peer inside other souls, we return at will to the past, we look from outside on an invented world. Nabokov deliberately exploits all these special conditions of the work of art. In life the present moment has the very stamp of "reality," but once the moment recedes we can never recall it in its fullness: it becomes almost as if it had never been. But works of art are available for endless reinspection, and Nabokov ensures that in *his* books the past we reexamine will continue to disclose complexities simply not visible at first. He tries to change our relation to time, and that, he suggests, might be one of our new freedoms, our new doors to "reality," if we ever escape the limitations of human consciousness.

In the world of art pain remains unreal and just as good as pleasure: the greater Lear's agony, the more our world is enriched. Perhaps beyond the human, that might be true of mortal hopes and fears, so that what ultimately matters might be not what we feel but the answering pity or delight our feelings arouse in whoever watches over us. Perhaps: but within this world we can never know, and Nabokov returns from metaphysical speculation to insist that in this life we have no choice but to act as if another's pain is as real as our own. Just as he chooses what sets art apart from life to define by contrast the conditions of being human, so he contrasts our moral immunity from the sorrows of art's invented worlds with the tangled world of "real, or at least responsible life" (*Ada* 97).

When characters like Humbert, Hermann, Axel Rex, or Van and Ada Veen claim that they are special, that they are artists, that they inhabit a different plane of being from those around them, they exaggerate a real condition of human life. Each of us exists in a sense on a different plane from everyone else: you are all outside my consciousness, the place where I *am*, as I am outside yours. But human consciousness also gives us the imagination to feel how immediate another's pain can be. Nabokov's artist-heroes dare to claim a special dispensation from ordinary morals only because they fail to imagine that others are also special, at least to themselves. Nabokov gives these "artists" all the imaginative scope they want to record their dubious pasts, but he condemns their strategies as mere cover-ups for their failure of imagination: in *his* world, in *this* life, there are no exemptions to be granted from responsibility. And if even those of gifted imagination do not imagine well enough, what of the rest of us?

Nothing could be more quintessentially Nabokovian than the sudden focal shifts in his sentence about his father as it rises up from a real memory to hover an instant in the world of art or eternity, among those painted paradisiac personages, before returning to this world, where Nabokov grieves for the man who taught him—as he puts it—the "moral "tradition, [the] principles of decency and personal honor deliberately passed from father to son" (Laansoo interview, 41). He needs to know more than this world holds, but he never shirks the fact that this may be the only world any of us can know.

And yet, and yet . . . Nabokov tilts the plane of literature—and of life. Reading him we no longer simply observe the drama of character against character; we become protagonists in a larger arena: the reader confronting the author, the mind confronting its world. In his best works Nabokov makes us recognize that his worlds are not ready made, that they are being created before our eyes, that the more we participate in their creation—observing their details, connecting up their parts, trying to solve all the problems they pose or feign not to pose—the more "real" these worlds become, and at the same time the more their reality seems only a step toward something realer still. As discoveries multiply, the pulse of excitement quickens, the sense of wonder deepens, until we stand on the threshold of new truth.

And that, says Nabokov, is how things are. If only we refuse to take our world for granted, we can detect something artful lurking at the heart of life, inviting us deeper into the world, allowing us to penetrate further and further into the mystery of its creation, perhaps even promising us a new relation to everything we know.

A great deal can be done by examining how Nabokov transformed the raw facts of his life into the art of *Speak, Memory*—not by misrepresenting the facts, which so far as I can ascertain he never willfully did, but simply by selection, style, and structure. But, on the other hand, as readers we inevitably wonder about the man behind this art. We can appreciate Nabokov's instinct for privacy, but at the same time we are deeply curious to know the original experiences behind what his imagination has transformed. In the case of the death of his father, half-assassination, half-accident, Nabokov seems to have had a particularly intense desire to control, to sublimate, to redeem the shock and horror of the initial event. That makes us wonder all the more about the way he reacted to the catastrophe before he could call on the power and consolation of his art.

I want now to cite Nabokov's own diary account of the most tragic evening of his life—an account that he would never have wanted published because it was too private, too painful, too raw. (For details about the context, which I explained in the Moscow talk, see *VNRY* 189–91.)

I want to stress the contrast between this straightforward diary account and that passage from *Speak, Memory* I lingered over. The finished art of that single sentence from *Speak, Memory* has an extraordinary range of implication missing from Nabokov's faithful transcript of a real-life scene, but it has very little of this scene's emotional power. As readers, as people interested in Nabokov, we want the art and its implications, but at moments we also want the rawness of raw life. Yet at the same time we will see that even as he records these events, Nabokov reveals the inherent artistry of his imagination: his accuracy of observation, his ability to recreate a scene in all its power not by the contrivances of false rhetoric, not by pumping the bellows of the emotions, but by his great respect for particulars and for the harmony—in this case the terrible, nightmarish harmony—of the way they interact.

28 March. I returned home about 9 p.m, after a heavenly day. After dinner I sat in the chair by the divan and opened a little volume of Blok. Mother, half-lying, was setting the cards out for patience. It was quiet at home—the girls were already asleep, Sergey was out. I was reading aloud those tender poems about Italy, about damp, resonant Venice, about Florence, like a smoky iris. "How splendid that is," Mother said, "yes, yes, exactly: a smoky iris." And then the phone rang in the hall. There was nothing unusual in its ring. I was simply annoyed that my reading was interrupted. I went to the phone. Hessen's voice: "Who's that?" "Volodya. Hello, Iosif Vladimirovich." "I am ringing because, . . . I want to tell you, to warn you . . ." "Yes, go on." "Something terrible has happened to your father." "What exactly?" "Something terrible. . . . A car is coming for you." "But what exactly has happened?" "A car is coming. Open the door below." "Fine." I hung up, got to my feet. Mother was standing in the door. She asked, eyebrows twitching, "What's happened?" I said, "Nothing special." My voice was cold, almost dry. "*Tell* me." "Nothing special. The fact is, father has been hit by a car. He's hurt his leg." I went through the living room to my bedroom. Mother followed. "No, I implore you, tell me." "Nothing to worry about. They're picking me up straight away." . . . She both believed me and did not. I changed, filled my cigarette case. My thoughts, all my thoughts, clenched their teeth. "My heart will burst," Mother said, "simply burst, if you are hiding anything." "Father has hurt his leg, rather seriously, Hessen said. That's all." Mother sobbed, went on her knees before me. "I implore you." I continued to calm her as I could. . . .

Yes, my heart *knew*, the end had come, but what exactly had happened was still a mystery, and in not knowing some hope could still flicker. Somehow neither Mother nor I linked Hessen's words with father's being that evening at Milyukov's lecture or that some sort of scene was expected there. . . . For some reason I remembered the afternoon: on the train with Svetlana [the girl who would within a few weeks become his fiancée] I had traced on the fogged-up carriage window the word "happiness"—and every letter trickled downwards in a bright line, a damp wriggle. Yes, my happiness has run. . . .

—At last a car drove up. Out came Shtein, whom I had never met before, and Yakovlev. I opened the doors. Yakovlev followed me, took me by the hand. "Keep calm. Shots were fired at the meeting. Your father was wounded." "Badly?" "Yes, badly." They stayed below, I went after Mother. Repeated what I had heard, knowing inside that the truth was softened. We went down. . . . Took off. . . .

That night journey I remember as something *outside life*, monstrously slow, like those mathematical puzzles that torment us in feverish half-sleep. I looked at the lights swimming past, at the whitish bands of lighted pavement, at the spiral reflections in the mirrory-black asphalt and it seemed to me that I was cut off from all this in some fateful manner—that the streetlights and the dark shadows of passersby were an accidental mirage, and the sole thing clear and significant and alive was the grief, tenacious, suffocating, compressing my heart. "Father is no more." These four words hammered in my brain and I tried to imagine his face, his movements. The night before he had been so happy, so kind. He laughed, he fought with me when I began to demonstrate a boxing clinch. Then everyone went off to bed, Father began to undress in his room and I did the same in mine next door. We chatted through the open door, talked of *Sergey*, of his strange, abnormal inclinations. Then Father helped me put my trousers under the press, and drew them out, turning the screws, and said, laughing: "That must hurt them." Dressed in pyjamas I sat on the arm of the leather chair, and Father, squatting, cleaned the shoes he had taken off. We were talking now about the opera *Boris Godunov*. He tried to remember how and when Vanya returns after his father has sent him off. Couldn't recall. At last I went to bed and hearing Father also going off asked him to give me the newspapers, he passed them through the slit of the parted doors—I didn't even see his hands. And I remember, that movement seemed creepy, ghostly—as if the sheets had thrust themselves through. . . . —And the next morning Father set off for *Rul'* before I woke and I didn't see him again. And now I was rocking in a closed car, the lights were shining—amber lights, screeching trams, and the route was long, long, and the tiny streets flashing by were all unfamiliar.

At last we arrived. Entrance to the Philharmonie. Hessen and Kaminka came across the street to us. They approach. I support Mother. "Avgust Isaakievich, Avgust Isaakievich, what's happened, tell me, what's happened?" she asks, seizing him by the sleeves. He spreads out his hands. "Something terrible." He sobs, cannot finish. "So it's all over, all over?" He says nothing, Hessen too says nothing. Their teeth chatter, their eyes dart away.—And Mother understood. I thought she would faint. She threw her head back somehow strangely, set off, looking fixedly before her, slowly opening her arms to something unseen. "So that's it?" she repeated quietly. She seemed to reason it out with herself. "How can it be?" and then: "Volodya, do you understand?" We walked up a long corridor. Through the open side door I saw the hall where *it* happened flash past. Some chairs were crooked, some overturned. . . . At last we went into a sort of entrance hall; people were crowded around; the green uniforms of the police. "I want to see him," Mother repeated in a monotone. From one door a black-bearded man with a bandaged hand came out, and somehow helplessly smiling muttered: "You see I . . . I am wounded too." I asked for a chair, sat Mother down. People crowded helplessly around. I understood that the police wouldn't allow us into the room where the body lay. In that room the man whom one of the madmen shot at kept vigil all night. I momentarily imagined him standing over the body—a dry, pinkish, gray-haired old man, fearing nothing, loving nothing. And suddenly Mother, sitting on the chair in the middle of an entrance hall full of embarrassed strangers, began to sob aloud and emit a kind of strained groan. I clung to her, pressed my cheek to her beating, burning temple and whispered one word to her. Then she began to recite "Our Father . . . ," and when she finished seemed to turn to stone. I felt there was no reason to stay any longer in that delirious room.

There the transcript Elena Nabokov made from her son's diary breaks off.

20. *Speak, Memory*: Nabokov, Mother, and Lovers

The Weave of the Magic Carpet

In the late 1990s Everyman and Knopf reissued major Nabokov titles with fresh introductions: Martin Amis for *Lolita*, David Lodge for *Pnin*, and Richard Rorty for *Pale Fire*. I was given *Speak, Memory*, which would be published, aptly, in 1999, the centennial of Nabokov's birth. I persuaded Dmitri Nabokov that we should also publish the hitherto unread chapter sixteen, which Nabokov had intended as a key to the rest but withheld from publication, perhaps because the fiction he adopts there of being an outside reviewer of his own book seemed too much at odds with the commitment to accuracy as well as artistry in the previous fifteen chapters. It was a tricky task introducing *Speak, Memory* and avoiding the evocation of it in the introduction to *Vladimir Nabokov: The Russian Years* and the introduction to it in *Vladimir Nabokov: The American Years*. In *this* introduction I focus on girls and women rather than fathers and sons, and on the chapter, the most important unit between the sentence and the structure of the whole, the two levels I had focused on in the biography.

Some facts, some figures. It is a hundred years since Vladimir Nabokov was born. It is fifty years since he wrote in his autobiography "I confess I do not believe in time" (*SM* 139). It is just under fifty years since he wrote *Lolita*, which has gone on to sell some fifty million copies, and ten years since this most American of his books could be published in the Russia he loved. And it seems an eternity since the worlds he calls up for us in *Speak, Memory* disappeared.

Speak, Memory is the one Nabokov work outside his finest novels—*The Gift*, *Lolita*, *Pale Fire*, *Ada*—that is a masterpiece on their level. Penelope Lively recently named it her book of the century. It has been rated the greatest of autobiographies, but since such judgments depend so much on the criteria we bring to them, I will call it only the most artistic of auto-biographies. It lacks the probing self-analysis of Saint Augustine or Tolstoy or the overt and the inadvertent self-display of Rousseau, the historical and categorical aplomb of Henry Adams, or the sparkling anecdotal flow of Robert Graves, but more than these and any other autobiographies, it fuses truth to detail with perfection of form, the exact with the evocative, an acute awareness of time with intimations of timelessness.

Nabokov confided to his friend Edmund Wilson in April 1947: "I am writing two things now 1. a short novel about a man who liked little girls—and it's going to be called *The Kingdom by the Sea*—and 2. a new type of autobiography—a scientific attempt to unravel and trace back all the tangled threads of one's personality—and the provisional title is *The Person in Question*" (*DBDV* 215). Adjacent in his mind and his bibliography, Nabokov's autobiography and his most famous novel seem to demand comparison.

He had planned to call his new novel *The Kingdom by the Sea* because Humbert sees Lolita, the first time he meets her, as a reincarnation of the girl he loved at thirteen, whom he names "Annabel Leigh" in honor of Edgar Allan Poe's poem ("It was many and many a year ago, / In a kingdom by the sea, / That a maiden there lived whom you may know / By the name of Annabel Lee"). Unlike the 1962 Stanley Kubrick film, Adrian Lyne's recent (1998) movie remake of *Lolita* attempts the Annabel Leigh sequence but aspires no higher than the slickest of advertising clichés when it shows long-limbed young models, one male, one female, in coolly elegant 1920s summer cottons, strolling through a soft-focus palmy beach before they withdraw for a slow striptease.

Lost loves and holiday romances may invite clichés, but Humbert's recollections could not be more idiosyncratic: "I was on my knees, and on the point of possessing my darling, when two bearded bathers, the old man of the sea and his brother, came out of the sea with exclamations of ribald encouragement, and four months later she died of typhus in Corfu" (*Lolita* 15). He reports their "unsuccessful first tryst," when one night Annabel managed "to deceive the vicious vigilance of her family" (16). The urgency and the moral muddle could only be Humbert's: "with a generosity that was ready to offer her everything, my heart, my throat, my entrails, I gave her to hold in her awkward fist the scepter of my passion" (17).

In his novels, not only can Nabokov ventriloquize his voice into the jitter and twitch of someone like Humbert, but he can also have all the freedom his formidable imagination allows to invent incidents, characters, names, relationships. Humbert's requited but still unfulfilled passion for Annabel can find a reprise in Lolita sunning herself on a lawn and then a mirage of promised consummation in the prospect of Lolita on the sands beside Hourglass Lake. But in his meticulously accurate autobiography Nabokov can draw only on facts, memories, and reflections, on his powers of expression and selection. He has often been rated the finest stylist of our times, and in *Speak, Memory*, more than in any other of his works, he has to rely on sheer style. No wonder anthologies of literary prose so often opt for *Speak, Memory*.

The particular "darling of the anthologists," as Nabokov wryly notes in his foreword, has been the chapter "First Love," since with its image of first love on a French beach early in the century, it prefigures and clearly inspires *Lolita*, especially its Annabel Leigh strain. Vladimir and his "Colette" are only ten, as opposed to the thirteen of Humbert and Annabel, and far more innocent, even though they elope, along with Colette's fox terrier, and have to be retrieved by Vladimir's tutor:

> Since my parents were not keen to meet hers, I saw her only on the beach; but I thought of her constantly. If I noticed she had been crying, I felt a surge of helpless anguish that brought tears to my own eyes. I could not destroy the mosquitoes that had left their bites on her frail neck, but I could, and did, have a successful fistfight with a red-haired boy who had been rude to her. She used to give me warm handfuls of hard candy. One day, as we were bending together over a starfish, and Colette's ringlets were tickling my ear, she suddenly turned toward me and kissed me on the cheek. So great was my emotion that all I could think of saying was, "You little monkey."
>
> I had a gold coin that I assumed would pay for our elopement. Where did I want to take her? Spain? America? The mountains above Pau? "*Là-bas, là-bas, dans la montagne*," as I had heard Carmen sing at the opera. One strange night, I lay awake, listening to the recurrent thud of the ocean and planning our flight. The ocean seemed to rise and grope in the darkness and then heavily fall on its face.
>
> Of our actual getaway, I have little to report. My memory retains a glimpse of her obediently putting on rope-soled canvas shoes, on the lee side of a flapping tent, while I stuffed a folding butterfly net into a brown-paper bag. The next glimpse is of our evading pursuit by entering a pitch-dark *cinéma* near the Casino (which, of course, was absolutely out of bounds). There we sat, holding hands across the dog, which now and then gently jingled in Colette's lap, and were shown a jerky, drizzly, but highly exciting bullfight at San Sebastián. My final glimpse is of myself being led along the promenade by Linderovski.

His long legs move with a kind of ominous briskness and I can see the muscles of his grimly set jaw working under the tight skin. My bespectacled brother, aged nine, whom he happens to hold with his other hand, keeps trotting out forward to peer at me with awed curiosity, like a little owl.

(SM 150–51)

The tenderness, the boy's total surprise at the sudden kiss, his absurd off-guard response, the naïve romanticism of the escape plan, the haunting duration of that night of solitary scheming to the sound of the sea, the flashes of unforgotten detail (rope-soled shoes, flapping tent, butterfly net in paper bag), the spaced glimpses of memory, so much truer to recollection than a glibly sustained narrative, the owl-like swiveling of the shamelessly curious younger brother's head—all these are worlds away from Humbert's lurid complaints, let alone Lyne's anodyne gloss.

In *Lolita*, Humbert attempts to consolidate his past by imposing it on what should be Lolita's fluid future. In *Speak, Memory*, Nabokov lets us feel the poignancy of his final parting from Colette in 1909. But as a healthy boy rather than a monster in the making, he accepts the reality of growth and change, and a succession of females stir his fancy: a young American woman at a Berlin skating rink in 1910, who suddenly loses her enchantment when he discovers she is a dancer on a music-hall stage, or Polenka, the daughter of the Nabokovs' head coachman, in 1911, or at last Tamara, his first real love, in 1915 and 1916, the subject of his first book of passionate poems, the object of his heartrending nostalgia when his family flees into the Crimea at the end of 1917 and her letters somehow reach him through the turmoil of the Russian civil war:

Tamara, Russia, the wildwood grading into old gardens, my northern birches and firs, the sight of my mother getting down on her hands and knees to kiss the earth every time we came back to the country from town for the summer, *et la montagne et le grand chêne*—these are things that fate one day bundled up pell-mell and tossed into the sea, completely severing me from my boyhood. I wonder, however, whether there is really much to be said for more anesthetic destinies, for, let us say, a smooth, safe, small-town continuity of time, with its primitive absence of perspective, when, at fifty, one is still dwelling in the clapboard house of one's childhood, so that every time one cleans the attic one comes across the same pile of old brown schoolbooks, still together among later accumulations of dead objects, and where, on summery Sunday mornings, one's wife stops on the sidewalk to endure for a minute or two that terrible, garrulous, dyed, church-bound McGee woman, who, way back in 1915, used to be pretty, naughty Margaret Ann of the mint-flavored mouth and nimble fingers.

The break in my own destiny affords me in retrospect a syncopal kick that I would not have missed for worlds.

(*SM* 249–50)

The incident of young Vladimir's attempted elopement with Colette is not quite typical of *Speak, Memory*. Nabokov can recall scenes from his past with perfect framing, focus, and lighting, but for the most part incidents are subordinate, as here, to epochs, phases of his life, pulses of feeling, and the sudden shifts of thought these phases and pulses can engender. Here his sense of loss is still more wistful than in the case of Colette, and like so many of his losses it has been, as it were, repeatedly rehearsed: in his verse that claims nothing could ever match the magic of his first summer with Tamara; in their frustrations over their first winter in St. Petersburg; in their discovery that their second summer indeed cannot relive the first; in their realization that they have drifted apart, even before the revolution sends them to different corners of Russia and then somehow revives the spell they cast over each other.

But even as he evokes loss layered upon anticipations of loss and a kind of recovery that only sharpens the initial loss, Nabokov cannot keep to the one plaintive note. Part of the special spell of *Speak, Memory* is the gap between his "perfect past" and the losses that would follow. Nabokov here registers the pain, the sharp severance from the past that would be characteristic of his destiny, yet affirms with wonderful humor that he would not have missed this shift, "this syncopal kick," for worlds. At the same time, by dint of the very gap between Russian exoticism and his homely image of the McGee woman, the old "naughty Margaret Ann," he shows how much he has now learned to feel at home in America—and incidentally anticipates the contrast between stay-at-home Shade and the wild romantic nostalgia of Kinbote in *Pale Fire*. Although *Speak, Memory* stops just when Nabokov and his family are about to leave Europe, America repeatedly shows through the scenery of his European past, like the foreglimpse of a second home, a solution to the problem of exile, a fulfillment of some of the fondest dreams of his childhood. He records the pangs of nostalgia, the anticipations of future loss that preceded them, and the compensations of memory, yet even here affirms the poignancy of his loss as a gain, a gain still more generously repaid once his destiny makes that surprise swerve toward America.

In the passage just quoted it is no accident that Nabokov's loss of Tamara and Russia stands beside the never-to-be-repeated but never-to-be-forgotten image of his mother kissing the earth on their return to the countryside for the summer. For the women in his life form a pattern that pervades his autobiography, starting long before Tamara or even Colette. Beginning with his mother, it moves, by way of the first governesses and pretty cousins he adored, to Colette's precursor, Zina, to Colette herself, to Polenka, Tamara, and ultimately to his wife, to whom he turns directly in the closing chapters ("the years are passing, my dear, and presently nobody will know what you and I know. Our child is growing" [*SM* 295]) and to whom he dedicated this and almost all his books.

While Véra stands as the crown of the series, Nabokov's sense of the privacy to which any living person is entitled—even "Colette" and "Tamara" are pseudonyms—keeps her both prominent and safely shielded behind that "you," leaving his mother to anchor and dominate the theme of the women who have mattered to him most.

When I addressed Nabokov's autobiography in the course of writing his biography, I focused especially on the roles of his father, Vladimir Dmitrievich Nabokov, and his son, Dmitri Vladimirovich Nabokov. Introducing *Vladimir Nabokov: The Russian Years*, I lingered over the extraordinary sentence at the end of *Speak, Memory*'s first chapter that pays tribute to Nabokov's father, anticipates his death, and seems to leave him suspended in the timelessness that the very shape of the autobiography's sentences somehow impart to their subjects. Introducing *Vladimir Nabokov: The American Years*, I drew together the patterns that converge on Dmitri at the end of *Speak, Memory*'s last chapter to suggest the intimation of America looming ahead as a solution to the problem of exile from Russia and even as a metaphor for the solution to the problem of our inevitable exile from our past.

Nabokov reflects his hunch that there must be something beyond time in both the texture of *Speak, Memory*'s individual sentences and the structure of the whole. Midway between these extremes stands the chapter. At this level, too, he finds ways to resist the relentless linearity of time, time as mere succession, time as implacable cause and effect. By exploring chapter 2 of the autobiography, entitled in its original *New Yorker* version "Portrait of My Mother," we can turn from the role of the males in his family (father and son as standard and stand-in) to the role of the females (his mother as source and stimulus, prefiguring the even richer role his wife will one day play as a kind of second self) and see how Nabokov shapes a single chapter to acknowledge and yet transcend time.

Speak, Memory's first chapter, "Perfect Past," revolves around his first memory, which he thinks may date from one of his mother's birthdays. As he walks along an avenue at Vyra, holding his parents' hands, he feels his first awareness of his self as distinct from theirs and his first awareness of time, when he discovers their age in relation to his and becomes "acutely aware that the twenty-seven-year-old being, in soft white and pink, holding my left hand, was my mother, and that the thirty-three-year-old being, in hard white and gold, holding my right hand, was my father" (*SM* 22).

Eschewing strict chronology, *Speak, Memory* strives to be less the slave of time than its master. True, each chapter introduces a new phase of his life: his first inklings of consciousness; his mother; his wider family; his early English governesses (from 1902 to 1905); his French governess (from 1905); his passion for butterflies (from 1906); his first love (1909); his Russian tutors (from 1906 to 1915); his school (from 1911 to 1917); his adolescent pursuit of his own masculinity and others' femininity; his first poem (1914); his first love affair and first taste of exile (from 1915 to 1919); his Cambridge years (1919 to 1922); his years in the Russian emigration (from 1922); his watching over the growth of his son (from 1934). Yet within each essay-like chapter Nabokov moves fluidly about in time.

"Portrait of My Mother" starts with a constant in Nabokov's psychic life; pauses for a second at a moment when he was six; shifts to summarize his mother's solicitude for him in his early childhood; lingers over another day when he was seven; leads to an overview of his mother's metaphysics; returns to her minute attention to the physical; shades naturally into a luminous but typical and timeless scene; summarizes her passions for games and gathering mushrooms; shifts to a portrait of the family's housekeeper, Elena Nabokov's old nurse; retraces the disappointment he caused his mother one Christmas morning; and glides forward to picture her as a wartime volunteer nurse, as a devotee of her dachshunds, as an exile in Berlin and in desolate bereavement in Prague. In the course of the chapter he surveys his life, zooms in on a moment, expands an incident, revives a setting, traces a passion or habit or quirk, scans ahead to a later loss, and gazes out toward timelessness.

Although organized around the subject the original titles announce, each chapter also has its riddling quality, especially in the melting vista with which so many end. Chapter 2 even *begins* with a double riddle: first, with the mild but inexplicable hallucinations that Nabokov can always remember being subject to, some aural, some optical, especially just before sleep, and then with the question why he should start a chapter called "Portrait of My Mother" with these solitary idiosyncracies. From there he segues into his colored hearing—an account that has become a classic, cited in scientific studies of synesthesia ever since its first publication—and toward his mother. For after spelling out and filling in the colors each sound of the alphabet evokes in him, he concedes that the

> confessions of a synesthete must sound tedious and pretentious to those who are protected from such leakings and drafts by more solid walls than mine are. To my mother, though, this all seemed quite normal. The matter came up, one day in my seventh year, as I was using a heap of old alphabet blocks to build a tower. I casually remarked to her that their colors were all wrong. We discovered then that some of her letters had the same tint as mine and that, besides, she was optically affected by musical notes. These evoked no chromatisms in me whatsoever.
>
> (*SM* 35)

Not only does he inherit special sensitivities from her, but he also then becomes the special object of her understanding and encouragement. Noticing his sharp responsiveness to the visual, she paints him aquarelle after aquarelle and even brings out her jewels for him to play with.

"My numerous childhood illnesses brought my mother and me still closer together," he declares (*SM* 36), before describing the strangest experience of his childhood. As he lies in bed while delirium ebbs, he seems to watch or accompany his mother as she enters a stationery shop and emerges with her footman, behind her, carrying the pencil she has purchased. Nabokov renders his vision so uncannily vividly and precisely that he seems to relive it now and allow us to relive it with him, as if we can transcend time and personality just as he seemed then to transcend space. As he watches the scene roll on, he cannot fathom why his mother does not herself carry something as small as a pencil, until she walks through his bedroom door, in reality now, carrying a four-feet-long model display pencil that he has often coveted and that the rational part of his mind has apparently "corrected" in size within his clairvoyant trance. "'Oh, yes,' she would say as I mentioned this or that unusual sensation. 'Yes, I know all that,' and with a somewhat eerie ingenuousness she would discuss such things as double sight, and little raps in the woodwork of tripod tables, and premonitions, and the feeling of the *déjà vu*" (*SM* 39).

Suddenly we can see why Nabokov starts this "Portrait of My Mother" with his own moments at the margins of consciousness: they, more than anything, link him to what is innermost in his mother. At the end of section 2, he describes her peculiar faith, in a way that recalls his own quirks of consciousness at the beginning of the chapter:

Her intense and pure religiousness took the form of her having equal faith in the existence of another world and in the impossibility of comprehending it in terms of earthly life. All one could do was to glimpse, amid the haze and the chimeras, something real ahead, just as persons endowed with an unusual persistence of diurnal cerebration are able to perceive in their deepest sleep, somewhere beyond the throes of an entangled and inept nightmare, the ordered reality of the waking hour.

(*SM* 39)

Section 3 turns from the metaphysical to the physical as it opens with Elena Nabokov's instructions to her son:

"*Vot zapomni* [now remember]," she would say in conspiratorial tones as she drew my attention to this or that loved thing in Vyra—a lark ascending the curds-and-whey sky of a dull spring day, heat lightning taking pictures of a distant line of trees in the night, the palette of maple leaves on brown sand, a small bird's cuneate footprints on new snow. As if feeling that in a few years the tangible part of her world would perish, she cultivated an extraordinary consciousness of the various time marks distributed throughout our country place.

(*SM* 40)

No wonder he thinks of entitling his autobiography *Speak, Mnemosyne*—until he is told it is unpronounceable—as if he were formally invoking Mnemosyne, memory, the mother of the muses. For it is his mother who teaches him to treasure Vyra, the home of *her* childhood, too, and to notice its fleeting details because they can be hoarded only within the sanctum of the mind. Just as she fosters his senses and his extrasensory intuitions, she trains him in memory and in her sense of the preciousness and precariousness of the world around, even as her love and her wealth enfold him in such security.

As so often, a stroll through the park turns a corner from space into time, as a glimpse of the overgrown old tennis court calls up the new court and the elaborately protracted picture of a typical game, Vladimir partnering his mother against his father and his younger brother, Sergey, with character sketches of principals and extras, action shots and comedy, landscapes and melting effects of light and shade, the seemingly effortless recreation of the presence of the past.

From this scene Nabokov slides into a summary—"She loved all games of skill and gambling" (*SM* 42)—that again suggests how much his passion for play owes to her, then leads into her zeal for the "very Russian sport of . . . looking for mushrooms" (*SM* 43), a drive that he understands and that enables *her* to understand when his own compulsion for collecting butterflies develops.

The fourth and final section of "Portrait of My Mother" opens with Nabokov's explanation of his mother's remoteness from the running of their large household ("fifty servants and no questions asked" [*SM* 46]). "Nominally," he explains, "the housekeeping was in the hands of her former nurse," but Elena Borisovna's encroaching senility means that the real organization of the household has to carry on behind her back, "with my mother deriving considerable comfort from the hope that her old nurse's illusory world would not be shattered" (*SM* 45–46). A little Christmas incident when Vladimir and Sergey shatter *her* illusions fades out into a picture of the First World War, with Elena Nabokov setting up a private hospital for wounded soldiers and playing the part of nurse. Another natural transition takes us to her fondness for dachshunds, and when we follow that to the end we find her in 1930 in Prague with her last dackel waddling far behind her "in a huff, tremendously old and furious with his long Czech muzzle of wire—an émigré dog in a patched and ill-fitting coat" (*SM* 48).

Rewinding a few years, Nabokov recalls sitting with his mother in the family apartment in Berlin, while on vacation from Cambridge, and reading her "Blok's verse on Italy—had just got to the end of the little poem about Florence, which Blok compares to the delicate, smoky bloom of an iris, and she was saying over her knitting, 'Yes, yes, Florence does look like a *dïmnïy iris*, how true! I remember—' when the telephone rang" (*SM* 49). He does not linger, does not explain, but the attentive reader can deduce: the call that interrupts them comes from the hall where Nabokov senior has just been assassinated. As I wrote in the biography and the previous chapter of this book, throughout *Speak, Memory* Nabokov returns obliquely to his father's death as if it were a wound he cannot leave alone but can hardly bear to touch.

He now advances to his mother's last years in Prague, without Vyra, without her husband, without her favorite son, in the "pitiable lodgings" where she has no large household to look after or to look after her:

> A soapbox covered with green cloth supported the dim little photographs in crumbling frames she liked to have near her couch. She did not really need them, for nothing had been lost. As a company of traveling players carry with them everywhere, while they still remember their lines, a windy heath, a misty castle, an enchanted island, so she had with her all that her soul had stored.
>
> (*SM* 49–50)

This sequence of treasured memories and anticipated losses, of disappointed hopes and new unexpected losses has not quite come to an end, for Nabokov's loss of his mother is still to come. Discussing his predormitary hallucinations at the start of the chapter, he had insisted, "What I mean is not the bright mental image (as, for instance, the face of a beloved parent long dead) conjured up by a wing-stroke of the will; *that* is one of the bravest movements a human spirit can make" (*SM* 33). Now at the end of the chapter, after a last image of the two wedding rings on his mother's fourth finger, her own and her husband's, too big for her, but tied to hers by a bit of black thread, he returns in a sense to that beginning, as he faces her death and his father's:

> Whenever in my dreams I see the dead, they always appear silent, bothered, strangely depressed, quite unlike their dear, bright selves. I am aware of them, without any astonishment, in surroundings they never visited during their earthly existence, in the house of some friend of mine they never knew. They sit apart, frowning at the floor, as if death were a dark taint, a shameful family secret. It is certainly not then—not in dreams—but when one is wide awake, at moments of robust joy and achievement, on the highest terrace of consciousness, that mortality has a chance to peer beyond its own limits, from the mast, from the past and its castle tower. And although nothing much can be seen through the mist, there is somehow the blissful feeling that one is looking in the right direction.
>
> (*SM* 50)

By structuring his chapters as he does, by decoupling chronology, by refusing to follow the strict sequence of before and after, Nabokov demonstrates the mind's power to range within and beyond its experience. He shows us storing up the present, aware that we will never have direct access to it again except in memory; he shows us anticipating loss and yet never able to foresee quite how it will happen; he saturates even the earliest phase of his past with the knowledge of future upheaval yet frees it from the tyranny of succession. He reflects that the time we live through, once it slips into the past, "ceases to mean the orderly alternation of linked events," as he phrases it in *Ada*, and becomes instead "a constant accumulation of images," out of which we can recall what we choose (*Ada* 545). He reveals human life as a complex interplay of anticipation and recollection, loss and restoration, incident and repetition, our previsions of future loss and our foreglimpses of later retrospection. Even in the way he shapes his chapters, Nabokov pits the powers of memory and imagination against time and suggests how much lies both within time and beyond it.

He ends the chapter with "the blissful feeling that one is looking in the right direction" in echo and honor of his mother's faith ("All one could do was to glimpse, amid the haze and the chimeras, something real ahead") and in anticipation of the triumphant end of *Speak, Memory*. There he and Véra will lead *their* son down another path, as his parents had once led him, in the direction of the boat that the boy cannot yet make out but that promises a new homeland and refuge ahead. Nabokov has lost his mother, but as he walks with Véra—mother to his son, muse, sharer of his most intimate memories—he also shares his mother's confidence in the ultimate generosity of things, in the recovery of losses in the past generation that seems somehow betokened by the gifts of the present and the promise looming ahead in the future. By the time *Speak, Memory* takes us down once more to the ocean's edge, we have come a long way indeed from Colette, let alone from Annabel Leigh and the Lolita who Humbert thinks will allow him to transcend *his* loss.

21. *Lolita*: Scene and Unseen

A fellow Nabokov scholar, Tadashi Wakashima, hosting me in a smoky, fishy student bar in Kyoto in 2003 was surprised to hear me say that I still did not think I understood *Lolita*. I still feel much that way, though I have taught the novel for many years. If I do ever get to understand it well enough (and something is stirring), I'll write a critical book on it. Meanwhile, my essay on the novel in *Vladimir Nabokov: The American Years* offers my fullest reading of the whole novel. But the three essays that follow here, each sparked by a different occasion, have made me feel as if a little less in *Lolita* has eluded me each time.

The Modern Languages Association has a series of Approaches to Teaching famous texts. Zoran Kuzmanovich and Galya Diment asked me to contribute to their *Lolita* volume. The following essay presents five different treatments of the same scene, in Nabokov's novel (1955), in his screenplay (1960, 1974), in the Kubrick film (1962), in the Stephen Schiff (and Harold Pinter) screenplay, and in the Adrian Lyne film (both 1998), to help students to read more actively and to learn about artistic media, ends, means, and effects.

Students today often have more experience "reading" films than novels and naturally incline to watch the film of the book if there is one. They may also tend to accept a literary text rather passively, as if it were somehow a record of prior, even if fictional, events. They can easily unlearn that habit when they see how choice shapes every element of a scene.

I approach *Lolita* by asking the class to dwell on a subscene in the novel, Humbert's first meeting with Lolita, and actual and possible film versions of such a scene, in order to engage the skills undergraduates already have; to block their inclination to think the film can substitute for the book; to draw on the critical independence of mind they readily exercise once shown different ways of telling the same story; and to develop their capacity to read and imagine actively.

Even apart from its recondite language and allusions, Lolita poses particular problems for students. The appeal of Humbert's intelligence, wit, and wry self-consciousness can seduce some, female as well as male, into seeing Humbert's and Lolita's story almost entirely from Humbert's point of view. Some even go as far as thinking that a girl as ordinary as Lolita is lucky to be loved so passionately by someone as discriminating and devoted as Humbert. Although students can be dislodged from such positions readily enough when made to consider Humbert's recurring interest in other nymphets or in the possibility of "a litter of Lolitas" (Lolita 302) or his repeated refusal to concern himself with Lolita's suffering, I think it better if from the outset they are primed for wariness and armed to resist Humbert's rhetoric. The ability to look from the viewpoint of those with less eloquence, confidence, or power is one that cannot be acquired too early, and learning how clearly Nabokov manages to see from a position outside his narrator's offers a salutary lesson in imaginative and moral independence.

In part 1, chapter 10, Humbert has arrived in Ramsdale, hoping that as a lodger in the McCoo house he can take advantage of his proximity to twelve-year-old Ginny McCoo. When he discovers the McCoo home has burnt down, he has no reason to remain in Ramsdale but cannot escape being shown over the home of the McCoos' friend, Charlotte Haze. Every detail of the Haze home hardens his indifference into positive revulsion, until this:

I was still walking behind Mrs. Haze through the dining room when, beyond it, there came a sudden burst of greenery—"the piazza," sang out my leader, and then, without the least warning, a blue sea-wave swelled under my heart and, from a mat in a pool of sun, half-naked, kneeling, turning about on her knees, there was my Riviera love peering at me over dark glasses.

It was the same child—the same frail, honey-hued shoulders, the same silky supple bare back, the same chestnut head of hair. A polka-dotted black kerchief tied around her chest hid from my aging ape eyes, but not from the gaze of young memory, the juvenile breasts I had fondled one immortal day. And, as if I were the fairy-tale nurse of some little princess (lost, kidnaped, discovered in gypsy rags through which her nakedness smiled at the king and his hounds), I recognized the tiny dark-brown mole on her side. With awe and delight (the king crying for joy, the trumpets blaring, the nurse drunk) I saw again her lovely in-drawn abdomen where my southbound mouth had briefly paused; and those puerile hips on which I had kissed the crenulated imprint left by the band of her shorts—that last mad immortal day behind the "Roches Roses." The twenty-five years I had lived since then, tapered to a palpitating point, and vanished.

I find it most difficult to express with adequate force that flash, that shiver, that impact of passionate recognition. In the course of the sun-shot moment that my glance slithered over the kneeling child (her eyes blinking over those stern dark spectacles—the little Herr Doktor who was to cure me of all my aches) while I passed by her in my adult disguise (a great big handsome hunk of movieland manhood), the vacuum of my soul managed to suck in every detail of her bright beauty, and these I checked against the features of my dead bride. A little later, of course, she, this *nouvelle*, this Lolita, *my* Lolita, was to eclipse completely her prototype. All I want to stress is that my discovery of her was a fatal consequence of that "princedom by the sea" in my tortured past. Everything between the two events was but a series of gropings and blunders, and false rudiments of joy. Everything they shared made one of them.

I have no illusions, however. My judges will regard all this as a piece of mummery on the part of a madman with a gross liking for the *fruit vert. Au fond, ça m'est bien égal.* All I know is that while the Haze woman and I went down the steps into the breathless garden, my knees were like reflections of knees in rippling water, and my lips were like sand, and—

"That was my Lo," she said, "and these are my lilies."

"Yes," I said, "yes. They are beautiful, beautiful, beautiful!"

(*Lolita* 41–42)

How does the passage work on us, from Humbert's viewpoint and from Nabokov's? How does it work as comedy? As romance? How do we respond to the gap between the mundane suburban setting and Humbert's extravagant expression of his feelings? How does Humbert's baroque style invite us into the privileged position of his private awareness and ask us to remain amused at the gap between his sense of the scene and Charlotte's and Lolita's inability to perceive what he feels? How do the shifting tones of Humbert's rhetoric operate to shape our responses? What part do the sliding times play? (And what times are there? Successively, Humbert with Annabel Leigh in 1923; first seeing Lolita in May 1947; the imagined time of fairytale; the immediacy of the moment's impact and the protractedness of the attempt to convey it; the near "future," first Lolita curing Humbert of all his aches then replacing Annabel; the courtroom scene Humbert still expects as he writes this in late 1952; the 1947 "present" again.) What role does fairytale play here and elsewhere in the novel? How does Nabokov work on us by inventing such a scene and establishing its connections with other parts of the book (in this case, especially via Lolita's precursor, Annabel) and through allowing Humbert such conscious control over our responses?

After this discussion, I then invite the students to draft a screenplay scene for this first glimpse of Lolita. I ask them to consider how they might deal with the possibility that the camera could show the scene quite differently from the way Humbert presents it in prose. In the Stephen Schiff screenplay used by Adrian Lyne for his 1998 movie, the scene takes only a hundred words. How much time would you give it? What would you want Humbert's first glimpse of Lolita to establish? (And what would you have already established, by this point in your film, of Humbert's feelings toward young girls or nymphets?) Do you wish to render the intensity of the moment for Humbert and, if so, how? Is it important to establish his sense that Lolita is Annabel revived and if, so, how could you do this? What attitude do you want viewers to take toward this meeting? How could you keep the comedy of the disparity between Humbert's feelings and Charlotte's unawareness of what has changed his mind?

I especially encourage students to think and script how we might see Humbert and Lo talk to each other alone for the first time. In the Schiff screenplay such a scene follows immediately, and takes another hundred and fifty words. How much screen time would you allow for this scene? What would you want to establish in their attitudes toward each other? What responses would you want the audience to have to each character, overall and in this scene?

We then consider the two film versions, directed by Stanley Kubrick (1962) and Lyne, to see what features of the scene they have dropped or added, and to see to what extent these differences can be attributed to the change of medium from prose to film, to the aims of the filmmakers, or to the circumstances of production.

Kubrick in 1962, I explain, had good reason to be wary of film censors and so to minimize Lolita's youth, maximize her readiness for Humbert, yet minimize the sexual element of the relationship. How do these aims affect his handling of the scene? How does the music contribute to impact of the moment? Lyne in 1998, by contrast, had little to fear from censors and could maximize Lolita's youth, minimize her invitation to Humbert, yet maximize the sexuality of the scene. How are these possibilities reflected in his version of the scene? And how do the conditions facing Kubrick in 1962 throw light on Nabokov's constraints, and his aims, in a novel begun more than a decade earlier?

Stephen Schiff wrote the published screenplay of the Adrian Lyne film, but Lyne had first hired others to draft his screenplay, including playwrights of the stature of Harold Pinter and David Mamet. Schiff incorporated a couple of scenes from Pinter, including the first conversation between Humbert and Lolita, which was to follow immediately in film time though not story time from Humbert's first seeing Lolita. The clothesline and pinging pebbles come from Humbert's first diary entry, in the chapter of the novel following his first vision of Lolita:

HUMBERT: Yes, yes. They are beautiful, beautiful. *(pause)* Uh, how much was the room?

THE BACK PORCH—DAY *Lolita taking clothes off a clothesline. Humbert—casually dressed, shoes off—is watching her. It is obvious he has moved in. Lolita puts the clothes in a tub, lazily brings the tub to the porch, glances at him.*

LOLITA: Hi.

Sitting on the step of the porch, she scoops peaches out of a can with her hand, and eats them. The syrup drips.

HUMBERT: You like peaches.

LOLITA: Who doesn't? You want one?

HUMBERT: No, no. I generally wait until after the sun goes down.

LOLITA: For what?

HUMBERT: Peaches.

He gazes at her bare arms. She begins to pick up pebbles with her feet and tosses them at the can. The sound of pebbles hitting the can: ping ping . . .

LOLITA: How come?

HUMBERT: Keeps the lions away. I learned that in Africa.

LOLITA: Learned what?

HUMBERT: About peaches.

She looks at him and grins.

LOLITA: You're nuts.

Since Schiff retained the scene and Lyne filmed it, although he excised it in the editing room, we can presume they had aims similar to Pinter's, at least in this scene. What do we infer of their sense of the relationship between Humbert and Lolita here? What aspects of Humbert and of Lolita in the novel does this illuminate or obscure?

We then look at the scene through one more lens, the most surprising of all. Nabokov traveled to Hollywood to write a screenplay for Kubrick in 1960, but his text was drastically rewritten at the end of the year by Kubrick and his producer, James B. Harris. Nabokov received full screenplay credit, nevertheless, so that his literary reputation could serve as yet another line of defense against the forces of censorship that they feared potentially massing over the horizon. In 1974 Nabokov published his own screenplay. There the scene of the first conversation between Lolita and Humbert takes six pages. Although it incorporates "She's a fright. And mean. And lame" from Humbert's first diary entry (*Lolita* 43), Nabokov makes the action follow directly from Humbert's decision to move into the Haze home. The new scene shows us Humbert not as seen by himself, debonair, impassioned, dramatic, wry but as seen from outside, creepily persistent, slyly circumspect, disconcertingly sleazy:

LOLITA: Did you see the fire?
HUMBERT: No, it was all over when I came. Poor Mr. McCoo looked badly shaken.
LOLITA: You look badly shaken yourself.
HUMBERT: Why, no. I'm all right. I suppose I should change into lighter clothes. There's a ladybird on your leg.
LOLITA: It's a ladybug, not a ladybird.
   She transfers it to her finger and attempts to coax it into flight.
HUMBERT: You should blow. Like this. There she goes.
LOLITA: Ginny McCoo—she's in my class, you know. And she said you were going to be her tutor.
HUMBERT: Oh, that's greatly exaggerated. The idea was I might help her with her French.
LOLITA: She's grim, Ginny.
HUMBERT: Is she—well, attractive?
LOLITA: She's a fright. And mean. And lame.
HUMBERT: Really? That's curious. Lame?

LOLITA: Yah. She had polio or something. Are you going to help me with my homework?

HUMBERT: *Mais oui*, Lolita. *Aujourd'hui?*

Charlotte comes in.

CHARLOTTE: That's where you are.

LOLITA: He's going to help me with my homework.

CHARLOTTE: Fine. Mr. Humbert, I paid your taxi and had the man take your things upstairs. You owe me four dollars thirty-five. Later, later. Dolores, I think Mr. Humbert would like to rest.

HUMBERT: Oh no, I'll help her with pleasure.

Charlotte leaves.

LOLITA: Well, there's not much today. Gee, school will be over in three weeks.

A pause.

HUMBERT: May I—I want to pluck some tissue paper out of that box. No, you're lying on it. There—let me—thanks.

LOLITA: Hold on. This bit has my lipstick on it.

HUMBERT: Does your mother allow lipstick?

LOLITA: She does not. I hide it here.

She indraws her pretty abdomen and produces the lipstick from under the band of her shorts.

HUMBERT: You're a very amusing little girl. Do you often go to the lake shore? I shaw—I mean, I saw that beautiful lake from the plane.

LOLITA: (*lying back with a sigh*): Almost never. It's quite a way. And my mummy's too lazy to go there with me. Besides, we kids prefer the town pool.

HUMBERT: Who is your favorite recording star?

LOLITA: Oh, I dunno.

HUMBERT: What grade are you in?

LOLITA: This a quiz?

HUMBERT: I only want to know more about you. I know that you like to solarize your solar plexus. But what else do you like?

LOLITA: You shouldn't use such words, you know.

HUMBERT: Should I say "what you *dig*"?

LOLITA: That's old hat.

Pause. Lolita turns over on her tummy. Humbert, awkwardly squatting, tense, twitching, mutely moaning, devours her with sad eyes; Lolita, a restless sunbather, sits up again.

HUMBERT: Is there anything special you'd like to be when you grow up?

LOLITA: What?

(LAS 42–45)

What is different—from the students' own versions, the film versions, the Schiff-Pinter screenplay, and the novel—in Nabokov' screenplay? What can we infer about Nabokov's aims in this scene in the screenplay? What does the scene suggest about his attitudes to Humbert and Lolita? How and why are these attitudes more difficult to infer from the novel? What does the difference between the screenplay and the novel suggest of Nabokov's attitude to the audiences for each form?

What do we gain, and what do we lose, from the screenplay's more objective view of Humbert? Although it is morally clearer—and may therefore help some of the more susceptible students not to succumb to Humbert's seductiveness of style—it is also artistically thinner. Why? Students are encouraged to think about the purpose of the novel's rich diction, imagery, and narrative self-consciousness; about the purpose and value of its characterization of Humbert from within; about the role of its humor. Why does Nabokov himself change the effect of the scene so dramatically from novel to screenplay? Because of a change of medium? For a different imagined audience? Because of a new attitude to the story? Does the screenplay scene make explicit what Nabokov would like his best readers to infer from the novel itself? Does it perhaps reflect his awareness that some readers had not inferred so well, that he had made Humbert even more persuasive than he intended?

How do we take the screenplay into consideration as evidence for reading the novel? Does it have the same evidentiary value as the Schiff screenplay or the Kubrick and Lyne films? If not, why not? What does our answer suggest about authors and authorial intentions and our response to them? How does it throw light on the Wimsatt-Beardsley notion of the intentional fallacy? How do Nabokov's changes (and he made others: minor ones for the Russian translation of *Lolita* he prepared between 1963 and 1965 and major ones during the novel's evolution from the 1939 Russian ur-*Lolita*, *The Enchanter*, to *Lolita*) affect the notion of the unity or finality of a work of art?

What does a comparison of these different versions of the first meeting and first conversation of Humbert and Lolita suggest about the way we should read the novel? Are there aspects of the novel that already prefigure the kind of reading of the scene, or of the relationship between Humbert and Lolita in general, that we infer from juxtaposing screenplay and novel? Or does reading with that kind of imaginative independence of Humbert prove almost impossible? If so, why has Nabokov made it so difficult?

What advantages are there of the more complex but potentially more misleading presentation of the novel over the less complex and perhaps less treacherous presentation in the film? Does it become a different story on page and screen? Should a story, in order to stay the same story, be transformed as it moves from one medium to the other? Does a story stay the same story when it is transformed in medium or emphasis? What creative potentials remain within the constraints of a given story or even a single scene?

22. Even Homais Nods

Nabokov's Fallibility; Or, How to Revise *Lolita*

Nabokov has a reputation for exactness, but as readers of the manuscript index cards of *The Original of Laura* now know, he could also be error-prone. A single mismatched detail in the internal dating of *Lolita* has led some good Nabokov critics and other keen readers, accustomed to unreliable narration and postmodern self-undermining, to see much in the late stages of *Lolita* as hallucinatory. Like most others aware of the discrepancy, I think it a simple mistake, and the various alternative readings that construe it as an intentional clue become more confused than Nabokov's text. But the discrepancy also offers a revelation.

The *New Yorker*'s wonderful research department several times saved Mr. Nabokov—who seems to combine a good deal of absentmindedness with his pedantism—from various blunders regarding names, numbers, book titles and the like.[1]

In *Pnin* Nabokov glances at one of the most famous mistakes in literature, when night after night Victor tries to induce sleep by sinking into fantasies of himself as a king about to flee, pacing, as he awaits rescue, a strand on the Bohemian Sea. Ben Jonson was the first to mock Shakespeare for having a ship wrecked on the coast of Bohemia in *The Winter's Tale*; Samuel Johnson assumes Shakespeare is "little careful of geography"; *Tristram Shandy* turns the point to its own advantage.[2]

But Coleridge more than once talked of having often dismissed as a fault in Shakespeare what he later saw as a "beauty." Just as Victor knew what he was doing in choosing this impossible sea coast—and this is probably Nabokov's particular point—so did Shakespeare in stressing the coast of Bohemia, since it would be hard to find a more landlocked region in Europe.[3] Shakespeare rewrote geography in order to emphasize the fantastic nature of his plot—as he did also in choosing *The Winter's Tale* for a title and in all the expressions of incredulity at the play's close—just as, for instance, he chose to violate history for other ends by fusing classical Rome and Renaissance Italy in *Cymbeline*.

In the twentieth century the professionalization of criticism and the ever-increasing prestige of Shakespeare have led critic after critic to resurrect as virtues in this or that play what had once seemed defects. This has yielded many valuable insights, but it has also led to a working principle that Shakespeare could not make a mistake. This of course, in the schizoid world of modern criticism, where some blithely combine Freud and Marx, is not incompatible with others insisting that Shakespeare always already contradicts himself. But the widespread assumption of Shakespeare's infallibility has often led to absurd consequences.[4]

In Nabokov's case, too, both the professionalization of criticism and the prestige of the author have encouraged critics to adopt as an article of faith that he also soars above error. He does, of course, let pass far fewer mistakes than Shakespeare. Where Shakespeare paid little if any attention to publishing works other than his poems, Nabokov kept meticulous control over his texts, in all the languages he knew. Aware that he was writing for an audience that would see a play only once, Shakespeare could distort the time scale of his stories to combine a sense of rapid pace and gradual development, since the dual calendar would be noticed only by careful rereaders. But such careful rereaders were precisely Nabokov's ideal audience.

Besides, Nabokov was of a notoriously precise, even pedantic temperament, hard on anyone else's mistakes, exigent about particulars, insistent on an exactitude of detail and a delicacy of interconnection that make it natural to expect him to ensure the accuracy of all his work. Nearly always, the expectation is justified. Line 3 of Humbert's poem "Wanted, wanted, Dolores Haze"—"Age: five thousand three hundred days" (*Lolita* 257)—seems only to combine the continuation of the "Wanted" poster format, an affectionate approximation, and a rhyme. But after we calculate the gap between Lolita's birth, January 1, 1935 and July 5, 1949, the day Humbert discovers her missing, and find it to be exactly 5,300 days, we will hesitate to attribute any discrepancy in Nabokov's work to oversight.

All the more so when we recall how fascinated he was by deception in nature, especially in mimicry, and how much he liked to find in his art equivalents for the sly playfulness he sensed behind things. He even wrote: "In art, as in nature, a glaring disadvantage may turn out to be a subtle protective device" (*KQK* viii). As if this were not enough, he has said, in discussing the editing of *Eugene Onegin*: "Even obvious misprints should be treated gingerly; after all, they may be supposed to have been left uncorrected by the author" (*EO* 1.15–16).

But even Homer nods, and so does Nabokov, and to build sweeping interpretations on details that seem much more explicable as errors is fraught with danger. I have in mind especially the thesis, first proposed in 1976 by Elizabeth Bruss, developed in 1979 by Christina Tekiner, in 1989 by Leona Toker, in 1990 by Alexander Dolinin, in 1995 by Julian Connolly, and soon perhaps by Dieter Zimmer—and independently by others who have spoken and written to me in the wake of the biography and still others on the Nabokov electronic bulletin board—that a hidden inconsistency in *Lolita*, in Toker's words, "untells Humbert's tale."[5] On the last page of the novel, Humbert says that he started work on his manuscript in captivity fifty-six days ago. In John Ray Jr.'s foreword, we discover that Humbert dies on November 16, 1952. Counting back fifty-six days from there, we reach September 22, the day Humbert receives the letter from Lolita. But since he is not in prison on that date, since over the next few days he drives first to Lolita in Coalmont, then to Ivor Quilty in Ramsdale, and finally to Clare Quilty at Pavor Manor, he has no time for these visits *and* composing the text we are reading. That is Nabokov's hint, say these attentive readers, that Humbert has merely invented the visit to seventeen-year-old Lolita and the murder of Quilty. In the Russian *Lolita*, some of these critics add, Nabokov has placed further stress on these dates.

To refute this reading, I will first show that Nabokov could indeed make mistakes, especially in dating, and that second thoughts often merely compounded the confusion. I will then show how little is required to eliminate the revisionist interpretation of *Lolita* (the emendation of a single typographical character would suffice) and how plainly it contradicts itself and the rest of the text.

First, some examples of Nabokov's fallibility. One of the reviewers of *Vladimir Nabokov: The American Years* listed as the "most intriguing fact" in the book my claim (*VNAY* 613) that Nabokov had committed twenty-one demonstrable errors in his autobiography, most of which I did not have space to list. Let me mention a few here.

Nabokov's map of the Vyra region in the endpapers of the revised *Speak, Memory* is thoroughly muddled. What looks like a small tributary coming past the Batovo estate is in fact the Oredezh itself; the river labeled "Oredezh" running past the Rozhdestveno estate is actually the Gryazno, a very short-lived little stream; and when the Oredezh passes the Vyra estate it does not continue west and away from Siverskaya but turns to flow east toward the town. Other errors in *Speak, Memory*, are equally close to home. Nabokov lists his father as the second son of Dmitri and Maria Nabokov and Sergey as the third when it was the other way around (59). But most of his autobiography's inaccuracies involve minor details of dating: the birth of his grandfather, his father's graduation, the sale of Batovo, the duration of the German occupation of Yalta, and the like.

Dates in fact are a common source of error in Nabokov, as he confesses in the foreword to *Speak, Memory*: "Among the anomalies of a memory, whose possessor and victim should never have tried to become an auto-biographer, the worst is the inclination to equate in retrospect my age with that of the century. . . . Mnemosyne, one must admit, has shown herself to be a very careless girl" (13). Protesting to Katharine White about the *New Yorker*'s wanting to change one of the visual details in *Speak, Memory*'s final chapter, he insisted "I very seldom err when recalling colors," but only after first making the concession: "As you have probably noticed I often make mistakes when recalling names, titles of books, numbers."[6] Very often Nabokov, like many of us, would date a letter in January to the previous year, but he could do this as late as October.[7] He could be quite wildly wrong about the dates of his works, as when he recorded the date of composition of "The Potato Elf" as 1929[8] rather than the correct April 1924, despite the vast stylistic gap between the stories he wrote in early 1924 and the mastery he had achieved by the time, five years later, that he was writing *The Defense*.

Errors of memory, especially when they involve dates, may, like casual slips of the tongue or the pen, seem of a different order from apparent inconsistencies in fictional worlds whose details Nabokov entirely controlled himself. But even there, although he was meticulous in the extreme in correcting his work for the smallest imprecisions of phrasing or fact, errors still persisted. Véra Nabokov, never one to denigrate her husband, told me he was very "absent-minded." When I asked her about resolving editorial problems by consulting the manuscripts, she told me the "manuscripts should not be trusted" as copy texts since "he would often write one word when he meant another" and "might not catch it until the galleys."[9]

Pnin is a novel where mistakes matter: Pnin's garbled English; his endearing errors like the one he discovers when, after laboriously returning a bulky library tome he cannot understand anyone else needing, he finds that the person who has recalled it was himself; Cockerell's false version of Pnin's mishap at Cremona; the discrepancies between Pnin's and the narrator's accounts of Pnin's past. In view of these and other meaningful mistakes,

Nabokov ought to have tried harder than ever to eliminate unintended errors. But he still does not succeed.

In February 1953 Pnin teaches Elementary Russian to a class that includes Frank Carroll (67). In September 1954 Pnin invites to his party "old Carrol, the Frieze Hall head janitor, with his son Frank, who had been my friend's only talented student and had written a brilliant doctor's thesis for him on the relationship between Russian, English and German iambics; but Frank was in the army" (147–48). Somehow in the space of a year Frank Carroll has advanced from Elementary Russian to having completed— some months ago, it seems, given his army service—a Ph.D. that requires a sophisticated command of the language and, presumably, could only have been envisaged by someone with a long-standing interest in Russian verse read in the original. He has also found the time to lose that letter from his surname.

Al Cook (Aleksandr Petrovich Kukolnikov) and his American wife Susan have a summer house, The Pines, to which they invite, "every even-year summer, elderly Russians . . . ; on odd-year summers they would have *amerikantsi*" (117). But only three pages later Varvara Bolotov is said to have visited The Pines for the first time "in 1951" (120), and finds that its birches and bilberries remind her of her "first fifteen summers" near Lake Onega in northern Russia. Are we to deduce that she is an American falsely posing as a Russian, a Russian whom Al Cook has mistaken for an *amerikanka*, or simply that Nabokov should have written "1950" or "1952"?

Nabokov was pressed for time, distracted by teaching, and publishing chapters serially over several years when he wrote *Pnin*. But there were no such excuses at the time of *Ada*.

Van recalls dining at a restaurant with Ada "on New Year's Eve, 1893" (515), in other words on December 31, 1893. But according to the novel's very precise calendar, Van and Ada do not meet between February 5, 1893 and October 11, 1905. Now we could deduce from this that Van has either fantasized this dinner with Ada, perhaps in desperate consolation, or that he has deliberately suppressed some of his time with Ada to exaggerate, for effect, the bleakness of their separation. Or we could simply decide that Nabokov made a natural error: he meant the day before New Year's Day, 1893, and should have written "on New Year's Eve, 1892."

Another much more serious error, or rather cluster of errors, was subsequently noticed by Nabokov himself. In part 1, chapter 26, Van describes the codes he and Ada use to correspond in the years between Ardis the First and Ardis the Second. One would expect Van and VN to have been utterly vigilant after a comment like this: "Again, this is a nuisance to explain, and the explanation is fun to read only for the purpose (thwarted, I am afraid) of looking for errors in the examples" (161–62). In fact, the first time the code was used, several pages earlier, Nabokov let slip a misprint ("*xlic*," [157]) which he corrected in later editions (to "*xliC*").[10]

But that is not the mistake I mean. Look at this tangle of thorns.

In describing the code, Van states: "The entire period of that separation was to span almost four years from September, 1884 to June 1888, with two brief interludes of intolerable bliss (in August, 1885 and June, 1886) and a couple of chance meetings" (160). The terminal dates are correct, but if the second interlude refers to Van's meeting feverish Ada at Forest Fork (178), that occurs on July 25, 1886, not in June. "The entire period of that separation" is also interrupted by the Brownhill visit, not a "chance meeting" but taking place in November or December 1884 (167: "he had not seen his Ada for close to three months"). The rest of the novel, then, implies that Van meets Ada between the summers of 1884 and 1888 only at Brownhill, in late 1884, anything but an "interlude of intolerable bliss," and at Forest Fork, in June 1886; but part 1, chapter 26, implies two trysts, August 1885—never mentioned elsewhere, though Van otherwise assiduously records his meetings with and partings from Ada as milestones and crossroads in his life—July 1886, and two other "chance" meetings. All four meetings seem either partially or totally incompatible with the rest of the novel's chronology.

But this short chapter, a mere two pages of solid text, is incompatible even with itself. Three paragraphs after the first passage, Van explains that "in the second period of separation, beginning in 1886, the code was radically altered" (161), This could be taken as implying that they changed the code at Forest Fork, in July, or is it June, 1886, but it ignores the August 1885 interlude which surely ought to start "the second period of separation." The next paragraph makes matters still worse: "Curiously enough, in their third period of separation, from January, 1887, to June 1888 (after a very long-distance call and a very brief meeting)" (162). The January 1887 meeting is not "chance," and since it marks the third of the three numbered periods in the four-year separation, it is perhaps one of the two "brief interludes of intolerable bliss," except that they have been dated 1885 and 1886.

No wonder, then, that Nabokov on his own copy of the novel, the one he marked on the recto of the front loose end-paper "*Author's copy*" and "Genial'naia kniga—perl' amerikanskoi literatury" ("A book of genius, the pearl of American literature"), lists on the half-title page thirty-odd corrections to be made, and this note: "p. 161 not worth correcting." Ingenious readers who had spotted these contradictions without seeing Nabokov's comment might perhaps have suggested that Van's aversion to the hints of betrayal in Ada's coded correspondence makes him recoil from close attention to codes or dates, or that Ada's Forest Fork fever somehow infects him so that he deliriously confuses this patch of their past. There is no end of possible conjectures, if all we need is an inconsistency as a springboard for fancy. That *Nabokov* might have become bored with or fatigued by his attempt to outline the codes and simply failed to scrutinize the dates sufficiently would strike some readers as methodologically impermissible, since it moves outside the world of the book, or as just plain heresy.

Nabokov could muddle things further in his attempts to correct real or imagined errors. In part 1, chapter 2, of *Ada*, for instance, Marina's "meeting with Baron O." (12) seems odd, sandwiched as it is between the first and third references to her opposite number in a stage travesty of *Eugene Onegin*: "a local squire, Baron d'O." and "Baron d'O., now in black tails and white gloves." Why, this second time, is he not also "d'O."? Things become no clearer when on the next page Demon, now occupying the role of Marina's real-life opposite, meets an art dealer—and soon, he discovers, her lover—called Baron d' Onsky, who in one of the three references to *his* name becomes ("simply"?) "d'O." (13). Why the solitary "Baron O." on the previous page? Is it to unsettle the bizarre equation between d'O. and d'Onsky? Does it suggest the theme of transfiguration with which Nabokov is preoccupied in his treatment of the *Eugene Onegin* travesty and even in these semi-interchangeable barons? Or is "O." a mere oversight for "d'O."?

In Nabokov's own master copy of *Ada*, he began to answer those questions when he changed the third reference to Marina's opposite, ten lines after the second, from "d'O." to "O."—but forgot to turn back to the previous page to alter that "d'O." to "O." But at least it was clear now what he wanted, that there should be *less* overlap than it had seemed between d'O. and d'Onsky. Accordingly, the three references to Marina's stage partner were changed to "O." in the German edition, which Nabokov checked through, for eleven days, in company with the German translators, while leaving the abbreviation of "d'Onsky" to "d'O." untouched.[11]

At last everything was correct. Or so it seemed. For in revising the French translation of *Ada*, which he did at his own pace and over a period of six intense months, Nabokov returned all three references to Marina's opposite to "d'O."[12] And this indeed seems what he originally, and finally, intended. In reading through his own master copy, he had noticed the inconsistency on page 12 and made the second instance conform to the first, not realizing that both now differed from the previous occurrence on page 11. His German translators, presumably, rectified the discrepancy by making the first occurrence conform to the other two, with no objections from Nabokov, who was never at his ease with (and almost never subjected himself to) teamwork. Only in rereading even more slowly and in his own time did Nabokov realize what had happened and restore what he had first meant. This, indeed, now seems the "obvious" reading since it links d'O. not only with d'Onsky but also with "the Don," Ada's opposite in *Don Juan's Last Fling*, pointedly associated with Marina's play as another orgasmically interrupted performance.[13]

One of the many curious features about this sequence of corrections and counter-corrections is that it shows Nabokov quite clearly forgetting what he had once meant. That is even more strikingly noticeable in another change in the *Ada* master copy where he "corrected" the account of a gambling evening during which Van notices Dick Schuler cheating on and winning a fortune off a pair of French twins. In "the unfortunate twins were passing to each other a fountain pen, thumb-pressing and repressing it in disastrous transit as they calculated their losses" (174), Nabokov changed "fountain pen" to "ball pen," which seems like a legitimate correction—we "thumb-press" only ball pens, not fountain pens—but destroys an incidental joke: that the twins are so drunk ("happily and hopelessly tight," 173) that they treat the fountain pen as *if* it were a ball pen.

Enough has been shown, surely, to prove that Nabokov not infrequently made mistakes, especially with dates, and that even second thoughts did not necessarily improve matters. Let's now start to move toward *Lolita*.

In Nabokov's published screenplay, act 1 opens: "The words LAST DAY OF SCHOOL are gradually scrawled across the blackboard" (*LAS* 21). Dialogue confirms it as the last day of school for Dolly and her classmates, and consistent time cues move the action forward by degrees to the next day, the day of Humbert's arrival in Ramsdale and his discovering that the McCoo house—in which he had hoped to enjoy Ginny McCoo's proximity— has just burned down. He finds himself steered to the Haze house and is about to reject it when he sees Lolita. While Charlotte happily pays for the taxi and installs his belongings in the house, Humbert chats up Lolita. He eagerly agrees to help her with her homework, but then she shrugs, "Well, there's not much today. Gee, school will be over in three weeks" (43). Shortly, Charlotte returns and calls Lolita to the phone: "It's Kenny. I suspect he wants to escort you to the big dance next month" (45). Two pages later, Nabokov headlines a jump in time: "THREE WEEKS LATER, THE DAY OF THE SCHOOL DANCE" (47). This appears not to be an intertitle, simply an objective indicator for the film's potential director, whether in studio or study. The dance ensues, with a cameo appearance by Clare Quilty.

Two clearly marked sequences, then, reinforce themselves and remain stubbornly incompatible with each other. In one, Humbert arrives at the Haze home on the last day of school. In the other, he has been at the Haze home for three weeks when Lolita's school year ends. In the time problem in the novel, there are almost three hundred pages between the incompatible dates, which involve a single indicator in each case. Here in the screenplay one elaborate series of time markers leads almost immediately into another quite incompatible with it.

Surely, some will chorus, a writer as attentive to detail and as wily as Nabokov could never have left such a glaring inconsistency without meaning it. (As far as I know, the discrepancy has never before been remarked on in print, more than twenty years after the screenplay was published. Inconsistencies tend to become "glaring" only when someone points them out.) Is one of the two time sequences unreal, invented perhaps by Humbert? If so, which one? Or is the whole sequence proof that Humbert *is* Quilty, or that Quilty is *only* Humbert's double, since both arrive on Lolita's (different) last days of school?

It is easy, all too easy, to invent fancy interpretations of this kind. Twentieth-century criticism has become expert, if that is the word, in strategies for retrieving a "higher" consistency from seeming inconsistency— although this often resembles a craft skill, an easily acquired habit, rather than real inquiry after explanation. Readers inclined, in this so-called postmodern era, to suppose a story will slyly undermine itself overlook other problems and possibilities. In the *Lolita* screenplay the inconsistent time sequences cannot be easily explained as Humbert's invention since the time indicators are objective, supplied in one case by Lolita's classmates before Humbert arrives in Ramsdale (although of course Humbert might have invented this scene, too, to say nothing of Lolita, and himself—this road can quickly lead to bog and fog) and in the other case by Nabokov himself in a "stage" direction.

But the screenplay's incompatible time schemes can easily be explained as a mere mistake. Nabokov composed a long first attempt at a *Lolita* screenplay in the spring and early summer of 1960.[14] It had a prologue, Humbert's killing of Quilty, and three acts, the first of which starts with Lolita on her last day at school, the day Humbert arrives. Nabokov here introduces Quilty to Ramsdale and to Lolita by way of Quilty's uncle, the dentist. But he then had the idea of reinstating a scene he had envisaged when he first composed the novel, of McCoo engaging Humbert in an irrelevant and comically spooky guided tour of the house where he would have had him as a lodger had lightning not just burnt it down (*LAS* x). Nabokov therefore wrote an alternative version of act 1 that begins with Humbert's arrival in Ramsdale and the scene at the McCoos'. This version then moves straight to Lawn Street and Humbert's conversation with sun-bathing Lolita, who runs off to talk on the phone to Kenny, the boy who will take her in three weeks' time to the end-of-school dance—which in this alternative version Nabokov uses as the means of introducing Quilty in Ramsdale.

Nabokov appears to have allowed Kubrick to decide between the two versions, for he offered both, one paginated normally, the other as "alternative 1," "alternative 2," and so on, together with the rest of the typescript. When Kubrick protested that he needed to cut drastically, Nabokov offered a much shorter and more filmable version, in which act 1 drew entirely on the alternative version (*LAS* x–xi). In late 1970, anxious to publish his screenplay before both Alan Jay Lerner's *Lolita* musical and the deadline for his multibook McGraw-Hill contract, Nabokov looked back over it and found that it included *three* versions of act 1, the original, the alternative, and the abbreviated (see *VNAY* 580). He decided he needed to introduce Lolita in Ramsdale before Humbert's arrival so returned to the original opening of act 1 but eliminated her clumsy encounter in the dentist's chair with Quilty and opted instead for Humbert at the McCoos', on the piazza with Lolita, and at the school dance with Quilty.

Nabokov conflated, for sound enough reasons, what seemed the best bits of each version, but he did so perfunctorily. He left very spare instructions for his secretary, Jaqueline Callier, to amalgamate the blocks as she retyped the manuscript. That he was anything but in command of dates in his own life, let alone in five versions of Humbert's (the novel and the ancestral, alternative, abbreviated, and amalgamated screenplays), is almost comically indicated in his record at the top of his instructions: "Added from Brown to Blue Oct 1930 Screenplay." The blue folder contained the shortened and revised version of the screenplay, which he had submitted to Kubrick in September, now remembered as "October," 1960, here misrecorded as "1930." Perhaps the "1930" date proves that everything subsequent, including the novel *Lolita* and Nabokov's meeting with Kubrick, was his invention? Or could we accept the simple proposition that he made a mistake here, as in the screenplay itself and, perhaps, in a much smaller way, in the novel?

Let us turn now to *Lolita* itself.

The argument that the final scenes of Humbert's story—his meeting with the married Lolita and his murder of Quilty—are his invention or fantasy depends on a single piece of evidence: that Humbert says on the last page of his book "When I started, fifty-six days ago, to write *Lolita*, first in the psychopathic ward for observation, then in this well-heated, albeit tombal seclusion, I thought I would use these notes in toto at my trial, to save not my head, of course, but my soul" (310). According to John Ray Jr.'s foreword, Humbert "died in legal captivity, of coronary thrombosis, on November 16, 1952, a few days before his trial was scheduled to start" (5). Flipping back fifty-six days, we arrive at September 22, the day Lolita's letter reached Humbert. Since the visit to Lolita, the discovery of the name of her abductor, and the murder of Quilty all take place over the next three days, when Humbert says he has been writing in a psychopathic ward, they are therefore, according to the revisionists, fabrications or delusions of Humbert Humbert.

In view of Nabokov's fallibility, it seems much sounder, let alone much more economical, to call into question a single numeral than to doubt the detailed reality of a whole series of major scenes. It seems especially peculiar to suppose that virtually everything in the last eighth of the novel is fabricated, except for the first nine words of the sentence quoted above: "When I started, fifty-six days ago, to write *Lolita*." Why, if even the trial mentioned in this sentence is Humbert's fiction (as it usually is for the revisionists),[15] if the psychopathic ward too is a fraud (as it is for Dolinin and sometimes for others), is the "fifty-six" swimming in this sea of falsity to be fished out as incontestable fact?

That Nabokov could err in dating his own life and the lives of his characters has already been amply demonstrated. But let us be clear that—as the revisionists know—*Lolita* itself is no zone of immunity. To take the life first: in his November 1956 "On a Book Entitled *Lolita*," Nabokov wrote that he had not "reread *Lolita* since I went through the proofs in the winter of 1954." He altered this to "in the spring of 1955" for the *Annotated Lolita* (318, 439), although in fact he received the first proofs only well into the summer of 1955 (July 12: *VNAY* 269). Only sixteen months after the event, in other words, he had been inaccurate by about eight months.

Within *Lolita*'s fictional world, he also made at least one incontrovertible error that immediately casts doubt on the value of the "fifty-six days." The morning Humbert comes down to check the mail is "early in September 1952" (266, 426), according to the 1955 and 1958 editions. Yet three pages later we find, "The letter was dated September 18, 1952 (this was September 22)" (269)—"this" being the day he receives the letter, hardly "early" in the month. Somebody, perhaps Nabokov himself, muted the mistake in the French translation, where the text has "vers la mi-Septembre."[16] In 1965 Nabokov altered the Russian translation by removing the "September 22" from the next chapter and bringing it forward to replace the vaguer initial reference: "for that particular morning, early in September 1952," became "ibo v to utro, 22-go sentiabria 1952-go goda" ("for that morning, September 22 1952").[17] Several years later Nabokov supplied to Alfred Appel Jr., for the *Annotated Lolita*, the correction to "late in September 1952" (266).

The undoubted mistake here, which persisted in Nabokov's manuscript, typescript, and through readings of at least two sets of proofs (Olympia's and Putnam's, though he also read the Crest edition, and presumably the Weidenfeld and Nicolson and Corgi editions), shows how little credence can be given to the unsupported testimony of "fifty-six days." Here a discrepancy of two weeks or so occurs within a space of three pages and was not picked up by Nabokov for over ten years. The "fifty-six days" as evidence depends on an error of only three days over a gap of over three hundred pages.

Not only on that, some might say. There is one other relevant change in the Russian—where, as Gennady Barabtarlo shows, dates have several times been supplied where there were none in the original.[18] In the English edition, Humbert, after finding it impossible to trace Lolita's abductor, begins a new chapter: "This book is about Lolita; and now that I have reached the part which (had I not been forestalled by another internal combustion martyr) might be called '*Dolorès Disparue*,' there would be little sense in analyzing the three empty years that followed" (255). In the Russian the last thirteen words become "podrobnoe opisanie poslednikh trekh pustikh let, ot nachala iiulia 1949 do serediny noiabria 1952, ne imelo by smysla [a detailed description of the last three empty years, from the beginning of July 1949 to the middle of November 1952, would make no sense]" (234). Alexander Dolinin cites this in support of his theory, as proof that there was nothing but blankness—no meeting with Lolita, no encounter with Quilty—in Humbert's life from Lolita's disappearance until this point near the end of his writing his book. Humbert is, "therefore, at home, at his writing desk but not in a cell awaiting trial, as he has tried to convince his gullible readers."[19] But if this were a major piece of evidence in the reading that Nabokov wanted to imprint on his book, why did he then not transfer it back into the *Annotated Lolita* when he incorporated corrections there that he saw as necessary in the Russian?

If the probability of a mistake in Nabokov's numerals seems high from the first, the improbability of the revisionist view seems overwhelming. Even a reader unaware of Nabokov's capacity for error will see an immediate objection to the revisionist theory: what of John Ray Jr.'s foreword? The November 16 date for Humbert's death, on which the whole case rests, comes from Ray, but Ray also confirms just what the case tries to deny—what Dolinin denies outright—that Humbert was in prison awaiting trial when he finished his manuscript and promptly died. Tekiner suggests that—since, presumably, Ray does not explicitly mention that Humbert's trial is for murder—the trial could be for his treatment of Lolita. But Ray declares that "references to 'H.H"s crime may be looked up by the inquisitive in the daily papers for September-October 1952" (6). There is nothing here or anywhere else in the foreword to imply that the inquisitive will find that the newspaper accounts utterly contradict Humbert's.[20]

In his long discussion of the implications of the "fifty-six days," Dolinin, of course, refers to the "November 16" date from which the countback starts, but curiously he never mentions the person who supplies that date and never addresses Ray's assumption that Humbert's story coincides with the known facts of the case, the details of the murder listed even in the newspapers. But to ignore evidence does not make it go away.

Connolly at least takes note of the conflicting evidence, even if only to will it into oblivion when he suggests that Humbert may have invented Ray's foreword.[21] But if that is the case, then of course Humbert does not die on November 16, 1952, and there is no firm date from which to count back fifty-six days, and the discrepancy on which the whole case rests becomes nonexistent or meaningless.

Nabokov intended to indicate that Humbert died just after putting the last words to his manuscript. That is why he supplied the number of days *Lolita* took Humbert to compose, why he has Dr. Ray supply the date of Humbert's death, and why he explains in his interview with Alfred Appel Jr. that in Humbert's final paragraph he meant "to convey a constriction of the narrator's sick heart, a warning spasm causing him to abridge names and hasten to conclude his tale before it was too late" (437). If there is a discrepancy between the number of days *Lolita* took Humbert to write and the number of days until Humbert's death, that seems an error all too easy to make. Either Nabokov simply used the wrong starting point, counting from September 22 (Humbert's receipt of the letter), the one concrete date given in the novel's concluding sequence of events, rather than from September 25 (the murder), which has to be inferred from the text, or he counted correctly but he—or the typesetter—put "November 16" rather than the intended "November 19" for Humbert's death, making no more than the very common slip of 6 for 9. If the text now read "November 19," the argument for Humbert's having invented the last fifty pages of *Lolita* would immediately collapse. Surely it is too much to base a major reinterpretation of a novel on a single typographic character?

Nabokov always aims for exactitude. He does not allow us simply to lean on evidence, as the revisionists have to do; he makes it click into place. He has made a mistake in the dating, but what he has tried to do has his customary precision and point. Humbert admits that he has "wanted," as he says in his final paragraph, just as he feels his heart twitch, "to exist at least a couple of months longer" (311) than Quilty. In fact, since he will have only a few more hours or even minutes, he will have outlasted Quilty by fifty-six days, or eight weeks: exactly two lunar months, but still just short of two strict calendar months. Playful Aubrey McFate, as it were, *pretends* to grant Humbert the two months he had asked for, then cuts him short, denying even that small request. That is the very exact, very Nabokovian irony of these final dates, except that somewhat—but not completely— uncharacteristically, and all too humanly, he has made a slight error.

I would not have written this article if only one critic had proposed the revisionist hypothesis. I would have stopped here if two or three had propelled me into print. But with six already advancing the argument, another thinking about doing so, and others inclined to entertain it, I will continue.

Dr. Ray's foreword records that Mrs. Richard Schiller dies in childbirth in Gray Star, "a settlement in the remotest Northwest" (6). How has she reached there, if Humbert does not respond to her letter that says, "I'm going nuts because we don't have enough to pay our debts and get out of here. Dick is promised a big job in Alaska" (268)? Why does Nabokov in the afterword think of Gray Star as "the capital town of the book" (318) if Lolita does not die there in childbirth? (Gray Star, presumably, is Juneau, Alaska's capital, in allusion to the old cartographic convention of stars for capital cities but also a play on Juno, the goddess of marriage.) If Ray's foreword is accepted—and to repeat, if it is not, "November 16" disappears as evidence and takes with it the whole revisionist argument—it explicitly or implicitly confirms Lolita's letter, Humbert's visit to her, Quilty's murder, and Humbert's composing the manuscript in prison while awaiting trial for the killing, all the things the revisionists try to discredit.

So too does *Lolita: A Screenplay.*

While the screenplay reinvents minor details of the novel, its main alterations seem designed precisely to convey what Nabokov regarded as crucial to the novel but likely to be lost without considerable adaptation.[22] First, and most important, Quilty's shadowy presence throughout the novel, which readers can discover only after Humbert has himself dropped the name, is signaled in the screenplay by opening with a flash forward to the murder scene and by then making him more prominent, once the narrative returns to the beginning, from the time of Humbert's arrival in Ramsdale (at the school dance, where Quilty is presented as author of *The Nymphet*; at the Enchanted Hunters, where he is named as the drunken guest; at Beardsley School, where he is again named as author of *The Enchanted Hunters*). Second, Nabokov stresses the Edgar Allan Poe allusions, at the cost of some strain, through Humbert's scholarly work and sometimes even Lolita's schooling. Third, as frame to and external commentator on Humbert's confession, John Ray Jr. becomes the sometimes comically obtrusive narrator of the whole film.

Humbert cannot narrate the film, as he does the book, for his utter ignorance of the identity of Lolita's abductor until the end is still crucial to the story. In the novel, he could introduce Quilty's presence and yet keep his identity hidden until the right moment, thereby having the satisfaction of keeping the reader in the darkness he had himself found so unlaughable. In the film, he could not be the narrator and allow Quilty to be seen on screen without repeatedly disclosing his present awareness of Quilty's role. By removing Humbert from the narration of the film and flashing forward right at the beginning to the murder, Nabokov alerts us to the identity of Humbert's foe from the start and therefore makes us vividly aware, whenever we later catch sight of Quilty, of Humbert's failure to recognize his rival until the very end.

The screenplay opens with Lolita telling Humbert where Quilty lives— showing him, in fact, a magazine photograph of Pavor Manor, which then comes to life as Humbert arrives and promptly, wordlessly, kills Quilty. Immediately afterward, the camera cuts to:

> *Dr. John Ray*, a psychiatrist, perusing a manuscript on his desk. He swings around toward us in his swivel chair.
>
> Dr. Ray: I'm Dr. John Ray. Pleased to meet you. This here is a bundle of notes, a rough autobiography, poorly typed, which Mr. Humbert Humbert wrote after his arrest, in prison, where he was held without bail on a charge of murder, and in the psychopathic ward for observation. Without this document his crime would have remained unexplained.
>
> (*LAS* 2–3)

After Ray explains that Humbert's memoir is "mainly an account of his infatuation with a certain type of very young girl," the camera cuts to

Humbert's Cell in The Tombs
He is writing at a table. Conspicuous among the reference books at his elbow are some tattered travel guides and maps. Presently his voice surfaces as he rereads the first sentences of his story.

Humbert's voice: I was born in Paris forty dark years ago . . .

(3–4)

Obviously, there are differences, but they seem designed primarily to make the major effects of the novel possible on the screen. Dr. Ray exists objectively before our eyes, and he describes Humbert's composing the manuscript in prison after committing murder (he does not explicitly specify Quilty as murder victim: does this leave a loophole for the desperate revisionist?). By indicating Humbert's reference books, Nabokov establishes his character's effort at reliability in retelling his past. And he lets us see the murder *before* Humbert sets down his story, even lets us see Quilty asleep in Pavor Manor before Humbert first appears on screen, before Humbert reaches the manor. The murder, unequivocally, is not a product of Humbert's narration.

The scene of Humbert's reading Lolita's letter, of which the revisionists make a great deal, is replaced by a parallel scene in the screenplay. Understandably, Nabokov has excised Rita from the screenplay as an unnecessary complication and instead shows Humbert, after he loses Lolita and all trace of her abductor's trail, teaching once again at Beardsley College. There he meets Mona Dahl, who quizzes him—years have passed—about Lolita. As Nabokov notes after this scene in an explanatory aside unimpeachably immune from revisionist skepticism: "It should now have been established that Mona has had a letter from Lolita, apparently asking her to find out if it is safe for her, Lolita, to write to Humbert" (198). Humbert picks up his mail at the university post office and heads straight to an examination he is to invigilate. He opens the letter, hears, just as in the novel "a small, matter-of-fact, agonizingly familiar, voice" (199)—and after reading through Lolita's letter, he dashes, dazed, from the exam room.

In the novel, Humbert prepares for his unpreparedness for Lolita's letter with the great passage about endowing "our friends with the stability of type that literary characters acquire in the reader's mind. No matter how many times we reopen 'King Lear,' never shall we find the good king banging his tankard in high revelry, all woes forgotten, at a jolly reunion with all three daughters and their lapdogs. Never will Emma rally, revived by the sympathetic salts in Flaubert's father's timely tear" (267). Obviously, something new is needed for the screenplay both to prepare us for the surprise and to show Humbert's unpreparedness: hence the device of introducing Mona's questions, whose import we can see but Humbert cannot, and Humbert's blandly opening the letter ("from a Mrs. Richard Schiller—some graduate student, I presume" [198], he had moaned in the mailroom) in the midst of the examination. And just as the novel stresses the shocked suddenness of Humbert's response—he leaves without even waking Rita from her solid morning sleep—so does the screenplay, when Humbert lurches away from his post as invigilator. For all the changes in the treatment of Lolita's letter, Nabokov has sought cinematic ways of stressing its credibility and of eliciting the same key responses in us and in Humbert.

Humbert heads for Coalmont, where the screenplay closely follows the novel. As soon as he finds Quilty's name from Lolita, ascertains that she will never return to him, and heads off to find Pavor Manor, the screenplay's visual action ends, as Dr. Ray's voiceover explains that

> Poor Lolita died in childbed a few weeks later, giving birth to a still-born girl, in Gray Star, a settlement in the remote Northwest. She never learned that Humbert finally tracked down Clare Quilty and killed him. Nor did Humbert know of Lolita's death when shortly before his own dissolution he wrote in prison these last words of his tragic life's story:
>
> Humbert's voice (*clear and firm*): . . . While the blood still throbs through my writing hand, you are still as much part of blest matter as I am. I can still talk to you and make you live in the minds of later generations. I'm thinking of aurochs and angels, the secret of durable pigments, prophetic sonnets, the refuge of art. And this is the only immortality you and I may share, my Lolita
>
> (212–13)

The screenplay ends with the final two sentences of the novel intact. Once again, it strives for the very effects that the novel achieves. The reader of the novel, anxious to know what exactly did happen to Lolita and vaguely remembering the fates of some characters given in Dr. Ray's foreword, can turn back there and appreciate the poignant ironies: Lolita's death, despite Humbert's wishes for her longevity; Humbert's sudden death, without ever learning of hers. The screenplay offers the connections that the novel invites; Nabokov planned nothing to undermine them, and a single slip in counting should not be allowed to destroy the world he created.

Revisionists could at this point try to shore up their sagging case by arguing that Nabokov would have been reluctant to undermine the status of the story in a Hollywood screenplay at the beginning of the 1960s. But he refused to undertake the screenplay at all while he could see no way to render the novel. Presumably when he *did* undertake it he thought he had found a means of conveying what mattered in the novel—and if the meeting with Lolita and the encounter with Quilty had never really happened in the novel, *that* would certainly matter.

Nor was Nabokov shy about undermining the status of dramatized events: the last act of *Death* (1923) may be, and almost all of *The Waltz Invention* (1938) certainly is, the delusion of the hero. He was hardly *less* bold in his sixties than he had been in his early twenties. The *Lolita* screenplay abounds in disruptive expressionist and self-conscious effects, like Humbert's mother flying up to heaven holding a parasol after her death by lightning, or Dr. Ray as narrator offering urgent advice to a driver in a scene he knows occurred more than a decade before ("Look out! Close shave. When you analyze these jaywalkers you find they hesitate between the womb and the tomb" [13]). Had Nabokov wanted to suggest the final scenes of the novel were Humbert's invention, he could have done so in the screenplay. There is nothing to suggest the idea ever occurred to him.

What surprises me most about the revisionists, the three most recent of whom are Nabokov scholars I greatly respect, is that they have not only so much against their case but so little going for it.

If their case were true, Humbert would have either invented or fantasized the visit to Lolita and the murder of Quilty. Surely invention is ruled out. Humbert, who is unrelentingly vain, would hardly choose to invent a Lolita who makes it perfectly plain he doesn't feature in her experience of love and never has and who says that the only person she has ever really loved is the rival whom Humbert detests and whom she herself has come to think rather squalid. Nor would Humbert be likely to fabricate the murder of his rival in such a fashion that he is made to look a fool in the very act of executing the revenge he has so longed for, as Quilty coolly mocks him ("Well, sir, this is certainly a fine poem. Your best as far as I am concerned" [*Lolita* 302]) and even orchestrates the whole show ("the ingenious play staged for me by Quilty" [307]) that Humbert so craves to direct himself.

Above all, it seems impossible to imagine a Humbert who could construct a scene as rich in independent life as the reunion with Lolita at Coalmont. He has no gift of narrative invention, apart from his penchant for vague self-indulgent fantasy—fondling Ginny McCoo, reliving his Mediterranean idyll with Annabel beside Hourglass Lake with Lolita, murdering Charlotte as she swims, siring a litter of Lolitas, savoring the bliss of sweet revenge on Lolita's abductor. Indeed, it is essential to Humbert's nature that in these brief projections on the screen of his indulgence he fails to take into account the live reality of others. Not that he is so obtuse as to be, like Hermann in *Despair*, incapable of perceiving it even after the fact—after Charlotte's discovery of the diary, after he has at last possessed Lolita, after he sees her burst into tears at the tenderness between Avis Chapman and her father. I cannot see what evidence the novel has offered that Humbert can invent a moment like this:

"And so," I shouted, "you are going to Canada? Not Canada"—I re-shouted—"I mean Alaska, of course."

He nursed his glass and, nodding sagely, replied: "Well, he cut it on a jagger, I guess. Lost his right arm in Italy."

(276–77)

Or this:

"What things?"

"Oh, weird, filthy, fancy things. I mean he had two girls and two boys, and three or four men, and the idea was for all of us to tangle in the nude . . ."

"What things exactly?

"Oh, things . . . Oh, I—really I"—she uttered the "I" as a subdued cry while she listened to the source of the ache, and for lack of words spread the five fingers of her angularly up-and-down-moving hand. No, she gave it up, she refused to go into particulars with that baby inside her.

(278–79)

Imagine that gesture, act it out. Nabokov, after decades of writing fiction and of deliberately studying gesture, can invent this, but Humbert surely cannot. Nor is there anything in these scenes that makes them smack, as Luzhin's or Hermann's or Kinbote's so plainly do, of a madman's visions.

Apart from the discrepancy in dating, the revisionists have no concrete evidence. They point to the tinge of fantasy surrounding the scenes that follow Humbert's reading the letter, especially the murder scene, and argue that this proves them his invention. In the murder scene, of course, Humbert has explicitly drunk too much and is even more agitated than usual. It would be astonishing if reality were *not* skewed a little. But the revisionists simply ignore the element of fantasy that surrounds almost every scene in *Lolita*, from as far back as Humbert's first memory, his mother's death ("picnic, lightning" [12]), through his first glimpse of Lolita ("And, as if I were the fairy-tale nurse of some little princess (lost, kidnapped, discovered in gypsy rags through which her nakedness smiled at the king and his hounds), I recognized the tiny dark-brown mole on her side. With awe and delight (the king crying for joy, the trumpets blaring, the nurse drunk) I saw again her lovely indrawn abdomen where my southbound mouth had briefly paused" [41]), to the morning Humbert finds Lolita gone and drives drunkenly to the hospital through the "cute little town" of Elphinstone, with "its model school and temple and spacious rectangular blocks, some of which were, curiously enough, just unconventional pastures with a mule or a unicorn grazing in the young July morning mist" (248). If a jittery jostling of reality sufficed to prove that Humbert invented a scene from scratch, we would have to conclude he had invented even his own childhood and Lolita's whole existence.

It further discredits the revisionists that they cannot agree on what the discrepant dates are supposed to show Humbert has invented: all that follows the letter but not the letter itself nor Ray's foreword? the letter, too? the foreword, too? Experienced Nabokovians should know that Nabokov does not allow dual or multiple solutions: his solutions, like those of his chess problems, are exact (and, of course, not self-contradictory, like an "invented" foreword).

The revisionists seem to want to avoid the implications of their theory for Clare Quilty. None of them wants to ditch Quilty, yet without Lolita's disclosing his name, there is no reason for Humbert to know the identity of her accomplice. The novel stresses Humbert's long frustration in attempting to track down his identity: the cryptogrammic paper chase; the absurd stalking of Ass. Prof. Riggs; the detective who turns up a Bill Brown near Dolores, Colorado (or in the screenplay, a "Dolores Hayes, H, A, Y, E, S, . . . a fat old dame selling homemade Tokay to the Indians" [188]). Until his visit to Lolita, both novel and screenplay insist, Humbert has no inkling of the abductor's identity, despite all the clues Quilty amuses himself and torments Humbert by scattering. If the visit to Lolita is invented, then so is the identification of Quilty.[23] But if Humbert does not know the real abductor, if he is simply inventing Quilty as a rival and victim, why does someone as vain as he, as sure of his own intellectual superiority to those around him, choose to invent someone who so easily frustrates and humiliates him? If Quilty were mere invention, would Humbert not concoct something less unflattering? If, on the other hand, he merely follows the facts, unpleasant though they are—and takes a kind of narrative revenge on Quilty and a kind of surrogate triumph over the reader by his manipulations of Quilty's concealed appearance—what we find in the text makes perfect sense.[24]

Nor do the revisionists agree on what their theory could prove. For Leona Toker, Humbert's having invented the conclusion of his story explains why throughout the earlier part of the story we hear the voice only of the old unreformed Humbert, not the new Humbert, who loves Lolita even in her post-nymphet phase, for, after all, the Humbert writing even the start of the story should be this "reformed" self. But this is an old problem in first-person narrative. The Gulliver of book 4 of *Gulliver's Travels* has come to hate humans and adore Houyhnhnms and horses, but none of that shows through the first three books, written after his return from that final voyage. Besides, Humbert explicitly says he has, until the point of her death, thought himself back into his initial relentlessly anti-Charlotte temper "for the sake of retrospective verisimilitude" (73). Why cannot he similarly mimic his unredeemedly nympholeptic state? And it suits his strategy to keep his "reform" a surprise. It wins over many of *Nabokov*'s readers, let alone Humbert's.

Dolinin and Connolly both suggest that Humbert's ability to invent a Lolita pregnant, independent, yet still loved by him reveals his new moral status, allows him to pass, in Dolinin's view, to another plane of "awareness."[25] But neither explains why Humbert should suddenly find this new moral power, in an uneventful moment in his deliberately, prophylactically bland and automatic life with Rita.

Nor does either notice how incompatible is Humbert's supposedly self-propelled leap to a higher moral plane with what Humbert actually records of his own behavior in the scene he supposedly invents. He comes to Coalmont knowing that Lolita is married and pregnant. But although he assumes that her husband is Lolita's abductor, he is ready to kill him, regardless of what that would do to Lolita and the child he realizes she is bearing and would be compelled to rear on her own. Nabokov accentuates the conjunction: "The moment, the death I had kept conjuring up for three years was as simple as a bit of dry wood. She was frankly and hugely pregnant" (271). Within Humbert's narrative strategy, of course, this serves a different purpose: to mislead us into thinking for a moment that it is Lolita whom he will kill, so that when he corrects us, we will be so relieved that we discount that he still plans to kill *someone*. He quickly disabuses us: "I could not kill *her*, of course, as some have thought. You see, I loved her" (272). Loved her enough, indeed, to plan to kill her husband. (He does not kill Dick Schiller only because he sees at once that this is not the man who spirited Lolita from Elphinstone.) How this planned murder of Lolita's unborn child's father would testify to Humbert's moral refinement, even within an invented scenario, I cannot conceive.

The revisionists indeed uniformly discount the significance of Humbert's overwhelming desire for revenge. But Humbert has always felt intense jealousy, even over the despised Valeria, let alone over Lolita, and he seethes with another kind of enraged pride at Quilty's manipulating him on the road to Elphinstone, though he himself has manipulated Lolita on roads across America for years. Humbert sees his desire for revenge as a positive, proof of his essential romanticism and dedication to Lolita, proof of his moral superiority to Quilty. He manages to convince many readers of this. Yet Nabokov has structured his whole novel to imply the parallelism between each of the quests—to possess Lolita, to erase his rival—that at the end of each part reaches its climactic and confusing satisfaction.

Despite the "moral apotheosis" of the scene above Elphinstone, Humbert harbors for the three years that follow a compulsion to kill Lolita's abductor, an urge as powerful as his desire for Lolita herself. Nabokov pointedly juxtaposes these two contrary impulses in Humbert in the very paragraph that introduces Humbert's dedication to murderous revenge. That paragraph ends: "To myself I whispered that I still had my gun, and was still a free man—free to trace the fugitive, free to destroy my brother" (249).[26] But it begins, in limpid prefigurement of the scene of the "moral apotheosis": "Elphinstone was, and I hope still is, a very cute little town. It was spread like a maquette, you know, with its neat greenwood trees and red-roofed houses over the valley floor and I think I have alluded earlier to its model school and temple" (248).[27] Humbert may choose for his own rhetorical purposes to make the scene of the moral apotheosis the last in his story, but Nabokov remembers that "apotheosis" was conjoined for three years with an absolute determination to revenge: "I wrote many more poems. I immersed myself in the poetry of others. But not for a moment did I forget the load of revenge" (259). Even Humbert juxtaposes the contrast: "To have him trapped, after those years of repentance and rage" (297). But far too few readers stop to think what that says about the quality of his repentance.

Nabokov—and even Humbert himself—manages to make Humbert seem funny in his plans for vengeance. "On the day fixed for the execution," Humbert writes (254), as he stalks not the Rev. Rigor Mortis but his near double, the visiting art teacher "Albert Riggs, Ass. Prof.," he discovers, of course, that although he seems to have ruled out everyone else, this, too, is not the man. Some discount the reality or the seriousness of Humbert's killing Quilty because he murders someone who is in a sense his own double, a writer, a nympholept, a manipulator. But Humbert does not merely shoot his mirror image. The murder scene will indeed end up "a silent, soft, formless tussle on the part of two literati" (301), but three years before he has the least inkling of Quilty's identity, of any similarity between himself and Lolita's abductor other than their interest in the girl, Humbert vows to destroy his foe as soon as he can track him down.

In Nabokov's world, murder matters because other people exist. A murderer acts as if another were only other, not a self in his or her own right. A lover, per contra, can treat the other as a self that matters at least as much as one's own. Nabokov structures *Lolita* around the contrasts and the comparisons between the girl Humbert loves and the man he hates, the one he tries to immortalize and the one he tries to obliterate, the one he at last realizes has a life of her own and the one he realizes, damn him, had such a life, was just as alive as himself, in fact far too like himself—and whom all the same he is still happy to have killed. Humbert at last loves Lolita, even though she has won free of him; he hates Quilty all the more, the more he finds him freer than himself. To reduce to Humbert's solipsistic fancies Lolita in her final proud but abashed independence and Quilty in his strutting irrepressibility is to gain nothing and lose almost everything—and all for the sake of one revisable digit.

23. Literature, Pattern, *Lolita*
Or, Art, Literature, Science

Brett Cooke, a Slavist at Texas A&M who has published on Nabokov, was also one of the earliest scholars to link evolution and literature and wrote the first monograph reading a literary work through evolutionary lenses, on Evgeny Zamyatin's science-fiction novel *We*, the inspiration for Aldous Huxley's *Brave New World*. He invited me to link my evolutionary interests and my Nabokovian ones at the annual conference of the American Association for the Advancement of Slavic Studies in Washington, D.C. I agreed, since I had realized that connecting my long-established interest in Nabokov and my newer interest in evolutionary approaches to literature offered a challenge and a test: if they worked for any literature, they should add new insights even for works I knew as well as Nabokov's.

But evolutionary criticism offers no readymade answers. I do not think I made much of Nabokov and evolution in my 2006 talk, but this expanded version offers one possible link, through pattern—which, in *On the Origin of Stories*, I take to be central to the evolution of cognition and of the arts. Here I focus on the patterns we notice in life, in art, and in science, then on the difference that some of the patterns concealed within patterns in *Lolita* can make to our sense of the novel.

I also discuss the greater importance in art, including storytelling, of attention over meaning—something appreciated, as I write in the essay, by artists and audiences, but not necessarily by academics, who habitually prioritize meanings that can be expressed in terms of generalizations. Nabokov has addressed this in his own inimitable way: "There is nothing wrong about the moonshine of generalization when it comes *after* the sunny trifles of the book have been lovingly collected" (*LL* 1). Despite having many of my attitudes to literature and life shaped by Nabokov, I needed to take an evolutionary perspective on literature to understand fully that there was more to Nabo-kov's statement than a bias and a bon mot.

Stories can offer so much pleasure that studying them hardly seems like work. Literary scholars have often atoned for enjoying the frissons of fiction by investigating literature as a form of history or moral education. And since the late 1960s, academic literature departments have tried especially to stress criticism as critique, as an agent of social transformation.

For the last few decades, indeed, scholars have often been reluctant to deal with literature as an art—with the imaginative accomplishment of a work or the imaginative feast of responding to it—as if to do so meant privileging elite capacities and pandering to indulgent inclinations. Many critics have sought to keep literary criticism well away from the literary and instead to arraign literature as largely a product of social oppression, complicit in it or at best offering a resistance already contained. No wonder academic literary scholarship now describes itself as "a profession suffering from an epochal loss of confidence."[1]

Literary academics have also been reluctant to deal with science, except to fantasize that they have engulfed and disarmed it by reducing it to "just another narrative," or to dismiss it with a knowing sneer as presupposing a risibly naïve epistemological realism. They have not only denied the pleasure of art and the power of science but also, like others in the humanities and social sciences, have denied that human nature exists, insisting against the evidence that culture and convention make us infinitely malleable.

I and others want literature to return to the artfulness of literary art and to reach out to science now that science has at last found ways to explore human nature and human minds. Since these are, respectively, the subject and the object of literature, it would be fatal for literary study to continue to cut itself off from science, from the power of discovery possible through submitting ideas to the rule of evidence. And indeed the publishing marketplace suggests that literary studies have begun to shift from a decidedly antiscientific and antinaturalistic ethos, long dominant but now exhausted, toward one that seeks to incorporate the discoveries and the methodological strengths of science.[2]

There are many ways in which science can return us to and enrich the art of literature. We could consider human natures and minds as understood by science and as represented in literature, not just as seen through the approved lenses of race, gender, and class but in terms, for instance, of the human life-history cycle or social cognition or cooperation versus competition. Or we could develop multileveled explanations that allow room for the universals of human nature, for the local in culture and history, for individuality in authors and audiences, and for the particular problem situations faced in this or that stint of composition or comprehension.

One way to use science to approach literature (and art in general) is to view it as a behavior in evolutionary terms. Why do art in general and storytelling in particular exist as species-wide behaviors? Asking the question in these terms makes possible a genuinely theoretical literary theory, one that depends not on the citation of purportedly antiauthoritarian authorities, but on the presence of evidence and the absence of counterevidence, on examining human behavior across time and space and in the context of many cultures and even many species.

The humanities have always accepted the maxim that biologist D'Arcy Thompson stated with sublime simplicity: "Everything is what it is because it got that way." How it got that way starts not with the *Epic of Gilgamesh* but much further back: with our evolving into art-making and storytelling animals. How did our capacities for art and story build and become ingrained in us over time? How do we now produce and process stories so effortlessly? What aspects of the mind do we engage, and how?

To consider art and story in evolutionary terms we have to decide whether they are biological adaptations: are they features that natural selection has designed into humans over time because they led to higher rates of survival and reproduction? I argue in my recent book *On the Origin of Stories: Evolution, Cognition and Fiction* that art and storytelling *are* adaptations. These behaviors are species-wide, engaged in spontaneously by all normal individuals and spontaneously encouraged in infants by their parents.

Art is a form of cognitive play with pattern. Just as communication exists in many species, even in bacteria, and human language derives from but redirects animal communication along many unforeseen new routes, so play exists in many species, but the unique cognitive play of human art redirects it in new ways and to new functions.

Play exists even in the brightest invertebrates, like octopi, and in all mammals in which it has been investigated. Its self-rewarding nature means that animals with flexible behavior—behavior not genetically programmed—willingly engage in it again and again in circumstances of relative security and thereby, over time, can master complex, context-sensitive skills. The sheer pleasure of play motivates animals to repeat intense activities that strengthen and speed up neural connections. The exuberance of play enlarges the boundaries of ordinary behavior, in unusual and extreme movements, in ways that enable animals to cope better with the unexpected.

Humans uniquely inhabit "the cognitive niche."[3] We have an appetite for information and especially for pattern, information that falls into meaningful arrays from which we can make rich inferences. We have uniquely long childhoods, and even beyond childhood we continue to play more than other species. Our predilection for the patterned cognitive play of art begins with what developmental psychologists call *protoconversation*, exchanges between infants and caregivers of rhythmic, responsive behavior, involving sound and movement, in playful patterns described as "more like a song than a sentence" and as "interactive multimedia performances."[4] Without being taught, children engage in music, dance, design, and, especially, pretend play.

Our adult compulsion for the cognitive play of art—from tribal work songs to tradesmen's transistors to urbanites' iPods—allows us to extend and refine the neural pathways that produce and process pattern in sonic, visual, and kinetic modes. Humans have not only a unique predilection for open-ended pattern but also a unique propensity to share attention (long before we learn language) and for that reason a unique capacity for learning from others. Our inclination for sharing attention and for social learning ensures that we readily master the rudiments of local artistic traditions. Participating in these traditions amplifies the pleasure we gain from social living. By helping to reduce the costs in tension and raise the rewards of sociality, art helps us to cooperate on a scale far beyond that of any other highly individualized animal.

The *Oxford English Dictionary* defines pattern as "an arrangement or order of things or activity . . . order or form discernible in things, actions, ideas, situations, etc." Pattern usually signals regularities in the world rather than mere chance: the pattern that my head and my feet turn up not far from one another is not coincidence but part of the regularity that is me.

Until recently computers have fared dismally at pattern recognition, but living organisms have long been expert at it. Pattern turns the data of the senses into information that can guide behavior. The more an organism depends on intelligence, the more it seeks pattern of multiple kinds at multiple levels. Frogs respond to the pattern of small objects flying across their field of vision by flicking out their tongues. That makes them more efficient than you or me at catching insects, but frogs cannot respond to new kinds of patterns. Humans can. In addition to the patterns evolution has programmed us to track, like the shapes or locations of objects, we search for patterns of many kinds. The chemical patterns of insecticides can, for instance, make us more efficient killers of insects than even frogs have evolved to be.

Because the world swarms with patterns, animal minds evolved as pattern extractors, able to detect the information meaningful to their kind of organism in their kind of environment and therefore to predict and act accordingly. Pattern occurs at multiple levels, from the stable information of spatial conditions and physical processes to highly volatile information about individuals and their moods, actions, and intentions. Pattern recognition allows us to distinguish animate from inanimate, human from nonhuman, this individual from any others, this attitude or expression from another. Identifying not only individuals but also the higher-order patterns in their behavior, personality, and powers allows for far more accurate social prediction.

If information is chaotic, it lacks meaningful pattern and can't be understood. If, on the other hand, it is completely patterned, we need not continue to pay attention, since the information is redundant: indeed, the psychological process of habituation switches attention off if a stimulus remains, if the pattern of information can be predicted. The most patterned novel possible would repeat one letter, say, *q*, over and over again—a queue no reader would want to wait in. But an unpredictable combination of patterns repays intense attention and can yield rich inferences, although finding how to ascertain what forms a meaningful pattern and what meaning the pattern implies may not be easy.

Committed to the cognitive niche, humans crave pattern because it can tell us so much. The more our minds can handle multiple patterns at multiple levels, the more successfully we can predict and act. We therefore have what physicist Edward Purcell calls an "avidity for pattern." As Stephen Jay Gould notes: "The human mind delights in finding pattern. . . . No other habit of thought lies so deeply within the soul of a small creature trying to make sense of a complex world not constructed for it."[5] Extreme informational chaos, the absence of pattern, as in whiteout or dense fog, can even cause distress and loss of sensory function.[6]

Art offers the opposite of chaos. It concentrates and plays with the world's profusion of patterns, with its patterns of interrelated or intersecting patterns. Our perception of pattern and of deviation from it produces strong emotional reactions.[7] Art engages us by appealing to our appetite for pattern at multiple levels, in producing or perceiving bodily movement, shapes, surfaces, sounds, words, or miniature worlds. Like play, art provokes us to continue the activities it offers long enough and to resume them often enough to modify our neural circuitry over time.

Our compulsion to engage in the behaviors we call art, in cognitive play with high-density pattern, enables us over many repetitions to produce or at least to process patterns in the perceptual and cognitive areas that matter most to us: movement, sound, sight, and sociality. And as in other primate species, the capacity to command attention correlates with status, which correlates in turn with access to resources and therefore with survival and reproduction rates. Those with an exceptional talent in some art can therefore earn status.

For both artists and audiences, art's capacity to ensnare attention is crucial: for the artist, to accrue status; for the audience, to motivate engagement. Exposure to a single story told once will not transform a mind substantially, but many repetitions, or many different stories, can improve our capacities for social cognition and scenario construction so valuable to us in the non-story world.

One conclusion I draw from this analysis of the origin of art and story is that attention—engagement in the activity—matters before meaning. Aristotle understood this. So do artists, authors, and audiences. Even children under the age of three grasp the crucial role of catching and holding the attention of listeners. At this age their stories are as much poems as narratives, focusing on striking characters and effects that violate expectations, but in a structure that resembles theme and variation, a simpler kind of pattern, rather than the event continuity that adults expect of stories:

> The monkeys
> They went up sky
> They fall down
> Choo choo train in the sky
> The train fell down in the sky
> I fell down in the sky in the water
> I got on my boat and my legs hurt
> Daddy fall down in the sky.[8]

The two-and-a-half-year-old boy who concocts this "story" has no idea yet that stories incorporate not just settings, characters, and events but also aims, goals, and outcomes. He cannot develop a story but seems to intuit the need to surprise, with his unusual characters in unusual places defying the principles of gravity he began to understand before he was three months old. Repetition is the simplest form of elaboration, but since pure repetition holds little interest, repetition of a bold idea with variation offers him the best prospects of holding the attention of listeners with the imaginative resources he has.

A four-year-old boy made up this story:

> Once there was a dragon who went poo poo on a house and the
>   house broke
> then when the house broke the people died
> and when the people died their bones came out and broke and got
>   together again and turned into a skeleton
> and then the skeletons came along and scared the people out of the
>   town
> and then when all the people got scared out of the town then skel-
>   eton babies were born
> and then everyone called it skeleton town
> and when they called it skeleton town the people came back and then
>   they got scared away again
> and then when they all got scared away again the skeletons died
> no one came to the town
> so there was no people ever in that town ever again.[9]

This story and others by young children are not plotless but unplanned and episodic, a series of opportunistic riffs, each aimed at catching attention: from the dragon as a conventional category-breaching monster to the decorum-breaching "poo poo" on the house and so on.

Yet if we normally engage in art simply because it can command our attention, meaning elbows its way to the fore in academic contexts because the propositional nature of meaning makes it so much easier to expound, circulate, regurgitate, or challenge than the fluid dynamics of attention.

"Examples," writes Nabokov, "are the stained-glass windows of knowledge (*SO* 312). *Lolita* offers a whole Sainte-Chapelle. How can we see its glowing colors better if we look at it in terms of cognitive play with pattern and its means for securing and refreshing attention?

Stories can earn attention through subject matter. Although house buying has become a stressful preoccupation in modern life, we have no genre of real-estate novels. But we do have stories about romantic love. An evolutionist can note the significance of reproduction and survival in the transmission of genes and the evolution of species to explain why, over countless generations, our emotions have been designed to respond so intensely to love and death and why romance stories so often focus on finding love while thrillers, mysteries, and adventure tales focus on avoiding death.

Precisely because who will partner whom matters so much to us, love stories have always flooded the story pool. Any new romance runs the risk of neglect through habituation, the fading of interest in repeated stimuli. But the passionate sexual love of a mature man for a girl is not an overfamiliar love story. As a novel about an unusual love and an unusual murder, *Lolita* appeals to immemorial interests but from unexpected angles. It surprised and shocked the public when it was first published, and it still does. At over 50 million copies sold, it is surely the most demanding novel ever to sell so well.

Let's dive from the overall design into the details of Humbert's story to see if they bear out the idea of art as cognitive play with pattern, and to see how Nabokov eliminates habituation and animates attention. Humbert begins:

1

Lolita, light of my life, fire of my loins. My sin, my soul. Lo-lee-ta: the tip of the tongue taking a trip of three steps down the palate to tap, at three, on the teeth. Lo. Lee. Ta.

She was Lo, plain Lo, in the morning, standing four feet ten in one sock. She was Lola in slacks. She was Dolly at school. She was Dolores on the dotted line. But in my arms she was always Lolita.

Did she have a precursor? She did, indeed she did. In point of fact, there might have been no Lolita at all had I not loved, one summer, a certain initial girl-child. In a princedom by the sea. Oh when? About as many years before Lolita was born as my age was that summer. You can always count on a murderer for a fancy prose style.

Ladies and gentlemen of the jury, exhibit number one is what the seraphs, the misinformed, simple, noble-winged seraphs, envied. Look at this tangle of thorns.

2

I was born in 1910, in Paris. My father was a gentle, easy-going person, a salad of racial genes: a Swiss citizen, of mixed French and Austrian descent, with a dash of the Danube in his veins. I am going to pass around in a minute some lovely, glossy-blue picture-postcards. He owned a luxurious hotel on the Riviera. His father and two grandfathers had sold wine, jewels and silk, respectively. At thirty he married an English girl, daughter of Jerome Dunn, the alpinist, and granddaughter of two Dorset parsons, experts in obscure subjects— paleopedology and Aeolian harps, respectively. My very photogenic mother died in a freak accident (picnic, lightning) when I was three, and, save for a pocket of warmth in the darkest past, nothing of her subsists within the hollows and dells of memory, over which, if you can still stand my style (I am writing under observation), the sun of my infancy had set: surely, you all know those redolent remnants of day suspended, with the midges, about some hedge in bloom or suddenly entered and traversed by the rambler, at the bottom of a hill, in the summer dusk; a furry warmth, golden midges.

No other novel that I can recall starts with more patterned prose than *Lolita*. And its initial patterns themselves form parts of other patterns, like Humbert's self-projection as an artist, a poet, an adoring lover, or his aestheticizing Lolita. But pattern and tantalizing hints of pattern saturate the text: Humbert's mother is "the granddaughter of two Dorset parsons, experts in obscure subjects—paleopedology and Aeolian harps." That in itself may be coincidence, or perhaps meaningful pattern; what are the odds of these two subjects containing the adjacent letters *a, l, e, o*? Is that accident or design, and if design, why?

Nabokov has been called the greatest prose stylist in English, and not, I think, for the likes of Humbert's patterned prose but for his mastery of the psychology of attention, his capacity to shift our imaginations so quickly. Lolita's name supplies the first word of Humbert's text and the last. His attention is obsessively on her, and he cannot introduce her name without caressing each syllable with lips and tongue. But even as he lingers on her in the second paragraph, the sudden images of Lo with different names and in different circumstances flash her into our mind's eye: "Lo, plain Lo, in the morning, standing four feet ten in one sock. . . . Lola in slacks. . . . Dolores on the dotted line." Nabokov knows how to catch our attention and fire our imagination by unexpected details and shifts.

Notice the saccadic jump in attention, without sensory detail but with the surprise revelation of "you can always count on a murderer for a fancy prose style." Or the shift again from summary to "I am going to pass around in a minute some lovely, glossy-blue picture postcards." Everyone sits up here, because Humbert suddenly breaks frame, as it were, and because of the sudden concreteness: the mere idea of passing around these polished postcards activates motor, tactile, and visual areas of the brain—as neuroscientists have only recently established.[10]

The average shot length in Hollywood movies has been shrinking as viewers have learned to assimilate film faster and to cope with the information rush of the modern world. Nabokov has influenced writers from acclaimed oldsters (Italo Calvino, W. G. Sebald, Salman Rushdie, Martin Amis, Orhan Pamuk) to feisty youngsters (Aleksandar Hemon, Zadie Smith, Marisha Pessl) by introducing into fiction something akin to modern film's reduction in shot length, its rapidity of changes of subject or perspective. I suspect that storytelling in general has speeded up our capacity to shift attention from one perspective to another. Homer generally moves from subject to subject slowly compared with modern storytelling, let alone Nabokov, but even Homer can swiftly shift level and focus when he suddenly backgrounds a warrior dying on the battlefield.

The intense sound patterning in Humbert's opening words may be unusual in fiction, but a high density of meaningful multiple patterns occurs everywhere in stories, even without Nabokovian alliterative play. Character is one kind of pattern particularly significant for social animals: identifying individuals and discerning consistent differences of personality (even animals as simple as guppies distinguish the personalities of others of their kind and interact with them accordingly). Character clues come thick and fast in fiction. That combination of Humbert's obsessive focus on Lolita and his capacity to shift attention so rapidly in the opening paragraphs of the novel arouses our interest in his lively, highly self-conscious mind—even if we soon find ourselves uneasy about what that mind intends.

Events can be unique and unprecedented in trivial details, but we understand them because they are similar enough in pattern to other situations we experience directly or indirectly: we recognize romantic love, for instance, as clearly in Humbert's first lines as we hear the pattern of his words.

In fiction we often find the compounding of event patterns: Humbert's love for his childhood sweetheart, "Annabel Leigh," the "certain initial girl-child. In a princedom by the sea," for instance, prefigures (and, as he wants to suggest, explains, intensifies the romanticism of, and helps excuse) his love for the girl-child Lolita. In Nabokov and many other authors, the relationship of life and art forms another kind of pattern: here, the relationship between the girl whom Humbert calls Annabel Leigh and Poe's poem "Annabel Lee," whose "kingdom by the sea" he also echoes. Such a pattern of characters' lives echoing art runs through the novel as a genre from *Don*

Quixote to *Northanger Abbey* and *Madame Bovary* and into modernism, post-modernism, and beyond.

Expectations are possible because the world and its objects and events fall into patterns. But we learn more from the surprising than from the expected since surprise signals something new and therefore potentially worth notice. Stories fall into patterns of patterns, which storytellers can play with to arouse, satisfy, defeat, or surprise expectations—and no wonder that expectation and surprise drive so much of our interest in story. When Humbert discloses that he is a murderer, certain patterns of events instantly spring to our minds, and, as we realize when we read on, our storyteller wishes to toy with storytelling expectations. The usual whodunit pattern of a murder mystery gives way to a whocoppedit pattern (see *VNAY* 243), as Humbert parades one possible victim after another before us and then finds out the name of the person he wishes to kill but refuses to tell us, although he unhelpfully notes he has sprinkled clues to the victim's identity throughout the story so far.

The most powerful patterns of all in fiction tend to be those associated with plot: with goals, obstacles, and outcomes, with expectations and surprises. Humbert's goal of obtaining Lolita powerfully shapes expectations and ironies throughout part 1 of the novel; his goal of venting his murderous hatred on the rival who took Lolita from him shapes much of part 2. These intensely human, albeit in Humbert's case perverse, goal patterns shape the narrative impetus of the novel. But Nabokov builds in other patterns, like those of Lolita's relationship to the stranger pursuing Humbert and Lolita out west: on a first reading we wonder with Humbert whether these signs signal a rival, a detective on his trail, or a paranoid projection of his fears or guilt. Quilty, the stranger, weaves a different set of elusive patterns into the hotel and motel ledgers along the way for the express purpose of tantalizing and taunting Humbert and us. And Humbert in telling his story then weaves into his manuscript the patterns pointing to Quilty's presence in order to tantalize and taunt us so that we cannot immediately identify the patterns he can now see, comprehend, and control.

In *On the Origin of Stories*, I note two examples of "early" story: one early in human history, Homer's *Odyssey*; the other early in individual development, Dr. Seuss's *Horton Hears a Who!*. I do not stress pattern in these two stories, but the openings of both books swarm with form. The *Odyssey* opens with the metrical pattern of dactylic hexameter, the structural pattern of the invocation to the muse and the proem, the focus on one hero amid larger events, and the verbal pattern of poly-adjectives surrounding Odysseus, even twice within the first line. In the opening four lines of

Horton Hears a Who! we find verbal pattern play at least as intense—alliteration, anaphora, anapestic tetrameter, antithesis, assonance, consonance, end rhyme, internal rhyme—usually in multiple doses and compounded by visual and narrative patterns.

Writers of fiction, from Homer, Dante, or Shakespeare to Dickens, Joyce, Nabokov, Beckett, and Dr. Seuss, produce patterns at many levels. Others produce fewer kinds of pattern but focus intensely on those that matter most to us in human terms, character and event, plus their own particular predilections: in Austen's case, for instance, generalizations about human conduct and character, in Tolstoy's, the patterns of an acutely observed physical and physiological world.

As "The monkeys / They went up sky" and dragons poo-pooing and Homer and Dr. Seuss show in their different ways, pattern saturates story from the start. But *Lolita*, a sophisticated late instance of story, not only proliferates patterns but also problematizes them. It protrudes pattern but sometimes provokes by suggesting significant implications it nevertheless withholds. The hotel name, The Enchanted Hunters, obtrudes in a first reading of *Lolita*, especially as the goal of Humbert's quest to possess Lolita, and because of the ecphrastic fresco at the hotel, whose enchanted hunters Humbert reimagines in terms of orgiastic incandescence, and because Humbert, although the hunter, feels enchanted when Lolita turns on him and suggests that they make love. A year and a half later Lolita is about to star in a school play called *The Enchanted Hunters* when she suggests to Humbert that they leave Beardsley and travel west together. In Elphinstone, a gem of a western state, as we later discover, she has an assignation with Quilty, the play's author, who also happened to be staying at The Enchanted Hunters the night Humbert tried to possess Lolita in her sleep and *did* possess her when she awoke.

The pattern seems charged with significance, yet it remains elusive, unlike the overt implications of, say, the motifs in *Ulysses*, such as the outsider Throwaway, the horse that wins the Ascot Gold Cup on Bloomsday and is associated with Bloom, and the ousted favorite, Sceptre, associated with Bloom's seemingly favored rival, Blazes Boylan.

One aspect of the Enchanted Hunters pattern I noticed many years ago was a series of covert links between the attempted rape of Lolita at the hotel and the killing of Quilty at his manor, where, as he stalks his prey, Humbert calls himself "an enchanted and very tight hunter." Despite this arch echo, Humbert fails to realize that fate (or Nabokov) has constructed a whole system of parallels between the Enchanted Hunters episode and the episode of the murder (*VNAY* 253). In *The American Years* I ask: What are we to make of this pointed pairing of ostensibly unrelated scenes?

And I answer:

Humbert carefully places after the murder that haunting and famous scene on the mountain trail overlooking the valley filled with the sound of schoolchildren at play: "I stood listening to that musical vibration from my lofty slope, to those flashes of separate cries with a kind of demure murmur for background, and then I knew that the hopelessly poignant thing was not Lolita's absence from my side, but the absence of her voice from that concord." In the position Humbert has given it, this becomes the last distinct scene of the novel. Even a fine reader like Alfred Appel, Jr., can treat this moment of epiphany for Humbert as his "moral apotheosis" (*Annotated Lolita* 326), a final clarity of moral vision that almost redeems him. Humbert does indeed feel profound and sincere regret here, albeit too late, but that is only one part of a complex whole. He places this image of himself to stand in contrast to Quilty, whom he has just murdered, though the vision itself occurred not then but three years earlier, when Quilty took Lolita from him. What difference does the timing make? For two years Humbert had been lucidly aware that he was keeping Lolita a prisoner and destroying her childhood and her spirit, but he continued to hold her in his power. So long as he could extract sexual delight from her, he could remain deaf to his moral sense. Only after her disappearance, when she was no longer available as the thrice-daily outlet for his lust, did he allow his moral awareness to overwhelm him as he looked down into that valley.

But that was a very selective insight. Humbert places the scene at the end of the novel to leave the closing impression that he can be self-lessly concerned for Lolita, and his rhetorical strategy persuades many readers. Nabokov assesses things differently, and although he gives Humbert complete control over his pen, he finds a way to inscribe his own judgment within and against what Humbert writes. By the covert parallels he constructs between the climaxes of the novel's two parts, he indicates that both scenes reflect the same romantic sense of the imperious dictates of desire, the same quest for self-satisfaction even at the expense of another life.

(*VNAY* 253–54)

The links between the scenes at The Enchanted Hunters and at Pavor Manor, where the murder occurs, are inconspicuous until noticed but then become insistently precise and pointed. Whether others agree with my interpretation of why Nabokov inscribed this particular covert pattern is another question. But the Enchanted Hunters pattern shows how Nabokov can continue to amplify the effects of the patterns of character and event that we register at once by planting further complementary patterns we can discover only on careful re-rereadings.

Another related pattern I noticed only recently. Ironies that ripple through the novel pervade the early scene at Hourglass Lake, where Humbert bathes with Charlotte and thinks of drowning her in what seems like ideal seclusion, but decides against it. Sunbathing with Charlotte afterward, he is surprised when Jean Farlow emerges from the bushes. The brief passage below, though funny in its own right, seems primarily preparation for other ironies:

> Charlotte, who was a little jealous of Jean, wanted to know if John was coming.
>
> He was. He was coming home for lunch today. He had dropped her on the way to Parkington and should be picking her up any time now. It was a grand morning. She always felt a traitor to Cavall and Melampus for leaving them roped on such gorgeous days. She sat down on the white sand between Charlotte and me. She wore shorts. Her long brown legs were about as attractive to me as those of a chestnut mare.
>
> (*Lolita* 88–89)

Notice the names of Jean Farlow's dogs, casually dropped in here, referred to once earlier as "two boxer dogs" but never mentioned again after the lines above. Cavall was not only King Arthur's favorite hound but the first of his hounds to turn the stag in a hunting episode in *The Mabinogion*.[11] Melampus is the name of the first hound of Actaeon, in Ovid's telling of the story of Diana and Actaeon in his *Metamorphoses*.[12]

The precision of these allusions startles: two hounds from different literary traditions that are the first to chase or turn a stag. Actaeon, remember, is the hunter who spies Diana, the virgin goddess of hunting, naked. Diana, enraged, transforms him into a stag, and his hounds pursue him, Melampus leading, and tear him to pieces. He still feels as a man, but he can express himself only as a deer, so his own hounds and his fellow hunters cannot respond to his strangled voice pleading for them to stop tearing him apart.

This leads us back to the Enchanted Hunters motif and the idea of the hunter hunted and of sex and chastity as linked with hunting and pursuit. Humbert, stalking Lolita, finds himself hunted by Charlotte and "captured" in marriage. Wanting to end Charlotte's life, but not daring to, he finds her suddenly killed, after a dog chases a car that swerves and kills her, as if his deadly plans have met with enchanted success. Stalking Lolita at The Enchanted Hunters, Humbert finds himself "hunted" by her when she proposes they try out what she discovered at camp. But Quilty, already at the hotel, witnesses Humbert and recognizes his designs on Lolita. This recognition inspires him to write the play *The Enchanted Hunters*, revolving around a character called Diana, whose role Lolita will take. The play itself turns out to be an enchanted device for Quilty's hunting down Lolita and then for stalking and hounding Humbert, now very much the hunted rather than the hunter, all the way across America. Just after Humbert gives up his hunt for Lolita's "kidnapper," he passes through Briceland (echoing Brocéliande, the home of Merlin the Enchanter) and The Enchanted Hunters Hotel, before writing a poem about Diana and the Enchanted Hunters. When he hears from Lolita about her marriage to a young American, Humbert resumes the hunt but finds himself chasing the wrong prey, and when at last Lolita gives him the scent he needs, he heads straight off to kill the man who had hunted and hounded him.

Nabokov was a scientist and had spent most of the decade before writing *Lolita* in charge of butterflies and moths at Harvard's Museum of Comparative Zoology. He was fascinated by pattern in nature, like the patterns of butterfly wings, the patterns of matching patterns in natural mimicry, and the complex patterns of relationships a scientist has to disentangle to work out the taxonomic relatedness within a genus or a family of butterflies. As a novelist he was also a shrewd intuitive psychologist, aware of how the mind processes pattern. He realized that the profusion of patterns in nature may obscure or distract us from other significant patterns. Beside Hourglass Lake, the character patterns of Charlotte's jealousy (of Lolita, of Jean) and of Humbert's scornfulness toward adult women, and the wry verbal patterns of free indirect speech, here ironically maximizing the mental distance between Humbert and Jean—all seem much more prominent than the incidental Cavall and Melampus.

Even if we track down Cavall and Melampus and link them to the Enchanted Hunters, and through Cavall as King Arthur's dog link to the Arthurian pattern that Nabokov seems to have attached from the first to the Lolita theme, I am not satisfied with what we can interpret of either the Enchanted Hunters or the Arthurian (and Merlinesque) pattern. Nabokov's patterns have powerful implications, once we trace them far enough, and in the case of *Lolita* I don't think I or anyone else has yet reached that point.

What do these examples from *Lolita* suggest? A writer can captu_
attention before, in some cases long before, we reach what academic critic
would accept as the "meaning" or "meanings" of works. The high density of
multiple patterns holds our attention and elicits our response—especially
through patterns of biological importance, like those surrounding character
and event, which arouse attention and emotion and feed powerful, dedicated, evolved information-processing subroutines in the mind.

Patterns in fiction, as in life, may proliferate and obscure other patterns. They can yield rich but sometimes far from evident implications.
They may be open-ended: they and their implications often do not come
preannounced and predigested. Sometimes they feed into efficient, evolved
pattern-detection systems, but often they have to be discovered through
attention and curiosity, and sometimes in ways that neither audiences nor
authors fully anticipate.

At a more general level, humans are extraordinary open-ended pattern
detectors because we so compulsively inhabit the cognitive niche. Art plays
with cognitive patterns at high intensity. The pleasure this generates is an
essential part of what it is to be human and matters both at the individual
level, for audiences and artists, and at the social level, for the patterns we
share (in design, music, dance, and story). The pleasure that art's intense
play with patterns affords compels our engagement again and again and
helps shape our capacity to create and process pattern more swiftly. Perhaps
it even helps explain the so-called Flynn effect,[13] the fact—and it seems to
be one—that IQs have risen with each of the last few generations: perhaps
as a consequence of the modern bombardment of the high-density patterns
of art through television, DVDs, music and iPods, computer games, You-
Tube, and the like.

And with their high intensity of pattern and their fixed form, works of art
should provide ideal controlled replicable experiments for the study of both
rapid and gradual pattern recognition in the mind.

Literary studies have no need to feel embarrassed at the art of literature or the pleasure we derive from it. Literature and other arts have helped
extend our command of information patterns, and that singular command
makes us who we are.

Four

"Pale Fire": Poem and Pattern

Pale Fire was the first Nabokov novel I read with rapture, in 1969, in my last year in high school. In *Vladimir Nabokov: The American Years*, I made an emphatic case for reading the whole novel as the invention of John Shade, an interpretation strongly influenced by Andrew Field's 1967 *Nabokov: His Life in Art* (which I read at an impressionable seventeen, in 1970) and by Julia Bader's 1972 *Crystal Land*. When the subject of the "Shadean" reading of *Pale Fire* rose again on the Nabokov listserv at the end of 1997, I found what I took to be additional evidence to support my Shadean reading and was asked by Zoran Kuzmanovich, the editor of *Nabokov Studies*, to expand this into an article. As I began to do so, I realized in pursuing clues that not only was a Shadean reading of the novel wrong but so were the terms of the debate. I found myself led by the evidence to a new interpretation that took me by surprise and exploded into *Nabokov's* Pale Fire: *The Magic of Artistic Discovery* (1999), which I wrote in six weeks of concentration that jarred my nerves and wrecked my back. In keeping with the strategy of that book, I will disclose nothing of the interpretation until readers work through a first reading and then a first rereading response to *Pale Fire*. I have since written a couple more pieces on the novel, extending the interpretation offered in my book. But I had never written on the poem "Pale Fire" by itself.

Early in 2007 Jean Holabird, the artist of *AlphaBet in Color* (2005), a painter's rendering of the colors letters had in Nabokov's synesthetic mind's eye, proposed to Gingko Press another novel book idea: an edition of John Shade's 999-line poem, "Pale Fire," as if handwritten on index cards—the very index cards that, according to the fiction of *Pale Fire*, his neighbor Charles Kinbote takes from him at his death, "annotates," and publishes. I was delighted to be asked to edit the volume and by the opportunity to focus intently on the poem, which I have loved for forty years, rather than to consider it within the mesmerizingly distracting context of Kinbote's commentary, which I have also loved for forty years. Shade takes the title of his poem from Shakespeare. I compare the intensity of patterning in "Pale Fire" to what we find in Shakespeare's sonnets.

"Pale Fire," John Shade's verse autobiography, credo, manifesto, and magnum opus, written in three weeks of sustained inspiration in July 1959, offers a clear retrospect on his quiet life and a confident prospect of a future in life and death that he knows he cannot know.

Pale Fire, Vladimir Nabokov's novel, written in a year of sustained inspiration from late November 1960 to early December 1961, discloses that "Pale Fire" is also Shade's unwitting last testament and the tragic target of a scholarly outrage perpetrated by his first editor, campus-town neighbor, and would-be friend K. Cruelly, the commentary continues to divert attention from the poem. Our edition returns the poem to readers as Shade left it, in his own hand, before unspeakable others intervened.

Writers as diverse as Penelope Lively, Edmund White, Orhan Pamuk, Martin Amis, and Zadie Smith have come to consider Nabokov the last of the great novelists, the most fertile fictionist of the last century. Many Nabokov admirers think *Pale Fire* his greatest novel—but there agreement ends, for the novel has spawned notoriously divergent and irreconcilable interpretations.

Nabokov as poet has earned much less acclaim. Indeed, because his Russian poetry was regularly dismissed by the leading Russian émigré critic, Georgy Adamovich, Nabokov adopted the pseudonym Vasily Shishkov for two poems that Adamovich then hailed as works of genius—until he discovered their true author. "Pale Fire" is not only Shade's but also Nabokov's longest poem, and in part, like the lyrics he wrote under that other nonce nom de plume, Nabokov's attempt to stake his patch on Parnassus. *Pale Fire* has sparked high praise but little critical agreement. "Pale Fire," by contrast, has earned radical evaluative disagreement—some think it a great poem, even "perhaps the finest single American poem of the past century";[1] some think it a great example of either intentionally or unintentionally poor poetry— but everyone seems to agree about how we *interpret* it.

I admire *Pale Fire* above all Nabokov's other work, which is saying something, but the greatness of the novel and its interpretive challenge have obscured both the greatness of the poem and *its* interpretive challenges. We have not paid Shade and his poem the respect, the care in reading, they deserve.

Let me quote from the opening of "Pale Fire" and from the opening of my discussion of the poem in my book about the novel:

John Shade's "Pale Fire" opens with an extraordinary series of images whose initial impact lingers in the mind as it expands in implication throughout the poem:

> I was the shadow of the waxwing slain
> By the false azure in the windowpane;
> I was the smudge of ashen fluff—and I
> Lived on, flew on, in the reflected sky.

As we learn more about Shade's lifelong attempt to understand a world where life is surrounded by death, we realize the full resonance of these opening lines: that he projected himself in imagination into the waxwing, as if it were somehow still flying beyond death, and into the reflected azure of the window, as if that were the cloudlessness of some hereafter, even as he stood looking at "the smudge of ashen fluff" of the dead bird's little body. Alvin Kernan comments that the bird "has died flying into the hard barrier of the image which promises freedom but only reflects the world it is already in,"[2] and that irony persists:

> And from the inside, too, I'd duplicate
> Myself, my lamp, an apple on a plate:
> Uncurtaining the night, I'd let dark glass
> Hang all the furniture above the grass,
> And how delightful when a fall of snow
> 10   Covered my glimpse of lawn and reached up so
> As to make chair and bed exactly stand
> Upon that snow, out in that crystal land!

The contrast between the mundaneness of Shade's room—"Myself, my lamp, an apple on a plate"—and the magic of the reflection reflects in turn off those other contrasts already intimated between real and imagined, between life and the hint of something beyond life in the "reflected sky," to create a tension sustained throughout the poem between the taken-for-granted, the freshly seen, the vividly projected, and the unseen beyond. This is major poetry, by any standard.

(*NPFMAD* 25–26)

Because Shade, like Nabokov, hides much of his design right under our noses, I will keep returning to these and other passages—as I did with others in *Nabokov's* Pale Fire: *The Magic of Artistic Discovery*—to show what we have missed.

Orhan Pamuk comments about his autobiography, *Istanbul*—perhaps the finest since Nabokov's own *Speak, Memory*—that like metaphor, it conflates two things not hitherto brought together: in his case, a personal autobiography and a history of his home town.[3] "Pale Fire" has that kind of originality: part autobiography, part philosophical credo, part artistic manifesto, part author's self-interview, it modulates between a narrative poem with a tragic drama at its center and a reflective lyric focused on space as much as time, on the poet's immediate surrounds and his sense of the unknown beyond. It slips back and forth between the everyday and the eternal, between Shade's paring his nails and his decision "to explore and fight / The foul, the inadmissible abyss" of death.

"Pale Fire" records Shade's lifelong attempt to peer past the bars of mortality. Canto 1 begins with the waxwing and ends with the brief bout of boyhood seizures that he now sees as perhaps a foretaste of death or something beyond. Canto 2 opens with his decision to explore death's abyss and closes, at the midpoint of the poem, with the harrowing account of his daughter Hazel's suicide, just over two years before he pens "Pale Fire." Canto 3 starts with wrong approaches to the hereafter, summed up in Shade's wry reflections on the Institute of Preparation for the Hereafter, I.P.H., and its inept attempts to probe death's "big if." It finishes with his own near-death experience, less than a year before writing "Pale Fire," the vision he had during that state, the futile attempt to corroborate that vision through another's similar experience, and the conclusion that

> > *this*
> Was the real point, the contrapuntal theme;
> Just this: not text, but texture; not the dream
> But topsy-turvical coincidence,
> 810 Not flimsy nonsense, but a web of sense.
> Yes! It sufficed that I in life could find
> Some kind of link-and-bobolink, some kind
> Of correlated pattern in the game,
> Plexed artistry, and something of the same
> Pleasure in it as they who played it found.

> > > > (*PF* 62–63)

Canto 4 begins with "Now," especially the now of composition, and ends as the poem catches up with the poet's present, with his serenity in the waning of the day and his life, and his affirmation that he feels he understands "Existence, or at least a minute part / Of my existence, only through my art, / In terms of combinational delight." He understands the mystery of life and death not through explicit conclusions but through a confidence in the playful and endless pattern he finds in his world and recreates in his work.

Why, apart from the fact that it comes wrapped in a novel, has "Pale Fire" received so little attention as a poem? Why has it even seemed to some intentionally poor poetry?

First, both Shade's stay-at-home life and his art seem too easy and too conventional for a century that often preferred its artists as tormented exiles or bohemians and its high art difficult and so new as to repudiate the art of the past.

Second, Shade's ideas as expressed in the poem may seem at odds with themselves, with the poem they form part of, and with their context. After he chases down Mrs. Z.—who, like Shade, seems to have seen a fountain as she hovered near death—only to find that her reported *fountain* was a misprint for *mountain*, Shade returns deflated, then suddenly realizes that *this* is "the real point, the contrapuntal theme," and concludes that he can understand his existence only through his art, through "combinational delight." Yet he expresses these realizations lucidly as text rather than as texture, and if we *do* seek surprises of texture, we readily find a far more tumultuous and tantalizing texture in *Pale Fire* the novel, in the relationship between calm poem and hysterical commentary, than in "Pale Fire" the poem. If "Pale Fire" surprises, it does so first by its limpidity, not by its density of texture or design.

Third, even if "Pale Fire" can fascinate us by the quality of Shade's imagery and imagination, the poignancy of his daughter's death, and the tirelessness of his quest for something beyond loss and death, can Shade's concluding confidence in design, in "some kind / Of correlated pattern in the game," still remain possible in a century that has had to face the chaos of recent history and to recognize the randomness in our evolutionary past? Has Shade not retreated into the false refuge of his own art? Is the waxwing he projects onto that azure sky only a Dedalian delusion? Does not the rejection of easy order in modern poetry come closer to the truth?

Nabokov knew that "Pale Fire" might look homely against its exotic commentary, flat and cool against the annotations' spiky impetuosity, meekly traditional within *Pale Fire*'s bold poem-and-apparatus experiment. But as he wrote not long after the novel itself, "in art, as in nature, a glaring disadvantage may turn out to be a subtle protective device" (*KQK* viii). If the texture of "Pale Fire" seems less rich than we might expect in view of the density of twentieth-century poetry and of Shade's "not text, but texture" motto, that is only because of Shade's and his master's mastery of the psychology of attention as well as the aesthetics of invention. They offer us immediately explicit sense and overt patterns while concealing for later discovery—further delayed by the distractions of the commentary—covert patterns and more poignant implications.

"Pale Fire" is easy to understand but hard to exhaust: its patterns continue to proliferate. And that not only bears out Shade's "not text, but texture," his search for "correlated pattern," but links his art with so much else in life and mind.

All art and all science make sense of our world through pattern. Minds of all kinds are highly efficient pattern extractors. They have evolved to detect effortlessly and almost instantly patterns especially appropriate to particular modes of life—smells for ants or dogs, ultrasound for bats, magnetic fields or nocturnal skies for migrating birds. But only humans have the curiosity to seek out patterns in the open-ended way that once led our ancestors to see constellations in the skies then to infer first the revolution of the earth from the motion of the stars and planets, then the expansion of the universe, then possibilities before or after or beyond or within our patch of our multiverse. As one distinguished chemist remarks, "Patterns are the lifeblood of science and the seeds of theories."[4]

Because life builds from the simple to the complex by endless recombination, we live in a world teeming with patterns. Art secures our attention by concentrating the multiple intersecting patterns that matter most to us and therefore stimulating our capacity to make the kinds of rich inferences patterns allow. In storytelling, the key patterns of social life are concentrated into character, event, and plot. In poetry, the indispensable pattern is the line, the poet's control of our attention in measured verbal doses. Poets can therefore invite our close scrutiny and amplify attention by offering more intense patterns within the line and from line to line.

Poetry need not focus on figures of speech, but it must always operate with patterns, and indeed patterns of patterns. Even metaphor offers a new link between one more or less familiar pattern and others: between, for instance, flight and freedom from the earth, between birds and the soul, between waxwings' propensity to fly into windows and the tendency of human thought to hurtle against its own limitations. And we understand such images through spreading patterns of neural activation that then offer us new starting blocks for swift-heeled thought.

The pattern folded on pattern that we call metaphor aids our imaginations both inside and outside poetry. But poetry has its own exclusive patterns, tied to the poetic line and the concentrated attention the line allows. In drama, whether in verse or prose, Shakespeare operates with an unequalled density of metaphor, but in his sonnets, to compensate for the patterns of character, event, scene, and plot he no longer has at his disposal, he makes the most of the new patterns the sonnet's line structure permits. His sonnets, the best-loved collection of lyrics in English, maximize the intensity of pattern that distinguishes lyric poetry. And Shade and Nabokov follow no one so closely as Shakespeare, who supplies the title for "Pale Fire" and the ambience for both Shade's New Wye and his commentator's fabled capital.

One of Shakespeare's most famous sonnets sets the pleasures of memory against its pains, the balm of recollection against the astringent recognition that what we have to recall we cannot have at hand:

> When to the sessions of sweet silent thought
> I summon up remembrance of things past,
> I sigh the lack of many a thing I sought,
> And with old woes new wail my dear time's waste:
> Then can I drown an eye, unused to flow,
> For precious friends hid in death's dateless night,
> And weep afresh love's long since cancelled woe,
> And moan the expense of many a vanished sight:
> Then can I grieve at grievances foregone,
> And heavily from woe to woe tell o'er
> The sad account of fore-bemoaned moan,
> Which I new pay as if not paid before.
>   But if the while I think on thee, dear friend,
>   All losses are restored, and sorrows end.

In statement, but not in effect, the poem could be condensed to: "When I think over the past, I grieve anew at all I have lost, but if I think of thee, dear friend, all losses are restored, and sorrows end." What makes this one of Shakespeare's greatest sonnets is that after its elaborations, after its long retrospectives of sorrow, even in the sweet backcast of memory, there comes, but only at the very end, the surprise of its final shift: a speaker who had seemed alone with his losses suddenly has a dear friend to address, who dispels all this reminiscential grief. Is that conclusion a sweet compliment, a fine hyperbole, a heartfelt tribute, or a particular mood, to be complicated by later moods?

Like most Shakespeare sonnets, sonnet 30 signposts the alignment of its structural, logical and syntactical patterns: "When . . . I" opens quatrain 1, "Then can I" quatrains 2 and 3, and "But if . . . I" the couplet. We usually think of verbs as concrete, but this sonnet swarms with verbs—almost all with the speaker as subject—that remain abstract or at least unimagistic, registering not so much action as emotion. The first thirteen lines have eleven finite verbs, all with *I* as subject (summon, sigh, sought, wail, can drown, weep, moan, can grieve, tell, pay, think). But once the speaker, seemingly isolated in retrospective sorrows, thinks of the unexpected "thee, dear friend," *I* drops out as subject and two new subjects in the sonnet's last line reverse the poem's entire direction: "All losses are restored, and sorrows end."

Unlike many other Shakespeare sonnets, sonnet 30 almost ignores the visual and the figurative. Instead, the poet saturates his poem with patterns of sound. And although he does demarcate structure, sense, and syntax, he does not differentiate the subject from quatrain to quatrain: each quatrain shows the speaker sunk in the repetitions of grief, since Shakespeare needs time to accumulate the apparent monotony of grief before suddenly dismissing it. Within and between quatrains, he amasses phonic repetitions: the *ss* and *ws* of quatrain 1; the "silent thought . . . sigh . . . sought" echoed by quatrain 2's "sight"; the "thought . . . thing . . . thing . . . sought" echoed in the couplet's "think"; and the first line's "silent *thought*" answered in the penultimate line's "wh*i*le I *think*." Quatrain 2's "*prec*ious . . . a*fresh*" meshes with the first quatrain's "*ses*sions." In the tour de force of quatrain 3, each line accentuates the repetition of griefs through the repetition of sound, "moan . . . many," "grieve at grievances," "woe to woe," and "fore-bemoaned moan," but the "*fore*- . . . *o'er* . . . *fore*- . . . *before*" pattern finds its requital in the last line's "res*tored*." And after the round of seemingly relentless repetition of word and sound, in the last line, suddenly, every word save "and" is new.

Shakespeare expresses the repetition of remembered woe and the restoration that present friendship allows not only in idea but in the patterns of word, sound, and structure, in ways that would draw unwelcome attention to their design in drama but that perfectly suit the sonnet's capacity to concentrate attention on a line, a quatrain, or a whole poem at once.

Helen Vendler, perhaps the best living critic of poetry in English (and an admirer of Shade's and Nabokov's verse) remarks that since Shakespeare's sonnets "often participate in several patterns simultaneously"—she specifies phonetic, syntactic, relational, and conceptual patterns—"their true 'meaning' is chartable only by charting their pattern-sets." She shows how "Shakespeare's elated variety of invention" "encourages alertness in his reader" and adds that in many of the sonnets he invents "some game or other and play[s] it out to its conclusion in deft and surprising ways . . . rarely amus[ing] himself the same way twice."[5] Everything she says here of Shakespeare applies at least as much to Shade.

Take the first fourteen lines of "Pale Fire": not a sonnet but, perhaps in homage to Shakespeare, forming three quatrains, a break to a new verse paragraph, and a new couplet—itself part of a new quatrain, but we can stop after line fourteen.

> I was the shadow of the waxwing slain
> By the false azure in the windowpane;
> I was the smudge of ashen fluff—and I
> Lived on, flew on, in the reflected sky.
> And from the inside, too, I'd duplicate
> Myself, my lamp, an apple on a plate:
> Uncurtaining the night, I'd let dark glass
> Hang all the furniture above the grass,
> And how delightful when a fall of snow
> 10 Covered my glimpse of lawn and reached up so
> As to make chair and bed exactly stand
> Upon that snow, out in that crystal land!
>
> Retake the falling snow: each drifting flake
> Shapeless and slow, unsteady and opaque.

(*PF* 33)

Each of the first three four-line groups, like each quatrain in many Shakespeare sonnets, supplies a self-contained variant on a common theme, in this case, Shade's exact but imaginative visions of the outside world from inside his house. In a passage in his Cornell lectures, Nabokov asks his students to envision the difference in a patch of countryside as apprehended by a stolid businessman on vacation, eager only to get via the nice new road to the nice new eating place in Newton that an office friend recommends, or a botanist who recognizes every plant, or a farmer who has lived there all his life and knows every trail and shadow (*LL* 252–55). Shade as poet stands as *antithesis* of the traveler, transforming his world in imagination rather than taking it as commonly received, and he *embodies* both the botanist—he is an astute naturalist, with a detailed knowledge of local insects, birds, flowers, and trees—and the farmer—everything he can see around his home comes amplified by the attachments of memory. Imagination, knowledge, and emotion, the three mental axes Nabokov's classroom example implies, enrich every feature of the world Shade's poem records.

In "Pale Fire" Shade can avail himself of the patterns of narrative—character, event, scene, and plot—as well as lyric's concentration on word, image, and line. Here his opening lines work inter alia as self-characterization, disclosing his acute observation and intense appreciation of the world around him, his inclination to transform what he sees, and his tendency to turn that transformation into an expression of his pleasure in this world, his apprehension at the prospect of losing it, his search for something permanent beyond.

There can be few more striking openings in poetry. Unlike "When to the sessions of sweet silent thought" but like other Shakespeare sonnets, Shade's poem focuses on the visual, recording exactly what he saw from his house but slightly shifting his stance each time: elaborate identification and metaphor in the first "quatrain," a playful role as coproducer of natural effects in the second ("I'd duplicate / . . . Uncurtaining the night, I'd let dark glass"), an enthusiastic spectator of nature's performance in the third. Even when he sat at his desk his imaginative response could turn the world outside into an elaborate show.

The rich observation-cum-reverie-cum-metaphor of Shade's opening introduces the thematic pattern that dominates the poem. The waxwing's hurtling itself against the illusion of continued cloudless blue stands for Shade's own attempts to project himself beyond himself and perhaps beyond death, flying on "in the reflected sky." That becomes more apparent near the end of canto 1, when an elegant echo ("I was the shadow of the waxwing slain / By feigned remoteness in the windowpane") introduces the boyhood fits he now sees as almost a foreglimpse of death, or at the start of canto 2 ("I decided to explore and fight / The foul, the inadmissible abyss"), or at the start of canto 3, with its amused resistance to I.P.H.'s nostrums.

Although the opening image continues to accumulate resonance, it remains vivid, immediate, accessible. Yet at the same time Shade also incorporates patterns he knows we will take time to see. Even on a first reading, we will notice the modulated reprise of the opening couplet later in canto 1 and the unfinished couplet at the end of the poem, "Trundling an empty barrow up the lane," which would offer a *rime riche*—Shade's admitted addiction—with the first line of the poem. It takes much longer to see that a pattern of rhymes in *ain* and *ane* or near equivalents (*-ains, -anes; -ained; -anned, -and*) weaves its strategic way through the poem, in ways I will shortly explore (see *NPFMAD* 191–95).

If most first-time readers notice the incomplete couplet at the end of the poem, and its possible completion by the opening line, few will register without help another link between start and finish: the waxwing in the opening and the butterfly the *Vanessa atalanta* (Red Admiral) at the close. Shade the naturalist knows and intends the link, the flash of bright red on the wings of each, explicit in the case of the butterfly ("A dark Vanessa with a crimson band"), left implicit in the waxwing. Readers will also discover only gradually that the various winged creatures—both birds and insects—that fly through the poem do more than reflect Shade as observant naturalist in a wooded suburban setting (or Nabokov as irrepressible lepidopterist) and in fact form part of another deliberate pattern that, like so much in the poem, revolves both around Hazel and around Shade's sense that pattern matters ("It sufficed that I in life could find / Some kind of link-and-bobolink"—a bobolink being another American bird). We will also soon follow some of these bird and insect trails.

Sensitive rereaders can see that Shade has Hazel in mind in the poem's first fourteen lines, even if he does not mention her there. He sees the waxwing smash itself against the "false *azure* of the windowpane." Hazel takes her own life after her first-ever blind date goes horribly wrong; when they arrive at the Hawaiian bar, in itself a kind of "false azure," an idyll that can never happen for her, her would-be partner makes a lame excuse and leaves her standing outside with the other couple, "Before the *azure* entrance for a while," until she takes a bus home, only to exit early from the bus and then from life itself.

The images of inside and outside the house through the first fourteen lines also anticipate the counterpoint Shade establishes on the night of Hazel's death, himself and Sybil inside, anxiously waiting for their daughter's return from this first date, and Hazel outside facing her fatal last humiliation. Outside, we know, Hazel has drowned herself; inside, her parents keep vigil:

> You gently yawned and stacked away your plate.
> We heard the wind. We heard it rush and throw
> 480 Twigs at the windowpane. Phone ringing? No.
> I helped you with the dishes. The tall clock
> Kept on demolishing young root, old rock.

"Midnight," you said. What's midnight to the young?
And suddenly a festive blaze was flung
Across five cedar trunks, snowpatches showed,
And a patrol car on our bumpy road
Came to a crunching stop. Retake, retake!

(PF 50)

Notice the details that recur from the opening passage: the explicit, emphatic link, "Retake, retake!"; the seemingly everyday but actually pointed recurrence of *windowpane* and *plate*; the even more covert link in the cedar trunks lit up by an ironically festive blaze, for the waxwing at the start of the poem can only be a cedar waxwing, *Bombycilla cedrorum* (and not the Bohemian waxwing, *Bombycilla garrulus*).[6]

In Shakespeare's sonnet 30, we tuned into the supple orchestration of sound, singular even by Shakespeare's standards. As part of a longer poem, the opening of "Pale Fire" can connect with multiple patterns in ways impossible within the small scope of a sonnet, but how do these lines compare with Shakespeare's sonnets in their *internal* phonic play? Because visual effects dominate so much, we may overlook the aural, but here, too, Shade voices his passion for pattern:

> I was the shadow of the waxwing slain
> By the false azure in the windowpane;
> I was the smudge of ashen fluff—and I
> Lived on, flew on, in the reflected sky.

Notice the unusual alliteration in *w* (*w*as, *w*axwing, *w*indowpane), reinforced by the terminal *w*s, and the repeated *dow*, in "sha*dow*" and "win*dow*pane," interlaced with the repeated *win* in "wax*win*g" and "*win*dowpane." Notice, too, that in addition to their end rhymes the first two lines, unusually, also have initial rhyme (*I/By*), and that this initial rhyme then becomes the rhyme for the second couplet (*I/sky*), and that the first line in this second couplet also continues the first couplet's initial rhyme, so that line 3 has both initial and end rhyme. If we add to these immediate rhymes the reprise at lines 131–32 ("I was the shadow of the waxwing slain / By feigned remoteness in the windowpane"—and notice here the new internal rhyme on "*feign*ed"), and the *-ain/-ane* rhyme pattern throughout the poem, and the shadow of a rich rhyme between the final line of the poem and the first, the opening couplet forms part of six rhyme patterns in addition to the immediately obvious end rhyme. "Some kind of link-and-bobolink," indeed!

Shade not only claims to understand his world through "combinational delight," to have "A feeling of fantastically planned, / Richly rhymed life," but he also takes issue with those who have rejected rhyme as if its possibilities had been exhausted. In *Four Quartets*—the most admired recent long poem at the time Shade was writing, and his one overt target[7]—T. S. Eliot alternates between mostly unrhymed and occasionally rhymed passages and explicitly articulates what he sees as the problems of modern poetry. Shade implicitly identifies the main problem as a failure to see new possibilities in fertile old forms. Eliot's sometime mentor and editor, Ezra Pound, famously rejected the crimes of rhyme, the evil of the cheville, and the anachronism of poetic inversion to secure a rhyme. I suspect that Shade has a polemic purpose at the end of his first line, in addition to all his other purposes, in placing "slain" after "waxwing," as if he were seeking the poetic elevation English poets have found from Milton's "with wandering steps and slow" to Arnold's "with tremulous cadence slow" and beyond, or as if he were placing the adjective after the noun in a way that modernists no longer tolerated but other poets of note could still use (Kathleen Raine, in "Passion" [1943], shows exactly what modernists had good reason to reject: "Then the sky spoke to me in language clear, / familiar as the heart, than love more near").[8] For a moment, Shade seems to have sinned—only to follow with an adverbial phrase, "By the false azure in the windowpane," that makes any other placement of "slain" unnatural.

Although Shade maintains the Shakespearean intensity of poetic craft of his first fourteen lines through all 999 lines of "Pale Fire," I will now jump to the end of the poem and the effects that he makes converge there.

The core of the concealed patterns that Shade embeds in his poem is an almost syllogistic series of images associating Hazel with phantoms and ghosts. He first refers to Hazel obliquely in terms of "The *phantom* of my little daughter's swing" under the shagbark tree in the garden. He next mentions her in terms of loving his wife most of all "When with a pensive nod you greet her *ghost*." After Hazel's death, his recollection of I.P.H. confirms for him that

> no *phantom* would
> Rise gracefully to welcome you and me
> In the dark garden, near the shagbark tree.

Nevertheless as he brings his poem to a close he admits, "I'm reasonably sure that we survive / And that my darling somewhere is alive." And, as we will see, he does his poetic utmost to call up Hazel's presence at his conclusion.

In part, his change from "no phantom . . . near the shagbark tree" to the sense of Hazel somehow near as his poem closes comes from the recognition that he reaches, more than a year after Hazel's death, in the epiphany after the fountain-mountain fiasco:

> take the hint,
> And stop investigating my abyss?
> But all at once it dawned on me that *this*
> Was the real point, the contrapuntal theme.

(PF 62)

He wishes to "play a game of worlds," and "Pale Fire" itself does so overtly through the counterpoint of parents and child one deadly March night. But throughout the poem he also weaves much stealthier webs of sense.

The "abyss-this" rhyme here has occurred once before, in Shade's report of the night he

> decided to explore and fight
> The foul, the inadmissible abyss,
> 180 Devoting all my twisted life to this
> One task. Today I'm sixty-one. Waxwings
> Are berry-pecking. A cicada sings.

Here Shade shifts back into the present from the resolution he came to so long ago. The details of his here and now are far from mere orientation: the waxwings confirm that the opening image of his poem already reflects his lifelong task, and the cicada will prove equally part of the pattern.

The lines that follow seem to dip near bathos as Shade pares his nails. But this, too, is far from casual since it leads to Maud Shade, to her slide toward death, to Shade's renewed anxieties about death, and to an empty cicada case that he and Sibyl see on the day Maud dies:

> Espied on a pine's bark,
> As we were walking home the day she died,
> An empty emerald case, squat and frog-eyed,
> Hugging the trunk; and its companion piece,

240   A gum-logged ant.

> That Englishman in Nice,
> A proud and happy linguist: *je nourris*
> *Les pauvres cigales*—meaning that he
> Fed the poor sea gulls!
>
> Lafontaine was wrong:
> Dead is the mandible, alive the song.
> And so I pare my nails, and muse, and hear
> Your steps upstairs, and all is right, my dear.
>
> (PF 41–42)

Shade leads us from his past self-dedication to exploring death and his present perception of waxwings and cicada, as he pares his nails, through Maud's death and another cicada—unmentioned in English but explicit in its description, in the French *cigales*, and in the allusion to La Fontaine's "La Cigale et La Fourmi"—back to him still paring his nails. Shade here confirms by texture what he affirms as text. "Dead is the mandible, alive the song," he claims—and as we know, a cicada indeed sings while he pares his nails.

Later, after discovering "fountain" should have been "mountain," Shade comes to the realization that he needs to find "some kind / Of correlated pattern in the game" of life. Here in the ring composition from cicada and nails via Maud's death back to cicada and nails, he has done just this, a fact he reinforces through "Lafontaine was wrong": the fabulist whose French name means "fountain" was wrong, as *fountain* was wrong in the report of Mrs. Z.'s near-death experience. Echoing texture underwrites text.

But Shade's key move within this associative chain is to smuggle in Hazel via the blunder (*cigale*, "cicada," for *sea gull*) made by the English tourist in Nice—where Hazel was conceived when her parents "visited in thirty-three, / Nine months before her birth." Why does Shade covertly implicate his daughter?

"Pale Fire" has a motif of metamorphoses, of which the tourist's inadvertent transformation of cicadas into seagulls is the most comical but not the least serious.[9] The pattern starts with Shade's imaginative transformation of himself into the waxwing in the first verse paragraph. It continues in the second verse paragraph with the poem's next bird, a ring-necked pheasant, a "torquated beauty" (*Phasianus colchicus torquatus*) playfully imagined as a "sublimated grouse." Discussing I.P.H., Shade asserts, "I'm ready to become a floweret, / Or a fat fly, but never, to forget," while I.P.H. itself offers

560   Precautions to be taken in the case
      Of freak reincarnation: what to do
      On suddenly discovering that you
      Are now a young and vulnerable toad
      Plump in the middle of a busy road,
      Or a bear cub beneath a burning pine,
      Or a book mite in a revived divine.

(PF 54)

Shade, in his recognition after the *fountain* fiasco, hopes to imitate those designers of life "Playing a game of worlds, promoting pawns / To ivory unicorns and ebon fauns." And the concentration of composition transforms his everyday world into one of magic metamorphosis: "I rhyme and roam / Throughout the house with, in my fist, a comb / Or a shoehorn, which turns into the spoon / I eat my egg with."

Through Hazel's conception in Nice, Shade incorporates his daughter into this pattern by way of the sea gulls absurdly becoming cicadas and the cicada whose empty case, in simple insect metamorphosis, suggests to him, "alive [is] the song""—an assertion whose structural centrality he quietly underscores by linking the cicada's singing with the waxwings' berry picking, and both with his determination to explore death's abyss: another "link-and-bobolink."

But he forges the central and saddest link in the failure of Hazel's looks to improve with time: "Alas, the dingy cygnet never turned / Into a wood duck." Here Shade puns on the scientific name of the wood duck, *Aix sponsa* (its species name means "bride, betrothed")[10] and plays with the Hans Christian Andersen fairytale of "The Ugly Duckling" through his wry recognition that the wood duck's spectacular colors outdo cygnet or even adult swan. (The Cornell Ornithology Laboratory notes that many consider the wood duck "the most beautiful of all waterfowl.")[11]

Just after the cicada digression, Shade returns to his present, paring his nails, and, hearing "your steps upstairs," he declares "all is right, my dear." At this point he introduces Sybil, as a way of leading into the Hazel theme that dominates the remainder of the canto. He describes Sybil's "loveliness," and invites her to "Come and be worshipped, come and be caressed, / My dark Vanessa, crimson-barred, my blest, / My Admirable butterfly!" Here Shade metaphorically metamorphoses his wife into a *Vanessa atalanta*, a sumptuous butterfly (once known as a Red Admirable but now called a Red Admiral). Affirming his love for her, he segues from the wife he now addresses to the daughter they can only recall:

I love you when you're standing on the lawn
Peering at something in a tree: "It's gone.
It was so small. It might come back" (all this
Voiced in a whisper softer than a kiss).
. . . .
                              And I love you most
290   When with a pensive nod you greet her ghost
And hold her first toy on your palm, or look
At a postcard from her, found in a book.
She might have been you, me, or some quaint blend:
Nature chose me so as to wrench and rend
Your heart and mine.

                                                      (PF 43)

In a poem as controlled as this, and as focused as this on death and beyond,
Shade does not bring Hazel explicitly into the poem with the phrase "her
ghost" by accident.

    As soon as he introduces her in these terms, he notes she does not take
after her mother's good looks and records how her unfortunate appearance
blights her personality and her happiness and ultimately drives her to suicide. But at the end of the poem, Shade does all he can to make a *Vanessa
atalanta* feature at least as an emblem of Hazel's surviving after death in a
happily transformed state.

Canto 4 opens with the word "Now" and closes in on Shade's here and
now, on the poet at work, and, in the final fifty lines, on the end of his last
day composing "Pale Fire," July 21, 1959. Shade draws us with him into his
present, as he treasures the evening scene around him. He responds serenely
to his immediate world with a steady glow of confidence in this world and
its patterns, and his art and *its* patterns, that gives him confidence in something more.

    After Hazel's death Shade had said that I.P.H. had taught him that "no
phantom would / Rise gracefully to welcome you and me / In the dark garden, near the shagbark tree." Nevertheless at the end of his poem, as he
looks at the world unwinding around him, he fuses together, through the
force of his art, the shagbark, the setting sun, the "phantom" recollection

of Hazel's swing, Sybil's "shadow" near the tree, and, explicitly, another but-terfly, the *Vanessa*: implicitly, his and Sybil's tenderly stored image of Hazel. What seems an ordinary evening turns out to be part of an intricate texture Shade has woven to celebrate all he shares with his wife and to commemo-rate what they have lost in their daughter. Here in his last evening so far with Sybil, more delicately and deceptively than in the starker scoring of the counterpoint of Hazel's last night, he plays his "game of worlds," answering the turmoil of that night with his own design and his own sense of confi-dence in ultimate design, even amid the accidents of the passing day.

We can see a larger Nabokovian context for the way Shade finds sense in the patterns his art can reveal in his life. In his autobiography Nabokov had posed himself the artistic challenge of affirming his confidence in life's ultimately generous design by taking as test case his own life, despite its routines and upsets, its incursions of anguish, and his lifelong frustration at the confines of human consciousness. *Speak, Memory* weaves intricate "the-matic trails or currents"[12] into his account of his life, and its horrors—his exile from his homeland, his father's assassination, his forced flight with his family from the sanctuary Western Europe had provided—and his own metaphysical quest. He admits planning his book "according to the way his life had been planned by unknown players of games,"[13] exactly as Shade feels it sufficed that in life he could find "some kind / Of correlated pattern in the game, / . . . and something of the same / Pleasure in it as they who played it found." Nabokov has poet and biographer Fyodor Godunov-Cherdyntsev, the Russian-speaking character in his work closest to himself, also pose and meet similar challenges, in very different ways, in *The Gift*. And he has poet and scholar John Shade, the English-speaking character closest to himself, pose himself a similar, perhaps even more formidable challenge: to affirm his confidence in life's design first by seeing his own life in terms of its whole pattern and rhythm, which he does especially in terms of *his* lifelong meta-physical quest; then by facing squarely his life's worst turn, his daughter's suicide, which he makes the heartrending centerpiece of his poem; and then by turning to the here and now, the unplanned circumstances of composing and closing his magnum opus.

Shade starts "Pale Fire" with abrupt action, the waxwing's fatal crash against the reflected azure sky. He ends the poem in calm, the end of a day and a season of composing. As he opens his last day's composition, he turns to his wife, with the kind of anaphoric patterns he has used again and again ("I was the shadow . . . I was the smudge . . . —and I . . ." at the start of canto 1; "There was a time . . . There was the day . . . And finally there was the sleep-less night" at the start of canto 2; "Now I shall spy . . . Now I shall cry out . . .

Now I shall try . . . Now I shall do . . ." at the start of canto 4). "And all the time, and all the time, my love" especially echoes the powerful anaphora in canto 2: "I love you when you're . . . I love you when you . . . And I love you most / When . . . you greet her ghost."

In the verse paragraph that starts his last day of composition ("And all the time, and all the time, my love, / You too are there, beneath the word, above / The syllable"), Shade plays with pattern in multiple ways. The previous day's composition had ended with "And that odd muse of mine, / My versipel, is with me everywhere, / In carrel and in car, and in my chair." *Versipel* both puns on *verse* and means "a creature capable of changing from one form to another" (see Nabokov's favorite dictionary, *Webster's Second New International*)—another metamorphic image, the imagination, perhaps, which allows him to become "the shadow of the waxwing," or "the smudge of ashen fluff," or to live on in the reflected sky. Shade prolongs this note into his last day's composition, as he turns to Sybil, and her contribution to his art, punning on her name in "above / The syllable," and resonating with *versipel*, which now seems to have an undertone of "*Sybil*" and "*syllable*."

At the end of canto 3, Shade had eloquently elaborated the conclusions he had reached in his recognition that "*this* / Was the real point, the contrapuntal theme." When he returns home from his quest for the fountain, eager to announce his new conviction, he finds the distracting rhythms of the real will not allow him to share his new confidence even with the woman who shares his life and his art:

> Making ornaments
> Of accidents and possibilities.
> 830 Stormcoated, I strode in: Sybil, it is
> My firm conviction—"Darling, shut the door.
> Had a nice trip?" Splendid—but what is more
> I have returned convinced that I can grope
> My way to some—to some—"Yes, dear?" Faint hope.
>
> (PF 63)

There ends canto 3, in apparent deflation, despite the brilliant quadruple rhyme—rare enough in itself, even rarer in such a serious context, rarer still in matching polysyllabic possibilities against monosyllables and high reflection against casual speech. But on his last day of composition Shade picks up on the "ornaments / Of accidents and possibilities" and "Sybil, it is" in the *syllable* play on *versipel* and *Sybil*, and the stress on his wife's inclusion in and inspiration for his art.

The verse paragraph devoted to Sybil plays not only on her name but also on the "you" by which Shade naturally calls her: "*You too*," "under*score* . . . *yore* . . . *your*," "And all in *you* is *you*th, and *you* make *new* / . . . old things I made for *you*." But Shade also puns on the tree, the *yew*, with which he has pointedly opened canto 3, at the midpoint of his poem, "*L'if*, lifeless tree"—a phrase itself punning on the French name for the tree, on "life" and this tree of death, on "lifeless" and "leafless" (the yew and cypress adorn cemeteries precisely because they do not become leafless), and on the outfit Shade dubs "I.P.H., a lay / Institute (I) of Preparation (P) / For the Hereafter (H), or If, as we / Called it—big if!" at a location he names as "Yewshade, in another, higher state." The *yew* enters the poem the moment after Hazel—herself named for a tree—steps to her death. And in playing so insistently on "you" near the end of the poem, Shade prepares for his final glimpse of Sybil, near another tree, the shagbark hickory that he and Sybil cannot help associating with Hazel and the "phantom" of her swing.

Shade brings us right into the present, into the end of this summer's day, in the antepenultimate paragraph:

> Gently the day has passed in a sustained
> Low hum of harmony. The brain is drained
> And a brown ament, and the noun I meant
> To use but did not, dry on the cement.
>
> *(PF 68)*

He begins here with "Gently," a word he first uses in the poem as he describes the white butterflies that "turn lavender as they / Pass through its [the shagbark's] shade where gently seems to sway / The phantom of my little daughter's swing." He has used the word once more, at the start of the verse paragraph that records the arrival of the patrol cars bringing news of Hazel's death: "You gently yawned and stacked away your plate. / We heard the wind. We heard it rush and throw / Twigs at the windowpane. Phone ringing? No."

He has written well all day, "in a sustained / Low hum of harmony." Harmony indeed, as he describes his present state and surroundings: not only the *ms* (and *hs*) in "hu*m* of har*m*ony," but the nasals throughout these lines (ge*n*tly, sustai*n*ed, hu*m*, har*m*o*n*y, brai*n*, drai*n*ed, a*m*e*n*t, *n*ou*n*, *m*ea*n*t, *n*ot, o*n*, ce*m*e*n*t); the *-ain* sound in sust*ain*ed, br*ain*, dr*ain*ed; the *-rain* sounds in b*rain* and d*rain*ed; the *brain-brown* consonance; the internal rhyme on *ament* harmonizing with the end rhymes in *meant* and *cement*; the complex "*brown ament-noun* I *meant*" echo, and the *drained-dry* match of sound and sense. And the noun Shade meant to use but did not, to maximize the possibilities of pattern his circumstances allow, is *catkin*, the much commoner homonym of *ament*. The only tree in the Shades' garden that has catkins or aments is the shagbark hickory so strongly associated with Hazel—although a tree more famous for its catkins is the hazel itself.

Shade explicitly thematizes the *meant/cement* rhyme in the remainder of this verse paragraph:

> Maybe my sensual love for the *consonne*
> *D'appui*, Echo's fey child, is based upòn
> A feeling of fantastically planned,
> 970　Richly rhymed life.

(PF 68)

The *consonne d'appui* (support consonant) is the consonant preceding the rhyming vowel, in this case the *m*s of the *m*eant-ce*m*ent rhymes. English versification tends to regard this as a blemish, a marring of the purity of the rhyme; French versification, by contrast, tends to see this as an enrichment, an extra grace. Indeed, Shade puns here on the French term "*rime riche.*"

In the next verse paragraph, the penultimate, he then expands on his "feeling of fantastically planned, / Richly rhymed life": "I feel I understand / Existence . . . / . . . only through my art." He states this as text, but he also shows it as texture, as correlated pattern. For the previous verse paragraph starts with the first of an unprecedentedly intense series of rhyme sounds harking back to the *-ain/-ane* rhyme that opens the poem and becomes a structural motif throughout: first, sust*ained*/dr*ained* at the start of the antepenultimate verse paragraph; then, slightly modulating sust*ained*/dr*ained* and marking the transition between the end of this paragraph and the start of the penultimate, pl*anned*/underst*and*; next, starting the final verse paragraph, and still more explicitly echoing the poem's first sl*ain*/windowp*ane* rhyme, att*ains*/windowp*anes*; one additional rhyme exactly echoing the pl*anned*/underst*and* rhyme, b*and*/s*and*, a rhyme I will return to; and finally the last line of the poem, ending in "lane," and missing a rhyme partner, though it would have not only a rhyme but even Shade's favorite *rime riche* if we were to return to the poem's first line and its rhyme word, sl*ain*. And in the paragraph that elaborates on "Richly rhymed life" by declaring "I feel I understand / Existence . . . / . . . only through my art, / In terms of combinational delight," Shade has ten consecutive rhymes that are not *rime riche* but begin with the same vowel, the diphthong *i*: del*ight*/r*ight*, div*ine*/l*ine*, surv*ive*/al*ive*, *I*/J*uly*, fifty-n*ine*/f*ine*. Supporting these end rhymes Shade incorporates a persistent pattern of assonance on the same sound, m*i*nute, my, my, my private, *I*, *i*ambic, *I*'m, my, *I*, *ni*neteen, myself, emphasizing, as it were, his own responsibility, or as if echoing an earlier burst of *i*-sounds: "It sufficed that *I* in life could find / Some kind of link-and bobolink, some kind / Of correlated pattern in the game."

The last paragraph comes closest of all to the present moment and, despite its seeming casualness, to the kind of pattern that makes Shade "reasonably sure" that his darling Hazel "somewhere is alive." Thinking first of Sybil, he asks "Where are you?" and answers himself:

> In the garden. I can see
> 990 Part of your shadow near the shagbark tree . . .
> . . . .
> A dark Vanessa with a crimson band
> Wheels in the low sun, settles on the sand
> And shows its ink-blue wingtips flecked with white.
>
> (*PF* 69)

Although Shade responds to chance circumstances around him, he also knows the pattern of his recent summer evenings and has presumably witnessed the recurrence of this *Vanessa atalanta*, a member of a sportive butterfly species, individuals of which fly most vigorously at dusk and may repeatedly frequent the same spot and engage with the same people at the same time day after day.[14] Shade, in other words, being a close observer of nature, could have expected he might end the poem this way, even as he looks out at his unplanned present: life, watched acutely, cooperates in the pattern of his art. And he knows that he can echo the unstated but implied pattern of bright red on the wing of the waxwing that starts his poem through the "dark Vanessa with the crimson *band*" settling here on the *sand*—the last of the pattern of rhymes in *ain-ane* and their congeners. For Shade, the Vanessa wheeling in the low sun also recalls the "nymph" who "came pirouetting" in the beauty-product advertisement on television the night Hazel dies, for lepidopterologically a *nymph* is any species of the subfamily *Nymphalinae*, especially of the genus *Vanessa*. The "nymph" in the beauty ad seems a sadly ironic counterpart to Hazel: Shade recoils from the television after seeing it, just at the time Hazel's blind date recoils from her, but the Vanessa in the poem's last paragraph seems almost Shade's evocation of or tribute to his daughter.

Sybil "In the garden" at this sunset hour and "near the shagbark tree" and the dark Vanessa evoke and conclude a series of patterns running through the poem and directed at memories of Hazel and at hopes of meeting her again: the shagbark Shade describes at sunset and the white butterflies that "turn lavender as they / Pass through its shade where gently seems to sway / The *phantom* of my little daughter's swing"; Shade's direct address to Sybil, in canto 2, "Come and be worshiped, come and be caressed, / My dark Vanessa, crimson-barred, my blest / My Admirable butterfly," and his "I love you when you're standing on the lawn / Peering at something in a tree," an insect or small bird, and his "I love you most / When with a pensive nod you greet her *ghost*"; the echo of *peer, tree,* and *ghost* here in Shade's last description of Hazel's action before she steps off the bank into the lake: "*she peered / At ghostly trees*"; and the conclusion Shade draws from the folly of his experience at I.P.H.:

> I learnt what to ignore in my survey
> Of death's abyss. And when we lost our child
> I knew there would be nothing:
> . . . .
> 650   no phantom would
> Rise gracefully to welcome you and me
> In the dark garden, near the shagbark tree.
>
> (*PF* 57)

In the final mention of the shagbark and the Vanessa, Shade resolves a pattern that, after his declaring his new confidence in pattern and in his darling Hazel's being "somewhere . . . alive," seems almost to rebut this "no phantom." Hazel, appropriately enough given her name, has been at the center of a pattern of trees, including the *shagbark*, the *cedars* that the patrol-car headlights illuminate just before her parents hear of her death (which, via the cedar waxwing, link to the poem's beginning), the *yew* at the start of the second half of the poem, and the *pine* with the cicada case that prompted Shade to declare: "Lafontaine was wrong: / Dead is the mandible, alive the song."

Shade seems to have made the Vanessa passing by Sybil's shadow near the shagbark tree just before his poem's end as close as he can get, in the texture and plexed artistry of his poem, to evoking Hazel herself as present with him and Sybil: the Vanessa, whose crimson stripe echoes the waxwing that killed itself in the poem's opening but that also, through Shade's imagination, "lived on, flew on, in the reflected sky"; the pattern of birds and insects, including Hazel associated with the shy butterfly, the Toothwort White,[15] or the "dingy cygnet" who never turned into a wood duck;[16] the pattern of trees, phantoms or ghosts associated with trees, and a cicada that has flown free of its case stuck to a pine's bark; the rhyme patterns, like the "band" and "sand" describing the final appearance of the Vanessa, that link the poem's opening and close and Shade's affirmation of his confidence in the implications of his patterned life and art. Shade has said he would like to try out the role of those "Playing a game of worlds, promoting pawns / To ivory unicorns and ebon fauns." He seems to have promoted Hazel from dingy cygnet to wood duck, from drab Toothwort White to splendid Sibylesque Red Admiral, from dull hazel grouse to the "torquated beauty" of the ring-necked pheasant.

Of course, Shade knows that his confidence and his command of pattern prove nothing. He knows that he will not know for sure until death writes the last line of his life. He pointedly evokes his own childhood foretastes of death—his fits at the age of eleven, the first as he lay on the floor watching "a clockwork toy— / A tin wheelbarrow pushed by a tin boy"—in the chance circumstances of the poem's close, as he winds his alarm clock, then, immediately after the Vanessa, notices

> through the flowing shade and ebbing light
> A man, unheedful of the butterfly—
> Some neighbor's gardener, I guess—goes by
> Trundling an empty barrow up the lane.

But by leaving his own last couplet incomplete here, Shade both affirms that there can be no closure, no end *within* life, and that nevertheless the poem of his life may somehow return, in a way consonant with the rhyme pattern, to the start. No one has seen such still untapped possibilities in the closed couplet, yet no one has waged the twentieth-century war against poetic closure so pointedly as Shade, when he insists that the pattern of his life and his poem cannot be completed until the unknown last line of death.

25. *Ada:* The Bog and the Garden
Or, Straw, Fluff, and Peat: Sources and Places in *Ada*

In November 2009, on the eve of publication of *The Original of Laura*, I spoke with Martin Amis at a Nabokov celebration at the Poetry Center in New York. Beforehand, I asked Martin about his review of *The Original of Laura*, which I had read just that day, where he confessed that despite his deep love of Nabokov he had tried to read *Ada* half a dozen times, unsuccessfully, before at last forcing himself through it earlier that year. He made it clear to me that he thought Nabokov not in control in *Ada* either ethically or aesthetically. I have written hundreds of pages on the precision of Nabokov's allusions and patterns in *Ada*, and the penetration of their ethical, psychological, and epistemological implications. This essay offers just one of many possible angles on *Ada*. I would be pleased if it converted anybody to an appreciation of a novel even some Nabokov admirers dislike but others recognize as his richest.

Nabokov confessed that "*Ada* caused me more trouble than all my other novels" (*SO* 138). At the time he was *most* troubled, in the second third of the 1960s, when plans for works tentatively entitled *Letters from* (or *to*) *Terra* and *The Texture of Time* seemed bogged down, he explained to an interviewer the process of preparing for a new novel: "At a very early stage of the novel's development I get this urge to garner bits of straw and fluff, and eat pebbles" (*SO* 31). This is already a kind of inspiration, he notes, but in his essay "Inspiration" he describes the forefeeling of a novel's approach, then a sudden flash, "a shimmer of exact details . . . a tumble of merging words" that the "experienced writer immediately takes . . . down" (*SO* 309). He cites the first surge of *Ada*, at the end of 1965:

Sea crashing, retreating with shuffle of pebbles, Juan and beloved young whore—is her name, as they say, Adora? is she Italian, Roumanian,

Irish?—asleep on his lap, his opera cloak pulled over her . . . in a corner
of a decrepit, once palatial whorehouse, Villa Venus.

(SO 310)

Nabokov comments on the contrast between the coloration of this passage and the finished *Ada* but draws attention to the "pleasing neatness"
of the fact that it "now exists as an inset scene right in the middle of the
novel (which was entitled at first *Villa Venus*, then *The Veens*, then *Ardor*, and
finally *Ada*)" (*SO* 310). He had settled on the name *Ada* by February 1966,
and over the next few months was astonished at the speed of the novel's
compositional flow.

Ada has many obvious sources: personal, like Nabokov's memories of
Russia, Vyra, and first love, and impersonal, like Chateaubriand, Tolstoy,
Proust, and the history of the novel. I want to focus on three unlikely pieces
of fluff and straw, whose appeal lay partly in their unlikeliness and whose
dates belong to the years immediately before Nabokov began writing *Ada*.

VEEN, BOG, VENUS

As Paul H. Fry first noted in 1985 and Wilma Siccama and Jack van der
Weide discussed again in 1995,[1] Nabokov discovered the Dutch meaning of
"*veen*" and rediscovered the Dutch surnames Veen and Van Veen in a detective novel published in 1964 by Nicolas Freeling, *Double-Barrel*.[2] Freeling,
who died in 2003, was "credited with elevating the crime genre by creating
probing examinations of complex personalities,"[3] but Nabokov had little
interest in crime fiction except for the purposes of parody, in *Despair*, *The
Real Life of Sebastian Knight*, and *Lolita*. Freeling's novel presumably came
to Nabokov's attention because at one point the detective and narrator,
Van der Valk, sifting through criminal records in a dreary little town in
Drente, the province in the north of the Netherlands to which he has
been sent from Amsterdam, notes: "The State Recherche—very very thorough indeed—had even unearthed the fact that the burgomaster, earlier in his career, had once been thought rather too fond of sitting little
girls on his lap. Charming; Burgomaster Humbert N. Petit of Larousse,
Ill." (*DB* 25).

The nod to *Lolita* and even to Quilty's alias in the cryptogrammic paper
chase (*Lolita* 250) follows a few pages after this:

The keyword in this north-eastern corner of Holland is 'Veen.' It
occurs as a suffix in place-names. Over to the west are Hoogeveen and

Heerenveen—larger towns these, around the twenty thousand mark. To the south, Klazinaveen, Vriezeveen—smaller, hardly more than villages. . . . 'Veen' means turf: the boggy peaty moorland that was cut for fuel in the depression days, before the oil pipelines and the natural gas.

(DB 17)

On first being assigned to Drente, Van der Valk remarks: "All I know about Drente is that it is up in the north-east corner of Holland. . . . A poor province; the ground is not much good for agriculture. Wet, peaty sort of moorland. What in Ireland is called 'the bog'" (DB 12). Two pages after commenting on "*veen*" in Drente place-names, Freeling returns again to the "boggy peaty moorland" theme: "The local people, and with them a swelling tide of strangers from congested metropolitan Holland, took with enthusiasm to easy work in sunny, canteen-and-canned-music factories. Pleasant change from trying to dig a living out of wet, black, stinking ground" (DB 19). Freeling seems less interested in the mystery story than in a sociological evocation of stifling provincialism and provincial resentment at the new influx from the cities: "None of this told me much about the people who lived there. Were they too just like the ones in metroland? Had a thousand years in the 'Veen' ground produced a local type? There were local names—I saw several 'Van Veen' and 'Van der Veen' nameplates on doors" (DB 20). As if in reply to Freeling, *Ada* stresses the Veens, inhabitants at Ardis of the Ladore region of "lovely rich marshes" (*Ada* 108) and "Ladoga bogs" (288), not as a "local type" but as a unique "happy famil[y] more or less dissimilar" (3) to any other on earth or Antiterra.[4]

Never one not to do his homework, Nabokov appears to have followed up Freeling's hint by consulting a map of the Netherlands. Freeling sets his novel in the province of Drenthe (as my atlas spells it), and there the concentration of *veen* towns common throughout the country—from Anerveen through Veendal, Veendijk, and Veenwouden to Witteveen—reaches its highest. Although Freeling's stress is on the province as a whole, he locates the action in the real town of Zwinderen and specifically mentions as an example of the *veen* towns the nearby Klazinaveen (Klazienaveen according to my atlas: the Dutch continually reform their spelling). Between the two, five kilometers from Klazienaveen by road, lies another village called Erica. When Nabokov saw, as he surely did, the town of Erica in Drenthe nestled among other places named *veen*, he must have thought of Venus Erycina, the temple to Venus as the goddess of prostitutes in the Sicilian town of Eryx, now Erice, and from that have developed Eric Veen, the boy "of Flemish extraction" (*Ada* 347) who dreams up a chain of palatial whorehouses, the Villa Venuses.

Eric Veen's grandfather, David van Veen, an architect, proceeds to realize his late grandson's "Organized Dream" (348) by designing and building "parodies of paradise" that include "imitating . . . the great-necessity houses of Dudok in Friesland," the province to the west of Drenthe. David van Veen's nephew and heir, "Velvet Veen," "an honest but astoundingly stuffy clothier" (350)[5] who takes over the final realization of the project, hails from a town in Drenthe located in the middle of a triangle formed by Wapserveen, Hoogeveen, and Kolderveen and bearing the suggestive name of Ruinen.[6]

The idea of decay here in "Ruinen" (plural of German *Ruine*, "ruin") becomes hauntingly dominant in the Villa Venus chapter, where Van even plays pointedly on the name's spelling "ruin,"[7] and echoes the theme in Latin, in Seneca's *subsidunt montes et juga celsa ruunt*.[8]

Already by the time Nabokov wrote down the first rush of the novel— "Juan and beloved young whore . . . in a corner of a decrepit, once palatial whorehouse, Villa Venus"—he seems to have picked up a number of hints from Freeling's *Double-Barrel* and a map of its locale: *Veen* as a surname, to echo Venus (and probably already *Van Veen*, to suggest a Don Juan or Don Giovanni), Erica among Drenthe's *-veens* as a reminder of Venus Erycina, Ruinen as an index of decay. He seems already focused, in other words, on images and myths of sexual love that he aims also to question or complicate, in the Villa Venus case, perhaps by a sense of excess, exhaustion, destruction, and decay.

If the "Veen" Nabokov found in Freeling suggested characters who evoke Venus, did the Dutch sense of *veen* as "peat, bog, marsh" that Nabokov found there also form part of his emerging sense of the story? The evidence suggests it does, and that indeed Nabokov saw as a central metaphor of the novel a garden of love that in places sinks into a bog.

Nabokov was well aware of the Western medieval tradition of the garden of love, especially from the *Roman de la Rose*, which he had studied at Cambridge, and as his play on the name of "Ardis Park" suggests, he also knew of the derivation of the word "paradise" from Greek *paradeisos*, "park," "paradise," itself derived from Persian. The most famous artistic play on the ambiguity of a garden of love that seems from one side paradisal, from another hellish, and centrally almost irresolvably ambiguous, is of course Hieronymus Bosch's *The Garden of Earthly Delights*. As many have felt, from even before Bobbie Ann Mason's *Nabokov's Garden: A Guide to Ada* (especially her appendix 1), Bosch's great triptych serves as a kind of parallel parody of paradise throughout *Ada*; it is explicitly introduced into the novel just at the point where a stern father figure is about to expel Ada and Van from their recreated paradise in Manhattan; and it is mentioned in a way that stresses

Bosch's Dutch origins—his unfamiliar birth name, Jeroen Anthoniszoon van Äken (438), which reflects the family's origins in Aachen—and plays on the Dutch meaning of the place-name that provided Bosch with his new name as an artist, that of his hometown, 's-Hertogenbosch (familiarly, Den Bosch), which in its full form means "the woods of the duke," or as Demon phrases it, "ducal bosquet":[9]

"If I could write," mused Demon, "I would describe, in too many words no doubt, how passionately, how incandescently, how incestuously—*c'est le mot*—art and science meet in an insect, in a thrush, in a thistle of that ducal bosquet. Ada is marrying an outdoor man, but her mind is a closed museum, and she, and dear Lucette, once drew my attention, by a creepy coincidence, to certain details of that other triptych, that tremendous garden of tongue-in-cheek delights, circa 1500, and, namely, to the butterflies in it—a Meadow Brown, female, in the center of the right panel, and a Tortoiseshell in the middle panel, placed there as if settled on a flower—mark the 'as if,' for here we have an example of exact knowledge on the part of those two admirable little girls, because they say that actually the *wrong* side of the bug is shown, it should have been the underside, if seen, as it is, in profile, but Bosch evidently found a wing or two in the corner cobweb of his casement and showed the prettier upper surface in depicting his incorrectly folded insect."

(436–37)

Nabokov had himself identified Bosch's Meadow Brown in a letter to *Life* magazine in 1949 (*SL* 93–94) and at the beginning of 1964 had replied to an approach from a publisher, asking would he have an idea for a lavishly illustrated book, that he would indeed like to compile a book on butterflies in art (*VNAY* 481–82). He may not have known Bosch's birth name until seeing it on the first page of Mario Bussagli's *Bosch* (1966),[10] from which he quotes at the end of this chapter of *Ada*, and he may not have thought about the Dutch sense of 's-Hertogenbosch until Nicolas Freeling had introduced him to the sense of *veen* in Dutch place-names, but he had of course known Bosch's painting a long time, and the way the two naked figures of Adam and Eve in the Edenic left panel multiply into crowds of naked revelers courting and cavorting in the formal garden of the central panel, only to reach a hell on earth in the right panel.

Nabokov remarks that his first foreglimpse of *Ada* "differs in coloration and lighting" (*SO* 310) from much of the finished novel, where Van invites us to join his long celebration of his love for Ada. As I observe elsewhere, years later, "Van still rejoices in the happiness of his and Ada's special destiny at Ardis: they had seemed charmed there, privileged to reenact not only myths of Edenic or Arcadian innocence but also—and only increasing the paradisal joy—myths of sexual experience, of Venus, Cupid, or Eros" (*NAPC* 153). It is as if, in evoking Ardis, Van pretends to paint only two panels of Bosch's triptych, the left-hand panel, pure paradise, and the central panel as an exuberant comic expansion of the first, although in fact, as we discover, he knows better: he knows and remembers the hellish implied *in* Ardis (the central panel as ominous) and following on *from* Ardis (the hell realized in the right panel). As the dark hues and shades of his initial vision of the novel indicate, Nabokov himself saw from the first the hell that complicates the heaven of love, the bog encircling the garden.

But just how does Bosch's ironic image of the Garden of Earthly Delights relate to the decrepit Villa Venus in Nabokov's first flash of *Ada*, and how does *Ada*'s garden of love subside into a bog?

Again, Freeling's novel may have lightly suggested the main ways *Ada* complicates and questions myths of love. As Siccama and van der Weide note, Freeling's Van der Valk observes that in Drente "the locals had ludicrous names. Ook and Goop and Unk. Surnames as bad, and clans of course—generations of intermarriage no doubt" (*DB* 20–21). Despite the veneer of Dutch Reformed Church respectability and restraint, Van der Valk finds in the police files "a lot of immorality—a bit too much. I had the file on the past year's police court cases behind-locked-doors. Incest, mm; never quite unknown in these ingrown inter-married districts" (*DB* 23). These brief early allusions (there are no more) to incest and intermarriage in a region of *veens* appear to have triggered Nabokov's imagination to parody myths of Venus and Eros through an incestuous family of Veens, whom he situates at Ardis (from Greek "point of an arrow" [*Ada* 225], and reminiscent of the arrows fired by Venus's son, Cupid) in the marshy Ladore region.[11] But it is not incest per se that complicates Van and Ada Veen's revisions of Venus.

Freeling's detective finds "a lot of immorality—a bit too much" in the police files of Drente because the neighbors eavesdrop and spy on one another inordinately. Van der Valk's French wife fulminates against the local "house-wives' snooping—incredible. If I lived here I'd turn into a window-peeper too" (*DB* 83). Van der Valk has been sent to Drente to discover a blackmailer, and in the course of his enquiries he interviews the director of a small electronics enterprise: "Your firm produces sensitive listening gadgets for various purposes. There's a lot of mention in the police reports of one that might have been useful in a blackmailer's hands" (*DB* 57). Van der Valk sets his wife to spying on the neighborhood, to testing the local networks of gossip, and later discovers that she herself in an amorous mood has been spied on by the blackmailer, whom he in turn spies on in a compromising situation—only to be caught himself in this act of tom-peeping.

The theme of multiple eavesdropping and spying (and as a minor variation, blackmail) also pervades *Ada*. In part it is a parody of eavesdropping as an immemorial device of narrative in general and of the novel in particular, an aspect of *Ada*'s general parody of the history of the novel.[12] But the spying on Van and Ada at their ardors in arbors at Ardis in a region of "lovely rich marshes" seems likely to have been triggered in part by Freeling's *Double-Barrel* and its eavesdropping, tom-peeping, and blackmail.[13]

Nabokov turns it, though, to a very different use. He establishes Van and Ada Veen as "children of Venus" (410), but their idyll at Ardis, which Van would like to present as "dream-bright . . . pure joyousness and Arcadian innocence" (588), is complicated by two persistent eavesdroppers or spies: Blanche and Lucette (as well as the blackmailer Kim Beauharnais). At first, the complications seem merely comic; both Blanche and Lucette introduce one or more tragic or hellish notes; and each time, Nabokov signals that the garden of love, the paradise of love, can also be a moral quagmire.

Blanche and Lucette are paired as spies on Van and Ada almost as soon as these young "cousins" have something to hide, as their feelings for each other catch fire even before their "first free and frantic caresses" (97). Both Van and Ada keep diaries, and at one point just after the Shattal Tree incident, both rush back separately

> to the house to hide their diaries which both thought they had left lying open in their respective rooms. Ada, who feared the curiosity of Lucette and Blanche (the governess presented no threat, being pathologically unobservant), found out she was wrong—she had put away the album with its latest entry. Van, who knew that Ada was a little "snoopy," discovered Blanche in his room feigning to make the made bed, with the unlocked diary lying on the stool beside it. He slapped her lightly on the behind and removed the shagreen-bound book to a safer place.
>
> (96)

The "*shagreen*-bound book" puns on *chagrin* (Van imagines that Blanche goes off somewhere to weep in her bower) and on *green with envy*, a color associated insistently with Lucette both because she wears green to tone with her red coloring, and because she herself is often green with envy as she watches Van and Ada (who, for instance, "frantically made love, while the child knocked and called and kicked until the key fell out and the keyhole turned an angry green" [213]). And just as Blanche here feigns to be making the bed she has already made, although she has in fact learned from the diary all she needs to know of Van's feelings for Ada and his first intimate contact with her, so Lucette, after being tied up by Van and Ada when they rush off to make love for the first time in her proximity, unties herself, spies on them, rushes back, and has almost retied herself when they return, although to them "writhing Lucette had somehow torn off one of the red knobbed grips of the rope and seemed to have almost disentangled herself when dragon and knight, prancing, returned" (143).

BLANCHE

Awed by what she has read of Van's feelings for Ada in the diary, and soon an eager witness of their activities, Blanche circulates exalted reports of their love. Ada in 1892 declares she had never realized

> that their first summer in the orchards and orchidariums of Ardis had become a sacred secret and creed, throughout the countryside. Romantically inclined handmaids, whose reading consisted of *Gwen de Vere* and *Klara Mertvago*, adored Van, adored Ada, adored Ardis's ardors in arbors. Their swains, plucking ballads on their seven-stringed Russian lyres under the racemosa in bloom or in old rose gardens (while the windows went out one by one in the castle), added freshly composed lines—naïve, lackey-daisical, but heartfelt—to cyclic folk songs. Eccentric police officers grew enamored with the glamour of incest. Gardeners paraphrased iridescent Persian poems about irrigation and the Four Arrows of Love. Nightwatchmen fought insomnia and the fire of the clap with the weapons of *Vaniada's Adventures*. . . . Virgin châtelaines in marble-floored manors fondled their lone flames fanned by Van's romance.
>
> (409)

It is no accident that the series of those affected by the "sacred secret and creed" begins with "romantically inclined handmaids," for handmaid Blanche is reading *Les Amours du Docteur Mertvago* when Van first arrives at Ardis; or that the list continues with "swains" and "nightwatchmen," for Blanche observes Van and Ada on her way to her own trysts with swains who include the nightwatchman, Sore, to whom she passes on her own clap, as she also passes on romantic secrets to others, to her sister, the handmaid Madelon (another romantically inclined handmaid who passes the "secret" of Van and Ada on to Percy de Prey), and to Van himself (the secret of Ada's love affairs with Rack and de Prey); or that the series ends with "virgin châtelaines," in mocking echo of Blanche's presenting herself to Van on his last night at Ardis as a kind of châtelaine ("C'est ma dernière nuit au château . . . 'Tis my last night with thee" [292]), only for her non-virginity to be stressed once again ("quite aside from the fear of infection (Bout had hinted at some of the poor girl's troubles)" [293]).

Blanche is central to the myths of Van and Ada's love at Ardis that saturate the Ladore countryside and *Ada* itself. But she also qualifies the myths she propagates. Sexually active with multiple partners on the Ardis staff—the butler, Bouteillan; his bastard son, the footman Bout; the nightwatchman, Sore; and the coachman, Fartukov—she represents the idea of sexual multiplicity so dominant in the central panel of Bosch's triptych and in the gardens of Ardis.

There are several ways in which Blanche's multiple sexual experiences comment on Van and Ada's. First, she sees *their* lovemaking on the way to her own trysts, and by gossiping about their ardor, she helps build the "sacred secret and creed" that exalts Ardis into a romantic and sexual paradise. Second, in 1888 she witnesses or learns from other servants and witnesses of Ada's affairs with Philip Rack and Percy de Prey, and she passes the news on to Van, which in effect expels him forever from an Ardis that he suddenly sees as hellish. Third, her protestations of sexual innocence are ironically undercut by her experience, indeed by her venereal disease, just as Trofim Fartukov's protestations that he would not touch her even through a leathern apron are undercut by his marrying her, and as Ardis's myths of Venus are cruelly undercut by the consequences Blanche's venereal disease has on their child, born blind as if in mocking replay of Venus's blind child, Cupid. Fourth, Blanche's combination of pretended sexual innocence and actual sexual damage, even as she offers herself to Van, contrasts so pointedly with Lucette, who is *actually* a virgin in the sense of never having made love to a man, but who has sustained sexual damage through her entanglement in the romps of Van and Ada, and who, after she offers herself one last desperate time to Van, and like Blanche is rebuffed, takes her own life.

As I have written elsewhere:

The Veens' surname not only hints at Venus but also, less glamorously, means "peat" in Dutch; Blanche, curiously, is "Blanche de la Tourberie"

(407) after her native village, Tourbière, the French for "peaty." Since she romanticizes Van and Ada's fervor, since her own love-making so often serves as a comic counterpoint to theirs, Blanche seems to have been positioned for some ironic comment on the myths of Ardis. . . . A negative Venus, lover of an inverse Eros, mother of a "hopelessly blind" Cupid, Blanche undermines completely the myths of love she has tried to disseminate.

(NAPC 153, 155).

From her first appearance in the novel, Blanche acts as ironic variation on the sexual paradise of Ardis, and the "peat" theme that mocks the venery of the Veens also sounds at once. On his first morning at Ardis, Van wakes early and wants to wander out to the garden, and he finds, "standing at a tall window, a young chambermaid whom he had glimpsed (and promised himself to investigate) on the preceding evening" (48). With a "savage sense of opportune license," he clasps the wrist of her raised arm. She disengages, and he asks her name:

Blanche—but Mlle Larivière called her "Cendrillon" because her stockings got so easily laddered, see, and because she broke and mislaid things, and confused flowers. His loose attire revealed his desire; this could not escape a girl's notice, even if color-blind, and as he drew up still closer, while looking over her head for a suitable couch to take shape in some part of this magical manor—where any place, as in Casanova's remembrances could be dream-changed into a sequestered seraglio nook—she wiggled out of his reach completely and delivered a little soliloquy in her soft Ladoran French:

"*Monsieur a quinze ans, je crois, et moi, je sais, j'en ai dix-neuf. Monsieur* is a nobleman; I am a poor peat-digger's daughter. *Monsieur a tâté, sans doute, des filles de la ville; quant à moi, je suis vierge, ou peu s'en faut. De plus*, were I to fall in love with you—I mean really in love— and I might, alas, if you possessed me *rien qu'une petite fois*—it would be, for me, only grief, and infernal fire, and despair, and even death, Monsieur. *Finalement*, I might add that I have the whites and must see *le Docteur Chronique*, I mean Crolique, on my next day off. Now we have to separate, the sparrow has disappeared, I see, and Monsieur Bouteillan has entered the next room, and can perceive us clearly in that mirror above the sofa behind that silk screen."

(49)

Notice the "Casanova" that introduces another archetype of sexual license, and the irony of Blanche's claiming to be almost a virgin in almost the same breath as she refers to an appointment with her gynecologist because she suspects the whites—which will turn out to be gonorrhea rather than leucorrhea. And notice that in her first direct speech Blanche identifies herself as "a poor peat-digger's daughter." Indeed, she will be named in full Blanche de la Tourberie: she has a surname that if translated into Dutch would become "van Veen."

On Van's last morning at Ardis the First, Bouteillan gives him advice:

> "Monsieur should be prudent. The winds of the wilderness are indiscreet. *Tel un lis sauvage confiant au désert—*"
> "Quite the old comedy retainer, aren't you?" remarked Van drily.
> "*Non, Monsieur,*" answered Bouteillan, holding on to his cap. "*Non. Tout simplement j'aime bien Monsieur et sa demoiselle.*"
> "If," said Van, "you're thinking of little Blanche, then you'd better quote Delille not to me, but to your son, who'll knock her up any day now."
> The old Frenchman glanced at Van askance, *pozheval gubami* (chewed his lips), but said nothing.
>
> (157)

Bouteillan presumably issues his warning because he has heard about Van and Ada's ardor and activities from Blanche. Van attempts to deflect Bouteillan's comments about himself and Ada by questioning Blanche's fidelity to Bouteillan, and he succeeds: the comment shuts Bouteillan up, and we can deduce, from the later evidence of Kim's blackmail album, that Blanche's relationship with Bout has indeed already begun. Van in this final chapter of Ardis the First is obsessed by the thought that Ada could be unfaithful to him in his absence, and although she has yet to be unfaithful, Blanche's infidelity anticipates what will happen in Ada's case by the time Van returns to Ardis.

On arriving at Ardis the Second, unexpectedly, Van witnesses Ada's hand being held and kissed twice by Percy de Prey. Stung with jealousy, he tears apart the diamond necklace he has brought for Ada. But she allays his suspicions, and they make love throughout a "strenuous 'Casanovanic' night" (198) only to be interrupted while "still fiercely engaged" by Blanche "back from a rendezvous with old Sore the Burgundian night watchman" (191). Again, the fact that Blanche once more has a new partner serves as an omen of Ada's own infidelities, whatever Ada may for the moment convince Van to believe.

During a Flavita (Russian Scrabble) game where Van takes notes "in the hope—not quite unfulfilled—of 'catching sight of the lining of time' (which, as he was later to write, is 'the best informal definition of portents and prophecies')" (227), Ada scores 383 points with a single word, TORFYaNUYu. Lucette objects:

> "It's a place name! One can't use it! It's the name of the first little station after Ladore Bridge!"
>
> "That's right, pet," sang out Ada. "Oh, pet, you are so right! Yes, Torfyanaya, or as Blanche says, *La Tourbière*, is, indeed, the pretty but rather damp village where our *cendrillon*'s family lives. But, *mon petit*, in our mother's tongue—*que dis-je*, in the tongue of a maternal grandmother we all share—a rich beautiful tongue which my pet should not neglect for the sake of a Canadian brand of French— this quite ordinary adjective means 'peaty,' feminine gender, accusative case."
>
> (228)

The portent will become clear later, when on what will be his last morning at Ardis Van discovers that it is Blanche who has slipped him a note warning him that he is being deceived by Ada. Visiting him as the night wanes, "in a wretched simulacrum of seduction," Blanche tells Van she loves him, "he was her 'folly and fever,' she wished to spend a few secret moments with him" (292). This time he is too preoccupied with the warning note to be stirred, "quite aside from the fear of infection" (293). Questioned, Blanche tells him of Ada's affair with Philip Rack. He stumbles out into the dawn, packs his bags, and confronts Ada, who, unaware that he has been referring to Rack, admits to her affair not with Rack but with Percy de Prey.

Van leaves Ardis, driven by the Russian coachman Trofim Fartukov, and drops off Blanche on the way (she has slipped him the note about Ada only because she, too, has decided to leave Ardis Hall). Offering him further vivid details about Ada's relations with Percy, she

> rambled on and on until they reached Tourbière. . . . Van let her out. . . . He kissed Cendrillon's shy hand and resumed his seat in the carriage, clearing his throat and plucking at his trousers before crossing his legs. Vain Van Veen.
>
> "The express does not stop at Torfyanka, does it, Trofim?"
>
> "I'll take you five versts across the bog," said Trofim, "the nearest is Volosyanka."

His vulgar Russian word for Maidenhair; a whistle stop; train probably crowded.

Maidenhair. Idiot! Percy boy might have been buried by now! Maidenhair. Thus named because of the huge spreading Chinese tree at the
end of the platform. Once, vaguely, confused with the Venus'-hair
fern. . . . Who wants Ardis Hall!

"*Barin, a barin*," said Trofim, turning his blond-bearded face to his
passenger.

"*Da?*"

"*Dazhe skvoz' kozhanïy fartuk ne stal-bï ya trogat' etu frantsuzskuyu
devku.*"

Bárin: master. *Dázhe skvoz' kózhanïy fártuk:* even through a leathern apron. *Ne stal-bï ya trógat':* I would not think of touching. *Étu:*
this (that). *Frantsúzskuyu:* French (adj., accus.). *Dévku:* wench. *Úzhas,
otcháyanie:* horror, despair. *Zhálost':* pity. *Kóncheno, zagázheno, rastér-
zano:* finished, fouled, torn to shreds.

(299–300)

Notice here the counterpointing of Blanche with Van's departure from Ardis
and Ada; the stress on Blanche as hailing from "Tourbière . . . Torfyanka . . .
the bog"; the phrase "Vain Van Veen," which also plays on the Dutch pronunciation of *veen*, close to English "vain"; the irony that at the very moment Van
is filled with outrage at Ada's multiple infidelities he can himself be stirred
with desire for Blanche; the sounding of the virginity and Venus/venereal
themes, by way of the place-name Volosyanka and thence "Maidenhair. . . .
Once, vaguely, confused with the Venus'-hair fern"; and at the very moment
Van rejects Ardis one last time ("Who wants Ardis Hall!"), Trofim's declaration that he would not touch Blanche "even through a leathern apron." In
fact, Trofim will marry her, and they will have a damaged child, just as Van
will return to Ada, and as a result another child, Lucette, will have her light
put out (*NAPC* 155).

Notice, too, that the unrecognized prophecy in the Scrabble game ("TOR-
FYaNUYu . . . Yes, Torfyanaya, or as Blanche says, *La Tourbière*, is, indeed,
the pretty but rather damp village where our *cendrillon*'s family lives. But,
mon petit, . . . French—this quite ordinary adjective means 'peaty,' feminine
gender, accusative case")—a prophecy of the disclosure that will end Ardis
the Second—returns in the reference now to Blanche's "Tourbière . . . Cendrillon's shy hand . . . Torfyanka . . . *Frantsúzskuyu:* French (adj., accus.)"
(*NAPC* 221). Blanche de la Tourberie's multiple partners and her desire to
have Van, too, as a partner lead her to pass him that note that alerts him to

Ada Veen's multiple partners and so turn Ardis the Second for Van from a paradise regained into a hell of infidelity and jealousy.

LUCETTE

If Blanche's active sexual experience presents one ironic comment on the idylls of Ardis and the myths of love that she does so much to disseminate, Lucette's innocence presents another: at first, apparently comic as Van and Ada try to evade her curious eyes, but ultimately tragic as she becomes embroiled in their amours. Blanche offers herself to Van, who is repulsed at the thought of her venereal disease. Lucette offers herself to Van, who knows how damaged she is, not from having *too many* lovers but from having had none. A witness to Van's amours with Ada since she was eight, an eavesdropper, a spy, Lucette wants only him.

Nabokov signals the Lucette-Blanche parallel and contrast in many ways, through the Cinderella and the deflower motifs and especially, as I show in *Nabokov's* Ada: *The Place of Consciousness*, through the ironic combination, in very different ways, of claims of virginity and signs of sexual damage (*NAPC* 152–55).[14]

Here I want to focus on another motif that links them and that suggests how central to Nabokov's conception of *Ada* was the idea of complicating our response to the venereal Veens: the motif of *peat, bog, marsh* in the name of Blanche's village and especially in the Dutch name of the Veens.

Marsh Marigold

Ada may collect "bog orchids," but the center of the *bog-peat-marsh* theme in the Veen name is Lucette, identified with the "marsh marigold" that Wallace Fowlie carelessly omitted from his 1946 translation of Arthur Rimbaud's "Mémoire." Fowlie, not realizing at the time that the phrase *souci d'eau* meant "marsh marigold," translated it word for word as "care of the water"—as Lucette, indeed, becomes the "care of the water" when she jumps to her death in the Atlantic (*Ada* 63–65).[15]

Nabokov collected this particular piece of straw in 1960 or soon after, when Bollingen Press, which was preparing his translation of *Eugene Onegin* for publication, sent him their reprint edition of Huntington Cairns's anthology *The Limits of Art: Poetry and Prose Chosen by Ancient and Modern Critics*. His copy preserves his outraged marginalia to Fowlie's translation of Rimbaud's poem on pages 1346–48, including beside an underlined "care of the water": "!! yellow flower le souci d'eau C. *palustris*!"[16]

Nabokov must have seen Fowlie's version of Rimbaud before reading Freeling's *Double-Barrel* and may well have followed Freeling's hint that the Dutch *veen* means "peat, bog, marsh," precisely because he remembered this "marsh marigold." As he admits, he prefers "obscure facts"—*veen* as Dutch "marsh," *souci d'eau* as French "marsh marigold"—"to clear symbols" (*SO* 7). And as someone who has a character define genius as "seeing . . . the invisible links between things" (*LATH!* 40), Nabokov appears to have anticipated that this link would somehow be fruitful, to have consulted an atlas, discovered Erica among the *-veen* place-names of Drenthe, and, recalling Venus Erycina, developed the idea for an ironic treatment of the myths of love that we find already foreshadowed in the passage he wrote down in a flash at the end of 1965.

I have discussed elsewhere the ironies of "deflowering"—Lucette's too-early sexual initiation by Van and Ada but her dying a virgin because she wants no one but Van—that Nabokov builds around the fact that Fowlie unwittingly "deflowers" Rimbaud's "Mémoire" by substituting for *souci d'eau* "the care of the water," a phrase that itself foreshadows Lucette's death, both because she dies by water and because her death is a suicide, a near-echo or anagram of *souci d'eau*.[17] As first-time readers we view Lucette as a minor comic complication of Van and Ada's love, a farcical but easily removed hindrance to their ardor, but we discover as we read on, and as we reread, how tragic her entanglement in their love has become. As in the case of Blanche, the other recurrent witness of the Veens' passions, Lucette shifts from comical witness to tragic victim of unrestrained ardor, and in her case also from the periphery to the center of the novel, precisely because her fate so complicates Van and Ada's presentation of their love as triumphant. If Nabokov saw these possibilities very soon after reading Freeling's novel, with its Veens and peat bogs, its whiff of incest, and its air of eavesdropping, if he saw from very early on the chance for an ironic exploration of myths of love—as seems the case from the decrepit Villa Venus in his first sketch for *Ada*—how nevertheless could he weave the peat-bog pattern through Lucette, when she has the same surname as Ada?

Images of Imitation

That indeed was a challenge, but Nabokov already had another piece of straw at hand for his nest. He encountered Fowlie's mistranslation of Rimbaud's *souci d'eau* at the beginning of the 1960s. He read Freeling's *Double-Barrel* some time in 1964 or 1965. In between, he noticed a *New Yorker* advertisement for Barton and Guestier wines in which two models in modern dress imitate the poses of two spectators in Henri de Toulouse-Lautrec's famous poster for the Divan Japonais cabaret, 75 rue des Martyrs, reproduced on the wall behind them, over the slogan "the wines you loved in Paris!" The advertisement appeared in the inside front cover of the *New Yorker* on March 23, 1963, an issue in which an excerpt from *The Gift* depicting Yasha Chernyshevsky's suicide was also published, and it ran for several years.[18]

The advertisement, of course, becomes the basis for Van's meeting with and description of Lucette in Paris on May 31, 1901 (3.3), at which she hears of his plan to cross the Atlantic on the *Tobakoff* in four days' time and determines to make one final effort to seduce him.

The advertisement was suggestive for Nabokov in many ways. It raises the question of the relationship between art and life, a central one throughout his thought and work and especially in *Ada*, where the relationship between the world of the book, Antiterra, and the world of the reader, Terra or Earth, confronts us on page after page and where the relationship between pictures (paintings, drawings, films, photographs) and events unsettles us again and again. The quiet but unmistakable contrast in period between the dress of the figures in the poster and the mimics in the photograph sounds the note of anachronism, which plays so insistently throughout *Ada*. The relationship between model and mimic also connects with the question of natural mimicry, a key point of contact between Nabokov's science and his art and a subject whose artistic treatment would reach its apotheosis in his work in *Ada* 1.16 (Ada painting imitations of mimetic orchids: more of this in a moment). Above all, the advertisement as a whole suggests the idea of imitation and doubling so important in *Ada*, from the imitation or doubling of planets (Antiterra and Terra, Venus and Earth) to the imitation or doubling of sisters or cousins (Aqua and Marina, Ada and Lucette, Walter D. Veen and Walter D. Veen) or eras or events (Ardis the First and Ardis the Second, the picnics on Ada's twelfth and sixteenth birthdays), most important of all in Lucette's imitative relationship to her sister, especially in her fatal love for Van.

There is no reason to suppose Nabokov saw all these possibilities as soon as he saw the advertisement. Indeed, he kept working on other things but sometime in 1964 or more probably 1965, read Freeling's *Double-Barrel*, where *veen* as a surname and the Dutch for "peat, bog, marsh" meshed with the "marsh marigold" of Fowlie's translation and with Venus and Venus Erycina. Now he could add the Barton and Guestier advertisement to his first ideas for a family of Veens as positive and negative embodiments of Venus, to Freeling's hints of incest and eavesdropping and Fowlie's inadvertent cue for a suicide by drowning ("the care of the water"). The advertisement's emphasis on imitation and doubling may have suggested a Veen who imitates her sister ("I knew it was hopeless," [Lucette] said, looking away. "I did my best. I imitated all her *shtuchki* (little stunts)" [386]), who becomes embroiled in her sister's love for their brother, whose image entangles with her sister's in her brother's mind and life. And the idea of a Veen who imitates a second Veen who makes love to a third Veen in an Ardis that imitates Eden but who ultimately commits suicide because of her entanglement evokes once again Bosch's triptych, with its Edenic image of Adam and Eve alone to the left, its frenzy of repetitive sensuality and sexuality in the center, its hellish consequences to the right.

Doubling and imitation pervade *Ada*. The most extraordinary example of mimicry in Nabokov, and perhaps the most extraordinary crossing of the boundary of art and science, art and nature, art and life, occurs when Ada, as she paints aquarelles on July afternoons in 1884, inventively imitates natural orchids that themselves imitate the females of insects whose males then copulate with the orchids. Nabokov here pointedly plays with the Venus theme, the *veen*-bog theme, and the idea of an endless repetition or imitation of sexuality in Ardis, in the Villa Venuses, and in the central panel of the *Garden of Earthly Delights*. Nabokov has Ada introduce odd changes and twists into her aquarelle of a mirror of Venus blossom (the genuine but extraordinary mirror of Venus or simply mirror orchid, *Ophrys speculum*), which Ada herself "seemed in her turn to mimic" (99). Van, leaning over her as she performs this mimicry, then rushes away with his mental image of her to masturbate over in a form of pseudo-copulation of his own, imitating the male wasps that copulate with the mirrory sheen of the orchid lip that mimics the metallic look of the female wasps. In a further mimetic mix, Ada paints a blend of *Ophrys scolopax* (= *speculum* under another name) and the invented *Ophrys veenae* (which one would expect to be a bog orchid, if the Dutch sense of *veen* supplied the grounds for the name).[19]

Four years later Lucette, trying to imitate her sister, shows how far she falls short of Ada's naturalistic and artistic brilliance as she tries merely to trace an orchid from one of the local bogs:

In the meantime obstinate Lucette kept insisting that the easiest way to draw a flower was to place a sheet of transparent paper over the picture (in the present case a red-bearded pogonia, with indecent details of structure, a plant peculiar to the Ladoga bogs) and trace the outline of the thing in colored inks. Patient Ada wanted her to copy not mechanically but "from eye to hand and from hand to eye," and to use for model a live specimen of another orchid that had a brown wrinkled pouch and purple sepals; but after a while she gave in cheerfully and set aside the crystal vaselet holding the Lady's Slipper she had picked. Casually, lightly, she went on to explain how the organs of orchids work—but all Lucette wanted to know, after her whimsical fashion, was: could a boy bee impregnate a girl flower *through* something, through his gaiters or woolies or whatever he wore?

(288–89)

As if Ada imitating mirror of Venus and Veen orchids, and Van imitating the insects that copulate with them, and Lucette in 1888 imitating Ada in 1884 were not enough, the discussion segues into Lucette's innocent but troubled reaction to her sitting atop Van on the way back from the picnic on Ada's 1888 birthday, itself the most remarkable imitation of the past, of Ada on Van's lap on the way back from the birthday picnic in 1884, in a novel saturated with such repetitions. Notice that the plant Lucette traces is an orchid peculiar to the Ladoga bogs and, as "a red-bearded pogonia, with indecent details of structure," calls to mind Lucette's red pubic hair, glimpsed and fondled by Van five years later in the disturbing *débauche à trois* scene.

(Notice, too, that the plant Ada wants Lucette to copy, a Lady's Slipper that is all she has collected while out ostensibly "botanizing" but in fact seeing Percy de Prey for the last time, is an orchid of the *Cypripedium* genus, probably the type species, *Cypripedium calceolus*, a bog orchid, and that Cypripedium derives from Greek *Cypros* for the island sacred to Venus, and means "Venus's slipper." As Liana Ashenden comments, "The veins, ripples, shape and color of the labellum of Ada's wilted specimen imitate the male scrotum in an outrageous parody of sexual symbolism as Van describes the orchid's 'brown wrinkled pouch and purple sepals' (289), when thinking about Percy de Prey."[20] The garden of Venus becomes a bog because of sexual jealousy, as well as because of the other damage it causes.)

Lucette in Paris steps suddenly into a picture as she seems to reenact a Toulouse-Lautrec poster and a Barton and Guestier photograph. On board the *Tobakoff* five days later, she has all but seduced Van when Ada herself steps into the picture, into the movie *Don Juan's Last Fling*. As soon as she recognizes Ada on screen, Lucette, so near success, tries to tear Van away from the ship's cinema and the image of Ada:

"Let's go, please, let's go. You must not see her *debasing* herself. She's terribly made up, every gesture is childish and wrong—"

"Just another minute," said Van.

Terrible? Wrong? She was absolutely perfect, and strange, and poignantly familiar. By some stroke of art, by some enchantment of chance, the few brief scenes she was given formed a perfect compendium of her 1884 and 1888 and 1892 looks.

The *gitanilla* bends her head over the live table of Leporello's servile back to trace on a scrap of parchment a rough map of the way to the castle. Her neck shows white through her long black hair separated by the motion of her shoulder. It is no longer another man's Dolores, but a little girl twisting an aquarelle brush in the paint of Van's blood, and Donna Anna's castle is now a *bog* flower.

(489; last italics added)

Reminded so vividly and poignantly of Ada, Van realizes he cannot allow himself to make love even once to Lucette and as a precautionary measure rushes off to masturbate, for the first time in seventeen years—since, in fact, the time that he last masturbated over the image of Ada painting her blend of the mirror of Venus and *Ophrys veenae* orchids: "And how sad, how significant that the picture projected upon the screen of his paroxysm, while the unlockable door swung open again with the movement of a deaf man cupping his ear, was not the recent and pertinent image of Lucette, but the indelible vision of a bent bare neck and a divided flow of black hair and a purple-tipped paint brush" (490).

The orchid and bog theme, then, indicates Lucette's doomed attempts to imitate or match or replace her sister and the fact that despite her being locked into the pattern of Ada and Van's avid sexuality, she will die a virgin. The only way she will be deflowered is like the unhappy marsh marigold in Fowlie's translation, by being eliminated, by being turned into nothing more than the care of the water.

The theme of imitation, doubling, and repetition, so striking in the advertisement that echoes Toulouse-Lautrec, in Bosch's *Garden of Earthly Delights*, in Van and Ada Veen's ardors at Ardis, and in Lucette's involvement in their fate, is signaled from Van's first approach to Ardis. It seems in one light that Ardis will be a Garden of Eden, a paradise of sexuality, and in Ardis the Second a paradise regained, but as Van drives for the first time from the train station to the manor of the Veens, he passes through "Torfyanka, a dreamy hamlet," then "Gamlet, a half-Russian village" (35). In both, the driver waves to someone; "Hamlet" (the prince or the play) is in Russian "Gamlet," and Torfyanka, we discover later, is half-Russian, half-French (it is also called Tourbière), so that the two villages seem to overlap in time as much as they succeed one another in space.[21] The odd repetition prefigures the doubling of the 1884 and 1888 picnic rides and Lucette's involvement in the pattern of Van and Ada's repetition since on both rides they pass through Gamlet.[22] But the prominence of Torfyanka here, which we do not pass through again until Van leaves Blanche there after she has told him about Ada's infidelities at the end of Ardis the Second, serves as a first "portent and prophecy" of the end of Ardis and shows how carefully Nabokov already integrates the "peat-bog-marsh" sense of *veen* as qualifications of the themes and myths of love even as he drives his hero for the first time to the Veen manor.

Paris

But if the imitation and repetition pattern that Nabokov chose to amplify from the Barton and Guestier advertisement affects the "*veen*" he discovered in Freeling, *veen* as "bog" also affects the treatment of Paris in the scene that imitates the advertisement that imitates Toulouse-Lautrec. After Van describes in minute detail the scene of Lucette standing at the bar, as if in imitation of the Barton and Guestier advertisement, speech is turned on:

"I'm so happy and sad," she murmured in Russian. "*Moyo grustnoe schastie!* How long will you be in old Lute?"

Van answered he was leaving next day for England, and then on June 3 (this was May 31) would be taking the *Admiral Tobakoff* back to the States. She would sail with him, she cried, it was a marvelous idea, she didn't mind whither to drift, really, West, East, Toulouse, Los Teques. He pointed out that it was far too late to obtain a cabin (on that not very grand ship so much shorter than [the] *Queen Guinevere*), and changed the subject.

(461)

Notice Lucette's question: "How long will you be in old Lute?" She means Paris, but on Antiterra characters sometimes refer to Paris as Lute. Why? From behind his Vivian Darkbloom mask, Nabokov explained the name "Lute" as "from 'Lutèce,' ancient name of Paris."

Why does Nabokov intermittently (six times out of twenty) rename Paris "Lute"? On Antiterra New York is *always* slightly defocalized as Manhattan, but that reflects the fact that for most people outside the city, right here on Terra, Manhattan is easily the city's most famous borough. But no one now thinks of Paris in terms of Lutèce. Why then does Nabokov?

There are two closely related answers. One is that the French name Lutèce derives from Latin Lutetia, which in turn derives from Latin *lutum*, "mud," because in Roman times Paris was "a collection of mud hovels" that Caesar called Lutetia Parisiorum ("mud town of the Parisii") (*Brewer's Dictionary of Phrase and Fable*). It is no accident that another place-name in *Ada* has the sense of what Freeling, glossing *veen*, calls "wet, black, stinking ground." And it is no accident that the name Nabokov cites as Darkbloom is the French version, Lutèce, for that almost spells "Lucette," and by far the most important scene in Paris in the novel is this scene where Lucette learns that Van will sail on the *Tobakoff*, which soon leads to her taking her own life when she fails in her last effort to seduce him on the ship.

Why does Nabokov not simply rename Antiterra's Paris "Lute" and leave it at that, as he renames New York "Manhattan" or Canada "Canady"? Why does he also call the city Paris?

After failing to entice Van to her Japanese divan in old Lute, Lucette proposes to him that since Ada is already married, he should marry *her* and get Ardis, too (left to Lucette by Marina), and they could then invite Ada there. "While she's there, I go to Aspen or Gstaad, or Schittau, and you live with her in solid crystal with snow falling as if forever all around *pendant que je shee* in Aspenis. Then I come back like a shot, but she can stay on, she's welcome, I'll hang around in case you two want me. And then she goes back to her husband for a couple of dreary months, see?" (466). When Van dismisses the idea, Lucette says she has "an important, important telephone call to make": she quietly phones Cordula to arrange a suite on the *Tobakoff* (Cordula's husband owns the liner) for her last attempt to win Van over.

It can be no accident that it is in Paris that Lucette makes her proposal that Van should marry her, despite her knowing Van's heart will always be Ada's, for two of the central stories of love in Western culture feature a "Paris" who loves someone already married. In the Trojan story, Priam's son Paris, after judging Aphrodite (Venus) as the fairest of the goddesses, is rewarded by Aphrodite with the fairest of mortal women, Helen, although Helen is already married to Menelaus and Paris's abducting her will give rise to the Trojan war.[23] In *Romeo and Juliet*, Count Paris arranges with Capulet to have Juliet's hand, although we know she is already married to Romeo.[24] Although Ada is officially married to Andrey Vinelander, both Lucette and Van regard her as Van's for life when Lucette proposes to Van that he should now marry *her*.[25]

He does not, and the next decision Lucette takes in Paris—to attempt a last amorous assault on Van aboard the *Tobakoff* and, failing that, to jump to her death and leave Van to read the letter she sends him from Paris "on June 2, 1901, 'just in case'" (146)—clinches the tragic ironies of love that surrounds "all three Veens, the children of Venus" (410). The irony of the "veen" or "peat, bog, marsh" in their name becomes the irony of Lucette, the marsh marigold missing from "Mémoire" and now forever the "care of the water."

And as if to indicate the irony, without losing the "Paris" allusions, Nabokov partially renames the city where she makes her fatal resolve "Lute," in echo of "Lutèce," in tribute to Lucette, *mon enfant favori*" (as he called her in his 1975 television interview with Bernard Pivot),[26] and in anticipation of the "mud" on which she would rest.

If Nabokov names Paris "Lute" because of Lucette, it is in accord with many other patterns in the novel, established long before Lucette's death but in fact proving to be related to her: the water pattern (Aqua and Marina and much, much more), the electricity-and-water pattern (the banning of electricity caused by the "L disaster"), the flower pattern, the mistranslation theme, and more. Bobbie Ann Mason was the first to suggest a Lucettocentric reading of *Ada*; I have taken it much further in *Nabokov's* Ada: *The Place of Consciousness* and the ongoing "Annotations to *Ada*"/*Ada*Online.

Nabokov himself was one of the first promoters of such a reading, writing to Mason in the early 1970s identifying the Barton and Guestier advertisement and adding that it "should be looked up by all admirers of Lucette,"[27] or referring in 1975 to Lucette as his favorite child. But he had made such a reading possible from the first, and the evidence of sources such as Fowlie's mistranslation of Rimbaud's *souci d'eau*, noted by Nabokov in 1960 or soon after; the Barton and Guestier ad, noted in 1963; the sense of *veen* as "peat, bog, marsh"; and the pattern of eavesdropping, in Freeling's 1964 *Double-Barrel*, suggest that Nabokov conceived her role as central to the novel from the start. From the first he linked the Veens with Venus and anticipated a decrepit Villa Venus, and from the first he seems to have sought a way of linking "marsh marigold" to the Veens to show the boggy substratum of their garden of Edenic love.

Nabokov always liked an element of wit and surprise in the overall design of his fiction. In his first novel, the twist is that *Mary*, the heroine of the novel, although fervently expected, never actually steps onto the novel's stage. In the novel before *Ada*, *Pale Fire*, the central irony, as I now read it, is that although Hazel is at the center of her father's poem, Kinbote wrenches the text and commentary out of the family's control to place himself at the center of the story, only for that very act itself to be under the deeper guidance of the dead Hazel (see *NPMAD*). And in *Ada*, the central irony of the novel is that the character who is relegated to the periphery by the intense ardor of the two older Veen children and our eagerness to watch their amours is actually the covert center, source, and standard of the novel.

CODA: REPLAYING LOVE

I may here have sometimes seemed to repeat what I have written elsewhere about *Ada*, but let me repeat myself again in order to say something new. I wrote above that "doubling and imitation pervade *Ada*"—referring especially to the fatal doubling of Ada's love for Van in Lucette's and the way this complicates the novel's myths of love. But there is another private myth of love that I think Nabokov also incorporates into *Ada* and its Boschean revision of Venus.

The replaying of a former love, whether in glory or despair, may be Nabokov's central myth, from the 1920s to the 1970s, from Chorb hopelessly and absurdly replaying his love for his dead bride in one of Nabokov's first fully mature stories or Ganin replaying his love for Mary in his first novel all the way to *Transparent Things* and *Look at the Harlequins!*. In Nabokov's second to last novel, Hugh Person woefully attempts to reenact his love for Armande by revisiting Switzerland, a reenactment that in the retelling also encompasses the replay of a Russian writer's prostitute in the same room as Hugh's, or Julia Moore recalling her former lover in the same room where she and Hugh make love, or R. recycling his former loves into his fiction. In his last finished novel, *Look at the Harlequins!*, Nabokov treats the myth most parodically, in the former wives that lead up to the You of the final section of the novel, thereby revisiting the myth he treated most personally and pointedly in the former loves that lead up to the You in the closing movement of *Speak, Memory*.

Nabokov, of course, reworks the myth most famously in Humbert's reembodying "Annabel Leigh" in *Lolita*. But he reworks it most rapturously and expansively—and complicatedly—in Van and Ada replaying the paradise of their Ardis the First love in Ardis the Second. For Van's celebration of their love at Ardis the Second already incorporates pangs of jealousy, anxiety, awkwardness, and regret, like the ambiguity of Bosch's central panel, with its lavish fruits that suggest an orgy of succulent ripeness and sweet delight but also endless reenactments of the forbidden fruit—and the implicit fatal follow-on—of the Fall. Ardis the Second explodes into a hell of despair when Blanche, herself a celebrant and an unwitting underminer of Ardis as a paradise of love, discloses Ada's infidelity and Van flees Ardis's garden via the bog beyond Blanche's Tourbière:

"I'll take you five versts across the bog," said Trofim, "the nearest is Volosyanka."

His vulgar Russian word for Maidenhair; a whistle stop; train probably crowded.

(299)

And Nabokov reworks his myth of love's repetition most helplessly in Lucette's trying to reenact Ada in order to have a share of Van but ending in her hell of emptiness. Standing on the platform of the Maidenhair station, self-consciously thinking of Anna Karenin's end, Van feels suicidal:

> Maidenhair. Idiot! Percy boy might have been buried by now! Maidenhair. Thus named because of the huge spreading Chinese tree at the end of the platform. Once, vaguely, confused with the Venus'-hair fern. She walked to the end of the platform in Tolstoy's novel. First exponent of the inner monologue, later exploited by the French and the Irish. N'est vert, n'est vert, n'est vert. L'arbre aux quarante écus d'or, at least in the fall. Never, never shall I hear again her "botanical" voice fall at biloba, "sorry, my Latin is showing." Ginkgo, gingko, ink, inkog. Known also as Salisbury's adiantofolia, Ada's infolio, poor Salisburia: sunk; poor Stream of Consciousness, marée noire by now. Who wants Ardis Hall!

(299–300)

Although Van thinks of Ada and the hell of never seeing or hearing her again, "Maidenhair," mistranslation, leavesdropping, the écus d'or, and especially the "sunk; poor Stream of Consciousness, marée noire by now" all point to Lucette and her virginal status, the "marsh marigold" or souci d'eau (the "forged louis d'or in that collection of fouled French" [64]), the closing lines of Rimbaud's "Mémoire," and Lucette's sinking beneath the "black . . . waters" of the Atlantic after a brief passage (493) of stream of consciousness (see also NAPC 149–52, 156–57). And the marée noire (black tide) here is surely a pun on marais noir (black bog) at the very moment Van expels himself from Ardis forever.

For Nabokov the tension between the singularity and the multiplicity of love is a central mystery: the singularity of love, love at its best, the passionate conviction that no one else will do, and the multiplicity of love, its repeatability with the same person or others. A single overwhelming love allows Van and Ada to transcend the isolation of their selves, and the rampant repeatability of the act of love only adds to the enchantment. Yet because we and others are ultimately on our own, we and they can wish to overcome our solitude: we can be aroused by many, as Van and Ada certainly are, in ways that cause each other intense pain, or as Blanche is, in an unintended ironic chorus. Or, conversely, Lucette, unable to have the one love she yearns for, despite her repeated lovemaking with Ada, feels only her ultimate emptiness. In the shift from the paradise of the left panel, two lovers in a world of bliss, to the crowded recapitulations and complicated ambiguities of the central panel and the torments of the right panel of Bosch's *Garden of Earthly Delights*, Nabokov found the richest straw for the boggy paradise of the Veens' venereal delights, and his most complex image of the triumphs and torments of love's singularity and repetitions.

26. A Book Burner Recants

The Original of Laura

The Original of Laura, as some reviewers observed, was the most eagerly awaited new novel of the twenty-first century. It disappointed me when I first read it, in 1987, as it disappointed many reviewers, and often for the same reasons. On the eve of publication, at the Poetry Center in New York's 92nd Street Y, I could not resist explaining why I first thought the book should not have been preserved, let alone published, and then why I had come around to being delighted by the publication of the index cards I had first reacted to so badly.

In 1973, four years before his death, Nabokov had the initial inkling of what became *The Original of Laura*, but first he had to finish *Look at the Harlequins!* and then, driven by a sense of personal honor, to revise and virtually rewrite the translation of *Ada* for the French publisher, after the first translator's breakdown. His intense work on the translation, from five A.M. each morning, at the age of seventy-six, drained him, as did severe falls, operations, and infections over the next two years, and he could not finish *The Original of Laura* before his death in 1977. Some time earlier, he had asked his wife to promise to destroy the manuscript should it be left uncompleted. She promised but could not bring herself to carry out his injunction.

Two years after his death, I finished my Ph.D. at the University of Toronto. After reading it, Véra invited me to visit her in Montreux; after the visit, she asked me to sort out Nabokov's archive for her. Although from late 1979 I had free access to the archive, I could not see other materials that Véra guarded in her bedroom: Nabokov's letters to his parents and to her, his diaries, and *The Original of Laura*. By mid-1981 she agreed even to condone my working on a biography and, in principle, to allow me access to all I wished to see. She gradually allowed me access first to Nabokov's letters to his parents, then to what she chose to read into my tape recorder of his letters to her. Not until February 1987, as I was already working on Nabokov's American years, did she at last agree to my entreaties to read Nabokov's final but unfinished fiction. She placed the little box of index cards on the maroon-and-silver striped period sofa on the west side of her narrow living room and monitored me from the matching sofa two meters away on the east side. I could read the manuscript once only and could take no notes. I also had to agree to delete anything she wished of what I might write on the novel as a result of this reading. The conditions could hardly have been worse.

Not long afterward, on Dmitri Nabokov's next visit to Montreux, Véra and Dmitri asked me what they thought I should do with the manuscript of *The Original of Laura*. I said, to my own surprise, "Destroy it." How glad I am now that they ignored my advice and that their attachment to Nabokov's work overrode even their respect for his last wish.

In 1950 Nabokov would have burned another manuscript of another still incomplete book, entitled *Lolita*, if Véra had not stopped him on his way to the incinerator. Of course, Nabokov, Véra, Dmitri, and the whole world have good reason to be thankful that that didn't happen. But he finished *Lolita*, and he came nowhere near finishing *The Original of Laura*. So why am *I* now thankful about *this* publication?

The Original of Laura could have been published badly, as if it were a new *Lolita* or at least a new *Pnin*. Instead it was better published than I could have imagined. Subtitled "A Novel in Fragments" on the cover and "(Dying Is Fun)" on the title page, the index cards now bound into book form rightly flaunt their unfinishedness. Readers should not expect a new story to rival *Lolita*'s intensity or a new character to match *Pnin*'s pathos but instead glimpses of a famously demanding writer still challenging his readers and himself, in his late seventies, with death closing in.

What troubled me so much when I first read *The Original of Laura* and recommended that VN's wishes should be followed and the text destroyed? And what has changed so much in my sense of the novel that I welcomed its publication?

All my initial dissatisfactions I have seen echoed in the responses of such gifted reviewers as Martin Amis, John Banville, Jonathan Bate, Alexander Theroux, and Aleksandar Hemon.

My first disappointment was that the fragments remain just that. I knew that Nabokov had had the first idea for the novel almost four years before his death and that when he still had more than fourteen months to live Véra had reported that he was "about half way" to completion.[1] I had expected much more than I found. Reading and understanding need trust. The embryonic nature of the text sapped my trust, especially when I could read it only once under Véra's wary eyes. For reviewers, their reluctance to trust an inchoate Nabokov text, too, was compounded by their suspicion of the rationale for its publication.

My second regret was that there were no sympathetic characters and no one who looms large in the imagination like Luzhin, Humbert, Pnin, Kinbote, or Van Veen.

The third was that the narrative driveshaft seemed broken. In *Lolita*, *Pale Fire*, and *Ada*, Nabokov reinvents fiction without forfeiting the pleasures of plot. *The Original of Laura* has a beginning, a middle, and an end, but it's hard to see how readers would have been impelled from one to the next even if the novel had been completed.

The fourth was the recurrence of unpleasantly heartless sex, as in *Transparent Things*, and the fifth, the recurrence of a *Lolita* theme. Nabokov had recycled the name of *Lolita*, or much more, in *Pale Fire*, *Ada*, and *Look at the Harlequins!* In *The Original of Laura* he introduces a character called Hubert H. Hubert, the partner of Flora's mother. When his hand touches twelve-year-old Flora's legs under the bedclothes, she kicks him in the groin. Do we really need a *fourth* reprise of *Lolita*, even with this twist?

The sixth disappointment was that the hero has a problem too strange to engage the imagination. Luzhin's love of chess haunts even readers who cannot play the game. Humbert's desire for Lolita compels readers despite their feelings about child rape. But in Nabokov's last completed novel, *Look at the Harlequins!*, Vadim Vadimych's maddening problem is merely that he can't imagine turning around to walk the other way along a street, an act that he can readily perform in real life but that sends his imagination spinning—and a problem that has always failed to turn *my* imagination. In *The Original of Laura* Philip Wild wants to find out how to *will* his own body dead, inch by inch, from his feet upward, so that dying becomes fun and a reversible relief from the itch of being. Most of us surely think about death, and most of us have times when we wouldn't mind redrawing our figures. But Philip Wild's obsessive quest to erase his body seems far from ordinary human preoccupations.

My seventh concern was the novel's style. In a 1974 review a stern young Martin Amis had greeted *Look at the Harlequins!*: "[Its] unnerving deficiency . . . is the crudity of its prose. . . . In the book's 250-odd pages I found only four passages that were genuinely haunting and beautiful; in an earlier Nabokov it would be hard to find as many that were not."[2] I, too, was sadly disappointed by *Look at the Harlequins!* and wondered if it marked an irreversible decline in Nabokov's powers. Yet he still sparkled in interviews and introductions. As his biographer, I sweated in 1987 as I picked up the first of the *Laura* index cards: would I be able to describe Nabokov's invention as undimmed, or would the manuscript confirm a decline? My fraught first reading, alas, bore out my fears. Above all, I felt that whatever *might* have become of the novel, the cards that survived fell far short of Nabokov's standards and should be destroyed as he wished.

If you have not yet bought *The Original of Laura* you will now be thinking that you need not bother. Read on: I want to change your minds. And rest assured that I'm not someone who approves of whatever Nabokov writes: I have sometimes been harsher than anyone on those of his works I think not up to his high standards.

My estimation of *The Original of Laura* has changed dramatically. It's not another *Lolita* or *Pale Fire*, but it could have been—it already is—another fascinating Nabokov novel and a priceless entry into his workshop. What's changed my mind? Not reading under impossible conditions. Not reading with wrong expectations. Reading for what's there and not for what's missing. Rereading. Trusting more. Re-rereading, and trusting still more.

My first disappointment was that the novel was so fragmentary, so unfinished. It still is, but there's a strong beginning, a vivid middle, a wry end, and an already intricate design. The more I reread the more I think that Nabokov may indeed have been nearly halfway to another short novel like *The Eye* or *Transparent Things*.

My second was with the characters. True, none is sympathetic. But the heroine, Flora, is deliciously unlikable, and her husband, the neurologist Philip Wild, is an unforgettable presence from his tartan booties and his ingrown toenails to his Buddha-like bulk and his brilliant brain trying to erase his feet.

My third lay with the plot. But if there's little plot tension there's also headlong action from reckless Flora and comic inertia from Wild's repeated self-erasures. Perhaps one in two of Nabokov's novels lacks a powerful plot impetus. Unless I'm mistaken, as you know by now I can be, *The Original of Laura* would have offered different pleasures from those of suspense: the contrasts of helter-skelter narration and meditative stasis and the puzzles of who has created and who has obliterated whom.

Three problems down, four to go. You'll still be far from persuaded.

My fourth and fifth: the frequent focus on sex and the replay of the *Lolita* theme. Why I thought the former disappointing on first encounter I now can't imagine. I now find Nabokov's descriptions of sex here hilariously unappetizing, prodigiously unsatisfying emotionally and often physically, comic in their painful shortcomings. Just forget the tension of *Lolita* or the ecstatic, "passionate pump-joy" release of *Ada* (*Ada* 286); forget, above all, the romance of first love in *Speak, Memory* or in *Mary*. Here's the different world of *The Original of Laura*:

> Flora was barely fourteen when she lost her virginity to a coeval, a handsome ballboy at the Carlton Courts in Cannes. Three or four bro-ken porch steps—which was all that remained of an ornate public toilet or some ancient templet—smothered in mints and campanulas and surrounded by junipers, formed the site of a duty she had resolved to perform rather than a casual pleasure she was now learning to taste. She observed with quiet interest the difficulty Jules had of drawing a junior-size sheath over an organ that looked abnormally stout and at full erection had a head turned somewhat askew as if wary of receiv-ing a backhand slap at the decisive moment. Flora let Jules do every-thing he desired except kiss her on the mouth, and the only words said referred to the next assignation.
>
> (77–79)

Nabokov has focused on sex before, but never has he shown it so divorced from feeling. But he surely amuses and appalls us in a new way with the sexual activity he depicts here.

My fifth concern yielded even greater surprises. Nabokov evokes Hum-bert Humbert not to replay *Lolita* but to mislead our expectations. Mr. Hubert H. Hubert lost a daughter at twelve, run over by a truck. He sees her in a sense resurrected in Flora, Daisy's age when she died, and wants to be nearer Flora than she wants him to be, wants, even, to brush her hair with his lips. But as far as I can see, he feels toward her only as the father of the lost daughter whom Flora keeps reminding him of. Flora, who knows about sex but not about love, misreads his intentions, as do readers misled by Nabokov's expert deception. The real link to *Lolita* we should make from Hubert H. Hubert is not to Humbert crushing Lolita under his memory of "Annabel Leigh," but to the Kasbeam barber, whom Nabokov identifies in his essay "On a Book Entitled *Lolita*" as one of "the nerves of the novel . . . the secret points, the subliminal co-ordinates by means of which the book is plotted" (*Lolita* 318). The barber appears in a sentence that, Nabokov reports, cost him a month of work:

> In Kasbeam a very old barber gave me a very mediocre haircut: he babbled of a baseball-playing son of his, and, at every explodent, spat into my neck, and every now and then wiped his glasses on my sheet-wrap, or interrupted his tremulous scissor work to produce faded newspaper clippings, and so inattentive was I that it came as a shock to realize as he pointed to an easeled photograph among the ancient gray lotions, that the mustached young ball player had been dead for the last thirty years.
>
> (*Lolita* 215)

Hubert H. Hubert feels tender love for his dead Daisy, and would like to offer the same to Flora, but Flora understands only sex, not love, not tenderness, and repays his attentions with a kick in the groin. Through the Hubert name and other *Lolita* echoes, Nabokov dupes us at first into misreading the scene just as hard-bitten Flora does. But in this novel of human erasures, Daisy's death has *not* been erased for her father, who remembers his lost child so painfully, so hopelessly. Nabokov has hidden under our noses the beating core of tenderness in this apparently heartlessly hard novel: Flora as potential Daisy, not as Lolita, is one of *this* novel's "secret points."

My sixth problem was that Philip Wild's obsession with willing his own death, erasing himself by inches so that he can restore himself by inches—so that death can dance to his tune—seems so remote from our experience and our desires. Wild's quest is certainly singular. But many of us have wished to shed intense pain or discard excess weight. Wild wants both. Many have sought to train the mind to control and transcend self, through meditation, and Wild has not only the shape of the fattest Buddha but the same urge to reach nirvana (the text makes reference to both) and to eliminate the self. In Wild's case life has pained him, with his vast bulk, abscessed toes, writhing gut, and the "anthology of humiliation" (219) his life has been since he married Flora. The word *anthology* derives from the Greek for "collecting flowers," but in Wild's case, his Flora casually plucks and casually or viciously jettisons other men.

Nabokov has some sympathy with Wild in his humiliation, and so should we, but he is no Pnin. All of us might wish at times we could control our own death or restoration, but Nabokov surely presents Wild's as exactly the wrong way to transcend death. Eliminating the self promises no worthwhile passage beyond life. The only transcending of death Nabokov could imagine wanting would take the self *through* death to a freer realm of being but not deny its accumulation of experience: "I am ready to become a floweret / Or a fat fly," John Shade writes in *Pale Fire*, "but never, to forget" (*PF* 52–53). In *Ada*, Van Veen explains "the worst part of dying": "the wrench of relinquishing forever all one's memories—that's a commonplace, but what courage man must have had to go through that commonplace again and again and not give up the rigmarole of accumulating again and again the riches of consciousness that will be snatched away!" (*Ada* 585).

Wild obsessively tries to will his own elimination, but for Nabokov self-elimination can only be the falsest kind of self-transcendence. Wild's ingrown toenails cause him agony. One time, as he lies in a mattress in his bath, again willing away what he can, he not only seems to erase his toes but decides not to restore them when he emerges from his hypnotrance. Opening his eyes, his heart sinks when he sees his toes are intact, but when he scrambles out of the tub, he falls flat on the tiled floor. To his "intense joy," his toes are "in a state of indescribable numbness. They looked all right, though . . . all was rubber and rot. The immediate setting-in of decay was especially sensational" (167).

For many over many millennia, but never more than for Nabokov, transcending death has seemed somehow akin to escaping earth's gravity. Fat Philip Wild flopping over on erased toes succumbs to gravity more grotesquely than ever. And his obsessive quest seems an apotheosis of self and of stasis, a self-fixated and self-enclosed attempt to circumvent the limits to the self that death imposes. To the extent that Nabokov imagines possibly passing through death—and that's to a very considerable extent—he sees it as a transition that hurtles the self into a state retaining accumulated selfhood but no longer subjected to "the solitary confinement of [the] soul" (*CE* 217)

Wild conjures up an image of an "I," "our favorite pronoun" (137), on his mental blackboard, its three bars representing his legs, torso, and head, and he sees his auto-hypnosis as akin to successively rubbing out each bar. Images of erasure or self-deletion pervade the whole novel in ways that reveal Nabokov's customary care in constructing and concealing his patterns. To take one example: Wild feels delight and relief at erasing his ingrown toenails. Flora, by contrast, wipes not a mental blackboard but her own flesh: she requires her menfolk to withdraw before ejaculation and promptly wipes the semen off her groin or, as the novel once phrases it, her "inguen" (121). How many know this word for "groin"? *Ingrown-inguen*: Nabokov covertly links Wild erasing his own life, rubbing out his toes, with Flora briskly wiping off the possibility of new life. The Roman Flora was a fertility goddess; Nabokov's Flora, a sterility goddess.

Art can offer a kind of immortality, a different promise of transcending death. But not here, not in this novel. Flora's grandfather, a painter of once-admired sentimental landscapes, falls forever out of favor: "What can be sadder than a discouraged artist dying not from his own commonplace maladies, but from the cancer of oblivion invading his once famous pictures such as 'April in Yalta' or 'The Old Bridge'?" (43–45) His son, a photographer, films his own suicide, *his* being rubbed out. The photographer's wife, Flora's mother, a ballerina known only as Lanskaya, finds her art fading as her body ages. Flora herself becomes the subject of a kiss-and-tell novel, *My Laura*, which aims not to immortalize but to expunge her: "The 'I' of the book is a neurotic and hesitant man of letters who destroys his mistress in the act of portraying her" (121). The laurel was associated with literary immortality because its leaves last so long after they detach. Flora, so eager to be deflowered, remains alive at the end of the novel; unlike her husband, obsessed with his own death, she ends *The Original of Laura* refusing to look at the novel *My Laura* lying on her lap and at what a friend recommends as "your wonderful death. . . . the craziest death in the world" (227).

We come to my seventh concern, the novel's style. For an older and still sterner Martin Amis, this by itself would be decisive. In 1999, for the centenary of Nabokov's birth, the oldest of the five journals devoted to him, the *Nabokovian*, decided to stage a Nabokov write-alike contest. A panel of judges selected three submissions, which appeared alongside what were announced as two "never before published pieces of Nabokov's prose"—both from *The Original of Laura*—that, readers were informed, Dmitri had supplied. Subscribers were invited to pick the original of Vladimir. Delightfully, most picked as Nabokov's a passage by Charles Nicol, an academic and writer who has been publishing superb work on Nabokov for more than thirty years, and *no one* picked the passages from *The Original Of Laura*. Nobody picked Nabokov as the one who wrote most like Nabokov.

What does that tell us? I think it indicates that even Nabokovians either misconstrue Nabokov's style or underestimate how new it can be from work to work. We can recognize on sight many hallmarks of his style when we see them "on site," and we can find many of them already on his construction site for *The Original of Laura*. But we have not sufficiently recognized how much Nabokov also modifies his style and reweights particular features in each work. To take his best English works: the high, controlled elegance of *Speak, Memory* differs radically from *Lolita*'s neurotic twitchiness, and both from *Pale Fire*'s would-be cloudless craziness, and all three from *Ada*'s rococo supersaturation—and all four from *The Original of Laura*.

That no one picked the *Laura* passages in the write-alike contest suggests to me not that Nabokov isn't writing up to par here but, on the contrary, that he's playing his usual game of *changing* or reinventing his game subtly to suit the special world of the work.

Nabokov has a reputation as a great prose stylist, perhaps even the greatest. *The Original of Laura* makes me want to rethink what constitutes the distinctively Nabokovian: not just elevated prose, a recondite lexicon, elegant quicksilver sentences, minute precision of visual detail, pointed allusion, foregrounded verbal combinatory play, lucid elusiveness. His style may be most extraordinary not so much as *prose* but as *story*. Unlike "Lolita, light of my life, fire of my loins," the thirteen words of the opening sentence of *The Original of Laura* would win no place in dictionaries of quotations and no prizes as prose. I won't quote them yet, but taken out of context, the first sentence offers plain words that muffle even their plain declarative force with a doubled concession—but as storytelling, the sentence astounds. It does more as *story* than we had any right to expect of a first sentence, until now.

All his writing life Nabokov stressed transition among character, description, report, speech, and reflection as the most demanding skill in storytelling. He sought new ways to shift from one to another, new ways to speed up the shifts or slow them down or highlight or veil them. He wanted both to extend the possibilities in narrative at every moment and to show readers how nimbly their minds can move from present to past or possible future, from outside a character to inside, from here to there, from actual to possible or impossible, counterfactual or suppositional. In *On the Origin of Stories*, I marshal the evidence that we have evolved into a storytelling species and that the key reason we have done so is because stories improve still further the social cognition and hence the perspectival shifts that had already reached such a high level in our species. From childhood pretend play to adult fiction, we speed up the capacity of our minds to leap beyond our here and now by taking on new roles, sidling and sliding this way and that through time, space, minds, and modalities, thanks to the intense doses of social information we deal with in fiction. No one has taken this further than Nabokov does in his last novel. Narratologists and novelists alike will focus for a long time on the opening chapter of *The Original of Laura* as proof of the new finds still to be made in fiction.

The Original of Laura starts with an answer, but we never learn the question, and we never quite keep up with the pace of the story. It reminds me of the myth of Atalanta and the golden apples. At top speed it picks up a stray fact, darts aside, nonchalantly drops one subject, gathers up another, and still races ahead—unless it slows down and all but stops, with Philip Wild, as he tries again and again to erase himself.

Nabokov not only rewrites narrative texture but from novel to novel reshapes narrative structure. In *The Original of Laura* he plays with the erasure of human selves. Philip Wild tries to dispense with his body by degrees. The author of *My Laura* aims to eliminate Flora. As you read the novel's first chapter, look for the unprecedented way Nabokov makes the narrator imply himself and conceal or erase himself throughout—while Laura disregards her new lover, dumps an old one, and ignores her husband.

Do not expect in *The Original of Laura* the high lyricism of sentiment and sentence found in *Lolita*, *Pale Fire*, and *Ada*. Instead, look for how much Nabokov does once again by inverting what he values most but, as always, in a new way. He inverts love as a path to self-transcendence (through procreation, through the tender attunement of lovemaking, through sharing a life with another) in Flora—as sterility goddess wiping the sperm off her groin, in her heartless promiscuity, in the "anthology of humiliation" she offers her husband. Art becomes not a way to self-transcendence here but, rather, the vengeful obliteration of others or the skulking effacement of the tattle-tale self. Nabokov sees death as a possible release from the confines of the self, not an erasing of the self like Philip Wild's or an evasion of its limits like Flora's.

Nabokov offers us, in the suppleness and speed of our imaginations as he sends us hurtling along the black trails of his story, a route beyond the rapacity of the sexual self in Flora or the stagnation of the cerebral self in Philip—and, if we invert his inversions, what he famously called "a sense of being somehow, somewhere, connected with other states of being where art (curiosity, tenderness, kindness, ecstasy) is the norm" (*Lolita* 316–17).

In some of the many interviews *The Original of Laura* has provoked I have sometimes illustrated the reasons for my reversal of judgment in terms of the excitement I now feel at the opening of the novel and its narrative novelty. David Gates, in the *New York Times Book Review*, quotes me and asks: "Does Boyd mean the device of beginning a novel *in medias res*, with a character answering a question we don't get to hear? Virginia Woolf did the same thing in the first sentence of *To the Lighthouse*." True, Woolf's landmark novel does begin "'Yes, of course, if it's fine tomorrow,' said Mrs. Ramsay.

'But you'll have to be up with the lark,' she added." The suddenness of that opening, and its clear announcement of a planned excursion, magnificently sets up the thwarted expedition to the lighthouse.

But Nabokov's openings are still more extraordinary, from "In the second place, because he was possessed by a mad hankering after Russia" ("The Circle") to "Lolita, light of my life, fire of my loins," to the parodic mistranslation and reversal of Tolstoy's famous first sentence of *Anna Karenina* in the first sentence of *Ada*, to the bizarre address from a dead narrator to a living character at the start of *Transparent Things*: "Here's the person I want. Hullo, person. Doesn't hear me" (*TT* 1).

And here's the opening sentence of *The Original of Laura*: "Her husband, she answered, was a writer, too—at least, after a fashion" (1). After those other famous first lines, what is it that strikes me as just as remarkable about this succession of individually unremarkable words?

Let me unpack my pleasure. The first word, "Her," a third-person possessive pronoun, already implies a female possessor we do not know and cannot identify as the narrator. "She" comes along at the third word, but she remains unidentified.

Over the last couple of centuries, fiction has tended to shorten exposition and even to begin in medias res. For that reason, direct speech as a more immediate and dramatic entry has become increasingly common in twentieth-century fiction. But indirect speech implies a narrator doing the reporting, and usually follows the narrator's establishment of the character's identity. Here we have neither the identity of the character nor the confident establishment of the narrator. Over the next few sentences the volubility of the still-unnamed woman continues to hold the narrator at bay.

As Tadashi Wakashima has also explained, we can infer what provokes "her" response: a preceding "I am a writer."[3] "She" then answers: "My husband is a writer, too—at least, after a fashion." Later in the long first paragraph we discover that "she" is Flora, that she is at a party, that she is drunk, that she "wished to be taken home or preferably to some cool quiet place with a clean bed and room service." Within another paragraph she has been offered and has eagerly accepted the apartment of friends and has begun to undress there to make love with someone whom she has picked up at the party, someone whom we cannot see clearly. As the lovemaking scene enfolds us and unfolds itself, we recognize Flora's sexual partner as the narrator, yet we also see that he avoids identifying or describing himself or reporting his actions as his, by dint of referring to them only through nonfinite verbs. The narrator, we infer, is the writer whom Flora has just met at the party, when she is already drunk, when she has asked what he does, when he has replied, and when she in turn answers, in the opening line of the novel. There she refers disparagingly to her husband—the very husband this new lover will return her to late in the chapter, after dawn, to add another rank flower to his "anthology of humiliation." She refers to her husband's being a writer, a profession she casually insults four short sentences later, despite being already in the process of picking up this other self-effacing writer—who in writing this very scene, in these very words, in his roman à clef *My Laura*, has his revenge on her heartlessness.

No one has ever packed so much story into the choice of the opening word ("Her"), the opening mode (indirect speech), and the opening declaration and its antecedents and consequences in terms of narrative action, narrative voice, and narrative aim. At the same time as he manages all this, Nabokov also shows the narrator *effacing* himself and *deleting* Flora as he portrays her (before killing her off fictively later in *My Laura*) mentioning her husband as "a writer of sorts," whose "mysterious manuscript" itself recounts how he *erases* himself, in another doomed attempt at transcending, or expunging, the self.

After reading Martin Amis's negative review of *The Original of Laura* on the day we were to appear in New York on the eve of the novel's publication, I gave him to read the printout of a review I had written for publication later that week. Handing it back, he had to say he disagreed with my claim that the opening shows Nabokov "at the peak of his powers." I stand by, and I can now explain, my claim.

NOTES

INTRODUCTION

1. Cornell Lepidoptera Collection, Cornell University.
2. Page numbers for *Lolita* are to the first edition of *The Annotated Lolita*, ed. Alfred Appel Jr. (New York: McGraw-Hill, 1970), whose page numbers are the same as the first U.S. edition (New York: Putnam, 1958). Page numbers of the 1989 edition (New York: Vintage) and the second edition of *The Annotated Lolita* (New York: Vintage, 1991) are always two less than the pages of these other editions.
3. See also Paisley Livingston, *Art and Intention* (Oxford: Oxford University Press, 2005); Peter Swirski, *Literature, Analytically Speaking: Explorations in the Theory of Interpretation, Analytic Aesthetics, and Evolution* (Austin: University of Texas Press, 2010); and *Of Literature and Knowledge: Explorations in Narrative Thought Experiments, Evolution, and Game Theory* (New York and London: Routledge, 2007).
4. VN to Roman Grynberg, 19 January 1957, VNA.

1. A CENTENNIAL TOAST

1. On the wall behind the high table stood a copy of the Holbein portrait of Henry VIII, founder of Trinity College, in doublet and hose.
2. Letter from John C. Downey to Kurt Johnson, 1997, private collection.
3. Zsolt Bálint and Kurt Johnson had been working together for a decade on the Latin American Blues, which Nabokov revised in a prescient paper of 1945. Although they had coauthored many papers and had named scores of butterflies after Nabokovian characters and places, they had met only the day before attending this memorial evening at New York's Town Hall. For a study of the context and consequences of Nabokov's 1945 paper, see Kurt Johnson and

Steven L. Coates, *Nabokov's Blues: The Scientific Odyssey of a Literary Genius* (Cambridge, Mass.: Zoland Books, 1999). The naming of newly discovered Latin American Blues in honor of Nabokov continues as I proofread this book in January 2011.

4. *CE* 217: "His best works are those in which he condemns his people to the solitary confinement of their souls"; *SM* 20: "Initially, I was unaware that time, so boundless at first blush, was a prison."

5. The patterns include the winged imagery that Shade weaves covertly into the poem, including the *Vanessa atalanta*, also with a red streak on its wing; the anticipation by Shade of the "azure" reflections in a puddle outside the bar on Hazel's last night; the homage by Shade to his parents, after whom a waxwing has been named; the "slain"-"pane" rhyme that permeates and punctuates Shade's poem; the color blue running through the novel, not least in "blue inenubilable Zembla"; the reflections, including Zembla as a "land of reflections"; the glass (glass pane, glass pain) imagery associated with Gradus; the winged imagery repeatedly flapping around Gradus; the "shadow" of a creature killed against glass and Gradus's being chosen to kill Charles II in a meeting of the Shadows, at the Onhava Glassworks, at the very moment this line is set down; the flight into the side of a building that results in death for Alfin, Charles II's father; the butterfly Blues (Icarus, implicit in the "waxwing," is the Common Blue, *Icaricia icarioides*, a genus named by Nabokov; the Azures are a subgroup of the Blues). For more on these patterns and their implications, see my *NPFMAD*.

6. Samuel Beckett, *Murphy*, in *Beckett: The Grove Centenary Edition*, ed. Paul Auster, Vol. 1: *Novels* (New York: Grove, 2006), 4.

7. VN to Elena Ivanovna Nabokov, November 25, 1921, Elena Sikorski Collection.

2. A BIOGRAPHER'S LIFE

1. Peter Medawar, BBC Radio 3, July 28, 1972, cited in Bryan Magee, *Popper* (London: Fontana, 1973), 9.

2. Andrew Field, *Nabokov: A Bibliography* (New York: McGraw-Hill, 1973).

3. Andrew Field, *Nabokov: His Life in Part* (New York: Viking, 1977).

3. WHO IS "MY NABOKOV"?

1. See his comments on Proust in chapter 14 of this volume, and his contrast of three perspectives on a patch of countryside in chapter 24.

2. See "Books," *Time*, May 23, 1969, 48–49, available from http://www.time.com /time/magazine/article/0,9171,900891,00.html.

3. *The Nabokovian*, 1993–; *Ada*Online, http://www.ada.auckland.ac.nz/.

4. THE NABOKOV BIOGRAPHY AND THE NABOKOV ARCHIVE

1. MS of *LRL*, VNA.
2. Published in *Rul'*, June 24, 1923, rept., Nabokov, *Stikhi* (Ann Arbor, Mich.: Ardis, 1979), 106–7.
3. On becoming dissatisfied with the title *Conclusive Evidence*, Nabokov had wanted to call his autobiography *Speak, Mnemosyne*, after Mnemosyne, goddess of memory, mother of the muses, and after the butterfly *Parnassius mnemosyne*, which he used to catch near his summer estate. *Look at the Harlequins!* repeats not only *Speak, Memory*'s imperative but also its oblique butterfly: harlequin is the popular name for a number of butterfly species.
4. Writing of himself in the third person, Nabokov declares that "his best works are those in which he condemns his people to the solitary confinement of their souls" (*CE* 217).
5. A later reflection: in this tribute to Véra as reader Nabokov seems to be endorsing in advance the thesis of Stephen Blackwell's fine *Zina's Paradox: The Figured Reader in Nabokov's* Gift (New York: Peter Lang, 2000), which proposes that Fyodor shapes the novel to position Zina, by now his wife, as his ideal reader.
6. Julian Moynahan, "Cards of Identity," review of Andrew Field, *Nabokov: His Life in Art*, *Partisan Review* (Summer 1968): 487.
7. Julian Moynahan, "Lolita and Related Memories," *Triquarterly* 17 (1970): 251.

5. FROM THE NABOKOV ARCHIVE: NABOKOV'S LITERARY LEGACY

1. Nabokov, "Professor Woodbridge in an Essay on Nature Postulates the Reality of the World," *New York Sun*, December 10, 1940, 15.
2. Nabokov, interview with George Feifer.
3. Unpublished lecture notes, VNA.
4. David Sexton, review of *VNAY*, *Sunday Telegraph*, January 5, 1992.
5. Roger Vila, Charles D. Bell, Richard McNiven, Benjamin Goldman-Huertas, Richard H. Ree, Charles R. Marshall, Zsolt Bálint, Kurt Johnson, Dubi Benyamini, and Naomi E. Pierce, "Phylogeny and Palaeocology of *Polyommatus* Blue Butterflies Show Beringia Was a Climate-Regulated Gateway to the New World," *Proceedings of the Royal Society B* (2011): 1–8, doi: 10.1098/rspb.2010.2213. See this volume, chapter 8, for more information on this research.
6. Nabokov, *Poems and Problems* (New York: McGraw Hill, 1971), 147.
7. Nabokov, *Stikhotvoreniya*, ed. Maria Malikova (St. Petersburg: Akademicheskiy Proekt, 2002); *Sobranie sochineniy russkogo perioda*, 5 vols. (St. Petersburg: Symposium, 1999–2000), *Sobranie sochineniy amerikanskogo perioda*, 5 vols. (St. Petersburg: Symposium, 1999); *Tragediya gospodina Morna, P'esy, Lektsii o drame*, ed. Andrey Babikov (St. Petersburg: Azbuka, 2008).

6. RETROSPECTS AND PROSPECTS

1. D. Barton Johnson, *Worlds in Regression: Some Novels of Vladimir Nabokov* (Ann Arbor, Mich.: Ardis, 1985); Pekka Tammi, *Problems of Nabokov's Poetics* (Helsinki: Suomalainen Tiedeakatemia, 1985); Sergey Davydov, *Teksty-Matryoshki Vladimira Nabokova* (Munich: Otto Sagner, 1982).
2. "Nabokov and *Ada*," Ph.D. dissertation, University of Toronto, 1979; "Nabokov's Philosophical World," *Southern Review* 14 (November 1981): 260–301; *NAPC*, chapters 4–5. In 1977 I sent what became chapters 1 through 5 of *NAPC* to Carl Proffer of Ardis, who sent a copy on to Véra Nabokov.
3. Nabokov, *Stikhi* (Ann Arbor, Mich.: Ardis, 1979), 3.
4. Dana Dragunoiu, *Vladimir Nabokov and the Poetics of Liberalism* (Evanston, Ill.: Northwestern University Press, 2011).
5. Vladimir E. Alexandrov, *Nabokov's Otherworld* (Princeton, N.J.: Princeton University Press, 1991).
6. Michael Wood, *The Magician's Doubts: Nabokov and the Risks of Fiction* (London: Chatto and Windus, 1994), 190.
7. See "Books," *Time*, May 23, 1969, 48–49, available from http://www.time.com /time/magazine/article/0,9171,900891,00.html.
8. I deal with this theme in *On the Origin of Stories: Evolution, Cognition, and Fiction* (Cambridge, Mass.: Belknap Press of Harvard University Press, 2009), chapters 8, 17, and the afterword.
9. From my 1992 review of *Nabokov's Otherworld* (1991), by the most distinguished of such readers, Vladimir Alexandrov:

> But is the "otherworld" Nabokov"s "main theme"? Nabokov himself declared that he "can't find any so-called main ideas, such as that of fate, in my novels." He was interested in the physical world, in the world of heart and mind and imagination, *and* in whatever might lie behind the human mind. To stress one of these as fundamental distorts and reduces Nabokov.
>
> In his introduction, Alexandrov acknowledges that to focus directly on the subject necessarily betrays Nabokov's obliqueness on these matters. But after his fertile, flexible, many-faceted introduction, Alexandrov becomes more rigid and much less sceptical on individual novels than he indicated he should be.
>
> Readers admire Nabokov's gift for vivid detail, his evident love of the things of this world. Alexandrov makes Nabokov out to be a neo-Platonist or almost a Gnostic, who prefers to escape the sordidness of materiality. He makes the "otherworld" a place of first resort rather than, as Nabokov made it, something that might offer an explanation when all others are exhausted.
>
> Take the first novel Alexandrov discusses. Because Luzhin cannot cope with the real world outside the chessboard, Alexandrov singles him out as the man attuned to the otherworld. . . . He overlooks both Luzhin's evident

blindness to most of life and Nabokov's emphatic distinction between chess problem composition, in which an element of timelessness can be achieved, and chess play, where the clock ticks on relentlessly.

When Luzhin leaves an uncompleted chess game in a state of stupor because he can no longer focus on the outside world, he tries to head home. He reaches a river and sees "great female figures" on a bridge. At this point, Alexandrov thinks of "the so-called guardians that heroes in many mythological quests must confront in order to complete their quests. . . . More specifically, the entire ominous realm through which Luzhin passes after the game recalls the Gnostic view of the world of matter as fallen." Alexandrov ignores the point that the statues indicate that this is a specific bridge in Berlin and not the simple bridge by the sawmill near Luzhin's Russian country home, which Luzhin in his confusion hopes to reach.

As he so often does, Alexandrov here disregards the fictional situation and the internal connections of the novel (in this case, a theme of "home" that if examined carefully *does* indicate the possibility of intervention from the beyond). Luzhin's suicide, according to Alexandrov, "seems less the act of a madman than an attempt to transcend an evil realm by releasing the soul from the fetters of the body." Suicide as an ideal, an escape from an evil realm? When Nabokov stresses his "belief in the goodness of man . . . goodness becomes a central and tangible part of one's world . . . This world I said was good" [*LL* 373–75]? Would it not be better to judge the works by their own workings, rather than by an automatic presumption in favor of an "otherworld"?

10. "Prof. Woodbridge in an Essay on Nature Postulates the Reality of the World," *New York Sun*, 10 December 1940, 15.

7. NABOKOV'S AFTERLIFE

1. See especially D. Barton Johnson, *Worlds in Regression: Some Novels of Vladimir Nabokov* (Ann Arbor, Mich.: Ardis, 1985); and Ellen Pifer, *Nabokov and the Novel* (Cambridge, Mass.: Harvard University Press, 1980); and Pifer, "Did She Have a Precursor: *Lolita* and Wharton's *The Children*," in *Nabokov's World*, vol. 2: *Reading Nabokov*, ed. Jane Grayson, Arnold McMillin, and Priscilla Meyer (London: Palgrave/School of Slavonic and East European Studies, 2002), 186–92.

2. Vladimir Nabokov, *The Eye*, trans. Dmitri Nabokov with Vladimir Nabokov (New York: Phaedra, 1965), 10.

8. NABOKOV, LITERATURE, LEPIDOPTERA

1. Ronald Wilkinson, perhaps the foremost recent historian of lepidopterology, had planned in the 1970s and 1980s to republish Nabokov's collected scientific

papers. In the course of the project he wrote this line to Edward Tenner of Princeton University Press (February 16, 1979, Princeton University Press archives).

2. Adalbert Seitz (1860–1938) began publishing his book, *The Butterflies of the World*, the most comprehensive ever attempted, in 1906. A last (sixteenth) installment was published in 1954, but the work was never quite finished.

3. As the lepidopterist Kurt Johnson has remarked to me, "There is no better place to get on a 'thought-wave' that just carries itself" than "out wandering about, collecting."

4. D. Barton Johnson, "The Butterfly in Nabokov's *Eye*," *Nabokov Studies* 4 (1997): 1–14.

5. Alexander B. Klots, *A Field Guide to the Butterflies of North America, East of the Great Plains* (Boston: Houghton Mifflin, 1951), 195, 164. Klots (1903–1989) was a professor of biology at the City College of New York and research associate at the American Museum of Natural History.

6. Kurt Johnson letter to Brian Boyd, July 24, 1995.

7. Diana Butler, "Lolita Lepidoptera," *New World Writing* 16 (1960): 58–84; repr., in *Critical Essays on Vladimir Nabokov*, ed. Phyllis A. Roth (Boston: G. K. Hall, 1984), 59–73, was the first to link the scene where Nabokov captured the female of *Lycaeides sublivens* with the scene in the novel, but she opted to read into the connection a strained symbolic rather than the plain topographical similarity.

8. The chapter in which this exchange occurs was rejected by the *New Yorker* for political reasons: Nabokov's frank criticism of Soviet prisons.

9. Dmitri Nabokov, "On Revisiting Father's Room," in *Vladimir Nabokov: A Tribute*, ed. Peter Quennell (London: Weidenfeld and Nicolson, 1979), 136.

10. Or, in a more explicit earlier formulation, "a seemingly incongruous detail over a seemingly dominant generalization" (*LL* 374).

11. Nabokov, *Stikhi* (Ann Arbor, Mich.: Ardis, 1979), 3.

12. As reported in Strannik (Archbishop Ioann), "Nachalo Nabokoviany," *Russkaya Mysl'*, June 1, 1978, 10.

13. For *The Gift*, see *VNRY* 468–78. I naively assumed *Thecla bieti* an invented butterfly discovered by Fyodor's father; Dieter Zimmer, *A Guide to Nabokov's Butterflies and Moths* (Hamburg: privately printed, 1998), 153, corrects and explains, and Zimmer, *A Guide to Nabokov's Butterflies and Moths 2001* (Hamburg: privately printed, 2001), 152–56, wonderfully expatiates. For *Pale Fire*, see *NPMAD*, chapters 9–10.

14. Nabokov had previously admired Howe's skill as an illustrator of Lepidoptera but was critical of his science (*SL* 367–69), as were many lepidopterists—including some of the volume's contributors—and of his editing of *Butterflies of North America*. But the section on Plebijinae, by Howe, Robert L. Langston, and John C. Downey, was technically one of the best in the book.

15. Kurt Johnson and Steve Coates, *Nabokov's Blues: The Scientific Odyssey of a Literary Genius* (Cambridge, Mass.: Zoland Books, 1999), 87.

16. Johnson and Coates, *Nabokov's Blues*, 87.

17. Johnson and Coates, *Nabokov's Blues*, 84.

18. Johnson and Coates, *Nabokov's Blues*, 89.

19. D. B. Stallings and J. R. Turner, "New American Butterflies," *Canadian Entomologist* 78 (1947): 135.

20. Klots, *A Field Guide*, 164. Klots would later write to William McGuire at Princeton University Press (November 22, 1981): "I know that I (not alone) was a bit worried as to what he might do when I first learned of his intention to work in the butterflies. It would have been so easy for an inspired, but untrained amateur to do a lot of damage that it would take more plodding workers years to repair. . . . I was greatly pleased with the intelligence and thoroughness of his work, which was published in a format that made it usable. (We have gifted amateurs who couldn't be bothered with such things as accurate references and bibliographies.) . . . Certainly we gained from his imaginative ability to see relationships and to trace postulated evolutionary trends. In fact I don't know anybody else who could have done this. . . . My own relations with Nabokov were always cordial. The inaccuracies he pointed out in my Field Guide were just that and needed to be exposed. And [in the 1960s] he very kindly collected for us some species in the south of France that we needed at the Museum."

21. Cyril F. dos Passos, *A Synonymic List of the Nearctic Rhopalocera* (New Haven, Conn.: The Lepidopterists' Society Memoir No. 1, 1964), iv. In a letter to Edward Tenner of Princeton University Press (February 21, 1979), dos Passos commented that Nabokov was "unfortunately not well known to most American entomologists."

22. Downey to Kurt Johnson, August 12, 1996.

23. Reported in Johnson and Coates, *Nabokov's Blues*, 98.

24. Obituary, *Journal of the Lepidopterists' Society*, 34, no. 2 (1980).

25. BB interview with Kurt Johnson, June 1996; Johnson to BB, August 16, 1996.

26. Johnson and Coates, *Nabokov's Blues*, 290.

27. Johnson and Coates, *Nabokov's Blues*, 90.

28. Kurt Johnson and David Matusik, "Five New Species and One New Subspecies of Butterflies from the Sierra de Baorucco of Hispaniola," *Annals of the Carnegie Museum* 57 (1988): 221–54; Albert Schwarz and Kurt Johnson, "Two New Butterflies (Lepidoptera: Lycaenidae) from Cuba," *Caribbean Journal of Science* 28 (1992): 149–57; and D. S. Smith, L. D. Miller and J. Y. Miller, *The Butterflies of the West Indies and South Florida* (Oxford: Oxford University Press, 1994). The preferability of Nabokov's Caribbean terminology to Riley's is summarized most recently in Zsolt Bálint and Kurt Johnson, "Polyommatine Lycaenids

of the Oreal Biome in the Neotropics, Part II: The *Itylos* Section (Lepidoptera: Lycaenidae, Polyommatinae)," *Annales Historico-Naturales Musei Nationalis Hungarici* 86 (1994): 53–77; and Johnson and Coates, *Nabokov's Blues.*

29. Bálint and Johnson, "Polyommatine Lycaenids," 54, 57.

30. Zsolt Bálint, "A Catalogue of Polyommatine Lycaenidae (Lepidoptera) of the Xeromontane Oreal Biome in the Neotropics as Represented in European Collections," *Reports of the Museum of Natural History, University of Wisconsin* 29 (1993): 2.

31. Vladimir Nabokov, "The Nearctic Forms of *Lycaeides* Hüb[ner]. (Lycaenidae, Lepidoptera)," *Psyche* 50 (September–December 1943): 88.

32. Robert Michael Pyle, my coeditor for *Nabokov's Butterflies*, adds the caveat of an experienced field naturalist: "Cladistic analysis sometimes suggests likely paths that might nonetheless be artificial because of plastic characters: exactly why Nabokov would have been likely to have stuck, as other good taxonomists do, to conservative traits observed precisely. Although cladistics uses *more* 'individuating details,' it is far less selective in doing so. Quantity of data is in, the 'good eye' is out."

33. Roger Vila, Charles D. Bell, Richard McNiven, Benjamin Goldman-Huertas, Richard H. Ree, Charles R. Marshall, Zsolt Bálint, Kurt Johnson, Dubi Benyamini, and Naomi E. Pierce, "Phylogeny and Palaeocology of *Polyommatus* Blue Butterflies Show Beringia Was a Climate-Regulated Gateway to the New World," *Proceedings of the Royal Society B* (2011): 1–8, doi: 10.1098/rspb.2010.2213.

34. Personal communication.

35. Kurt Johnson to BB, July 24, 1995.

36. Now considered to be not *Lysandra cormion*, a new species, but a cross between *Lysandra coridon* and *Meleageria daphnis*; see Klaus G. Schurian, "Bemerkungen zu '*Lysandra cormion*' Nabokov 1941 (Lepidoptera: Lycaenidae)," *Nachrichten des entomologischen Vereins Apollo* [Frankfurt] n.s. 10 (1989): 183–92; Schurian, "Nachtrag zu den Bemerkungen zu '*Lysandra cormion*' (Lepidoptera: Lycaenidae)," *Nachrichten des entomologischen Vereins Apollo* [Frankfurt] n.s. 12 (1991): 193–95; and Zimmer, *A Guide* (1998), 53.

37. Edward O. Wilson, *The Diversity of Life* (New York: Norton, 1992), 132–33.

9. NETTING NABOKOV: REVIEW OF DIETER E. ZIMMER, *A GUIDE TO NABOKOV'S BUTTERFLIES AND MOTHS 2001*

1. David Sexton, "The True Loves of Nabokov," review of *Nabokov's Butterflies*, *Evening Standard*, March 20, 2000, 55.

10. THE PSYCHOLOGICAL WORK OF FICTIONAL PLAY

1. Sir Peter Medawar, *Pluto's Republic* (Oxford: Oxford University Press, 1982), 140.
2. Marco Iacoboni, *Mirroring People: The New Science of How We Connect with Others* (New York: Farrar, Straus and Giroux, 2008).
3. Michael Tomasello, *Origins of Human Communication* (Cambridge, Mass.: Bradford/MIT Press, 2008).
4. Lawrence W. Barsalou, "Grounded Cognition," *Annual Review of Psychology* 59 (2008): 617–45.
5. Daniel Goleman, *Social Intelligence: The New Science of Human Relationships* (New York: Bantam, 2006).
6. Barsalou, "Grounded Cognition"; Lisa Aziz-Zadeh et al., "Congruent Embodied Representations for Visually Presented Actions and Linguistic Phrases Describing Actions," *Current Biology* 16 (2006): 1818–23.
7. Frederic C. Bartlett, *Remembering: A Study in Experimental and Social Psychology* (Cambridge: Cambridge University Press, 1932).
8. Daniel L.Schacter and Donna Rose Addis, "The Cognitive Neuroscience of Constructive Memory: Remembering the Past and Imagining the Future," *Philosophical Transactions of the Royal Society B* 362 (2007): 773–86.
9. John Tooby, and Leda Cosmides, "Does Beauty Build Adapted Minds? Toward an Evolutionary Theory of Aesthetics, Fiction, and the Arts," *Substance* 30 (2001): 6–27.
10. See chapter 20; see also Galdys Reichard, Roman Jakobson, and Elizabeth Werth, "Language and Synesthesia" *Word* 5 (August 1949); Richard Cytowic and David Eagleman, *Wednesday Is Indigo Blue: Discovering the Brain of Synesthesia* (Cambridge. Mass.: Bradford/MIT Press, 2009).
11. Rebecca Saxe and Simon Baron-Cohen, *Theory of Mind*, special issue of *Social Neuroscience*, 2006 (Hove, U.K.: Psychology Press, 2007); Dan Sperber, "Metarepresentations in an Evolutionary Perspective," in *Metarepresentations: A Multidisciplinary Perspective*, ed. D. Sperber (Oxford: Oxford University Press, 2000), 117–38.
12. Norman Doidge, *The Brain That Changes Itself: Stories of Personal Triumph from the Frontiers of Brain Science* (New York: Penguin, 2007).
13. See Peter Swirski, *Of Literature and Knowledge: Explorations in Narrative Thought Experiments, Evolution, and Game Theory* (New York, London: Routledge, 2007).

11. STACKS OF STORIES, STORIES OF STACKS

1. Richard Dawkins, *The Ancestor's Tale: A Pilgrimage to the Dawn of Life* (London: Weidenfeld and Nicolson, 2004), 158.

2. Michael Tomasello, quoted in David Sloan Wilson, *Evolution for Everyone: How Darwin's Theory Can Change the Way We Think About Our Lives* (New York: Delacorte, 2007), 169.

3. BB, *On the Origin of Stories: Evolution, Cognition, and Fiction* (Cambridge, Mass.: Belknap Press of Harvard University Press, 2009), 104, citing Michelle Scalise-Sugiyama, "Narrative Theory and Function: Why Evolution Matters," *Philosophy and Literature* 25 (2001): 238.

4. Marek Kohn and Steve Mithen, "Handaxes: Products of Sexual Selection?" *Antiquity* 73 (1999): 518–26.

5. Barry Powell, *Homer and the Origin of the Greek Alphabet* (Cambridge: Cambridge University Press, 1991).

6. "Confabulation" is the filling in by fiction of gaps in our knowledge, most strikingly demonstrated in those who have right-hemisphere strokes that, say, paralyze a limb that the patient's mind refuses to recognize as paralyzed, or those who have had cerebral commisurotomies, severing the corpus callosum that normally acts as the information interchange between the two cerebral hemispheres. When doctors ask stroke victims to move a paralyzed limb or commisurotomy patients to explain why they made a choice in tests where each hemisphere has been offered different information, the left hemisphere immediately invents or confabulates an answer, without the individuals' apparent recognition of their invention. Like the writers of recent "neurofiction," who create characters with conditions like autism, de Clérambault's syndrome, Tourette's syndrome, Nabokov would have been fascinated.

7. Ángel Gurría-Quintana, "Orhan Pamuk: The Art of Fiction Interview No. 187," *Paris Review* 175 (Fall–Winter 2005): 119.

8. Marie Nyreröd, *Ingmar Bergman—3 dokumentärer om film, teater, Fårö och livet,* 2004.

9. Robert Root-Bernstein, "The Art of Innovation: Polymaths and Universality of the Creative Process," in *International Handbook on Innovation,* ed. Larisa Shavinin (Amsterdam: Elsevier), 267–78; Root-Bernstein, "The Sciences and the Arts Share a Common Creative Aesthetic," in *The Elusive Synthesis: Aesthetics and Science,* ed. A. I. Tauber (Dordrecht: Kluwer, 1996), 49–82.

10. Daniel Dennett, *Darwin's Dangerous Idea: Evolution and the Meanings of Life* (London: Penguin, 1996).

12. NABOKOV'S HUMOR

1. Sir Philip Sidney, *A Defence of Poetry,* ed. J. A. Van Dorsten (Oxford: Oxford University Press, 1966), 44.

2. Unpublished letter to Véra Nabokov, 10 January 1924.

13. NABOKOV AS STORYTELLER

1. For the metaphysics, see chapters 6 and 7 and their notes. Among work on Nabokov's morals, see Ellen Pifer, *Nabokov and the Novel* (Cambridge, Mass.: Harvard University Press, 1980); Boyd, *NAPC*; Leona Toker, *Nabokov: The Mystery of Literary Structures* (Ithaca, N.Y.: Cornell University Press, 1989); and Richard Rorty, "The Barber of Kasbeam: Nabokov on Cruelty," in *Contingency, Irony, and Solidarity* (Cambridge: Cambridge University Press, 1989), 141–68.

2. D. Barton Johnson and Brian Boyd, "Prologue: The Otherworld," in *Nabokov's World*, vol. 1: *The Shape of Nabokov's World*, ed. Jane Grayson, Arnold McMillin, and Priscilla Meyer (London: Palgrave/School of Slavonic and East European Studies, 2002), 18–25; also see this volume, chapter 7.

3. For a particularly comprehensive and subtle but uninvitingly formalistic analysis of Nabokovian narrative, see Pekka Tammi, *Problems of Nabokov's Poetics* (Helsinki: Suomalainen Tiedeakatemia, 1985).

4. Letter to Katharine White, March 17, 1951: "Most of the stories I am contemplating (and some I have written in the past . . .) will be composed on these lines, according to this system wherein a second (main) story is woven into, or placed behind, the superficial semitransparent one" (*SL* 117).

5. For Nabokov's brief but important references to preparation and transition as items in the storyteller's toolkit, see his "Commentary to Eugene Onegin," *EO* 3.80; *SIC* 10; *LL* 151; *LRL* 73.

6. See Josef Perner, *Understanding the Representational Mind* (Cambridge, Mass.: Bradford/MIT Press, 1991), and Dan Sperber, ed., *Metarepresentations: A Multidisciplinary Perspective* (Oxford: Oxford University Press, 2000).

7. Nabokov, *Mary*, trans. Dmitri Nabokov with Vladimir Nabokov (New York: McGraw-Hill, 1970), 1.

8. Helmut Bonheim, *The Narrative Modes: Techniques of the Short Story* (Woodbridge, Suffolk: D. S. Brewer, 1982).

9. Dieter E. Zimmer argues that the ordered sequence of Ganin's recollections in *Mary* reflect a psychological truth in line with F. C. Bartlett's 1932 demonstration of memory as "constructional" ("*Mary*," in *The Garland Companion to Vladimir Nabokov*, ed. Vladimir E. Alexandrov [New York: Garland, 1995], 354–55). But this seriously misreads Bartlett. The mind does reconstruct memories as they emerge into consciousness rather than upload exactly from a veridical databank, but memory does not and could not suppress details as they emerge to consciousness in order to recollect them only in the correct sequence. Nabokov does explain Ganin's deliberate private reconstruction of his past with Mary in order to motivate the narrative sequence (*Mary*, 33), but he carries on the orderly retelling of Ganin's past even unprompted by Ganin's memory (*Mary*, 99–102), only to provide an after-the-fact motivation

in terms of memories that are explicitly not orderly: "All this now unfolded in his memory, flashing disjointedly, and shrank again into a warm lump when Podtyagin, with a great effort, asked him 'How long ago did you leave Russia?'" (*Mary*, 102).

10. The text should read "passions," as here and in the manuscript in VNA, not "passing" as in the published version.

11. See my analysis of this layering of past on past in the afterword to *Ada* (London: Penguin, 1999), rpt., in *NAPC*.

14. NABOKOV'S TRANSITION FROM RUSSIAN TO ENGLISH: REPUDIATION OR EVOLUTION?

1. Alexander A. Dolinin, "Nabokov as a Russian Writer," in *Cambridge Companion to Vladimir Nabokov*, ed. Julian Connolly (Cambridge: Cambridge University Press, 2005), 49–64; hereafter cited by page number in the text.

2. "Anniversary Notes," Supplement to *Triquarterly* 17 (1970); reprinted in *SO*.

3. Boyd, *Vladimir Nabokov: Russkie gody*, trans. Galina Lapina (Moscow and St. Petersburg: Nezavisimaya Gazeta and Symposium, 2001), 470. Martin Amis and I agreed, after an April 1999 talk at the Town Hall in New York in which he had named Nabokov rather than Joyce his novelist of the century, that *Ulysses* was the greatest single novel of the century but, as Martin added and I concurred, it has its longueurs.

4. See *KQK* x; *LL* 144, 147; VN to Mark Aldanov, May 6, 1942, Bakhmeteff Collection, Columbia University Library.

5. On *Hamlet* as a "miracle," see unpublished lecture notes, cited in *VNAY* 100; and on its not being "flawless," see unpublished lectures notes for Russian Survey course, VNA.

6. Véra Nabokov to Rebekka Candreia, December 29, 1966, VNA.

7. Nabokov, *Glory*, trans. Dmitri Nabokov with Vladimir Nabokov (New York: McGraw-Hill, 1971), x–xi.

8. Nabokov, *Mary*, trans. Dmitri Nabokov with Vladimir Nabokov (New York: McGraw-Hill, 1970), xii.

9. Nabokov to Guggenheim Foundation, October 8, 1951, VNA.

10. Nabokov to Elena Sikorskiy, October 25, 1945, in *Perepiska s sestroy* (Ann Arbor, Mich.: Ardis, 1985), 18; *SO* 89, 190; *PP* 14.

11. Another claim Dolinin makes is that he de-Russianized his Russian works, sometimes substituting for Russian references in the originals English or "international" references. But Nabokov had done the same in translating Romain Rolland's *Colas Breugnon* from French into Russian in 1922 as *Nikolka Persik* or in translating his own *Lolita* from English into Russian in the early 1960s. For the former example, see Stanislav Shvabrin, "Vladimir Nabokov

as Translator: The Multilingual Works of the Russian Period," Ph.D. diss., UCLA. 2007: "Nabokov amplifies the 'Russianness' of *Nikolka Persik* not only by means of addition, but also by means of subtraction" (146); Shvabrin characterizes Nabokov's practice, as early as 1922, as "resolute imaginative conversion of the traits peculiar to the native literary tradition to those specific to the literary tradition active in the target language" (180).

12. Andrew Field, *Nabokov: Life in Art* (Boston: Little, Brown, 1967), 381; *VNAY* 515–16.

13. Unpublished, from Lectures on Russian Literature MS, VNA.

14. Unpublished letter, Nabokov to Andrew Field, September 26, 1966, VNA.

15. Nabokov responded after reading the book at the galley stage: "A marvelous achievement . . . and a fascinating story": unpublished letter, Nabokov to Field, February 3, 1967, VNA.

16. Unpublished lecture for Russian Survey course, VNA.

17. Unpublished letter, Véra Nabokov to Heinrich-Maria Ledwig Rowohlt, January 30, 1966, VNA: "The translator should follow faithfully the English text [of *The Gift*], and the English text only. Whenever there is a discrepancy between the English and the Russian texts, it was done by my husband himself quite deliberately."

18. Daniil Pasmanik, cited in *VNRY* 156.

19. *Daily Dispatch and Manchester Morning Chronicle*, March 31, 1922, 6; *VNRY* 34.

20. Among other ideas Nabokov may have found congenial were Spencer's stress on benevolent design and Haeckel's stress on monism and on evolution's achieving artistic perfection.

21. Nabokov, "The Lermontov Mirage," *Russian Review* 1, no. 1 (1941): 32.

22. Nabokov, "The Lermontov Mirage," 32.

23. Unpublished lectures for Russian Survey course, VNA.

24. Unpublished lectures for Russian Survey course, VNA.

25. Unpublished lectures for Russian Survey course, VNA.

26. Unpublished lectures for Russian Survey course, VNA.

27. Unclear in original; perhaps "considerations."

28. Unpublished lectures for Russian Survey course, VNA.

29. In original, "stops to be."

30. Unpublished lectures for Russian Survey course, VNA.

31. Also known as "Russian Writers, Censors, and Readers" (*LRL*).

32. Nabokov, *The Eye*, trans. Dmitri Nabokov with Vladimir Nabokov (New York: Phaedra, 1965), 8; *Gift* 9, *Glory*, xii.

33. Boyd, *Russkie gody*, 284, 328.

34. Among the challenges to Joyce: a portrait of an artist as a young man, providing ample rather than insufficient evidence of the artist's artistic growth, even to the point where he writes the work in question; close confinement in a

closely observed city and a natural motivation for fabulous voyages beyond; and a subtle Odyssean parallel, a son brooding on his father's apparent failure to return from distant voyages, and his search for him, incorporated within the story rather than imposed from without. Among the challenges to Proust: lost time regained both in small witty ways throughout the course of the story and unexpectedly at a higher level and to a deeper degree at the end of the work, and assertion of the significance of voluntary over involuntary memory.

15. NABOKOV, PUSHKIN, SHAKESPEARE: GENIUS, GENEROSITY, AND GRATITUDE IN *THE GIFT* AND *PALE FIRE*

1. For excellent discussions of the presence of Pushkin in *The Gift*, which, however, come short of identifying Pushkin as part of the fate Fyodor senses surrounding him, see Simon Karlinsky, "Vladimir Nabokov's Novel *Dar* as a Work of Literary Criticism: A Structural Analysis," *Slavonic and East European Journal* 7 (1963): 284–96; Sergei Davydov, "Weighing Nabokov's *Gift* on Pushkin's Scales," in *Cultural Mythologies of Russian Modernism: From the Golden Age to the Silver Age*, ed. Boris Gasparov et al. (Berkeley: University of California Press, 1992), 419–30; Davydov, "Nabokov and Pushkin," in *The Garland Companion to Vladimir Nabokov*, ed. Vladimir Alexandrov (New York: Garland, 1995), 482–96.; and Alexander Dolinin, "*The Gift*," in *The Garland Companion to Vladimir Nabokov*, ed. Vladimir E. Alexandrov (New York: Garland, 1995), 135–69; and the first of his "Tri zametki o romane Vladimira Nabokova 'Dar,'" in *V. V. Nabokov: Pro et Contra*, ed. B. Averin, Maria Malikova, and T. Smirnova (St. Petersburg: Russkiy Khristianskiy Gumanitarniy Institut, 1997), 697–740.
2. Pushkin (1828), *Sobranie sochineniy v desyati tomakh*, vol.2: *Stikhotvoreniya 1824–1836* (Moscow: Pravda, 1981), 125 (translation by BB). Dolinin, "*The Gift*," 166n. 29. Dolinin follows "*dar*" as a theme throughout the novel, in its relation to Pushkin and Lermontov and to Dovid Knut and Adamovich in "Tri zametki," and shows that Nabokov all but explicitly had "Dar naprasnyy, dar sluchaynyy" in mind at the end of the "Vtoroe dopolnenie k 'Daru'" (698n).
3. See Davydov, "Weighing Nabokov's *Gift*," 420.
4. Cf. Clarence Brown, "Nabokov's Pushkin and Nabokov's Nabokov," in *Nabokov: The Man and His Work*, ed. L. S. Dembo (Madison: University of Wisconsin Press, 1967), 207: "Fate and Pushkin are identical. Pushkin is Nabokov's fate." Brown means this, though, in a different sense from mine.
5. Unpublished lecture notes, VNA.

16. NABOKOV AS VERSE TRANSLATOR: INTRODUCTION TO *VERSES AND VERSIONS*

1. To follow the lead of Nabokov (see below) and the lilt of his friend Dr. Seuss. Nabokov met Theodore Seuss Geisel at a writers conference in Utah in the summer of 1949. During the conference, "Dr. Seuss" wrote a butterfly poem for Nabokov; years later, in *Horton Hears a Who!* (1954), he introduced an incidental "black-bottomed eagle named Vlad Vlad-i-koff," after Vladimir Vladimirovich Nabokoff (as Nabokov once spelled his name).
2. Page a Day Diary, November 11, 1958, VNA.
3. Jason Epstein to VN, December 2, 1958, VNA.
4. VéN to Jason Esptein, January 18, 1959, VNA.
5. VN to Jason Epstein, June 6, 1959, VNA.
6. VéN to Ray Mantle, October 22, 1968, VNA.
7. Cited in Ljuba Tarvi, *Comparative Translation Assessment: Quantifying Quality* (Helsinki: University of Helsinki, 2004), 230.
8. I kicked myself when, after the publication of *Verses and Versions*, while writing obituaries for both Alfred Appel Jr., and Simon Karlinsky, I came across Nabokov's translation of a four-line poem by Marina Tsvetaeva that I should have noted or recalled in time. Appel and Karlinsky coedited a special issue of *Triquarterly* (27–28 [1973]), published in book form as *The Bitter Air of Exile: Russian Writers in the West, 1922–1972* (Berkeley: University of California Press, 1973). Nabokov knew both editors and, recalling Karlinsky's book on Tsvetaeva, translated for him, on November 12, 1972, this verse, the last quatrain of an untitled poem (first line, "Moim stiham, napisannym tak rano," "To my poems composed so early"), which Tsvetaeva composed in 1913 (*Bitter Air*, 93):

    Amidst the dust of bookshops, wide dispersed
    And never purchased there by anyone,
    Yet similar to precious wines, my verse
    Can wait: its turn shall come.

9. Tarvi, *Comparative Translation*, 228.
10. In Tarvi, *Comparative Translation*, 234.
11. Douglas Hofstadter, *Le Ton beau de Marot* (New York: Basic Books, 1997), 548, 268, 270, 269.
12. Unpublished. From TS note, VNA, which may have been the beginning of a talk that Nabokov was invited to delivered to the English Institute on September 14, 1954, as he wrote Edmund Wilson on July 30, "on the Art of Translation" (*DBDV* 317).
13. Nabokov, "Problems of Translation: 'Onegin' in English," *Partisan Review* 22 (1955): 498.

14. Elaine Feinstein, ed., *After Pushkin* (London: Folio Society, 1999), 18.

15. Alexander Zholkovsky, " 'Ya vas lyubil . . .' Pushkina: invarianty i struktura" (Pushikin's "I loved you . . . ": variants and structure), http://college.usc.edu /alik/rus/ess/bib21.html.

17. TOLSTOY AND NABOKOV

1. *LRL* manuscript, VNA.

2. Gary Saul Morson, *Hidden in Plain View: Narrative and Creative Potentials in War and Peace* (Stanford, Calif.: Stanford University Press, 1987).

3. Unpublished letter, Nabokov to Mark Aldanov, May 6, 1942, Bakhmeteff Collection, Columbia University.

4. *LRL* manuscript, VNA.

5. Unpublished Russian survey course lecture, VNA.

6. I have placed this word in square brackets, because the Russian *"ekonomka"* can be translated only as "housekeeper," but does not belong to the *dom* (house, home)—*domochadtsy* (household) pattern I have translated via the English "house."

7. Cited in Richard F. Gustafson, *Leo Tolstoy: Resident and Stranger* (Princeton, N.J.: Princeton University Press, 1986), 3:53, 94.

8. National Educational Television interview with Robert Hughes, 1965.

9. John Bayley, *Tolstoy and the Novel* (1966; Chicago: University of Chicago Press, 1988), 242.

10. Stephen Jay Gould, *Bully for Brontosaurus: Further Reflections in Natural History* (Harmondsworth: Penguin, 1992), 476.

11. Leona Toker, *Nabokov: The Mystery of Literary Structures* (Ithaca, N.Y.: Cornell University Press, 1989), 198–227.

12. Bayley, *Tolstoy and the Novel*, 207.

13. Roman Jakobson and Morris Halle, *Fundamentals of Language* (The Hague: Mouton, 1956).

14. Quoted in Gary Adelman, *Anna Karenina: The Bitterness of Ecstasy* (Boston: Twayne, 1990), 109.

15. Craig Raine, "Craig Raine Fondles Vladimir Nabokov," *London Review of Books*, May 14, 1992, 6.

16. Isaiah Berlin, *The Hedgehog and the Fox: An Essay on Tolstoy's View of History* (1953; New York: Simon and Schuster, 1967).

18. NABOKOV AND MACHADO DE ASSIS

1. Joaquím Maria Machado de Assis, *The Posthumous Memoirs of Brás Cubas* (1881), trans. Gregory Rabassa. New York: Oxford University Press, 1997; hereafter, *BC*.

2. Joaquím Maria Machado de Assis, *Dom Casmurro* (1899), trans. John Gledson (New York: Oxford University Press, 1997), 186; hereafter *DC*.

3. Joaquím Maria Machado de Assis, *Quincas Borba* (1891), trans. Gregory Rabassa (New York: Oxford University Press, 1998), 102; hereafter *QB*.

4. Joaquím Maria Machado de Assis, *The Devil's Church and Other Stories*, trans. Jack Schmitt and Lorie Ishimatsua (Austin: University of Texas Press, 1984), 102–3; hereafter *DCh*.

5. Joaquim Maria Machado de Assis, *Obras Completa*, 3 vols. (Rio de Janeiro: Editora José Aguilar, 1962), 3:398, cited in Maria Manuel Lisboa, "Machado de Assis and the Beloved Reader: Squatters in the Text," in *Scarlet Letters: Fictions of Adultery from Antiquity to the 1990s*, ed. Nicholas White and Naomi Segal (New York: St Martin's Press, 1997), 160.

6. Unpublished lecture on Soviet drama, VNA.

7. Not "passing," as *MUSSR* incorrectly transcribes.

8. "Actually, of course, any genuinely new trend is a knight's move, a change of shadows, a shift that displaces the mirror" (*Gift* 239).

9. For this at the cultural level, see chapter 14.

10. Cited by Helen Caldwell, *The Brazilian Othello of Machado de Assis* (Berkeley and Los Angeles: University of California Press), 1960, 150.

11. Nabokov wrote "between the author and the world," but corrected this in memory in *SO* 183 to "between the author and the reader."

19. *SPEAK, MEMORY:* THE LIFE AND THE ART

1. See my "In Memory of Simon Karlinsky," *The Nabokovian* 63 (Fall 2009): 7–14.

22. EVEN HOMAIS NODS: NABOKOV'S FALLIBILITY; OR, HOW TO REVISE *LOLITA*

1. From Nabokov's pseudo-review of *Conclusive Evidence*, intended at the time of writing to form a sixteenth chapter in the book version, but then omitted; published in *SM* 1999.

2. "'And there happening through the whole kingdom of Bohemia, to be no seaport town whatever'
   "'How the deuce could there—Trim?' cried my uncle Toby; 'for Bohemia being totally inland, it could have happened no otherwise.'
   "'—It might,' said Trim, 'if it had pleased God'" (Sterne, *Tristram Shandy*, book 8, chap. 19).

3. There were a couple of occasions when Bohemia had a brief toe hold on the Adriatic, in the thirteenth and sixteenth centuries, and Shakespeare's source

for *The Winter's Tale*, Robert Greene's *Pandosto* (1588), did once mention the coast of Bohemia. But Greene does not make it a turning point of the plot, as Johnson observes Shakespeare has made it.

4. Ably exposed by Richard Levin in *New Readings vs. Old Plays* (Chicago: University of Chicago Press, 1979) and many subsequent articles, most collected in *Looking for an Argument: Critical Encounters with the New Approaches to the Criticism of Shakespeare and His Contemporaries* (Madison, N.J.: Fairleigh Dickinson University Press, 2003).

5. Elizabeth Bruss, *Autobiographical Acts: The Changing Situation of a Literary Genre* (Baltimore, Md.: Johns Hopkins University Press, 1976), 145–46; Christina Tekiner, "Time in *Lolita*," *Modern Fiction Studies* 25 (1979): 463–69; Leona Toker, *Nabokov: The Mystery of Literary Structures* (Ithaca, N.Y.: Cornell University Press, 1989), 198–227, esp. 208–11, quotation at 209; Alexander Dolinin, "Dvoinoe vremia u Nabokova: ot *Dara* k *Lolite*," revised in "Nabokov's Time Doubling: From *The Gift* to *Lolita*," *Nabokov Studies* 2 (1995): 3–40 (see his n. 1); Julian Connolly, "'Nature's Reality' or Humbert's 'Fancy'? Scenes of Reunion and Murder in *Lolita*," *Nabokov Studies* 2 (1995): 41–61; Dieter Zimmer, in a forthcoming limited edition, to be published in Switzerland, of the German *Lolita* (personal communication); Barbara Wyllie, "'Guilty of Killing Quilty': The Central Dilemma of Nabokov's *Lolita*," NABOKV-L, November 21, 1994.

6. Note in *Conclusive Evidence* MS, VNA, cited *VNAY* 147.

7. VN to Morris Bishop, October 12, 1947 (marked "46"), VNA.

8. Nabokov, *A Russian Beauty and Other Stories* (New York: McGraw-Hill, 1973), 220.

9. Interview of June 28, 1979.

10. Cf. Maurice Couturier, *Textual Communication: A Print-Based Theory of the Novel* (London: Routledge, 1991), 89.

11. Nabokov, *Ada oder Das Verlangen*, trans. Uwe Friesel and Marianne Therstappen (Reinbek: Rowohlt, 1974).

12. Nabokov, *Ada ou l'ardeur*, trans. Gilles Chahine with Jean-Bernard Blandenier (Paris: Fayard, 1975).

13. Cf. my "Annotations to *Ada*, 2: Part 1 Chapter 2," *Nabokovian* 31 (1993): 39, and *Ada*Online.

14. MSS, VNA.

15. Tekiner, "Time in *Lolita*," 468, writes however that "the chronology implies that Humbert is in jail for his actions toward Lolita, rather than Quilty," but does not explain how or why Humbert has been tracked down or at what point before the supposed arrest for his treatment of Lolita (an arrest, of course, entirely without textual foundation) he began, as this conjecture would require, to suppress what was really happening to him, or why the conjecture does not square with the foreword (see below). Toker, *Nabokov: The Mystery*,

218, suggests as one possibility (though she seems to prefer another) that "Humbert may have been arrested on the same day, almost immediately after reading Dolly's letter, and placed in a psychiatric ward 'for observation' . . . prior to being scheduled for trial," but though she rules out the murder of Quilty she does not suggest why he is being tried.

16. Nabokov, *Lolita*, trans. into French by Eric Kahane (Paris: Gallimard, 1959).

17. Nabokov, *Lolita*, trans. Vladimir Nabokov (New York: Phaedra, 1967), p. 245.

18. Gennady Barabtarlo, *Aerial View: Essays on Nabokov's Art and Metaphysics* (New York: Peter Lang, 1993), 135–38. The dates become more specific for several reasons: Nabokov's style evolved consistently towards greater chronological detail; he felt he needed to identify for Russian readers in the late 1960s a period that was more self-evident to the Americans for whom he was writing in the early 1950s; and to correct inconsistencies he had noticed.

19. Dolinin, "Dvoinoe vremia u Nabokova," 39.

20. Tekiner, "Time in *Lolita*," 468. Nabokov's reason for having Ray not mention murder, of course, is to avoid spoiling the sublime surprise of Humbert's first page: "You can always count on a murderer for a fancy prose style" (11).

21. Connolly, "'Nature's Reality,'" 45.

22. Toker, *Nabokov: The Mystery*, 210, realizes the awkwardness of the screenplay to her case, but rules it out as "a totally new work. . . . The screenplay, therefore, cannot be used to settle moot points in the novel." It is indeed, as Nabokov says, "a vivacious variant" (*LAS* xiii) on the novel, not a bland transposition, but as the examples will make clear, the screenplay strives even in its changes to be true to the novel.

23. Toker is particularly confused. According to her version, Humbert does not plan ahead; his slightly reformed feelings for Lolita develop only as he suddenly begins to fantasize, from the point he writes about receiving Lolita's letter to the end of his composing the narrative (*Nabokov: The Mystery*, 211, 217, 218). But in that case Humbert does not discover who Quilty is until he writes the Coalmont scene, yet at the very moment she tells him who her abductor was, he comments: "Quietly the fusion took place, and everything fell into order, into the pattern of branches that I have woven throughout this memoir with the express purpose of having the ripe fruit fall at the right moment" (*Lolita* 274). In other words, he has planned Quilty's peek-a-boo presence from the first.

24. Tekiner, "Time in *Lolita*," 466 (followed by Connolly, "'Nature's Reality,'" 51–52), suggests that Humbert identifies Quilty from *Who's Who in the Limelight* in the psychiatric institution where—according to her—Humbert writes up his manuscript. (Rejecting the murder, Tekiner, "Time in *Lolita*," 468, rules out prison but does not explain why Humbert suddenly finds himself in a psychiatric institution, when his life with Rita seems perfectly stable; Dolinin is convinced that Humbert is happily sitting in his study, hoodwinking the

reader.) Why Humbert should have read through the thousands of entries in *Who's Who in the Limelight* and realized the relevance of the brief Quilty entry, when he has for years come nowhere near to suspecting Quilty, seems anything but clear. True, Lolita did lie that "Quilty" was the "gal author" (*Lolita* 223), but why would Humbert persist in reading through a fat biographical tome until he found this one clue when he had never made any connection between Lolita's disappearance and the playwright of the play in which she was to star?

25. Dolinin, "Dvoinoe vremia u Nabokova," 37.
26. Quilty, of course, has posed as Lolita's uncle in taking her from the Elphinstone hospital.
27. He has: and that description on p. 243 confirms the equation between Elphinstone and the vista of the moral apotheosis.

23. LITERATURE, PATTERN, *LOLITA*; OR, ART, LITERATURE, SCIENCE

1. William Deresiewicz, "Professing Literature in 2008," *The Nation*, March 24, 2008, http://www.thenation.com/article/professing-literature-2008; also see *Critical Inquiry* Symposium Special Issue, *Critical Inquiry* 30 (2004); Louis Menand, "Dangers Within and Without," *Profession* (2005): 10–17.

2. See, for instance, Patrick Colm Hogan, *The Mind and Its Stories: Narrative Universals and Human Emotion* (Cambridge: Cambridge University Press, 2003); Joseph Carroll, *Literary Darwinism: Evolution, Human Nature, and Literature* (New York: Routledge, 2004); Jonathan Gottschall and David Sloan Wilson, eds., *The Literary Animal: Evolution and the Nature of Narrative* (Evanston, Ill.: Northwestern University Press, 2005); Marcus Nordlund, *Shakespeare and the Nature of Love: Literature, Culture, and Evolution* (Evanston, Ill.: Northwestern University Press, 2007); David Bordwell, *Poetics of Cinema* (New York: Routledge, 2008); Jonathan Gottschall, *The Rape of Troy: Evolution, Violence, and the World of Homer* (Cambridge: Cambridge University Press, 2008); Gottschall, *Literature, Science, and a New Humanities* (New York: Palgrave, 2008); Edward Slingerland, *What Science Has to Offer the Humanities* (Cambridge: Cambridge University Press, 2008); Denis Dutton, *The Art Instinct: Beauty, Pleasure, and Evolution* (New York: Bloomsbury, 2009); Brian Boyd, *On the Origin of Stories: Evolution, Cognition, and Fiction* (Cambridge, Mass.: Belknap Press of Harvard University Press, 2009); Harold Fromm, *The Nature of Being Human: From Environmentalism to Consciousness* (Baltimore, Md.: Johns Hopkins University Press, 2009); Blakey Vermeule, *Why Do We Care About Literary Characters?* (Baltimore, Md.: Johns Hopkins University Press, 2009); Brian Boyd, Joseph Carroll, and Jonathan Gottschall, eds., *Evolution, Literature, and Film: A Reader* (New York: Columbia University Press, 2010).

3. The term was coined by John Tooby and Irwin DeVore, "The Reconstruction of Hominid Behavioral Evolution Through Strategic Modelling," in *The Evolution of Human Behavior: Primate Models*, ed. W. G. Kinzey (Albany: State University of New York Press, 1987), 183–237.

4. Daniel Goleman, *Social Intelligence: The New Science of Human Relationships* (New York: Bantam, 2006), 361; Ellen Dissanayake, *Art and Intimacy: How the Arts Began* (Seattle: University of Washington Press, 2000), 29.

5. Stephen Jay Gould, *The Flamingo's Smile: Reflections in Natural History* (New York: Norton, 1985), 199; Gould, *Bully for Brontosaurus: Further Reflections in Natural History* (Harmondsworth: Penguin, 1992), 268, also supplies the Purcell quotation.

6. Robert Solso, *Cognition and the Visual Arts* (Cambridge, Mass.: Bradford/MIT, 1994), 52.

7. John Sloboda, "Power of Music," *New Scientist*, November 29, 2003, 38.

8. Brian Sutton-Smith, *The Folk-Stories of Children* (Philadelphia: University of Pennsylvania Press, 1981), 53–54.

9. Sutton-Smith, *The Folk-Stories of Children*, 110–11.

10. See, for instance, Lisa Aziz-Zadeh et al., "Congruent Embodied Representations for Visually Presented Actions and Linguistic Phrases Describing Actions," *Current Biology* 16 (2006): 1818–23.

11. See Alfred, Lord Tennyson, "The Marriage of Geraint" (1857), ll. 184–86: "And while they listened for the distant hunt, / And chiefly for the baying of Cavall, / King Arthur's hound of deepest mouth" (*The Poems of Tennyson*, ed. Christopher Ricks, 2nd ed. [London: Longman, 1987], 3:330). Although the detail derives ultimately from the tale of "Geraint the Son of Erbin" in the *Mabinogion*, Nabokov may have encountered it in Thomas Bulfinch, *The Age of Chivalry and The Legends of Charlemagne, or Romance of the Middle Ages* (1858; New York: New American Library, 1962), 229: "Now this is how Arthur hunted the stag. The men and the dogs were divided into hunting-parties, and the dogs were let loose upon the stag. And the last dog that was let loose was the favorite dog of Arthur; Cavall was his name. And he left all the other dogs behind him and turned the stag."

12. Ovid, *Metamorphoses*, trans. Frank Justus Miller (Cambridge, Mass.: Harvard Univ. Press, 1921), 3.206–8.

13. James R. Flynn, *What Is Intelligence? Beyond the Flynn Effect* (Cambridge: Cambridge University Press, 2007).

24. "PALE FIRE": POEM AND PATTERN

1. Ron Rosenbaum to Mo Cohen, June 7, 2010.

2. Alvin Kernan, "Reading Zemblan: The Audience Disappears in Nabokov's *Pale Fire*" (1982), in *Vladimir Nabokov: Modern Critical Views*, ed. Harold Bloom

(New York: Chelsea House, 1987), 106. Shade's image strikingly recalls an even more extended image that the narrator Fyodor Godunov-Cherdyntsev paraphrases from a *Discourse on Shades* by the invented French thinker Pierre Delalande, in Nabokov's last Russian novel, *The Gift*: "I know that death in itself is in no way connected with the topography of the hereafter, for a door is merely the exit from the house and not a part of its surroundings, like a tree or a hill. One has to get out somehow, 'but I refuse to see in a door more than a hole, and a carpenter's job' (*Delalande, Discours sur les ombres*, p. 45). And then again: the unfortunate image of a 'road' to which the human mind has become accustomed (life as a kind of journey) is a stupid illusion: we are not going anywhere, we are sitting at home. The other world surrounds us always and is not at all at the end of some pilgrimage. In our earthly house, windows are replaced by mirrors; the door, until a given time, is closed; but air comes in through the cracks" (*Gift*, 321–22).

3. Ángel Gurría-Quintana, "Orhan Pamuk: The Art of Fiction Interview No. 187," *Paris Review* 175 (Fall–Winter 2005): 139–40.

4. Peter Atkins, *Galileo's Finger: The Ten Great Ideas of Science* (Oxford: Oxford University Press, 2003), 139.

5. Helen Vendler, *The Art of Shakespeare's Sonnets* (Cambridge, Mass.: Belknap Press of Harvard University Press, 1997), 29, xvii, 12, 28, 31.

6. See D. Barton Johnson, "A Field Guide to Nabokov's *Pale Fire*: Waxwings and the Red Admiral," in *The Real Life of Pierre Delalande: Studies in Russian and Comparative Literature to Honor Alexander Dolinin*, 2 vols., ed. David M. Bethea, Lazar Fleishman, and Alexander Ospovat (Stanford: Stanford University Press, 2007), 2:652–73.

7. The words Hazel asks her parents to gloss, "grimpen," "chthonic," and "sempiternal," identify what Shade dismisses as "some phony modern poem that was said / In English Lit to be a document 'Engahzay and compelling'—what this meant / Nobody cared" (*PF* 46). For more on Shade's polemical engagement with Eliot, see *NPFMAD*. For Nabokov's, see his chapter "First Poem" (written in July–August 1948), which in the first version of his autobiography contains this passage: "For I did not know [as a poet in his mid-teens] that beyond the archipelago there was the continent; that beyond mere verse, rime-bangled or blank, fettered or free, falsely clear or falsely recondite (concealing triteness beneath *ashen* obscurities—the *waste* product of some recognized religion) there existed a Russian prose which borrowed its romantic sweep from science and its terse precision from poetry" (*CE* 158; italics added); see also the parodies of "Gerontion" and "Ash Wednesday" in *Lolita*, and more jabs in *Ada*. Interestingly, although Shade singles out three rare words as a means of referring obliquely but unequivocally to Eliot, his diction in "Pale Fire" is actually more diverse than Eliot's in *Four Quartets*: 369

unique words per 1,000, versus 287 unique words per 1,000 for *Four Quartets* (2,821 types [different words] in the 7,632 tokens [occurrences of any word] of Shade's poem, 1,937 types in the 6,732 tokens of Eliot's), and despite the apparent homeliness of Shade's poem and the foregrounded exoticism and stylistic innovation in Eliot's.

8. Kathleen Raine, *The Collected Poems of Kathleen Raine* (Washington, D.C.: Counterpoint, 2001).

9. "Transformation . . . Transformation is a marvelous thing," Nabokov used to tell his students: see *N'sBs* 472.

10. As first noted by Johnson, "A Field Guide to Nabokov's *Pale Fire*," 2:652–73.

11. http://www.birds.cornell.edu/AllAboutBirds/BirdGuide/Wood_Duck_dtl .html.

12. Nabokov, *Speak, Memory: An Autobiography Revised*, ed. Brian Boyd (New York: Knopf, 1999), 248.

13. Nabokov, *Speak, Memory: An Autobiography Revised*, 250.

14. Robert Michael Pyle (personal communication).

15. Better known as the West Virginia White, *Pieris virginiensis*; see *NPFMAD* 135–37.

16. Note the species names: the Toothwort White is *Pieris virginiensis* (Hazel, like Lucette in *Ada*, drowns herself because she feels doomed to remain a *virgin*); the wood duck is *Aix sponsa*, *sponsa* meaning "bride."

25. *ADA:* THE BOG AND THE GARDEN; OR, STRAW, FLUFF, AND PEAT: SOURCES AND PLACES IN *ADA*

1. Paul H. Fry, "Moving Van: The Neverland Veens of Nabokov's *Ada*," *Contemporary Literature* 26, no. 2 (1985): 123–39; Wilma Siccama and Jack van der Weide, "Een sleutel in Meppel: Nederlandse aantekeningen bij Vladimir Nabokovs *Ada*," *Maatstaf* 6 (1995): 17–27.

2. Nicolas Freeling, *Double-Barrel* (London: Victor Gollancz, 1964). Citations will be from the Penguin edition (Harmondsworth: 1967), hereafter *DB*. Nabokov "rediscovered" the surname because "there was a Cornell professor van Veen whose name was painted on the letterbox of a home in Highland Road, Cayuga Heights, Ithaca, when Nabokov was living further along Highland Road in 1957" (BB, "Annotations to *Ada* 1: Part 1 Chapter 1," *The Nabokovian* 30 [Spring 1993]: 26); also see *Ada*Online.

3. *Time*, August 4, 2003, 12.

4. The Nabokov summer estates of Vyra, Rozhdestveno, and Batovo were surrounded by bogs and by places whose names reflected that terrain, like Gryazno ("Muddy," a village just to the north of Vyra: see Nabokov's not-always-reliable map in *SM*), Chornaya Rechka ("Black Brook," after its peaty

water), Gryaznaya ("Muddy," again: the sluggish short river running past the Rozhdestveno manor). See Dmitri Ryabov, *Toponimiya Verkhnego Pooredezh'ya: Slovar'-spravochnik* (St. Petersburg: Muzey-usad'ba "Rozhdestveno," 1995).

5. Which makes him sound exactly like the background characters in *Double-Barrel*.

6. Further confirmation of how closely Nabokov consulted the area of Drenthe in a detailed map of the Netherlands can be seen in the name Valthermond, a town lying between three *veen* towns to the north (Eexterveen, Gieterveen, and Gasselternijeveen) and three to the south (Emmer-Erfscheidenveen, Klazien-aveen, and Barger-Oosterveen). To anyone who knows *Ada* the town's name suggests both Walter (Demon) Veen and Van's nom de plume in *Letters from Terra*, Voltemand. And since Voltemand is a courtier in *Hamlet*, and the most *Hamlet*-saturated chapter of *Ada* takes place while Van is at Voltemand Hall, we should note in *Ada* book 1, chapter 5, the doubling of *Gamlet* (a village in the boggy area near Ardis but also the Russian transcription of "Hamlet") and *Torfyanka* (or Tourbière), whose name means "peaty": in other words, a veen-*Hamlet* conjunction from Van's first arrival at Ardis. Also see note 21 and text.

7. "All the hundred floramors opened simultaneously on September 20, 1875 (and by a delicious coincidence the old Russian word for September, '*ryuen*,' which might have spelled 'ruin,' also echoed the name of the ecstatic Neverlander's hometown)" (*Ada* 350). Van notes that Ruinen is "somewhere near Zwolle, I'm told" (350): Zwolle is indeed the nearest city, and a Nabokovian hint that we really should consult a map. An additional significance may be that the family of the great art dealer Joseph Duveen, certainly in Nabokov's mind while composing *Ada*, hailed from Meppel, between Ruinen and Zwolle; for the Duveen theme, see Siccama and van der Weide, "Een sleutel in Meppel," 23–25.

8. From Lucius Annaeus Seneca's *Omnius tempus edax depascitur, omnia carpit*; translated by Nabokov in his Vivian Darkbloom notes as "mountains subside and heights deteriorate." See J. E. Rivers and William Walker, "Notes to Vivian Darkbloom's Notes to *Ada*," 289–90.

9. Discussed in a Nabokv-L posting, August 25, 1998. Available at http://listserv.ucsb.edu/lsv-cgi-bin/wa?A2=ind9808&L=nabokv-l&P=R4027.

10. Mario Bussagli, *Bosch* (Florence: Sadea, 1966), 3; trans. Claire Pace (London: Thames and Hudson, 1967). The source was first identified by Julia Bader, *Crystal Land: Artifice in Nabokov's English Novels* (Berkeley: University of California Press, 1972), 147.

11. Siccama and van der Weide, "Een sleutel in Meppel," 25, notes the theme of multiple intermarriage also present in the Duveen clan.

12. In various places outside *Ada*, Nabokov discusses eavesdropping in other writers, including in Lermontov (translator's foreword, *A Hero of Our Time*,

trans. Vladimir Nabokov with Dmitri Nabokov [Garden City, N.Y.: Double-day, 1958], x–xii), in Proust (*PF* 87 and *LL* 230), and in Pasternak (Gilliat interview, 279).

13. It is also a brief minor theme in Nabokov's autobiography, where he reports that a tutor spied on his dalliances with "Tamara" (Valentina Shulgina) and a gardener reported to his mother on the snooping. Nabokov added more details on this matter in each version of the autobiography, the last between November 1965 and January 1966, as he made final revisions to *SM*, at the time *Ada* was beginning to take shape in his mind: see *VNAY* 506.

14. See also BB, "Annotations to *Ada*, 7: Part 1 Chapter 7," *The Nabokovian* 37 (Fall 1996): 63–64; also see *Ada*Online.

15. See *NAPC* 51–57, 291–97; BB, "Annotations to *Ada*, 10: Part 1 Chapter 10," *The Nabokovian* 39 (Fall 1997): 43–63; *Ada*Online.

16. BB, "Annotations to *Ada*, 10," 50; *Ada*Online.

17. *NAPC* 51–57, 150–51, 154–55, 215–16, 294–95; "Annotations to *Ada*, 10," 57–60; *Ada*Online.

18. For discussion, and a black-and-white reproduction, see *NAPC* 129–31; that book's cover reproduces in color the photograph of models and poster.

19. See BB, "Annotations to *Ada*, 16: Part 1 Chapter 16," 54–76, and Liana Marie Arangi Ashenden, "Mimicry, Mimesis, and Desire in Nabokov's *Ada*," M.A. thesis, University of Auckland, 2000.

20. Nabokov twice associates Eric Veen's Villa Venuses with Cypros: "Cyprian party" (*Ada* 399), "Cyprian dreams" (419). Ashenden, "Mimicry, Mimesis, and Desire," 89.

21. See note 6.

22. See BB, "Annotations to *Ada*, 5: Part 1 Chapter 5," *The Nabokovian* 35 (Fall 1995): 56–57; also see *Ada*Online.

23. In a bitter moment, when Ada decides to stay with the dying Andrey Vine-lander, Van will explode in scorn: "Helen of Troy, Ada of Ardis!" (*Ada* 530).

24. On the night of the Burning Barn, Ada turns around to Van, "naively ready to embrace him the way Juliet is recommended to receive her Romeo" (*Ada* 121).

25. The Paris–"already married" theme is played in two other keys in the chapter preceding Van's meeting with Lucette at Ovenman's bar. In Paris, Van encoun-ters first Greg Erminin, whom he discovers to be already married (a theme strikingly emphasized by the sustained echoes of *Eugene Onegin*, where One-gin in the final chapter finds that Tatyana has already married Prince N.), and then Cordula, whom he happily, hurriedly makes love to, despite knowing she is already married to Ivan Tobak.

26. Nabokov, interview with Bernard Pivot, "Apostrophes," TF-1, May 30, 1975.

27. Cited in Bobbie Ann Mason, *Nabokov's Garden: A Guide to* Ada (Ann Arbor, Mich.: Ardis, 1974), 163.

26. A BOOK BURNER RECANTS: *THE ORIGINAL OF LAURA*

1. Véra Nabokov to Fred Hills, April 20, 1976, cited *VNAY* 654.
2. Martin Amis, review of *Look at the Harlequins!*, *New Statesman*, April 25, 1975.
3. Tadashi Wakashima, "Watashi no Keshikata" [The effaced I], *Gunzo* 11 (2009).

BIBLIOGRAPHY

ARCHIVES

Bakhmeteff Collection, Columbia University Library
Cornell Lepidoptera Collection, Cornell University
Princeton University Press Archives, Princeton, New Jersey
Vladimir Nabokov Archive, Henry W. and Albert A. Berg Collection, New York Public
  Library.

BY VLADIMIR NABOKOV

Ada oder Das Verlangen. Trans. Uwe Friesel and Marianne Therstappen. Reinbek:
  Rowohlt, 1974.
Ada or Ardor: A Family Chronicle. New York: McGraw-Hill, 1969.
Ada ou l'ardeur. Trans. Gilles Chahine with Jean-Bernard Blandenier. Paris: Fayard,
  1975.
"Anniversary Notes." Supplement to *Triquarterly* 17 (1970); rpt. in *SO*.
The Annotated Lolita. Ed. and annot. Alfred Appel Jr. New York: McGraw-Hill, 1970.
  2nd rev. ed. New York: Vintage, 1991.
Bend Sinister. 1947. Repr., with intro. VN. New York: Time, 1964.
Conclusive Evidence: A Memoir. New York: Harper and Brothers, 1951.
The Enchanter. Trans. Dmitri Nabokov. New York: Putnam, 1986. New York: Vintage,
  1991.
Eugene Onegin, by Alexander Pushkin. Trans. with commentary by Vladimir Nabo-
  kov. 4 vols. Rev. ed. Princeton, N.J.: Princeton University Press, 1975.
The Eye. Trans. Dmitri Nabokov with Vladimir Nabokov. New York: Phaedra, 1965.

Foreword to *A Hero of Our Time*, by Mikhail Lermontov. Trans. Vladimir Nabokov with Dmitri Nabokov. Garden City, N.Y.: Doubleday, 1958.

The Gift. Trans. Michael Scammell with Vladimir Nabokov. 1963. New York: Vintage, 1991.

Glory. Trans. Dmitri Nabokov with Vladimir Nabokov. New York: McGraw-Hill, 1971.

A Hero of Our Time, by Mikhail Lermontov. Trans. Vladimir Nabokov with Dmitri Nabokov. Garden City, N.Y.: Doubleday, 1958.

Invitation to a Beheading. Trans Dmitri Nabokov with Vladimir Nabokov. New York: Putnam, 1959.

King, Queen, Knave. Trans. Dmitri Nabokov with Vladimir Nabokov. New York: McGraw-Hill, 1968.

Lectures on Don Quixote. Ed. Fredson Bowers. New York: Harcourt Brace Jovanovich/Bruccoli Clark, 1983.

Lectures on Literature. Ed. Fredson Bowers. New York: Harcourt Brace Jovanovich, 1980.

Lectures on Russian Literature. Ed. Fredson Bowers. New York: Harcourt Brace Jovanovich, 1981.

Lectures on Ulysses. Bloomfield Hills, Mich.: Bruccoli Clark, 1980.

"The Lermontov Mirage." *Russian Review* 1, no. 1 (1941): 31–39.

Lolita. New York: Putnam, 1958.

Lolita. New York: Vintage, 1989.

Lolita. Trans. into French by Eric Kahane. Paris: Gallimard, 1959.

Lolita. Trans. into Russian by Vladimir Nabokov. New York: Phaedra, 1967.

Lolita: A Screenplay. New York: McGraw-Hill, 1974.

Look at the Harlequins! New York: McGraw Hill, 1974.

Mary. Trans. Dmitri Nabokov with Vladimir Nabokov. New York: McGraw-Hill, 1970.

The Man from the USSR and Other Plays. Trans. and ed. Dmitri Nabokov. New York: Harcourt Brace Jovanovich/Bruccoli Clark, 1984.

Nabokov's Butterflies: Unpublished and Uncollected Writings. Ed. Brian Boyd and Robert Michael Pyle. Boston: Beacon, 2000.

"The Nearctic Forms of *Lycaeides* Hüb[ner]. (Lycaenidae, Lepidoptera)." *Psyche* 50 (September–December 1943): 87–99.

Nikolai Gogol. Norfolk, Conn.: New Directions, 1944.

Novels, 1955–62, Lolita, Pnin, Pale Fire, Lolita: A Screenplay. Ed. Brian Boyd. New York: Library of America, 1996.

The Original of Laura. New York: Knopf, 2010.

Pale Fire. New York: Putnam, 1962.

Perepiska s sestroy. Ann Arbor, Mich.: Ardis, 1985.

Pnin. Garden City, N.Y.: Doubleday, 1957.

Poems and Problems. New York: McGraw Hill, 1971.

"Problems of Translation: 'Onegin' in English." *Partisan Review* 22 (1955): 496–512.

"Professor Woodbridge in an Essay on Nature Postulates the Reality of the World." *New York Sun*, 10 December 1940, 15.

Pushkin, Lermontov, Tyutchev. London: Editions Poetry London, 1947.

The Real Life of Sebastian Knight. Norfolk, Conn.: New Directions, 1941.

A Russian Beauty and Other Stories. New York: McGraw-Hill, 1973.

Selected Letters, 1940–1977. Ed. Dmitri Nabokov and Matthew J. Bruccoli. New York: Harcourt Brace Jovanovich/Bruccoli Clark Layman, 1989.

Sobranie sochineniy amerikanskogo perioda. 5 vols. St. Petersburg: Symposium, 1999.

Sobranie sochineniy russkogo perioda. 5 vols. St. Petersburg: Symposium, 1999–2000.

The Song of Igor's Campaign. Trans. with notes Vladimir Nabokov. New York: Vintage, 1960.

Speak, Memory: An Autobiography Revisited. New York: Putnam, 1967.

Speak, Memory: An Autobiography Revisited. Ed. Brian Boyd. New York: Knopf, 1999.

Stikhi. Ann Arbor, Mich.: Ardis, 1979.

Stikhotvoreniya. Ed. Maria Malikova. St. Petersburg: Akademicheskiy Proekt, 2002.

The Stories of Vladimir Nabokov. Ed. Dmitri Nabokov. New York: Knopf, 1995.

Strong Opinions. New York: McGraw Hill, 1973.

Three Russian Poets. Norfolk, Conn.: New Directions, 1944.

Tragediya gospodina Morna, P'esy, Lektsii o drame. Ed. Andrey Babikov. St. Petersburg: Azbuka, 2008.

Transparent Things. New York: McGraw-Hill, 1972.

Verses and Versions: Three Centuries of Russian Poetry. Ed. Brian Boyd and Stanislav Shvabrin. New York: Harcourt, 2008.

"Vladimir Nabokov Reads His Own Prose and Poetry and His Translations of Russian Poets in English and Russian." Tape recording. Ed. Stratis Haviaras and Michael Milburn. Cambridge, Mass.: Harvard, 1988.

The Waltz Invention. Trans. Dmitri Nabokov with Vladimir Nabokov. New York: Phaedra, 1966.

Nabokov, Vladimir, and Edmund Wilson. *Dear Bunny, Dear Volodya: The Nabokov-Wilson Letters, 1940–1971.* Ed. Simon Karlinsky. 1979. Rev. ed., Berkeley and Los Angeles: University of California Press, 2001.

——. *The Nabokov-Wilson Letters.* Ed. Simon Karlinsky. New York: Harper & Row, 1979.

Nabokov Interviews

Interview with George Feifer. "Vladimir Nabokov: An Interview." *Saturday Review*, November 27, 1976, 20–26.

Interview with Penelope Gilliatt. "Nabokov." *Vogue*, December 1966, 224–29, 279–81.

Interview with Christopher Givan, "Cocktails with Nabokov: 'The Thing Is to Avoid the Cliché of Your Time.'" *Los Angeles Times*, August 7, 1977.

Interview with Anne Guérin. *L'Expres*, January 26, 1961, 26–27.

Interview with Mati Laansoo, March 1973. *Vladimir Nabokov Research Newsletter* 10 (1983): 39–48.

Interview with Kathleen Lucas. "Nabokou [sic] Condemns Classification; Says No Art Exists, Only Artists," *Wellesley College News*, March 5, 1942, 5.

Interview with Phyllis Meras. "V. Nabokov Unresting." *Providence Sunday Journal*, May 13, 1962.

Interview with *Newsweek*. "*Lolita*'s Creator—Author Nabokov, a 'Cosmic Joker.'" *Newsweek*, June 25, 1962, 51–54.

Interview with Bernard Pivot. "Apostrophes." TF-1, May 30, 1975.

BY OTHERS

Adelman, Gary. *Anna Karenina: The Bitterness of Ecstasy*. Boston: Twayne, 1990.

Alexandrov, Vladimir. *Nabokov's Otherworld*. Princeton, N.J.: Princeton University Press, 1993.

Amis, Martin. Review of *Look at the Harlequins! New Statesman*, April 25, 1975.

Appel, Alfred, Jr., ed. and annot. *The Annotated Lolita*. New York: McGraw-Hill, 1970.

——. *Nabokov's Dark Cinema*. Oxford: Oxford University Press, 1974.

Armel, K. C., and V. S. Ramachandran. "Acquired Synaesthesia in Retinitis Pigmentosa." *Neurocase* 5 (1999): 293–956.

Ashenden, Liana Marie Arangi. "Mimicry, Mimesis, and Desire in Nabokov's *Ada*." M.A. thesis, University of Auckland, 2000.

Atkins, Peter. *Galileo's Finger: The Ten Great Ideas of Science*. Oxford: Oxford University Press, 2003.

Atran, Scott. *Cognitive Foundations of Natural History: Towards an Anthropology of Science*. Cambridge: Cambridge University Press, 1990.

Aziz-Zadeh, Lisa, Stephen M. Wilson, Giacomo Rizzolatti, and Marco Iacoboni. "Congruent Embodied Representations for Visually Presented Actions and Linguistic Phrases Describing Actions." *Current Biology* 16 (2006): 1818–23.

Bader, Julia. *Crystal Land: Artifice in Nabokov's English Novels*. Berkeley: University of California Press, 1972.

Bálint, Zsolt. "A Catalogue of Polyommatine Lycaenidae (Lepidoptera) of the Xeromontane Oreal Biome in the Neotropics as Represented in European Collections." *Reports of the Museum of Natural History, University of Wisconsin* 29 (1993): 1–42.

Bálint, Zsolt, and Kurt Johnson. "Polyommatine Lycaenids of the Oreal Biome in the Neotropics, Part II: The *Itylos* Section (Lepidoptera: Lycaenidae, Polyommatinae)." *Annales Historico-Naturales Musei Nationalis Hungarici* 86 (1994): 53–77.

Barabtarlo, Gennady. *Aerial View: Essays on Nabokov's Art and Metaphysics*. New York: Peter Lang, 1993.

——. *Phantom of Fact: A Guide to Nabokov's Pnin*. Ann Arbor, Mich.: Ardis, 1989.

Barnes, Julian. *Flaubert's Parrot*. London: Jonathan Cape, 1984.

Barsalou, Lawrence W. "Grounded Cognition." *Annual Review of Psychology* 59 (2008): 617–45.

Bartlett, Frederic C. *Remembering: A Study in Experimental and Social Psychology*. Cambridge: Cambridge University Press, 1932.

Bayley, John. *Tolstoy and the Novel*. 1966. Chicago: University of Chicago Press, 1988.

Beaujour, Elizabeth Kosty. "Translation and Self-Translation." In *Garland Companion to Vladimir Nabokov*, ed. Vladimir E. Alexandrov, 714–24. New York: Garland, 1995.

Beckett, Samuel. *Murphy*. In *Beckett: The Grove Centenary Edition*, ed. Paul Auster. Vol. 1: *Novels*. New York: Grove, 2006.

Berlin, Isaiah. *The Hedgehog and the Fox: An Essay on Tolstoy's View of History*. 1953. New York: Simon and Schuster, 1967.

Blackwell, Stephen H. *The Quill and the Scalpel: Nabokov's Art and the World of Science*. Columbus: Ohio State University Press, 2009.

——. *Zina's Paradox: The Figured Reader in Nabokov's Gift*. New York: Peter Lang, 2000.

Borges, Jorge Luis. *Labyrinths: Selected Stories and Other Writings*. Ed. Donald A. Yates and James E. Irby. New York: New Directions, 1962.

Bonheim, Helmut. *The Narrative Modes: Techniques of the Short Story*. Woodbridge, Suffolk: D. S. Brewer, 1982.

Bordwell, David. *Poetics of Cinema*. New York: Routledge, 2008.

Boyd, Brian. *Ada*Online, http://www.ada.auckland.ac.nz/.

——. "Annotations to Ada, 1: Part 1 Chapter 1." *The Nabokovian* 30 (Spring 1993): 9–48.

——. "Annotations to *Ada*, 2: Part 1 Chapter 2." *The Nabokovian* 31 (Fall 1993): 8–40.

——. "Annotations to Ada, 5: Part 1 Chapter 5." *The Nabokovian* 35 (Fall 1995): 41–60.

——. "Annotations to Ada, 7: Part 1 Chapter 7." *The Nabokovian* 37 (Fall 1996): 56–66.

——. "Annotations to Ada, 10: Part 1 Chapter 10." *The Nabokovian* 39 (Fall 1997): 38–63.

——. "Annotations to Ada, 16: Part 1 Chapter 16." *The Nabokovian* 45 (Fall 2000): 54–76

——. "In Memory of Simon Karlinsky." *The Nabokovian* 63 (Fall 2009): 7–14.

——. "Nabokov and *Ada*." Ph.D. diss., University of Toronto, 1979.

——. *Nabokov's* Ada: *The Place of Consciousness*. 1985. 2nd rev. ed., Berkeley: Cyber-editions.com, 2001.

——. *Nabokov's* Pale Fire: *The Magic of Artistic Discovery*. Princeton, N.J.: Princeton University Press, 1999.

——. "Nabokov's Philosophical World." *Southern Review* 14 (November 1981): 260–301.

——. *On the Origin of Stories: Evolution, Cognition, and Fiction*. Cambridge, Mass.: Belknap Press of Harvard University Press, 2009.

——. *Vladimir Nabokov: The American Years.* Princeton, N.J.: Princeton University Press, 1991.

——. *Vladimir Nabokov: The Russian Years.* Princeton, N.J.: Princeton University Press, 1990.

——. *Vladimir Nabokov: Russkie gody.* Trans. Galina Lapina. Moscow and St. Petersburg: Nezavisimaya Gazeta and Symposium, 2001.

Boyd, Brian, Joseph Carroll, and Jonathan Gottschall, eds. *Evolution, Literature, and Film: A Reader.* New York: Columbia University Press, 2010.

Brown, Clarence. "Nabokov's Pushkin and Nabokov's Nabokov." In *Nabokov: The Man and His Work*, ed. L. S. Dembo, 195–208. Madison: University of Wisconsin Press, 1967.

Bruss, Elizabeth. *Autobiographical Acts: The Changing Situation of a Literary Genre.* Baltimore, Md.: Johns Hopkins University Press, 1976.

Bulfinch, Thomas. *The Age of Chivalry and The Legends of Charlemagne, or Romance of the Middle Ages.* 1858. New York: New American Library, 1962.

Bussagli, Mario. *Bosch.* Florence: Sadea, 1966. Trans. Claire Pace. London: Thames and Hudson, 1967.

Butler, Diana. "Lolita Lepidoptera." *New World Writing* 16 (1960): 58–84. Repr., in *Critical Essays on Vladimir Nabokov*, ed. Phyllis A. Roth, 59–73. Boston: G. K. Hall, 1984.

Cairns, Huntington, ed. *The Limits of Art: Poetry and Prose Chosen by Ancient and Modern Critics.* 1948. Bollingen Series 12. New York: Pantheon, 1960.

Carroll, Joseph. *Literary Darwinism: Evolution, Human Nature, and Literature.* New York: Routledge, 2004.

Comstock, William, and E. Irving Huntington. "Lycaenidae of the Antilles (Lepidoptera, Rhopalocera)." *Annals of the New York Academy of Sciences* 45 (December 1943): 49–130.

Connolly, Julian. "'Nature's Reality' or Humbert's 'Fancy'? Scenes of Reunion and Murder in *Lolita*." *Nabokov Studies* 2 (1995): 41–61.

Cooke, Brett. *Human Nature in Utopia: Zamyatin's We.* Evanston, Ill.: Northwestern University Press, 2002.

Couturier, Maurice. *Textual Communication: A Print-Based Theory of the Novel.* London: Routledge, 1991.

Critical Inquiry Symposium Special Issue. *Critical Inquiry* 30 (2004).

Cytowic, Richard, and David Eagleman. *Wednesday Is Indigo Blue: Discovering the Brain of Synesthesia.* Cambridge, Mass.: Bradford/MIT Press, 2009.

Darwin, Charles. *On the Origin of Species by Means of Natural Selection.* 1859. Ed. Joseph Carroll. Peterborough, Ont.: Broadview, 2003.

Davydov, Sergey. "Nabokov and Pushkin." In *The Garland Companion to Vladimir Nabokov*, ed. Vladimir Alexandrov, 482–96. New York: Garland, 1995.

——. *Teksty-Matryoshki Vladimira Nabokova.* Munich: Otto Sagner, 1982.

——. "Weighing Nabokov's *Gift* on Pushkin's Scales." In *Cultural Mythologies of Russian Modernism: From the Golden Age to the Silver Age*, ed. Boris Gasparov et al., 419–30. Berkeley: University of California Press, 1992.

Dawkins, Richard. *The Ancestor's Tale: A Pilgrimage to the Dawn of Life*. London: Weidenfeld and Nicolson, 2004.

——. *The Selfish Gene*. 1976. 2nd ed., Oxford: Oxford University Press, 1989.

Dennett, Daniel. *Darwin's Dangerous Idea: Evolution and the Meanings of Life*. London: Penguin, 1996.

Deresiewicz, William. "Professing Literature in 2008." *The Nation*, March 24, 2008. http://www.thenation.com/article/professing-literature-2008.

De Vries, Gerard, D. Barton Johnson, and Liana Ashenden. *Nabokov and the Art of Painting*. Amsterdam: Amsterdam University Press, 2006.

Dissanayake, Ellen. *Art and Intimacy: How the Arts Began*. Seattle: University of Washington Press, 2000.

Doidge, Norman. *The Brain That Changes Itself: Stories of Personal Triumph from the Frontiers of Brain Science*. New York: Penguin, 2007.

Dolinin, Alexander A. "*The Gift*." In *The Garland Companion to Vladimir Nabokov*, ed. Vladimir E. Alexandrov, 135–69. New York: Garland, 1995.

——. "Nabokov as a Russian Writer." In *Cambridge Companion to Vladimir Nabokov*, ed. Julian Connolly, 49–64. Cambridge: Cambridge University Press, 2005.

——. "Nabokov's Time Doubling: From *The Gift* to *Lolita*." *Nabokov Studies* 2 (1995): 3–40.

——. "Tri zametki o romane Vladimira Nabokova 'Dar.'" In *V. V. Nabokov: Pro et Contra*, ed. B. Averin, Maria Malikova, and T. Smirnova, 697–740. St. Petersburg: Russkiy Khristianskiy Gumanitarniy Institut, 1997.

dos Passos, Cyril F. *A Synonymic List of the Nearctic Rhopalocera*. New Haven, Conn.: The Lepidopterists' Society Memoir No. 1, 1964.

Dostoevsky, Fyodor. *Brat'ya Karamazovy*. Novosibirsk: Zapadnoe-Sibirskoe Knizhnoe Izdatel'stvo, 1984.

Dragunoiu, Dana. *Vladimir Nabokov and the Poetics of Liberalism*. Evanston, Ill.: Northwestern University Press, 2011.

Dutton, Denis. *The Art Instinct: Beauty, Pleasure, and Evolution*. New York: Bloomsbury, 2009.

Feinstein, Elaine, ed. *After Pushkin*. London: Folio Society, 1999.

Field, Andrew. *Nabokov: A Bibliography*. New York: McGraw-Hill, 1973.

——. *Nabokov: His Life in Art*. Boston: Little, Brown, 1967.

——. *Nabokov: His Life in Part*. New York: Viking, 1977.

Flynn, James R. *What Is Intelligence? Beyond the Flynn Effect*. Cambridge: Cambridge University Press, 2007.

Freeling, Nicholas. *Double-Barrel*. 1964. Harmondsworth: Penguin, 1967.

Fromm, Harold. *The Nature of Being Human: From Environmentalism to Consciousness*. Baltimore, Md.: Johns Hopkins University Press, 2009.

Fry, Paul H. "Moving Van: The Neverland Veens of Nabokov's *Ada*." *Contemporary Literature* 26, no. 2 (1985): 123–39.

Funke, Sarah, and Glenn Horowitz, eds. *Véra's Butterflies*. New York: Glenn Horowitz, 1999.

Goleman, Daniel. *Social Intelligence: The New Science of Human Relationships*. New York: Bantam, 2006.

Gottschall, Jonathan. *Literature, Science, and a New Humanities*. New York: Palgrave, 2008.

———. *The Rape of Troy: Evolution, Violence, and the World of Homer*. Cambridge: Cambridge University Press, 2008.

Gottschall, Jonathan, and David Sloan Wilson, eds. *The Literary Animal: Evolution and the Nature of Narrative*. Evanston, Ill.: Northwestern University Press, 2005.

Gould, Stephen Jay. *Bully for Brontosaurus: Further Reflections in Natural History*. Harmondsworth: Penguin, 1992.

———. *The Flamingo's Smile: Reflections in Natural History*. New York: Norton, 1985.

Grayson, Jane. *Nabokov Translated: A Comparison of Nabokov's Russian and English Prose*. Oxford: Oxford University Press, 1977.

Green, Geoffrey. *Freud and Nabokov*. Lincoln: University of Nebraska Press, 1988.

Gurría-Quintana, Ángel. "Orhan Pamuk: The Art of Fiction Interview No. 187." *Paris Review* 175 (Fall–Winter 2005): 115–41.

Gustafson, Richard F. *Leo Tolstoy: Resident and Stranger*. Princeton, N.J.: Princeton University Press, 1986.

Haeckel, Ernst. *Kunstformen der Natur: Artforms in Nature: The Prints of Ernst Haeckel*. Trans. Michaele Schons. New York: Prestel, 1998.

———. *Die Weltraetsel: Gemeinverständliche Studien über Monistische Philosophie*. 1899. Rev. ed., Leipzig: Kröner, 1909.

Hofstadter, Douglas. *Le Ton beau de Marot: In Praise of the Music of Language*. New York: Basic Books, 1997.

Hogan, Patrick Colm. *The Mind and Its Stories: Narrative Universals and Human Emotion*. Cambridge: Cambridge University Press, 2003.

Howe, William H., ed. *The Butterflies of North America*. Garden City, N.Y.: Doubleday. 1976.

Iacoboni, Marco. *Mirroring People: The New Science of How We Connect with Others*. New York: Farrar, Straus and Giroux, 2008.

Jakobson, Roman, and Morris Halle, *Fundamentals of Language*. The Hague: Mouton, 1956.

James, William. *Principles of Psychology*. 2 vols. London: Macmillan, 1890.

Johnson, D. Barton. "The Butterfly in Nabokov's *Eye*." *Nabokov Studies* 4 (1997): 1–14.

———. "A Field Guide to Nabokov's *Pale Fire*: Waxwings and the Red Admiral." In *The Real Life of Pierre Delalande: Studies in Russian and Comparative Literature to Honor Alexander Dolinin*, 2 vols., ed. David M. Bethea, Lazar Fleishman, and Alexander Ospovat, 2:652–73. Stanford, Calif.: Stanford Slavic Studies, 2007.

——. *Worlds in Regression: Some Novels of Vladimir Nabokov*. Ann Arbor, Mich.: Ardis, 1985.

Johnson, D. Barton, and Brian Boyd. "Prologue: The Otherworld." In *Nabokov's World*, vol. 1: *The Shape of Nabokov's World*, ed. Jane Grayson, Arnold McMillin, and Priscilla Meyer, 18–25. London: Palgrave/School of Slavonic and East European Studies, 2002.

Johnson, Kurt, and Steve Coates. *Nabokov's Blues: The Scientific Odyssey of a Literary Genius*. Cambridge, Mass.: Zoland Books, 1999.

Johnson, Kurt, and David Matusik. "Five New Species and One New Subspecies of Butterflies from the Sierra de Baorucco of Hispaniola." *Annals of the Carnegie Museum* 57 (1988): 221–54.

Karlinsky, Simon. "Vladimir Nabokov's Novel *Dar* as a Work of Literary Criticism: A Structural Analysis." *Slavonic and East European Journal* 7 (1963): 284–96.

Karlinsky, Simon, and Alfred Appel Jr., eds. *The Bitter Air of Exile: Russian Writers in the West, 1922–1972*. *Triquarterly* 27–28 (1973). Berkeley: University of California Press, 1973.

Kernan, Alvin. "Reading Zemblan: The Audience Disappears in Nabokov's *Pale Fire*." 1982. In *Vladimir Nabokov: Modern Critical Views*, ed. Harold Bloom, 101–25. New York: Chelsea House, 1987.

Klots, Alexander B. *A Field Guide to the Butterflies of North America, East of the Great Plains*. Boston: Houghton Mifflin, 1951.

Kohn, Marek, and Steve Mithen. "Handaxes: Products of Sexual Selection?" *Antiquity* 73 (1999): 518–26.

Kubrick, Stanley, dir. *Lolita*. MGM/Seven Arts, 1962.

Kyoto Reading Circle. "Annotations to *Ada* (1)." *Krug O.S.* 1, no. 2 (2000): 16–24.

Levin, Richard. *Looking for an Argument: Critical Encounters with the New Approaches to the Criticism of Shakespeare and His Contemporaries* Madison, N.J.: Fairleigh Dickinson University Press, 2003.

——. *New Readings vs. Old Plays*. Chicago: University of Chicago Press, 1979.

Leving, Yuri. *Vokzal—Garazh—Angar: Vladimir Nabokov i poetika russkogo urbanizma*. St. Petersburg: Ivan Limbakh, 2004.

Lisboa, Maria Manuel. "Machado de Assis and the Beloved Reader: Squatters in the Text." In *Scarlet Letters: Fictions of Adultery from Antiquity to the 1990s*, ed. Nicholas White and Naomi Segal, 160–73. New York: St Martin's Press, 1997.

Livingston, Paisley. *Art and Intention*. Oxford: Oxford University Press, 2005.

Lyne, Adrian, dir. *Lolita*. Pathe, 1998.

Machado de Assis, Joaquím Maria. *A Chapter of Hats: Selected Stories*. Trans. John Gledson. London: Bloomsbury, 2008.

——. *Counselor Ayres' Memorial*. 1908. Trans. Helen Caldwell. Berkeley and Los Angeles: University of California Press, 1972.

——. *The Devil's Church and Other Stories*. Trans. Jack Schmitt and Lorie Ishimatsua. Austin: University of Texas Press, 1984.

——. *Dom Casmurro*. 1899. Trans. John Gledson. New York: Oxford University Press, 1997.

——. *Esau and Jacob*. 1904. Trans. Elizabeth Lowe. New York: Oxford University Press, 2000.

——. *Obra Completa*. 3 vols. Rio de Janeiro: Editora José Aguilar, 1962.

——. *The Posthumous Memoirs of Brás Cubas*. 1881. Trans. Gregory Rabassa. New York: Oxford University Press, 1997.

——. *The Psychiatrist and Other Stories*. Trans. William L. Grossman and Helen Caldwell. Berkeley and Los Angeles: University of California Press, 1963.

——. *Quincas Borba*. 1891. Trans. Gregory Rabassa. New York: Oxford University Press, 1998.

Magee, Bryan. *Popper*. London: Fontana, 1973.

Manolescu, Monica, and Anne-Marie Paquet-Deyris. *Lolita: Cartographies de l'Obsession (Nabokov, Kubrick)*. Paris: CNED/Presses Universitaires de France, 2009.

Mason, Bobbie Ann. *Nabokov's Garden: A Guide to* Ada. Ann Arbor, Mich.: Ardis, 1974.

Medawar, Sir Peter. *Pluto's Republic*. Oxford: Oxford University Press, 1982.

Menand, Louis. "Dangers Within and Without." *Profession* (2005): 10–17.

Morris, Paul. *Vladimir Nabokov: Poetry and the Lyric Voice*. Toronto: University of Toronto Press, 2010.

Morson, Gary Saul. *Hidden in Plain View: Narrative and Creative Potential in* War and Peace. Stanford, Calif.: Stanford University Press, 1987.

Moynahan, Julian. "Cards of Identity." Review of Andrew Field, *Nabokov: His Life in Art. Partisan Review* (Summer 1968): 483–88.

——. "*Lolita* and Related Memories." *Triquarterly* 17 (1970): 247–52.

Murray, Isabel. "'Plagiatisme': Nabokov's 'The Vane Sisters' and *The Picture of Dorian Gray.*" *Durham University Journal* 39 (1977): 69–72.

Nabokov, Dmitri. "On Revisiting Father's Room." In *Vladimir Nabokov: A Tribute*, ed. Peter Quennell, 126–36. London: Weidenfeld and Nicolson, 1979.

Nordlund, Marcus. *Shakespeare and the Nature of Love: Literature, Culture, and Evolution*. Evanston, Ill.: Northwestern University Press, 2007.

Nyeröd, Marie. *Ingmar Bergman—3 dokumentärer om film, teater, Fårö och livet*. 2004.

Ovid. *Metamorphoses*. Trans. Frank Justus Miller. Cambridge, Mass.: Harvard University Press, 1921.

Perner, Josef. *Understanding the Representational Mind*. Cambridge, Mass.: Bradford/ MIT Press, 1991.

Pifer, Ellen. "Did She Have a Precursor: *Lolita* and Wharton's *The Children.*" In *Nabokov's World*, vol. 2: *Reading Nabokov*, ed. Jane Grayson, Arnold McMillin, and Priscilla Meyer, 186–92. London: Palgrave/School of Slavonic and East European Studies, 2002.

——. *Nabokov and the Novel*. Cambridge, Mass.: Harvard University Press, 1980.

Popper, Karl. *Unended Quest: An Intellectual Autobiography.* 1974. London: Fontana, 1976.

Powell, Barry. *Homer and the Origin of the Greek Alphabet.* Cambridge: Cambridge University Press, 1991.

Propertius, Sextus. *Properce, Élégies.* Trans. D. Paganelli. Paris: Les Belles Lettres, 1929.

——. *Propertius: Elegies.* Ed. and trans. G. P. Goold. Cambridge, Mass.: Harvard University Press, 1990.

Pushkin, Aleksandr. *Eugene Onegin.* Trans. with commentary Vladimir Nabokov. 4 vols. Princeton, N.J.: Bollingen, 1964. 2nd ed., Princeton, N.J.: Princeton University Press, 1975.

——. *Sobranie sochineniy v desyati tomakh.* Vol.2: *Stikhotvoreniya 1824–1836.* Moscow: Pravda, 1981.

Raine, Craig. "Craig Raine Fondles Vladimir Nabokov." *London Review of Books,* May 14, 1992, 6–8.

Raine, Kathleen. *The Collected Poems of Kathleen Raine.* Washington, D.C.: Counterpoint, 2001.

Rampton, David. *Vladimir Nabokov: A Critical Study of the Novels.* Cambridge: Cambridge University Press, 1984.

Reichard, Gladys, Roman Jakobson, and Elizabeth Werth. "Language and Synesthesia." *Word* 5 (August 1949).

Richardson, L., Jr., ed., *Propertius: Elegies I–IV.* Norman: Oklahoma University Press, 1977.

Rivers, J. E., and William Walker. "Notes to Vivian Darkbloom's Notes to Ada." In *Nabokov's Fifth Arc,* ed. J. E. Rivers and Charles Nicol, 260–95. Austin: University of Texas Press, 1982.

Rosenbaum, Ron. "Nabokov's Pale Ghost: A Scholar Retracts." *New York Observer,* April 26, 1991, 39.

Root-Bernstein, Robert. "The Art of Innovation: Polymaths and Universality of the Creative Process." In *International Handbook on Innovation,* ed. Larisa Shavinin, 267–78. Amsterdam: Elsevier.

——. "The Sciences and the Arts Share a Common Creative Aesthetic." In *The Elusive Synthesis: Aesthetics and Science,* ed. A. I. Tauber, 49–82. Dordrecht: Kluwer, 1996.

Rorty, Richard. "The Barber of Kasbeam: Nabokov on Cruelty." In *Contingency, Irony, and Solidarity,* 141–68. Cambridge: Cambridge University Press, 1989.

Rowe, William Woodin. *Nabokov's Deceptive World.* New York: New York University Press, 1971.

——. *Nabokov's Spectral Dimension.* Ann Arbor, Mich.: Ardis, 1981.

Ryabov, Dmitri. *Toponimiya Verkhnego Pooredezh'ya: Slovar'-spravochnik.* St. Petersburg: Muzey-usad'ba "Rozhdestveno," 1995

Saxe, Rebecca, and Simon Baron-Cohen. *Theory of Mind*. Special issue of *Social Neuroscience*, 2006. Hove, U.K.: Psychology Press, 2007.

Scalise-Sugiyama, Michelle. "Narrative Theory and Function: Why Evolution Matters." *Philosophy and Literature* 25 (2001): 233–50.

Schacter, Daniel L., and Donna Rose Addis. "The Cognitive Neuroscience of Constructive Memory: Remembering the Past and Imagining the Future." *Philosophical Transactions of the Royal Society B* 362 (2007): 773–86.

Schiff, Stacey. *Véra (Mrs Vladimir Nabokov)*. New York: Random House, 1999.

Schiff, Stephen. *Lolita: The Book of the Film*. New York: Applause, 1998.

Schurian, Klaus G. "Bemerkungen zu '*Lysandra cormion*' Nabokov 1941 (Lepidoptera: Lycaenidae)." *Nachrichten des entomologischen Vereins Apollo* [Frankfurt] n.s. 10 (1989): 183–92.

——. "Nachtrag zu den Bemerkungen zu '*Lysandra cormion*' (Lepidoptera: Lycaenidae)." *Nachrichten des entomologischen Vereins Apollo* [Frankfurt] n.s. 12 (1991): 193–95.

Schwartz, Albert, and Kurt Johnson. "Two New Butterflies (Lepidoptera: Lycaenidae) from Cuba." *Caribbean Journal of Science* 28 (1992): 149–57.

Seitz, Adalbert. *Die Gross-Schmetterlinge der Erde*. 16 vols. Stuttgart: Lehmann, then Alfred Kernen, 1906–54.

Seuss, Dr. *Horton Hears a Who!* 1954. Repr., New York: Collins, 1998.

Sexton, David. Review of *Vladimir Nabokov: The American Years*, by Brian Boyd. *Sunday Telegraph*, January 5, 1992.

——. "The True Loves of Nabokov." Review of *Nabokov's Butterflies*. *Evening Standard*, March 20, 2000, 55.

Shapiro, Gavriel. *The Sublime Artist's Studio: Nabokov and Painting*. Evanston, Ill.: Northwestern University Press, 2009.

Shvabrin, Stanislav. "Vladimir Nabokov as Translator: The Multilingual Works of the Russian Period." Ph.D. diss., University of California at Los Angeles, 2007.

Siccama, Wilma, and Jack van der Weide. "Een sleutel in Meppel: Nederlandse aantekeningen bij Vladimir Nabokovs Ada." *Maatstaf* 6 (1995): 17–27.

Sidney, Sir Philip. *A Defence of Poetry*. Ed. J. A. Van Dorsten. Oxford: Oxford University Press, 1966.

Slingerland, Edward. *What Science Has to Offer the Humanities*. Cambridge: Cambridge University Press, 2008.

Sloboda, John. "Power of Music." *New Scientist*, November 29, 2003, 38–42.

Smith, D. S., L. D. Miller, and J. Y. Miller. *The Butterflies of the West Indies and South Florida*. Oxford: Oxford University Press, 1994.

Spencer, Herbert. *First Principles of a New System of Philosophy*. 1862. 6th ed. London: Williams & Norgate, 1904.

Sperber, Dan, ed. *Metarepresentations: A Multidisciplinary Perspective*. Oxford: Oxford University Press, 2000.

——. "Metarepresentations in an Evolutionary Perspective." In *Metarepresentations: A Multidisciplinary Perspective*, ed. D. Sperber, 117–38. Oxford: Oxford University Press, 2000.

Stallings, D. B., and J. R. Turner. "New American Butterflies." *Canadian Entomologist* 78 (1947): 134–37.

Stevan, Megan S., and Colin Blakemore, "Visual Synesthesia in the Blind." *Perception* 33 (2004): 856–68.

Strannik (Archbishop Ioann). "Nachalo Nabokoviany," *Russkaya Mysl'*, June 1, 1978, 10.

Sutton-Smith, Brian. *The Folk-Stories of Children*. Philadelphia: University of Pennsylvania Press, 1981.

Swirski, Peter. *Literature, Analytically Speaking: Explorations in the Theory of Interpretation, Analytic Aesthetics, and Evolution*. Austin: University of Texas Press, 2010.

——. *Of Literature and Knowledge: Explorations in Narrative Thought Experiments, Evolution, and Game Theory*. New York and London: Routledge, 2007.

Tammi, Pekka. *Problems of Nabokov's Poetics*. Helsinki: Suomalainen Tiedeakatemia, 1985.

Tarvi, Ljuba. *Comparative Translation Assessment: Quantifying Quality*. Helsinki: University of Helsinki, 2004.

Tekiner, Christina. "Time in *Lolita*," *Modern Fiction Studies* 25 (1979): 463–69.

Tennyson, Alfred, Lord. *The Poems of Tennyson*. 3 vols. Ed. Christopher Ricks. London: Longman, 1987.

Toker, Leona. *Nabokov: The Mystery of Literary Structures*. Ithaca, N.Y.: Cornell University Press, 1989.

Tolstoy, Leo. *Sobranie sochineniy*. 10 vols. Moscow: Khudostvennaya Literatura, 1974.

——. *What Is Art?* Trans. Richard Pevear and Larissa Volokhonsky. London: Penguin, 1996.

Tomasello, Michael. *Origins of Human Communication*. Cambridge, Mass.: Bradford/MIT Press, 2008.

Tooby, John, and Leda Cosmides. "Does Beauty Build Adapted Minds? Toward an Evolutionary Theory of Aesthetics, Fiction, and the Arts." *Substance* 30 (2001): 6–27.

Tooby, John, and Irwin DeVore. "The Reconstruction of Hominid Behavioral Evolution Through Strategic Modelling." In *The Evolution of Human Behavior: Primate Models*, ed. W. G. Kinzey, 183–237. Albany: State University of New York Press, 1987.

Vendler, Helen. *The Art of Shakespeare's Sonnets*. Cambridge, Mass.: Belknap Press of Harvard University Press, 1997.

Vermeule, Blakey. *Why Do We Care About Literary Characters?* Baltimore, Md.: Johns Hopkins University Press, 2009.

Vila, Roger, Charles D. Bell, Richard McNiven, Benjamin Goldman-Huertas, Richard H. Ree, Charles R. Marshall, Zsolt Bálint, Kurt Johnson, Dubi Benyamini, and

Naomi E. Pierce. "Phylogeny and Palaeoecology of *Polyommatus* Blue Butterflies Show Beringia Was a Climate-Regulated Gateway to the New World." *Proceedings of the Royal Society B* (2011): 1-8. doi: 10.1098/rspb.2010.2213.

Wakashima, Tadashi. "Watashi no Keshikata" [The effaced I]. *Gunzo* 11 (2009).

Wheeler, R. H., and Timothy D. Cutsforth. "Synaesthesia, a Form of Perception." *Psychological Review* 29 (1922): 212–21.

Wilson, David Sloan. *Evolution for Everyone: How Darwin's Theory Can Change the Way We Think About Our Lives*. New York: Delacorte, 2007.

Wilson, Edward O. *The Diversity of Life*. New York: Norton, 1992.

Wimsatt, William K., and Monroe Beardsley. "The Intentional Fallacy." *Sewanee Review* 45 (1946): 469–88. Rpt., in *The Norton Anthology of Theory and Criticism*, ed. Vincent B. Leitch et al., 1374–87. New York: Norton, 2001.

Wood, Michael. *The Magician's Doubts: Nabokov and the Risks of Fiction*. London: Chatto and Windus, 1994.

Wyllie, Barbara. "'Guilty of Killing Quilty': The Central Dilemma of Nabokov's *Lolita*." NABOKV-L, November 21, 1994.

——. *Nabokov at the Movies*. Jefferson, North Carolina: McFarland, 2003.

Zholkovsky, Alexander. "'Ya vas lyubil . . .' Pushkina: invarianty i struktura." http://college.usc.edu/alik/rus/ess/bib21.html.

Zimmer, Dieter E. *A Guide to Nabokov's Butterflies and Moths*. Hamburg: privately printed, 1998.

——. *A Guide to Nabokov's Butterflies and Moths 2001*. Hamburg: privately printed, 2001.

——. "*Mary*." In *The Garland Companion to Vladimir Nabokov*, ed. Vladimir E. Alexandrov, 354–55. New York: Garland, 1995.

——. *Nabokov reist im Traum in das Innere Asiens*. Reinbek bei Hamburg: Rowohlt, 2006.

——. "Nabokov's Lepidoptera." In *Les Papillons de Nabokov*, ed. Michel Satoris. Lausanne: Musée Cantonal de Zoologie, Bibliothèque Cantonale et Universitaire, 1993.

——. *Nabokov's Berlin*. Berlin: Nicolai, 2001.

——. *Wirbelsturm Lolita: Auskünfte zu einem epochalen Roman*. Reinbek bei Hamburg: Rowohlt, 2008.

INDEX